Fundamentals of Investments for Financial Planning

Huebner School Series

Walt J. Woerheide, Editor

Huebner School Series

Fundamentals of Investments
for Financial Planning

Second Edition

Robert S. Graber
Walt J. Woerheide
Lynn Hayes, Managing Editor

The American College/*Bryn Mawr, Pennsylvania*

This publication is designed to provide accurate and authoritative information about the subject covered. While every precaution has been taken in the preparation of this material, the authors, the editor, and The American College assume no liability for damages resulting from the use of the information contained in this publication. The American College is not engaged in rendering legal, accounting, or other professional advice. If legal or other expert advice is required, the services of an appropriate professional should be sought.

Contents

Preface

A basic and inescapable principle of economics is the law of scarcity: In every society, human wants are unlimited, whereas the resources available to fill those wants are limited. The available resources must somehow be rationed among the wants. This rationing problem creates the need for financial planning even in affluent societies, such as the United States, and even among the most affluent members of such societies. To put it bluntly, there is never enough money to go around.

In today's economy, available financial resources are rationed through markets, and these markets operate in a dynamic environment in which the only certainty is change. It is in this environment that financial planners endeavor to practice their profession. Volatile economic conditions create greater demand for financial planning services. They also emphasize the need for financial planners to continually monitor their clients' financial circumstances and to adjust the plans as circumstances dictate. A major part of the financial planner's challenge in today's economic environment is to help clients overcome obstacles that could impede the achievement of their financial goals. To this end, the planner needs to educate clients about managing their money so that they will derive the maximum benefit from what they earn. To accomplish this purpose, financial planners must understand the securities markets and the investment alternatives that comprise it.

This is a basic or fundamentals textbook that is designed to help both financial planners and individual investors understand the nature of the securities markets and investment opportunities. It presupposes no prior knowledge of these subjects, yet it covers all the topics that constitute the foundation for the study of more specialized aspects of investments. Those who seriously study the information contained herein should find the book to be a useful guide. Practical aspects of investing are stressed. Abstract theoretical issues are introduced only when they are relevant to actual investing.

Investing is seen by many as a worthwhile "game." Those who are going to play the game may as well play it to win. Whether or not the game is worth playing, it is certainly worth winning. This book should help both financial planners and individual investors learn the rules of the game and learn something about the strategies that are most likely to prove effective in winning the game.

The book includes numerous pedagogical features designed to help students focus their study of investments. Among the features found in every chapter of the book are

- *Learning objectives:* Statements at the beginning of each chapter are designed to provide direction to students studying the subject matter in the chapter.
- *An outline:* Following the learning objectives, the subject matter is organized and listed in the order in which it appears in the chapter.
- *Key terms:* In the margins where the terms first appear, as well as grouped together at the end of each chapter, certain terms or phrases are singled out because of their importance to the specific subject matter.
- *Examples:* Problem sets interspersed throughout the chapter are designed to help students see how difficult concepts are applied in specific situations.
- *Review questions:* Essay-style questions at the end of each chapter are designed to test the student's knowledge of the learning objectives.
- *Self-test questions:* True-false statements following the review questions at the end of each chapter are designed to provide students with a quick assessment of their grasp of the subject matter.

Features located in the back of the book are

- *A glossary:* Key terms found in each chapter are defined and included in the back of the book.
- *An answer section:* Answers to all the review questions and self-test questions are located in this part of the book.
- *An index:* The book has a comprehensive index to help identify pages on which various topics are found.

Robert S. Graber
Walt J. Woerheide

Acknowledgments

We would like to especially thank Ben Branch, professor of finance in the school of management, the University of Massachusetts at Amherst, for his contributions to this book. Its foundation and starting point was the second edition of *Investments: Principles and Practices* by Ben Branch, which was published in 1989 by Longman Financial Services Publishing. In addition, Ben made several contributions to the first edition of The American College's version of this textbook.

We would like to thank the following professors at The American College for their contributions to the first edition: Roger C. Bird, professor of economics and holder of the Frank M. Engle Distinguished Chair in Economic Security Research; Thomas A. Dziadosz, associate professor of economics; Paul Hoffman, assistant professor of finance, and C. Bruce Worsham, associate vice president and director of educational development.

We would also like to thank these three individuals for their contributions in revising and/or updating parts of the second edition:

- Paul Hoffman, assistant professor of finance, The American College, for writing chapters 7 and 15
- Barbara Poole, associate professor of finance and insurance, The American College, for writing chapter 4
- Robert Zweig, senior financial analyst at the Securities and Exchange Commission, for his contribution to chapter 12, particularly for providing information regarding mutual fund loads and 12b-1 fees

We gratefully thank the members of The American College's editorial and production departments. Two of these individuals must be singled out for their noteworthy contributions to the project—Lynn Hayes, editorial director, and Evelyn M. Rice, production assistant.

All of these individuals made this a better book. In spite of their help, however, some errors have undoubtedly been successful in eluding our eyes. For these we are solely responsible. At the same time, however, we accept full credit for giving those readers who find these errors the exhilarating intellectual experience produced by such discovery. Nevertheless, each of the authors acknowledges that any errors discovered are the fault of one of the other authors.

Robert S. Graber
Walt J. Woerheide

About the Authors

Robert S. Graber, PhD, is an assistant professor of finance at The American College. He obtained his BS in economics from the Massachusetts Institute of Technology and his MBA, MA in economics, and PhD in financial economics from the University of New Orleans. He also has taught at Moorhead State University, the University of Houston, and Villanova University. In addition, his experience includes serving as a financial analyst with the Securities and Exchange Commission and as a financing specialist with Louisiana Power and Light Company.

Walt J. Woerheide, PhD, is the vice president and dean of academic affairs at The American College. His bachelor's degree is from Brown University, and his MBA and PhD are from Washington University in St. Louis. He previously served on the faculties at the Rochester Institute of Technology for 11 years, University of Michigan—Flint for 6 years, and University of Illinois at Chicago for 10 years. He is a past president of both the Academy of Financial Services and the Midwest Finance Association. He has authored two other books, the most recent a college textbook, *Introducing Personal Finance,* and has published about 24 articles, mostly in refereed academic publications.

Fundamentals of Investments
for Financial Planning

1

Introduction to Investments

Learning Objectives

An understanding of the material in this chapter should enable the student to

---

1-1. Identify the three separate but related processes of investing.

1-2. Compute holding period returns, geometric mean returns, and effective annual yields.

1-3. Explain the risk-expected return trade-off.

1-4. Distinguish between liquidity and marketability.

1-5. Describe the tax treatment of investments.

1-6. Describe the psychological aspect of investing.

Chapter Outline

INTRODUCTION TO INVESTMENTS

The first three chapters of this book lay the groundwork for a practical approach to investment and money management. The following hypothetical case raises many of the issues with which these three chapters deal.

The Newleys: A Young Couple's Finances

Ralph and Evelyn Newley have decided to take a careful look at their finances. They were married immediately after graduation from college 5 years ago and now have two children aged 3 and 1 1/2. Ralph earns $37,000 per year as a history teacher at Metropolis High School. He expects modest salary increases if he remains a teacher. He may, however, move into school administration, in which case his income should rise somewhat faster. Evelyn is a CPA with the prestigious accounting firm of Earnest Anderson, earning $54,500 a year. She seems to be on a fast track and may become a partner in 10 to 15 years. Even junior partners in Earnest Anderson earn in excess of $200,000.

The Newleys' principal assets are a home (estimated market value of $200,000 with a $140,000 mortgage), $45,000 in savings, and a tract of land left to them by Evelyn's parents. Evelyn's father was a real estate developer who died 3 years ago. Her mother is in ill health, and she is supported from a large trust whose principal asset is her late husband's development firm. This firm will be sold, and the principal of the trust (after deducting taxes) will be divided among Evelyn and her two brothers upon her mother's death.

Ralph's parents are in good health and have relatively modest assets. Ralph and Evelyn both have small amounts of life insurance through their respective employers. They are currently adding about $7,000 per year to their savings.

The Newleys are already relatively well off financially. They have a sufficiently large combined income to meet most of their needs. They have also begun to accumulate some assets (for example, their house and savings). Nonetheless, they believe that a careful examination of their situation will reveal a variety of ways to prepare better for the future.

Consider the following questions that relate to the Newleys' situation:

- A substantial portion of the Newleys' joint income goes for taxes. How might they reduce that tax burden?
- They maintain a balance of about $3,000 in their NOW checking account. Should they switch to a super NOW, money market, or cash management account?
- Their $45,000 in savings is currently in a passbook savings account at their bank. That money serves as an emergency reserve, but they could also borrow against the *equity* in their house (the excess of its market value over the mortgage is $60,000). Thus, they are now ready to begin investing the money in the savings account for growth and are willing to take some risks. What are some appropriate investments?
- Evelyn's share of her parents' estate will probably exceed $300,000. She would like to learn more about investment opportunities. What types of investments should she consider when this money is received?
- After some thought, the Newleys concluded that they should begin to invest some of their savings in the stock market. How should they go about selecting a broker?
- Having selected a brokerage firm, they now would like to buy stock in a company recommended by one of Evelyn's colleagues. How might they analyze this company?
- The Newleys have heard about such aspects of stock market trading as short selling, buying on margin, and using limit orders. What do they need to know about each of these issues?

equity

Many of these questions do not have single or simple answers, but the first three chapters of this book will provide the basic knowledge to deal with these types of questions.

The Investment Process

Effective financial management inevitably involves some investment-like decisions. We decide how much to spend on current consumption, how much to spend on durable goods like a car or stereo (which will provide long-term value), and how much to save for later. Moreover, most people do periodically put aside some portion of their current income. Investment choices are virtually limitless. Each investment opportunity has advantages and disadvantages. Each investor has a unique set of needs, goals, attitudes, and resources that influence the relative attractiveness and suitability of particular investments.

Investing involves three separate but related processes: selection, implementation, and timing. The investor must decide which investments to buy or sell, how to go about implementing the transactions, and when to make these transactions. This book is designed to help current and prospective investors make each of these decisions.

The Separate Processes of Investing

- Selection: what to buy or sell
- Implementation: how to buy or sell
- Timing: when to buy or sell

CHARACTERISTICS OF INVESTMENTS

Many types of investments are available, each of which has unique features. Indeed, some types of investments have been tailor-made to appeal to specific types of investors. Obviously, investors themselves have a diverse array of interests and characteristics. They range from unsophisticated individual investors with modest resources to huge institutions (banks, mutual funds, insurance companies, and so on) with literally billions of dollars to invest. Individual investors differ in such dimensions as age, wealth level, income level, tax bracket, risk tolerance, financial sophistication, access to commission discounts, ability to spend time researching and managing their investments, need for current income, access to relevant investment information, and ethical and moral attitudes toward particular investments. Institutional investors also differ in some of these dimensions. Accordingly, the different investments will appeal to different investors.

liquid assets

marketable assets

Some assets promise nearly certain rates of return. More risky investments offer higher expected returns. Some investment areas require detailed management, whereas others are virtually trouble free. *Liquid assets* can be quickly converted into cash at little cost or risk, while *marketable assets* can usually be bought and sold in quantity at the current market price. That market price, however, may or may not be an attractive price to the current holder. Some investment areas are open to people with minimal cash to invest, while other areas require large minimum commitments. Some investments finance activities to which many people object, while other investments are more innocuous. Finally, investment income may be subject to a variety of different types of tax treatments, depending upon how the return is generated. Clearly, investments vary in a number of important dimensions.

Return

People invest because they hope—and expect—to earn a satisfactory return on their investment. The expected return on an investment is a key factor in determining its relative attractiveness. Returns generally take two forms: current income and price appreciation. Many investments are structured to yield periodic and relatively dependable income payments (such as dividends, interest, rents, or royalties). Other investments (such as common stock) are structured to provide returns primarily in the form of price appreciation. Many investments offer both current income and expected price appreciation.

Determining an Investment's Overall Return

- Periodic payments: dividends, interest, rents, or royalties
- Changes in market value: capital gains or losses

Although investments are expected to yield a positive return, their actual return may be different from the expected level. Indeed, many investments produce a negative return. The potential difference between expected and actual returns is a function of risk, which we shall address shortly. First, however, we need to explore the definition and computation of returns.

The Holding Period Return

holding period return (HPR)

holding period return relative (HPRR)

The overall profitability of an investment is often expressed in the form of a relatively simple concept called the *holding period return (HPR)*. The HPR relates the profit on an investment directly to its beginning value. A concept called the *holding period return relative (HPRR)* is useful in its own right, as well as being helpful in introducing the HPR. The HPRR is the ratio of the current value of the investment (including any income received during the holding period) divided by its initial cost or value:

HPRR = [Current value of investment + income received]/ Initial value of investment

---

Example: If an investment is purchased for $10, has paid $1 in dividends, and is now worth $20, its HPRR is computed as follows:

$$\text{HPRR} = \frac{\$20 \text{ (current value)} + \$1 \text{ (dividend)}}{\$10 \text{ (initial value)}} = 2.1$$

In other words, this investment is now worth 2.1 times its initial cost.

profit

The HPR is the *profit* for the holding period relative to the initial investment. Mathematically, the HPR is simply the HPRR minus 1. The "1" reflects the initial amount invested. In equation form:

$$\text{HPRR} - 1.00 = \text{HPR} = \text{Holding period profit (or loss)/ Initial value of investment}$$

Example:

Suppose an investment cost $1,000, provided a payment of $100 during the holding period, and was sold for $1,500.

The HPRR and HPR can then be computed as

$$\text{HPRR} = \frac{\$1,500 + \$100}{\$1,000} = 1.6$$
$$\text{HPR} = \text{HPRR} - 1 = 1.6 - 1 = .60, \text{ or } 60\%$$

Alternatively, we could also compute the HPR directly. The total holding period profit would be the sum of the appreciation in value of $500 ($1,500 – $1,000) plus the interim payment of $100. Thus, the total profit would be $600 ($500 + $100). Dividing this sum ($600) by the initial cost ($1,000) gives us:

$$\text{HPR} = \$600/\$1,000 = .60, \text{ or } 60\%$$

expected HPR

When the HPR is measured using expected values, it is referred to as an *expected HPR* or expected return. When it is measured using actual (historical) values, it is referred to as an actual HPR. An HPR computation must always state the period of the computation. To say an investment has an expected HPR of 30 percent is much less meaningful than saying that it has an expected one-year HPR of 30 percent.

Per-Period Return

per-period return (PPR)

A better way to measure returns is to compute the *per-period return (PPR),* where a period represents a standard-length holding period, such as one year. An asset's PPR is defined as the sum of that period's income payments and price appreciation divided by its beginning-of-period market value or price:

$$PPR = \frac{\text{Period's income} + \text{price change}}{\text{Beginning-of-period value}}$$

Computing a single-period return with the PPR formula produces the same value as a one-period return computed by the HPR formula. The two formulas, however, produce different values when the holding period differs from the standard-length holding period. PPRs are generally expressed for standard periods of one year's length. Thus, a one-year PPR is the same as an HPR for a one-year holding period.

Impact of Compounding

Returns are compounded when an investment earns a return for more than one period and the return from each period is added to the initial investment. The investment earns a return on both the initial sum invested and on the returns that accumulate from earlier periods. In other words, compounding reflects the impact of earning a return on both the amount initially invested and the returns that have been earned on the initial investment in prior periods.

$100,000 – Initial Investment
10% Rate
Compounded Annually is $110,000
Compounded Quarterly – take
the 10% and devide by 4 (/4)
t get 2.5% Per Period.

100,000   Quarterly   2   3   4
——————— ———— ———— ——————
102,500   105062   107689   110,381

Compounding Quarterly is a better
deal – The more often you
compound, the better off you are.

Example:

Consider an investment that yields 10 percent per year for 2 years. It earns 10 percent during the first year. At the end of that first year, the investment will show an HPRR of 1.10. Earning another 10 percent during the second year will generate an HPRR of 1.21 for the 2 years. This compound value results from earning 10 percent on the initial principal in the first year, another 10 percent on principal during the second year, and 10 percent on the first year's 10 percent return (.10 x .10 = .01, or 1%). The sum is 10% + 10% + 1% plus the initial investment, or 121 percent of the original amount. A simpler way of making this computation is to take 110 percent of 110 percent (1.10 x 1.10 = 1.21).

We can also work backward from the appreciated value to the interest rate that produced it. Therefore, an investment that, after one year, was worth 110 percent of its initial value is said to have yielded a return of 10 percent. Similarly, an investment that appreciated by 21 percent over a 2-year period is said to have generated a 10 percent annual return compounded annually.

Measuring the Mean Return

mean return

The *mean return* (or average return) often needs to be computed for two different types of circumstances: an investment (single asset or portfolio) over time and a group of investments over the same time. We may, for example, know the PPRs for each year and wish to know the average return for the entire holding period. That is, we might have an investment that earned 10 percent, 7 percent, and 12 percent per year over a 3-year period. Alternatively, we may know the individual returns for the components of a portfolio and wish to compute the portfolio's overall return.

The Per-Period Return of a Portfolio. The per-period return for a portfolio is the arithmetic average of the returns of the individual components, if equal amounts are invested in each component.

Example: Suppose we have a portfolio of five investments that individually had annual returns of 3 percent, 7 percent, 9 percent, 11 percent, and 15 percent. Assume that there is $20,000 invested in each of these five securities.

To compute the per-period return of this five-investment portfolio, we need to add the five separate returns and divide by 5:

$$(3\% + 7\% + 9\% + 11\% + 15\%)/5 = 45\%/5 = 9\%$$

The above example is frequently referred to as an unweighted or equally weighted rate of return.

If different amounts are invested in the various securities, then the portfolio's per-period return is computed as a weighted average.

$$\text{Weighted average} = W_1 \times R_1 + W_2 \times R_2 + \ldots + W_n \times R_n$$

where W_i = percentage of portfolio invested in security i
R_i = the per-period return on security i

Handwritten margin notes:

R
S
T

%
.50 x 10 = 5
.25 x 6 = 1.5
.25 9 = 2.25
.25   8.75%
1.00

Weighted avg.

(This is asset allocation)

This computation is frequently referred to as a weighted average rate of return.

Example: Suppose a portfolio consists of 50 percent of investment R that earned 10 percent, 25 percent of investment S that earned 6 percent, and 25 percent of investment T that earned 9 percent. The portfolio's per-period return would be

$$(.5 \times 10\%) + (.25 \times 6\%) + (.25 \times 9\%) = 8.75\%$$

The Mean Return for a Single Investment. We may also know the returns for a single investment over several periods and wish to compute its mean, or average, return over the entire period. Clearly, if the same per-period return were earned in each period, that PPR would also be the mean return. Frequently, however, the investment will produce different PPRs during different periods. An arithmetic average of these returns can be computed by adding the PPRs and dividing by the number of periods. This average is simple to compute, reasonably useful when the individual returns are similar, but misleading when the individual returns are dissimilar.

Example: An investment that earned successive returns of 7 percent, 7.5 percent, and 8 percent would grow to a compound value equal to 1.24227 times its initial level. The arithmetic average of these three returns is 7.5 percent. Had the investment actually earned 7.5 percent per period for 3 years, its compound value would be 1.24230. Thus, the actual compound value and the value derived from using the *arithmetic mean return* are very similar.

arithmetic mean return

When the individual returns are dissimilar, however, the arithmetic average of returns earned over time can paint an overly optimistic picture. Conceptually, the number reported for the overall return should be one that, if earned every period, would produce the same end-of-period value as has resulted from the separate per-period returns actually earned. The arithmetic mean does not have that property.

Example: To see just how misleading the use of this arithmetic mean can be, consider an investment of $1,000 that doubles in value (to $2,000) in the first period (a return of 100 percent) and then falls to half of its value (to $1,000) during the next period (a return of –50 percent). This investment would have the same value at the end of the second period ($1,000) as it had at the start of the first ($1,000). Most people would agree that an investment with the same beginning and ending value has an HPR of 0 percent over the two periods. Yet if we average +100 percent and –50 percent, we obtain +25 percent.

The Geometric Mean Return use this most of the time since it uses compound interest

geometric mean return

Unlike the arithmetic mean return, the *geometric mean return* (GMR) has the desirable property that an investment that earns its GMR each period will grow to the same end value as it would have from earning the separate returns used to compute that mean. The GMR for N-periods is obtained by first computing the holding period return relatives for each of the N-periods. These N values of HPPRs are all multiplied together and the nth root is calculated. Remember, taking the nth root of a number is the same as taking that number to the 1/n power.

For example, suppose we want to take the fifth root of 7. The calculation is as follows:

$$\sqrt[5]{7} = 7^{1/5} = 7^{.2} = 1.4758$$

On a typical hand-held calculator, we simply input "7," then hit the "y^x" key, then enter ".2." This result minus 1 is the geometric mean return (GMR). Stated as equations:

$$HPRR = HPRR_1 \times HPRR_2 \times \ldots \times HPRR_n$$

where $HPRR_i$ = holding period return relative for period i
$HPRR$ = holding period return relative for the entire N-period

$$GMR = \sqrt[n]{HPRR} - 1$$

(Note: The symbol "$\sqrt[n]{}$" is to be read as "the nth root of . . .")

In the previous example where n = 2:

$$\text{PPR}_1 = 1.00\,(100\%) \text{ and } \text{PPR}_2 = -.50\,(-50\%)$$
$$\text{HPPR}_1 = 2.00 \text{ and } \text{HPPR}_2 = .50$$
$$\text{HPRR} = 2.00 \times .50 = 1.00$$
$$\text{GMR} = \sqrt[2]{1.00} - 1.00 = 1.00 - 1.00 = 0\%$$

This is exactly the result that we would expect for an investment that doubled its value in the first period, then lost half of its value in the second period. Thus, a 0 percent return is consistent with our expectations.

***Example*:** Now let us consider a more complicated example. Suppose we want to determine the GMR for an investment that generated annual returns of 13 percent, 17 percent, 2 percent, 8 percent, and 10 percent. We could start the search by computing its HPRR based on its PPRs:

$$\text{HPRR} = 1.13 \times 1.17 \times 1.02 \times 1.08 \times 1.10 = 1.6021$$

To find the GMR we must take the nth root of the HPRR. In this instance n is 5:

$$\text{GMR} = \sqrt[5]{1.6021} - 1.00 = 1.0988 - 1.00 = .0988,$$
$$\text{or } 9.88\%$$

The arithmetic mean is

$$(13\% + 17\% + 2\% + 8\% + 10\%)/5 = 10\%$$

Note that in this relatively straightforward case the arithmetic mean is a reasonable approximation of the geometric mean.

There are three points to remember about the relationship between the GMR and the arithmetic mean return. First, only when *all* the PPRs are identical will they be equal. Second, if the PPRs are not identical, then the GMR will always be less than the arithmetic mean return. Third, this difference increases as the variability among the PPRs increases.

Compounding Interest within a Period

In a previous section, we discussed the effect of compounding over multiple time periods. Let us now consider the effect of compounding interest multiple times *per* period. When interest is compounded multiple times per period, it creates a distinction between what is known as the **nominal** (or stated) **interest rate** and the **effective annual rate.** The effective annual rate is the true annual interest rate in a problem.

The concept we use in computing an effective annual interest rate requires us to break down the period of one year into the number of periods that interest is compounded. We then determine the compounding effect of these multiple periods. The formula for this is

$$r_{eair} = \left(1 + \frac{r_{nom}}{m}\right)^m - 1$$

where r_{eair} = effective annual interest rate

r_{nom} = stated nominal annual interest rate

m = number of times per year compounding occurs

As an example, you look at your credit card statement and note that the interest rate is 18 percent. As the interest on credit cards is charged each month on the unpaid balance, the interest is compounded monthly, or 12 times per year. The effective annual rate would then be computed as

$$r_{eair} = \left(1 + .18/12\right)^{12} - 1 = 1.015^{12} - 1 = .1956, \text{ or } 19.56\%$$

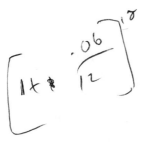

Example: You are considering two different banks for your savings account. The first bank pays 4 percent compounded daily, and the second bank pays 4 1/4 percent compounded annually. Which bank offers the higher effective annual rate?

For the bank that pays interest compounded annually, no adjustment is necessary. Any interest rate compounded annually is automatically stated as an effective annual rate. To adjust the interest rate that is compounded daily, we start by noting that daily compounding means 365 times per year. We can thus compute the effective annual rate for the first bank as

$$r_{eair} = (1 + .04/365)^{365} - 1 = .0408 \text{ or } 4.08\%$$

This makes it clear that the bank offering 4 and 1/4 percent compounded annually has a much better deal in terms of the interest rate paid.

Risk

In popular usage, the term risk refers to the probability of some undesirable event. Thus, a risky investment is one that might produce a return that is less than expected. Investors may talk of the downside risk (that an investment's return will be less than anticipated), perhaps coupled with the upside potential (that the return will exceed expectations). No doubt such statements convey information.

The element of risk that troubles investors is the possibility of downside fluctuations in value and return. Yet using the term risk in this way is imprecise. What units are used to measure the amount of risk? How is the risk of one investment compared with another?

pure risk
speculative risk

To help clarify the meaning of risk, we can begin by classifying risk as either *pure risk* or *speculative risk*. Pure risks involve only the chance of loss or no loss, whereas speculative risks involve the chance of loss, no loss, or gain. Pure risks are "pure" in the sense that they do not mix both profits and losses. Insurance is concerned mainly with the economic problems created by pure risks. This text deals primarily with speculative risks, which involve an element of both profit and loss.

risk

The common terminology in finance and economics is that *risk* refers to the dispersion of potential variation in possible returns. Thus, we relate risk to the likelihood that realized returns will differ from those that were expected. An asset with a wide range of possible returns is considered risky, while an asset with a narrow range of potential returns is considered more secure.

For example, an asset that could easily double its value or become worthless in a year would be viewed as quite risky. On the other hand, a one-year U.S. government bond with a 5 percent yield would be viewed as having practically no risk. A person who holds the government bond until it matures is virtually certain of receiving the promised yield.

expected return

The range of returns is generally measured in terms of the distance or dispersion from the mean or expected (per-period) return. An asset's *expected return* is the average of its possible returns weighted by their respective likelihoods. Thus, the probabilities of below-expectation and above-expectation returns balance out. The actual yields of risky assets almost always differ from the market's expectations. The owner of a (relatively risky) asset whose return is expected to be between 2 percent and 18 percent bears the "risk" that the actual return could be anywhere within this range. The investor who owns a (relatively secure) asset with a 99+ percent probability of earning exactly 7.5 percent has little risk about which to be concerned. Simply stated, risk refers to the magnitude of the range of possible returns.

Risk-Expected Return Trade-off

Some people thrive on speculative risk. They love to gamble even when they know the odds are heavily against them. Most, however, prefer to limit their exposure to unpleasant surprises. The profitability and success of the insurance industry illustrate the demand for risk reduction.

There is also a risk-expected return trade-off for investors. Most investors are willing to sacrifice some potential return if they can thereby obtain a sufficiently large reduction in risk. Accordingly, to be salable, risky assets must offer a high enough expected return to offset their risk. Thus, corporate bonds, having some risk of default, yield a higher return than otherwise similar U.S. government bonds. Likeswise, higher-risk corporate bonds provide a higher expected return than otherwise similar low-risk corporate bonds. When an investment offers too low an expected return to justify its risk, the asset's price will fall until the market views its risk to be in line with its expected return.

Liquidity

liquidity

Liquidity is the ability to quickly convert an asset to cash with little or no uncertainty as to value. The most liquid of assets is cash (paper money, checking account balances, and coins). Other types of liquid assets are close to cash—bank certificates of deposit (CDs) and Treasury bills—but cannot be spent in their present form. A department store or gas station may accept currency, checks, or credit cards but will not let someone pay for a purchase with a CD or Treasury bill. These assets can, however, be readily converted to spendable form with relatively little sacrifice for the investor. That is, the owner who wishes to sell the asset to obtain immediately spendable cash can do so at little or no cost, inconvenience, or danger of receiving less than the

---

Other Types of Investment Risks

(It is important to consider all risks in investment analysis. The following risks are present to some degree in every monetary investment.)

- Loss-of-principal risk: the risk of losing the initial investment
- Loss-of-income risk: the risk that the investment may not provide the income anticipated
- Timing risk: the possibility of getting into or out of an investment at a disadvantageous time
- Marketability risk: the possibility of being unable to convert an investment to cash when needed
- Interest rate risk: the risk associated with changes in the interest rate

sum of the purchase price and accrued interest. These "investments" are immediately redeemable or, at most, require a minimum amount of effort to make them so. Bonds with short maturities or the right to be redeemed upon demand are also quite liquid because of the high degree of certainty as to price. The more distant the redemption date (that is, the longer until its maturity), the less liquid the investment is considered to be because of the greater uncertainty as to price.

Marketability

marketability

Marketability refers to the ease of (buying or) selling an asset for its market value. The market value of an investment is the price that a willing buyer and willing seller would reach if neither were under immediate pressure to trade. Investments differ substantially in their degree of marketability. Shares in large firms like Exxon or General Motors are highly marketable. They trade nearly continuously at prices that vary little from transaction to transaction. Assets that are exchanged in active high-volume markets generally sell at or close to the current market price.

The advantage of marketable assets is that they will sell easily for their market prices, whatever those prices might be at the time. These market prices, however, may or may not yield an acceptable return for the investor. Investments with poor marketability present their owners with another kind of problem: They are difficult and costly to sell.

Example: Difficult-to-market assets such as a house, rare painting, or certain one-of-a-kind investments appear on the market rather infrequently. Potential buyers of such investments are relatively scarce. Sellers must either be patient or be willing to trade at a substantial discount from the theoretical market value. Suppose the owner of a house that should sell for $200,000 (according to current conditions in the local real estate market) needs a lot of cash in a hurry. He or she might have to accept a sacrifice price of $150,000 to make a quick sale. To obtain a reasonable price (fair to the seller), the seller would need to be prepared for a potentially significant wait for the right customer to come along.

All liquid assets are marketable because marketability is a component of liquidity. But not all marketable assets are liquid. A widely held stock can generally be sold for the current market price (marketable), but that price will vary from day to day. Note that the term "liquid" is often used interchangeably with "marketable" in the press. Thus, a stock that is referred to as liquid is one for which an active competitive market exists.

Investment Effort

Selecting and managing some types of portfolios require little or no special knowledge, facilities, or time commitment. For instance, the investor need not be an expert on short-term debt securities to understand the relevant characteristics (risk, expected return, liquidity, marketability, and tax treatment) of Treasury bills and similar securities. Moreover, the certificates of ownership can be conveniently held by a brokerage firm or in a safe deposit box. Those who invest in other assets, such as real estate, collectibles, soybean futures, or mink farms need special knowledge, talent, and/or facilities. Similarly, some types of assets may be maintained with little or no effort (bonds), whereas others require constant management (an apartment complex). Accordingly, would-be investors need to carefully consider the expertise, talent, facilities, and time required to assemble and manage the particular type of investment portfolio effectively.

Minimum Investment Size

Portfolios of some types of investments may be assembled with small sums, whereas others require a much larger minimum commitment. Moreover, some investments have such low risk that a portfolio consisting of a single asset is an appropriate holding. For instance, a savings account can be opened for as little as $100 and some higher-yielding bank certificates are available in $500 denominations. Most mutual funds will accept initial deposits of $1,000. Indeed, mutual funds offer an attractive way for small investors to participate in the stock and bond market with relatively small sums of money. Many collectibles sell for a few hundred dollars or less. On the other hand, several thousand dollars are generally needed to purchase a single stock or bond position efficiently. Such a holding, however, would be very much at the mercy of the market for that particular stock or bond. A reasonably well-diversified stock or bond portfolio would require several times as much of an initial investment. Later in this text we will discuss the use of mutual funds and other investment company products that allow for well-diversified stock and bond portfolios at low cost. A single real estate purchase (to say nothing of a diversified real estate portfolio) is likely to require at least several thousand dollars (or more likely several tens of thousands of dollars) for just the down payment. Similarly, most brokers will not accept commodity accounts having less than $20,000 to $50,000 in investor capital.

Obviously, the capital requirements of different types of investments differ appreciably. Those beginning with relatively small sums are restricted to investments that are available in modest size units. Over time, however, investors may be able to shift into investments that are traded only in larger increments. For instance, a beginning investor may start with a savings account and then move into certificates of deposit. Later, he or she may buy into a mutual fund and still later begin assembling a portfolio of stocks and/or buy some rental property.

Ethical and Moral Appeal

Investments may also differ substantially in their ethical and moral appeal, particularly to certain groups of investors. Many investors take the attitude that if an activity is legal, it is a proper area in which to seek investment profits. Other investors, however, want their investment dollars associated only with activities of which they personally approve. What is socially unacceptable for some, however, is not socially unacceptable for others. Social responsibility is largely in the eye of the beholder. No doubt many investors would draw the line at pornography and prostitution even where they are allowed by the law. Others would refuse to become slumlords even if all health and safety codes are adhered to and the profit potential is substantial. Still others would object to investments in companies involved with one or more of the following types of products or activities: alcohol, tobacco, armaments, war toys, major pollutants, nonunionized employees, unionized employees, child labor, misleading advertising, and poor safety records.

TAX TREATMENT OF INDIVIDUALS

Investors are able to retain only the after-tax component of their returns. The after-tax return of an investment is similar to a worker's take-home pay. It is the part of the return available to the investor after various governments take their cut. Because not all types of investment income are taxed equivalently, tax considerations are an important factor in deciding which investments to purchase. The tax treatment of an investment is particularly relevant for investors in high tax brackets. To understand how investment income is taxed, we need to examine our tax system's basic makeup.

The individual federal tax return on Form 1040 has a relatively complex structure. First, income from wages, salaries, and most other sources (including investment income) is added to compute gross income. (Certain items of income, such as municipal bond interest, are excluded because they are tax free at the federal level.) Gross income is then reduced by certain adjustments, such as alimony paid by the taxpayer, to arrive at adjusted gross income (AGI). AGI is then reduced by personal exemptions ($3,000 per exemption in 2002) and either itemized deductions or the standard deduction. **taxable income** The result of this series of calculations is called *taxable income*. This sum is the amount on which tax liability is based. The actual tax liability incurred depends on both the individual's taxable income and filing status (joint, individual, head of household, and so forth). The computation uses a schedule such as that of table 1-1, which shows the relevant figures for married individuals filing jointly and for unmarried individuals.

TABLE 1-1
Individual Tax Rate Schedules for 2002

Filing Status	If Taxable Income Is	The Tax Is
Married individuals filing joint returns	Not over $46,700 Over $46,700 but not over $112,850 Over $112,850 but not over $171,950 Over $171,950 but not over $307,050 Over $307,050	15% of the taxable income $6,405 plus 27% of the excess over $46,700 $24,265 plus 30% of the excess over $112,850 $41,995.50 plus 35% of the excess over $171,950 $89,280.50 plus 38.6% of the excess over $307,050
Unmarried individuals	Not over $27,950 Over $27,950 but not over $67,700 Over $67,700 but not over $141,250 Over $141,250 but not over $307,050 Over $307,050	15% of the taxable income $3,892.50 plus 27% of the excess over $27,950 $14,625 plus 30% of the excess over $67,700 $36,690 plus 35% of the excess over $141,250 $94,720 plus 38.6% of the excess over $307,050

Itemizing deductions is advantageous to the taxpayer if the deductions exceed the standard deduction. Deductions are allowed for charitable contributions, certain employee business expenses (above a threshold), some types of interest payments, unreimbursed medical expenses (above a threshold), and casualty and theft losses (above a threshold), as well as most state and local income and property taxes (but not sales taxes). At higher income levels, the tax shelter that itemized deductions as well as personal and dependency exemptions provides begins to be reduced, thereby effectively raising the marginal tax rate at these income levels.

Taxation of Extra Income

Additions to total income almost always increase taxable income. Moreover, for taxpayers in all but the 15 percent tax bracket, extra taxable income is taxed at a marginal rate that is higher than the average rate.

An individual's taxable income results from adding investment income to other forms of income (after subtracting appropriate adjustments and deductions). We normally view investment income as the last increment of income. If the investment income had not been received, total income would have been less by that amount. Taxes would then be reduced by the amount of the investment income not received multiplied by the tax rate on that incremental income. The last increment of income is taxed at the marginal rate. Therefore, the marginal rate is the relevant rate to use in assessing the tax implications of most investment decisions.

Example: Jan Q. Investor's $70,000-per-year income is the sole support for her family of four. The three dependents (including her husband) and her personal exemption permit her to exclude $12,000, while the standard deduction for married couples filing jointly of $7,850 reduces her taxable income to $50,150. Table 1-1 shows that joint filers (Jan and her husband file jointly) with taxable incomes between $46,700 and $112,850 pay (2002 rates) $6,405 plus 27 percent of the excess over $46,700. This formula yields a tax liability of $8,686.50 ($6,405 + $2,281.50). Any additional income would be taxed at the marginal tax rate of 27 percent. If Mrs. Investor's income increased by $1,000 to $71,000 without changing deductions, her taxable income would increase by $1,000 to $51,150, and her tax would rise by $270, or 27 percent of the $1,000 income increase.

average tax rate   In the above example, we can compute Mrs. Investor's *average tax rate.* It is initially 17.32 percent ($8.686.50/$50,150) before the increase in income, and 17.85 percent after the increase in income. However, the average tax rate is a meaningless number for decision-making purposes.

Different tax brackets apply to the various filing statuses. For example, single filers reach the higher tax brackets at lower levels of income than joint filers do. Although Congress may change the tax rates from time to time, each investor's marginal rate (whatever its current level) remains the relevant rate for investment decisions.

While tax laws are frequently revised, most revisions are relatively minor, although some have resulted in substantial changes. The possibility of tax law changes increases both the complexity and the desirability of tax planning. Serious investors need to stay abreast of the current tax laws. Investors may well want to change their strategies and adjust their portfolios in light of tax law changes or even in light of expected changes.

Taxation of Investment Income

Whether, and if so how, the income from an investment is taxed has a major impact on the net return that the investor receives. Interest income on savings accounts, corporate bonds, and U.S. government bonds is taxed as ordinary income (that is, like wages and salaries), whereas state and local (municipal) government bond interest is (with a few exceptions) untaxed at the federal level. Capital gains on municipal bonds, however, are subject to capital gains tax. After any relevant expenses are deducted, rents, royalties, and most dividends are fully taxed like income from wages and salaries.

capital distributions

Sometimes corporations will provide payments to their stockholders that look like dividends but are actually *capital distributions*. A capital distribution is a return *of* investment (and is technically paid from the sale of assets), and a dividend is a return *on* investment (and is technically paid from profits).

Capital Gains and Losses

capital gains and losses

Capital gains and losses arise whenever capital assets (essentially, any assets such as stocks or bonds that are held for investment purposes) are bought and sold for different amounts. Normally, the taxable gain equals the sale price (minus commission) less the purchase price (plus commission).

cost basis

The purchase price and its associated commission are referred to as the *cost basis*. Any capital distributions must, however, be subtracted from the purchase price to determine the basis.

Example: Suppose 100 shares of the BDC Company are purchased for $25 per share and sold for $35 per share. The taxable gain (ignoring commissions) would normally be $1,000 ($3,500 – $2,500). Prior capital distributions of $500 would, however, reduce the cost basis from $2,500 to $2,000. Such distributions would have the effect of increasing the taxable gain to $1,500 ($3,500 – $2,000).

Capital gains and losses are subject to rather complicated tax treatment. The basic rule is that short-term gains (gains on assets sold after being held one year or less) are taxed as ordinary income, whereas long-term gains (gains on assets sold after being held for more than a year) are subject to a tax rate of 10 or 20 percent, depending on one's marginal tax rate. The long-term capital gains tax rate is 10 percent if one's marginal tax rate is 15 percent; otherwise it is 20 percent. Unrealized gains (appreciation on assets that have not yet been sold) are not subject to tax. Gains become taxable only if and when they are realized, which would normally occur only if the underlying asset is sold.

Taxes are applied to the net gain. A taxpayer who has some capital losses may deduct the losses from any gains on other transactions to arrive at the net gain or loss. A separate net figure is computed for both short- and long-term gains or losses.

If both short- and long-term gains are positive, the taxpayer is taxed at his or her ordinary income tax rate on the short-term gains and at the 10 or 20 percent rate on the long-term gains.

Things get more complicated if the taxpayer has net losses for either the short or long term. If either short- or long-term transactions result in a net loss figure, that amount is netted against the opposite gain. That is, short-term losses are subtracted from long-term gains, or long-term losses are subtracted from short-term gains. If this overall net number shows a gain, it is subject to tax based on its term. If the net gain is short term, it is taxed as ordinary income, and if it is long term, the 10 or 20 percent rate applies.

If the overall net number shows a loss or if there are only short-term and long-term losses, the taxpayer may use these losses to offset ordinary income. Generally, up to $3,000 of capital losses may be deducted from ordinary income (married, filing separately taxpayers are limited to $1,500) in any one year. If the net capital loss is greater than $3,000, the excess must be carried forward and used to offset capital gains and/or ordinary income in subsequent years.

Note that the law on the taxation of capital gains has been changed frequently in the past. At different times long-term capital gains have been fully taxed, taxed at half the ordinary rate, and subject to a 6-month or 18-month (as opposed to 12-month) holding period.

The Alternative Minimum Tax

Individuals with large amounts of tax-sheltered income (accelerated depreciation, for example) or high itemized deductions may be subject to the alternative minimum tax (AMT). To determine whether the AMT applies, tax liability is first computed in the regular way. Then all of the includible tax-sheltered items are added back to adjusted gross income, and certain allowable deductions are subtracted to obtain the income subject to the AMT. The AMT tax equals 26 percent (or 28 percent of the taxable amount exceeding $175,000) of this sum. The individual's tax liabilities computed for the two different ways (regular and AMT) are then compared. The higher of the two tax figures is the one that must be paid. In other words, the AMT can raise but cannot lower an individual's tax liability.

State and Local Taxes

The interest income on U.S. Treasury issues is exempt from state and local income taxes. Interest income from state and local bonds is not taxed within the state that issues them. In contrast, the interest income on those bonds issued by other jurisdictions is fully taxed in the owner's own state and local residence jurisdiction.

Tax Treatment Summary

The taxation of the four basic types of investment income for federal tax purposes is as follows:

- Capital distributions on stock and the interest on state and local government bonds are tax free.
- Unrealized capital gains are untaxed.
- Dividend and nonmunicipal bond interest income, net rents, royalties, other investment income, and short-term capital gains are taxed at ordinary tax rates.
- Long-term capital gains are taxed at 10 or 20 percent.

Table 1-2 summarizes these tax categories.

Implications of Investment Tax Treatment

Investments that offer a tax-free or tax-sheltered return are priced to offer a lower before-tax return than otherwise equivalent investments whose returns are fully taxed. Thus, for example, the before-tax yields of tax-free bonds are well below otherwise equivalent (in terms of risk) taxable bond

TABLE 1-2
Tax Treatment of Investment Income

Capital distributions on stock Interest on state and local (municipal) bonds	Not subject to federal income tax
Unrealized capital gains	Tax deferred until realized
Dividend and interest income (other than municipal bond interest) Rents, royalties, and any other investment income payments Short-term capital gains and short-term capital gain distributions (from mutual funds) Payments from deferred income plans, 401(k) plans, IRAs, and so forth	Taxed at ordinary income tax rate
Long-term capital gains and long-term capital gain distributions (from mutual funds)	10% or 20%

holding it for more than 1 year

returns. A lower tax-free return may or may not be more attractive than a higher taxable return for a particular investor. Which investment offers the highest after-tax return depends on both the level of the two pre-tax returns and on the investor's tax bracket.

The market-determined trade-off between fully taxed and tax-deferred income reflects the average tax impact on the relevant investors. Different investors, however, face different tax rates. Some investors (for example, nonprofit charities and college endowment funds) do not incur taxes on their investment income, while others pay taxes at various marginal rates (15 percent, 27 percent, 30 percent, 35 percent, and 38.6 percent at the federal level). A fully taxable return of 10 percent might be equivalent to an after-tax return of 8.5 percent, 7.3 percent, 7.0 percent, 6.5 percent, or 6.2 percent, depending on the investor's tax bracket. State and local income tax rates further complicate the after-tax cash flow comparisons, as does the AMT and the phaseout of exemptions for higher-income taxpayers. Thus, the after-tax return on a given investment depends, among other things, on the particular investor's tax bracket.

tax equivalent yield

In general, for an investor with a marginal tax rate of T, the *tax equivalent yield* on a tax-exempt bond paying a coupon of C can be expressed as follows:

Handwritten marginalia:

What this says is:

I have to earn 10% to earn what a 7% taxable investment would give me.

Ex:

$$\frac{7}{1-.30} = \frac{7}{.70} = 10\%$$

$$TE = \frac{Y}{1 - T}$$

Handwritten marginalia: Compare municipal Bond with a taxable Bond or CD.

where   TE = tax equivalent yield

T   = investor's marginal tax rate

Y   = tax-exempt municipal yield

Table 1-3 shows the fully taxable yield that is necessary to produce a 10 percent after-tax return (2002 rates).

TABLE 1-3
Tax Equivalent Yield Equating to 10% Tax-Exempt Yield
(Joint Return, 2002 Rates)

Taxable Income (Married Filing Jointly)	Marginal Tax Rate	Tax Equivalent Yield
$0–$46,700	15%	11.8%
$46,700–112,850	27%	13.7%
$112,850–$171,950	30%	14.3%
$171,950–$305,050	35%	15.4%
Over $305,050	38.6%	16.1%

PSYCHOLOGICAL ASPECTS OF INVESTING

Investors need to take account of their own psychological tendencies. Otherwise, such factors may unduly influence their decisions. Investors are subject to all of the shortcomings and biases inherent in human judgment. Individuals who evaluate their own biases and tendencies may be better able to control and perhaps offset those that could otherwise lead them astray.

Example: A tendency to invest impulsively could cause the investor to trade too frequently. Overly active trading may be profitable to the broker (in commissions) but is usually rather costly for the investor. This tendency might be reduced if the investor could agree to take a day to think over each trade. That approach would allow for a cooling-off period to rethink the decision.

Paul Slovic and his coworkers at the Oregon Research Institute have studied human judgment biases and their impacts on investor decisions. His classic work, "Psychological Study of Human Judgment: Implications for Investment Decision Making," synthesizes the investment implications of a number of psychological studies.[1] For example, Slovic observes that the human mind frequently makes random judgmental errors. This trait may be dealt with by programming individual decision processes. The decision maker would use mathematical models of the considerations, weights, and estimates to check the logic of the decision. Random human error can cause the unprogrammed approach to yield different results from the programmed approach. The programmed result may or may not be superior to the unprogrammed one, but knowledge of the differences is generally helpful.

Slovic also reports that people usually react to new information by revising their opinions in the correct direction but more conservatively than is warranted by the new information. On the other hand, people tend to extrapolate from a small nonrandom sample to an unsupportable generalization.

Complex decisions may be divided into a series of smaller decisions, combining the judgments on each decision into a solution for the initial major problem. Systematic biases in the smaller decisions, however, may lead to a biased decision on the larger question.

Note that systematic biases are different from random errors. For example, suppose that an investor can interpret new information in an overly optimistic, overly pessimistic, or accurate manner. Someone who makes random errors will be sometimes overly optimistic and sometimes overly pessimistic, but on average will interpret new information accurately. An investor with systematic biases, however, will have either an overly optimistic or an overly pessimistic interpretation of events most of the time. This distinction will be important to remember later when the efficient market hypothesis is discussed.

Selective recall is one typical human bias. People remember some events more easily than others. People also tend to see patterns where none exist and to attribute a result to a particular cause even when there is no real correlation. The claimed success of many investment chartists may be due to such tendencies. Another common fallacy is to attach undue importance to recent events, relative to other events that occurred in the more distant past but are relevant nonetheless.

Individuals also sometimes respond differently to the same question if it is asked in different ways. For example, an individual might simultaneously predict a 10 percent increase and a $5 price rise on a $40 stock (10 percent of $40 is $4, not $5). Questions, therefore, should be structured to elicit the most accurate approach to answering them. If available data are in percentages, for example, a question asked in terms of percentage may elicit a more reliable response.

Apparently, the degree of risk aversion is not a universally generalizable characteristic. People may be quite risk averse in their investment decisions but much less so in their driving, or vice versa. Moreover, decisions made by a group tend to be riskier than individual decisions. Finally, many people tend to overrate the reliability of their own judgments. Others, however, tend to follow the herd and seem to have little confidence in their own judgment.

SUMMARY AND CONCLUSIONS

The expected return and its associated risk are key factors in most investment decisions. Other relevant characteristics include liquidity (the ease of converting the asset into cash with little or no loss in value), marketability (the ability to trade at the current price), effort (the time and expertise required of a serious investor), capital requirements (the minimum sum needed to purchase one unit and/or a diversified portfolio), appeal to socially responsible investors, and tax treatment.

Investments differ appreciably in the way that they are taxed. Some investment returns, such as municipal bond interest and capital distributions, are not taxed. Most other types of investment income are fully taxed. Long-term capital gains are taxed at lower rates than ordinary income.

CHAPTER REVIEW

Answers to the review questions and the self-test questions start on page 501.

Key Terms

equity	geometric mean return
liquid assets	pure risk
marketable assets	speculative risk
risk	risk
holding period return (HPR)	expected return
	liquidity
holding period return relative (HPRR)	marketability
	taxable income
profit	average tax rate
expected HPR	capital distributions
per-period return (PPR)	capital gains and losses
mean return	cost basis
arithmetic mean return	tax equivalent yield

Review Questions

1-1. Describe what is meant by return and risk.

1-2. Explain the various return concepts, including holding period return relative (HPRR), holding period return (HPR), per-period return (PPR), annualized return, compound interest, arithmetic mean return (AMR), and geometric mean return (GMR).

1-3. Compute the HPRR and HPR for each of the following:
   a. an investment in land purchased for $5,000 and sold for $7,000
   b. a $3,000 noninterest-bearing note purchased for $1,800 and held until maturity, at which time it is paid off at its face value
   c. a building that is held for 9 months, during which time it generates $3,500 in rental income (in excess of costs), and then sold for a $30,000 profit. Its original purchase price was $195,000.

1-4. Compute the annual return for each of the following investments:
   a. an investment in 100 shares of stock that cost $10 per share, sold one year later for $11 per share, during which time a 30-cent-per-share dividend is received. Ignore commissions in your computations.
   b. a $1,000 one-year CD with a stated yield of 7 percent compounded quarterly
   c. a long-term bond purchased for $890 and sold a year later for $850. The bond pays a coupon of 8 percent on its $1,000 face value. The first coupon (one-half of the annual rate) is payable in the middle of the one-year holding period.

1-5. Compute the appreciated value of an investment held for 2 years with 10 percent return compounded annually, semiannually, quarterly, and monthly.

1-6. a. Compute the AMR of a portfolio that consists of equal amounts invested in assets yielding returns of 7.8 percent, 9.3 percent, 4.5 percent, and 11.5 percent, respectively.
   b. Now suppose the amounts invested (in a. above) are in the proportions of .2, .3, .4, and .1. What would this portfolio's PPR be?

1-7. a. Compute the GMR for an investment with the following per-period returns: 5.6 percent, –8.9 percent, 10.0 percent, 7.7 percent, and 13.0 percent.
   b. Compare the result (in a. above) with the AMR.

1-8. a. Explain what is meant by the risk-return trade-off.
   b. Does the risk-return trade-off imply that all risky investments offer high returns? Explain.

(Handwritten margin notes:)

$.08 \times 1000 = 80 / 2 = \$40$

$\frac{890}{1000} \approx 8.9 \approx 9\%$

$40 \times 1.09 = \frac{43.60}{40.00}$ $\frac{3.60}{360} \div 2 = \$1.80$

40 interest
40 interest
1.80 interest from compound of first $40
$1.80 first $40

$\frac{81.80 + 850}{890} = \frac{931.80}{890} = 1.0469$

$1.0469 - 1 = \boxed{.0469}$ answer

1-9. a. Define and compare liquidity and marketability.
      b. Are liquid investments always marketable; are marketable investments always liquid? Explain.

1-10. Explain what is meant by investment effort. Give specific examples.

1-11. Describe the roles of minimum investment size and ethical and moral appeal in investment selection and portfolio management.

1-12. Explain the various ways in which investment income may be taxed at the federal level.

Self-Test Questions

T   F   1-1. Investing involves three separate but related processes: selection, implementation, and timing.

T   F   1-2. Marketable assets can be quickly converted into cash at little cost or risk.

T   F   1-3. The holding period return (HPR) relates the profit on an investment directly to its beginning value.

T   F   1-4. An asset's per-period return (PPR) is defined as the sum of that period's income payments and price appreciation minus its beginning-of-period price.

T   F   1-5. Accumulating returns over time and earning a return on the return of prior periods is called compounding.

T   F   1-6. In finance and economics, the term risk refers to the dispersion of possible returns.

T   F   1-7. Insurance companies are in the business of selling protection from speculative risk.

T   F   1-8. Long-term debt securities are considered to be very liquid.

T   F   1-9. The tax treatment of an investment is particularly relevant for investors in high tax brackets.

T   F   1-10. Itemizing deductions is advantageous to the taxpayer if allowable deductions fall below the standard deduction.

T   F   1-11. Deductions are allowed for sales taxes.

T   F   1-12. The last increment of income is always taxed at the marginal rate.

T   F   1-13. The marginal rate of taxation is the relevant rate to use in assessing most investment decisions.

T   F   1-14. State and local government bond interest for residents of that state is usually taxed as ordinary income.

T   F   1-15. The basic rule is that short-term capital gains are taxed at a maximum tax rate of 20 percent.

T   F   1-16. If a taxpayer is in the 15 percent tax bracket on total taxable income, then long-term gains would be taxed at a 10 percent rate.

T   F   1-17. Individuals with large amounts of tax-sheltered income or high itemized deductions may be subject to the alternative minimum tax (AMT).

T   F   1-18. The lower of the regular tax or the AMT is the tax amount that a taxpayer must pay.

T   F   1-19. People may be very risk averse in their investment decisions but much less so in their driving, or vice versa.

NOTE

1. P. Slovic, "Psychological Study of Human Judgment: Implications for Investment Decision Making," *Journal of Finance*, September 1972, pp. 779–799.

Types of Investments

Learning Objectives

An understanding of the material in this chapter should enable the student to

2-1.   Describe nonmarketable and marketable short-term debt investments.

2-2.   Describe the various types of bonds.

2-3.   Describe the various types of equity securities.

2-4.   Describe the differences between calls, puts, warrants, rights, and futures contracts.

2-5.   Identify other investment types, including real estate, collectors' items, and nontraditional investments.

Chapter Outline

The preceding chapter laid the necessary groundwork so that we can now effectively explore some of the more important types of investments. This chapter discusses investments in three categories: debt securities, equity investments, and less common investments including real estate, commodities, collectors' items, and nontraditional investments. The chapter is designed as an overview. A more detailed discussion of many of these investments is presented later in the book.

DEBT INSTRUMENTS

Many of us are introduced to the concept of investing when a savings account is opened in our name. Such an account is a debt instrument, basically an IOU. The bank (or other type of financial institution) holding the account is in debt to the depositor for the balance in the account. The provisions of a savings account illustrate the nature of a debt instrument. The borrower and lender enter into a legally enforceable contract. The lender agrees to provide the borrower with a sum of money for a period of time. The borrower agrees to pay interest at a prespecified rate and repay principal (amount borrowed) according to the terms of the debt instrument. Failure of the borrower to fulfill any of the contract's provisions (such as missing a scheduled interest or principal payment) constitutes a default. If the default itself is not cured, the lender may take appropriate legal action. This action may eventually result in a seizure of assets (collateral), bankruptcy, and/or liquidation of the borrower's assets.

Equity investments, by contrast, involve a share of ownership in an asset. The holder of an equity instrument (such as stock) has no more than a residual claim on the property of the instrument's issuer. The claims of the issuer's creditors have priority over those of the equity holders. On the other hand, the equity holders own all of the firm's value in excess of the creditors' claims. (Creditors in this context include employees, suppliers of raw materials, the IRS, and the electric company, as well as lenders).

Short-Term Debt Securities

maturity

Debt securities are classified in several different ways. The most common is according to the length of time until the creditor must be paid back (time until *maturity*). Securities that mature within a year are classified as short term. One of the most popular of these types of investments is the savings account offered by banks and thrift institutions.

depository institution

Savings accounts offered by any *depository institution* are both liquid and safe. A depository institution is one that accepts deposits of any sort, and the term usually refers to banks, mutual savings banks, savings and loan institutions, and credit unions. Funds can normally be deposited into or withdrawn from a savings account at any time, and most accounts are insured up to a maximum of $100,000 by the Federal Deposit Insurance Corporation *(FDIC)*. Accordingly, depositors need not spend any time shopping around for a "safe" bank or thrift. Rather, they should focus on convenience, service, and rate of return. Savings institutions have generally paid similar rates, although credit unions usually offer a slightly higher rate.

FDIC

certificates of deposit (CDs)

Most depository institutions also issue debt instruments called *certificates of deposit (CDs)*. CDs are typically offered with maturities varying from 30 days to 10 years. There is enough variation in CD rates to make shopping around a worthwhile activity. Like savings accounts, CDs are insured up to $100,000. Some CDs have minimum deposit amounts that range up to $10,000.

**Short-Term Debt Securities
(Available to Small Investors)**

- Deposits in banks and thrift institutions
- Money market mutual funds
- Money market accounts
- U.S. savings bonds

---

money market mutual fund

Yet another type of short-term marketable debt instrument available to an investor is the *money market mutual fund*. Money market mutual funds are designed to serve small investors who want to invest in money market funds but cannot afford the large minimum denominations of many money market instruments. Money market mutual funds pool the resources of many individual small investors to invest in the high-denomination money market securities that would otherwise be unavailable to these investors. Thus, money market funds assemble a diversified portfolio of money market instruments. They then package these portfolios into a form that allows small investors to participate.

After subtracting administrative expenses, money market funds yield slightly less than the rates on the money market instruments themselves. If, for example, money market returns are averaging 6 percent, a $1,000 money market fund account might earn about 5.75 percent. Money market fund deposits are readily accessible by check or wire transfer. Because most money market funds buy only high-quality short-term securities (that is, money market instruments), they are considered quite safe.

The saving accounts and CDs described above are known as nonmarketable securities in the sense that an investor cannot sell these to someone else. They can only be redeemed. There are two other nonmarketable investments that people with minimum cash might consider. The first is the money market deposit account (MMDA) offered by banks. MMDAs were created to allow banks to compete directly with money market mutual funds. The rates MMDAs pay are usually below those offered by money market funds, and these accounts typically require a $1,000 minimum balance and allow six withdrawals (three by check) per month. They are, however, protected by FDIC insurance (up to the $100,000 maximum).

savings bond

The other nonmarketable investment is the U.S. government *savings bond*. The savings bonds currently issued include the EE, HH, and I bonds. Rates tend to be below but close to the market rates on other short-term instruments. Although they are not really short-term securities, the early redemption feature of U.S. savings bonds offers a similar degree of liquidity. The EE savings bond, the most popular of the three, does not pay periodic interest but rather accumulates in value over time. HH bonds pay a steady amount of interest income, and the interest rate on I bonds is adjusted regularly to reflect the recent rate of inflation. Early redemption leads to a yield sacrifice. The EE savings bonds allow investors to defer federal income taxes on their returns until maturity. In addition, no state and local income taxes are assessed on interest earned on savings bonds.

**Money Market Debt Securities
(Available in Large Denominations That Appeal
Primarily to Large Investors)**

- Treasury bills
- Banker's acceptances
- Eurodollars
- Commercial paper
- Short-term municipals

---

money market

There are several marketable short-term debt instruments from which an investor may choose. Collectively, these investments define what is known as the *money market*. They include Treasury bills, bankers' acceptances, Eurodollar deposits, commercial paper, and short-term municipals. Unfortunately, all but one of these are available only in large denominations. The Treasury bill (or T-bill) has a $1,000 minimum denomination, and all the rest have minimum denominations of at least $100,000. Once these securities are purchased, the owner must either hold them until their maturity or sell them in the marketplace. Such a sale will usually require the payment of a commission. Because of their minimal risk and their short term to maturity, there is not much fluctuation in their market prices.

Some money market instruments are sold at a discount and mature at their face value. For example, a one-year Treasury bill might be sold at 95 and mature at 100, thereby providing an HPR of 5/95, or 5.26 percent. Other short-term instruments make periodic payments. For example, a one-year CD could be structured to pay interest each month.

In summary, short-term debt securities usually offer a secure return. Little or no time commitment or special expertise is required to purchase or manage portfolios of many types of short-term debt securities. Their returns are usually lower than those available on less liquid investments.

Bonds and Similar Long-Term Debt Instruments

bond

par value
face value
note

A *bond* is an obligation to pay interest periodically and to pay principal at the end of a specified period. The principal due at maturity is known as the *par value* or *face value* of a bond. A bond with a maturity of one to 10 years is referred to as intermediate term and is usually called a *note*. Bonds with maturities more than 10 years in the future are long term. The issuer's "guarantee" makes any bond less risky than the stock of the same issuer. Corporate bonds are as secure as the financial condition of the issuing company. The extensive taxing power of the federal government means that there is no *default risk*—the risk the issuer will fail to make an interest payment or principal payment when it is due.

default risk

municipal bond
general obligation
bond
revenue bond

A bond issued by any state or local government is known as a *municipal bond*. A municipal bond backed by the "full faith and credit" of the municipality and referred to as a *general obligation bond* is usually considered quite safe. The other type of municipal, known as a *revenue bond*, can be repaid only from the revenue of a particular project (such as bridge tolls) and may have some default risk.

Long-Term Debt Securities

- Corporate bonds
- Federal government notes and bonds (governments)
- State and local bonds (municipals)

---

investment-grade
bonds

Relatively few bonds default, and those that have were almost always rated as speculative shortly before their default. Thus, an investor can largely avoid default risk by investing only in nonspeculative bonds, known as *investment-grade bonds,* and selling any issues that get downgraded to speculative. Even in a default, the bondholder will often receive a portion of the promised principal and accrued interest. Moreover, the promised return on a bond tends to rise with its perceived risk.

interest rate risk

price risk

purchasing power risk

callable bonds

In addition to default risk, bond investors must worry about *interest rate risk*. Interest rate risk consists of both price risk and reinvestment rate risk. *Price risk* is the fact that as interest rates rise, the values of bonds (which yield a fixed-dollar amount) decline. Reinvestment rate risk refers to the impact of changes in interest rates on the reinvestment of future coupon payments. *Purchasing power risk* is the risk that, due to unexpected increases in the rate of inflation, the bond's proceeds will purchase fewer goods than expected. *Callable bonds* permit the issuer to repurchase its issues prior to maturity, usually for a premium above their face value.

A bond's vulnerability to interest rate fluctuations usually varies directly with its maturity. Although short- and intermediate-term debt instruments are less sensitive to adverse interest rate movements, their yields are usually, but not always, below those on long-term bonds with comparable default risk.

Major Risks of Investing in Long-Term Corporate Bonds

- Default risk: issuer's failure to pay its interest and/or principal when due
- Interest rate risk: losses associated with changes in market interest rates
- Purchasing power risk: losses in purchasing power resulting from increases in the inflation rate

---

Corporate bonds are almost always issued with $1,000 face values and are usually issued to new investors at the face value. Bond prices are generally quoted in percentages of 100. Therefore, a bond selling at 90 is priced at $900.

In summary, most bonds are riskier and less liquid than most short-term debt securities, but they are typically less risky and in some cases more liquid than equity instruments. Because U.S. government bonds have no default risk, their yields are almost always below those of similar-maturity corporate bonds. Moreover, corporate bond yields vary appreciably with their respective risks. Bonds of well-known issuers are generally quite marketable, whereas bonds of small corporations and governmental units often trade in rather thin markets. Relatively little time or effort is required to manage most bond portfolios.

EQUITY INSTRUMENTS

Equity securities represent ownership shares. The owners have a residual claim (creditors' claims come first) on the corporation's assets and earnings.

Equity-related assets include publicly traded common stock, preferred stock, options, convertibles, and mutual funds, as well as ownership positions in small firms and venture capital investments. Each of these investments represents direct or indirect ownership in a profit-seeking enterprise. Equity holders' claims are subordinate to those of all debtors but include all residual value and income in excess of the claims of the senior securities.

Common Stock

Common stock is by far the most important type of equity-related security. Approximately 23 percent of United States households own stock directly, while many more participate indirectly in the stock market. Such vehicles as mutual funds, trust funds, insurance company portfolios, and the invested reserves of pension funds all provide indirect access. As the residual owners, shareholders are paid *dividends* out of their firm's profits. The portion of profits not paid out (earnings retained) is reinvested in the company, thereby helping it grow. Growth in sales, assets, and particularly profits should lead to a higher overall value for the firm. The benefit of any appreciation in the firm's value accrues to its owners, the stockholders. A company's stockholders theoretically control it by electing its board of directors. The board, in turn, selects upper-level management and makes major policy decisions. Most stock ownership groups are, however, widely dispersed and unorganized. Existing management usually fills the resulting power vacuum by nominating and electing friendly slates of directors. In general, stock returns compare favorably with those of all the investments discussed so far (see table 2-1). However, their variability of returns, as measured by the standard deviation of their returns, is also greater than that of the other investments. Standard deviations will be discussed in chapter 7.

Dividend payments on stocks are not assured or contractually guaranteed, and common stock never matures. Investors who own stocks that reduce or eliminate their dividends are likely to see a dramatic decline in the values of their shares. Bond prices generally fluctuate much less than stock prices. Moreover, firms are legally obligated to pay interest on bonds, whether they have a profitable year or not. Bonds, therefore, almost always have less downside risk than stocks of the same or similar-risk firms.

Because stocks can be bought and sold effectively in increments of as little as a few hundred dollars, an investor with relatively little cash can hold a diversified stock portfolio. Commissions may be disproportionately high, however, on very small transactions (less than about $1,000 and/or fewer than 100 shares).

In summary, common stock offers somewhat higher but more risky expected returns than bonds. Small investors can begin to assemble a stock portfolio with relatively modest sums.

dividends

TABLE 2-1
Basic Series: Summary Statistics of Annual Total Returns (From 1926 to 1999)

Series	Geometric Mean	Arithmetic Mean	Standard Deviation
Large Company Stocks	11.3%	13.3%	20.1%
Small Company Stocks	12.6	17.6	33.6
Long-Term Corporate Bonds	5.6	5.9	8.7
Long-Term Government Bonds	5.1	5.5	9.3
Intermediate-Term Government Notes	5.2	5.4	5.8
U.S. Treasury Bills	3.8	3.8	3.2
Inflation	3.1	3.2	4.5

Source: Stocks, Bonds, Bills, and Inflation Yearbook, © 2000 Ibbotson Associates, Inc. Based on copyrighted works by Ibbotson and Sinquefield. All rights reserved. Used with permission.

Preferred Stock

Preferred stocks have more price variability than bonds do but less than common stock does. Although preferred is technically a form of ownership, preferred shareholders usually have no real control of the company. All preferred stock carries a promised annual dividend payment. Virtually all preferred stock is *cumulative,* which means that any missed dividends must be made good before common shareholders can receive dividends. Preferred shareholders, as a group, can elect directors only if a certain number of dividend payments have been missed. Moreover, in any reorganization of the company, the preferred shareholders must be paid the liquidation value of their stock before common stockholders receive anything.

cumulative

Preferred dividend yields are usually below the average long-term total return (dividend plus capital gains) on common stocks. As fixed-income securities, preferreds are subject to the same type of interest rate risk as bonds. The preferred stock of a weak company may be riskier and have a higher expected yield than the common stock of a strong company. Preferred stock is not particularly liquid, but it is generally marketable.

Most preferred stock is owned by corporations. This is because dividend income to a corporation is 70 percent tax exempt. In fact, preferred stock is usually priced to reflect this tax treatment. This means that preferred stock would normally be considered overpriced to individual investors for whom dividends are fully taxable as ordinary income.

Example: The Crunch Auto Insurance Company has an extra $100,000 to invest. High Roller Realty has asked Crunch if it would like to buy $100,000 worth of a new issue of preferred stock (this is referred to as a private placement). This preferred stock has a dividend yield of 8 percent. What will Crunch's after-tax return on this investment be? Assume a 25 percent corporate tax rate.

The 8 percent dividend yield means Crunch will receive $8,000 per year in dividends. Of these, $5,600 (70% x $8,000) is tax exempt. The taxes owed on the remaining $2,400 are $600 ($2,400 x 25%). Therefore, Crunch's after-tax income is $7,400 ($8,000 – $600) and its after-tax return is 7.4 percent ($7,400/$100,000).

Limited Partnerships and Master Limited Partnerships

Most businesses are organized as corporations. The corporate form of organization provides limited liability for owners (shareholders), but its income is first taxed at the corporate level and its shareholders are taxed again on their dividends and capital gains when the stock is sold.

Some businesses are organized as partnerships. The income of a partnership is taxed only once. Partnership profits, whether distributed or retained by the partnership, are treated for tax purposes as the imputed income of the partners, where the allocation of income is based on the partnership agreement.

limited partnership

The *limited partnership* is an alternative way of organizing a business enterprise. These partnerships combine the benefits of a corporation's limited liability with the single taxation advantage of a partnership. A single general partner, who is usually the organizer and may be a corporation, *does* have unlimited liability. The limited partners, however, are not generally liable for the partnership's debts and obligations beyond their initial capital contribution. Most limited partnerships have one major drawback: Because they are relatively small, their ownership units trade in very thin markets. In addition, there may be legal or contractual restrictions on the sale of a limited partnership interest.

master limited partnership (MLP)

The *master limited partnership* (*MLP*) is designed to overcome this drawback. Most MLPs are relatively large (compared to limited partnerships). Their ownership units are designed to trade actively in the same types of markets as stock.

MLPs have generally been organized around oil and gas holdings. Others are designed for real estate. Investing in MLPs involves many of the same advantages and disadvantages as investing in common stock.

Equity-Related Securities: Direct Ownership of a Company

- Common stock: provides residual ownership of a corporation
- Preferred stock: receives preference over common to dividends and liquidation of assets
- Master limited partnership (MLP): combines the tax advantage of a partnership with the limited liability and ease of trading of a corporation

---

Venture Capital

Venture capitalists provide risk capital to otherwise undercapitalized companies that they believe have attractive growth prospects. In exchange, venture capitalists receive ground-floor equity positions in what may turn out to be highly lucrative ventures.

venture capital

Venture capital may be used to help fund both start-up firms and undercapitalized going concerns. Most types of direct venture-capital investing are available only to institutions and wealthy individuals. New ventures generally require substantial capital. Investors of more modest means can participate indirectly through public venture-capital funds, venture-capital limited partnerships, venture-capital clubs, small business investment companies (SBICs) geared toward venture-capital investing, and newly public companies needing venture capital. Regardless of how investors participate, they will find venture capital to be a risky business. Nevertheless, the potential rewards may sometimes justify the risk.

Options: Calls, Puts, Warrants, and Rights

derivative securities

Options are a derivative security. *Derivative securities* (derivatives) are securities whose values are derived from other securities or assets (for example, bushels of corn). The special feature of options is that they give the owner (holder) the choice of whether or not to engage in a particular transaction in the future. Stock options give the holder the right to acquire or dispose of stock. The owner of a *call* option has an option to **buy** a specified number of shares of stock at a specified price (called the *strike price* or *exercise price*), prior to a specified date (called the *expiration date*). A *put* option is an option to **sell** a specified number of shares of stock at a specified price, prior to a specified date. Exercising an option is solely at the owner's

call
strike price
exercise price
expiration date
put

(not the seller's) discretion. Anyone buying a call option expects the price of the underlying asset to rise. People who buy put options expect the price of the underlying asset to fall.

Example: Suppose an investor pays $200 for a call option to buy 100 shares of stock at a strike price of $20 per share. If the stock's price subsequently rises to $30, the investor can exercise the option, buy the stock at $20, and then immediately sell that same stock at $30. That trade would produce a gain of $1,000 ($3,000 – $2,000). After deducting the cost of the option, the set of transactions would yield a net profit of $800 ($1,000 – $200) before commissions, compared with an initial cost of $200 for the call.

The same $200 could, in contrast, have purchased 10 shares at $20. This would have produced a $100 gain when the stock rose to $30 per share.

Standardized option trading began with the 1973 opening of the Chicago Board Option Exchange (CBOE) and soon spread to other exchanges. Listed options now exist for a large number of different stocks. Other options are written on stock indexes and commodities futures contracts. Most options have relatively short lives (9 months or less).

warrants   *Warrants*, like calls, permit their owners to purchase a specified amount of stock at a specified price prior to a specified date. Unlike calls, warrants are generally exercisable for relatively long periods, such as several years. Warrants are issued by the company whose stock underlies the warrant. When exercised, warrants result in newly created shares and generate cash for the issuer. Calls are contracts between individual investors and do not involve the underlying company.

rights   *Rights*, like warrants, are company-issued options to buy stock. Rights differ from warrants in two ways: First, rights have short lives. They usually expire within a few weeks of the time of their issue. Second, the exercise price on a right is usually set substantially below the market price of the stock when the rights are issued. The exercise price of warrants is frequently set substantially above the market price of the stock at the time of issue. Most rights are exercised, therefore, while the eventual exercise of warrants is more uncertain.

Example: A right might allow an investor to buy stock at $25 when the market price is $45. Failure to exercise or sell such rights is like throwing away $20 multiplied by the number of shares of stock underlying those rights. Stockholders normally receive one right for each share they own. Stockholders do not pay for the rights. They are issued because the company wants to raise new money and allow existing stockholders to maintain their percentage ownership of the company.

Equity-Related Derivative Securities

- Call option: option-to-buy contract
- Put option: option-to-sell contract
- Warrant: long-term company-issued to buy option
- Right: short-term company-issued to buy option

Convertible Bonds

convertible bonds

Convertible bonds (convertibles) are debt securities that can be exchanged for the issuing company's stock at a specified exchange ratio. Although they are technically debt instruments, their conversion feature gives them an equity-related component. Their value tends to increase with increases in the underlying stock's price. As a result, they offer a combination of the relatively assured income of bonds and the upside potential of stock. Convertibles generally sell for more than their *conversion*

conversion value

value. Conversion value is the product of the exchange ratio multiplied by the current price of the company's common stock. Consequently, with a set amount of money, the investor can usually buy more shares of the underlying stock directly than by purchasing convertibles. Accordingly, direct stock ownership is normally more profitable in a rising market. Moreover, their conversion feature allows convertibles to be sold with lower yields than equally risky *straight bonds*. Straight bonds are any bonds that have no

straight bonds

conversion feature. They are generally more attractive in declining stock markets. Convertibles offer a compromise between investing in a company's stock and its nonconvertible (straight) bonds.

Convertible bonds tend to be less risky than common stock but more risky than straight bonds. Their liquidity, marketability, and minimum investment requirements are similar to those of straight bonds.

Mutual Funds, Closed-End Investment Companies, and Similar Investments

Many investors have neither the time nor the inclination to manage and monitor their investments carefully. These investors can leave most of this

mutual fund

**net asset value
  (NAV)**

**load funds
no-load funds**

load

closed-end fund

**unit investment
  trusts
variable annuities**

work to a *mutual fund*. The fund's shares represent proportional ownership of its managed investment portfolio. Funds pool the resources of many small investors. Their fund holders' money is used to assemble and manage a diversified portfolio of investments. Funds may invest in a large variety of types of investments. Most funds, however, hold portfolios of debt or equity securities. The price of a mutual fund share is its *net asset value (NAV)*. A fund's NAV equals the market value of its portfolio less any liabilities, divided by the number of shares outstanding.

Some mutual funds—*load funds*—are sold by agents who receive a fee (up to 8.5 percent of the purchase price). *No-load funds*, in contrast, deal directly with their investors, thereby eliminating the need for a sales force and *load* fee. No-load fund portfolios usually offer about the same average risk-adjusted returns on their portfolios as those of load funds.

Mutual funds are also known as open-end investment companies. New shares of these funds are issued to anyone who wants to buy them. Alternatively, the funds redeem all shares being sold by their investors. Closed-end investment companies, by contrast, neither issue additional shares nor redeem them on demand. The number of outstanding shares of a *closed-end fund* is established at the time the fund is founded and generally remains constant. These shares are usually publicly traded. The operations of exchanges and the over-the-counter market are discussed in the next chapter. Unlike mutual funds, closed-end share prices can vary substantially from their net asset values, although they usually trade at a discount.

Unit investment trusts and *variable annuities* are additional types of pooled portfolio arrangements. Unit investment trusts generally hold unmanaged portfolios. Variable annuities are much like mutual funds, but they usually offer a life guarantee component and are organized and managed by insurance companies.

Equity-Related Securities

- Convertible bond
- Convertible preferred stock
- Mutual fund
- Closed-end investment company
- Unit investment trust
- Variable annuity

The investment goals and portfolio compositions of mutual funds differ widely. Portfolios may be made up of low-risk or speculative bonds or stocks, tax-exempt securities, combinations of stocks and bonds, and so on. If the portfolio consists of short-term, highly liquid securities, then the fund is known as the money market mutual fund discussed earlier. Thus, mutual fund investors can choose from a wide array of characteristics.

Most mutual funds are well diversified and, as such, are considerably less risky than most individual common stocks or small portfolios consisting of a few different stocks. Investors with sufficient resources can assemble their own diversified portfolios of common stocks tailored to their own particular circumstances, although the commitment of time and effort may be substantial. While mutual funds require less time and expertise than individually managed portfolios, selecting a suitable fund does require some effort.

OTHER INVESTMENTS

In addition to debt and equity securities, there are two other important investment types to consider: real estate and futures contracts. Other somewhat less common investments (in terms of total market values) are collectibles and noncollectibles.

Real Estate

Many large fortunes have been built from small initial investments in real estate. Real estate investing offers the potential of large percentage profits, as well as a number of tax advantages. However, many small investors' life savings were wiped out by the Florida land-boom bust in the 1920s and other less spectacular real estate market collapses. Many bank failures in the late 1980s and early 1990s (for example, First Republic Bank in Texas and the Bank of New England) can be traced to a collapse in real estate values.

Real estate investors have good reasons to be cautious:

- The more debt (leverage) used to finance real estate purchases, the greater the risks. Yet one of the primary attractions of real estate as an investment is the ability to use debt to finance a large percentage of the cost.
- Determining a fair value for a prospective real estate investment requires considerable expertise.
- Managing improved property is a time-consuming task.
- Real estate commissions are considerably higher than those on securities. Therefore, real estate is more difficult, time consuming, and costly to buy and sell than most other types of investments.
- Most real estate purchases require a relatively large initial investment (down payment).

Real estate may offer attractive returns to investors with the required talents, but securities markets demand less time and expertise, offer greater liquidity, and are generally less risky. The stock of real estate-related companies provides an interesting compromise. The real estate investment trust (REIT) is yet another way of participating. Like MLPs, REITs offer the tax advantages of partnerships and the limited liabilities and ease of trading of the corporate form or organization. (See chapter 15.)

Futures Contracts

Futures contracts, like options, are derivatives. Their values are derived from the values of the underlying assets on which the contracts are based. Futures speculators and hedgers buy (go "long") and sell (go "short") contracts for future delivery of a prespecified amount of some asset, such as so many ounces of silver, bushels of corn, or thousands of dollars worth of Treasury bills at the full futures contract value.

To execute a trade, market participants are required only to deposit between 5 percent and 15 percent of the contract's value. As a result, any given percentage price fluctuation is magnified 7 to 20 times in terms of profit or loss.

Example: Buying a 6-month contract valued at $100,000 (a "long" position) might require a 10 percent deposit ($10,000 in earnest money). A 20 percent increase in the contract's value (to $120,000) would produce a profit of $20,000 (less commissions), or 200 percent of the original $10,000 deposit. A 10 percent fall in the contract's price would, however, wipe out the original $10,000 deposit.

Most brokerage firms require individuals seeking to open a commodity trading account to establish a relatively large beginning balance (initial deposit of funds) and to have a substantial net worth. Commissions on commodity trades are only a tiny fraction of the potential gains or losses.

speculator
hedger
There are generally two types of people who trade futures contracts: speculators and hedgers. A *speculator* believes he or she can predict better than others where the price of a contract is headed. A *hedger* uses futures markets to hedge his or her risks. For example, a soybean farmer might sell soybean futures to tie down a price for his or her expected soybean harvest.

Commodity speculation is generally quite risky. Futures contracts are marketable but illiquid. Substantial expertise, time, and resources are required. Still, some investors find the fast-paced action and potential for rapid riches (coupled with at least as great a potential for disaster) appealing.

Collectibles

Although a relatively minor investment medium, collectibles have grown substantially in popularity in recent years. Coins, stamps, art, and antiques have long been of interest to collectors. As an indication of their importance, both *Barron's* and *Forbes* report the Sotheby Index of prices on a variety of types of art, ceramic, silver, and furniture collectibles.

A bewildering assortment of items is now considered collectible. Collectibles are usually extremely speculative and illiquid. They are generally sold at a high markup, subject to a substantial fraud risk, and involve all of the uncertainties present in the more traditional types of investing. Selling is one of the most difficult aspects of investing in collectibles. Investors may, of course, use the same outlets to sell as they used to buy, but this approach may not always be best. Transaction costs are likely to be quite high.

Noncollectibles

Collectibles constitute one class of nontraditional investments. Additional nontraditional investments include Broadway shows, movies, California vineyards, discos, coal mines, computerized home-delivery groceries, racehorses, baseball clubs, and freight cars. All of these can be quite legitimate, but they are so specialized that only the aficionados should even think about them. While most traditional investments (securities, real estate, and commodities) are risky, at least the investor has a better idea of past history and a modicum of regulatory protection.

Investments Other Than Debt or Equity Securities

- Real estate: land and property that is permanently attached to it
- Commodity futures: contracts calling for deferred delivery of some physical commodity
- Collectibles: diverse array of tangible assets
- Noncollectibles: diverse array of investments, including Broadway shows, coal mines, race horses, sports clubs, freight cars, and the like

Investment Scams

Ponzi scheme

One of the most common investment scams is the *Ponzi scheme.* Promoters of Ponzi schemes promise high "yields" that they plan to finance from later investors' capital, at least as long as the money holds out. These schemes are inverted pyramids that need ever larger new "investments" to pay returns on earlier "investments." Eventually, not enough new money is brought in, and the scheme collapses. Those holding such "investments" are left with little or nothing.

SUMMARY AND CONCLUSIONS

Generalizing about the various types of investments is difficult. Conservative investors may prefer fixed-income investments, such as savings accounts, bonds, and preferred stock. Commodities futures or options may be attractive to more speculative investors. Those with the time and special expertise may find real estate, collectors' items, or small businesses appealing. Investors with limited time, funds, expertise, and willingness to take risks may find common stock and related securities (convertible bonds, convertible preferreds, warrants, mutual funds) an attractive investment.

Investors should carefully consider any investment opportunity before making a commitment. In particular, whenever an unrealistically high return is offered, the investor should be wary of a possible Ponzi scheme or other undisclosed risks, or even outright fraud.

CHAPTER REVIEW

Answers to the review questions and the self-test questions start on page 501.

Key Terms

maturity	purchasing power risk
depository institution	callable bonds
FDIC	dividends
certificates of deposit (CDs)	cumulative
money market mutual fund	limited partnership
savings bond	master limited partnership (MLP)
money market	venture capital
bond	derivative securities
par value	call
face value	strike price
note	exercise price
default risk	expiration date
municipal bond	put
general obligation bond	warrants
revenue bond	rights
investment-grade bonds	convertible bonds
interest rate risk	conversion value
price risk	straight bonds

mutual fund   unit investment trusts
net asset value (NAV)   variable annuities
load funds   speculator
no-load funds   hedger
load   Ponzi scheme
closed-end fund

Review Questions

2-1.   a.   Identify the dimensions of risk, expected return, liquidity, marketability, minimum investment size, and investment effort (using L for little, M for moderate, H for high, and N for neutral) for the following types of fixed-income securities: savings deposits, savings bonds, money market mutual funds, Treasury bonds, corporate bonds, and municipal bonds.

       b.   Describe any special tax treatments that apply to any of the fixed-income securities listed in a. above.

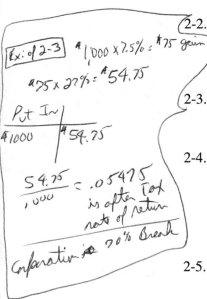

2-2.   a.   Describe the major characteristics of limited partnerships that make them attractive to investors.

       b.   What major drawback of limited partnerships inspired the development of master limited partnerships?

2-3.   Compute the after-tax yield for a preferred stock with a before-tax return (all in the form of dividends) of 7.5 percent for an individual in the 27 percent tax bracket and a corporation in the 36 percent tax bracket.

2-4.   Assume equal amounts are invested in venture capital opportunities with the following returns: 80 percent, –25 percent, –15 percent, 12 percent, 105 percent, –80 percent, 350 percent, –100 percent, and 0 percent.
       a.   What would the overall return from venturing be?
       b.   If these returns were earned over a 5-year period, what would the per-period (annual) geometric mean return be?

2-5.   Compare warrants to each of the following:
       a.   calls
       b.   rights

2-6.   a.   Compute the holding period return for a fund purchased with an NAV of 10 and sold when the NAV reached 12. Assume an 8.5 percent front-end load is charged at purchase time.

       b.   How much would the holding period return be if the fund (in a. above) were no-load?

2-7.   Give several reasons why real estate investors should be cautious.

2-8.   Assume an investor purchases a futures contract having a value of $150,000 with a 10 percent deposit. Ignoring commissions and taxes, assume the investor closes out his or her position right after its value rises to $200,000. In this situation, what is the gain as a percentage of the amount originally invested?

Self-Test Questions

non regulated

T **F** 2-1. Depository institutions are subject to maximum rate limitations on most of their accounts and certificates.

T F 2-2. Most money market securities have relatively high minimum denominations ($100,000 or more).

T F 2-3. EE savings bonds do not pay periodic interest but rather accumulate value over time.

T F 2-4. The possibility of a rise in market interest rates is a major risk that long-term bond investors face.

T **F** 2-5. Approximately 75 percent of U.S. households own stock directly.

T **F** 2-6. Stock prices generally fluctuate much less than bond prices.

T **F** 2-7. Preferred stock is not very marketable, but it is generally liquid.

T F 2-8. Master limited partnerships (MLPs) have generally been organized around oil and gas holdings.

T F 2-9. Warrants are generally exercisable for relatively long periods, such as several years.

T **F** 2-10. Calls are sold by the company whose stock underlies the call. *Rights are sold by Co.*

T F 2-11. A mutual fund's net asset value (NAV) equals the market value of its portfolio less its liabilities, divided by the number of its shares outstanding.

T **F** 2-12. Mutual funds are classified as closed-end investment companies, which neither issue new shares nor redeem outstanding shares.

T F 2-13. Futures contracts are derivatives whose values are derived from the values of the underlying assets on which the contracts are based.

T **F** 2-14. Commissions on commodity trades are a large portion of the potential gains or losses.

T F 2-15. Ponzi schemes are inverted pyramids that need ever larger new "investments" to pay returns on earlier "investments."

Bond

Pen example   *10yr 5yr 1yr*

Int rates

as int rates go down, the bond rate go up - vice versa. The longer bond is worse off if int rates increase

3

The Securities Markets

Learning Objectives

An understanding of the material in this chapter should enable the student to

---

3-1.   Explain the role of brokers and investment managers, and describe the markets where securities are traded.

3-2.   Explain the mechanics of executing transactions, and describe the methods for minimizing trading costs.

3-3.   Describe the mechanics of margin trading and short selling.

3-4.   Explain the various institutional arrangements for handling new issues and large trades.

3-5.   Explain the nature of securities regulation, and describe the emerging central market system.

Chapter Outline

This chapter explores the mechanics and regulation of the securities markets. Although common stocks are the principal focus, preferred stocks and warrants are traded in virtually identical fashions. Moreover, the listed option, mutual fund, and bond markets have much in common with the stock market. Thus, the topics this chapter covers apply to much of the investment scene.

THE MECHANICS OF THE SECURITIES MARKETS

Unlike the purchase of a can of beans at the supermarket, buying and selling stocks and bonds frequently involves a variety of relatively complex trading arrangements. For example, brokers, exchanges, third and fourth markets, limit orders, specialists, margin purchases, stock certificates, and commissions may play a role.

Brokers and Brokerage Firms

An investor's principal link to the securities market is through his or her broker. The term broker is frequently used to refer to both the individual employee and the employing firm. To minimize such confusion, here the term *broker* will mean the employee, and *brokerage firm* (or brokerage house) will refer to the employer. In securities industry jargon, the term "broker" or "broker-dealer" applies to the brokerage firm. A broker is also referred to as a *registered representative* (RR).

Brokers and their firms perform a number of functions, the most basic of which is linking investors to the securities markets. Stockbrokers implement their customers' trading instructions and act as the customer's agent. A *dealer*, in contrast, trades for his or her own accounts and makes markets by advertising a willingness to buy and sell.

In addition to facilitating trades, most full-service brokerage firms work as investment bankers (marketing new security issues and large blocks of already outstanding securities called secondary offerings). One easy way to remember the distinction is to think of an investment banker or underwriter as a wholesaler of securities, while a broker-dealer is like a retailer of securities. Some brokerage firms also manage and sell mutual funds, make a market in unlisted securities, sell life insurance, offer and manage various types of pension plans, manage some customer accounts individually, provide access to commodity exchanges, deal in government securities, sell tax-sheltered annuities, and so on. As brokerage firms have expanded into new areas, other types of financial service firms have expanded into their areas. The lines between brokerage and other types of financial services firms, particularly commercial banks, are quickly eroding, and the erosion is likely to accelerate since the repeal of the *Glass-Steagall Act* (the Bank Act of 1933). The Glass-Steagall Act prohibited investment banks from being commercial banks and vice versa. Indeed, some nonfinancial firms have entered the field, mainly through acquisitions. Some of these financial conglomerates offer an entire array of financial services, including checking, credit cards, travelers' checks, personal loans, insurance, pension packages, and real estate trading and management, as well as the traditional brokerage functions.

What Should Investors Expect of a Broker?

The brokerage industry can be divided into two general groups: **full-service brokers** and **discount brokers.** In full-service brokerage firms, a specific individual handles each account. The emphasis is on personalized service, including such things as investment research advice. Full-service brokers will contact their customers to suggest trades. In some cases, these brokers will actually encourage their customers to open what is known as a

broker
brokerage firm

registered
representative

dealer

Glass-Steagall
Act

discretionary account

discretionary account. A discretionary account is defined as an arrangement by which the holder of an account gives written power-of-attorney to someone else, often a broker, to buy and sell without the holder's prior approval. These accounts are also known as managed accounts or controlled accounts. There are generally two rationales for opening a discretionary account. One is that, although the investor continues to be the primary decision maker, he or she does not want to miss an attractive trading opportunity if the broker cannot reach the investor in a timely manner. In this case, the broker places the order at his or her own discretion. The other rationale for a discretionary account is that the investor is asking the broker to act as the portfolio manager and to make the trades that he or she deems appropriate for the account.

Payment of the vast majority (if not all) of the stockbrokers who work at full-service brokerage firms is based solely on the commissions they generate. The commission income the investor pays is split between the firm and the broker. Generally, the higher the total commissions a broker produces in a year, the higher the percentage of those commissions the broker gets to keep.

In a discount brokerage firm, accounts are with the firm, not a specific broker. Customers simply place an order with the firm rather than with a specific broker. A discount broker never calls a customer to initiate a trade. Accounts at discount brokerage firms are for investors who really want to manage their own accounts and seek to minimize the cost of maintaining their accounts.

Until a few years ago, the level of service was easy to distinguish between a full-service broker and a discount broker. In recent years, the distinction has blurred. Many of the traditional full-service brokerage firms are moving to implement discount service operations for those customers who want substantially discounted commissions. In addition, many of the discount brokerage firms are seeking ways to provide higher levels of service for those customers who want more personalized contact. It should be noted that to have more personalized service at a discount brokerage firm typically requires the customer to have in the account a minimum amount of assets that is nontrivial. Some firms require at least $500,000 or $1 million in assets for personalized service.

Bankruptcy of Brokerage Firms

SIPC

As part of the Securities Investor Protection Act of 1970 Congress set up the Securities Investor Protection Corporation *(SIPC)*. The SIPC is neither a government agency nor a regulatory authority. Rather, it is a nonprofit, membership-owned corporation patterned after the Federal Deposit Insurance Corporation (FDIC) that protects deposits in banks. The SIPC protects brokerage customers against losses that would otherwise result from the failure of their brokerage firm. Of course, customers are not protected against losses due to market fluctuations. SIPC liquidates troubled firms at the SEC's request. Customers are insured up to $500,000, not more than $100,000 of which may be in cash. Any claims above those sums are applied against the firm's available assets during liquidation. Most brokerage firms, however, have purchased additional insurance.

Integrity of Brokerage Houses

Most brokers and brokerage firms are honest. The exchanges, the National Association of Securities Dealers (NASD), and the Securities and Exchange Commission (SEC) monitor the brokerage industry closely. Those found guilty of serious wrongdoing can lose their license to work in the industry. Still, improprieties such as the following are uncovered with some frequency: conflicts of interest, kickbacks, misuse of customer assets, embezzlement, and improper use of discretionary authority.

Investment Managers

Professional investment management services are offered by brokerages, mutual funds, and many other financial service providers, such as banks, insurance companies, insurance agents, and financial planners. Individuals with $100,000 or more have long been able to hire a portfolio manager. Many investment advisory firms and banks will handle portfolios as small as $10,000, making professional advice available to investors of rather modest means. Accounts of less than $100,000 are generally managed as part of a pool. Accounts of $100,000 or more may be managed individually.

The risk-adjusted returns of the average mutual fund are generally comparable to but no higher than those of the market averages before consideration of fees. Advisers charge an annual management fee of up to 3 percent of assets (on small accounts) compared with annual fees of about 0.5 percent for most mutual funds.

Whether the investor wants to manage his or her own investments, hire an investment manager, or purchase mutual fund shares is an individual decision. The investor should take into account the sum to be invested, the time available, and his or her goals.

TYPES OF SECURITIES MARKETS

Regardless of how the portfolio is managed, securities must be bought and sold. Potential buyers could try to find sellers themselves, but relatively few people wish to trade any one stock at a particular time. The need to bring buyers and sellers together efficiently led to centralized facilities (exchanges), as well as to the less organized over-the-counter markets.

The Stock Exchanges

NYSE

Companies listed on the *NYSE* (New York Stock Exchange) produce a large percentage of the economy's gross domestic product. Most other exchanges tend to follow NYSE rules. Only members can transact business on the exchange, and only listed securities may be traded. Large established firms are generally traded on the *Big Board* (NYSE). The NYSE has about 3,000 listed companies and about 3,500 listed securities, including preferred shares.

Big Board

AMEX

Smaller firms may be listed on the *AMEX* (American Stock Exchange), which in terms of primary listings is the second largest floor-based exchange in the nation. Still smaller firms have their primary listing on the regional exchanges. Some of the regional exchanges' trading volume, however, involves NYSE-listed securities.

dual listing

Some exchanges permit trading other exchanges' listings, and many stocks are listed on more than one exchange (*dual listing*). To become listed, a firm meeting the requirements must apply, pay a fee, and not engage in any practice prohibited by the exchange.

NASDAQ and the Over-the-Counter Market

OTC

Many publicly owned firms are actively traded but are unlisted. Their stocks trade in the *OTC* (over-the-counter) market, an informal network of market makers who offer to buy and sell unlisted securities. Many listed companies (which trade primarily on an exchange) are also traded OTC. To trade in the OTC market, an investor would have his or her broker ask the brokerage firm's trading department to contact an appropriate OTC dealer or market maker.

NASDAQ

Until the National Association of Securities Dealers (NASD) set up the National Association of Securities Dealers Automated Quotations (*NASDAQ*), OTC stocks were relatively difficult to trade. Now, however, NASDAQ connects the quoting dealers and brokers and reports the best available prices for NASDAQ issues.

NMI

NASDAQ securities are listed in one of three categories. The National Market Issues (*NMI*) list contains the largest and most actively traded issues. National Market Issue newspaper quotations use the same format as NYSE and AMEX securities. About 4,000 firms are "listed" on the NMI. More than 1,100 smaller firms appear on the NASDAQ's SmallCap List. Another group of much smaller NASDAQ OTC issues is included on the Bulletin Board.

―――――――――――――――――――――――――――――――――

Three Categories of NASDAQ OTC Quotations

―――――――――――――――――――――――――――――――――

- National Market Issues (NMI): largest and most actively traded stocks
- SmallCap List: smaller firms
- Bulletin Board: much smaller issues

―――――――――――――――――――――――――――――――――

Table 3-1 shows some of the company listing requirements for the NYSE, the AMEX, and the NMI category of NASDAQ.

TABLE 3-1
Company Listing Requirements (as of 2001)

	NYSE	NASDAQ/NMI	AMEX
Pretax income (most recent year)	$2.5 million	$1 million	$.75 million
Stockholders' equity	None	$15 million	$4 million
Shares publicly held	1.1 million	1.1 million	.5 million
Market value of public shares	$100 million	$8 million	$3 million
Number of round-lot holders	2,000	400	None
Minimum share price	None	$5	$3

pink sheets

The National Daily Quotation Service reports the bid and ask prices for all actively traded OTC issues (about 6,000 NASDAQ and 22,000 other issues). These price quotations appear daily in the *pink sheets*, copies of which are available at most brokerage firms.

In 1999, NASDAQ and AMEX merged. As a result, they now have a common governance board and a common web site.[1] Nonetheless, the two markets continued to operate much as before. AMEX remains an exchange for medium-size companies, and NASDAQ continues to facilitate unlisted trading in the OTC market.

Other Securities Markets

Preferred stocks, warrants, and rights are traded on the same exchanges and OTC markets as common stocks. Standardized options (specifying strike price and delivery date) are also traded on a number of exchanges. Some corporate bonds are listed on exchanges; most are traded over-the-counter. Moreover, unlike warrants and preferred stock, bonds have a different commission structure, and bond trading on an exchange is generally physically separated from equity trading.

Although some U.S. government bond trading takes place on exchanges, the vast majority of trades are handled by a small number of OTC government bond dealers. Commercial paper, large CDs, municipal bonds, and other money market instruments trade primarily in similar OTC markets.

The Third and Fourth Markets

third market
fourth market

Ex: mutual funds banks

Most trading and virtually all trades involving individual investors take place on an exchange or in the traditional OTC market for unlisted issues. Institutional investors, on the other hand, make significant use of two other markets. OTC trading of listed stocks takes place in what is called the *third market*. The *fourth market* is an informal arrangement for direct trading between institutions. Both third and fourth markets involve off-exchange trading of what are usually large blocks of exchange-traded stock. The third market grew up in response to the exchanges' then-fixed commission schedules.

Third-market dealers were not bound by exchange-set commissions. Thus, they were usually able to (and, in fact, did) charge high-volume institutional traders much less than the commissions charged on the exchanges. By the time the exchanges stopped setting commissions, the third market was already established. Third-market dealers often offer a more attractive overall price (stock price and commission) than is available on the exchanges.

The fourth market provides its institutional participants with an even less costly way of trading. Because the institutions trade directly with each other, no commission is incurred. Those who help put the two sides of the trade together usually receive a finder's fee. This finder's fee is, however, much lower than the commission on a trade of equivalent size.

Two Other Markets Institutional Investors Use

- Third market: OTC trading of listed stocks
- Fourth market: direct trading between institutions via an informal arrangement

---

Dually Traded Securities

arbitrageur

Many high-volume stocks trade simultaneously on the NYSE, several regional exchanges, and OTC. Each market's bid and ask prices may differ somewhat and an *arbitrageur* tries to take advantage of these differences.

Arbitrageurs are people who seek profits from price disparities. While they do tend to drive the prices on different markets together, there may be some temporary disparities. Moreover, the quantities available on a single market may be more limited than needed. Shopping around, therefore, may be worthwhile for traders who seek to execute large orders.[2]

Pricing Points

Historically, stocks, bonds, options, and similar securities have been priced in dollars and fractions of a dollar. Until recently, most stocks were priced in eighths. Thus, investors encountered prices like 21 1/8, 25 1/2, and 30 3/4. As this textbook is written, however, most stocks are now priced in dollars and cents (decimal points).

The Ticker Tape

ticker tape

Actual transactions for listed securities are reported on the *ticker tape*. Many brokerage houses display the ticker tape on a large electronic screen in their offices. The ticker tape is also available on a few cable television stations, such as those of the Consumer News and Business Channel (CNBC). Each stock has an identifying ticker symbol. For example, the symbol "T" stands for telephone (American Telephone and Telegraph). Volume and price information for each transaction appears below the company ticker symbol. A typical ticker tape reading is shown in figure 3-1. The first entry, DCX with 6.7 below, reports a single round-lot sale of Daimler Chrysler Corporation at $66.70 per share. A *round lot* is 100 shares, and an *odd lot* is any trade of less than 100 shares. The second entry, X with 2s 9 below, indicates a trade of two round lots of USX at $29 per share. The entry LDW with 2700 7.5, reports that 2,700 shares of Laidlaw traded at $7.50 each. Those who follow the tape are expected to know the general price range for the stocks they follow. The full number of shares is displayed for trades of 1,000 shares or more. Company names and the corresponding ticker symbols are contained in some investment references, such as the *S&P Stock Guide*, and most brokerage houses keep booklets with the same information.

round lot
odd lot

FIGURE 3-1 Typical Ticker Tape Reading			
DCX	X	LDW	
6.7	2s 9	2700	7.5

TRANSACTION COSTS

Most books and articles on investing deal with what and when to trade. How to trade effectively at the lowest costs is often ignored or treated only briefly. Nevertheless, execution techniques are not only worthwhile but are also considerably more straightforward to apply than the various approaches to successful timing and selection. The sections that follow deal with the two major costs of executing a trade:

- commissions (broker fees)
- spreads (wholesale/retail markups)

commissions

Commissions

Security market commission rates were long fixed by agreement among the brokerage firms. Indeed, the so-called Buttonwood agreement setting up the original New York Stock Exchange in the late 18th century had a rate-fixing clause. In the 1930s, the SEC assumed regulatory authority over the rate structure. Thirty years later, rates were still being fixed.

Deregulated Rates

By the late 1960s, institutional traders made up a large and growing percentage of stock market volume. These institutional traders began to find various ways around the high fixed commissions. The brokerage industry was forced to respond by making commission setting competitive. Since

May Day

May 1, 1975 (known in the industry as *May Day*), each brokerage firm has set its own schedule rather than agreeing to some common formula.

Discount Commissions

The end of fixed commissions greatly expanded potential competition among brokerage firms. At first, this reform primarily benefited institutional customers, such as mutual funds, insurance companies, and bank trust departments. Although full-service firms are willing to negotiate discounts with their large individual customers, most do not compete openly on a price basis. Small investors will generally find more attractive rates at discount brokers—and today, Internet trading offers the least expensive (and fastest-growing) method for the small investor.

In addition to executing trades, a few discounters offer services similar to retail houses. Thus, investors should shop for the combination of discounts and services (including the quality and quantity of investment information) that best suits their needs.

Bid-Ask Spreads

bid-ask spread

OTC dealers and their stock exchange equivalent, the specialist, quote both a bid price at which they will buy and an ask price at which they will sell the securities in which they make a market. The difference between the buy and sell prices, or *bid-ask spread,* is the dealer's markup. Spreads tend to represent a smaller percentage of the price for higher-priced and more actively traded stocks. Listed stocks generally have lower bid-ask spreads than those traded over-the-counter.

Market and Limit Orders

market order

A customer wishing to trade a security begins by placing an order with his or her broker. The investor is likely to use either a market or a limit order. A *market order* requires an immediate execution at the best available price. Normally, this type of order results in a trade at the highest unexercised bid for a sale and at the lowest unexercised ask for a purchase. If a stock is quoted 23 bid and 23.25 ask, a buy market order would generally result in a purchase at 23.25 and a sell market order in a sale at 23. Sometimes, however, a buy and sell order will arrive simultaneously and be crossed with each other, usually at a price within the bid-ask range.

limit order

By contrast, customers using limit orders specify the prices at which they are willing to do business. Thus, a *limit order* is executable only at the limit price (or better). A good way to remember this is to think of a limit order as an order that sets a limit on how much the customer is willing to pay. A market order ensures a transaction, whereas a limit-order transaction must await an acceptable price. The vast majority of trading is done with market and limit orders.

posts

Brokerage firm representatives take their customers' orders to the section of the exchange where stocks are traded (trading stations, or *posts*) and attempt to execute the orders.

Example: A representative may seek to fill a client's limit order to purchase 100 shares of XYZ at 23. If the stock is available at 23 or less, the trade will be executed immediately. In fact, the order will be filled at less than 23 if possible. A limit order stipulates only the least favorable price that will be accepted. Normally, a limit order is entered at a level that is more favorable to the initiator than the current price. Thus, the order to buy XYZ at 23 might be entered when the bid and ask prices are 23.25 and 23.50.

After waiting a short time, the representative will leave any unexecuted limit order with the specialist who makes a market in that stock. The order will then be put on the specialist's book for later execution, if possible. The role of the specialist will be discussed in a later section.

Stop-Loss and Stop-Limit Orders

stop-loss order

Occasionally, people will use stop orders (both stop-loss and stop-limit) to limit exposure to an adverse price move. Most stop orders are designed to sell a position before the stock goes any lower. A *stop-loss order* to sell implements a sale at market (which means the best immediately available price) if the price falls to the prespecified level. These orders seek to protect the investor from a further fall. Because the stock must be traded immediately after the stop price is reached, the realized price is usually relatively close (but not necessarily identical) to the stop-loss price. Therefore, a stop-loss order at 20 might result in a sale at 20, but it could result in a sale at 19.95 or even 19.50 or lower if the stock is dropping rapidly.

stop-limit order

A *stop-limit order*, in contrast, activates a limit order when the market reaches the stop level. Thus, when the stop level is reached, a stop-limit order may not liquidate the position. The vast majority of stop orders are set to sell a position if the price drops. Buy stop orders, in contrast, are triggered by a price rise. Such an order might be used to protect a short position. (Short positions are discussed later.) A stop-loss buy order at 30, therefore, might be placed on a stock trading at 25. As long as the price stays below 30, nothing is done. Once it touches 30, the stock is bought.

Principal Types of Orders

- Market order: requires an immediate execution at the best available price
- Limit order: stipulates the minimum (sell) or maximum (buy) price acceptable for a trade to take place
- Stop-loss order: requires an immediate trade if the specified price is reached
- Stop-limit order: activates a limit order if a specified price is reached

---

More trades occur and more prices are quoted at whole numbers than at halves, and both are more common than tenths. Tenths, in turn, are more common than hundredths (pennies). Most investors prefer to think and trade in what they view as round numbers. Their placement of limit orders reflects this preference. Some people argue that one could earn extra profits by taking advantage of this tendency.

Good-'Til-Canceled, Day, Fill-or-Kill, and All-or-Nothing Orders

GTC orders

day orders

fill-or-kill orders

Because market orders require immediate execution, specifying how long to keep trying to fill the order is not normally necessary. Limit, stop-loss, and stop-limit orders, in contrast, may be entered either as *GTC orders* (good 'til canceled) or as executable for a specified period. An order can be placed to remain on the books for a day, a week, or for some other period. *Day orders* are canceled automatically at the close of the day's trading, whereas the broker must remember to cancel other orders on the prespecified day. *Fill-or-kill orders* must be either executed immediately or canceled.

Period for Which an Order Is Executable

- GTC order (good 'til canceled): executable until filled or canceled
- Day order: executable only during the day the order is placed
- Fill-or-kill order: canceled if not immediately executed

---

all-or-nothing orders

Commission charges are based on trades of the same security that take place during the same day. If an order to purchase 500 shares is executed in several pieces throughout the same day, the commission will (or should) be computed for a single 500-share trade. If that same trade took several days to be executed, however, the commissions would be computed separately on each day's trade. The total commission on a stretched-out trade would appreciably exceed that on a single 500-share transaction. A customer who wishes to trade more than one round lot may either allow the order to be filled a bit at a time or stipulate an all-or-nothing order. *All-or-nothing orders* must trade as a unit incurring a single commission (with any volume discount applying) but can be executed only when sufficient volume is available. A regular order might be filled in pieces when insufficient volume exists for a single fill. Moreover, all-or-nothing orders are automatically superseded by any other limit orders placed by other customers at the same price. Thus, those who would use all-or-nothing orders need to realize that the potentially lower commission is accompanied by a reduced likelihood of execution.

Versus Purchase Orders

Investors sometimes sell only a portion of their holdings of a particular issue. For example, an investor might sell 200 shares from a 1,000-share *versus purchase order*

You can decide which stocks you want to sell — it's a tax issue.

versus purchase

position. The holdings may themselves have been accumulated at different prices over an extended period. The tax implication of the trade will depend heavily on the price applied to the purchase side of the trade. The higher the cost basis, the lower the gain or the higher the loss that is reported to the IRS. Normally, the shares purchased earliest are recorded as the ones sold (first in, first out: FIFO). The seller may, however, prefer to utilize a trade with a different purchase price. Identifying securities that were purchased at a later date as the ones that were sold may produce a higher basis (reducing the profit or increasing the loss for tax purposes). Making the order *versus purchase* allows the seller to specify which block of shares is to be sold.

specialist

The Specialist

Specialists manage the markets in listed stocks. They do so primarily by quoting bid and ask prices on the securities assigned to them. They maintain an inventory of their assigned stocks and buy for and sell from that inventory. A given specialist may make markets in a dozen or so securities, and a few actively traded securities are handled by more than one specialist. Most securities, however, are assigned to a single specialist. Securities that are traded on more than one exchange have an assigned specialist for each exchange.

Specialists record limit and stop orders in their order books. They are responsible for executing these orders whenever the prespecified limit prices are reached. Orders entered at the same price level are executed chronologically.

Example: A particular limit order to purchase 100 shares at 23 may be preceded by another limit buy order at 23 for 500 shares, and another limit purchase order for 300 shares at 23 may follow the 100-share buy order. Once the 500 shares at 23 are purchased, the 100-share order will be crossed with any incoming market sell order or limit order with a minimum sale price of $23 or less. However, if any offer to pay more than 23 should arrive prior to the 100-share order's being executed, it would immediately supersede the 100-share order.

Individual specialists are members of specialists' firms. These firms may handle up to 70 stocks. Under most types of market conditions, these specialists' firms perform their jobs effectively. They are supposed to ensure that the market for each of their stocks is always orderly and well managed. Prices are not supposed to swing too widely from transaction to transaction.

The specialist is expected to fill any temporary gaps by offering to buy or sell as necessary. Specialists are supposed to be net buyers when the public wishes to be net sellers. Under normal circumstances, specialists' firms may be managing a few stocks that are under selling pressure while others have more public buyers than sellers. During the October 1987 crash, however, almost all of the public orders were on the sell side. Most of the specialists' capital was quickly committed. Some firms were unable to provide an orderly market as they were hit with more and more sell orders at lower and lower prices.

Floor Traders or Registered Competitive Market Makers (RCMMs)

Specialists, who make markets, and unexecuted limit orders, which represent potential demand or supply, both have an influence on stock prices.

floor traders

RCMMs

Individuals called *floor traders* or registered competitive market makers (*RCMMs*) also have a modest role in the price-formation process. RCMMs own exchange seats and trade for their own account. They benefit from quick access to the market and the information that is available at the center of the action. As recently as the 1960s, a substantial fraction of NYSE members were floor traders. Since that time, however, various restrictions have substantially reduced their ranks. In 1999, only 10 floor traders remained. The options and commodity exchanges, however, continue to have many floor traders.

MANAGING EQUITIES

Buying on Margin

Marketable securities provide excellent collateral for lenders. The Federal Reserve Board (the Fed) allows most stocks to be bought using borrowed funds for part of the purchase price. This is referred to as buying on margin. To be purchasable on margin, an OTC stock must have at least 1,200 shareholders and a market value of $5 million or more. Listed companies are marginable unless specifically excluded by the SEC. However, most brokerage firms will not extend margin loans on low-priced shares (below $5).

A margin rate of x percent permits marginable stock to be purchased with x percent cash (called the initial margin) and (100 − x) percent borrowed funds. Thus, a 60 percent margin requirement would allow the purchase of $10,000 worth of stock with as little as $6,000 in cash. In the past, the Fed

**margin account
buying power**

net equity

lowered and raised the margin requirement on stocks as part of its economic policy. Since 1974, the margin requirement on stocks has remained at 50 percent.

A *margin account* is said to have *buying power* based on the net equity in the account and the amount of margin borrowing already outstanding. A margin account, as opposed to a cash account, is one in which the investor is allowed to buy on margin. Buying power is the amount of additional stock an investor could buy without having to come up with additional cash.

The buying power of a portfolio of marginable stocks is equal to the *net equity* of the portfolio divided by the initial margin rate, less the current account value. In equation form:

$$BP = \frac{E}{MR} - MV \qquad \text{(Equation 3-1)}$$

where BP = buying power
E = equity (marginable stocks)
MR = margin requirement (initial)
MV = market value of the assets in the account

The equity value of an account is the market value of all the securities in an account, less the loan balance. In equation form:

$$E = MV - L \qquad \text{(Equation 3-2)}$$

where L = current loan balance

Example 1: An investor with $20,000 worth of marginable stocks and no margin debt outstanding could, with a 50 percent margin rate, buy another $20,000 worth of marginable stocks with the account's buying power.

$$BP = \frac{20,000}{.50} - 20,000$$
$$= 20,000$$

Example 2: An investor with $35,000 in marginable stocks, a 50 percent margin rate, and an outstanding loan balance of $10,000, would be able to purchase another $15,000 worth of marginable stock with the account's buying power.

$$E = 35,000 - 10,000$$

$$= 25,000$$

and

$$BP = \frac{25,000}{.50} - 35,000$$

$$= 15,000$$

Margin Calls

Margin loans may remain outstanding as long as the borrower's equity position does not fall below the *maintenance margin percentage.* Maintenance margin is the minimum amount of equity an investor can have, as a percentage of the portfolio. Maintenance margin requirements are set by the Federal Reserve, although individual brokerage firms may set higher rates. Maintenance margin rates are always less restrictive than initial margins. Margin borrowers are not required or expected to make payments according to any particular schedule. The only time that the borrower may be required to make a payment is when the equity in the account falls below the maintenance margin rate. In other words, the equity in an account must always satisfy the following relationship:

$$\frac{MV - L}{MV} \geq MMR$$

where MMR = maintenance margin rate

Margin accounts are structured to limit the danger of becoming undercollateralized (having an outstanding loan balance greater than the value of the securities collateralizing it). As long as the value of the collateral comfortably exceeds the amount of the loan, the outstanding loan is considered to be relatively secure.

The current maintenance margin percentage set by the Federal Reserve Board is 25 percent. Many brokerage firms set their rates at 35 percent. An investor whose equity falls below this percentage of the value of his or her portfolio (counting only marginable securities) will receive a margin call.

Example: A 50 percent initial margin requirement allows $10,000 in marginable stocks to be purchased with $5,000 in cash and $5,000 in credit. Any fluctuation in the portfolio's value will be reflected in a change in the equity position (equity equals portfolio value less margin debt). If the value of the portfolio rises to $12,000, the equity rises to $7,000 ($12,000 – $5,000). If, however, the value of the margined stock falls to $7,700, the equity position declines to $2,700 ($7,700 – $5,000) or slightly over 35 percent ($2,700/7,700). If the brokerage firm has a 40 percent maintenance margin requirement, the investor will receive a margin call

A margin call can be either a "house call" or a "Fed call." The brokerage firm has the option of enforcing or waiving the enforcement of a house margin call. However, a Fed call must be enforced. In either instance, the brokerage house may give the customer a modest amount of time to restore the account to the compliance level.

A margin call may be settled in any of several ways. One way is to deposit sufficient cash into the account to pay down enough of the loan so that the maintenance margin requirement is met. A second way to settle up is to deposit other securities into the account. A third way is to sell a sufficient number of shares from the portfolio until the maintenance margin requirement is met. The cash from the sales is applied to the loan.

Ways to Satisfy a Margin Call

- Add more money to the account.
- Add more collateral (marginable securities) to the account.
- Sell stock from the account and use the proceeds to reduce the margin debt.

In each case, the result must raise the equity percentage above the margin maintenance minimum to satisfy the margin call.

If the investor opts to add cash to the account, then the amount of cash needed is the amount necessary to meet the maintenance margin requirement. In mathematical terms:

$$\text{Cash added} = \text{LOAN} - \text{MV} \times (1 - \text{MMR})$$

where LOAN = loan balance at the time of the margin call
MV = market value at the time of the margin call
MMR = maintenance margin rate

Example: An investor buys $10,000 worth of stock using $5,000 in cash and a $5,000 loan. The stock falls to a market value of $6,000. If there have been no deposits to offset the loan, what is the amount of the margin call if the maintenance margin rate is 25 percent?

$$\text{Cash added} = \$5,000 - \$6,000 \times (1 - .25)$$
$$= \$5,000 - \$4,500 = \$500$$

Concentrated Positions

Investors with margin accounts should have relatively well-diversified portfolios of marginable stocks. These accounts are vulnerable to a general market decline, but they tend to be rather well protected against price declines limited to a few individual stocks. If one or two stocks in a diversified portfolio decline sharply, the overall account value will generally be able to withstand the pressure and thereby avoid a margin call.

Example: If a single stock position representing 10 percent of a portfolio's value falls to half its previous value, that fall would cause the portfolio's overall value to fall by 5 percent. If the account had met the initial margin requirement (50 percent) prior to the stock's decline, it should still be considerably above any maintenance rate.

If, however, a large percentage of the account's value is concentrated in one or a very few stocks, the risk to the margin borrower (and the margin lender) goes up. If the one or a few stocks on which most of the account value is derived suffer a serious decline, the danger of a margin call becomes much greater than with a well-diversified portfolio.

Example: Suppose a stock representing 50 percent of the portfolio's value falls to half its previous value. The portfolio's value would fall by 25 percent (.5 x .5 = .25), which could easily trigger a margin call.

The Leverage of Margin Borrowing

Margin loans are normally used to allow the investor to purchase more stock than cash alone could buy. The use of such leverage tends to magnify both gains and losses. With $5,000, the investor could buy outright 50 shares of a marginable stock trading at $100 per share or (with a 50 percent margin rate) 100 shares by borrowing the additional $5,000. Table 3-2 illustrates some possible results (neglecting the impact of dividend payments and interest charges) from a cash versus a margin purchase. Clearly, margin purchases increase both the upside potential and the downside risk.

TABLE 3-2
Margin Example: $5,000 Available to Invest in Stock Selling for $100 per Share

Stock Price Moves to	Purchase 100 Shares Using 50% Margin at $100 per Share		Purchase 50 Shares for Cash at $100 per Share	
	Change in Holding's Value	Change Relative to Equity	Change in Holding's Value	Change Relative to Equity
70	−$3,000	−60%	−$1,500	−30%
80	−2,000	−40%	−1,000	−20%
90	−1,000	−20%	−500	−10%
100	0	0	0	0
110	+1,000	+20%	+500	+10%
120	+2,000	+40%	+1,000	+20%
130	+3,000	+60%	+1,500	+30%

To understand the relationship among the numbers in table 3-2, we must distinguish between two measures of return: return on assets (ROA) and return on equity (ROE). ROE is the same as the HPR of the investment. It is the performance of the security itself. If a stock is bought on an all-cash basis, there is no difference between the HPR (or ROE) of the investor and the ROA of the stock. ROE is the return on the investor's cash investment. The relationship between these two terms is

$$ROE = \frac{ROA}{MR}$$

where MR = margin rate (initial)

Example: As illustrated in table 3-2, an investor buys 100 shares of a stock trading at $100 per share. If the stock falls to $70 per share, then the stock's ROA is

$$ROA = \frac{(100 \times \$70) - (100 \times \$100)}{100 \times \$100} = -30\%$$

If that same stock is bought with a 50 percent initial margin, then

$$ROA = \frac{(100 \times \$70) - (100 \times \$100)}{50\% \times 100 \times \$100} = -60\%$$

Note that

$$ROE = \frac{-30\%}{.50} = -60\%$$

The relationship between ROA and ROE must be adjusted for the interest rate charged on the loan. Assume the margin loan costs 9.5 percent. If a year later the stock illustrated in table 3-2 had risen to $120, the cash purchase would have appreciated by $1,000 ($20 x 50), compared with a $1,525 gain on the margin purchase ($20 x 100 = $2,000; 9.5% x $5,000 = $475; $2,000 − $475 = $1,525). Should the stock fall to 80, the losses would be $1,000 and $2,475, respectively. Interest costs on the margin position would, however, be at least partially offset by dividend payments. Commissions and taxes also affect the amounts modestly but leave the basic point unaffected. The use of margin credit to purchase stock tends to magnify both gains and losses. As long as the stock's return (net of commissions and taxes) exceeds the financing cost of the loan, leverage will enhance the overall return. Mathematically, the payment of interest on margin loans can be incorporated with the following:

$$ROE = \frac{ROA}{MR} - i \times t$$

where i = interest rate on the loan
      t = time (measured in years) the loan is outstanding

Using margin credit may also provide some tax advantages. Interest costs are an itemized deduction (but only against investment income) as incurred, whereas any price appreciation is taxable only when the asset is sold. Thus, the interest charges incurred on margin borrowing may shelter other investment income, while the price appreciation goes untaxed until realized.

    Brokerage firms finance some of their margin lending from other customers' credit balances, such as those generated through short sales. A positive balance in a customer's account is called a *credit balance*; a negative one (a margin loan) is referred to as a *debit balance*. Additional loan funds are obtained from commercial banks at the *broker call-loan rate*. Interest charges on margin loans are based on the exact length of each part of the loan. If, for example, $10,000 is borrowed and then $750 is repaid a week later, interest will be calculated on $10,000 for a week and on $9,250 thereafter. Margin loan interest rates are usually determined by a sliding scale added to the broker call-loan rate. Table 3-3 is typical.

credit balance
debit balance
broker call-loan rate

TABLE 3-3
Typical Margin Loan Rates

Net Debit Balance	Call Rate Plus
$ 0 – 9,999	2 1/4%
$10,000 – 29,999	1 3/4%
$30,000 – 49,999	1 1/4%
$50,000 and over	3/4%

    Banks generally set their broker call-loan rate equal to or below their prime rate (the lowest advertised business rate). Margin loan rates are normally no more than 2 percent above the prime business rate. Relatively favorable interest rates and flexible payment schedules make margin loans an attractive credit source.

    Preferreds, warrants, and convertibles are subject to the same margin requirements as common stocks. Margin restrictions also apply to corporate bond purchases, although their proportional collateral value is typically higher (25 percent margin rate on most nonconvertible bonds). A 10 percent margin requirement applies to government bonds with a 10-year or greater maturity. The margin requirement is lower for shorter-term governments.

    While brokerage houses specialize in margin loans, banks and other financial intermediaries also accept securities as collateral. If these loans finance other security purchases, the Fed's margin restrictions apply. Otherwise, the lender can determine the maximum loan value on such collateral.

Short Selling

    Most stock trades involve the purchase and sale of securities that the seller owned prior to the transaction. Unlike offering to sell the Brooklyn Bridge, however, an investor who sells stock that he or she does not own

short selling

(*short selling*) is involved in a perfectly legal practice. The short seller borrows the shares from his or her broker and immediately sells them at the current market price. The short seller's broker simply sells someone else's shares. The short seller then owes the brokerage firm the shorted shares. The customer whose stock is borrowed is as secure as a bank depositor whose funds are loaned. If the lender wishes to sell the loaned stock, the brokerage firm will simply borrow replacement shares from another customer or brokerage firm.

The short seller hopes the price will fall far enough so that when the stock is repurchased, he or she will make a profit after covering expenses. This gain would be reduced somewhat by commissions on the short sale and the covering (repurchase) transaction. Furthermore, the short seller must pay any dividends accruing on the borrowed stock. Moreover, the short sale proceeds and an additional percentage (margin) of the sale price must be left in a non-interest-bearing account at the brokerage house. A still larger margin deposit may be required by an adverse price move.

Example: Shorting 100 shares at 50 and then repurchasing them (covering the short position) at 35 produces a gross profit of $1,500 (100 x [$50 – $35]) less commissions and accrued dividends. However, should the stock price increase to 65, the seller would show a loss of $1,500 ($100 x [$50 – 65] plus commissions and accrued dividends.

The short seller may legally remain short indefinitely. The dividend payment and margin deposit requirements, however, could make such a position costly to maintain. Moreover, stock prices have no ceiling. Thus, losses are technically unlimited on a short sale. Clearly, short selling is a relatively risky practice.

One limit to short selling is the brokerage firm's ability to obtain stock that can be used to facilitate the short sale. For widely held stocks, this need to find shares to sell is generally not much of a problem. Sometimes, however, the interest in selling a less widely held stock short is so great relative to the shares available to short that brokerage firms run out of available shares. This situation is particularly likely for small companies in which the shares are closely held by a few people or the shares' price has dropped to such a low level that it is not marginable. Investors tend only to

street name

hold stock in the name of the brokerage house, referred to as *street name* (where it is available for shorting), if the stock is marginable. Investors who wish to sell short a stock that is in short supply may not be able to do so. Similarly, an investor who sells such a stock short may be required by his or her brokerage firm to close the position if the firm finds that it can no longer borrow the shares needed to maintain the short position.

In the past, unscrupulous investors have used a rapid series of large short sales to attempt to force a rapid decline in a stock's price. This was known as a *bear raid*. Any type of effort to manipulate the market, however, is illegal. For example, using short sales to drive a stock's price down is considered an illegal attempt to manipulate the market. To forestall such attempts, the SEC does not allow traders to sell short after a negative price change (*downtick*) in a stock. If the last price change was a decline, therefore, a would-be short seller must wait until the price begins to rise again (two or more successive trades at rising prices, which is called an *uptick*) before implementing a short sale.

As the preceding discussion indicates, to short (or sell short) stock is to sell stock that is not owned with the intention of covering (buying it back) later—preferably, at a lower price. The act of executing a short sale may be described as shorting or, in the past tense, as having shorted the stock. To be short or have a short position is to have executed such a trade and not yet covered. Similarly, an investor can be long or go long or have a long position. This is just another way of saying that the investor owns the stock.

bear raid

downtick

uptick

Easier to trade ———→

Street Name

Securities bought on margin must be left on deposit with the shareholder's brokerage house, and securities bought with cash may be. Broker-held securities are generally registered in street name although the customer retains beneficial ownership. Street-name registration offers secure storage to the investor and allows securities to be traded without new certificates having to be issued. Furthermore, a customer who holds a diversified portfolio of securities and who changes addresses needs to file only one change of address notice with the brokerage firm, rather than notifying all the companies separately.

Advantages of Street-Name Registration

- Offers secure storage
- Lets securities be traded without new certificates being issued
- Allows customers who move frequently to file only one change of address with brokerage firm instead of notifying all companies separately

---

Street-name registration has a number of disadvantages. Assets held in street name may be tied up during a bankrupt brokerage firm's reorganization. Moreover, dividends and interest on street-name securities are sometimes credited to an improper account. The customer must discover and report the error before it is likely to be corrected. Even a properly credited dividend may be retained by the broker in a non-interest-bearing account for a few days before being sent to the shareholder. Furthermore, all company reports (annual reports, quarterly reports, proxy materials, class-action suit notices, and so on) for street-name securities are sent initially to the brokerage firm. Thus, street-name holders will receive their company reports only after the brokerage firm has forwarded them. Also, some companies will send discount coupons and sample products to investors who own the shares directly, but not to street-name accounts. Clearly, street-name registration has both advantages and disadvantages.

Disadvantages of Street-Name Registration

- Assets may be tied up during the reorganization of a bankrupt brokerage firm.
- Dividends and interest may be credited to an improper account.
- Properly credited dividends may be retained by the broker in a non-interest-bearing account for a few days before being sent to the shareholder.
- Because all company reports are sent to the brokerage firm, the shareholder will receive them only after they have been forwarded.
- Discount coupons and sample products are not sent to street-name accounts.

The Stock Certificate

stock certificates

In this day of computerized accounting and electronic transfers, using *stock certificates* to prove ownership is similar to a cash-only payment system. Stock certificates must be issued whenever a stock is registered in an individual's name. Because the certificates require a great deal of paperwork and may be stolen or forged, many experts have advocated substituting computer cards or bookkeeping entries. Individuals might still receive a stock certificate upon request or at least be given some proof of ownership, such as a receipt or a bill of sale.

Institutions are involved in a large percentage of securities transactions as either the buyer or seller or both. Many other trades involve individuals who leave the stockholding function to their brokerage firm. With such trades, appropriately safeguarded bookkeeping entries have largely eliminated the need for stock certificates. Stock certificate reissues are minimized by the National Securities Clearing Corporation (NSCC). It records all members' transactions, verifies the consistency of their accounts, and reports net positions daily. NSCC members settle within the clearinghouse rather than between individual brokerage firms. Moreover, the Depository Trust Company (DTC) immobilizes many certificates by holding member firms' securities. Securities traded between members can be handled internally by simply debiting one account and crediting another. Although institutional and street-name accounts benefit from these facilities, investors with non-street-name securities continue to experience all the inconveniences inherent in a stock certificate transfer system.

THE PRIMARY MARKET

primary market

When corporations want to raise new money, they issue new securities. Corporations' sale of these securities to investors is referred to as the *primary market*.

Once an issue has been sold in the primary market, all subsequent trades take place in the secondary market. Some shares of a primary distribution may already be actively traded in the secondary market. Alternatively, the stock of the issuing firm may have heretofore been privately held (owned by a small number of people). A private firm that sells a substantial block of additional shares and thereby creates a more active and diverse ownership is said to *go public*. This is known as an *initial public offering (IPO)*. Normally, an *investment banker* (usually also a brokerage firm) is retained to assemble a syndicate to *underwrite* the issue.

go public
initial public offering (IPO)
investment banker
underwrite

prospectus

Investment bankers usually facilitate new-issue sales of debt and equity by agreeing to buy the securities for resale (underwriting). Together, the issuing firm and its investment banker compose a registration statement and a *prospectus* detailing all of the relevant material information. These statements must be filed with the SEC and supplied to every buyer. The investment banker deducts its underwriting fee from the offering price. The investment-banking syndicate generally guarantees to sell the issue, although the job might be taken on a *best-effort basis*, in which case the investment banker acts as an agent for the issuing firm. Most underwriting is done on a *firm-commitment basis*, which means the investment banker buys the securities from the issuer and then sells them to the public.

best-effort basis

firm-commitment basis

Shelf Registration

shelf registration

While most primary sales are marketed quickly after their registration, *shelf registration* is permitted by the SEC's Rule 415. Under this rule, a firm can file one registration statement for a relatively large block of stock and then sell parts of it over a 2-year period. The shelf registration option tends to reduce red tape and expenses, and because the stock can be sold directly to institutional investors, it sometimes eliminates the underwriting fee.

Private Placements

private placement

lettered stock

New issues are sometimes sold in large lots to a small group of buyers in what is called a *private placement*. These placements allow start-up firms to demonstrate viability by successfully raising some capital on their own. Additional shares may subsequently be marketed to the public through an underwriter. The private placements are usually sold below the public offering price. In exchange for a favorable price, the initial investors may agree to accept *lettered stock*. Under SEC Rule 144, such securities can be resold only after a holding period of at least 2 years and in a gradual manner that does not disrupt trading markets.

Debt issues may also be placed privately, usually to large buyers such as insurance companies.

LARGE SECONDARY MARKET TRADES

The vast majority of secondary market trades can be handled comfortably by the specialists on the exchange or the dealers in the OTC market who earn their living positioning the stock. Other institutional arrangements are, however, used to handle trades that would strain the specialist's or market maker's capital resources. Really large amounts of stock usually require a secondary distribution (sale) or tender offer (buy); intermediate-sized trades may go through a block trader or be handled as a special offering.

block trades

Block Trades

Attempting to buy or sell 10,000 shares or more in the ordinary channels might result in an unfavorable price for the trader. For example, an attempt to purchase 10,000 shares of a less actively traded stock could temporarily raise its market price appreciably while the buying is under way. Therefore, these trades are often implemented by a professional who specializes in handling large quantities in ways designed to minimize the market disruptions: the block trader.

For a large sell order, the block trader first obtains buyer commitments for part or all of the shares. He or she then offers to buy and resell the lot slightly below the current price, charging commissions to both sides of the trade. The block trader may purchase some of the lot to facilitate the transaction. This facilitating purchase may ultimately have to be sold at a loss. While block traders are usually given the task of selling large quantities of stock, they sometimes are asked to assemble large blocks for single buyers.

Special Offerings

Special offerings or spot secondaries are also sometimes used to sell relatively large blocks of stock. Brokers who buy the securities for their clients receive a special incentive fee. The exchange must approve the offering, which is then announced on the ticker. It must remain open for at least 15 minutes. The offering price must generally equal or exceed the current bid but not exceed either the last sale price or the current ask.

Secondary Distributions

Extremely large blocks generally require relatively long periods to be sold at reasonable prices. These unusually large blocks are generally sold in *secondary distributions* that are handled in much the same way as new issues. A syndicate or the original seller or sellers directly market the issue over time at a price somewhat below the previous level. The offering price includes a discount to the selling syndicate. No direct commission is charged.

Tender Offers

If the buyer is an outside party, then the purpose is usually to acquire control of the company. If the buyers consist primarily of management, then the purpose is usually to take the company private. A *tender offer* is generally used for these large purchases. For a limited period, the buyer offers to purchase a substantial block of stock, normally at a premium price. The tenderer usually pays an additional fee to brokers who handle their customers' trades. If the offer is oversubscribed and the buyer does not want the excess, stock may be bought on a pro rata basis. If too little is tendered, the buyer may reject all bids or purchase what is offered.

SECURITIES MARKETS REGULATION

Because they are "clothed with the public interest," the securities markets are regulated. It is important that investors understand the nature and direction of this regulation. The exchanges, led by the NYSE, engage in a great deal of self-regulation. Until 1975, the NYSE fixed commissions, prohibited exchange members from trading listed shares off the exchange, and prohibited the AMEX from trading NYSE-listed securities. After a long struggle and rearguard action to preserve them, fixed commission rates were ended by SEC order. Although the AMEX no longer automatically de-lists companies that obtain NYSE listings, only a relative handful of the NYSE's listings are dually traded with the AMEX, and most of the volume in those issues takes place on the NYSE. Therefore, the two New York exchanges still do not compete head-on. Off-exchange member trading of listed securities is no longer prohibited *per se*, but restrictions still discourage such activity.

Some NYSE regulations help both the exchange and its customers. For example, protecting customers from fraud or bankruptcy consequences of member firms inspires public confidence.

Securities Act of 1933
Securities Exchange Act of 1934

The SEC has been diligent in protecting investors against fraud, misrepresentation, financial manipulation, and trading on inside information. Full and frank disclosure is a top priority. As part of the *Securities Act of 1933,* public security offerings must be accompanied by a prospectus that fully discloses all material information. As part of the *Securities Exchange Act of 1934*, publicly traded firms must file periodic financial statements with the SEC, the exchanges where they are traded, and their stockholders. Trading by insiders must be reported to the SEC. In spite of the SEC's efforts, however, substantial insider-informed trading continues. Any attempt to manipulate security prices runs afoul of both SEC regulations and the antitrust laws. The SEC has also extended its jurisdiction to many nonstock investments and has pushed for greater corporate disclosure. The current security regulation controversy involves the central market.

DEVELOPMENT OF A CENTRAL MARKET

Congress has mandated that all of the exchanges and other securities markets (third and fourth) be fully linked. If and when that mandate is realized, buyers and sellers in all submarkets will be able to trade directly with each other. The more numerous alternatives should move buying and selling prices closer together (narrower bid-ask spreads), and the greater diversity of reachable markets should allow larger blocks to be more easily absorbed. Not surprisingly, this vision requires a number of difficult changes.

Consolidated Reporting

Until the mid-1970s securities trading was highly segmented. To obtain the best available price, each market had to be checked separately, and NYSE members could not trade in the third market. Most NYSE brokers simply funneled their orders to the market with the greatest volume. In 1974, consolidated trades began to be reported on a common ticker tape. The financial press initiated consolidated quotation reporting in 1976.

Consolidated reporting without fully consolidated trading is confusing, however. Investors expect a buy limit order to be executed if the subsequent

Composite Limit Order Book (CLOB)

low falls below the limit price. If, however, the limit order is entered on the Big Board (New York Stock Exchange), and the low occurs on the third market or another exchange, the trade may not take place. A *Composite Limit Order Book (CLOB)* and free order flow would allow all orders to be executed in any market where the security is traded. Thus, investors would always have access to the best available price, regardless of where the order was entered. Not surprisingly, however, NYSE specialists, regional specialists, and third-market dealers are each interested in preserving their existing advantages. The various submarkets cannot be linked without exposing the participants to additional competition. These conflicts, coupled with the SEC's unwillingness to impose a solution, have slowed the pace of reform.

Rule 390

Rule 390

As with the CLOB and market-link controversy, rules barring member off-exchange trading of listed securities have been fiercely defended by the securities profession. NYSE Rule 394, which prohibited such trading, was replaced with *Rule 390*, which restricts such trading. In 1977, the SEC announced that it intended to require the repeal of Rule 390 by January 1, 1978. That deadline was moved forward a number of times until December 2, 1999, when the NYSE finally voted to repeal Rule 390.

Industry sources had argued that if Rule 390 were repealed prior to the complete establishment of a central market, off-exchange markets made by the larger brokerage houses would cause some exchanges to close and others to shrink. According to this argument, brokerage houses too small to make markets for their customers would be unable to obtain competitive prices on the exchanges. Some industry sources went so far as to advocate concentrating trading on a single exchange. Similar self-serving arguments were used to oppose the end of fixed commissions. In actuality, the repeal of fixed commission rates left the overall security trading system intact. In any case, it might prove beneficial to hasten the linkup of the various markets. Easy access to the third and fourth markets should increase competition and lead to more efficient pricing.

The intermarket information system, which facilitates an exchange of price quotations, is a small step toward centralized trading. Fortunately, Congress has mandated that trading on and off the exchanges be unrestricted and that orders be allowed to flow freely from market to market.

SUMMARY AND CONCLUSIONS

This chapter explores the trading mechanisms and regulation of the securities markets. A wide array of mechanisms may be used to buy and sell securities. Most trading involves the larger companies listed on the various exchanges. Smaller companies are generally traded OTC. Newly issued securities may be sold through an underwriting syndicate, by private placement, on the exchanges, or OTC. Large blocks of already issued securities are normally marketed through a block trader, special offering, or secondary offering. A tender offer is generally used for a large purchase. Short sales are employed by investors seeking to profit from an expected price decline, while margin purchases leverage investors' equity positions.

A variety of orders are used in securities trading. Market orders require immediate execution, whereas limit orders await an acceptable price. Stop orders (stop-loss and stop-limit) offer protection from adverse price moves.

As for the development of the central market, reform forces are quite powerful, much progress has been made, opposition to additional reform is intense, and further reforms have been recommended and will probably be enacted. The principal unresolved issues involve the consolidation of trading and limit-order access.

CHAPTER REVIEW

Answers to the review questions and the self-test questions start on page 501.

Key Terms

broker	fourth market
brokerage firm	arbitrageur
registered representative	ticker tape
dealer	round lot
Glass-Steagall Act	odd lot
discretionary account	commissions
SIPC (Securities Investor Protection Corporation)	May Day
	bid-ask spread
NYSE (New York Stock Exchange)	market order
Big Board	limit order
AMEX (American Stock Exchange)	posts
dual listing	stop-loss order
OTC (over-the-counter)	stop-limit order
NASDAQ (National Association of Securities Dealers Automated Quotations)	GTC orders
	day orders
	fill-or-kill orders
NMI (National Market Issues)	all-or-nothing orders
pink sheets	versus purchase
third market	specialist

floor traders

RCMMs (registered competitive market makers)

margin account

buying power

net equity

maintenance margin percentage

credit balance

debit balance

broker call-loan rate

short selling

street name

bear raid

downtick

uptick

stock certificates

primary market

go public

initial public offering (IPO)

investment banker

underwrite

prospectus

best-effort basis

firm-commitment basis

shelf registration

private placement

lettered stock

block trades

special offerings

secondary distributions

tender offer

Securities Act of 1933

Securities Exchange Act of 1934

Composite Limit Order Book (CLOB)

Rule 390

Review Questions

3-1. Explain the purpose of the Securities Investor Protection Corporation (SIPC).

3-2. Explain the purpose of the National Daily Quotation Service.

3-3. Explain the four principal types of orders.

Versus Purchase Order example

3-4. Assume that over a period of time, an investor purchases XYZ stock in five 300-share blocks at prices of $15, $18, $31, $23, and $40 per share, respectively.

a. If the investor then sells 700 shares of XYZ, how would the basis in these shares normally be determined?

b. Explain how the investor could achieve a much higher basis for the 700 shares of XYZ than would normally be the case as determined in a. above.

(handwritten margin notes):
300 × 15 = 4500
300 × 18 = 5400
100 × 31 = 3100
$13,000 moving left
Lot the Versus Purchase order allows you to sell the whatever ones ya want so you would take the highest cost
300 × 40 = 12000
300 × 31 = 9300
100 × 23 = 2300
$23,600

3-5. Explain the roles of the third and fourth markets.

3-6. a. Describe the two types of margin calls.
b. Explain the various ways to satisfy a margin call.

3-7. Jo Ann Investor uses $5,000 plus maximum margin (50 percent) to buy stock in the Up Up Corporation at $10 per share. The stock is a clear winner. It rises to $15 per share after one month, and she continues to hold it. It then splits three for two (that is, for every two shares owned by Jo Ann, she will now have three shares) and continues rising in price until it reaches $20 per share after another 4 months have passed. Jo Ann then buys as many more shares as her position allows. Six months later, the stock pays a 25 percent stock dividend and rises to $30 per share. Jo Ann again increases her holdings to the maximum allowed by her equity. Up Up then goes to $50 per share one year later. Ignoring the impact of taxes, regular dividends, interest, and commissions, answer the following questions about Jo Ann's position after 23 months' experience with the Up Up Corporation stock.

    a. How many shares does Jo Ann own?

    b. What is the value of Jo Ann's stock?

    c. How much does Jo Ann owe in margin?

    d. What is Jo Ann's equity position?

3-8. Joe Investor uses $50,000 plus maximum margin (50 percent) to buy stock in the Down Down Corporation at $50 per share. After 6 months, the stock falls to the point where he gets a margin call (35 percent equity). To satisfy the call, he sells enough of his position to bring his equity back up to 50 percent. Two months later, Joe gets a second margin call (35 percent equity) and repeats the process. When he gets the third margin call (35 percent equity) one month later, Joe liquidates his position. Ignoring the impact of taxes, dividends, interest, and commissions in answering this question, how much of Joe's original $50,000 investment is left?

3-9. Assume the broker call-loan rate is 8 1/2 percent and that the margin loan rates of table 3-3 apply. Compute the cost of margin for each of the following, using monthly compounding:

    a. $53,000 borrowed for 6 months

    b. $27,000 borrowed for 3 months

    c. $7,000 borrowed for 10 months

3-10. Investment bankers facilitate new-issue sales of debt and equity securities. Describe the two underwriting approaches they use to accomplish this objective.

3-11. Explain what the creation of a central market for securities would accomplish.

Self-Test Questions

T F   3-1. The most basic function that brokers and their firms perform is to link investors to the securities markets.

T F   3-2. The lines between brokerage and other types of financial service firms, particularly commercial banks, are quickly eroding, and the erosion is likely to accelerate.

T F   3-3. The Securities Investor Protection Corporation (SIPC) protects brokerage customers against losses due to market fluctuations.

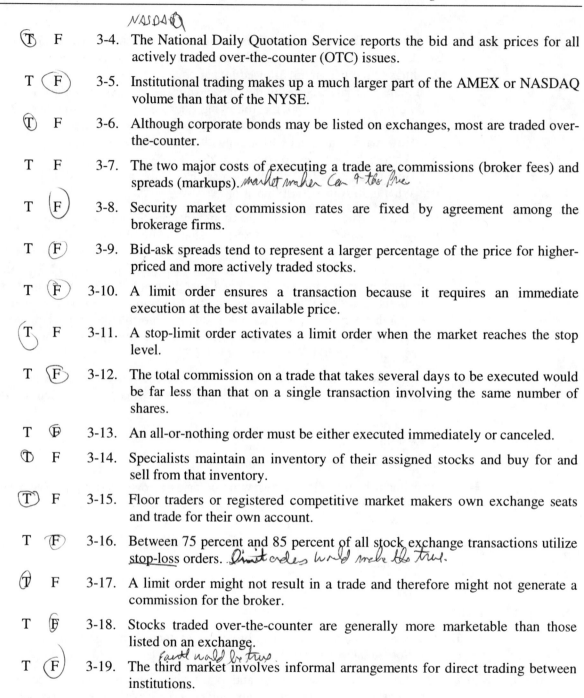

NASDAQ

(T)   F   3-4.   The National Daily Quotation Service reports the bid and ask prices for all actively traded over-the-counter (OTC) issues.

T   (F)   3-5.   Institutional trading makes up a much larger part of the AMEX or NASDAQ volume than that of the NYSE.

(T)   F   3-6.   Although corporate bonds may be listed on exchanges, most are traded over-the-counter.

T   F   3-7.   The two major costs of executing a trade are commissions (broker fees) and spreads (markups). *market maker can 9 the price*

T   (F)   3-8.   Security market commission rates are fixed by agreement among the brokerage firms.

T   (F)   3-9.   Bid-ask spreads tend to represent a larger percentage of the price for higher-priced and more actively traded stocks.

T   (F)   3-10.   A limit order ensures a transaction because it requires an immediate execution at the best available price.

(T)   F   3-11.   A stop-limit order activates a limit order when the market reaches the stop level.

T   (F)   3-12.   The total commission on a trade that takes several days to be executed would be far less than that on a single transaction involving the same number of shares.

T   (F)   3-13.   An all-or-nothing order must be either executed immediately or canceled.

(T)   F   3-14.   Specialists maintain an inventory of their assigned stocks and buy for and sell from that inventory.

(T)   F   3-15.   Floor traders or registered competitive market makers own exchange seats and trade for their own account.

T   (F)   3-16.   Between 75 percent and 85 percent of all stock exchange transactions utilize stop-loss orders. *limit orders would make this true.*

(T)   F   3-17.   A limit order might not result in a trade and therefore might not generate a commission for the broker.

T   (F)   3-18.   Stocks traded over-the-counter are generally more marketable than those listed on an exchange.

T   (F)   3-19.   *fourth would be true.* The third market involves informal arrangements for direct trading between institutions.

(T)   F   3-20.   Many high-volume stocks trade simultaneously on the NYSE, several regional exchanges, and over-the-counter.

[handwritten: This is the maintenance #]

[handwritten: 50 %]

T (F) 3-21. The Federal Reserve Board set the initial margin requirement on stocks at 25 percent.

(T) F 3-22. To be purchasable on margin, an OTC stock must have at least 1,200 shareholders and a market value of $5 million or more.

(T) F 3-23. Margin loans may remain outstanding as long as the borrower's equity position does not fall below the maintenance margin percentage.

(T) F 3-24. Preferreds, warrants, and convertibles are subject to the same margin requirements as common stock.

T (F) 3-25. Traders typically use short sales to drive a stock's price down. *[handwritten: This is illegal]*

(T) F 3-26. Margined securities must be left on deposit with the shareholder's brokerage house. *[handwritten: Borrowing securities at too]*

(T) F 3-27. Stock certificates must be issued whenever a stock is registered in an individual's name.

T (F) 3-28. Investment bankers generally agree to sell a new issue on a best-effort basis where they act as agents for the issuing firm.

T (F) 3-29. Off-exchange member trading of listed securities is strictly prohibited. *[handwritten: (OTC market)]*

(T) F 3-30. Congress has mandated that trading on and off the exchanges be unrestricted and that orders be allowed to flow freely from market to market.

NOTES

1. The two separate web addresses (www.amex.com and www.nasdaq.com) still work, but both bring up the same page.
2. I. Friend, "The Economic Consequences of the Stock Market," *American Economic Review,* May 1972, pp. 212–219.

started on 9/19/02 — This Chapter.

4

Securities Valuation

Learning Objectives

An understanding of the material in this chapter should enable the student to

4-1. Explain the application of time value of money to the valuation of securities.

4-2. Value a bond.

4-3. Value a stock using the appropriate model.

4-4. Explain the various factors that affect discount rates.

4-5. Describe the relationship between a stock's value, its expected earnings per share, its expected payout ratio, and the discount rate.

Chapter Outline

time value

The primary tool in finance is the concept of the *time value* of money. Time value of money is used to calculate how much some lump sum or series of payments will accumulate to at some later time. This tool is also used to determine how much money should be set aside today to fund a future payment or cash flow. Finally, time value of money is used to price a security by determining the present value of all expected cash inflows. In this chapter, we will review the basics of time value of money and show how these calculations can be used to price various types of securities.

Many of these applications of time value of money can be obtained more simply by using a financial calculator. In addition, the use of a financial calculator can significantly improve the speed and ease of solving time value problems.

THE BASICS OF TIME VALUE OF MONEY

Suppose you were offered the choice of receiving $100 now or $100 a year from now. Which would you choose? Everyone would choose to have the money now rather than later. Even those who did not intend to use the money for a year would not want to wait. Any funds that are available now but are not needed until a year from now can be invested and used at some later time. The notion that the $100 today is preferable to $100 one year from today is the basis for the time value of money concept.

present value

A dollar today can begin to earn interest immediately. Thus, a currently payable dollar should be worth more than a promise to pay a dollar in the future. The *present value* of a future payment depends on how much is to be received, when it is to be received, and how much of a discount is applied to future values compared to present values. Similarly, the value of a stream of payments to be received over time depends on the amounts, timing, and *discount rate* applied to the payments.

discount rate

The Present Value of a Future Payment or Stream of Payments Depends On . . .

- How much is to be received
- When is (are) the payment(s) to be received
- How much of a discount rate is to be applied to the payment(s)

Application to Securities Pricing

valuation

The value of any security is the present value of the expected future payments derived from ownership of that security. Such a *valuation* enables an individual to compare a security price in the market today to the present value of the future payments. The present value today of the future payments is referred to as the intrinsic value of the security. This intrinsic value is based on expected future payments that may include dividends or interest, plus a sale or maturity value.

As indicated earlier, an understanding of time value of money concepts is required to understand securities pricing. These concepts are necessary to calculate the present value of expected future cash flows. They also may be necessary to project the future value of expected payments, such as dividends, based on growth rate expectations. Therefore, both present value and *future value* calculations will be reviewed in this chapter.

future value

Compounding and Discounting

compound interest

Money grows over time to some future value as a result of compounding interest. *Compound interest* is interest on both the original principal and the interest that has been credited throughout the period. As a result of compounding, the future value will always exceed the present value, as long as the interest rate exceeds 0 percent.

opportunity cost

Interest accrues as compensation for delay in using the money. This compensation can be referred to as *opportunity cost*—the interest that could have been earned if the money had been invested elsewhere. For example, if you deposit $1,000 in a savings account and leave it there for one year, you expect your account to earn interest as compensation for your opportunity cost.

discounting

Likewise, some value in the future can be reduced to an equivalent value as of today using *discounting*. When a future value is discounted at some interest rate greater than 0 percent, the resulting present value is less than the future value. For example, in order to have $1,000 one year from today, you can expect to deposit less than that $1,000 in your bank account today.

There are two important variables that you will need to determine the future value or present value of some sum. The first is the number of periods over which compounding or discounting occurs. The greater the number of periods that an amount is compounded, the higher the future value. Likewise, the greater the number of periods that an amount is discounted, the lower the present value.

The second important variable is the interest rate used in the compounding or discounting process. The higher the interest rate for compounding, the higher the future value. Likewise, the higher the interest rate for discounting, the lower the present value.

Let's summarize these relationships. The future value is higher than the present value. The future value *increases* when the number of periods (n) *increases* or the interest rate (i) *increases*. The present value has an inverse relationship with these variables—that is, the present value *decreases* when the number of periods (n) *increases* or the interest rate (i) *increases*.

So far, we've talked about relationships among variables for compounding and discounting. The four key variables in time value of money problems are the number of periods, the interest rate, the present value, and the future value. Given three of the variables, we can always solve for the fourth.

Future Value of Single Sums

Let's consider a specific example of how to compute the future value of some single sum today. Let's say that we deposit $100 in a savings account that earns 3 percent annually and let all the cash ride for 4 years. Each year, the account will earn 3 percent on the principal sum of $100 plus the interest that has accrued on that principal. Each year our account will accrue interest as follows, starting from today, year 0:

Year 0   Deposit $100
Year 1 $100 + 3% (100) = $103
Year 2 $103 + 3% (103) = $106.09
Year 3 $106.09 + 3%(106.09) = $109.27
Year 4 $109.27 + 3% (109.27) = $112.55

This approach can quickly become tedious when many years are involved. We can determine the future value more directly by using a general equation that takes into account each year of compounding. The general equation for future value is

$$FV = PV (1 + i)^n$$

where FV = future value
PV = present value
i = interest rate for compounding
n = number of periods of compounding

Let's use the equation to verify the results of our example. In this case, FV is our unknown, PV is $100, i is .03, and n is 4 years. We will round our result to two decimal places.

$$FV = PV (1 + i)^n$$
$$FV = \$100 (1.03)^4$$
$$FV = \$100 (1.125509)$$
$$FV = \$112.55$$

Example: Calculate the future value of $8,000 today, invested for 19 years at 7 percent.

$$FV = PV (1 + i)^n$$
$$FV = \$8,000 (1.07)^{19}$$
$$FV = \$8,000 (3.616528)$$
$$FV = \$28,932.22$$

So far, we have assumed that compounding takes place once a year (annually). Unless told otherwise, you can assume that compounding or discounting takes place on an annual basis. However, compounding or discounting may take place more frequently than annually. When that occurs, the same equation can be used, but the n and i variables must be adjusted. The following relationships apply to the frequency of compounding. First, the more frequent the compounding, the higher the future value. The more frequent the discounting, the lower the present value. Let's take a look at calculating a future value when compounding occurs more frequently than annually.

Let's say that your $100 will receive 3 percent interest, but this time compounding will be on a monthly basis, or 12 times a year. We can expect that after a 4-year period, we will end up with more than $112.55—the amount we would receive on an annual basis. Before we begin, remember that we will need to make adjustments both to n and to i. The adjustments can be expressed as follows:

n = number of years multiplied by the frequency of compounding
i = annual interest rate divided by frequency of compounding

In this case,

$$n = 4 \times 12 = 48$$
$$i = .03/12 = .0025$$

Now we can use our formula as usual:

$$FV = PV (1 + i)^n$$
$$FV = \$100 (1.0025)^{48}$$
$$FV = \$100 (1.127328)$$
$$FV = \$112.73$$

If compounding had been semi-annual (twice a year), we would have multiplied the number of years by 2, and divided the interest rate by 2. If compounding had been quarterly (four times a year), we would have multiplied the number of years by 4, and divided the interest rate by 4.

Adjustments to n and i are the same, regardless of whether you are calculating a future value or a present value.

Example: Determine the future value of $8,000 invested for 19 years at 7 percent quarterly.

$$n = 19 \times 4 = 76$$
$$i = .07/4 = .0175$$

$$FV = PV (1 + i)^n$$
$$FV = \$8,000 (1.0175)^{76}$$
$$FV = \$8,000 (3.737797)$$
$$FV = \$29,902.38$$

Note that the quarterly compounding has increased the future value by $29.84, compared to the annual compounding of the previous example.

Present Value of Single Sums

So far, we've taken single sums of today's dollars and compounded them to various amounts. Now we will work in the opposite direction, discounting future values back to the present. Let's say that we expect to receive $100 4 years from now and we would like to discount it at 3 percent annually. We may select that discount rate because we could have earned this rate in an investment if the money were available to us now, rather than 4 years from now. We will discount our future value back to today, year 0, as follows:

Year 4	$100
Year 3	$100/(1 + 3%) = $97.09
Year 2	$97.09/(1 + 3%) = $94.26
Year 1	$94.26/(1 + 3%) = $91.51
Year 0	$91.51/(1 + 3%) = $88.84

We can obtain the same result using an equation based on the future value equation. Remember that $FV = PV (1 + i)^n$. We can restate this equation for the present value by solving for PV:

$$FV = PV(1+i)^n$$

$$\frac{FV}{(1+i)^n} = PV$$

$$PV = \frac{FV}{(1+i)^n}$$

Let's use the equation to verify the results of our example. In this case, PV is our unknown, FV is $100, i is .03, and n is 4 years. We will round our result to two decimal places. You will notice that our answer is one cent different from our answer using the prior method. This difference is due to rounding and should not be a concern.

$$PV = \frac{FV}{(1+i)^n}$$

$$PV = \frac{\$100}{(1+.03)^4}$$

$$PV = \frac{\$100}{1.125509} = \$88.85$$

Example 1:   Discount an asset promising $100 3 years from now back to today at a discount rate of 6 percent.

$$PV = \frac{\$100}{1.06^3} = \frac{\$100}{1.1910} = \$83.96$$

Example 2:   Determine the present value of $10,000 9 years from now, discounted semi-annually at an annual rate of 5 percent.

$$n = 9 \times 2 = 18$$

$$i = .05 / 2 = .025$$

$$PV = \frac{FV}{(1+i)^n}$$

$$PV = \frac{\$10,000}{(1+.025)^{18}}$$

$$PV = \frac{\$10,000}{1.559659} = \$6,411.66$$

Periodic Payments

So far, we have talked about compounding and discounting a single payment. We can also compound or discount a series of payments made at the end of each period. These cash flows may be of equal or different amounts. We can solve for the future value or present value of a series of periodic payments by using the previous equations for each payment and totaling the results.

Example 1:	Determine the future value at the end of 5 years of five annual payments, starting in one year, of $700 each compounded at 6 percent annual.

For each payment, $FV = PV(1 + i)^n$

The first payment will compound for 4 years, the second payment for 3 years, and so on. The fifth payment at the end of the 5 years will receive no interest.

$$FV = PV(1 + i)^n + PV(1 + i)^n + PV(1 + i)^n + PV(1 + i)^n + PV(1 + i)^n$$

$$FV = \$700(1 + .06)^4 + \$700(1 + .06)^3 + \$700(1 + .06)^2 + \$700(1 + .06)^1 + \$700(1 + .06)^0$$

$$FV = \$700(1.262477) + \$700(1.191016) + \$700(1.123600) + \$700(1.06) + \$700(1)$$

$$FV = \$883.73 + \$833.71 + \$786.52 + \$742.00 + \$700 = \$3,945.96$$

Example 2:	Discount an asset promising three annual payments of $100 each back to today at a discount rate of 6 percent.

For each payment,

$$PV = \frac{FV}{(1+i)^n}$$

$$PV = \frac{\$100}{1.06} + \frac{\$100}{(1.06)^2} + \frac{\$100}{(1.06)^3}$$

$$PV = \frac{\$100}{1.06} + \frac{\$100}{(1.123600)} + \frac{\$100}{(1.191016)}$$

$$PV = \$94.34 + \$89.00 + \$83.96 = \$267.30$$

annuity

An *annuity* is a series of equal single sums, as in the examples above. These examples are not complex, but they do become tedious. Fortunately, when the stream of periodic payments consists of a series of equal amounts, the following equations may be used for future and present value calculations. These equations are summations of the single sum equations for more than one single sum.

$$FV = \text{payment} \times \left[\frac{(1+i)^n - 1}{i} \right]$$

$$PV = \text{payment} \times \left[\frac{1 - \dfrac{1}{(1+i)^n}}{i} \right]$$

In the following example, we will restate the prior examples using the formulas.

Example 1:   Determine the future value in 5 years of five annual payments of $700 each, starting in one year and compounded at 6 percent annually.

$$FV = \text{payment} \times \left[\frac{(1+i)^n - 1}{i} \right]$$

$$FV = \$700 \times \left[\frac{(1 = .06)^5 - 1}{.06} \right]$$

$$FV = \$700 \times 5.637093$$

$$FV = \$3,945.97$$

Example 2:   Discount an asset promising three annual payments of $100 each back to today at a discount rate of 6 percent.

$$PV = \text{payment} \times \left[\frac{1 - \dfrac{1}{(1+i)^n}}{i} \right]$$

$$PV = \$100 \times \left[\frac{1 - \dfrac{1}{(1+.06)^3}}{.06} \right]$$

$$PV = \$100 \times \left[\frac{1 - \dfrac{1}{(1.191016)}}{.06} \right]$$

$$PV = \$100 \times \frac{(1 - .839619)}{.06}$$

$$PV = \$100 \times \frac{(.160381)}{.06}$$

$$PV = \$100 \times (2.673017) = \$267.30$$

BOND VALUATION

Let us see how the concept of time value can be applied to the income stream of a bond. A bond is a debt security that makes periodic interest (coupon) payments and then returns a face value at maturity. For the vast majority of bonds, the periodic interest payment is fixed at a set amount, called the coupon rate. Additionally, most corporate bonds pay interest every 6 months.

Example: A 10-year, 8 percent, $1,000 corporate bond would promise the following income stream:

- coupon payments of $40 every 6 months (1/2 x 8% x $1,000) for 10 years, for a total of 20 coupon payments *plus*
- a principal payment of $1,000 at the end of 10 years

A bond that promises a constant income stream, known as an annuity, can be valued by combining the present value formulas for the annuity stream with the present value of the principal repayment:

$$PV = \text{payment} \times \left[\frac{1 - \dfrac{1}{(1+i)^n}}{i}\right] + \frac{FV}{(1+i)^n}$$

There are several important ideas to note about valuing a bond. First, the coupon is payable on a semi-annual basis (twice a year). Therefore, the number of periods is n x 2 where n is the number of years to maturity.

Second, because the discounting will take place on a semi-annual rather than annual basis, the discount rate must be adjusted. The discount rate will be one-half the annual discount rate.

Finally, the cash flows will be discounted back at some rate that is not necessarily the same as the coupon rate. In fact, in most instances, the discount rate will not equal the *coupon rate* because the discount rate is based on market conditions and other factors at the time of the bond valuation.

coupon rate

In general, the discount rate on a bond can be thought of as the market-determined interest rate that would be paid on a bond of comparable risk and maturity that trades at par. Trading at par means that the bond sells for the maturity value of $1,000 and has a present value equal to its face value. We will discuss this more in a later section.

Example: A $1,000 (face value) bond with a 5 percent coupon rate will mature in 3 years. Therefore, the bond will pay semi-annual coupons of $25 (1/2 x 5% x $1,000). The present value of this income flow at an 8 percent discount rate is

$$PV = \text{payment} \times \left[\frac{1 - \dfrac{1}{(1+i)^n}}{i}\right] + \left[\frac{FV}{(1+i)^n}\right]$$

$$PV = \$25 \times \left[\frac{1 - \dfrac{1}{(1+.04)^6}}{.04}\right] + \left[\frac{\$1,000}{(1+.04)^6}\right]$$

$$PV = \$25(5.242137) + \$790.31 = \$921.36$$

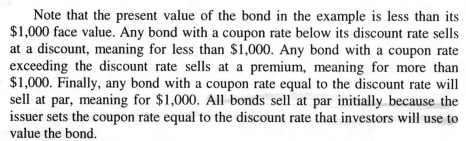

Note that the present value of the bond in the example is less than its $1,000 face value. Any bond with a coupon rate below its discount rate sells at a discount, meaning for less than $1,000. Any bond with a coupon rate exceeding the discount rate sells at a premium, meaning for more than $1,000. Finally, any bond with a coupon rate equal to the discount rate will sell at par, meaning for $1,000. All bonds sell at par initially because the issuer sets the coupon rate equal to the discount rate that investors will use to value the bond.

Now, suppose that the bond in the example is valued using a 3 percent (annual) discount rate. We already know, therefore, that the bond will sell for more than $1,000, because the coupon rate is higher than the discount rate. At a 3 percent annual discount rate, the bond's present value would be $1,056.97. You can verify this by following the steps in the example above using a semi-annual discount rate of 1.5 percent.

The vast majority of debt obligations promise to repay principal at some future date. Britain, however, has issued some infinite-maturity bonds called consols. They can be valued in a manner similar to preferred stock, which will be discussed in a later section.

DETERMINANTS OF THE DISCOUNT RATE

As shown above, the discount rate is critical to bond valuation. The appropriate discount rate varies both over time and from investment to investment. Many factors influence discount rates for bond valuation.

Default Risk

A particular asset's appropriate discount rate depends on the perceived risk of the investment. In general, the more certain the expected outcome, the lower the appropriate discount rate. Because the lower the discount rate, the higher the present value, low-risk expected income streams are valued more highly than high-risk expected streams of equivalent magnitude and timing.

Default risk is the risk that the issuer will not fulfill the obligation to pay all coupons plus the maturity value. The default risk of municipal and corporate debt securities depends on the income-producing and/or liquidation values of the issuers' assets and on the amount of other debt outstanding.

The federal government guarantee of Treasury-issued securities results in virtually no default risk for these securities. The market trusts the federal guarantee because the government has extensive taxing power, and the Federal Reserve Board (the Fed) can facilitate sales of government securities.

Price Risk

Interest rate risk is the risk that the value of a bond will decline as a result of an increase in market rates. Market rates may change as a result of changing economic conditions, and they vary inversely with the relative supply of loanable funds. At times, the supply of funds available for borrowing (relative to the demand) is tight, while at other times loanable funds are more plentiful. An increase in the demand for funds can fuel an increase in market rates, resulting in a decrease in the value of bonds. The prices of longer-maturity debt issues are much more sensitive to interest rate shifts than are the prices of shorter-term debt issues.

Reinvestment Rate Risk

Reinvestment rate risk is the risk that the income from a bond portfolio will be reinvested at rates of return lower than the current rates. That is, if interest rates fall (which is good news with respect to price risk), then as future coupon payments are received, the returns available will be less attractive for the investor.

STOCK VALUATION

As stated earlier, the value of any security is the present value of the expected income stream. We have seen how this valuation technique is applied to bonds. Now we will explain how the value of stock can be determined by finding the present value of the stream of expected future cash flows from the stock.

The stream of cash flows from stocks differs from that of bonds in two ways. First, while bonds pay interest, or coupon, payments, stocks generally pay dividends. Second, stocks do not have a specified maturity date but rather are assumed to have a perpetual life with a perpetual stream of cash flows.

Zero Growth Model

Preferred shares are usually expected to pay a stream of equal annual dividend payments.[1] The expected stability of the income stream is similar to the expected stability of the coupon payment of bonds. However, as noted earlier, stocks do not mature like bonds but are expected to continue dividend payments in perpetuity.

zero growth model

For situations where the rate of dividend growth is expected to remain the same, the *zero growth model* is used to price the security. Thus, the value of preferred stock can be modeled as follows:

$$V = \frac{d}{k}$$

where V = intrinsic value of the bond
d = constant annual dividend
k = discount rate

required rate of return

For stock valuation, k, the discount rate, is also referred to as the investor's *required rate of return*. We will discuss this more thoroughly in a later section.

Example: A preferred stock pays a dividend of $1.50 annually. If the appropriate discount rate is 5 percent, determine the value of the stock.

$$V = \frac{d}{k} = \frac{\$1.50}{.05} = \$30.00$$

---

constant growth model

Constant Growth Model

As stated earlier, stocks pay a portion of profits to shareholders in the form of dividends. Holders of common stock own a share of the company, as well as receive the dividends. Profits not paid out as dividends are reinvested in the company. The additional resources acquired with these investments are expected to lead to growth and increased future earnings and dividends. This growth is also expected to result in increased share value. Figure 4-1 illustrates the relationship between earnings and stock prices.

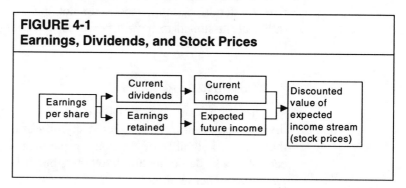

FIGURE 4-1
Earnings, Dividends, and Stock Prices

When dividends are expected to grow at a constant rate, g, then the dividend for any year, n, is expected to equal the prior year's dividend times one plus that growth rate. Thus, $d_1 = d_0(1 + g)$, $d_2 = d_1(1+g) = d_0(1+g)^2$, and so on. This relationship can be defined as

$$d_n = d_{n-1}(1+g) \text{ or } d_n = d_0(1 + g)^n$$

where d_n = dividend in year n
d_{n-1} = dividend in year prior to year n
d_0 = dividend just paid yesterday
g = growth rate

If we are willing to make this one assumption with regard to future dividends, then we can state the value of a share of stock as

$$V_0 = \frac{d_1}{(1+k)} + \frac{d_2}{(1+k)^2} + \frac{d_3}{(1+k)^3} + \ldots$$

$$= \frac{d_0(1+g)}{(1+k)} + \frac{d_0(1+g)^2}{(1+k)^2} + \frac{d_0(1+g)^3}{(1+k)^3} + \ldots$$

It turns out that some nifty mathematical manipulation can reduce this complex formula to the rather simple formula:

$$V_0 = \frac{d_1}{(k-g)} = \frac{d_0(1+g)}{(k-g)} \qquad \text{for } g < k$$

In this equation, V_0 is the intrinsic value of the stock today (at year 0) d_1 is the dividend projected for the coming year (year 1), k is the required rate of return, and g is the growth rate.

As indicated by the constant growth formula, the price of a stock rises with both its dividend and its growth rate and falls as the discount rate is increased. This formula applies only when expected growth rates are below the discount rate. Stocks with dividends that have expected growth rates exceeding the discount rate in perpetuity would have theoretically infinite prices. That nonsensical result would occur because each successive expected dividend would have a higher present value than the one before it. Clearly, stock prices are finite.

For short periods, companies may grow more rapidly than their market-determined discount rate. These growth rates are, however, temporary phenomena that exist only when a company is in a stage of rapid growth. In the long run, dividends are always expected to grow more slowly than the rate at which they are discounted. A modification of the constant growth model, referred to as the supernormal growth model, can be used to price such a security.

Obviously, not all stocks experience rising earnings, dividends, and stock prices. Some companies experience losses, pay no dividends, or experience declines in their stocks' price. In extreme cases, a company may be forced to declare bankruptcy. The shareholders may be left with nothing but some worthless stock certificates and a tax write-off. Nevertheless, those who buy stock, at the time that they make the investment, expect to receive a return in the form of dividends and/or price appreciation.

Example 1: Assume that Acme Corp. experiences constant dividend growth at a rate of 5 percent per year. Its required rate of return (discount rate) is 15 percent. The dividend that was just paid was $2/share. Using the constant growth model, we can value Acme Corp. common stock as follows:

$$d_1 = d_0(1+g) = \$2(1.05) = \$2.10$$

$$P_0 = \frac{d_1}{k-g} = \frac{\$2.10}{.15-.05} = \$21.00$$

Example 2: Use the same assumptions as in Example 1, except assume that Acme's dividend growth rate is now 7 percent. To find the value:

$$d_1 = d_0(1+g) = \$2(1.07) = \$2.14$$

$$P_0 = \frac{d_1}{k-g} = \frac{\$2.14}{.15-.07} = \$26.75$$

Example 3: Use the same assumptions as in Example 1, except assume that now Acme's required return is 20 percent. To value the security:

$$d_1 = d_0(1+g) = \$2(1.05) = \$2.10$$

$$P_0 = \frac{d_1}{k-g} = \frac{\$2.10}{.20-.05} = \$14.00$$

Example 4: Assume Baker Co. just paid a dividend of $3/share. It is expected to pay $3.15/share next year and to maintain a constant rate of growth. The value of Baker stock is $25/share. Determine the investor's required rate of return.

$$d_1 = d_0(1+g)$$
$$\$3.15 = \$3(1+g)$$
$$1.05 = 1 + g$$
$$.05 = g$$

$$P = \frac{d_1}{k-g} = \frac{3.15}{k-.05} = 25$$
$$\$3.15 = \$25(k-.05)$$
$$\$3.15 = \$25k - 1.25$$
$$4.4 = \$25k$$
$$.176 = k = 17.6\%$$

(Handwritten margin notes:)

$$\frac{3.15}{3} = 1.05$$

$$P = \frac{3.15}{k - .05} =$$

$$P = \frac{3.15}{k - .05}$$

$$25 = \frac{3.15}{k - .05}$$

$$3.15 = 25(k - .05)$$

In the above problems, we used a discount rate to calculate the present value of anticipated cash flows. The discount rate used, k, represents the investor's required rate of return. The investor arrives at this rate based on the risk of the security, as well as the returns available in the market for other securities. As with bonds, many factors influence the discount rate for stock valuation.

risk-free rate

One factor in securities valuation is known as the *risk-free rate*. This is the compensation that investors need, to induce them to forgo current consumption. The rate on U.S. government debt is considered the risk-free rate, because there is virtually no risk that the United States government will default on its debt obligations. The appropriate rates for risky assets are scaled up from the current market rate (the risk-free rate) on riskless assets.

real risk-free rate

The risk-free rate is generally thought to equal a *real risk-free rate* that assumes no inflation expectations, plus an inflation rate that is related to the long-term *inflation expectations* of the economy. The inflation premium is compensation for the loss in future purchasing power due to expected future inflation.

inflation expectations

risk premium

Another factor in the discount rate is the *risk premium*—the extra compensation that an investor demands for making an investment that is not risk free. For stocks, this risk will be discussed in more detail in chapter 7.

nominal rate

The *nominal rate* on an investment is the rate unadjusted for inflation. Nominal rates are the rates we see and work with every day. To understand the actual inflation-adjusted rate on an investment, the nominal rate must be adjusted. The following equation adjusts the nominal rate to obtain a real inflation-adjusted rate:

$$\frac{1 + \text{nominal rate}}{1 + \text{inflation rate}} - 1 = \text{real rate}$$

The nominal rate can be approximated as follows:

$$\text{Nominal rate} - \text{inflation rate} \approx \text{real rate}$$

MARKET PRICES

Common stock can generate income streams that are much less predictable than the income streams of bonds and preferred shares. Although investors may use market analysts' forecasts or historical experience to estimate future cash flows, the market's true (unobservable) expectations may differ. The market price does not reveal the market's earnings stream expectations *per se*. Rather, the price is jointly determined by the expected payments and the rate used to discount them. Nevertheless, the price, which is observable, does provide some insight into the market's earnings stream expectations, which are not observable.

We can use the constant growth model to find the market's expected rate of return, in the form of the discount rate, for the firm. We already know the prior year's dividend. If we make an assumption about the expected growth rate, g, we can determine the rate at which the market discounts the income stream by solving for k.

Example: Assume that Acme Corp. experiences constant dividend growth at a rate of 5 percent per year. The dividend that was just paid was $2/share and the security sells for $25 per share.

$$d_1 = d_0(1+g) = \$2(1.05) = \$2.10$$

$$P_0 = \frac{d_i}{(k-g)}$$

$$\$25 = \frac{\$2.10}{k - .05}$$

$$k = .134$$

P/E Ratio

earnings per share (EPS)

price-earnings (P/E) ratio

Investors and investment analysts often focus on the price of a stock in relation to its *earnings per share (EPS)*. The per-share price divided by the per-share earnings is called the *price-earnings (P/E) ratio*. The P/E ratio puts stock prices into perspective by relating the stock's price per share to its earnings per share. The more optimistically the market views the prospects for a particular stock, the more it is prepared to bid up the price of the stock relative to its current earnings. Thus, the stocks of companies with favorable growth opportunities (often called growth stocks) tend to have high P/E ratios. Stocks with less promising earning potentials have lower P/Es.

The P/E ratio can be expressed as

$$PE = \frac{\text{Price per share}}{\text{Earnings per share}} = \frac{P_0}{EPS}$$

In this equation, P_0 represents the price of the security today. The denominator may represent either last year's (actually the sum of the last 4 quarters) earnings per share, or next year's earnings per share. If the historical earnings are used, the number is referred to as the past P/E ratio or price-to-current-earnings ratio. If the future earnings are used, it is the price-to-future-earnings ratio or future P/E ratio. Most people are sloppy when using this term and simply say "P/E ratio." An investor should always be sure he or she understands which ratio is being described or discussed. Remember, a future P/E ratio depends on whose forecast of earnings is being used. Furthermore, even the task of forecasting earnings one year ahead is incredibly complex. The preferred P/E ratio is the one that uses the prior year's earnings. There should never be any debate as to this value at any point in time.

SECURITIES SELECTION

dividend payout ratio

Evaluating an investment involves forecasting its income stream and assessing the corresponding risk. Many firms try to maintain a stable long-term relationship between dividends and earnings, known as the *dividend payout ratio*. Dividend payouts do, however, tend to vary from firm to firm and over time for the same firm. More specifically, they tend to move inversely with growth, risk, and earnings volatility. A company with rapidly growing, volatile, and uncertain earnings tends to pay out a smaller fraction of its income than a slower-growth firm with a more dependable earnings stream. Most mature companies have a relatively high, stable, long-run payout ratio. Typically, between 50 percent and 60 percent of corporate after-tax earnings are paid out as dividends.

The market's weighted average opinion of a particular investment (as reflected by the price that the market determines from the interplay of supply and demand) is, by itself, little help in investment selection. Market expectations may or may not be accurate. The investment selection process as typically performed by fund managers or security analysts can be viewed largely as a search for assets that the market has improperly valued. In other words, investment analysts generally attempt to understand and find errors (overvaluations or undervaluations) in the market's evaluation.

The predictions and recommendations of investment analysts are notoriously uneven. Two basic problems with most investment analysts are their tendency to utilize similar approaches and their reluctance to recommend sales. Thus, those rare analysts who do not follow the herd and who sometimes recommend selling may deserve close attention.

Studies have generally concluded that analysts do slightly better than naive models of simple extrapolation of past growth rates. Even though there are errors in analysts' forecasts, because they have more information on which to base a forecast, analysts can still do a better job at forecasting earnings than can a simple mechanical model based on past earnings growth.

Security analysts and other professional investors can compare their own discounted dividend forecasts with the market's or compare their assessments of the company's growth prospects with the market's expectations. With either approach, theoretically, investors can identify "undervalued" and "overvalued" securities by contrasting their valuations with the market's. Selections based on this analysis, however, can fail to produce the expected result for a variety of reasons:

- The income stream forecasts can be inaccurate. If the investor's income stream forecast is too high, the investment is likely to do less well than expected.
- Even if the income forecasts are on target, errors in the assumed discount rates can account for the apparent difference between the investor's and the market's evaluations.
- The anticipated earnings increase can be offset by an increase in risk. An increase in risk will cause the discount rate to rise, thereby tending to decrease the investment's value.
- The investor may need to sell the asset before the market (favorably) reevaluates it. The investor may be correct on value but incorrect on timing.
- The investor may correctly identify undervalued securities but subsequent revaluations are offset by a general market decline.

Therefore, a security identified as undervalued may not necessarily earn a superior return for its owners, relative to other investments of comparable risk.

SUMMARY AND CONCLUSIONS

The fundamental idea behind the time value of money is that people prefer to receive money sooner rather than later. Therefore, the value of an expectation of receiving $1,000 at some future time must be less than $1,000. The concept of the time value of money allows us to quantify the time value, or present value, of an expected future cash flow or stream of cash flows.

Fundamental to determining the present value of future cash flows is the idea of discounting. The discount rate is the rate by which the value of expected future cash flows is reduced to reflect the time one has to wait to receive them. Just as the interest rate increases the future value of money available now, the discount rate reduces the present value of money one expects to receive in the future.

The factors that make up the discount rate are the same as the factors that make up the interest rate. First, there is the real risk-free rate, which reflects the preference for present consumption over future consumption. Then there is the expectation of inflation over the time horizon until the cash flows are received. Finally, there is the risk premium, which factors in any uncertainty of the expected cash flows being received at the expected times and in the expected amounts.

CHAPTER REVIEW

Answers to the review questions and the self-test questions start on page 501.

Key Terms

time value	required rate of return
present value	constant growth model
discount rate	risk-free rate
valuation	real risk-free rate
future value	inflation expectations
compound interest	risk premium
opportunity cost	nominal rate
discounting	earnings per share (EPS)
annuity	price-earnings (P/E) ratio
coupon rate	dividend payout ratio
zero growth model	

Review Questions

4-1. Explain what is meant by time value. How does the concept enter into investment valuation?

4-2. Compute the present value (PV) for the following income streams:
   a. $50 annually, forever discounted at 10 percent.
   b. $200 annually for 20 years, discounted at 20 percent

Question 4-3

A   C   e
20   20

N 20
       10%
1/YR 7%
        1317.82 1000   289.26
PV _____
pmt 100   100   100
       1000   100   1000
FV   1000   1000
                  1
P/YR 1   1

when int rates (like?) are lower then the nominal rate (10%) 4-3a) the bond is selling at a Premium.

Bond A
        10
N
1/YR   12
        773.99
PV _____
PMT   80
FV   1000
P/YR   1

c. a bond with a $150 annual coupon for 12 years, maturing at $1,070, discounted at 16 percent

d. a payment stream discounted at 8 percent of $200 in year 1, $300 in year 2, $400 in year 3, $500 in year 4, and 0 in subsequent years

1000×10%<r

4-3. Compute the price of a 20-year bond with a par value of $1,000 and a 10 percent annual coupon when comparable market interest rates are

a. 7 percent
b. 9 percent
c. 10 percent
d. 11 percent
e. 13 percent

1000×10% = 100 PMt   20N   2I < 1059.40
1000 FV   20N   2I =   → 258.42
                                        1317.82

4-4. Look at the following income streams:

Year	A	B	C
1	$100	$500	$200
2	200	400	300
3	300	300	500
4	400	200	300
5	500	100	200

a. Which of these will have the least present value and why? Which will have the greatest present value?

b. Find the present value of the income streams discounted at 12 percent.

c. What would the present value of the income streams be if they were discounted at 0 percent?

4-5. Compute the present value of the following bonds. Assume a principal payment of $1,000 and annual interest payments.

	Coupon Rate	Years to Maturity	Discount Rate
Bond A	8%	10	12%
Bond B	16	10	12
Bond C	8	2	12
Bond D	16	10	10

4-6. How is an approach based on the present value of the expected future income stream used to value investment assets?

4-7. Explain how a 20-year bond with a $1,000 face value could sell for $600 or $1,200. What would cause such bonds to rise or fall in value?

4-8. Explain the various ways that inflation might affect the value of a bond.

4-9. The American Pig Company (ticker symbol PORK) currently pays a dividend of $3.00 per share, which is expected to rise by $.25 per share for the next 5 years. The stock currently sells for $36 per share, a ratio of 12 times its current dividends. The same ratio of dividends to price is also expected at the end of 5 years. Compute the present value of PORK's expected income stream for discount rates

a. of 8 percent
b. of 10 percent
c. of 12 percent
d. of 15 percent
e. of 18 percent
f. at a constant dividend of $3.00 (at a discount rate of 8 percent)

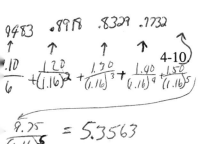

4-10. Evaluate the stock of ZYX Corporation using the following information:
- current dividend: $1.00
- respective annual dividend over next 5 years: $1.10, $1.20, $1.30, $1.40, $1.50
- current discount rate: 16 percent
- current and future market price/dividend rate: 6.5

4-11. Repeat question 4-10 using discount rates of
a. 10 percent
b. 20 percent

4-12. Assuming constant growth, compute the market price for the following sets of information:
a. $d_0 = \$1$; k = 12%; g = 10%
b. $d_0 = \$2$; k = 12%; g = 11%
c. $d_0 = \$1.50$; k = 12%; g = 8%

4-13. Assuming a payout of 55 percent, what would the P/E ratios in question 4-12 be?

4-14. Compute the market-implied expected long-term growth rate for the following information (assuming both growth and the dividend payout ratio are constant):
a. PE = 8; p = 40%; k = 12%
b. PE = 10; p = 50%; k = 12%
c. PE = 15; p = 60%; k = 12%

4-15. Why do investment analysts concentrate on earnings predictions rather than dividend predictions?

Self-Text Questions

T   F   4-1. For the vast majority of bonds, the periodic interest payment varies directly with the current market rate of interest.

T   F   4-2. Any bond with a coupon rate below the discount rate is worth more than its face value.

T F   4-3. Yields on government bonds are often used to proxy for the risk-free rate.

T F   4-4. The appropriate rate for discounting any income stream equals the risk-free rate plus a risk premium associated with the asset's risk.

T F   4-5. Nominal interest rates are stated in inflation-adjusted terms, and real interest rates are stated in current dollar terms.

T F   4-6. An investor who is planning to hold stock only for a short time need not be concerned about the stock's expected dividend stream after the time he or she plans to sell the stock.

T F   4-7. The required return on stock is equal to the risk-free rate plus the stock's risk premium.

T F   4-8. The discount rate used to evaluate the expected future dividend stream is the same as the required return.

T F   4-9. Dividend payments on common stock tend to remain constant over time.

T F   4-10. The price of common stock should reflect the present value of its expected future stream of dividends.

T F   4-11. When using the constant growth model, the price of a stock should equal its current dividend divided by (k − g), where k is the required rate of return.

T F   4-12. For the constant growth model to apply, the discount rate must exceed the growth rate.

T F   4-13. In equilibrium, the price-earnings model should yield the same result as the constant growth model, assuming the dividend payout ratio remains constant.

T F   4-14. The expected income stream from common stock is much more difficult to determine than that of bonds.

T F   4-15. A security that is undervalued will always earn a superior return for its owners, relative to other investments of comparable risk.

T F   4-16. An appropriate dividend payout ratio for a rapidly growing start-up company may be too low for a mature company.

T F   4-17. Any net earnings not paid out in dividends are retained earnings, which should be used to finance the company's future growth and future income.

T F   4-18. Dividend increases are often interpreted as a sign of management's confidence in the firm's future prospects.

T F   4-19. Past earnings growth is an excellent predictor of future earnings growth.

NOTE

1. Actually, the payments are usually on a quarterly basis, but this has no real significance for the valuation process.

5

Fixed-Income Securities

Learning Objectives

An understanding of the material in this chapter should enable the student to

5-1. Describe the characteristics of the various short-term debt instruments that trade in the money market.

5-2. Describe the characteristics of the various long-term debt instruments and preferred stock issues that trade in the financial market.

Chapter Outline

TYPES OF FIXED-INCOME SECURITIES

fixed-income securities

The federal government, state and local governments, corporations, foreign governments, and international organizations all issue *fixed-income securities*. Most fixed-income securities promise to pay a fixed periodic coupon amount and return their face value at a prespecified time. They vary in a number of ways, including time to maturity, coupon rate, type of collateral (if any), convertibility, tax treatment, and restrictions placed on the borrower. This chapter explores the characteristics of the various types of short- and long-term debt instruments, along with the mutual funds that invest in these securities.

THE MONEY MARKET AND OTHER SHORT-TERM DEBT SECURITIES

Securities maturing in a year or less are considered short term. High-quality, short-term debt obligations constitute what is called the money market. Money market instruments are usually highly liquid, quite marketable, and generally very secure. The principal money market instruments are Treasury bills, commercial paper, large bank CDs, bankers' acceptances, and Eurodollar deposits. In addition, money market mutual funds, short-term unit investment trusts, and certain securities and accounts of banks and other financial institutions compete in the short-term debt security market.

Treasury Bills and Other Short-Term Governments

Treasury bills (T-bills)

Short-term U.S. government securities (governments) make up one of the money market's largest segments. This market consists of bills and other securities maturing within a year. *Treasury bills (T-bills)* are issued at a discount and mature at par (face value), whereas other governments are sold initially at or near par and pay a semiannual coupon.

Most T-bills are issued in $1,000 minimum denominations. Short-term governments are frequently offered for sale (original offerings) and possess excellent OTC (over-the-counter) marketability, low risk, and competitive yields. Moreover, governments are not subject to state and local income taxes. This feature enhances their relative after-tax yield, particularly for investors in high tax states. A number of non-Treasury U.S. government agencies also issue short-term securities.

New issues of T-bills can be bought through a broker or bank for a commission, or they can be purchased directly from the nearest Federal Reserve bank at a weekly auction. Bills with maturities of 13 weeks and 26 weeks are offered each week, while 52-week bills are typically offered once every fourth week. Bids may be entered on either a competitive or a noncompetitive basis. All noncompetitive bids are accepted by the Treasury, and buyers who enter these bids agree to pay the price (yield) that corresponds to the lowest price (highest yield) of all the competitive bids that are accepted. Buyers entering competitive bids state a price (yield) they are willing to pay and the Treasury accepts these bids, taking the highest prices (lowest yields) first until the issue is sold out. However, the price (yield) that all buyers who have accepted competitive bids actually pay is the same as the price (yield) that noncompetitive buyers pay. In other words, once the lowest price (highest yield) that the Treasury is willing to accept is determined, then all buyers (both competitive and noncompetitive) pay that price (receive that yield).

Example 1:   Suppose the Fed wants to sell $8 billion of 13-week T-bills. It receives $14 billion in bids, $5 billion of which are noncompetitive. The $5 billion of noncompetitive bids are accepted. The remaining $9 billion in bids are put in order, from the highest price (lowest yield) to the lowest price (highest yield). The Fed then accepts $3 billion worth of these competitive bids (to round out its goal of $8 billion), taking the highest prices (lowest yields) first. It is the last bid in this group, which is the lowest price (highest yield) bid accepted, that determines the price paid (yield received) by all. All bids are provisional until this final step of the auction when the price (yield) is determined.

Example 2:   A buyer enters a competitive bid for a 13-week T-bill at a rate that translates into a price of 985.52.

If this bid is accepted and happens to coincide with the auction price, the buyer will pay $985.52 for a $1,000 (face value) bill. If the bill is held until it matures 13 weeks later, the buyer will receive $1,000 for an investment of $985.52.

Dealers in government securities maintain an active secondary market in T-bills. The terms offered by these dealers are reported daily in the financial section of most major newspapers, as well as on-line at the Federal Reserve's Web site. Dealers trade T-bills prior to maturity by quoting discount percents. The actual dollar prices for which a dealer will buy and/or sell a T-bill are obtained from the discount.

Example 1: A T-bill with 60 days left to maturity is listed as 5.62 percent bid and 5.58 percent ask. Both of these discount percents were computed by multiplying the actual discount by 360/60 (the reverse of the portion of a 360-day year involved). (Note: The convention is to use a 360-day year for T-bill calculations.) To obtain the actual discount associated with the 5.62 percent bid, the bid is multiplied by 60/360. This results in .937 percent. In other words, the dealer is bidding 99.063 percent of face value (100% – .937%). This translates into a price of $990.63 that a dealer is willing to pay for a $1,000 T-bill that matures in 60 days.

Example 2: A dealer will sell the T-bill in Example 1 at a discount of .930 percent (5.58% x 60/360). In dollar terms, the dealer is willing to sell the T-bill for $990.70 [$1,000 x (100.00% –.930%)], a discount of $9.30 off the $1,000 face. The difference between the prices at which a dealer is willing to sell and buy the T-bill (that is, $990.70 – $990.63 = $.07) is called the dealer's spread, and it compensates the dealer for maintaining an inventory of bills, taking the associated risks, and incurring the necessary costs.

bond equivalent yield

Besides the bid and ask discounts, *The Wall Street Journal* and several other media provide a *bond equivalent yield* that is based on the ask price. The bond equivalent yield is computed by first dividing a security's dollar discount (based on its ask price) by its purchase price (what a dealer will sell the security for). The resulting figure is the rate of return associated with buying the security. This rate is then annualized by multiplying it by 365, and dividing the product by the number of days until maturity. This gives the equivalent yield.

Example: The bond equivalent yield for the T-bill in Examples 1 and 2 is calculated by taking the $9.30 discount (from Example 2) and dividing it by its purchase price of $990.70 (from Example 2). The result of .939% is the rate of return associated with purchasing the security ($93/$9,907 = .939%). This rate of .939% is then annualized by multiplying it by 365 and then dividing it by 60, the number of days until maturity. The answer is 5.71% (.938% x 365/60 = 5.71%).

Example of a Treasury Bill Quotation

Maturity	Days to Mat.	Bid	Ask	Chg.	Ask Yld.
Jun 01 '00	49	5.64	5.60	−0.04	5.72

- Maturity: the date on which the Treasury bill will be paid off
- Days to Mat.: the number of days remaining (from the previous trading day) until the T-bill matures
- Bid: the price (as a discount percentage) that a dealer is willing to pay for the T-bill (as of mid-afternoon of the previous trading day)
- Ask: the price (as a discount percentage) that a dealer is willing to sell the T-bill for (as of mid-afternoon of the previous trading day)
- Chg.: the change between the bid price as listed in bid column and the bid price from the previous trading day (which is really two trading days previous); −0.04 indicates a decrease of 4/100)
- Ask Yld.: the bond equivalent yield for the T-bill based on its ask price

Commercial Paper

commercial paper   Corporations that seek to raise short-term debt capital in the public markets often sell what is called commercial paper. *Commercial paper* is a short-term IOU issued by large corporations with solid credit ratings. The paper is secured only by the issuer's good name. The issuer usually has a backup line of credit at a bank. This credit line is available to repay the commercial paper issue when due if sale of new paper is not possible in the existing market environment. Commercial paper issuers are generally able to pay slightly less than bank rates (the prime rate) on their borrowings. They will also incur a fee on their backup credit lines. Even adding in this fee, the commercial paper issuer's borrowing costs are typically below the alternative cost of bank borrowings, while the return to investors is slightly higher than the interest rate they would get by buying a bank's CDs.

Commercial paper is rated, but as a practical matter, only high-grade issues are marketable. Paper is marketed in round lots of $250,000, and it is seldom available in smaller than $100,000 denominations. Commercial paper always has a maturity of less than 9 months; usually it is 6 months or less.

Large CDs

The interest rates on bank and thrift-issued negotiable CDs (certificates of deposit) of $100,000 and above usually exceed the rates payable on smaller balances. Several New York-based CD dealers handle most secondary market trading. CDs are subject to the same government guarantee of up to $100,000 as other bank and thrift institution issues. Most of the principal of high-denomination CDs ($1 million or more) is uninsured, but most CDs are considered quite safe. Those issued by troubled banks may be risky, however. Troubled banks generally have difficulty selling uninsured CDs even at high interest rates. Moody's Investors Service rates the quality of some CDs. Most CDs have short-term maturities.

Their relatively high minimum denomination ($100,000) puts large CDs beyond the range of most investors. Funds for one large CD may be assembled from several investors, however. Moreover, many banks will lend individuals the funds needed to reach the minimum. Typically, the loan rate slightly exceeds the CD rate, but the holding's net yield may still be relatively attractive.

Banker's Acceptance

banker's acceptance

A *banker's acceptance* involves an obligation to pay a certain amount at a prespecified time. This type of instrument is usually created as a result of international trade. Once the obligation is accepted (guaranteed) by a bank, it becomes an acceptance. The acceptance is a liability of the bank. As such, the bank is required to redeem it whether or not the issuer funds the redemption. With this possibility in mind, banks are inclined to check carefully the credit standing of the issuers of these obligations.

Example: An American firm wishes to finance the importation of sombreros using a banker's acceptance. After negotiating with the foreign exporter of these hats, the American importer arranges with its U.S. bank for the issuance of an irrevocable letter of credit (L/C) in favor of the foreign exporter.

The L/C specifies the details of the shipment and states that the exporter may draw a time draft for a certain amount on the U.S. bank. In conformity with the terms of the L/C, the foreign exporter draws a draft on its local bank, receiving immediate payment. The foreign bank forwards the draft and the shipping documents conveying title to the sombreros to the U.S. bank that issued the L/C. The U.S. bank stamps the draft accepted (accepts an obligation to pay the draft at maturity), and an acceptance is created.

The new acceptance is either returned to the foreign bank or sold to a dealer with the proceeds credited to the foreign bank's account. The acceptance can then be traded on the secondary market. The shipping documents conveying title to the sombreros are released to the American importer so that it can take delivery of the goods for resale to customers. The proceeds of the sales are deposited by the American importer at the accepting U.S. bank in time to honor the acceptance. At maturity, the acceptance is presented for payment by its owner, whether that be the foreign bank or someone else who purchased it from a dealer, and the transaction is completed.

The purpose of an acceptance is to substitute the creditworthiness of a bank, which is known and respected both nationally and internationally, for that of a local merchant, who may be relatively unknown, especially in the international market.

Once an acceptance is created, it trades like other money market securities. Acceptances are available in a wide variety of denominations and maturity dates. A small number of dealers buy and sell acceptances, quoting spreads of about 1/4 of 1 percent. Acceptances are also known as *two-name paper* because both the importer and the bank guarantee the payoff at maturity.

two-name paper

Eurodollar Deposits

Eurodollar deposits

Eurodollar deposits are dollar-denominated liabilities of banks located in Europe or anywhere else outside the United States.

Eurodollar yields are usually slightly higher than other money market rates. Eurodollar deposits of U.S. investors may occasionally be difficult to repatriate. Moreover, disputes between borrower and lender must be settled without reliance on the protections of the U.S. legal system. Finally, the issuing bank's depositors are rarely as protected by insurance and government regulation as those of U.S. banks. In fact, one reason that many foreign banks can afford to pay a higher interest rate than U.S. banks is that they do not have the reserve requirements and other costs of complying with government regulations that U.S. banks face. Many issuers are subsidiaries of U.S. banks, and others are large institutions with long histories of sound operations. Thus, risks in the Eurodollar market should be considered but not overrated. Defaults have been very rare.

Short-Term Debt Securities: Money Market

Type	Issuer	Minimum Denomination
Treasury bill	U.S. Treasury	$1,000
Commercial paper	Large corpo- rations	$250,000
Negotiable CD	Banks and thrifts	$100,000
Banker's acceptance	Export/import companies; bank-guar- anteed	Varies
Eurodollars	Foreign-based banks	$250,000

Federal Funds, Repurchase Agreements, and Discount Loans

federal funds market

Banks and other types of financial institutions also participate in several active short-term debt markets. The *federal funds market* arose to facilitate overnight bank borrowing and lending of excess reserves. Subsequently, other financial institutions and even some foreign banks and government security dealers entered the market. Federal funds are bank deposits at Federal Reserve banks. A federal funds loan is an agreement to move the cash from one bank's account to another bank's account. The federal funds rate is the interest rate for these overnight loans.

discount rate

A key rate that affects the federal funds rate is the *discount rate*. This is the rate the Federal Reserve charges its members for loans. Sometimes the discount rate is above the federal funds rate, and sometimes it is lower. When the discount rate is the higher of the two, banks borrow more federal funds. When the discount rate is lower than the federal funds rate, banks tend to borrow more from the Federal Reserve. Banks always have a slight preference for borrowing federal funds because excessive borrowing from the Federal Reserve may invite additional auditing by the Fed. The Federal Reserve uses changes in the discount rate to make dramatic statements about changes in the direction of monetary policy.

repurchase agreements (repos)

Repurchase agreements (repos) are sales of securities with guaranteed repurchase at a prespecified price and date (often one day later). The relationship between the purchase and sales prices establishes the instrument's return. For example, a guaranteed resale in 6 months at 5 percent above the purchase price would generate a 10 percent annual rate of return (actually 10.25 percent if compounding is considered). This is an indirect way for banks to borrow from other banks, using the security as collateral. Payment is generally required to be in immediately available reserve-free funds transferred between financial institutions. These arrangements are extremely safe.

prime rate

One other rate that is usually quoted along with the yields on money market securities is the *prime rate*. Banks charge their best and safest customers prime rate or less. Everyone else is charged a rate higher than prime. Each bank sets its own prime rate and can change it at will. Most banks adjust their primes almost simultaneously, and some banks set their prime equal to someone else's prime. Many use Citibank's prime rate.

Money Market Mutual Funds

Money market mutual funds and short-term unit investment trusts (discussed next) were developed several years ago in response to interest rate ceilings on many bank savings instruments (known as Regulation Q) coupled with generally higher money market rates. These money funds invest resources from many small investors in a large portfolio of money market securities. While some funds have no minimum account size, many funds set a $1,000 or larger minimum. Still other funds have implemented a rate structure that pays higher rates for larger balances. The net income of the portfolio is distributed to the fund's owners and may be paid monthly or reinvested.

Money market funds can be redeemed in whole or in part on short notice without a redemption charge. Most funds permit several types of redemption: The fund holder can write, e-mail, or call toll free for an immediate check-mailing or wire transfer into the fund holder's bank account. Most funds also permit checks to be written on the fund holder's account. Use of this feature allows the investor's funds to earn interest until the check clears.

The returns paid on money market funds are slightly below the prevailing rates in the money market because of the expenses of the fund. Yields among money market funds differ because of differences in portfolio allocation among money market instruments and differences in maturities. Some money market funds invest only in Treasury bills, whereas other portfolios contain slightly riskier money market investments (for example, Eurodollars or commercial paper). Some funds hold only very short-term instruments. Others are willing to incur the somewhat reduced liquidity of slightly longer maturities. Still others vary their average maturity on the basis of their interest rate expectations. Some short-term municipal funds offer (lower) tax-free yields. Thus, different types of money market funds appeal to various types of investors.

Most money market funds of a given class (general, governments only, or municipal) offer similar risks and returns, but they do differ slightly. There are organizations that rate the safety and performance of these funds, such as Moody's Investors Service and Standard and Poor's.

Short-Term Unit Investment Trusts

Short-term unit investment trusts offer many of the same advantages as money market funds: low-risk, low-denomination investment and money market yields. The key difference is that money market funds are managed and perpetual investments; unit investment trusts are unmanaged and mature at a prespecified time. Furthermore, unit investment trusts are less convenient than money market funds, but their yields are higher. Units must be held until maturity (generally 6 months) or sold in a relatively inactive secondary market.

Unlike money market funds, unit investment trust yields are established when they are purchased. Yields on existing units do not change when market interest rates change. For example, if market rates move up, the trustholder continues to earn the rate originally promised. He or she must wait until the units mature to reinvest at the higher rate available in the market. On the other hand, if interest rates decline, the holder will receive an above-market rate until the trust matures.

Low-Denomination Short-Term Securities of Banks and Other Intermediaries

money market deposit accounts

Banks and depository institutions offer a variety of low-denomination securities. To compete with money market funds, banks can offer *money market deposit accounts*. These accounts are federally insured up to

$100,000 but are limited to a specified number of withdrawals per month and a nontrivial minimum balance requirement. The rates paid on these accounts fluctuate with money market rates.

The investor response to money market deposit accounts has been quite favorable. One drawback is that the interest on these accounts is subject to state and local income taxes. Thus, the after-tax yield on T-bills is generally higher than the yield on otherwise equivalent depository institution certificates.

Banks also sell short-term certificates of deposit with a variety of maturities. These small-denomination CDs are nontransferable. Holders can redeem their CDs before maturity at the issuing bank, but they sacrifice a substantial amount of interest. Alternatively, holders may borrow up to the amount represented by the investment using the CD as collateral, even though the rate of interest charged exceeds the interest rate paid on the CD. Before redeeming a CD early, therefore, the holder should compare the interest sacrifice with the net cost of such a loan.

Money Market Rates

The yields on CDs, bankers' acceptances, and commercial paper tend to move together. Treasury bills generally offer a slightly lower yield because of their somewhat greater security and marketability. Commercial paper yields are always less than prime, and the yields on bankers' acceptances are only slightly higher than yields on T-bills. Eurodollar rates tend to exceed other money market rates by a modest increment, reflecting their slightly greater risk as well as the avoided costs of complying with U.S. banking regulations.

Sample Money Market Rates

Prime rate	6.0%
Federal Reserve Board discount rate	2.5
Federal funds rate	2.5
G.E. commercial paper	2.4
Euro commercial paper	3.7
Dealer commercial paper	2.6
3-month certificates of deposit	2.5
Bankers' acceptances	2.6
LIBOR (London interbank offered rate)	2.6

Money market rate quotations for key U.S. annual interest rates are found in the financial section of most major newspapers. At a minimum, these sources provide the latest quotes from the previous or most recent business day. Some sources also provide rates from 6 months and/or one year ago for comparison purposes. In addition, the Federal Reserve provides daily updates of selected rates on its web site.

LONG-TERM DEBT INSTRUMENTS

Long-term debt securities fall into three categories: government bonds (including agencies), municipals (state and local), and traditional corporate bonds. Other categories include mortgage loans and mortgage-related securities, bank CDs, bond funds, income bonds, floating-rate securities, zero-coupon bonds, Eurobonds, and private placements. Preferred stock also competes for the same income-oriented investor dollars that might otherwise go into long-term debt securities.

Before reading on, it may be helpful to remember that for all its complex language and provisions, a bond or other debt instrument is basically an IOU. That is, it is a contract by which one party (which may be a business corporation, bank, municipality, or even the federal government) borrows money from another party or group of parties. The contract may, in some cases, be rather complex. It specifies the amount of the loan, when the loan must be repaid (maturity date), the rate of interest, and the frequency with which interest payments are to be made. The contract may specify whether certain particular property of the borrower is to serve as collateral to guarantee repayment, what is to happen in case of default, the priority of repayment obligations of a borrower with multiple debts (subordination), whether the borrower has the option of repaying the debt before it is due (call provision), whether the lender has the option of exchanging the financial obligation for an ownership interest in an agreed-upon percentage of the borrower's net assets (conversion provision), and any number of other provisions. Still, for all its potential complexity, a bond is basically just an IOU between two parties or groups of parties.

Treasury Notes and Bonds

Besides short-term (T-bills) debt instruments (covered earlier in this chapter), the U.S. Treasury Department also auctions debt instruments that have intermediate (notes) and long-term (bonds) maturities. Notes are issued with maturities from one to 10 years; bonds have maturities greater than 10 years at the time of issuance. Both notes and bonds are issued in denominations of $1,000 or more, and both are traded in an active secondary market made by dealers in U.S. government securities. Price quotations for notes and bonds in the over-the-counter market are contained daily in *The Wall Street Journal* and other media sources of financial information. Unlike T-bill quotes, which are in hundredths, note and bond quotes are expressed in 32nds.

Example: A bond has bid and ask price quotes of 99:31 and 100:01, respectively. Because these quotes are expressed in 32nds, they correspond to 99 31/32 and 100 1/32, giving the bond a spread of 2/32 or 1/16. In dollar terms, the bid is equivalent to $999.6875 per $1,000 of par value. Alternatively, the ask quote is equivalent to $1,000.3125 per $1,000 of par value.

**Treasury Note and Bond Quotations
(Sample Quotes from the OTC Market)**

Rate	Maturity Mo./Yr.	Bid	Ask	Chg.	Ask Yld.
6 5/8	May 07n	112:05	112:09	−5	4.16
9 1/8	May 09	113:20	113:24	−3	6.79

- Rate: the coupon rate at which interest is paid as a percentage of par value
- Maturity Mo./Yr.: the month and year in which the note/bond will be paid off (a small n after the maturity date identifies the security as a note, while a range of years given as the maturity date identifies the security as a callable bond)
- Bid: the price (in 32nds) that a dealer is willing to pay for the note/bond (as of mid-afternoon of the previous trading day)
- Ask: the price (in 32nds) that a dealer is willing to sell the note/bond for (as of mid-afternoon of the previous trading day)
- Chg.: the change (in 32nds) between the bid price as listed in the bid column (see Bid above) and the bid price from the previous trading day (which is really 2 trading days previous) (for instance, a −1 means a decrease of 1/32)
- Ask Yld.: the yield to maturity for the note/bond based on its ask price

Since mid-1983, all newly issued Treasury notes and bonds are in registered (payable only to the registered owner) form. Prior to mid-1983, some notes and bonds were issued in bearer (payable to bearer) form. All notes that were issued in bearer form have long since matured, but some **bearer bonds** still remain outstanding. An advantage to having securities issued in the registered form is that if they are lost or stolen, they will be replaced by the issuer.

Treasury notes and bonds make coupon payments semiannually with the par or face value paid at maturity. Unlike notes, some bonds have call provisions that allow them to be called during a specified period prior to maturity (although no callable Treasury bonds have been issued since 1984). This period usually begins 5 to 10 years before maturity and ends at the maturity date. This means that at any scheduled coupon payment date during the callable period, the Treasury can require the bondholders to sell the bonds back to the government at par.

The yield to maturity for Treasury securities typically is calculated using the ask price. However, if the ask price for a callable bond is greater than par, then the yield to call is calculated on the assumption that the bond will be called at the earliest allowable date. The relevant yield for callable bonds is the lesser of the yield to maturity or yield to call.

Treasury notes and bonds are generally traded in an over-the-counter market composed of about two dozen dealers. Most of these dealers are New York investment or commercial bankers. Treasury notes and bonds are also traded on the NYSE. Finally, the Treasury conducts an active original-issue auction for notes and bonds. Banks and others may bid for newly issued notes and/or bonds at this auction.

Treasury securities (that is, bills, notes, and bonds) will continue to be considered secure as long as the government is willing and able to raise sufficient tax revenues to finance the debt. Because the risk of default is virtually nonexistent, these securities yield less than even the safest corporate bonds.

Agency Issues

In addition to the Treasury department, several federal agencies, as well as federally sponsored agencies, issue debt obligations. The federally sponsored agencies are privately owned agencies that issue securities and use the proceeds to support the granting of certain types of loans to farmers, homeowners, and others. Although the securities of these federally sponsored agencies are rarely guaranteed by the federal government, federal control does ensure that these securities are relatively safe. Moreover, it is generally presumed that federal assistance would be forthcoming if there were any danger of default on these securities. For the sake of analysis, all federal and federally sponsored agencies are lumped together and simply referred to as federal agencies. Like Treasury bonds, the interest from most federal agency issues is not subject to state or local income taxes. The most significant exceptions include the bonds of the Federal National Mortgage Association (Fannie Mae) and the Government National Mortgage Association (Ginnie Mae).

Agency securities bear a slightly higher interest rate than Treasury securities of comparable maturity. Their somewhat lower marketability is the major reason for the yield differential. Also, because the trading volume for most agency issues is less than that for Treasury securities, the market is thinner and bid-ask spreads are wider. This results in greater trading costs for agency issues and forces investors to demand a higher return.

Mortgage Loans and Mortgage-Backed Securities

mortgage-backed securities

mortgage

Many agency and some types of nonagency securities are either backed by or represent ownership in a pool (portfolio) of *mortgage* loans. The vast majority of outstanding mortgage debt is collateralized by a first claim (first mortgage) on developed real estate, such as single family homes, apartments, or commercial property. Most such mortgage loans require a minimum initial down payment of 10 percent to 20 percent. These mortgages are generally amortized with level monthly payments over an extended period (20 to 30 years is typical). Thus, the amount owed usually declines over time. Moreover, the property securing the mortgage loan usually (but not always) appreciates as time passes, as inflation drives up real estate prices. As a result, the ratio of *collateral* value to mortgage debt tends to rise over time. Accordingly, first mortgages are usually declining-risk investments. Even in a default and distress sale of the property, the mortgage holder is likely to recover a high percentage of the outstanding debt.

collateral

Financial intermediaries, such as banks, savings and loan associations (S&Ls), and insurance companies, write the vast majority of mortgages. Some mortgages are backed by the federal government through the *VA (Veterans Administration)* guarantee program or the *FHA (Federal Housing Administration)* insurance program, which adds further protection. Several federal agencies and some other groups promote mortgage lending by purchasing mortgage loans from the originator.

VA (Veterans Administration)
FHA (Federal Housing Administration)

Virtually all actively traded mortgage-backed or mortgage-related securities are issued by federal agencies and a handful of large banks. The oldest and largest of these agencies is the *FNMA (Federal National Mortgage Association)*. It purchases mortgages from original mortgage lenders (mortgage bankers, commercial banks, S&Ls, and savings banks) with the proceeds of its own debt security sales. Its bonds have fixed coupons and maturities and trade in a secondary market much like other bonds.

FNMA (Federal National Mortgage Association)

GNMA (Government National Mortgage Association)

The *GNMA (Government National Mortgage Association)* bundles together packages of similar mortgages. These mortgage packages are created by private institutions (mortgage bankers, commercial banks, S&Ls, and savings banks) and contain only individual mortgages insured by the FHA or guaranteed by the VA. Once a package is bundled together, an application is made to GNMA for a guarantee on the pass-through securities. Once guaranteed, GNMA *pass-through* securities are backed by the full faith and credit of the U.S. government and therefore are nearly riskless debt instruments.

pass-through

The principal drawbacks of GNMA pass-throughs are a relatively high minimum denomination ($25,000, but they may be bought in $5,000 units thereafter) and an uncertain amortization rate. Pass-through owners literally own a part of a mortgage pool. They receive monthly interest and amortization payments (less a small service fee to GNMA and the financial institution that administers the mortgage).

Mortgages written for specific periods are often prepaid, and the prepayment rate cannot be predicted with certainty. As a result, a typical GNMA pass-through security with a stated life of 30 years may actually have a much shorter life. This can cause a loss for an investor who buys an existing GNMA pass-through that is selling at a premium. If, for whatever reason, homeowners decide to prepay their mortgages, the investor will then receive par value on the security, thereby incurring a loss. In spite of this drawback, GNMA's relatively secure high yields make GNMA pass-throughs quite attractive to income-oriented investors.

Freddie Mac (Federal Home Loan Mortgage Association)

The *Freddie Mac (Federal Home Loan Mortgage Association)* also sells mortgage-related securities. Freddie Mac purchases conventional (not government-backed) mortgages, pools them, and sells participations that have much in common with GNMA pass-throughs. Freddie Mac participations trade in $100,000 minimum denominations. Substantial collateral generally underlies the mortgages, and Freddie Mac guarantees them; therefore, participations are also quite safe.

Because of the success of FNMA, GNMA, and Freddie Mac, several large banks started packaging and marketing their own mortgage pools. These pools offer somewhat higher yields and are a bit more risky than the agency securities. Although they are not government backed, these private pass-throughs are backed by the underlying mortgage collateral, and most have a partial guarantee from a private insurer.

Some depository institutions also sell mortgage-backed bonds. These securities are, however, just another type of corporate bond that happens to have mortgages as collateral. Finally, some mutual funds invest only in mortgage-backed security portfolios, thereby allowing small investors relatively easy access to the mortgage market.

Securitization

securitization

The various categories of mortgage-related securities are an example of a broader phenomenon called *securitization*. Securitization involves taking assets that heretofore were not easily traded in a secondary market and structuring a marketable security or group of securities from them. The goal of the process is to convert assets with poor marketability into assets with much greater market acceptance. If the effort is successful, the institution doing the converting will be able to acquire the less marketable assets for appreciably less than the corresponding securitized assets can be sold for.

The difference, less the cost of the conversion, represents the fee or profit paid for the conversion. Looked at from another perspective, securitization allows an institution to turn over its capital much more frequently than is possible with the more traditional buy-and-hold approach to the intermediation process. Thus, a bank that is only able to make and service loans equal to a percentage of its deposit base can securitize, earn an origination fee, and earn a service fee on a multiple (several times 100 percent) of its deposit base.

One major benefit of securitization, from the standpoint of the investor, is that it effectively creates a diversified pool of loans, thus reducing the overall risk to the investor (risk reduction through diversification will be discussed in greater detail in chapter 7). While the risk of default would deter most investors from providing a large loan to an unknown individual, investing in a diversified pool of such loans is relatively safe.

Most of the activity in securitization has been based on first mortgage real estate loans. More recently, however, other types of assets have been securitized. For example, auto loans, credit card loans, second mortgages, sovereign loans to Third World countries, student loans, and a variety of other types of loans are (or are suggested as) the basis for securitization. Moreover, real estate mortgages themselves are coming in for further securitization, as discussed in the following section.

Collateralized Mortgage Obligation (CMO)

A basic feature of mortgages and traditional mortgage pass-throughs is their uncertain rate of repayment. When the underlying property is sold or refinanced, the original debt instrument is generally paid off. The borrower may also have the option of prepaying part of the principal. Thus, a typical 25- or 30-year mortgage is paid off in 7 to 10 years. The rate of prepayments will, however, vary with a number of factors, including market interest rates compared to the stated rate on the mortgage, the amount of labor mobility (and the divorce rate) in the community, inflation, the stage of the business cycle, economic conditions (for example, the bankruptcy rate) in the area originating the mortgages, and so on. Many investors prefer a more certain time frame of payments than is provided by the typical mortgage. The *CMO (collateralized mortgage obligation)* was devised to deal with this problem. CMOs are multiclass pass-through securities. They offer a potentially improved way of securitizing mortgage loans.

Owners of the various classes (known as tranches) of CMO securities are paid out at different but defined rates. Thus, one class might receive payments equivalent to a one-year zero-coupon bond, a second class might

CMO (collateralized mortgage obligation)

receive payments equivalent to a 5-year zero-coupon bond, and a third class might receive payments equivalent to a 10-year zero-coupon bond. The CMO issuer would be left with the residual cash flow, which might itself be sold as another security. In this way, the uncertain cash flows of a pool of mortgages are restructured into a series of bond-like predictable cash flows and a residual. Virtually all of the uncertainty of the payment timing is impounded into the residual security. Because of the market's general preference for predictable payments, the total value of a mortgage pool subdivided into CMOs can be substantially higher than as a single-class pass-through.

State and Local Government Debt Obligations

A large number of state and local government securities are also part of the debt security market. These securities are called municipals or municipal bonds. Municipals may be revenue bonds (which are backed by revenues from a designated project, authority, or agency, or by the proceeds from a specific tax) or general obligation bonds (which are backed by the taxing power of the issuing government). The issuing government or authority may be as well known as the State of New York or the New York Port Authority or as obscure as a small rural water district. Obviously, the adequacy of the tax or revenue bases of these units varies enormously. A major determinant of municipal bond quality is the unit's ability to pay, as measured by its tax or revenue base.

Even well-known, long established issuers of municipals can default. Issuers of municipals can purchase insurance for the benefit of investors, with the municipalities benefiting from lower interest costs due to lower default risks. A lower default risk on a bond would cause an increase in its rating, as well as its marketability. In addition, traders, bond dealers, and institutional investors can purchase insurance for municipal bonds traded in the secondary market.

Municipal Bond Funds

A rather large investment would be required to spread the risks of a municipal bond portfolio effectively. Because of the commission structure and the time devoted to picking a single security, an investor would not want to purchase municipals in smaller than 10-bond units. This means that a diversified municipal bond portfolio would cost at least $100,000 and would be out of reach for most investors.

Fortunately, investors who have relatively limited resources have an alternative to assembling their own municipal bond portfolios. Municipal bond funds assemble and manage well-diversified portfolios. These funds appeal to investors with moderate means who seek tax-exempt income. Many portfolios of these funds are, however, weighted toward high-risk securities. Prospective investors may have to do a substantial amount of digging through a fund's prospectus to determine the fund's average risk level.

Like the money market mutual funds, municipal bond funds compete with unit investment trusts that assemble and hold portfolios of municipals. There are several similarities. The risk-adjusted yields of municipal unit investment trusts are somewhat higher, but the units are somewhat less convenient to own than municipal bond funds. A number of funds invest only in the securities of a single state. Thus, their residents can take full advantage of the tax-free status of the income at the federal, state, and local levels.

Corporate Debt Obligations

debentures

Corporations are the largest issuers of bonds. They issue both secured bonds (bonds backed by specific collateral) and *debentures* (bonds backed only by the issuer's full faith and credit). Corporate bonds, like government and municipal bonds, have a coupon rate and mature on a specified date. In addition, some corporate bonds may, at the owner's option, be exchanged at some fixed ratio for stocks of the issuing corporation. These corporate bonds, known as convertibles, are discussed in greater detail in a later chapter.

Most bond trades involve both the price of the bond and an adjustment for accrued interest. The buyer pays and the seller receives a sum to reflect the portion of interest that has already been earned but not yet paid.

Example: A bond that is quoted at 93 would initially cost the buyer \$930 in principal plus the pro rated amount of accrued but unpaid interest. If the bond has a 10 percent coupon and made its last coupon payment 3 months ago, unpaid interest would have accrued as follows:

$$(1/2 \text{ x } .10) \text{ x } \$1,000 \text{ x } 3/6 = .05 \text{ x } \$1,000 \text{ x } 1/2 = \$25$$

That is, the bond pays interest every 6 months. Since 3 months have elapsed, half of one coupon payment has accrued. This corresponds to 3/6 (or 1/2) of the semiannual interest payment.

As with dividends on stock, interest is paid to the one who holds the bond on the day of record. When the issuer makes the coupon payment, the new owner will receive and get to keep the entire amount of interest for that period.

flat

Bonds trading for a net price that does not reflect any accrued interest are said to trade *flat*. Typically, bonds that are in default or whose interest payments are considered uncertain trade flat. While the number of bonds that are traded flat is relatively small, if these bonds do make their interest payments, the full amount of the payments goes to the holder of record on the record date. Thus, the owner of these bonds on the day of record receives all of that period's interest payments, regardless of length of ownership. In the bond quotations, bonds that trade flat have an "f" following the abbreviation for their name.

Some corporate bonds are listed on an exchange, but most of the trading takes place in an active OTC market. Investors who wish to buy or sell a large amount of bonds should obtain several quotations to see which market maker offers the best price. In addition to NYSE listings, some bonds are traded on some other exchanges, including the AMEX.

Examples of Corporate Bond Quotations

Bonds	Cur. Yld.	Vol.	Close	Net Chg.
Att6s09	6.6	4	90 1/2	– 1/8
Hilton5s06	cv	130	82	– 1
Polaroid11 ½ f		489	14 1/2	–1/2

- Bonds: the name of the company issuing the bond, the interest or coupon rate as a percentage of the face or par value (typically $1,000), and the year in which the bond will be paid off (the s that sometimes appears between the interest rate and the year of maturity has no significance other than to separate the interest rate from the year of maturity when the interest rate does not include a fraction—read the explanatory notes given in the financial media for the meaning of other letters used)
- Cur. Yld.: the current yield or annual percentage return to the purchaser at the current price (as of 4 p.m. Eastern Time of the previous trading day when the exchanges closed, calculated by dividing the coupon amount by the current price). Flat bonds show no current yield and convertible bonds have the letters cv listed here.
- Vol.: the number of bonds traded (as of 4 p.m. Eastern Time of the previous trading day when the exchanges closed)
- Close: the price, which is a percentage of par value (as of 4 p.m. Eastern Time of the previous trading day when the exchanges closed)
- Net Chg.: the difference between the closing price as listed in the close column (see Close above) and the closing price from whatever day the bond previously traded, which is usually the previous trading day (which is really two trading days previous)

corporate bond funds

A convenient alternative to the direct purchase of corporate bonds is a *corporate bond fund*. With the stock market depressed and interest rates at historic highs, bond fund yields became increasingly attractive in the early 1970s. The high interest environment of the early 1980s further enhanced their yields and attractiveness. Markets are, of course, always changing. Later in the 1980s, interest rates fell, making bonds and bond funds somewhat less attractive. Their yields were still lower throughout the 1990s as the stock market boomed. As a result, bonds have lost some of their luster.

Bond Ratings

**Standard & Poor's
Moody's Investors
Service**

The best way to avoid the uncertainty and potential losses from a default and possible bankruptcy is to invest in low-risk bonds. This strategy requires a method for assessing the risk level. Bond ratings offer a risk-assessment method. The default risks of both municipal and corporate bonds are rated by several rating services. The best known services are *Standard & Poor's* and *Moody's Investors Service*. Two other important ratings firms are Duff & Phelps and Fitch Investors Service. Each service's ratings are based on its evaluation of the firm's financial position and earnings prospects. Table 5-1 describes the primary rating categories of these four agencies. Pluses and minuses are used to discriminate within a rating category.

Rating services do not release their specific rating formulas or analyses, but a number of academic studies do reveal a rather predictable pattern. Ratings tend to rise with profitability, size, and earnings coverage (earnings before interest and taxes, divided by total interest expense). They decrease with earnings volatility, leverage, and pension obligations; they vary with industry classification. Ratings sometimes differ among the rating agencies; these differences usually reflect a close call on fundamentals.

For issues of the same company, a subordinate issue usually receives a lower rating than a senior security. The rating agencies follow the fortunes of issues over time and will change ratings on occasion. However, these rating changes occur relatively infrequently and often take place long after the underlying fundamentals change.

High-Yield Corporates (Junk Bonds)

junk bonds

Bonds were once thought of as secure, low-risk investments. More recently, since the 1980s' merger and acquisition wave, the issue volume and marketability of *junk bonds* have increased manyfold. Many of these bonds are viewed as risky, and thus bear commensurate risk premiums, even though most junk bonds will pay off. Table 5-2 illustrates some yield differentials

TABLE 5-1
Bond Rating Categories

Moody's	Standard & Poor's	Fitch	Duff & Phelps	Definition
Aaa	AAA	AAA	AAA	Prime, maximum safety
Aa1 Aa2 AA3	AA+ AA AA–	AA+ AA AA–	AA+ AA AA–	High grade, high quality
A1 A2 A3	A+ A A–	A+ A A–	A+ A A–	Upper medium grade Medium grade
Baa1 Baa2 Baa3	BBB+ BBB BBB–	BBB+ BBB BBB–	BBB+ BBB BBB–	Lower medium grade Minimum investment grade
Ba1 Ba2 Ba3	BB+ BB BB–	BB+ BB BB–	BB+ BB BB–	Noninvestment grade
B1 B2 B3	B+ B B–	B+ B B–	B+ B B–	Highly speculative
Caa	CCC+ CCC CCC–	CCC	CCC	Substantial risk, in poor standing
Ca				Extremely speculative
C				May be in default
	D	DDD DD D	DD DP	Default

from May 19, 1982. This was a time of relatively high interest rates. Risk premiums also tended to be high at that time. For comparison, the table also shows some rates for January 18, 1988, and September 25, 2001.

Clearly, these substantial yield differentials reflect appreciable differences in risk. Indeed, the higher the "promised" yield, the greater the default risk is likely to be. Although junk bonds are ill-suited to the needs of

TABLE 5-2
Differential Bond Yields

May 19, 1982				
Company	Coupon	Maturity	Price	Current Yield
Very Secure:				
AT&T	13 1/4	1991	96 1/4	13.7
GE Credit	13 5/8	1991	97 1/4	14.0
Risky:				
Eastern Airlines	17 1/2	1998	92 7/8	18.8
Rapid American	11 1/4	2005	57 5/8	18.9
World Airlines	11 1/4	1994	52 7/8	22.3
Very Risky:				
International Harvester	9 1/4	2004	28 1/2	31.6
In Default:				
Braniff	10 1/4	1986	32 1/2	30.8 (if paid)

January 18, 1988				
Company	Coupon	Maturity	Price	Current Yield
Very Secure:				
AT&T	8 5/8	2026	89 1/2	9.6
General Motors	8 5/8	2005	91 1/2	9.4
Risky:				
Bethlehem Steel	8 3/8	2001	74 1/2	11.3
Commonwealth Edison	11 3/4	2015	103 1/2	11.4
Very Risky:				
Texas Air	15 3/4	1992	94 1/2	16.7
Resorts International	11 3/8	2013	62 1/4	18.3
In Default:				
LTV	8 3/4	2004	25 1/4	35.0 (if paid)

September 25, 2001				
Company	Coupon	Maturity	Price	Current Yield
Very Secure:				
AT&T	6 3/4	2004	102 3/8	6.6
Bellsouth	5 7/8	2009	99 5/8	5.9
Risky:				
Chesapeake Electric	8 1/2	2012	95 1/2	8.9
Conseco	10 1/2	2004	101	10.4
Very Risky:				
Bethlehem Steel	8.45	2005	51 1/4	16.5
US Timber	9 5/8	2007	75 3/4	12.7
In Default:				
Polaroid	11 1/2	2006	14 1/	79.0 (if paid)

more cautious investors, many investors with a greater tolerance for risk are attracted to them. Risk and potential return can be comparable to that of many stocks. Indeed, a risky firm's bonds sometimes offer a more attractive way of speculating than its stock does, since the bonds represent a stronger claim on the firm's assets in case of liquidation or bankruptcy. To realize an attractive return, the junk bond investor needs the troubled firm only to avoid bankruptcy or to maintain substantial value in a reorganization. The stockholder's return may not be attractive unless the firm becomes relatively profitable, because stocks represent only a residual claim on the firm's assets.

During the late 1980s and early 1990s, rates of return on junk bonds were often low and sometimes even negative. While always an important investment goal, diversification is crucial for junk bond investors. A defaulting issue may eventually pay off, but the wait can be long and nerve-racking. Having a diversified bond portfolio substantially dilutes the impact of a single default. Junk bond mutual funds provide small investors with an effective diversification vehicle. In fact, these funds' growth has encouraged some firms with relatively low credit ratings to return to the bond market.

Long-Term Debt Securities: Primary Types

- Treasury notes and bonds: lowest risk category
- Agency issues: slightly higher risks and yields than Treasuries—prepayement risk
- Mortgage-related securities
  - FNMA: mortgage-backed (VA and FHA)
  - GNMA: mortgage pass-throughs (VA and FHA)
  - Freddie Mac: conventional mortgages, with Freddie Mac guarantee
  - Bank issued: conventional mortgages, often with a private guarantee
- Direct mortgage, seller financing: risk varies; second mortgages usually quite risky
- Municipals: tax-free; risk varies
  - Municipal bond funds—diversified: may be open- or closed-end
- Corporates: vary greatly in risks and yields
  - Corporate bond funds: diversified; may be open- or closed-end
- Junk bond funds: high-risk portfolios

Income Bonds

income bonds   Most bonds must either pay the agreed-upon sums (coupon rate) or go into default. *Income bonds*, on the other hand, pay interest only if the issuer earns it. Passed coupons do not accumulate. Specific indenture provisions indicate when earned income is sufficient to require an interest payment. Most income bonds originate in a reorganization exchange (that is, bankruptcy). Some, however, are sold initially as income bonds. The volume of income bonds outstanding is negligible in comparison to preferred stock.

Floating-Rate Securities

floating-rate securities

Bonds can be issued with variable or floating rates of interest. These *floating-rate securities* are a form of long-term debt, but they are subject to short-term interest rate changes. The floating or variable rate feature of these bonds generally allows their prices to remain relatively close to their par values. Just how close their prices remain to their par values is a function of how frequently the coupon rate is adjusted, as well as the rate to which it is pegged. Because the changes in the interest rate tend to reflect changes in the inflation rate, these bonds keep their *real* rate of return relatively constant. Thus, their prices can stay relatively constant as interest rates fluctuate.

The characteristics of these floating-rate bonds vary somewhat. Some adjust their coupon rates once every 6 months; others adjust them weekly. Some peg the coupon rates to one percent over the base rate; others peg them to .75 percent over the base rate or even lower. Some peg the coupon rates to 90-day T-bills; others use the prime rate or the federal funds rate as the base rate. Although floating-rate bonds do appear in the United States, they appear more often in the international market, especially in Asia. A few companies even issue floating-rate preferred stock.

Zero-Coupon and Other Types of Original-Issue Discount Bonds

zero-coupon bonds

Most bonds' coupon rates are initially set so that the price of the bonds will be close to their face or par value. Original-issue discount bonds, however, are sold for appreciably less than their par value. These bonds either pay no coupon or have a coupon rate that is well below the market rate. Bonds that do not make coupon interest payments are called *zero-coupon bonds*, or zeros. The return on these securities is derived from the difference between their purchase price and maturity value.

Zero-coupon bonds have precisely identifiable maturity values. This feature has an appeal for IRA and Keogh accounts. Investors in zeros know at the outset exactly what the value will be at maturity. The end-period value of funds invested in coupon-yielding bonds, in contrast, is uncertain, as it depends on the rate earned on the reinvested coupon payments.

The uncertainty associated with the return on reinvested coupon payments is called reinvestment rate risk. Because of their lack of reinvestment rate risk and relative scarcity, zero-coupon bonds have tended to sell for somewhat lower yields than equivalent-risk coupon bonds.

Like other long-term bonds, long-term zero-coupon bonds lock both the buyer and the issuer into a long-term rate. If rates go up after the purchase, the buyer will end up receiving a below-market return. The issuer, in contrast, will pay an above-market rate if market interest rates decline after the issue is sold. Moreover, for a given change in interest rates, the prices of zeros change more than those of most coupon bonds. Owners of coupon bonds are at least able to reinvest their coupon income at higher rates when market interest rates rise. Owners of zeros receive no coupon payments and thus have no interim payments to reinvest.

Even though zeros pay no coupons, they nevertheless impose an annual tax liability on their owners. Determining a zero-coupon bond's tax liability first involves determining the relevant amount of imputed interest, which is the bond's yield to maturity. This is the amount that is accrued but not received each year. The imputed interest rate is computed as if the bond made annual coupon payments equal to its yield-to-maturity rate at the time of its purchase. Thus, a zero-coupon bond that was sold to yield 8 percent would be treated for tax purposes as if it did, in fact, earn 8 percent each year. The issuer is allowed to deduct the imputed interest cost each year, while the owner incurs an equivalent tax liability. As a result, the issuer obtains a tax deduction, while the owner must pay taxes prior to receiving the associated income.

Example: XYZ Corp. zero coupon bonds, par value $1,000, due to mature in September 2021, sell for $240 in September 2001. The holding period return is $1,000/$240 − 1 = 4.167 − 1 = 3.167.

The holding period is 20 years. Therefore, the imputed annual interest is $\sqrt[20]{4.167}$ (the 20th root of 4.167) − 1, or $4.167^{.05}$ (to the 1/20 or .05 power) − 1 = 1.074 − 1 = 7.4%.

The tax computation on coupon-paying original-issue discount bonds is even more complex. The owner is, of course, liable for taxes on the coupon payments. In addition, taxes are assessed on the appropriate imputed interest (amortization of the discount) as the bond moves closer to maturity. The basis on both types of original-issue discount bonds is increased each year by the amount of the accumulated imputed interest. Therefore, the basis on an original-issue discount bond would equal the initial purchase cost plus the sum of the imputed interest amounts.

By contrast, when bonds that were originally issued at par are bought at a discount, only the actual interest payments are taxed as ordinary income.

When such bonds mature, the difference between the face value and the purchase price is taxed as a capital gain.

In 1985, the Treasury introduced a program call STRIPS (Separate Trading of Registered Interest and Principal Securities). Under this program, the Treasury prestrips certain interest-bearing Treasury securities so that investors who purchase a *strip bond* can keep whatever cash payments they want and sell the rest. For example, a 20-year coupon bond could be stripped of its 40 semiannual coupons, and each of these coupons would then be treated as a stand-alone zero-coupon bond. The maturities of these 40 bonds would range from 6 months to 20 years. The final payment of principal would also be treated as a stand-alone zero-coupon bond.

strip bond

Sample U.S. Treasury STRIPS Quotations

Mat.	Type	Bid	Ask	Chg.	Ask Yld.
May 06	ci	68:15	68:19	− 10	6.29
May 02	np	98:14	98:15	− 1	2.34
May 11	bp	71:19	71:23	− 2	3.50

- Mat.: the month and year in which the principal will be paid off
- Type: ci—indicates stripped coupon interest; bp—indicates Treasury bond, stripped principal; np—indicates Treasury note, stripped principal
- Bid: the price (in 32nds) that a dealer is willing to pay for the security (as of 3 p.m. Eastern Time of the previous trading day)
- Ask: the price (in 32nds) that a dealer is willing to sell the security for (as of 3 p.m. Eastern Time of the previous trading day)
- Chg.: the change (in 32nds) between the bid price as listed in the bid column (see Bid above) and the bid price from the previous trading day (which is really two trading days previous) (for instance, a −10 indicates a decrease of 10/32)
- Ask Yld.: the yield to maturity for the security based on its ask price

Eurobonds

Eurobonds

Eurobonds are bonds that are offered outside the country of the borrower and outside the country in whose currency the bonds are denominated. Therefore, if a U.S. corporation issues bonds that are denominated in U.S. dollars (or in Japanese yen for that matter) but sold in France (and perhaps some other countries as well), the bonds would be considered Eurobonds. These foreign bonds differ from U.S. or foreign bonds that are traded in only one country. The Eurobond issuer benefits from the wider distribution and the absence of restrictions and taxes that are placed on single-country bonds. Eurobond buyers may obtain greater diversification than is available from U.S. bonds alone. Moreover, bonds denominated in a foreign currency offer investors an opportunity to speculate on exchange rate fluctuations.

One of the most attractive features of Eurobonds (at least for some investors) is the ease with which some of these bonds allow investors to avoid taxes. Two features of many Eurobonds facilitate tax evasion. First, unlike domestic bonds, no backup withholding is applied to Eurobond interest payments. Second, many Eurobonds have been issued in bearer (unregistered) form. Without either registration or backup withholding, Eurobond owners find that taxes are relatively easy to avoid. Because of this appeal, Eurobonds tend to yield less than domestic bonds of comparable risk. More recently, however, Eurobonds have generally been issued in registered form, and thus the tax evasion opportunity has disappeared for newer issues.

Most Eurobonds are issued by multinational corporations, governments, and international organizations, and most are denominated in dollars, yen, or deutsche marks. They may take on any of the forms of regular bonds: straight bonds, convertibles, floating-rate notes, zero-coupon bonds, and so on.

Private Placement

Approximately one-third of the debt instruments sold are placed privately to a few large buyers (often insurance companies) and publicly announced in the financial press. Announcements are generally referred to as "tombstones" because of the large amount of white space and small amount of lettering. Even if the size (tens of millions of dollars) of typical private placements rules out direct purchases, individuals may participate indirectly through one of the closed-end funds that specialize in such investments.

Private placements generally yield 1/2 percent to one percent more than equivalent-risk bonds because they lack marketability. Private placements offer greater flexibility to issuers. They can be tailored for specific buyers and do not require a prospectus. Moreover, the underwriting cost savings largely offset their somewhat higher coupon. Finally, the relatively small number of owners makes terms easier to renegotiate if necessary.

Private placements do not have to comply with the standards of disclosure that the SEC requires of public offerings. The absence of disclosure of material risk factors makes the investment more risky to potential investors. Therefore, private placements can be suitable investments only for those with both the know-how and the financial resources to discover risk factors for themselves.

Preferred Stock

Although preferred stock is a type of equity security, it has much in common with debt instruments. The issuer of the preferred stock is not required to declare dividends. However, the payment of preferred stock dividends is required before common stock dividends can be paid. Moreover, most preferreds are cumulative, which means that accumulated (unpaid) dividends must be made up before any common stock dividend can be paid. Thus, most companies' preferred stock dividends are almost as dependable as their bond interest. In addition, many preferred stock charters call for the preferred stockholders to gain voting rights if two consecutive dividend payments are missed, giving preferred stockholders some control over the management of the company. The preferreds of a weak company may, however, be almost as risky as its common stock. Some preferreds may receive an extra dividend payment if earnings or common stock dividends are high enough. These are known as *participating preferred stock*.

participating
preferred stock

Preferred stockholders are residual claimants only one step ahead of common stockholders. Unless the creditors' claims are fully satisfied, nothing will be left for either class of stockholders. Unlike corporate interest payments, 70 percent of the dividends received by a domestic corporation (incorporated in the United States) from another domestic corporation are tax exempt. This exemption applies to both common stock dividends and preferred dividends. Moreover, the exemption may be 80 percent or even 100 percent of dividends received if the receiving corporation owns specified percentages of the stock of the paying corporation. For a corporation in the 34 percent tax bracket eligible for the 70 percent exemption, a 9 percent preferred yield is equivalent to an after-tax yield of 8.08 percent (9% − [9% x (1 − .70) x .34]). In contrast, a fully taxable yield of 12.24 percent would be needed to generate the same after-tax yield of 8.08 percent [12.24% x (1 − .34)].

Preferreds have always been popular with corporate investors. Because their tax advantage is available only to corporations, individual investors should avoid them.

SUMMARY AND CONCLUSIONS

At a minimum, investors should consider the wide variety of risks, returns, marketabilities, liquidities, and tax treatments the bond market offers. A well-diversified portfolio that contains both equity and debt securities is likely to be less risky than a well-diversified portfolio of stocks or bonds alone. Investors should have little difficulty finding issues bearing risk-expected return characteristics that correspond to their own preferences.

The money market provides relatively attractive short-term rates on high-quality securities, such as T-bills, commercial paper, large bank CDs, bankers' acceptances, and Eurodollar loans. Small investors can participate in this market through money market mutual funds, short-term unit investment trusts, and the money market certificates and accounts of commercial banks and thrift institutions.

Treasury and federal agency securities make up a large part of the long-term debt security market. Most of these issues are untaxed at the state and local level. The agencies tend to offer slightly higher yields but are somewhat less marketable than Treasury issues. A large part of the agency security market is mortgage related. The various bonds, pass-throughs, and participations of FNMA, GNMA, Freddie Mac, and the large bank pools offer default-free monthly income combined with a somewhat uncertain maturity (prepayment and reinvestment risk).

The interest payments of state and local issues are usually untaxed at the federal level. Thus, municipals offer relatively low before-tax yields. These securities appeal primarily to investors in high tax brackets. Municipal bond funds and municipal unit investment trusts give small investors various ways to enter this market. Municipal bonds are also generally exempt from the state income tax in their state of issue.

Long-Term Fixed-Income Securities: Specialized Types

- Income bonds: interest paid only if earned
- Floating-rate securities: coupon varies with market interest rates
- Zero-coupon bonds: sold at a discount; pay no coupon
- Eurobonds: traded internationally
- Private placements: large and flexible; do not have to comply with SEC disclosure standards; low liquidity
- Preferred stock: 70% tax sheltered to domestic corporations

---

Corporate securities vary greatly in risk. Some high-risk issues offer very high yields. Corporate bond funds (including high-risk bond funds) and closed-end bond funds permit small investors to own part of a diversified debt security portfolio.

Some bonds have special features. These bonds include income bonds, floating-rate securities, and zero-coupon bonds. The final segment of the discussion of fixed-income securities includes Eurobonds, privately placed issues, and preferred stock (an equity asset but one paying a fixed amount periodically). Each of these securities appeals to specialized segments of the marketplace.

CHAPTER REVIEW

Answers to the review questions and the self-test questions start on page 501.

Key Terms

fixed-income securities	GNMA (Government National Mortgage Association)
Treasury bills (T-bills)	
bond equivalent yield	pass-through
commercial paper	Freddie Mac (Federal Home Loan Mortgage Association)
banker's acceptance	
two-name paper	securitization
Eurodollar deposits	CMO (collateralized mortgage obligation)
federal funds market	
discount rate	debentures
repurchase agreements (repos)	flat
prime rate	corporate bond fund
money market deposit accounts	Standard & Poor's
bearer bonds	Moody's Investors Service
mortgage-backed securities	junk bonds
mortgage	income bonds
collateral	floating-rate securities
VA (Veterans Administration)	zero-coupon bonds
FHA (Federal Housing Administration)	strip bond
	Eurobonds
FNMA (Federal National Mortgage Association)	participating preferred stock

Review Questions

5-1. Compute the equivalent yield for a 52-week T-bill priced at 95.

5-2. Construct a table that briefly itemizes the advantages and disadvantages of T-bills, commercial paper, and money market mutual funds.

5-3. Describe the three principal types of bonds by issuer. How do they differ? In what ways are they similar?

5-4. With respect to mortgages and mortgage-related securities:
   a. What is meant by securitization?
   b. What is the advantage to the issuer, individuals, and to the marketplace of the securitization of assets?

5-5. a. What is the function of a rating service? Discuss bond ratings and default risks.

    b. What are the principal bond rating agencies?

    c. What is the main drawback to relying on bond ratings to assess default risks?

5-6. How do yields vary with bond ratings?

5-7. Summarize the characteristics of
    a. income bonds
    b. floating-rate notes
    c. zero-coupon bonds

5-8. Discuss the relevance to individual investors of
    a. Eurobonds
    b. private placements
    c. preferred stock

5-9. Discuss alternative ways (to direct investment) that the individual investor can participate in the various fixed-income investments introduced in this chapter. Briefly indicate advantages and disadvantages.

Self-Test Questions

T   F   5-1. T-bills are sold initially at or near par value and pay a semiannual coupon.

T   F   5-2. New issues of T-bills come with maturities of 13 weeks, 26 weeks, or 52 weeks.

T   F   5-3. All auction bids for new issues of T-bills are entered on a competitive basis.

T   F   5-4. Dealers in government securities maintain an active secondary market in T-bills.

T   F   5-5. Commercial paper is usually issued by large corporations to finance their short-term needs.

T   F   5-6. Commercial paper is typically secured by real estate or high-quality securities.

T   F   5-7. Commercial paper issuers usually have to pay 1 or 2 percent above the prime rate on their borrowings.

T   F   5-8. The principal of negotiable CDs issued by bank and thrift institutions does not qualify for protection by government deposit insurance.

T   F   5-9. Once a banker's acceptance is created, it trades like other money market securities.

T   F   5-10. The federal funds rate is the interest rate that banks charge other banks for overnight loans.

T   F   5-11.   Discount loans are extended by the Federal Reserve to member banks for the purpose of covering a short-term reserve deficiency.

T   F   5-12.   Adverse interest rate moves are likely to affect a money market fund's share prices significantly.

T   F   5-13.   Most money market funds permit checks to be written on the fund holder's account.

T   F   5-14.   Short-term unit investment trusts are managed and perpetual.

T   F   5-15.   The yields on existing short-term unit investment trusts increase when market interest rates rise.

T   F   5-16.   For all its potential complexity, a bond is basically just an IOU between two parties or groups of parties.

T   F   5-17.   U.S. Treasury bonds are issued with maturities from one to 10 years.

T   F   5-18.   Treasury note and bond price quotations are expressed in hundredths.

T   F   5-19.   All newly issued Treasury notes and bonds are in bearer form.

T   F   5-20.   The yield to maturity for Treasury securities typically is calculated using the ask price.

T   F   5-21.   Treasury securities are subject to state and local taxes.

T   F   5-22.   Most federal agency issues are not subject to state and local taxes.

T   F   5-23.   Agency issues generally bear a slightly higher interest rate than Treasury securities of comparable maturity.

T   F   5-24.   The principal drawbacks of Government National Mortgage Association (GNMA) pass-through securities are their relatively high minimum denomination and an uncertain amortization rate.

T   F   5-25.   The goal of the securitization process is to convert assets with poor marketability into assets with much greater market acceptance.

T   F   5-26.   The category of municipal bonds known as revenue bonds is backed by the taxing power of the issuing government.

T   F   5-27.   Corporate bonds known as debentures are backed by specific collateral.

T   F   5-28.   A bond with a rating of A has greater risk of default than a bond with a rating of B.

T   F   5-29.   Bonds that are in default or whose interest payments are considered very uncertain typically trade flat.

T   F   5-30.   Income bonds must pay the coupon rate of interest or go into default.

T   F   5-31.   Original-issue discount bonds are sold for appreciably less than their value at maturity (par).

T   F   5-32.   A bond that is separated from its coupons is called a junk bond.

T   F   5-33.   The maturity value of a zero-coupon bond is difficult to calculate.

T   F   5-34.   There is no annual tax liability associated with zero-coupon bonds.

T   F   5-35.   Eurobonds are bonds that are offered outside the country of the borrower and outside the country in whose currency the bonds are denominated.

T   F   5-36.   Debt instruments that are privately placed lack marketability.

T   F   5-37.   The payment of preferred stock dividends is required before common stock dividends can be paid.

T   F   5-38.   Preferred stockholders' claims to corporate assets receive the lowest priority.

T   F   5-39.   Corporations would generally prefer to issue preferred stock rather than bonds.

6

The Determinants of Fixed-Income Security Yields

Learning Objectives

An understanding of the material in this chapter should enable the student to

6-1. Describe the parameters of the default risk facing debt security instruments, and explain how rating services assess the risk.

6-2. Describe the term structure of interest rates, and explain the investment implications of the term structure.

6-3. Describe the concept of duration, and explain how immunization is used to achieve a desired duration level.

6-4. Describe several factors that affect bond prices and yields.

6-5. Describe several aspects of assembling and managing a bond portfolio.

Chapter Outline

The terms fixed-income security and debt security are often used interchangeably. This is because the initial interest rate or coupon rate on debt instruments, such as bonds, is stated in a contractual agreement at the time that the debt instrument is issued. Although there are other types of debt instruments, most debt takes the form of bonds. Therefore, unless stated otherwise, the terms *bond yield, debt security yield,* and *fixed-income security yield* can be used interchangeably.

The yield to maturity on a debt security instrument is based on its market price and coupon rate. The coupon rate on a debt security instrument is initially determined by the general level of interest rates and by the factors specific to the particular instrument, such as its level of risk. As discussed in chapter 4, the general level of interest rates is determined both by the real (purchasing power) rate of interest and by inflationary expectations. The real rate of interest is determined by the supply and demand for loanable funds (credit), which in turn are, respectively, determined by consumers' willingness to forgo present consumption in return for greater consumption in the future (time preference for consumption) and by the production and investment opportunities in the economy. This chapter explores the impacts of a variety of factors that affect individual debt security yields.

DEFAULT RISK

No investor wants to buy bonds in what appears to be a secure company and later see the company get into financial difficulty. The market price of these bonds would adjust downward to reflect their increased risk. Unless the financial problems facing the firm are corrected quickly, the issuing company may default on its debt obligation. The bonds might eventually pay off part or all of the principal amount plus accrued interest, but that is uncertain when default occurs. It is even possible that the bondholders will be left with nothing.

As discussed in the previous chapter, it is possible for an investor to achieve high yields from investing in a portfolio of risky bonds. Some investors are even willing to bear the risk of investing in a diversified portfolio of bonds that are near default, since they can purchase these bonds at a substantial discount below their face value. Such a strategy, while potentially quite profitable, is also risky. To understand how bonds differ in riskiness, let us start with the bond *indenture*, which is the issuer's contract with the bondholders.

indenture

Indenture Provisions

[handwritten margin notes:]
If A Company goes Under The following Are Paid off In the following order

Creditor { Collateralized-Mortgage Company
Senior Debt
Debenture-Non-Secured Note }

Equity { Preffered Common }

Bond indentures are contracts and, as such, contain a variety of provisions. Most important are those specifying the coupon rate and the maturity date. The indenture may also contain a number of other provisions. For example, some debt obligations are backed by specific collateral. The indenture for such a security will specify the nature of the collateral obligation. The provision will typically state that the issuer agrees to maintain any pledged assets in good repair.

Most corporate bonds, known as *debentures*, do not have specific property serving as collateral but, rather, are backed by the full faith and credit of the issuer. In the event of bankruptcy, holders of debentures are treated the same as any other creditors of the issuer.

Some other fairly common indenture provisions include subordination, a sinking fund, call or conversion provisions, and restrictions on the company, such as restrictions on the amount of dividends that can be paid. *Subordination* means that the company's obligation to the bondholders is subordinate to some specified other financial obligations, called *senior debt*. The company's obligations to the holders of senior debt take precedence over its obligations to the holders of subordinate debentures. This means that if the company becomes insolvent and unable to pay all of its debts, the holders of the subordinated bonds will not be paid even a penny until after the holders of the senior debt are paid in full.

subordination

senior debt

To protect the bondholders from the risk of default, it is not uncommon for an indenture to contain a provision that restricts the amount of additional debt that the issuing firm can incur. For example, an indenture might restrict the total amount of long-term debt to a specified percentage of the company's total assets.

call provision

call price

call premium

A *call provision* gives the issuer the option of redeeming the bonds prior to maturity, usually at a specified amount above the par value, called a *call price*. The difference between the call price and par is the *call premium*. When a bond has a call provision, the indenture generally specifies when the company may call the bond and what the call premium will be at any given point in time. There is no common rule as to how a company will set the call premium.

Example: A hypothetical bond has an initial maturity of 30 years. The indenture specifies that the issuer may call the bond 20 or more years after the date of issue and that the call premium is 1 percent of the face value for each remaining year until the bond matures. If the company issued a $1,000 bond in 1999, the soonest the bond could be called is 2019, in which case the company would have to pay bondholders $1,100 per bond. If the company were to redeem the bonds in 2024, it would have to pay $1,050 per bond.

Usually, a company will call bonds prior to maturity only if market interest rates decline sufficiently that it will be cost effective for the company to call the bonds, even with a call premium, and refinance at a lower interest rate. Although less likely, there are also situations in which a company will become less risky over time, so that even if market conditions do not change, the company will be able to issue bonds with a lower risk premium than before. There have even been cases in which a company has called a mortgage bond because the corporation wants to sell the assets that are pledged as collateral. Some bond indentures contain a provision stipulating that when bonds are called because of the sale of the mortgaged property rather than to refinance, the bonds are callable at par rather than at the call price.

Example: Imagine a start-up company with very little operating history. Since the company's financial performance is uncertain, the market may require a substantial risk premium on the company's debt obligations. But 20 years later, if the company establishes an admirable track record of profitable operations and financial stability, its debt might be regarded as quite safe, and therefore it may be able to borrow money at a much lower interest rate. It might then make sense for this company to call its outstanding bonds and issue new bonds at a lower interest rate.

An investor who is considering purchasing a bond should be careful of call provisions, especially if the bond is paying a high coupon rate and trading at a price greater than the call price. An early call would cost the bondholder the difference between the bond's market price and the call price. Therefore, an investor considering purchasing a bond at a premium should check for call provisions and never pay more than the present value (based on prevailing interest rates on comparable bonds) of the stream of payments until the first call date plus the call price.

Some restrictions contained in the indenture are intended to ensure that the company remain solvent and able to make interest and principal payments when due. For example, an indenture may specify that a company limit its dividend payments to a specified percentage of its net income. The indenture may also specify that the company maintain at least a certain current ratio (current assets divided by current liabilities) or that its total debt be limited to a specified percentage of its total assets.

trustee

The indenture also specifies a *trustee,* usually the trust department of a large bank, who is appointed to represent the bondholders and ensure that the company abides by the provisions of the indenture.

Contract

Typical Indenture Provisions

- Principal and maturity: specifies amount and timing of principal payment
- Coupon: specifies amount and timing of each coupon (interest) payment *What Rate is & When it will be Pd.*
- Collateral (first mortgage bond, equipment trust certificate, or other collateralized bond): identifies pledged collateral and specifies obligation of the issuer to maintain collateral's value
- Full faith and credit (debenture): backs bond with the pledge of the issuer
- Subordination: gives interest payment and liquidation priority to other specified debt issues
- Sinking fund: provides for periodic redemption and retirement over the life of the bond issue, or for an escrow account to ensure repayment of the principal amount when due *Company sets aside $ each yr to be able to buy back the Bond at maturity*
- Call provision: specifies length of no-call protection and call premiums payable over life of the bond *Bond can be Called before maturity.*
- Dividend restrictions: restrict dividend payments, based on earnings and/or amount of equity capital
- Current ratio minimum: requires that the ratio of current assets to current liabilities not fall below a specified minimum
- Me-first rule: restricts the amount of additional (nonsubordinated) debt that may be issued (usually as a percentage of total assets)
- Trustee: specifies the institution responsible for enforcing the indenture provisions
- Grace period: specifies the maximum period that the firm has to cure a default without incurring the risk of a bankruptcy filing

sinking fund

Some indentures require a sinking fund. A *sinking fund* is a fund into which the company periodically deposits a portion of its debt obligation to the bondholders. The purpose of this fund is to make certain that when the bonds mature, the company will have sufficient money available to repay the principal amount of the bonds. In order to meet the sinking fund requirements, the company may buy back some of the bonds on the open market, call some of the bonds (assuming the indenture contains a call provision), or put funds into an escrow account.

Defaults and Near-Defaults

Firms rarely fail to pay required interest and principal when they have a choice. Sometimes, however, they have no choice. The recent years of prosperity have tended to lower this level of concern, but because the economy tends to move in cycles, understanding some of the aspects of defaults is still important.

technical default

A firm is in *technical default* whenever any of the indenture provisions of its bonds are violated. Many technical defaults, however, involve relatively minor matters. For example, if the current ratio falls below the stipulated minimum, the firm is technically in default of the relevant indenture provision. Rarely, if ever, does a default in such a matter in itself lead to a bankruptcy filing. The trustee may grant a waiver for the violation, or the matter may be quickly cured.

Even a failure to make an interest payment on time does not necessarily lead to bankruptcy. The firm may rectify the situation within a grace period; the indenture usually provides for such grace periods. In addition, defaults and near-defaults generally result in a mutually acceptable resolution that stops short of bankruptcy and liquidation.

When a few large creditors (such as banks who have extended substantial loans) can be identified, the troubled borrower may seek concessions that will give it a reasonable chance of avoiding a bankruptcy filing. Big lenders have an important stake in their debtors' survival. An interesting oversimplification of the borrower-lender relationship is seen in the following two sentences:

- A borrower who owes $1,000 and cannot pay is in trouble.
- A borrower who owes $1 million and cannot pay puts the lender in trouble.

The weakness of a troubled borrower is, in fact, a strength in any negotiations with the lender. Accordingly, lenders with large exposures are likely to be asked to accept a payment stretch-out, an interest rate reduction, a swap of debt for equity or tangible assets, a reduction in loan principal, or a change or waiver of certain default provisions. Lenders often agree to such restructurings in the hope of eventually recovering more than they would in a formal bankruptcy.

Of course, a firm that is in financial difficulty will have serious trouble obtaining additional financing. Therefore, it is in a firm's self-interest to avoid even a technical default or near default, however slim the risk of a formal bankruptcy may be.

Although the stock price of firms that are struggling will generally already be quite low, when a firm formally files for bankruptcy, there is usually an additional substantial drop in stock value.

Example: Enron Corporation, an interstate marketer of natural gas, electricity, and related products, was trading as high as $84.87 as recently as December 2000. The stock's price began a gradual decline in 2001 as bad news about the company circulated. In August 2001, Enron's CEO resigned, and the stock price declined from $42.80 to $36.80 (a 14 percent drop) during the subsequent 11-day period.

Thompson

The stock price decline continued in October and November as news about the company's financial difficulties hit the market. On October 31, there was a news release to the effect that the SEC had begun an investigation into the company's financial dealings with affiliated partnerships. The decline in stock price accelerated in November.

On November 28, Enron's stock opened at $3.69, which was the low for the year until that point. On November 28, there was news to the effect that Standard and Poor's had lowered Enron's bond rating from BBB– (the lowest rating that is still considered investment grade) to B– (a speculative grade bond rating).

Enron Corporation formally filed for Chapter XI on November 29. Its stock price reached a low of $.25 on November 30. This was a drop of over 93 percent in just 2 days.

Bankruptcy Filings

Even though bankruptcy should be avoided if at all possible, the reorganization of a financially troubled firm is not always possible without filing for bankruptcy. Bankruptcy proceedings may begin with a petition from a creditor, a creditor group, an indenture trustee, or the defaulting firm itself.

If the firm chooses to file for reorganization under Chapter XI, it intends to emerge from bankruptcy as a continuing entity. Chapter XI permits the firm to retain its assets and to restructure its debts under a plan of reorganization. A Chapter XI proceeding can give the firm respite from creditors' claims, as it has 120 days after filing the petition to formulate a plan of reorganization.

Reorganizations under Chapter XI, however, are not always successful in salvaging financially troubled firms, plus they are very expensive. An unsuccessful Chapter XI reorganization effort usually leads to Chapter VII liquidation proceedings.

Filing for Bankruptcy

- Chapter XI reorganization

  - The proceeding is designed to preserve potentially profitable elements of the business in a recapitalized form.

  - It permits the firm to keep its assets and restructure its debts, provided a plan of reorganization is drafted within 120 days after filing the petition.

  - During that 120-day period, the company is protected from the claims of creditors.

- Chapter VII liquidation

  - A bankruptcy trustee, appointed by the court, is given the responsibility for selling the firm's assets and distributing the proceeds under the absolute priority of claims principle. Following this principle, the valid claims of each priority class must be satisfied in full before the next priority class receives any proceeds.

  - To regain possession of the company from the trustee, the debtor firm must file an appropriate bond.

---

liquidation

bankruptcy trustee

absolute priority of claims principle

If a defaulting firm is thought to be worth more dead than alive, bankruptcy proceedings may begin as a Chapter VII *liquidation*. Under Chapter VII, the *bankruptcy trustee* is responsible for selling the firm's assets and distributing the proceeds according to the *absolute priority of claims principle*. Under this principle, the valid claims of each priority class are fully satisfied before the next class receives anything. The marginal priority group receives proportional compensation. The classes below the marginal priority class receive nothing because the funds available for distribution will have already been exhausted.

A few companies do successfully emerge from Chapter XI bankruptcy proceedings after a careful review of their financial and competitive situation. The process is designed to preserve the potentially profitable elements of their businesses in a recapitalized form. Unproductive assets are liquidated. The bankruptcy trustee and courts seek to preserve as much value as possible for distribution to the creditors. They also try to minimize the risk that the firm will have to return for court protection or seek additional lender concessions.

Many troubled firms would be financially viable if their debt load were sufficiently reduced. Thus, an objective of many Chapter XI bankruptcy proceedings is to reduce the company's debt load, and since bankrupt firms generally have little or no excess cash to distribute to creditors, most creditors are prevailed upon to accept lower-priority securities of the reorganized firm as payment. Senior creditors may receive subordinated debentures or preferred shares, whereas junior creditors could be given common stock and warrants.

Several factors, however, limit the applicability of the absolute priority of claims principle. The going-concern value of a firm experiencing a bankruptcy process is quite subjective. The securities to be issued by the reorganized firm will not have an established market price until it emerges from bankruptcy. Therefore, the relevant values are rather uncertain at the time (in the course of the bankruptcy proceeding) the securities distribution is set. Not surprisingly, the ability of these securities to satisfy claims is often subject to dispute.

Generally, the lower-priority claimants argue for a higher overall valuation for the company and its securities. In this way, they seek to increase the estimated value of the securities that are available for distribution to their priority class. The greater the firm's overall estimated value, the greater the proportion of that estimated value available to satisfy the lower-priority claimants.

Example: Suppose a company's high-priority claimants have claims of $95 million and the company's value is estimated at $100 million. The high-priority claimants will be awarded securities representing 95 percent of the firm's value. Only 5 percent will be available to the lower-priority claimants. Now suppose that the lower-priority claimants are able to get the company's estimated value raised to $110 million. At that valuation, the higher-priority claimants will receive about 86 percent (95/110) of the firm's value. The lower-priority claimants will, in contrast, see their share rise to about 14 percent (15/110).

Unless the low-priority claimants are given something, however, they may use various legal maneuvers to delay the proceedings. As a result, most informal workouts and reorganizations ultimately allocate lesser-priority claimants somewhat more than what the absolute priority of claims principle requires. In practice, unsecured and subordinated creditors can usually make enough noise to obtain some share of the assets even when senior creditors' claims exceed the firm's remaining asset value. When a company emerges from Chapter XI bankruptcy, the reduced debt burden generally permits it to remain solvent.

Bond Ratings and Performance

In the previous chapter, we discussed bond ratings. Now let us consider the performance of bonds with different ratings. How well do bonds of the various risk classes perform? Bonds in the top four rating categories (Aaa, Aa, A, or Baa) are considered investment grade. Bonds with ratings below investment grade are referred to as junk bonds or, euphemistically, as high-yield bonds. In principle, the lower the rating, the higher a bond's interest rate, because investors require a risk premium that is roughly proportional to the riskiness of an investment.

Some argue that a diversified portfolio of Baa-rated bonds is a sensible investment, since the likelihood of any bond's defaulting is low and the expected return is higher than that of safer (Aaa-rated) bonds. In other words, at least down to Baa-rated bonds, some have argued that the historical differences in default risk have not justified the historical differences in return. That is, even after subtracting default losses, investors can achieve a significantly higher return with Baa than with Aaa issues. Whether this disproportionate relationship between return and default risk will continue in the future is something that only time will tell. What is clear is that the yield differential between Baa and Aaa bonds moves inversely with the economy. Thus, when the economy is strong, the yield differential is narrow, and when the economy is weak, it widens.

The issues are less clear for lower-rated bonds. The realized (after default loss) yield experience of below-Baa bonds is of considerable interest in light of the growing numbers of these issues. Since many institutional investors are not permitted to own below-Baa bonds, these securities may well offer superior risk-adjusted yields. Thus, diversified portfolios of medium-to-high-risk bonds might outperform similarly diversified high-quality bond portfolios. Diversification across industries would spread the default risk, and the higher promised yield might more than offset any default losses. In fact, extensive studies in the mid-1980s found that the yield premium on junk bonds substantially exceeded the loss from default.[1] These results, however, were derived from studies that covered relatively prosperous times. Experience during severe recessions might be quite different.

TERM STRUCTURE OF INTEREST RATES

Impact of Maturity on Bond Prices

term structure

The relationship between a bond's time to maturity and its interest rate (assuming all other factors, such as default risk, are equal) is known as the *term structure* of interest rates. To understand why bonds of different maturities have different interest rates, let us first consider how differences in maturity can affect the value of bonds.

The longer the maturity of a bond (all other things being equal), the greater the bond's price sensitivity to changes in market interest rates. Therefore, any change in market interest rates, such as an overall increase in the rate of inflation, will have a larger impact on the price of a bond with 10 years remaining to maturity than on a bond with only one year remaining to maturity.

Since most investors are risk averse, the possibility of an interest rate rise and the consequent capital loss generally causes them concern. Furthermore, a bond's call feature limits its upside potential if interest rates fall. The imminent return of principal limits the interest rate sensitivity of short-term issues, however.

A doubling of interest rates would cause the price of the long-term bond to fall to nearly half its previous value, while the price of the shorter-term issue would decline by much less. Thus, short-term issues are less sensitive to interest rate risk than longer-term securities are. On the other hand, borrowers (bond issuers) may prefer the security of a fixed long-term rate and therefore find distant-maturity issues less risky. If they issue shorter-maturity debt, they factor in the risk that interest rates will rise when the debt matures, and they will have to pay a higher rate of interest to refinance the debt when it comes due.

Example 1: Consider a hypothetical bond that has a coupon rate of 8 percent paid annually, or $80 per year. For simplicity, assume that interest payments are made once a year. Assume that because of an increase in the inflation rate, the yield to maturity for bonds of comparable risk is now 10 percent. The bond with one year to maturity has one more interest payment of $80 plus the principal amount of $1,000, both due in one year. Since the discount rate of future cash payments is now 10 percent, the present value of future cash flows is $80/1.1 + $1000/1.1 = $1,080/1.1 = $981.82, which should be the market price of the bond if the bondholder were to sell it in the secondary market rather than hold it to maturity. In other words, a 2 percent increase in the market interest rate would cause the market value of the bond to decrease by $18.18 or 1.82 percent ($1,000 − 981.82)/1,000).

Example 2:   Now consider a similar 8 percent coupon bond that has 10 years to maturity in an environment in which the required rate of return on comparable bonds is 10 percent. Again, for simplicity, assume that interest is paid only once a year. The present value of the stream of cash flows is now $80/1.1 + $80/1.1^2 + $80/1.1^3 + $80/1.1^4 + . . . +$1,080/1.1^{10} = $72.73 + 66.12 + 60.11 + 54.64 + 49.67 + 45.16 + 41.05 + 37.32 + 33.93 + 416.39 = $877.12, which should also be the market price of the bond in the secondary market. Therefore, for a bond with 10 years to maturity, a 2 percent increase in market interest rates causes the value of the bond to decrease by $122.88 or 12.29 percent ($1,000 − 877.12)/1,000). (To make the same calculations with semi-annual coupon payments, double the number of payments, let each coupon payment be $40 instead of $80, and use 5 percent as the discount rate instead of 10 percent, since only half a year elapses between each payment.)

Sensitivity to interest rate changes implies upside potential as well as downside risk. To see this, assume that market interest rates decline by 2 percent, and compute the market value of both the 8 percent bond with one year to maturity and the bond with 10 years to maturity. While both will now trade at a premium, the premium on the bond with 10 years to maturity will be much higher. This calculation should also demonstrate how the call feature could work to the detriment of bondholders.

To see this clearly, assume that the bond with 10 years to maturity has a call feature, allowing the issuer to redeem the bond in 2 years at a 5 percent premium over par ($1,050). The present value of the stream of cash flows will now be $80/1.06 + ($80 + $1,000 + $50)/1.06² = $75.47 + $1,005.70 = $1,081.17. Although this bond will still trade at a premium, its market value will be far less than the $1,147.20 it would be worth if there were no call feature and the bondholders were assured of receiving the $80 annual coupon for 10 years while bonds of comparable risk paid 6 percent.

yield curve

Term to maturity is a major determinant of a debt security's yield to maturity. The relationship between term to maturity and yield to maturity is illustrated with a *yield curve*. A yield curve is the graphic representation of the term structure of interest rates—that is, the relationship between yield and term to maturity for debt securities with otherwise similar characteristics (default risk, coupon, call feature, and so on). The yield curve reveals a pattern that at various times rises, falls, does not vary, or rises and then falls (see figure 6-1). It is critically important that any investor understand why the yield curve takes on different shapes at different times.

Major Determinants of a Debt Security's Yield to Maturity

- length of time to maturity
- general credit conditions
- default risk

Term Structure Hypotheses

The following term structure hypotheses are all designed to explain the various shapes of the yield curve:

- market segmentation
- preferred habitat
- liquidity preference
- unbiased expectations

Although there are different yield curves for different classes of bonds, the most commonly discussed yield curve is the one for Treasury bonds. This is probably because Treasury bonds have virtually no risk of default, and thus any difference in yield between two Treasury bonds results solely from the difference in their maturities. Hence, this discussion will focus on the Treasury bond yield curve.

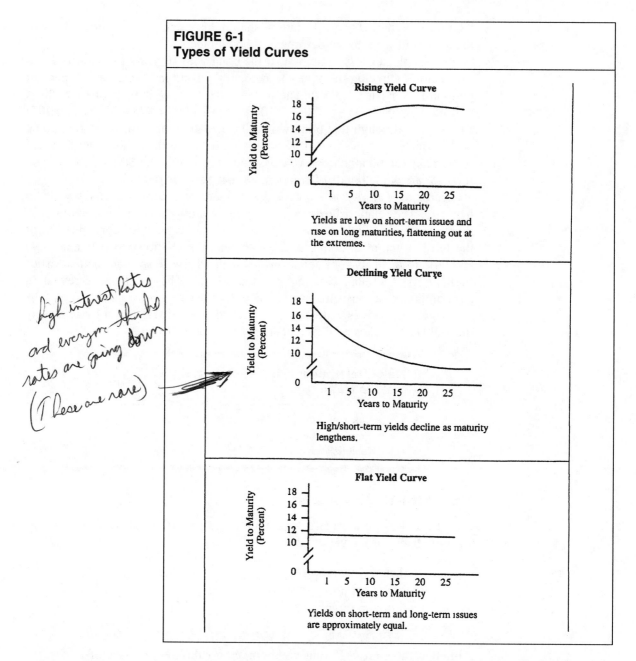

FIGURE 6-1
Types of Yield Curves

Rising Yield Curve

Yields are low on short-term issues and rise on long maturities, flattening out at the extremes.

Declining Yield Curve

High/short-term yields decline as maturity lengthens.

Flat Yield Curve

Yields on short-term and long-term issues are approximately equal.

[handwritten note in margin: high interest rates and everyone thinks rates are going down (These are rare)]

market segmentation hypothesis

    The *market segmentation hypothesis* asserts that supply and demand within each market segment determine interest rates for that maturity class. According to this hypothesis, the yield curve simply reflects the supply and demand for each maturity class. Because most investors are thought to prefer to lend for short time periods, and most borrowers prefer to borrow long term, we would expect to see upward-sloping yield curves almost all of the time.

preferred habitat hypothesis

A related but somewhat less restrictive term structure hypothesis is the *preferred habitat hypothesis*. According to this hypothesis, borrowers and lenders prefer certain maturities. They can be induced to accept other maturities only if the rates are significantly more attractive. The preferred habitat hypothesis provides more likelihood for any shape of yield curve.

The difference between the two theories is that the market segmentation hypothesis states that there are completely separate markets for debt instruments of different maturities, so the interest rates of bonds of a particular maturity should have no effect on the interest rates of bonds of another maturity. By contrast, the preferred habitat hypothesis allows for the possibility of substitution of maturity by borrower and lender if the interest rates on debt instruments of different maturities differ sufficiently. The preferred habitat hypothesis allows for differences between interest rates of different maturities, but it recognizes that there are limits to the extent by which those rates can differ. Under the market segmentation hypothesis, there can be substantial differences in the yields of bonds of different maturities.

As long as there is an active secondary market for bonds and other debt instruments, it is difficult to argue that the markets for debt instruments of different maturities are distinct, and that investors cannot be attracted to bonds of different maturities by interest rate differentials.

liquidity preference hypothesis

The *liquidity preference hypothesis* assumes that because price risk (the impact of interest rate changes on the bond price) increases with maturity, investors demand a premium to hold longer-term securities. Hence, the yield curve would always be upward sloping. The difference between long-term and short-term interest rates due to liquidity preference is called the liquidity premium.

unbiased expectations hypothesis

The *unbiased expectations hypothesis* asserts that long-term rates reflect both current short-term rates and the market's expectation of future short-term rates. Thus, the 2-year rate is simply the geometric average of the current one-year rate and the expected one-year rate one year from now. Suppose that the 2-year rate is Y percent. The unbiased expectations hypothesis asserts that this rate has embedded in it the market's anticipated one-year rate one year from now. That expected rate is, in fact, the rate necessary, when combined with the current one-year rate, to yield an average annual rate of return over 2 years of Y percent.

Example: Consider one-year and 2-year yields of 8 percent and 9 percent, respectively. Taken together, these yields imply a specific value for the expected one-year yield for a security to be issued in one year. Thus, the rate for the second one-year period will cause an investment that yields 8 percent for the first year to generate an overall average annual return of 9 percent.

An (annualized) 8 percent return that is earned for one year corresponds to a return relative of 1.08. A 9 percent return that is earned for 2 years corresponds to a return relative of 1.09^2. Thus, we first seek the return relative for the second one year that will produce the appropriate 2-year return relative. Once we obtain the return relative, the corresponding annualized return is easy to compute. The appropriate formula is as follows: $1.08 \times X = 1.09^2$. Therefore, solving for X is $1.09^2/1.08 = 1.100$.

A return relative of 1.100 for one year corresponds to a one-year return of 10 percent.

The unbiased expectations hypothesis asserts that the market's expectations for future interest rates are reflected by the rates it establishes for debt securities of various maturities. According to this view, potential arbitrage activity (riskless buying and selling to gain a profit) always drives the yield curve into the shape that is appropriate for that set of expectations.

If long-term rates seem too high vis-à-vis expected future short-term rates, some short-horizon investors will move toward longer-term issues while some longer-horizon lenders will switch toward shorter-term borrowing. This activity should quickly drive rates into the appropriate relation. Although the preferred habitat, liquidity preference, and unbiased expectations hypotheses all recognize the existence of this arbitraging activity, only the unbiased expectations hypothesis asserts its overriding power.

Each hypothesis explains the various yield curve shapes slightly differently and has somewhat different implications. According to liquidity preference, yield curves are typically rising because of investor risk aversion. Segmented markets and preferred habitat are also consistent with a tendency for yield curves to rise. Lenders may be relatively more numerous at the short end of the maturity spectrum and borrowers more numerous at the long end.

The unbiased expectations hypothesis, in contrast, asserts that yield curves rise only when interest rates themselves are expected to increase. A flat yield curve indicates neutral expectations—that is, expectations that interest rates will remain constant. A falling yield curve reflects an expectation that rates will fall. This expectation causes borrowers (bond issuers) to rely on short-term financing until the expected fall occurs. Accordingly, borrowers anticipating a decline in interest rates tend to shift demand from the long- to the short-term market. As a result, short-term rates tend to be bid up relative to long-term rates.

Term Structure of Interest Rates Hypotheses

- Segmented markets: Yields reflect supply and demand for each maturity class.
- Preferred habitat: Investors and borrowers can be induced out of their preferred maturity structures only by significantly more attractive rates.
- Liquidity preference: Borrowers are risk averse and demand a premium for buying long-term securities. As a result, yield curves tend to be upward sloping.
- Unbiased expectations: Long-term rates reflect the market's expectation of current and future short-term rates.

[handwritten margin note: There are buyers and lenders which deal w/ certain markets. You will have to give me a higher rate. To get me out of my normal period. Give me 5 yr w/ higher rate vs 3 yr w/ normal rate]

Lenders' expectations have a similar effect. Lenders (bond buyers) want to profit from the expected interest rate decline by owning long-term bonds. Falling rates would cause the prices of outstanding long-term bonds to rise relative to shorter-term issues. Thus, investors who expect rates to fall will tend to favor the longer maturities, thereby pushing long-term rates downward and short-term rates upward.

None of the term structure hypotheses has gained overwhelming acceptance or been completely ruled out. On theoretical grounds, the unbiased expectation hypothesis is generally favored. Liquidity preference may also be useful in explaining the data. Most academicians believe that modern debt markets are not segmented *per se* but that appreciable numbers of borrowers and lenders may have preferred habitats. More than one hypothesis may be useful in explaining the relationship between yield and maturity.

Investment Implications of the Term Structure

Yield curve relationships may give bond traders two opportunities. First, securities whose yields are some distance from curves plotted with otherwise-similar issues may well be misvalued. Thus, bonds whose yields exceed their respective yield curve values may be underpriced. If their market prices adjust more quickly than the curve itself shifts, the strategy could produce an above-market return. Of course, a trader who detects such underpriced bonds will need to act very quickly because other investors will be following the same strategy, thus driving the price of undervalued bonds up to their intrinsic value. Also, the trader should make certain that the underpricing does not represent a risk premium, perhaps for a risk that has only recently been discovered and is not yet reflected in the bond's rating. (This is, of course, assuming that the bond in question is not a Treasury bond, which has virtually no default risk.)

riding the yield curve

A second strategy involves what is called *riding the yield curve.* A steeply rising yield curve may offer an attractive trading opportunity. To ride the yield curve, an investor buys a bond whose term to maturity corresponds to the "top" of the curve, and then holds this bond as the maturity shortens to a flatter part of the curve. The holding period return from such a strategy may dramatically exceed the yield to maturity of the bond that was purchased. The only way one "loses" on this strategy is if the yield curve rises dramatically or flips to a declining slope during the investment period.

Example: For a simple example, let's assume that T-bills can have maturities of up to 2 years. Assume further that 2-year T-bills have a yield to maturity of 7 percent and one-year T-bills have a yield to maturity of 5 percent. If the investor buys the one-year T-bill and holds it to maturity, the HPR is 5 percent. But if the investor buys the 2-year T-bill, holds it one year and then sells it, and the yield curve does not change, then his purchase price is $873.44 ($1000/1.07^2), the selling price is $952.38 ($1000/1.05), and the HPR is 9.04 percent [($952.38 − $873.44)/$873.44)].

DURATION

All 12-year bonds promise to return principal in 12 years. Not all 12-year bonds are alike, however. Measuring their length by maturity or the amount of time remaining before the principal is to be repaid may be quite misleading to an investor. The term to maturity does not fully reflect the timing of a debt security's payment stream. The final payment on a debt security is usually only one of the promised payments. Each of these coupon payments may be viewed as a partial payment of the instrument, and the higher (lower) the coupon rate is, the smaller (larger) the percentage of the total cash flow the principal represents.

The greater the proportion of the return coming from the coupon, the more of the debt security's promised cash flows will be paid prior to its maturity. Thus, a higher coupon is somewhat akin to a shorter maturity. The owner of such a security will receive back a higher proportion of his or her investment prior to the return of principal at maturity.

duration

The concept of *duration* allows the investor to make an appropriate adjustment for different maturities and coupon rates. Like maturity, duration is a measure of time. Duration is defined as the weighted average of the lengths of time until the present values of all remaining payments are made. In other words, it is the weighted average time until recovery of the present value of the bond's future cash flows (principal and interest). The weight of each promised payment's time to receipt is based on its present value relative to the sum of the present values of the entire payment stream (the intrinsic value of the bond). That is, each weight equals the present value of that payment divided by the bond's market price. The total of the present values of expected future cash flows equals the bond's market price. Duration thereby captures the impact of differing coupon rates and recognizes that the earlier coupon payments have a higher present value than later coupon payments. For a bond paying annual interest, the general formula for the duration (D) of a bond with N remaining payments left in its life is as follows:

$$D = \frac{\displaystyle\sum_{t=1}^{N} \frac{t \times C_t}{(1+i)^t}}{\displaystyle\sum_{t=i}^{N} \frac{C_t}{(1+i)^t}} \qquad \text{(Equation 6-1)}$$

where C_t = the cash flow in period t (coupon or principal)

t = the time period when the cash flow is to be received

i = yield to maturity (discount rate)

Several alternative formulations are commonly used to express the computation of the duration statistic. One is

$$D = \frac{\displaystyle\sum_{t=1}^{N} PV(C_t) \times t}{P_0} \qquad \text{(Equation 6-2)}$$

where $PV(C_t)$ = the present value of the cash flow at time t

P_0 = price of the bond

Consider the durations of two bonds maturing in 7 years. Bond A has a 6 percent coupon, whereas bond B has a 10 percent coupon. Table 6-1 shows the results of computing the durations of both bonds when the market-determined interest rate for new bonds of comparable risk is 8 percent.

TABLE 6-1
Durations of Two Bonds Maturing in 7 Years
(Assume annual interest payments)

Bond A

(1) Year(s) Until Receipt t Where N = 7	(2) 6% Cash Flow	(3) Present Value at 8%	(4) Year(s) x Present Value [Column (1) x Column (3)]
1	$ 60	$ 55.56	$ 55.56
2	60	51.44	102.88
3	60	47.63	142.89
4	60	44.10	176.40
5	60	40.83	204.15
6	60	37.81	226.86
7	1,060	618.50	4,329.50
Total	$1,420	$895.87	$5,238.24

Duration for Bond A is equal to $5,238.24/$895.87 = (5.8470984 years rounded to) 5.85 years

Bond B

(1) Year(s) Until Receipt t Where N = 7	(2) 10% Cash Flow	(3) Present Value at 8%	(4) Year(s) x Present Value [Column (1) x Column (3)]
1	$ 100	$ 92.59	$ 92.59
2	100	85.73	171.46
3	100	79.38	238.14
4	100	73.50	294.00
5	100	68.06	340.30
6	100	63.02	378.12
7	1,100	641.84	4,492.88
Total	$1,700	$1,104.12	$6,007.49

Duration for Bond B is equal to $6,007.49/$1,104.12 = (5.4409756 years rounded to) 5.44 years

Better deal since you are recapping your $ sooner

Dividing the total in table 6-1 column 4 by the total in table 6-1 column 3 gives us the duration of each bond, which is approximately 5.85 years for Bond A and 5.44 years for Bond B. Thus, although both bonds have maturities of 7 years, they have durations of only 5.85 years (Bond A) and 5.44 years (Bond B).

Bond A's lower coupon rate corresponds to a duration of about 5 months longer than Bond B's. For equivalent maturities, the lower the coupon

coupon effect

interest rate, the longer the duration. This is called the *coupon effect*. The sensitivity of bond price movements to interest rate changes varies proportionately with duration, and when market interest rates change, the duration of all bonds changes in the opposite direction. A bond's duration reflects its sensitivity to interest rate changes more accurately than the bond's time to maturity does. This is because duration takes into account all expected future cash flows, while maturity considers only the final cash flow (repayment of principal).

The mathematical link between bond price and interest rate changes involves the concept of modified duration, which is discussed later in this chapter.

Still another formula for computing duration is

$$D = \frac{1+Y}{Y} - \frac{(1+Y)+T(C-Y)}{C\left[(1+Y)^T - 1\right]+Y} \qquad \text{(Equation 6-3)}$$

where Y = yield to maturity
C = coupon rate per period
T = term to maturity

(The reason that the symbol for yield to maturity is Y in this equation and i in the prior equation is because both of these formulas are on the Formula Sheet for the CFP™ exam, and this is the way each formula is presented.)

Using this alternative formula, the duration statistics for Bonds A and B can be computed as

$$D_A = \frac{1+.08}{.08} - \frac{(1+.08)+7(.06-.08)}{.06\left[(1+.08)^7 - 1\right]+.08}$$
$$= 5.847$$
$$D_B = \frac{1+.08}{.08} - \frac{(1+.08)+7(.10-.08)}{.10\left[(1+.08)^7 - 1\right]+.08}$$
$$= 5.441$$

A zero coupon bond will always have a duration equal to its remaining life N because it has only one payment, the principal, associated with the bond. In other words, since $P_0 = PV(C_t)$ for a zero coupon bond, equation 6-2 reduces to

$$D = \frac{PV(C_N) \times N}{P_0} = \frac{P_0}{P_0} \times N = 1 \times N = N$$

The duration of a bond that has coupons will always be less than its remaining life N because in equation 6-2 the largest value that t can have is N, and since each value of t is multiplied by a weight equal to $PV(C_t)/P_0$ (as is done in table 6-1, column 3), it follows that D must be less than N.

[handwritten marginal notes: 150 PV, 1000 FV, = 20.89%, 10 N, solve for I]

Major Characteristics of Duration *[handwritten: Pay $50 + in ten years pay me $1000 = 20.89%]*

- The duration of a zero-coupon bond is equal to its term to maturity. *[handwritten: You buy at a discount, doesn't pay interest until maturity]*
- The duration of a coupon bond is always less than its term to maturity.
- There is an inverse relationship between coupon rate and duration.
- There is an inverse relationship between yield to maturity and duration.

From the calculation of the duration of individual bonds like Bond A and Bond B, it is a simple matter to calculate the duration of a whole portfolio of bonds. The duration of a bond portfolio is equal to the weighted average of the durations of the individual bonds in the portfolio, where the weights are based on market values.

Example: If a portfolio has one-fourth of its funds invested in Bond A with a duration of 5.85 years and three-fourths in Bond B with a duration of 5.44 years, then the portfolio itself has a duration of 5.54 years $[D_p = (1/4 \times 5.85) + (3/4 \times 5.44) = 1.46 + 4.08 = 5.54$ years, where D_p is the duration of the portfolio].

One of the most important uses of the duration concept is in a strategy that is known as bond portfolio immunization. This strategy is discussed below.

Immunization of a Portfolio

For an investor holding a bond, there is always both good news and bad news when interest rates change, regardless of the direction of change. When interest rates rise, the coupon payments can be reinvested at higher rates, but the price of the bond falls. When interest rates fall, reinvested coupons will receive lower rates of return, but the price of the bond will rise. The impact of the interest rate change on the yield of reinvested coupon payments is known as reinvestment rate risk. The impact of this interest rate change on the price of the bond is known as price risk.

The important feature about price risk and reinvestment rate risk is that they work in opposite directions. As noted above, a rise in interest rates raises reinvestment rates but lowers the price of the bond. The reverse is true when market interest rates decline. A portfolio is said to be immunized when the benefits from one of these changes exactly offset the losses from the other change.

immunization

Components of Interest Rate Risk

- Price risk: the risk of an existing bond's price changing in response to unknown future interest rate changes. If rates increase, the bond's price decreases, and if rates decrease, the bond's price increases.
- Reinvestment rate risk: the risk associated with reinvesting coupon payments at unknown future interest rates. If rates increase, the coupons are reinvested at higher rates than previously expected, and if rates decrease, the coupons are reinvested at lower rates than previously expected.

Immunization allows an investor to earn a specified rate of return from a bond portfolio over a given period of time, regardless of what happens to market interest rates. In other words, the investor is able to immunize his or her bond portfolio from the effects of changes in market interest rates over a given planning horizon. The objective of immunization is to have opposing effects exactly offset each other, and this is accomplished by frequently rebalancing the portfolio so that its duration is always equal to the investor's planning horizon—that is, when the investor needs to receive funds from the portfolio.

There are two methods available to the investor for immunizing his or her portfolio. The easiest of these methods is to purchase a series of zero-coupon bonds that mature at times and in amounts that correspond to the investor's need for funds. This strategy encounters two basic problems, however. First, the need for funds can rarely be forecast precisely, and second, zero-coupon bonds may not be available in the exact maturities needed.

The typical method of immunizing involves assembling and appropriately managing a diversified portfolio of bonds. The portfolio is structured and managed with the objective of keeping its duration equal in length to the investor's planning horizon. This requires continual portfolio rebalancing on the part of the investor because every time interest rates change, the duration of the portfolio changes. Since immunization requires that the portfolio have a duration equal to the remaining time in the investor's planning horizon, the composition of the investor's portfolio must be rebalanced every time interest rates change. When an imbalance occurs, the investor may have to replace some portfolio components with others whose durations more closely match the planning horizon target.

Even in the absence of market rate changes, immunizing a portfolio once does not ensure that it will remain immunized for all time. The mere passage of time can unbalance a portfolio because duration declines more slowly than term to maturity. This means that the investor must periodically rebalance the portfolio to reduce its duration to equal the remaining time horizon.

Example: An investor's planning horizon is presently 5 years. Assume that the investor's bond portfolio has only one coupon bond and that its duration is computed at 5 years when the market interest rate for new bonds of comparable risk is 10 percent. One year later with the market rate unchanged at 10 percent, the duration of the bond is computed to be about 4.2 years. In other words, although the bond's term to maturity declined by one full year, its duration declined by only 0.8 years. Thus, assuming no change in the market interest rate, the investor must rebalance the portfolio by reducing its duration to 4 years so that it will again equal the remaining time horizon. As noted in the previous section on duration, only a zero-coupon bond's duration decreases at the same rate as its term to maturity.

Moreover, as cash flows are received from coupon payments, the proceeds can be used to purchase new bonds to maintain the target duration. These cash inflows, however, may not be adequate to rebalance the portfolio. To accomplish rebalancing under these circumstances, the investor may have to sell some bonds in the secondary market to obtain the additional funds.

Example: Jane Smith plans to retire in 7 years (her planning horizon). At retirement, she plans to use her savings to buy an annuity so that she will have a guaranteed lifetime income. Her savings are invested in a portfolio of coupon bonds that currently has a 7-year duration.

Even though the portfolio's duration currently equals Jane's planning horizon, she will have to sell some bonds and buy others to maintain the desired immunization for the next 7 years. These transactions will be necessary for two reasons. First, every time market interest rates change, the duration of the portfolio will change. Second, in the absence of market interest rate changes, the mere passage of time will unbalance the portfolio because duration declines more slowly than term to maturity (except in the unique case of zero-coupon bonds).

Whatever immunization method is chosen, the strategy is to ensure that the duration of the bond portfolio matches the planning horizon because when that happens, the price and reinvestment effects of changing market interest rates exactly offset each other. As is evident from the discussion, portfolio immunization is a powerful investment tool that is clearly not a passive strategy. Under the typical immunization method, a portfolio requires frequent rebalancing to keep its duration equal to the remaining time horizon. Finally, it must be mentioned that the effectiveness of immunizing a portfolio must take into account transaction costs. Frequent rebalancing can be very expensive.

Immunizing a Portfolio

- Purchasing a series of zero-coupon bonds whose maturities correspond with the planning horizon
- Assembling and managing a bond portfolio whose duration is kept equal to the planning horizon

Estimating a Bond's Price Volatility

modified duration   An adjusted measure of duration, called *modified duration,* can be used to estimate the interest rate sensitivity of a noncallable bond. That is, modified duration can be used to estimate the percentage change in a bond's price resulting from a relatively small change in market interest rates. To find a bond's modified duration, calculate its duration using equation 6-1, 6-2, or 6-3, and adjust it for the bond's yield to maturity as follows:

$$D^* = \frac{D}{1+Y} \qquad\qquad \text{(Equation 6-4)}$$

where D^* = the bond's modified duration
  D = the bond's duration
  Y = the bond's yield to maturity

[handwritten note in left margin: Question #15 or test in Syllabus or test (pg 4 or test)]

Once having determined a bond's modified duration, it is relatively easy to estimate the bond's percentage price change resulting from a small change in the market interest rate. Thus, the bond's modified duration is first multiplied by –1 (to reflect the inverse relationship between bond prices and interest rates) and then by the amount of change in the market rate. In equation form, this is expressed as follows:

$$\frac{\Delta P}{P} = -D\left[\frac{\Delta(1+Y)}{1+Y}\right]$$

$$= -D^* \times \left[\Delta(1+Y)\right]$$

(Equation 6-5)

where P = price of the bond
ΔP = change in the price of the bond
$\Delta(1 + Y)$ = change in bond's yield to maturity

Example: Continuing with the previous discussion of duration, Bond A's modified duration would be

$$D^* = \frac{5.85 \ \text{years}}{1 + .08} = 5.42 \ \text{years}$$

where 5.85 years is Bond A's duration, calculated using a yield to maturity of 8 percent (the market-determined interest rate for new bonds of comparable risk) when its coupon rate is 6 percent.

Assuming the market interest rate for new bonds of comparable risk increases from 8 to 8.5 percent, the price of Bond A would decrease by approximately 2.71 percent (or $24.28 [2.71% x $895.87]) in value. This is computed as follows:

$$\text{Percent change in bond price} = -5.42 \times 0.5\% = -2.71\%$$

The actual dollar value decline in price is $23.83. Had the magnitude of the change in the discount rate been smaller, the approximation would have been even more accurate.

The concept of modified duration is a useful tool for bond investors. It enables them to estimate bond price changes for small changes in market interest rates. The accuracy of price change estimates deteriorates with larger changes in interest rates because the modified duration calculation is a linear approximation of a bond price-yield relationship that is convex in nature. When interest rates increase, the approximations will always overestimate the dollar value of the decline in price. When interest rates fall, the approximations will always underestimate the dollar value of the increase in price.

Tax Implications of the Coupon Effect

The relative amounts of coupon and price appreciation in the return on a bond also have tax implications. Most bond interest income is fully taxed when received by individuals. For bonds originally sold at par, capital gains are taxed only when they are realized as the bonds either mature or are sold in the secondary market. Thus, the capital gains income on such bonds is both tax deferred and taxed at a lower rate. An investor in a high tax bracket may therefore prefer to buy bonds that pay a below-market coupon rate of interest and are sold at a discount in the secondary market. Note, however, that the imputed yield from price appreciation on zero-coupon and original-issue discount bonds is taxed as if it were received periodically. Only bonds originally issued at or near par generate a capital gains tax treatment. Still, the market generally contains many low-coupon bonds that were initially **deep discount bonds** sold at par but are now priced at a deep discount. These are known as *deep discount bonds*.

Accordingly, private investors in high tax brackets often tend to prefer deep-discount bonds to higher-coupon issues. The before-tax yields to maturity on low-coupon, deep-discount issues are usually somewhat below yields on otherwise similar issues trading nearer to par. This relationship is also called the coupon effect. When capital gains are taxed at a lower rate than ordinary income, as they are currently, the coupon effect has an even greater impact.

It should be remembered that while interest on municipal bonds is not taxable, capital gains are. A high-tax-bracket investor would therefore prefer to purchase municipal bonds that trade at par, or even at a premium, rather than at a discount.

OTHER FACTORS THAT AFFECT BOND PRICES AND YIELDS

The characteristics already discussed (general interest rate levels, risk of default, maturity/duration, coupon effect, tax status) constitute the principal price/yield determinants of specific bonds. Other relevant characteristics include marketability, seasoning, call protection, sinking fund provisions, and "me-first" rules.

Factors Affecting Bond Yields

- General credit conditions: Credit conditions affect all yields to one degree or another.
- Default risk: Riskier issues require higher promised yields.
- Term structure: Yields vary with maturity, reflecting expectations of future interest rate changes.
- Duration: The weighted average of the amount of time until the present value of the purchase price is recouped.
- Coupon effect: Low-coupon issues offer yields that are partially taxed as capital gains.
- Seasonings: Newly issued bonds may sell at a slight discount to otherwise-equivalent established issues.
- Marketability: Actively traded issues tend to be worth more than otherwise-equivalent issues that are less actively traded.
- Call protection: Protection from an early call tends to enhance a bond's value.
- Sinking fund provisions: Sinking funds increase demand and reduce the probability of default, thereby tending to enhance a bond's value.
- Me-first rules: Bonds protected from the diluting effect of additional borrowings are generally worth more than otherwise-equivalent unprotected issues.

Seasoned issues are established in the marketplace. They have been traded for at least a few weeks beyond completion of the initial (offering) sale. As with new stock issues, new issues of bonds tend to be priced a bit below equivalent seasoned issues.

Call protection varies appreciably from issue to issue. Some bonds are callable when sold. Many others may not be called for the first 5 or 10 years of their life. Callable issues that are reasonably likely to be redeemed due to their high yields should be evaluated on their *yield to earliest call* rather than their yield to maturity.

yield to earliest call

A sinking fund's presence increases demand slightly and reduces the probability of default. Thus, a sinking fund generally adds modestly to the value of a bond.

Me-first rules are designed to protect existing bondholders. These rules prevent their claims from being weakened by the issuance of additional debt with a priority higher than or equivalent to theirs. Research has found that these rules significantly enhance the market values of the protected bonds.[2]

Transaction Costs for Bonds

The cost of trading bonds is affected by brokers' commissions and the bid-ask spread. Accrued interest also needs to be taken into account.

Compared to commissions on stock trades, commissions on bond trades are relatively low as a percentage of the principal amount involved. This is because most bonds are fairly marketable, which makes it easier for brokers to find counterparties to the trades.

Small trades may be particularly costly to an investor. Brokers generally have a minimum commission that they charge. For a particularly small trade, this minimum charge could be a sizable percentage of the value of the bonds traded. Also, a trade involving deep-discount bonds may incur a high commission relative to the dollar value of the trade.

Bid-ask spreads are important to consider as well. On actively traded bonds, these spreads tend to be quite narrow. For example, on government bonds, the spread can be less than one-tenth of one percent of the price of the bond. On the other hand, a small, inactively traded corporate bond may have a spread of 5 percent of the bond's price.

ASSEMBLING AND MANAGING A BOND PORTFOLIO

Diversified bond portfolios should be managed to meet their owners' needs. A good portfolio contains bonds that are issued by firms in different industries that have different basic attributes (size, location of company, and so on). Bonds should also be selected to produce the desired level of maturity/duration, default risk/quality rating, coupon/price appreciation, and taxable income.

Bond Swaps

bond swap

Portfolio managers frequently finance a bond purchase with the funds freed up by liquidating another position. A *bond swap* may be designed to increase yield to maturity, increase current yield, adjust duration or risk, or establish a tax loss.

Many swaps are not executed simultaneously. Thus, swap traders risk making one side of the swap (say, the sell) only to encounter an adverse price move before the other side of the swap is accomplished. Moreover, transaction costs absorb some of the anticipated benefits of the swap. Nonetheless, a variety of circumstances make swaps attractive.

Example 1: A bond originally purchased as a long-term issue may be approaching maturity. Swapping it for a longer-term bond would restore the desired duration level.

Example 2: In another type of swap, an investor might sell one bond issue that had decreased in value since it was purchased and then purchase another very similar

tax swap

issue. Such a pure *tax swap* establishes a tax-deductible capital loss while leaving the basic character of the portfolio unchanged.

However, under the wash sale tax rules, a loss sustained on the sale of a bond issue is not allowed if the investor purchases a "substantially identical" issue from the same issuing company within a period beginning 30 days before the sale and ending 30 days after the sale. If a bond purchased as a replacement was issued by a company different from the one that issued the bond being replaced, it will not be considered substantially identical.[3]

Other Aspects of Bond Portfolio Management

Managing a bond portfolio effectively can involve much more than the simple types of swaps mentioned above. The investor might, for example, speculate on a bond upgrade by buying an issue that the market views pessimistically. Margin borrowing may be used to magnify potential gains and/or to leverage a high yield. Some bonds may have higher promised long-term yields than the current cost of margin money. Whether such apparently attractive yield spreads should be exploited depends on both the likelihood that they will persist and the default risk of high-yielding issues. If market interest rates rise, the margin borrowing rate will increase and bond prices will decline.

Bond Returns Compared with Stock Returns

Many investors keep both stocks and bonds in their portfolios. There are advantages and disadvantages to each. Stocks' expected returns are higher, but bonds are less risky. A balanced portfolio of stocks and bonds may offer the risk-expected return tradeoff appropriate to the needs and risk-tolerance levels of many investors.

THE MATHEMATICS OF YIELDS

The term yield is often used as if its meaning were unambiguous, but it can actually be taken to mean a number of different things. For example, the current yield reported in the newspaper quotation is simply the coupon rate divided by the current price. Thus, an 11 percent coupon on a bond quoted at 85 would have a current yield of 12.94 percent, as calculated below:

$$\text{Current yield} = 11\%/85 = \$110/\$850 = 12.94\%$$

yield to maturity

Such a computation does not, however, take account of the discount or premium in the price of the bond. A more complex concept, the *yield to maturity* does consider the impacts of premiums and discounts. To compute the yield to maturity one would solve for the discount rate that would make the present value of the interest payments and par equal to the price of the bond. The yield to maturity is comparable to the internal rate of return concept used in capital budgeting.

Since some bonds are likely to be called before maturity, the yield to first call is often computed for such issues. The computation is similar to that for the yield to maturity except the earliest call date and the call price are used rather than the maturity date and face values.

Those who sell their investment prior to maturity may compute yet another yield: the holding period or realized yield. This is the rate that makes the present value of the payments and sale price equal the purchase price.

Most yields, especially long-term yields, are quoted in coupon-equivalent terms. Short-term yields, in contrast, are often stated in what is called the discount basis. The two yields are computed differently and can produce rather different numbers. Coupon-equivalent yields assume that interest payments take place semiannually and are based on a 365-day year. Discount yields, in contrast, work with a 360-day year and assume that the interest is deducted at the outset. As a result, stated discount-basis yields are somewhat below the coupon-equivalent yield computed for the same security.

The formula for a discount-basis yield of a one-year security is

$$d = D/F$$

where d = discount-basis yield
F = face value
D = discount in face value

SUMMARY AND CONCLUSIONS

There are a number of factors that influence bond yields. General market conditions, especially the inflation rate and expectations about inflation rate changes, affect both the level of yields in general and the term structure of interest rates. For any given market environment, default risk plays the largest role in determining the interest rate of a particular issue of bonds.

Four hypotheses attempt to explain the term structure of interest rates. The unbiased expectations hypothesis holds that long-term interest rates are based on the average of present and expected future short-term rates. The liquidity preference hypothesis argues that investors prefer to invest short term, while borrowers prefer to borrow long term, so long-term interest rates tend to be higher than short-term rates in order to attract investors. The preferred habitat and segmented markets hypotheses argue that both borrowers and lenders (investors) have specific planning horizons, so there are, in effect, different supply-and-demand functions for bonds of different maturities.

Duration is the weighted average of the time it takes to receive the present value of the bond's expected stream of future payments. It is a measure of a bond's sensitivity to interest rate changes. Duration matching is a strategy that investors can use to immunize their bond portfolios by matching the duration of their portfolio with their planning horizon, thus allowing the price risk and reinvestment rate risk to offset each other.

Investors should consider tax implications when purchasing bonds. Coupon payments on municipal bonds are tax exempt, which may make these bonds particularly attractive to investors in high tax brackets. Investors may prefer to purchase taxable bonds at a discount in the secondary market, rather than bonds that trade at par and pay higher coupons, because coupon payments are taxable when they are received, while the capital gain on a bond purchased at a discount is not taxable until the bond matures.

Other factors that influence the price and yield of bonds are marketability, call provisions, priority in the event of default, collateral, and sinking funds. Managing a bond portfolio includes ensuring that there is adequate diversification, rebalancing the portfolio to match the portfolio's duration with the investor's desired time horizon, and using bond swaps when appropriate. Although the expected return to a portfolio of stocks is higher than that of a bond portfolio, stocks are also a more risky investment. A balanced portfolio that contains both stocks and bonds is considered to have good risk-expected return characteristics suitable to the needs, desires, and risk-tolerance level of most investors. A bond portfolio may be particularly desirable to an investor who has a specific time horizon and seeks the relative certainty of bonds' cash flows. Tax-exempt bonds are also attractive to many investors. A diversified portfolio of high-risk bonds may well offer expected returns similar to those of stocks.

CHAPTER REVIEW

Answers to the review questions and the self-test questions start on page 501.

Key Terms

indenture	call price
subordination	call premium
senior debt	trustee
call provision	sinking fund

technical default   riding the yield curve
liquidation   duration
bankruptcy trustee   coupon effect
absolute priority of claims principle   immunization
term structure   modified duration
yield curve   deep discount bonds
market segmentation hypothesis   yield to earliest call
preferred habitat hypothesis   bond swap
liquidity preference hypothesis   tax swap
unbiased expectations hypothesis   yield to maturity

Review Questions

6-1. Which bond indenture provisions are most important to the bondholder?

6-2. What is a default? How does it relate to bankruptcy?

6-3. What is meant by the absolute priority of claims principle? What is its relevancy to most bankruptcies? How is it generally applied in practice?

6-4. Describe the four proposed explanations for the term structure of interest rates. How would each explain the normal (rising) yield curve?

6-5. Recompute the duration for bonds A and B in table 6-1 using an appropriate discount rate of 20 percent. Compare the results with those derived from the 8 percent rate.

6-6. Explain the coupon effect.

6-7. What is immunization? Explain the two methods of immunization.

6-8. Discuss the impacts on yields of
    a. marketability
    b. seasoning
    c. call protection
    d. sinking fund provisions
    e. How should an investor assess the importance of these factors?

6-9. a. What should be considered when assembling a bond portfolio?
    b. What are bond swaps?
    c. What trading costs are involved in buying and selling bonds?

Self-Test Questions

Ⓣ F   6-1. The terms *fixed-income security* and *debt security* can be used interchangeably.

T Ⓕ   6-2. The current yield is the contractually stated interest rate on a bond.

T (F)   6-3.   A bond's coupon rate and yield to maturity are always equal.

(T) F   6-4.   The yield to maturity on a debt instrument is based on both its market price and its coupon rate.

T (F)   6-5.   Aside from general credit conditions, the most significant factor that influences the coupon rate of a bond is duration.

(T) F   6-6.   The market uses Moody's and Standard & Poor's ratings to assess the riskiness of bonds.

(T) F   6-7.   The indenture is a detailed contract between the bond's issuer and the bondholders.

T (F)   6-8.   Debentures are bonds backed by specific collateral.

(T) F   6-9.   In the case of liquidation, the claims of senior creditors must be satisfied before any money is paid to the holders of subordinate debt.

T (F)   6-10. A call provision gives the bondholder the option of receiving the principal amount of the bond prior to maturity.

(T) F   6-11. A call provision is most likely to be exercised if market interest rates decline appreciably while the bond is outstanding.

T (F)   6-12. In the case of bankruptcy, preferred stockholders have priority over unsecured creditors.

(T) F   6-13. The term structure of interest rates describes the relationship between maturity and market interest rates.

(T) F   6-14. The yield curve is a graphical representation of the term structure of interest rates.

T (F)   6-15. Under the liquidity preference hypothesis, borrowers prefer to borrow short-term rather than long-term.

(T) F   6-16. Under the unbiased expectations hypothesis, if long-term interest rates are higher than short-term interest rates, one can conclude that the consensus expectation is that interest rates will increase in the future.

T (F)   6-17. Maturity is a better measure of a bond's sensitivity to interest rate changes than duration.

(T) F   6-18. For bonds of the same maturity, the lower the coupon rate, the greater the duration.

(T) F   6-19. The duration of a zero-coupon bond is equal to its maturity.

(T) F   6-20. Immunizing a portfolio reduces the portfolio's interest rate risk.

(T) F   6-21. All other things being equal, investors in high tax brackets are likely to prefer to purchase bonds at a discount in the secondary market (even though they pay a lower coupon rate) and hold them to maturity rather than purchase bonds at par.

T (F)   6-22. Capital gains on municipal bonds are not taxable.

(T) F   6-23. A bond's sinking fund reduces the risk of default.

T (F)   6-24. As a percentage of the market value of the asset (stock or bond) purchased or sold, commissions on bond trades tend to exceed those on stock trades.

(T) F   6-25. When a bond is <u>traded flat</u>, the purchaser does not receive the accrued interest on the bond.   *not paying interest*

(T) F   6-26. The expected return to stocks tends to be higher than the expected return to bonds, but stocks also tend to be more risky than bonds.

NOTES

1. E. Altman and S. Nammacher, "The Default Rate Experience on High-Yield Corporate Debt," *Financial Analysts Journal* (July/August 1985, pp. 25–41; J. Fons, "The Default Premium and Corporate Bond Experience," *Journal of Finance* (March 1987), pp. 81–97.
2. G. Brauer, "Evidence of the Market Value of Me-First Rules," *Financial Management* (spring 1983), pp. 11–18; M. Brody, "Controversial Issue: A Leveraged Buy-Out Touches Off a Bitter Dispute," *Barron's* (September 19, 1983), pp. 15, 19–22.
3. *See* I.R.C. §1091(a).

Risk and Diversification

Learning Objectives

An understanding of the material in this chapter should enable the student to

---

7-1. Explain the differences between individual, portfolio, nonmarket, and market risk.

7-2. Explain the parameters of portfolio risk determination.

7-3. Describe the risk-reduction potential of diversification.

7-4. Describe the efficient frontier and its implications.

7-5. Explain the theory and uses of the capital asset pricing model.

7-6. Explain other portfolio theories.

Chapter Outline

Most investors have a basic understanding of investment risk. They generally (1) realize that risk is related to the confidence placed in expectations regarding the returns their investments are likely to pay, (2) are willing to accept a lower expected return to obtain a reduction in risk, and (3) understand that the discount rate applied to the valuation of any expected income stream should vary directly with its risk. This chapter expands on that base, focusing primarily on risk's role in investment analysis and portfolio management. First, the definition of risk is explored and then its primary forms (individual and portfolio) are introduced. Next, portfolio risk is analyzed. Finally, the evolution of portfolio theory is explored.

SIMPLE EXAMPLE OF INVESTMENT RISK

Consider the following investment alternatives. Suppose investment A guarantees a return of precisely 5 percent. Now consider investment B with a 5 percent chance of a 0 percent return, a 90 percent chance of a 5 percent return, and a 5 percent chance of a 10 percent return. B's expected return is 5 percent $[(.05 \times .00) + (.90 + .05) + (.05 \times .10) = .00 + .045 + .005 = .05]$, which is the same as A's. B's actual (or realized) return is less likely to equal its expected return than A's is. Ten percent of the time investment B will not earn 5 percent. Investment A offers an equivalent expected return and lower risk than investment B does. Thus, risk-averse investors would prefer A to B.

risk averse To be *risk averse* simply means that, for a given expected return, an individual would prefer less risk to more risk. A vast majority of people fit that definition. Comparing A to B is very straightforward.

Now consider asset C with a 5 percent chance of a 3 percent return, a 90 percent chance of a 5 percent return, and a 5 percent chance of a 7 percent return. Like A and B, C offers an expected return of 5 percent $[(.05 \times .03) + (.90 \times .05) + (.05 \times .07) = .05]$. Because B's actual return is uncertain, risk averters would prefer A. On the other hand, because C's return variation (or range of possible returns) is less than B's, C is less risky than B, yet still riskier than A. That is, the possible returns for B are 0 percent, 5 percent, and 10 percent; for C, they are 3 percent, 5 percent, and 7 percent. B's actual return could be 5 percent above or below its expected value, whereas C's can differ only 2 percent from its mean in either direction.

histogram Return possibilities such as these are often illustrated graphically, as shown in figure 7-1, as a *histogram* of investment return possibilities. The vertical axes in figure 7-1 report the probability of each event; the horizontal axes identify the event (such as the realized return).

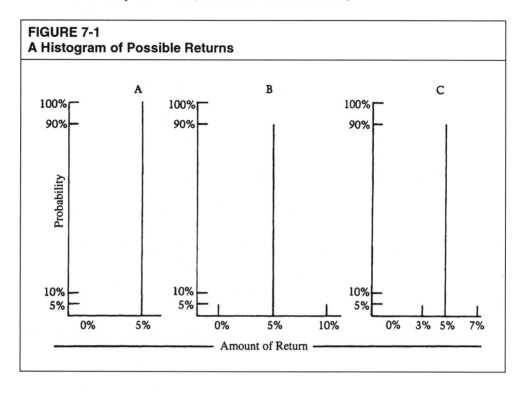

FIGURE 7-1
A Histogram of Possible Returns

RISK OF A DISTRIBUTION OF POSSIBLE RETURNS

Although determining the expected (average) value of a distribution of returns is rather straightforward, measuring its risk is more complex. B's return could vary from 0 percent to 10 percent, compared with 3 percent to 7 percent for C. Because B's range of possible returns is greater, most people would rate B as riskier. This comparison suggests that a measure of risk could be based on the difference between the maximum and minimum possible returns. Such an approach would capture at least some of the flavor of what people mean when they talk about an investment's risk. Viewed in isolation, the magnitude of the range of possible returns, however, ignores possible differences in the shape of the distribution between the two extremes, which would demonstrate the likelihood of obtaining an exceptionally high or exceptionally low return. For example, imagine an investment D with a 50 percent chance of a 10 percent return and a 50 percent chance of a 0 percent return. It has the same range as investment B, yet it is clearly a riskier investment.

Rather than use the range of possible returns, a risk measure could be based on the dispersion or deviation from the expected return. The simple average deviation from the mean is precisely zero (the negative differences exactly offset the positive differences).

Example: An investment offers a 30 percent probability of a –2 percent return, a 40 percent probability of an 8 percent return, and a 30 percent probability of an 18 percent return. The expected return is 8 percent (.30 x –2% + (.40 x 8%) + (.30 x 18%). The deviations from the mean are –10 percent (–2% – 8%), 0 percent (8% – 8%), and 10% (18% – 8%). The sum of the three deviations is zero (–10% + 0% + 10%).

---

mean absolute deviation

Alternatively, the absolute value of the deviation could be calculated without regard to positive or negative signs. The average of the absolute values of the deviations from the mean would measure the average distance of the actual return from the expected return. This computation is known as the *mean absolute deviation*. The mean absolute deviation is statistically difficult to work with, however, so an alternative method of taking the average of the squared deviations (producing nonnegative values) has become standard practice. This average is called the *variance*. Another measure of dispersion, *semivariance,* is occasionally used by financial analysts and others. Semivariance resembles variance but differs by considering only deviations below the mean. The motivation is that investors are primarily concerned with the risk associated with below-average returns. Use of this statistic is relatively rare.

variance
semivariance

standard deviation

Statisticians have found the variance a convenient statistic to work with. The variance and its square root, the *standard deviation*, are frequently employed as descriptive statistics for a distribution of random variables. To understand how the standard deviation serves as a risk measure, we first need to explore its relationship to probability distributions.

Probability Distributions

probability distributions

Histograms such as those in figure 7-1 relate possible discrete events to their likelihoods or frequencies. *Probability distributions* are used for continuous phenomena, which are phenomena with infinite possible outcomes. Figure 7-2, a symmetrical probability distribution, illustrates the relation between expected returns and their probabilities. The probabilities rise to a peak at return $\overline{R}$ (the mean, or expected return) and decline symmetrically thereafter. With a symmetrical distribution, the probabilities for returns equidistant from $\overline{R}$ are equal. The simple average of these paired returns is $\overline{R}$.

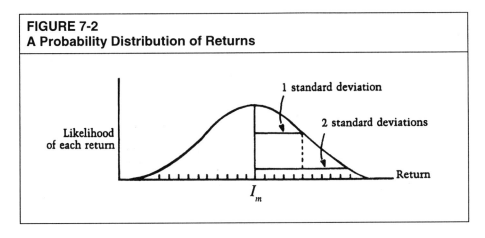

FIGURE 7-2
A Probability Distribution of Returns

Figure 7-2 also illustrates returns one and two standard deviations from the average. For most commonly encountered distributions (the most prevalent example is the normal distribution), the actual value will be within one standard deviation of the mean approximately two-thirds of the time; about 95 percent of the time it will be within two standard deviations. Thus, the standard deviation of the return distribution is a useful measure of a distribution's spread. It may be used as an index of the degree of confidence (or risk) in the expected return.

Simple Example

Suppose we had N equally likely returns denoted by R_t. The mean or expected return for R_t is shown in the following formula:

$$E(R) = \overline{R} = \sum_{t=1}^{N} R_t / N = \frac{1}{N} \sum_{t=1}^{N} R_t \qquad \text{(Equation 7-1)}$$

Similarly, the formula for the variance is

$$\sigma^2 = \sum_{t=1}^{N} \frac{\left[R_t - E(R) \right]^2}{N} = \frac{1}{N} \sum_{t=1}^{N} \left[R_t - E(R) \right]^2 \qquad \text{(Equation 7-2)}$$

$\sum_{t=1}^{N}$ followed by a formula such as R_t/N means "the sum of" that formula for each value of t from 1 through N; $\sum_{t=1}^{N} R_t/N$ means $R_1/N + R_2/N + R_3/N + \ldots + R_n/N$.

The standard deviation is the square root of the variance:

$$\sigma = \sqrt{\sigma^2} = \text{standard deviation} \qquad \text{(Equation 7-3)}$$

For unequal weights, the mean and standard deviation computations are somewhat more complex. Rather than take the simple (unweighted) average of returns, a weighted average is computed as follows, where $P(R_t)$ = probability of return R_t:

$$E(R) = \sum_{t=1}^{N} P(R_t) R_t \qquad \text{(Equation 7-1a)}$$

Similarly,

$$\sigma^2 = \sum_{t=1}^{N} P(R_t) \left[R_t - E(R_t) \right]^2 \qquad \text{(Equation 7-2a)}$$

Note that these are essentially the same formulas used in equations 7-1 and 7-2. For N equally weighted returns, the probability of any return t is simply 1/N, so P (R_t) can be expressed as 1/N. Then equations 7-1a and 7-2a become identical to equations 7-1 and 7-2.

Example: Assume equal probabilities of returns of –2 percent, 4 percent, 10 percent, and 16 percent:

$$P(R_1) = P(R_2) = P(R_3) = P(R_4) = .25$$

R_1	R_2	R_3	R_4
–.02	.04	.10	.16

We begin by computing the average or expected return for this set of possible returns:

$$E(R) = \left(\frac{-.02 + .04 + .10 + .16}{4} \right) = \frac{.28}{4} = .07$$

Next, we form the deviations of each possible return from its expected value:

$$X_t = R_t - E(R)$$

$$X_1 \qquad X_2 \qquad X_3 \qquad X_4$$
$$(-.02 - .07)\ (.04 - .07)\ (.10 - .07)\ (.16 - .07)$$
$$(-.09) \qquad (-.03) \qquad (.03) \qquad (.09)$$

These values are then squared:

$$(X_t)^2 = [R_t - E(R)]^2$$

$$X_1^2 \qquad X_2^2 \qquad X_3^2 \qquad X_4^2$$
$$(-.09)^2 \quad (-.03)^2 \quad (.03)^2 \quad (.09)^2$$
$$.0081 \qquad .0009 \qquad .0009 \qquad .0081$$

The results are then totaled and averaged. (Had the probabilities not been equal, a weighted average would have been taken.) The result of this computation is the variance (σ^2):

$$\text{Sum} = .0081 + .0009 + .0009 + .0081 = .0180$$

$$\sigma^2 = \frac{.0180}{4} = .0045$$

The standard deviation is simply the square root of the variance:

$$\sigma = \sqrt{.0045} = .0671 \text{ or } 6.71\%$$

Thus, this investment has an expected return of 7 percent and a standard deviation of 6.71 percent. This means that the best guess for this investment's return is 7 percent. If its returns are normally distributed, about two-thirds of the time the yield should be between .29 percent (.29% = 7% − 6.71%) and 13.71 percent (13.71% = 7% + 6.71%).

ex ante

ex post

The above examples are all what are known as *ex ante* (before the fact) data. That is, we defined all the possible future returns and the probabilities of each of those returns. In practice, the statistics discerned above are usually calculated from *ex post* (after the fact) or historical data. When statistics are calculated with historical data, there are some adjustments to the formulas. Fortunately, the mechanics of the expected return calculation are the same. It is the calculation of the variance that is different. The difference is that the sum of the squared differences is divided by N – 1 rather than by N. This is shown in equation 7-2b:

$$\sigma^2 = \frac{1}{N-1} \sum_{t=1}^{N} \left[R_t - E(R) \right]^2 \qquad \text{(Equation 7-2b)}$$

The standard deviation calculation shown above is called the sample standard deviation because it is based on the sample of observed outcomes, rather than on the universe of possible outcomes. Note that the subscript used is the letter t to represent time periods, and previously we used the letter i to represent each potential return.

Example: You are looking at a stock and note that the returns for the last 5 years are –15 percent, 5 percent, 10 percent, –3 percent, and 28 percent. You believe these returns are representative of future returns, and you are willing to base your estimate of expected return and standard deviation on these historical data. What would the expected return and standard deviation be? The expected return is

$$E(R) = \frac{-15\% + 5\% + 10\% - 3\% + 28\%}{5} = 5\%$$

The standard deviation is derived from the variance as

$$\sigma^2 = \frac{1}{5-1} \times \left[(-15-5)^2 + (5-5)^2 + (10-5)^2 + (-3-5)^2 + (28-5)^2 \right]$$

$$= \frac{1}{4} \times \left(400 + 0 + 25 + 64 + 529 \right)$$

$$= 254.5$$

$$\sigma = \sqrt{254.5} = 15.95\%$$

RISK AVERSION

Most people are risk averse. Risk-averse investors dislike the prospect of an unexpectedly low (perhaps negative) return more than they like the possibility of a favorable return of similar magnitude above the mean. For example, if the mean return is 10 percent, they view a –10 percent return (20 percent below the mean) as more undesirable than they view a return of +30 percent (20 percent above the mean) as desirable. To avoid the possibility of experiencing the pain of an unexpectedly low return, risk-averse investors prefer assets whose expected returns are more certain.

Individual investor circumstances can differ greatly from investor to investor. These different circumstances tend to affect investors' attitudes toward risk. Their degree of risk aversion varies, however. Some have good reasons for being cautious about their investments. For example, many retired couples depend on their investments for a substantial fraction of their income. Their budgeting decisions are relatively simple if they have a dependable source of investment income. As another example, a young unmarried professional with a substantial income and some money to invest may well be less risk averse than the average investor. This individual may believe he or she is better able to absorb losses and therefore is more willing to take large risks for large potential gains. Still, even this type of investor would probably prefer less risk to more risk if the expected returns were nearly the same.

Different individual investor circumstances can explain some, but by no means all, differences in investor risk aversion. A second major factor is the investor's personal preference. Some individuals are, by their very nature, risk takers. These individuals may be quite comfortable taking large risks. They may still be risk averse but only modestly so. Other individuals may be much more cautious in their approach to risk taking. Notwithstanding their circumstances, these investors are willing to tolerate only a low level of risk and only if the potential reward from risk taking is substantial.

Risky investments must be priced low enough relative to their prospective payoffs to attract risk-averse investors. In practice, this means that a higher discount rate is applied to the investment's expected cash flow streams. The market accomplishes this process as follows: In order for the market to clear, an equilibrium price must be established. This principle applies to investments, just as it applies to goods and services. An equilibrium price is a price at which the quantity supplied is equal to the quantity demanded. This is also known as the market-clearing price. If a particular investment with very little or no risk (for example, a Treasury bond) is priced to yield 5 percent, an otherwise similar investment with more risk (for example, a corporate bond of comparable maturity) must be priced to yield a higher expected return, such as 6 percent or 7 percent. A still riskier but otherwise similar investment would need to offer a still higher expected return, such as 8 percent or 10 percent, in order to attract enough buyers for the market to clear. The riskier the investment, the higher the discount rate applied to it and, thus, the lower its market value.

Example: An investment that is expected to be worth $1,000 in 5 years could now sell for $700, $500, or $300, depending on its risk and the corresponding discount rate. At $700, the market is applying (approximately) a 7.4 percent discount rate; $500 corresponds to a 14.9 percent rate, and $300 implies a rate of 27.2 percent. The greater the risk, the higher the discount rate applied to the investment and the lower the current (present) value, hence the lower price.

INDIVIDUAL VERSUS PORTFOLIO RISK

As discussed earlier, the standard deviation is a useful measure of an individual investment's risk. The standard deviation of an individual asset's expected return is an inadequate risk measure, however, if the asset is part of a larger portfolio. An investor's wealth and investment income stem from his or her entire portfolio. If poor performance by some parts of the portfolio tends to be offset by more favorable performance in the rest of the portfolio, the investor's overall wealth position may not suffer. The investor is unlikely to know ahead of time which investments will do well and which will not, but he or she will know that some investments will do better than others. The more diversified the portfolio, the more likely individual losses in the portfolio are offset by other investments that are doing well. Accordingly, investors should concern themselves primarily with portfolio risk, rather than the risks of each of the portfolio's individual components. If the values of two investments fluctuate by offsetting amounts, the owner is no worse off than if neither had varied. This example shows the benefits of diversification.

Example: Imagine a sunscreen business and an umbrella business at the beach. Let's say there is a 50 percent chance that it will rain and a 50 percent chance that it will be sunny. The sunscreen business will have a 20 percent return if it is sunny but a 0 percent return if it rains. The umbrella business will have a 20 percent return if it rains but a 0 percent return if it is sunny. Each business will have an expected return of 10 percent (.5 x 20%) and a standard deviation of 10 percent. Now imagine a diversified portfolio consisting of equal weights of the sunscreen and umbrella businesses. It will still have an expected return of 10 percent, but the standard deviation is now zero since there will be a 10 percent return whether it is sunny or rainy.

As the simplified example above shows, diversification is used to create a riskless portfolio out of two risky investments. Note that risk has been eliminated without any reduction in the expected return.

TWO-ASSET PORTFOLIO RISK

diversification

The simplest type of portfolio contains a single asset, such as stock in one company. This portfolio is, by definition, totally undiversified. The next simplest portfolio contains two assets, such as stock in two different companies. A two-asset portfolio begins to take advantage of the risk-reduction potential of *diversification*. First, we define the expected return of the two-asset portfolio:

$$E\left(R_p\right) = W_i\left[E\left(R_i\right)\right] + W_j\left[E\left(R_j\right)\right] \qquad \text{(Equation 7-4)}$$

where W_i = portfolio weight of asset i
W_j = portfolio weight of asset j

portfolio variance

The risk of the portfolio depends on both the individual risk of its two components and the degree to which the two components' return variations are related. The *portfolio variance* for a two-asset portfolio is shown in equation 7-5:

$$\sigma_p^2 = W_i^2\sigma_i^2 + 2W_iW_jCOV_{ij} + W_j^2\sigma_j^2 \qquad \text{(Equation 7-5)}$$

where σ_i^2 = variance of asset i

σ_j^2 = variance of asset j

COV_{ij} = covariance of asset i with j

For simplicity, the weights W_i and W_j are restricted to the 0–1 range (ruling out short selling and borrowing). The terms $W_i^2\sigma_i^2$ and $W_j^2\sigma_j^2$ are the squares of each component's weight multiplied by its respective variance. Recall that W_i and W_j are the proportions of the portfolio invested in assets i and j. Therefore, both W_i and W_j are fractions between zero and one that sum to one. That is, $W_i + W_j = 1$ where $0 \leq W_{ij}, W_j \leq 1$. If, for example, half of the portfolio is invested in each asset, both W_i and W_j equal 0.50.

The remaining term, $2W_iW_j COV_{ij}$, requires further explanation. The first part of the term, $2W_iW_j$, is twice the product of the proportions W_i and W_j. The key—indeed a central aspect of portfolio risk in general—is the covariance term COV_{ij} (the symbol σ_{ij} is also sometimes used). The covariance reflects the impact of portfolio diversification.

Covariance

The *covariance*, like the mean and standard deviation, is a statistic that is almost always estimated from ex post (historical) values of the relevant variables. It measures the comovement or covariability of two variables. Thus, the covariance of two assets' returns is an index of their tendency to move relative to each other. For example, the market prices of stocks of two similar companies that operate in the same industries would probably tend to move together. On the other hand, stock prices of two different types of companies would probably tend to move largely independently of each other. The former pair of stocks would have a relatively high positive covariance with each other; the latter pair would have a covariance near zero. Stocks with low covariances with each other are better diversification vehicles than those with high covariances.

To understand how the covariance statistic is defined, first consider the difference between asset i's period t return (R_{it}) and its mean value $E(R_i)$. Because a mean value is generally located near the center of the distribution, this difference $[R_{it} - E(R_i)]$ may be either positive or negative, and it is equally likely to be one as it is to be the other. The same is true for the difference $[R_{jt} - E(R_j)]$. Now consider the product of the differences $[(R_{it} - E(R_i)][R_{jt} - E(R_j)]$. When the two asset returns are either both above or both below their means, the product is positive. The product of two positives is positive, and the product of two negative numbers is also positive. The product of these two differences is negative when one is above its mean and the other below. The covariance is defined as the average of the products $[R_{it} - E(R_i)][R_{jt} - E(R_j)]$.

The covariance of a two-asset portfolio based on ex ante returns is

$$COV_{ij} = \sum_{t=1}^{N} [R_{it} - E(R_i)][R_{jt} - E(R_j)]/(N-1)$$

$$= \frac{1}{(N-1)} \sum_{i=1}^{N} [R_{it} - E(R_i)][R_{jt} - E(R_j)] \qquad \text{(Equation 7-6)}$$

Example: To explore how a covariance of two returns is computed, suppose we have the following five observations on variables R_i and R_j:

$$(R_{i1}, \ R_{j1}) \ = \ (5\%, 4\%)$$
$$(R_{i2}, \ R_{j2}) \ = \ (10\%, 15\%)$$
$$(R_{i3}, \ R_{j3}) \ = \ (-7\%, -12\%)$$
$$(R_{i4}, \ R_{j4}) \ = \ (-2\%, 2\%)$$
$$(R_{i5}, \ R_{j5}) \ = \ (19\%, 16\%)$$

First, we must compute the average values for i and j:

$$\overline{R}_i = E(R_i) = \left(\frac{5 + 10 - 7 - 2 + 19}{5} \right) = \frac{25}{5} = 5\%$$

$$\overline{R}_j = E(R_j) = \left(\frac{4 + 15 - 12 + 2 + 16}{5} \right) = \frac{25}{5} = 5\%$$

Next, we must compute the value for the differences $\left(R_{it} - \overline{R}_i \right)$ and $(R_{jt} - \overline{R}_j)$, and their product for each t value:

$R_{it} - \overline{R}_i$	$R_{jt} - \overline{R}_j$	$(R_{it} - \overline{R}_i)(R_{jt} - \overline{R}_j)$
$5 - 5 = 0$	$4 - 5 = -1$	$(0)(-1) = 0$
$10 - 5 = 5$	$15 - 5 = 10$	$(5)(10) = 50$
$-7 - 5 = -12$	$-12 - 5 = -17$	$(-12)(-17) = 204$
$-2 - 5 = -7$	$2 - 5 = -3$	$(-7)(-3) = 21$
$19 - 5 = 14$	$16 - 5 = 11$	$(14)(11) = 154$

Finally, we can determine the covariance by averaging these values:

$$COV_{ij} = \frac{0 + 50 + 204 + 21 + 154}{5 - 1} = 107.25$$

Note that in this example, the R_i and R_j values tended to move together, producing a positive covariance. The result is a relationship like that in figure 7-3.

Correlation

correlation coefficient

An even more important statistic than the covariance is the *correlation coefficient* of i and j, denoted as ρ_{ij}, which is their covariance divided by the product of their standard deviations. The divisor scales the correlation coefficient between a maximum of +1 and a minimum of –1.

$$\rho_{ij} = COV_{ij} / \sigma_i \times \sigma_j \qquad \text{(Equation 7-7)}$$

As is true of the variance, the correlation between assets i and j, ρ_{ij}, is a measure of the degree to which the returns of these two assets change together. If the returns change at the same time, in the same direction, and are perfectly proportional, then $\rho_{ij} = 1$. If the returns change at the same time and are perfectly proportional but change in opposite directions, then $\rho_{ij} = -1$. If there is no relationship between the two returns, then $\rho_{ij} = 0$. Therefore, the range of possible values for ρ_{ij} is $1 \le \rho_{ij} \le 1$. Readers should note that proportionality does not imply that returns are necessarily equal, only that they exhibit a constant relationship. If, for example, an asset i always has returns two times greater than asset j, the returns are exactly proportional and their correlation is 1. The following example illustrates the effects of correlation on two-asset portfolios.

Example: Assume that asset A has a return of 4 percent and a standard deviation of 1.5 percent. Asset B has a return of 6 percent and a standard deviation of 2 percent. Assets A and B have a correlation of +1. Also assume that asset C has the same return and standard deviation as asset B, but its correlation with asset A is −1. If an investor holds a two-asset portfolio that is composed of 50 percent of asset A and 50 percent of asset B, then the return on the portfolio is 5 percent, and the portfolio's standard deviation is 1.75 percent. However, if the two-asset portfolio is composed of 50 percent of asset A and 50 percent of asset C, the portfolio's return remains at 5 percent, but its standard deviation is now .25 percent. Therefore, the second portfolio is substantially less risky than the first portfolio. The more correlated the returns of the two assets, the larger the portfolio standard deviation. As the correlation decreases and approaches −1, the portfolio standard deviation becomes smaller. These characteristics form the core of the diversification effect, which is a fundamental building block of portfolio theory.

Figures 7-3, 7-4, and 7-5 help to illustrate the meaning of the correlation coefficient. Suppose we are interested in the comovements of assets i and j. We might explore this relation by plotting $(r_{it} - \overline{R}_i)$ and $(r_{jt} - \overline{R}_j)$ over time. Whenever investments i and j are above their averages together, we will plot the point in the upper right-hand quadrant. When they are simultaneously below their means, we will plot the point in the lower left-hand quadrant. Investments that tend to vary together in this way will largely plot in an area concentrated in those two quadrants (figure 7-3). Most asset pairs exhibit this positive covariance.

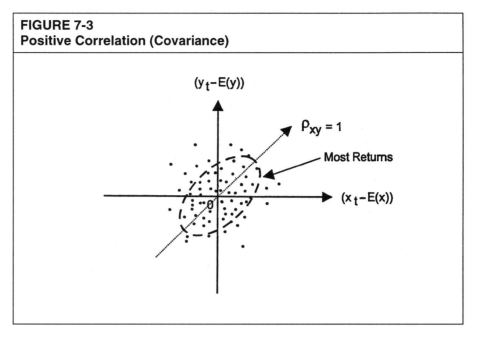

FIGURE 7-3
Positive Correlation (Covariance)

An investment may, however, experience above-average returns while another is below average (upper left and lower right quadrants). If the returns move in opposite directions more than they move together, the correlation will be negative (figure 7-4). Finally, if the returns move in a totally

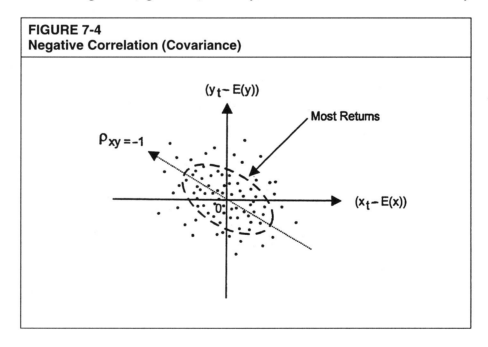

FIGURE 7-4
Negative Correlation (Covariance)

independent fashion, a zero correlation coefficient will result (figure 7-5). When assets have a zero correlation, they are termed as being independent of each other.

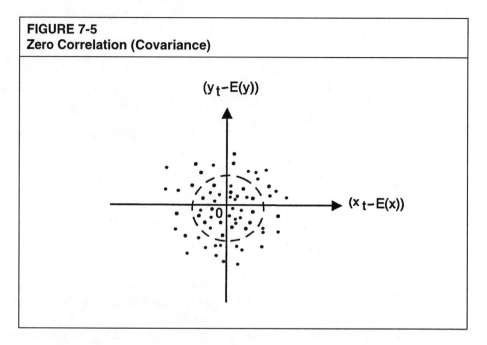

FIGURE 7-5
Zero Correlation (Covariance)

Remember our earlier example of umbrellas and sunscreen. That is an example of two assets whose returns (sales) are negatively correlated. On the other hand, suppose the two assets under consideration are bread and butter. We would expect their returns (or sales) to have a high positive correlation.

Example of a Two-Asset Portfolio's Risk

Returning to equations 7-4 and 7-5, consider a simple example. Suppose i and j have standard deviations of .10 and .15 respectively, and a covariance of .01. We could form a portfolio composed half of i and half of j. If the expected returns of i and j are .09 and .11, the portfolio's expected return would be .10. This is calculated as follows:

$$E(R_P) = .5(.09) + .5(.11) = .45 + .55 = .10$$

We might think that the portfolio's standard deviation would also be a weighted average of .10 and .15 (.125). The formula for the variance, however, reveals a different result. Consider:

$$\sigma_p^2 = W_i^2 \sigma_i^2 + 2W_i W_j COV_{ij} + W_j^2 \sigma_j^2$$
$$\sigma_i = .10$$
$$\sigma_j = .15$$
$$W_i = .5$$
$$W_j = .5$$
$$COV_{ij} = .01$$

Thus, the variance is calculated as follows:

$$\sigma_p^2 = (.5)^2 (.10)^2 + 2(.5)(.5)(.01) + (.5)^2 (.15)^2$$
$$\sigma_p^2 = .0025 + .0050 + .005625 = .013125$$

Since the standard deviation is the square root of the variance,

$$\sigma_p = \sqrt{.01325} = .115$$

In this case, diversifying the portfolio has clearly reduced the risk below the average of the two components' risk. The average risk (as measured by the standard deviation of the expected return) of the two components is .125, compared with the portfolio's overall risk of .115. The next section will consider the issue in greater detail.

Three Special Cases

Exploration of the standard deviation formula of a two-asset portfolio renders some important insights. These results will provide a foundation for subsequent discussions of portfolio theory.

When the correlation is at its maximum value of 1, the standard deviation formula reduces to

$$\sigma_P = W_i \sigma_i + W_j \sigma_j$$

In this case, the standard deviation is a weighted average of the individual standard deviations of i and j. The graph of this function is a straight line connecting the points corresponding to i's and j's return and standard deviation.

When the correlation is at its minimum value of −1, the portfolio formula has two solutions:

$$\sigma_P = \begin{cases} -W_i \sigma_i + W_j \sigma_j \text{ or} \\ W_i \sigma_i - W_j \sigma_j \end{cases}$$

When the correlation is −1, it is possible to choose weights W_i and W_j so that $\sigma_P = 0$. Incorporating these results produces two lines originating at i and j that meet at f, the zero risk portfolio. Figure 7-6 demonstrates that portfolios possessing minimum and maximum correlations lie on lines making up a triangle anchored at f, i, and j.

FIGURE 7-6
Portfolio Risk: The Two-Asset Case

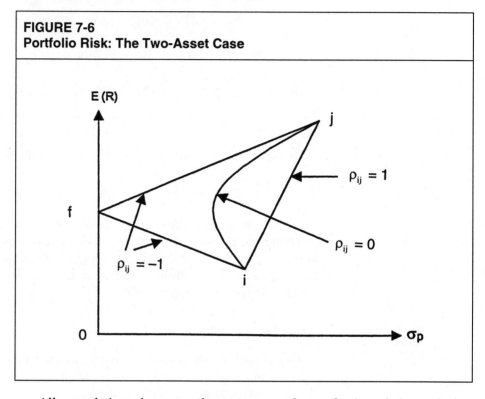

All correlations between the extreme values of −1 and 1 result in portfolios in the interior of the triangle. In these cases, the portfolio formula cannot be reduced and remains

$$\sigma_P = \sqrt{W_i^2\sigma_i^2 + 2W_iW_j\rho_{ij}\sigma_i\sigma_j + W_j^2\sigma_j^2}$$

Graphing this function for a single fixed correlation results in a curve anchored at assets i and j. Curvature becomes more pronounced as the correlation decreases. Correspondingly, the curves move closer to the minimum correlation lines.

N-ASSET PORTFOLIO RISK

The N-asset equivalent of equation 7-5 contains variance and covariance terms for every asset and asset pair in the portfolio.

$$\sigma_P^2 = \sum_{i=1}^{N} W_i^2 \sigma_i^2 + \sum_{i=1}^{N} \sum_{\substack{j=1 \\ i \neq j}}^{N} W_i W_j COV_{ij} \qquad \text{(Equation 7-8)}$$

This formula is merely an extension of the two-asset case. The first summation gives the variances and their weights. The double summation gives every covariance with the appropriate weights. Note that there are N (N − 1)/2 covariance terms, and they incorporate the covariance of every asset with every other asset.

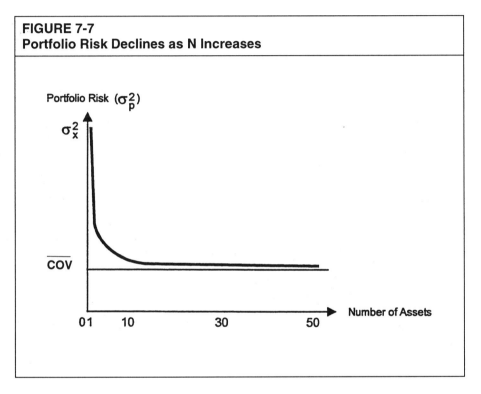

FIGURE 7-7
Portfolio Risk Declines as N Increases

The N-asset risk formula demonstrates that the number of covariance terms increases exponentially faster than the number of variance terms. The implication is that diversification benefits quickly increase due to the direct link between covariance and diversification. As the number of assets increases, the covariance effect will dominate, causing the portfolio's variance to approach its theoretical minimum—the average covariance of all securities.

For randomly selected stocks, a large portfolio will have between 30 percent to 40 percent of the risk of a typical one-stock portfolio. Once the diversified portfolio's risk is reduced to this level, it cannot be reduced further by adding still more stocks. Research has repeatedly shown that a relatively small number of stocks (about 30) is sufficient to obtain most of the risk-reduction potential of diversification. It is important to remember that diversification is not just a matter of numbers. A portfolio of 100 firms in the same industry and location, subject to the same risks, would have relatively large covariance terms and thus would not provide much diversification benefit.

Estimating Variances and Covariances

Covariance and variance statistics can be estimated from past (historical) data. That is, a data series for the past returns of a group of investments can be used to compute variance and covariance estimates. When possible, however, these estimates should also utilize future-oriented information. For example, the stock of a firm whose future environment is expected to be similar to its past is likely to behave much as its historically estimated variance and covariance statistics imply. On the other hand, some firms may have recently experienced a major change, such as a merger, new product introduction, different regulatory environment, or large capital infusion. These firms are more likely to behave differently than they had prior to the changes. If the change has a tendency to increase risk, historical risk estimates should be adjusted upward. Similarly, a change that decreases risk should lead to a downward adjustment in the historically based measure of risk.

EVOLUTION OF PORTFOLIO THEORY

The Efficient Frontier

portfolio theory

Portfolio theory, sometimes referred to as modern portfolio theory, or MPT,[1] began to take shape in the 1950s with the pioneering efforts of Harry Markowitz and others. Markowitz's groundbreaking research centered on the risk and return of N-asset portfolios. He was one of the first to recognize that portfolio risk can be quantified by taking into account the means, variances, and covariances of the individual risky assets. Equation 7-8 (repeated below) formed the framework for Markowitz's investigations:

$$\sigma_P^2 = \sum_{i=1}^{N} W_i^2 \sigma_i^2 + \sum_{i=1}^{N} \sum_{\substack{j=1 \\ i \neq j}}^{N} W_i W_j COV_{ij}$$

Although straightforward in concept, this formula can be extremely difficult to work with. The first step involves the estimation of N means, N variances, and $N(N-1)/2$ covariances. The second step involves incorporation of weights. This step is potentially unmanageable because the number of possible weights is nearly infinite. In practice, a few standard weights are chosen. Even with this simplification, the computational demands made the calculation of portfolio variance an extremely demanding process, given the nascent state of computing in the 1950s.

Computational concerns aside, there are important implications of this formula. These become evident when viewed graphically in mean-variance space. When portfolio means and corresponding variances are plotted, the results occupy a clearly defined space. The outer edge of this area represents the highest expected return that can be achieved for a fixed level of risk. Markowitz called this boundary the *efficient frontier*. Portfolios located on the efficient frontier are efficient because no higher return can be found at any given risk level. Similarly, interior portfolios are inefficient. Rational investors should consider only efficient portfolios. This is an important insight because portfolio composition has now been reduced to a manageable number of choices.

efficient frontier

The efficient frontier is concave (curved downward). This characteristic affects the risk/return trade-off. If the investor were to observe returns of rising fixed increments of variance, he or she would find that each succeeding increment of expected return is a bit smaller than the previous. If the investor wanted to maintain constant increments of return, he or she would have to take larger and larger increases in risk. These are examples of what economists call diminishing returns to risk (which is directly related to a concave graph). Figure 7-8 illustrates the efficient frontier.

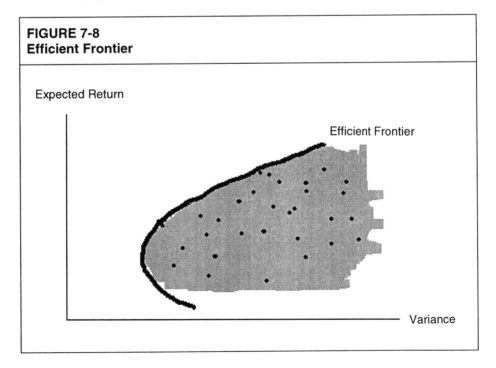

**FIGURE 7-8
Efficient Frontier**

The Separation Theorem

Markowitz's analysis dealt with portfolios consisting of risky assets. In 1958, James Tobin extended the analysis by considering the effects of adding a riskless asset that has a return of R_f, the risk-free rate. In practical terms, most people think of the risk-free asset as a 90-day Treasury bill. The riskless asset can be added to any combination of risky assets. This is demonstrated in figure 7-9. If the riskless asset, R_f, is combined with the risky portfolio H, possible portfolios lie on the line connecting the two points. Similarly, portfolios made up of varying proportions of R_f and A are made possible by rotating the line beginning at R_f upward. For any given level of risk, the returns offered by this combination are greater than the returns offered by the appropriate combination of R_f and H. Similarly, the trial-and-error process of rotating the line upward could continue until the line reaches its highest level that still retains contact to the efficient frontier of risky portfolios. This is the line R_fM, which is tangent to the efficient frontier at the single portfolio T. The line R_fM can be extended beyond M if borrowing at the risk-free rate is allowed (giving the riskless asset a negative weight). The borrowed funds are then invested in further shares of the risky portfolio M (resulting in its weight being greater than one).

The addition of a riskless asset results in a new efficient frontier that consists of a straight line that begins at R_f and passes through risky portfolio M. M will now be the only risky asset that rational investors will hold.

FIGURE 7-9
Efficient Frontier with Lending and Borrowing at the Risk-Free Rate

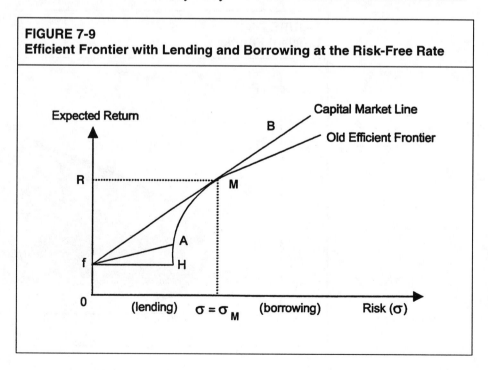

Investors with varying degrees of risk tolerance will attain their desired risk levels by adjusting the relative proportions of R_f and M.

separation theorem

Tobin's insight simplified portfolio choice to selecting the relative proportions of the risk-free asset and a single risky portfolio. This is the essence of the *separation theorem*—that an investor's risk preferences do not affect his or her choice of risky assets (M is the only rational choice). This was a valuable theoretical innovation, but practical problems remained. The primary one was that the optimum risky portfolio, M, was not specified.

The Capital Market Line

The preceding innovations were subsequently applied to portfolios' expected returns—specifically, finding that a portfolio's return is a function of the risk-free rate, the expected return of a single efficient portfolio M, and the expected standard deviations. The explicit relationship is

$$E(R_p) = R_f + \sigma_p \left(\frac{E(R_M) - R_f}{\sigma_M} \right)$$

(Equation 7-9)

capital market line

market portfolio

This is the equation of a line that has come to be called the *capital market line* (CML). In this model of the securities market, portfolio M must represent what is referred to as the *market portfolio*. The market portfolio is the portfolio of all assets. Such a portfolio is obviously a theoretical concept. In practice, most people think of the Standard & Poor's 500 Index as a surrogate for the market portfolio. The reason that portfolio M must be the market portfolio is that, as noted before, in this model everyone would hold some combination of M and the risk-free asset—nothing more, nothing less. Furthermore, all assets are owned by someone (there are no ownerless assets). The only way to reconcile these two statements is if M represents the market portfolio.

The bracketed term in equation 7-9 (repeated below) is, of course, the slope of the capital market line:

$$\text{Slope}_{CML} = \left(\frac{E(R_M) - R_f}{\sigma_M} \right)$$

This slope represents the market price of risk in our financial markets. It signifies the equilibrium trade-off between risk and return at any point in time. Keep in mind that this slope changes any time any of the three parameters that define it change.

Figure 7-10 illustrates the capital market line.

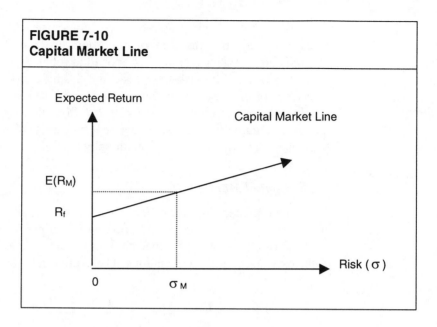

FIGURE 7-10
Capital Market Line

The Capital Asset Pricing Model

William F. Sharpe approached the unknown risky portfolio problem by postulating that returns are related through a common relationship with a basic underlying factor. The foundation of his capital asset pricing model begins with 10 assumptions. These range from everyone's possessing the same expectations about the risk and return of assets to a market consisting of all assets, including those that are not usually thought of as an asset, such as human capital (the skills a worker can offer to the marketplace). Many of these assumptions have been relaxed by subsequent research without unduly altering the implications of Sharpe's conclusions.

Proceeding from these assumptions, Sharpe's model enters familiar territory by constructing an efficient frontier for risky assets. Introduction of a riskless asset leads to a new efficient frontier (a straight line) made up of varying proportions of the risk-free asset and the market portfolio.

Sharpe then posed the question of what would determine the expected return on an individual asset. Remember, the CML defines the expected return only on effectively diversified portfolios. Portfolios that are not effectively diversified, which would include single securities, would plot somewhere below the capital market line. Sharpe mathematically proved that the expected return was a function of how the individual asset affected the variability of a portfolio's returns. The greater the contribution to a portfolio's variability, the greater the expected return should be. An asset's contribution to a portfolio's variability could then be measured by a term known as the *beta* coefficient (or beta statistic). It can be computed as follows:

beta

$$\beta_i = \frac{COV_{iM}}{\sigma_M^2} \qquad \text{(Equation 7-10)}$$

where β_i = market risk of asset i

COV_{iM} = covariance between asset i and the market portfolio

σ_M^2 = variance of the market portfolio

capital asset pricing model

Note the similarity between beta and correlation coefficient. The full model is known as the *capital asset pricing model*, or CAPM. It is formally stated as

$$E(R_i) = R_f + \beta_i \left(E(R_M) - R_f \right) \qquad \text{(Equation 7-11)}$$

In our earlier discussions of N-asset portfolio risk, we learned that as N increases, portfolio variance approaches the average covariance of the component assets. Similarly, under CAPM, a portfolio's risk is a weighted average of the component assets' betas. Calculation of a portfolio's risk is thereby simplified to computing the weighted average of betas of the N securities in a portfolio.

Use of CAPM

Since its unveiling in the 1960s, the applicability of CAPM has been extended by finding ways to relax Sharpe's original assumptions. The model has thereby gained enough versatility that it can be applied in a great variety of situations (for example, corporate finance). Its utility has garnered it wide acceptance among both academics and the financial industry. Sharpe, along with the other developer of the model, earned a Nobel prize in economics for his work.

Betas are calculated by using the statistical tool of regressing an asset's returns against the market's returns. In practice, a proxy such as the S&P 500 is used in place of the theoretical market portfolio. The process begins by pairing returns by time (M_t, R_{it}) where t is the time period. (See figures 7-11 and 7-12.)

The regression calculations attempt to find a regression line that passes through ($E(M)$, $E(R_i)$)) while minimizing the distance from data points to the line. By minimizing the distances, the process finds the best-fitting line. Beta is the slope of the regression line and alpha (α) its intercept.

coefficient of determination (R^2)

A statistic that is sometimes mentioned in conjunction with betas is the *coefficient of determination (R^2)*. R^2 is a measure of how well the regression line fits the data. R^2 is a percentage and therefore ranges from 0 to 1 (that is, 100 percent). In relation to betas, R^2 can be interpreted as the percentage of a

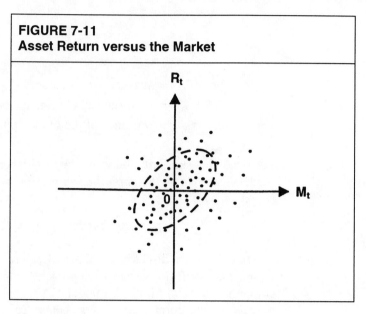

FIGURE 7-11
Asset Return versus the Market

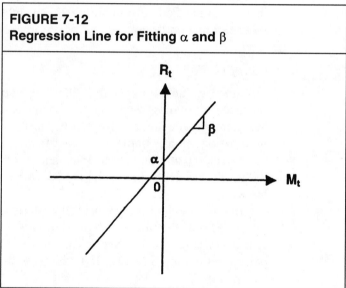

FIGURE 7-12
Regression Line for Fitting α and β

stock's variability in return that can be attributed to the variability in the market's return. It is therefore just another measure of relatedness.

The CAPM equation has very important implications. First, expected returns for all assets can be estimated once we know their respective betas. Second, an asset's expected return is related only to its market risk; in other words, *nonmarket risk* (individual and all other types of risk) is not rewarded with higher expected returns because it can be diversified away.

nonmarket risk

Example: If beta $\beta_i = 1.3$, $R_f = 5.0\%$, and $E(R_M) = 10.0$ percent, applying equation 7-11 yields

$$
\begin{aligned}
E(R_i) &= 5.0\% + 1.3(10.0\% - 5.0\%) \\
&= 5.0\% + 1.3(5.0\%) \\
&= 5.0\% + 6.5\% \\
&= 11.5\%
\end{aligned}
$$

Thus, a stock with a beta of 1.3 would be expected to return 11.5 percent when the risk-free rate is 5 percent and the market portfolio's return is expected to be 10 percent.

Equation 7-11 is represented graphically as a line that crosses the $E(R_i)$-axis (y-axis) at R_f and has a slope of $(E(R_M)-R_f)$. The line is called the *security market line (SML)*.

security market line

Note that the security market line extends to the left of the $E(R_i)$-axis. Since betas are based on the covariance between the asset and market portfolio, they can, in theory, have negative values. Simply put, any asset whose beta is negative would have an expected return **lower** than the risk-free rate of return. If the beta has a large enough negative value, then the expected return would actually be negative! Investors would be willing to hold such assets because the negative betas indicate that these assets would do really well when the rest of the market is collapsing. Think of a negative-beta asset as analogous to term life insurance. If you live, the payment of the premiums was a waste of money. If you die, the policy is incredibly valuable.

Expected Asset Returns for Different Betas and Market Returns

Range	Expected Asset Return for Positive Market Return	Expected Asset Return for Negative Market Return
$\beta > 1$	Above market	Below market
$\beta = 1$	Market	Market
$0 < \beta < 1$	Below market	Above market
$\beta = 0$	Risk-free rate	Risk-free rate
$\beta < 0$	Less than risk-free rate, or even negative	Positive

As can be seen in figure 7-13 and equation 7-11, return is a linear function of risk (constant returns to risk). Investors who desire greater expected return must accept greater risk as measured by beta. Correspondingly, investors who desire less risk must accept lower expected returns. In short, an investor's risk preferences determine his or her preferred beta, which in turn determines the expected returns.

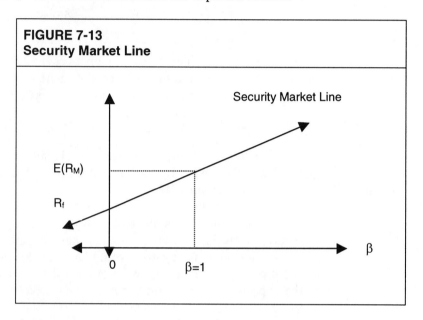

FIGURE 7-13
Security Market Line

Arbitrage Pricing Theory

The advent of CAPM revolutionized financial theory, but many researchers were not convinced that this single-index model fully explained the variability of asset returns. Various multi-index models were proposed, culminating in Stephen Ross's 1976 paper outlining his *arbitrage pricing theory* (APT). APT is derived from the economic principle that perfect substitutes must have the same price, or arbitrage profits will be available to traders. Through the action of arbitrage, all prices of financial assets remain in equilibrium.

Multi-index models are based upon the belief that an asset's risk is a linear function of its correlation with a variety of risk factors. APT postulates that asset returns are affected by various basic economic forces, such as industrial production, interest rates, inflation rates, and so on. The *arbitrage pricing model* (APM) is based upon APT and is as follows:

$$E(R_i) = \alpha_i + \beta_{i1}F_1 + \beta_{i2}F_2 + ... + \beta_{iM}F_M \qquad \text{(Equation 7-12)}$$

alpha

where the F_1 to F_M are the relevant economic factors influencing R_i. In this model, *alpha* (α) represents the expected return when all of the independent variables (F_1, F_2, . . . F_M) are equal to 0. For example, in CAPM, alpha would be the risk-free rate. Note that CAPM is just a special case of the more general multi-index model. A graph of this equation is conceptually similar to that of CAPM; the major addition is that it is multidimensional. If there are two factors, the graph is a plane in three dimensions; models with more than two factors cannot be visualized.

A significant problem with APT is that the factors are not specified by the theory. Moreover, empirical investigation for relevant factors has been inconclusive. APT has offsetting positive attributes, such as not requiring the use of a market portfolio, allowing for different expectations of market participants, and pricing that may exceed CAPM in accuracy.

The important question in comparing the two approaches: Does the greater complexity of APT add appreciably to our understanding of markets and our ability to explain real-world prices? APT's initial tests failed to demonstrate clear superiority to CAPM, and subsequent research has resulted in mixed assessments. Nonetheless, the APT model has continued to generate much interest.

Approaches to Portfolio-Risk Estimation

Model	Requirements to Analyze Portfolio of N Securities
Markowitz's full model	N variances and N(N − 1)/2 covariances
CAPM	N betas (N covariances and the market variance as inputs)
APT	(N x M) betas corresponding to M factors

SUMMARY AND CONCLUSIONS

The portfolio theory discussed in this chapter yields a number of interesting conclusions: A single asset's risk may be defined as the standard deviation or variance of its expected return. Portfolio risk depends crucially on the covariance between terms. Covariance is the driving force behind diversification effects. If only risky assets are considered, investors should choose only from portfolios along the curved efficient frontier, thus giving them the highest expected return for a given level of risk. Once a riskless asset becomes available, the efficient frontier becomes a straight line connecting the riskless asset and a single risky portfolio (lying on the old efficient frontier). Investors are thereby freed from choosing which risky assets to hold; this is the essence of Tobin's separation theorem. CAPM identifies the single portfolio as the market portfolio. It further identifies market risk, measured by beta, as the only relevant risk in portfolio construction. Betas measure market risk by quantifying the relatedness between expected asset returns and those of the market. An asset's expected return may be computed once the asset's beta, the risk-free rate, and the market's expected return are known. The APM states that an asset's expected return is a function of its covariance with a number of economic risk factors.

CHAPTER REVIEW

Answers to the review questions and the self-test questions start on page 501.

Key Terms

risk averse	efficient frontier
histogram	separation theorem
mean absolute deviation	capital market line
variance	market portfolio
semivariance	beta
standard deviation	capital asset pricing model
probability distributions	coefficient of determination
ex ante	(R^2)
ex post	nonmarket risk
diversification	security market line
portfolio variance	arbitrage pricing theory
covariance	arbitrage pricing model
correlation coefficient	alpha
portfolio theory	

Review Questions

7-1. Contrast the common concept of risk with the definition introduced in this chapter.

7-2. Compute the expected return and standard deviation for the following:
   a. equally probable returns of –5%, 0%, 5%, 10%
   b. 10% chance of a 0% return
       15% chance of a 5% return
       25% chance of a 10% return
       25% chance of a 15% return
       15% chance of a 20% return
       10% chance of a 25% return

c. 100% chance of a 10% return

7-3. Compute the covariance estimate for the following observations (assume equal probabilities):

$(R_{i1}, R_{j1}) = (.03, .05)$
$(R_{i2}, R_{j2}) = (.05, .03)$
$(R_{i3}, R_{j3}) = (-.01, -.05)$
$(R_{i4}, R_{j4}) = (.10, .08)$
$(R_{i5}, R_{j5}) = (0, 0)$
$(R_{i6}, R_{j6}) = (.01, -.01)$

7-4. Discuss the three simplifications for estimating portfolio risk.

7-5. For three separate stocks having alphas and betas of .01, .7; .05, 1.1; and −.02, 1.5, respectively, compute their expected returns for market returns of .05, .10, .15, −.05, and −.10.

7-6. Define alpha and beta, and discuss their relevance in portfolio management.

7-7. Explain the capital asset pricing model.

7-8. a. Define market and nonmarket risk.
    b. How are the two types of risk related to diversification?

7-9. a. Define the efficient frontier, first without borrowing or lending allowed and then with both allowed at the risk-free rate.
    b. What does the efficient frontier look like with riskless lending only (no borrowing)?
    c. What happens if the two rates differ?

7-10. For efficient portfolios (100 percent invested in the market portfolio) with risk-free rates and market rates of .07 and .14; .09 and .16; and .05 and .1 respectively; what would be the expected returns with portfolio betas of .7, 1.0, 1.3, and 1.6?

Self-Test Questions

T F 7-1. The realized return from an investment is subject to uncertainties that may or may not occur.

T F 7-2. The realized return received by an investor is, by itself, the appropriate measure to assess and compare the performance of several investments.

T F 7-3. Risk can be defined as the chance that the actual outcome from an investment will be less than the expected outcome.

T F 7-4. The standard deviation is a measure of an asset's riskiness.

T   F   7-5.   The riskiness of a portfolio is greater than the riskiness of the securities it contains.

T   F   7-6.   A portfolio's return is the average of the returns of the assets included therein.

T   F   7-7.   A correlation coefficient of −1 between two assets would result in an increased variability of the portfolio's return.

T   F   7-8.   Market risk is the risk caused by factors independent of a given security or property investment.

T   F   7-9.   The total risk of an investment is the sum of the general (market) risk and the specific (nonmarket) risk.

T   F   7-10. If investors are to hold only risky assets, they could hold a portfolio of assets that lies on the efficient frontier.

T   F   7-11. The introduction of risk-free assets enables every investor to choose the same risky portfolio.

T   F   7-12. Any portfolio on the capital market line is an undiversified portfolio.

T   F   7-13. If the beta of a stock is 1.1, the risk-free rate is 4 percent, and the return on the market is 10 percent, then according to the capital asset pricing model, the expected rate of return for the stock is 15.4 percent.

T   F   7-14. The arbitrage pricing model treats the required return to a stock as a function of its correlation with various economic factors.

NOTE

1. Portfolio theory is sometimes referred to as modern portfolio theory, or MPT, for short. That title, however, may be somewhat inappropriate, as the theory was developed in the 1950s and 1960s. In this book, we will refer to this theory as portfolio theory. Nevertheless, students should be familiar with the term MPT, because it is still used in some textbooks and other financial literature.

8

Efficient Market Hypothesis

Learning Objectives

An understanding of the material in this chapter should enable the student to

8-1. Explain the difference between fundamental analysis and technical analysis.

8-2. Explain the three forms of the efficient market hypothesis.

8-3. Explain the relationship between risk premiums and nonmarket risk.

8-4. Explain the usefulness of beta estimates as a guide to subsequent performance.

Chapter Outline

This chapter considers three interesting and important implications of portfolio theory:

- First, no trading method can consistently generate risk-adjusted returns that exceed those implied by the efficient market model.
- Second, nonmarket risk does not affect the discount rate (required rate of return) applied to risky assets.
- Third, returns tend to vary linearly (the security market line) with (nondiversifiable) market risk.

If these implications hold well enough for practical use, then practitioners in the fields of investment analysis and portfolio management have a powerful theoretical and scientific underpinning upon which to base their studies and recommendations. It is, in fact, because of these wide-ranging practical implications that several Nobel Laureates have been awarded to some of the most famous names in these fields over the last decade or so (Harry Markowitz, James Tobin, Merton Miller, Franco Modigliani, William Sharpe, and Myron Scholes).

TYPES OF INVESTMENT ANALYSIS

efficient market hypothesis (EMH)

fundamental analysis

To discuss the *efficient market hypothesis (EMH)* in a meaningful fashion we need a basic understanding of the two primary types of investment analysis: fundamental analysis and technical analysis. *Fundamental analysis* consists of analyzing the factors that affect the amount and value of expected future income streams. Thus, fundamental security analysts assess a firm's earnings and dividend prospects by evaluating such factors as its sales, costs, and capital requirements. Fundamental commodity analysts base their futures forecasts on the relevant demand and supply factors. Fundamental real estate analysts generate price and rental value expectations from anticipated future construction costs and demand growth estimates.

technical analysis

Technical analysis, in contrast, concentrates on past price and volume relationships of a security or commodity (narrow form) or technical market indicators applicable to that security or commodity (broad form). Both types of technical analysis attempt to identify evolving investor sentiment, but neither has a sound theoretical base. Technical analysts are not particularly concerned with a theoretical justification for their method. They are more inclined to argue that results are what ultimately matter. A wealth of available data facilitates the application of technical analysis to the security and commodity markets. The techniques of technical analysis are discussed in chapter 11.

One major distinction between technical and fundamental analysis is that technical analysis looks at prices and volume of trade in isolation without concern for the type of company whose stock is being traded (its financial strength, the quality of its management, the nature of its competition, and so on). Fundamental analysis is more inclusive and takes into account both quantitative and qualitative factors.

THE EFFICIENT MARKET HYPOTHESIS

random walk

The efficient market hypothesis questions the usefulness of technical analysis and, in some versions, fundamental analysis. Many natural phenomena follow a *random walk*, or what the physical sciences call Brownian motion. If applied to stocks, the random walk concept would imply that the next price change of a randomly moving stock is unrelated to past price behavior. Obviously, if prices move randomly, the repeating price patterns that technical analysts claim to observe have no predictive ability. Of course, stock prices tend to rise over time, so it might be more accurate to describe their movement as a "random walk with drift." In other words, it seems pretty safe, based on historical evidence, to predict that the market will be higher 10 years from now than it is today, but it might not be safe to predict that the market will be higher (or lower) tomorrow than it is today.

Price movements need not be precisely random for past price data to lack predictive ability. Marginally associated relations between past and future price changes may be either too small or too unreliable to generate returns that consistently exceed transaction costs. Indeed, commissions, search costs, and bid-ask spreads would generally offset any expected price change of less than 2 percent or 3 percent.

Weak Form of the Efficient Market Hypothesis

weak form EMH

The *weak form of the efficient market hypothesis* states that knowledge of past price behavior has no value in predicting future price movements. That is, such knowledge cannot be used to construct a portfolio that consistently outperforms the market on a risk-adjusted basis. The weak form implies that once we know the most recent price quote, we know as much about possible subsequent returns as those who know the full price history up to that point. In other words, prices do not move in predictable patterns. Weak form adherents further argue that, if prices did move in dependable patterns, the reactions of alert market participants would rapidly eliminate any resulting profit opportunities. If a particular price pattern was thought to forecast a rise, enough market participants would react to take advantage of the move. Such actions would eliminate the value of any recognized patterns, because the market would very quickly be driven to its predicted value.

Example: Suppose a stock sells for $6 per share. Also suppose that based on some technical formula, it is possible to predict that next month the price of the stock will be $10 per share. Other people would also use that formula and make the same prediction. Therefore, everyone would want to buy the stock, and nobody would want to sell it. The stock would move immediately to almost $10 per share. (To be exact, it would move to the present value of $10 discounted one month at the risk-free interest rate.)

In other words, if it were really possible to find trends and predict future stock prices, the forces of supply and demand would immediately bring present prices in line with expected future prices.

Semistrong Form of the Efficient Market Hypothesis

semistrong form EMH

The weak form of the efficient market hypothesis implies that technical analysis is useless, but it does not address the effectiveness of fundamental analysis. The *semistrong form EMH*, on the other hand, asserts that the market quickly and correctly evaluates all relevant publicly available information, which is quickly reflected in market prices.

Tests of the semistrong form must distinguish between anticipated and unanticipated information. Investors may correctly anticipate new information that has not yet become public. For instance, based on careful fundamental analysis, an investor may anticipate an increase in a firm's dividend. Generally, anticipated information will already be incorporated into security prices.

Unanticipated information, although not incorporated in a security price, will be quickly assimilated as soon as it is publicly available. If markets are semistrong form efficient, then risk-adjusted returns can exceed those of the market only due to unexpected developments.

Strong Form of the Efficient Market Hypothesis

strong form EMH

According to the *strong form of the efficient market hypothesis*, the market also incorporates information that so-called monopolists of information (usually called insiders) have about security prices. Professional money managers, such as mutual funds or investment advisory services, are one group alleged to have special knowledge about companies they follow. Specialists who make a market in stocks on the organized exchanges are also supposed to have knowledge of their stocks. Since they are granted a monopoly in making a market in specific stocks, they have short-term knowledge of the flow of buy and sell orders on those stocks. In particular, knowing what orders are outstanding may give them insight into future price movements.

Corporate insiders comprise the main group of information monopolists. Corporate insiders—defined as managers, board members, and those who own 10 percent or more of the stock of a company—certainly have access to information that is not yet made public. However, SEC rules and federal law prohibit them from profiting from that information or sharing it with outsiders selectively prior to a public announcement. Insiders are permitted to trade the stocks of their own companies, but they are subject to some restrictions. For example, they are prohibited from engaging in short-term trading. Strong-form efficiency maintains that even the information known by these monopolists quickly gets reflected in security prices, thus eliminating the potential for abnormal gains.

It is possible for an investor to earn an abnormally high return, just as it is possible to make money at a gambling casino. Some people make the mistake of thinking that if the market is efficient, then one can never earn an abnormally high return. That is not the case. Market efficiency simply means that technical and fundamental analysis should not *consistently* earn an investor an abnormally high return once risk and transaction costs are taken into account. (The costs of obtaining information, including the opportunity cost of forgoing other productive uses of one's time, should also be taken into account when deciding whether to use fundamental analysis techniques.)

Forms of the Efficient Market Hypothesis

- Weak form: Future returns are unrelated to past return patterns. (Charting and other types of technical analysis do not consistently result in superior returns.)
- Semistrong form: Future returns are unrelated to any analysis based on public information. (Fundamental analysis does not consistently result in superior returns.)
- Strong form: Future returns are unrelated to any analysis based on public or nonpublic data. (Insider trading does not consistently result in superior returns.)

Adjusting Returns for the Impacts of Risk and the Market

Theoretical and empirical studies of market efficiency need to take proper account of the impact of both risk and market returns. We have already seen how a tendency toward risk aversion causes investors to require higher returns on more risky investments. Virtually everyone who studies the securities markets realizes that actual returns generally do increase with risk. Thus, any type of market performance study needs to take account of the impact of risk on expected and actual returns. Similarly, individual security returns tend to be higher when the overall market is strong than when it is weak. Failing to adjust for the impacts of risk and the market could lead to misleading results. Calculation of differential returns and risk-adjusted returns are standard methods that are used to adjust actual returns for these effects.

Differential Return

differential return

A first step to truly understand a stock's or portfolio's performance is to compute what is known as the *differential return*. A differential return is defined as

$$d_{it} = r_{it} - r_{Mt}$$

where d_{it} = differential return for firm i during period t
r_{it} = actual return for firm i during period t
r_{Mt} = market return for period t

This calculation measures the performances of a firm, or portfolio of firms, relative to the market as a whole. It is always better to consider differential returns rather than actual returns when doing an analysis. But an even better analysis would adjust performance for risk.

Risk-Adjusted Return

risk-adjusted return

Thanks to the development of portfolio theory, we have a model that allows us to effectively adjust for both risk and the return to the market. The security market line (SML) can be written as

$$\overline{r}_i = r_f + \beta_i(\overline{r}_M - r_f)$$

where $\overline{r}_i$ = the equilibrium or expected return of security i
r_f = the risk-free rate of return
$\overline{r}_M$ = the expected return on the market portfolio

Actual returns r_i in this framework are then described in equation 8-1 as composed of three components:

$$r_i = \overline{r}_i + \overline{\alpha}_i + \varepsilon_i \qquad \text{(Equation 8-1)}$$

where r_i = actual return
$\overline{r}_i$ = the expected return
$\overline{\alpha}_i$ = the average difference between actual returns and expected returns
ε_i = a random error term with expected value of 0

Jensen's alpha

Sometimes α_i is called *Jensen's alpha*. It is a measure of how well or poorly a particular security or portfolio performs relative to its expected performance, considering the market-related risk characteristics of the security or portfolio. The estimate of alpha, as shown in equation 8-2, is a measure of the risk-adjusted performance of the security:

$$\overline{\alpha}_i = r_i - \overline{r}_i = (r_i - r_f) - \beta_i (r_M - r_f) \qquad \text{(Equation 8-2)}$$

Jensen's alpha is also sometimes expressed as[1]

$$\alpha_p = r_p - \left[r_f + \left(r_M - r_f \right) \beta_p \right]$$

where the subscript for security i is replaced by p (for portfolio p)

Two other measures are also commonly used for risk-adjusted performance evaluation in studies of market efficiency: the Sharpe ratio and the Treynor ratio.

**Sharpe ratio
reward to
   variability (RVAR)**

The *Sharpe ratio*, or the *reward to variability (RVAR)* ratio as it is sometimes called, is defined as follows in equation 8-3:

$$S_i = \frac{r_i - r_f}{\sigma_i} \qquad \text{(Equation 8-3)}$$

Note that the numerator of this ratio is the excess above the risk-free rate of return, while the denominator is simply the standard deviation of the security's returns (noted first in chapter 7 as the Markowitz model's measure of risk). Here, actual returns adjusted by the risk-free rate are compared with total risk, rather than only market risk.

**Treynor ratio
reward to
   volatility (RVOL)**

The *Treynor ratio*, called the *reward to volatility (RVOL)* ratio, shown in equation 8-4 is also used:

$$T_i = \frac{r_i - r_f}{\beta_i}$$
(Equation 8-4)

Note that the numerator is the same as in the Sharpe ratio, but the denominator's measure of risk is now the beta of the security—which means that only *market-related risk* is considered. In other words, the Treynor ratio is a measure of risk to an investor who holds a diversified portfolio of assets. The Sharpe ratio is a measure of risk to an investor who does not hold a diversified portfolio of assets.

All three measures of risk-adjusted performance—Jensen's alpha, and the Sharpe and Treynor ratios—are commonly used to evaluate the performance of securities and portfolios (including mutual funds), and they are also used in studies of market efficiency.

Essentially, all the measures of risk-adjusted performance relate the actual return to some measure of the level of riskiness of the investment. Virtually all serious securities market research utilizes risk- and market-adjusted returns such as those described.

Example of Performance Measurement

Suppose the following data are available for the 1985–1999 period for several mutual funds (the S&P 500 Index and the 90-day T-bill rate will serve as proxies for the market return and the risk-free rate, respectively):

Mutual Fund	Average Return	Standard Deviation	Beta	R^2
Dreyfus Growth	19.20	18.50	.83	.472
Fidelity Magellan	31.92	18.57	1.08	.532
Wellington Fund	15.19	9.57	.65	.877
S&P 500 Index	17.16	13.18	1.00	1.000
90-day T-Bill rate	8.31	2.56	0.0	

Then, using the formulas for the Sharpe and Treynor ratios and Jensen's alpha, we can derive the following:

Mutual Fund	Sharpe	Treynor	Jensen's Alpha
Dreyfus Growth	.589	13.120	3.545
Fidelity Magellan	1.271	21.861	14.052
Wellington Fund	.719	10.585	1.127
S&P 500 Index	.671	8.850	–0–

The interpretation is that Fidelity Magellan is clearly superior among the funds on all three measures of risk-adjusted performance. Dreyfus Growth and Wellington Fund have different rankings, depending on the measure chosen. When total risk is considered as measured by the standard deviation, as with the Sharpe ratio, the Wellington Fund appears superior. However, when the beta measure of risk is chosen, which reflects market risk only, Dreyfus Growth is better. All three funds are superior to the S&P 500 Index on a risk-adjusted basis, judging by the Treynor ratio and alpha measure. It is important to note that the Wellington Fund did not achieve as high an average return as the market, but because the return it achieved involved less risk on a risk-adjusted basis, its performance is superior to the market.

The meaning of the R^2 (R-squared), the coefficient of determination, is as follows: It is the square of the simple correlation coefficient between the mutual fund's returns and the S&P 500 Index returns. An R^2 can range between zero and one. As such, it measures the degree of "goodness of fit" of the relationship between the fund and the market index. It also indicates the percentage of the variation in the fund's return that is "explained by" the market index. The greater the degree of diversification of the fund, the closer it approximates the market and the higher the coefficient of determination R^2 will be. Conversely, the lower the R^2, the less diversified the fund is, and the more the fund is subject to nonsystematic or nonmarket risk. In the example shown, Wellington Fund appears to have the highest degree of coincidence with the market as measured by R^2.

Outperforming the Market

As we have seen, the returns generated from applying both technical and fundamental analysis should be judged relative to the returns on the market. If the market is rising, most investment strategies will produce positive returns; a declining market tends to have the opposite effect. The market return may be used as a benchmark against which to judge the usefulness of a particular type of analysis. To be judged successful, a trading strategy needs to generate returns that, after an appropriate adjustment for risk, must, in the aggregate, exceed the market returns of the corresponding periods. Thus, the techniques of both technical and fundamental analysis need to be tested against real-world data. These data can be used to generate hypothetical returns for various investment strategies and then compared with the market's returns for the same period. Normally, a conformable stock market index such as the S&P 500 Index or the New York Stock Exchange Composite (a weighted average of all NYSE listings) is used to represent overall market performance. If the technique to be tested leads the investor to assemble a portfolio whose average market risk (average beta) differs appreciably from that of the market's (hence a beta appreciably different from one), the market benchmark should be chosen to better represent the types of investments in the portfolio. For example, the portfolio's return can be compared with that of mutual funds of comparable risk, or adjustment can be made for the portfolio's beta. Differential or risk-adjusted returns (or some other adjustment) should be used to examine the effectiveness of any strategy based on fundamental or technical analysis. Virtually all academic studies of market efficiency utilize such risk-adjusted returns data.

Weak Form Tests of EMH

Technical analysis techniques have been explored empirically in two basic ways. First, the relationship between past and future price changes has been tested for statistical dependence (relatedness) or independence (unrelatedness). Second, filter rules analogous to technical trading rules have been applied to historical data. If past price patterns help forecast future price change, past and future price changes should be related, and filter rules should help identify profitable trading opportunities.

Some studies have examined serial correlation (relationship between past and present price changes); others investigated runs of price changes. A

run

run is an uninterrupted series of price increases or decreases. Many different studies have consistently failed to find any significant relationship in successive price changes. Thus, past price patterns do not appear to forecast

chartists

future price movements. *Chartists* point out that these statistical tests look largely for linear relations and say that the tests are much too crude to capture subtleties. Moreover, chartists assert that their "craft" is as much art as science because it depends heavily on judgment, interpretation, and experience; that is, beneath the apparent randomness of stock price movements is a distinct nonrandom pattern that can be discerned from charts. They argue that these patterns are difficult to quantify by standard statistical methods. Nonetheless, most nonlinear dependencies that they claim to see should show up in the tests as linear approximations. Chartists have offered no convincing counterevidence (to academicians) as to why standard statistical proofs of forecast reliability cannot be applied.

filter rules

Filter rules attempt to capture the momentum/resistance-level factors that technical analysts claim are important. (Technical terms, such as momentum and resistance level, are discussed in greater detail in later chapters.) Momentum indicates the tendency of a stock price to continue to rise or fall, whereas resistance level refers to a stock price at which either a large number of sell orders (upper resistance level) or a large number of buy orders (lower resistance level) would be expected to appear. Filter rules mechanically identify supposed buy-and-sell situations.

The standard filter rule flashes a buy signal whenever a stock increases by x percent. After an x percent decline from a subsequent high, a sell signal is given. For instance, a 5 percent filter would signal to buy whenever a stock rose 5 percent from the previous low. When transaction costs are taken into account, the filter rule approach fails to outperform a buy-and-hold strategy.

Semistrong and Strong Form Tests of EMH

General tests of the semistrong and strong form are difficult to devise and perform. Moreover, test procedures are not all that powerful in identifying market efficiency. Market efficiency cannot be directly proven. Rather, we can only infer efficiency by showing that specific inefficiencies do not exist. The market pricing process generates so much random movement, or "noise," that prices can stray quite a bit from their intrinsic values without detection by tests that are commonly used. Nevertheless, various subhypotheses of the efficient market hypothesis have been examined. Many studies have found market anomalies or imperfections. An *anomaly* suggests that a specific type of fundamental analysis is profitable in consistently outperforming the market on a risk-adjusted basis.

anomaly

For instance, a number of studies suggest that stocks with low price-earnings ratios, small market capitalizations, low per-share prices, or related characteristics tend to outperform the market. With so much conflicting evidence, the extent of semistrong-form efficiency is decidedly debatable. Some academicians suggest that, since institutional investors—with all their professional expertise—rarely outperform the market on a risk-adjusted basis, individual investors are unlikely to do better. Others claim that there are enough market imperfections that talented investment analysts can outperform the market. Even if the market eventually evaluates public information accurately, they claim that some investor/analysts may be able to take advantage of lags in the price-adjustment process.

Many strong-form supporters concede that insider information is sometimes useful, but they contend that such instances are rare and therefore the conclusions of the strong form generally hold up. Research on the profitability of insider information is somewhat mixed. Several of the early studies found little evidence of excess returns to insiders. More recent studies showed that insiders earned more than outsiders on the same purchase or sale transaction in the same company's stock; results also indicated that, as the information became public knowledge, excess insider returns decreased as the length of the holding period increased.

The mixed results may be due to different definitions of "insiders." The advantages of professional money managers and specialists may be somewhat limited. However, corporate insiders such as senior managers and directors clearly have access to information about a company's prospects that is not available to the general public. In the absence of laws against insider trading, they would be able to reap excessive profits from that information.

Market Efficiency Debate

Although some academicians hold extreme positions, few who have examined the issue believe that the market is strong-form efficient or is always semistrong-form efficient. On the other hand, virtually all serious finance scholars agree that the weak form of the efficient market hypothesis is essentially correct. The principal disagreements relate to the importance, extent, and causes of the imperfections of the semistrong form. These imperfections are largely viewed as departures or exceptions to normal behavior defined by portfolio theory.

Causes of Persistent Market Imperfections

Why, if the market contains many talented rational investors, do imperfections persist? As yet, there is no consensus on the issue. These imperfections can have numerous causes.

Conventional theory assumes that market prices are formed by a homogeneous group of investors who analyze the same sources of information in identical fashions. Although market efficiency does not require perfect homogeneity of investor expectations, marginal investors must behave as if they accurately analyze all relevant public information and are unaffected (or identically affected) by such matters as tax status, costs of trading, risk orientation, borrowing power, liquidity preference, familiarity with local markets, and total available funds. In the real world, however, the resources of investors who are best positioned to profit may be insufficient to eliminate some mispricings.

Because investment analysts and periodicals concentrate on the larger, better known firms, the security prices of many smaller firms may depart from the values that a careful analysis would yield. These firms generally trade in localized markets; therefore, few investors are positioned to observe the mispricings. This is known as the *small firm effect*.

small firm effect

Other types of mispricings may be exploited only by investors who can purchase control of the company. An investor who acquires control of a firm that is worth more out of business than in business could liquidate its assets for more than the firm's value as a going concern. Such takeovers, however, are not usually easy to accomplish. The effort tends to bid up prices and provoke vigorous defensive efforts by those whose interests are threatened. Investors with the necessary resources to eliminate the mispricing may frequently have inadequate incentives to do so. Still other imperfections (arbitrage opportunities) may require quick and low-cost access to several markets. Only if enough investors are able to take advantage of these imperfections will their actions correct the price imbalances.

THE RISK PREMIUM ON NONMARKET RISK

According to portfolio theory, the risk premiums applied to the expected returns of individual investments should be solely determined by each asset's market risk. Thus, two assets with the same level of market risk should have equal expected returns even if they have different levels of nonmarket risk. A number of studies have found, however, that risk premiums are also related to nonmarket risk. This apparent conflict between the theory and the evidence has spawned a number of hypotheses.

If, for instance, effective diversification were relatively difficult or costly, many investors would diversify incompletely rather than incur the high costs of achieving a fully diversified portfolio. Because nonmarket risk would contribute to overall portfolio risks for these investors, they would consider it relevant.

Studies have found that various possible sources of estimation error could account for the price effect of nonmarket risks. The results suggest two factors: inefficiently estimated betas and a positive correlation between actual betas and nonmarket risk. If betas are inefficiently estimated, the true effect of market risk will not be fully captured by the beta estimate. If the true beta and the estimate for nonmarket risk are correlated, the nonmarket risk variable may act as a second proxy for market risk.

Estimates of beta are based on a firm's historical correlation with the market. But the nature of the firm's business, competitors, sources of supply, customer base, influence of government regulation, and other factors that influence its riskiness change over time. In some more extreme examples, a company can merge with another firm, diversify into another line of business, acquire a foreign subsidiary, divest itself of an unprofitable division, undergo a complete change of management, or experience similar major changes. In such cases, historical beta might not even be a close approximation of current beta.

Another explanation for the apparent premium paid for nonmarket risk relates to the borrowing and lending assumption: If investors cannot borrow and lend at the same riskless rate, effective diversification of nonmarket risk may be impossible.

The possibility that returns are not normally distributed provides yet another possible explanation. The mean and variance completely specify the shape of normal distributions. All normal distributions have the same basic shape. Like circles, normal distributions differ from each other only in scale.

skewed distributions   Nonsymmetric or *skewed distributions*, in contrast, may have identical means and variances and yet have different shapes. Portfolio theory assumes that expected returns are normally distributed. When expected returns are not normally distributed, the model's implications may not apply. For example, distributions A and B (figure 8-1) have the same mean and standard deviation; yet they offer markedly different return possibilities.

Distribution A's returns have some probability of being high and almost no chance of being more than one standard deviation below the mean. This type of distribution is called positive skewness. Distribution B's returns could well be more than one standard deviation below the mean but are unlikely to be even one standard deviation above its mean. This distribution is said to be negatively skewed. The mode (point of greatest probability) of B exceeds the mode of A, however. While individual preferences vary, most investors prefer positive skewness. Stocks with highly variable returns also tend to have highly skewed returns. An investor preference for skewness may cause high-risk stocks to be priced to offer a lower expected return than less risky stocks. Moreover, investors who seek to achieve their desired skewness level might hold too few securities to be fully diversified.

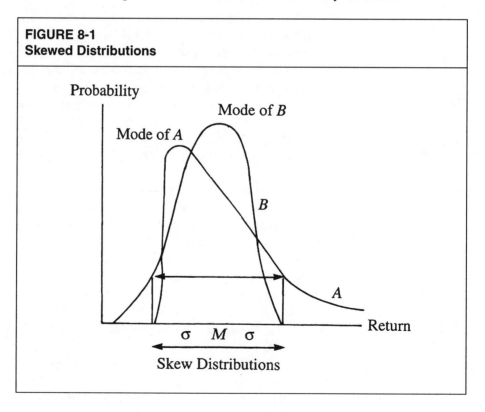

FIGURE 8-1
Skewed Distributions

Real-world distributions may differ from the normal form in several respects. We have already discussed the degree and direction of skewness.

Normal distributions are symmetrical; skewed distributions are not. Another area of potential difference relates to the relative distribution of the probabilities. All normal distributions have the same probability associated with each distance (scaled in standard deviations) from the mean: 68 percent within one standard deviation of the mean; 95 percent within two standard deviations; and 99.9 percent within three deviations. There are some distributions that are symmetrical like the normal distribution but do not have its famous "bell shape." Such distributions may have as little as 50 percent to as much as 80 percent of the returns within one standard deviation. These distributions are known as leptokurtic and platokurtic.

Factors Contributing to Nonmarket Risk

- Errors in estimated betas may be correlated with nonmarket risk contributing to an apparent empirical relationship.
- Estimates of beta are based on the past and fail to
- take major changes in the company or its business environment into account.
- Investors who are unable to lend and borrow risklessly may find that inefficient portfolios are the most effective way of achieving their desired risk levels.
- Nonnormal expected return distributions, coupled with an investor preference for skewness, may further compound the difficulty of assembling efficient portfolios and thus increase the relevance of nonmarket risk.

ESTIMATED BETAS AND SUBSEQUENT PERFORMANCE

Estimated betas are potentially useful statistics. Investors who expect the market to move in a particular direction would like to assemble a portfolio that will take full advantage of the expected market move. If the market is expected to rise, the portfolio manager would like to be concentrated in high-beta stocks. Alternatively, if a market decline is anticipated, the portfolio manager would prefer to be invested in low-beta stocks. A large number of advisory services seek to service these investors. They sell their lists of beta estimates to investors and portfolio managers. Betas are normally estimated by regressing historical security returns on market returns. Investors who use these beta estimates as a guide to sensitivity to market moves need to know how well they explain individual security performance. A number of tests have been developed to assess the usefulness and accuracy of beta estimates.

One approach is to compare actual security returns with those implied by the market model estimates and actual market returns.

A security's performance can be simulated by adding its estimated alpha to the product of its estimated beta and the corresponding period's market return. Equation 8-5 determines the simulated risk-adjusted return as follows:

$$SRAR_i = \alpha_i + \beta_i \, (r_M) \qquad \text{(Equation 8-5)}$$

where $SRAR_i$ = simulated risk-adjusted return
α_i = estimated α for firm i
β_i = estimated β for firm i
r_M = market return

and α_i and β_i are estimates from the fitted characteristic line of the security

This simulated return is the amount that is subtracted from an actual return to produce the corresponding risk-adjusted abnormal return. In an efficient market, risk-adjusted abnormal returns should have an average value very close to 0. In other words, the actual returns and the simulated risk-adjusted returns should be approximately equal. The accuracy of any individual security return simulation is related to both random nonmarket influences and the appropriateness of the simulation process. A sufficiently sizable sample, however, should largely eliminate individual random influences and reveal any biases and inefficiencies in the estimation process. Thus, a comparison of actual returns with simulated risk-adjusted returns should shed light on the accuracy of estimated betas.[2] Therefore, we will now consider some properties of estimated betas.

Properties of Beta Estimates

For most publicly traded stocks, estimated betas have an average value of 1, and most beta estimates are relatively close to one. The vast majority of estimates of beta are between zero and two. Individual beta estimates have been found in several different tests to be relatively unreliable. Portfolio betas, in contrast, appear to be much more dependable. Apparently, errors inherent in individual company beta estimates are largely offsetting. The inconsistency between actual returns and those implied by individually estimated betas could be due to instability in the underlying betas and/or errors in the estimation process. An important question to consider: Does the estimation process introduce systematic errors, and if so, can an improved process be devised?

Improved Beta Estimates

A number of statistical phenomena, including beta estimates, exhibit a tendency to move toward the grand mean (regression toward the mean). For example, in baseball, individual high and low first-month batting averages generally move toward the overall all-player average. Note, however, that this phenomenon describes the behavior of extreme values, not the entire population. Thus, batting averages and betas near the mean tend to move randomly away from the mean with sufficient frequency to repopulate the extremes as the prior-period extremes move in. Several estimation techniques take account of the regression-toward-the-mean phenomena.

adjusted beta

M.E. Blume suggests adjusting the beta for next year as follows: *Adjusted beta = .35 + .68 x beta estimate (based on data for the past 3 years).*[3] Others have proposed more sophisticated adjustments. Extensive study of these various beta-adjustment techniques shows that they are better than naively assuming no change in future betas. On the other hand, beta adjustments appear to be less necessary for large portfolios even though several mutual fund advisory services create adjusted betas for each fund as a regular part of their service. Substituting fundamental factors for or combining them with historically estimated betas is a further effort to generate more reliable beta estimates. Although all of these efforts may have improved the resulting beta estimates, the best estimates are still not perfect.

Barr Rosenberg was able to predict betas for companies using fundamental operating data—that is, accounting numbers taken from either historical or projected income statements and balance sheets.[4] Rosenberg argues that the problems with applications of the capital asset pricing model (CAPM) arise from the unrealistic assumptions of the simple model based on the EMH. For instance, the standard version of the CAPM is based on the clearly unrealistic assumption that investors have immediate access to all information needed to establish a security's price.

uncertain information hypothesis (UIH)

Brown, Tinic, and Harlow present a modified version of the EMH called the *uncertain information hypothesis (UIH)*, that attempts to extend efficient market theory to show how investors respond in a situation of major uncertainty.[5] Greater uncertainty among investors leads to heightened price volatility and thus produces greater risk for investors. Since investors require higher expected returns to compensate for bearing increased risk, they tend to respond to unexpected information by setting stock prices below their expected values. As the uncertainty over an expected outcome diminishes, subsequent price changes tend to be more favorable, regardless of whether the initial unexpected event was good or bad. The UIH theory sets forth the following propositions:

- On average, stock return variability will increase following the announcements of major unanticipated events.
- The average price adjustments following the initial market reactions to both "negative" and "positive" events will be positive.
- To the extent that the market's risk aversion decreases as the level of stock prices increases, post-event price increases will be larger for negative events than for positive ones. In other words, the market may initially overreact to bad news, in which case the stock price is likely to rise later to correct for the overreaction.

The main point is that portfolios are priced rationally in both situations; thus, based on anticipated changes, there are no opportunities for investors to earn riskless abnormal returns from alleged price overreactions or under-reactions. Therefore, markets only appear to *consistently* overreact to bad news and underreact to good news, because the market's response to bad news may be viewed as a combined response to both the news itself and the increase in uncertainty (risk) resulting from the news.

mean reversion

Another type of market efficiency test focuses on the mean reversion of security prices. The *mean reversion* process can be visualized by picturing a path of stock prices that swing excessively back and forth across some trend line that somehow measures the underlying or intrinsic value. Hence, the theory suggests a long-run pattern of overreactions followed regularly by market corrections. The general conclusion drawn from recent evidence is that there appear to be predictable return components in securities prices. It has been shown that 25 percent to 45 percent of the variability of stock returns over a 3-to-5-year time period can be predicted from returns in previous periods. These results can be explained in two different ways: (1) Investors are irrational and thus prices often depart from fundamental values that may provide an opportunity for abnormal profits, or (2) both the risks borne and risk premiums demanded by rational investors change with varying levels of uncertainty, which is consistent with the UIH discussed above.

The most recent important attack on the use of market beta was posited in an article by Fama and French in 1991.[6] They found evidence that the CAPM does not explain why returns of different types of risky stocks differ, and they argued that beta is not sufficient to describe the risk-return relationship in markets. They examined transactions by major U.S. stock exchanges between 1963 and 1990 and found that better predictors of stock returns were size of the firm and the ratio of the firm's book value to its market value. Critics of the Fama-French results argue that investors may simply have a preference for large capitalization firms not explained by economic rationality, or that investors may not have sufficient capital to diversify risk completely so that systematic risk may not fully explain market returns.

The Market Index

The market index used in the beta estimating equation may also introduce error into the estimation process. The theoretical model assumes that betas are estimated with an index that reflects all capital assets in proportion to their relative contribution to investor wealth. In practice, however, the NYSE composite or an even less broad index (such as the Standard and Poor's 500 Index) is usually employed. The NYSE index is an acceptable measure of U.S. stock movements, although the smallest firms are omitted from the index. NYSE-listed securities are a large part of the total U.S. stock market, and NYSE, NASDAQ, AMEX, regional, and OTC stocks all tend to move together. Moreover, option, warrant, and convertible prices also tend to change in the same direction as stock prices. Thus, the NYSE composite reflects the movements of U.S. stocks reasonably well.

The NYSE index's acceptability declines, however, as the relevant universe expands progressively to include U.S. debt securities, real estate, futures contracts, foreign securities, collectibles, precious metals, and so on. Even though many of these assets are influenced by the U.S. equity market, the correlations are relatively weak for most assets and essentially zero for others. Investments other than U.S. stocks (especially home ownership) represent an appreciable part of most investors' total wealth. Accordingly, using only U.S. stocks in the market index may result in bias in the resulting beta estimates. Indexes of varying quality do exist for debt securities, foreign securities, commodities, some collector's items, real estate, and non-NYSE equities.

Although no one has yet been able to make all the assumptions needed to assemble a complete, broad-based market index, the inclusion or exclusion of a particular asset class seems to have relatively little impact on an expanded index.

International Diversification

The stock markets in different countries appear to have a large component of independent variability. That is, a large part of the variability in their returns is unrelated to fluctuations in domestic markets. Thus, a strategy of adding foreign securities to a portfolio of domestic securities can be used to reduce the impact of the home country's business cycle. An international portfolio of debt and equity securities offers even greater diversification gains. Figure 8-2 shows the risk-reduction potential of international diversification.

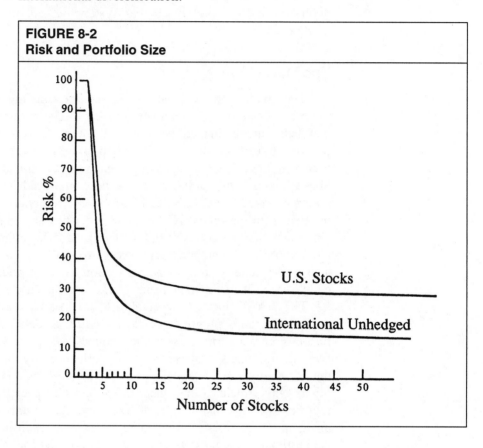

FIGURE 8-2
Risk and Portfolio Size

American depository receipts (ADRs)

Investors can diversify internationally in a variety of ways. They can purchase shares in an international mutual fund, a U.S.-based multinational company, a foreign company's stock, or *American depository receipts (ADRs)* representing ownership of such securities. Well over 500 foreign firms are tradable as ADRs. ADRs are denominated in dollars, which offers the benefit of indirectly holding stock in foreign companies without the risk of adverse currency fluctuations. Many mutual fund families (Fidelity, Vanguard, and so on) offer both foreign and international funds. A foreign fund holds only stocks and bonds of foreign countries. An international fund holds both foreign and domestic securities. A potential problem with international funds is that their relative composition of domestic and foreign securities may change dramatically without the investor's awareness.[7]

The ownership expenses of both foreign and international funds tend to be somewhat higher than those of domestic funds because transaction costs abroad are higher, and it is more difficult to obtain information on the securities of foreign firms. Furthermore, offshore mutual funds are less closely regulated than U.S. funds. Finally, investing in foreign securities exposes the investor to exchange rate risk and political risk.

Implications of Statistical Tests

As a whole, the research presents a relatively discouraging picture for these implications of statistical tests: (1) The markets are not as efficient as the theory assumes; (2) contrary to the theory, nonmarket risk may affect prices; and (3) relative return forecasts based on the market model are unreliable. In view of these shortcomings, why does the theory continue to receive so much attention? The answer to this question has three parts.

First, portfolio theory is an elegant simplification of complex phenomena. The theory's defenders can make useful explanations of a great deal of portfolio behavior, and there is a huge amount of literature (and correspondingly huge investment of time, money, and reputations) behind the theory. Not surprisingly, portfolio theory proponents would prefer to preserve as much of that investment as they reasonably can.

Second, the theory offers a useful point of departure. Economists, for example, need to understand the model of pure competition even though few markets are perfectly competitive. Similarly, most physicists are quite familiar with the properties of a frictionless world and perfect gas. These idealized models yield interesting insights and testable predictions. A particular nonidealized effect may be observed in the difference between the model forecast and the actual event (ex post forecast analysis) and thereby yield useful information for the next (ex ante) forecast period. Remember, for rational investment, forecasting is unavoidable. Therefore, finance theorists and empiricists are expected to know the implications of portfolio theory even if the real world often behaves differently.

Third, and most important, there is no better alternative model for the relationship between risk and expected return. If we do not use the portfolio theory framework to think about and analyze security returns, then the investment world becomes nothing but mumbo-jumbo observations.

Of course, we need to keep in mind one of the original reasons for developing portfolio theory—especially the CAPM—was to evaluate the risk-adjusted past performance of professional portfolio managers. Prior to the CAPM approach, there was no formal way to evaluate the performance of a portfolio of securities relative to the risks taken to earn those returns. Thus, the CAPM approach may be best suited to evaluating past performance, rather than as a predictive model. In this respect, the model performs admirably.

Finally, the beta estimates for diversified portfolios are relatively reliable, even though the estimates for individual stocks are imprecise. Until a demonstrably superior theory is devised, therefore, the standard form of portfolio theory will continue to provide the foundation for the study of finance.

SUMMARY AND CONCLUSIONS

We have explored predictions of portfolio theory dealing with market efficiency, nonmarket risk, and the properties of estimated betas. Some of the evidence appears to be in conflict with the theory's predictions. Various inefficiencies are observed; nonmarket risk does appear to affect prices; and the relationship for securities between market risk and expected return is not demonstrably linear. The chapter discusses a number of real world violations of the model's assumptions. Historical beta may be an imprecise indicator of a stock's current beta. Too few investors may be appropriately situated to eliminate some mispricings; different investors borrow and lend at differing rates; return distributions may be nonnormal; some investors may be concerned with skewness; most empirical work with the market portfolio utilizes an index that excludes everything but U.S. equity securities; and imperfections such as taxes and transaction costs influence market prices. In spite of the drawbacks, portfolio theory continues to be studied and utilized. The portfolio theory model is appreciably ahead of whatever is in second place, it offers a useful point of departure, and it fits some aspects of the real world reasonably well.

CHAPTER REVIEW

Answers to the review questions and the self-test questions start on page 501.

Key Terms

efficient market hypothesis (EMH)	risk-adjusted return
fundamental analysis	Jensen's alpha
technical analysis	Sharpe ratio
random walk	reward to variability (RVAR)
weak form EMH	Treynor ratio
semistrong form EMH	reward to volatility (RVOL)
strong form EMH	run
differential return	chartists

filter rules   uncertain information hypothesis
anomaly   (UIH)
small firm effect   mean reversion
skewed distributions   American depository receipts
adjusted beta   (ADRs)

Review Questions

8-1.   Compare the two principal types of investment analysis.

8-2.   Discuss the three forms of the efficient market hypothesis. What do each imply about the types of investment analysis? Summarize the relevant evidence on each.

8-3.   Discuss the possible causes of persisting market imperfections.

8-4.   a.   Compare the theoretical price impact of nonmarket risk with real world experience.
       b.   Discuss the possible explanations for the apparent inconsistency.

8-5.   a.   What does portfolio theory usually assume for return distributions?
       b.   How do most investors feel about skewness?

8-6.   a.   How are betas estimated?
       b.   What problems arise?
       c.   How may betas be adjusted?

8-7.   Compute Blume-adjusted betas for each of the following unadjusted betas: 1.34, .57, .78, and 1.20.

8-8.   a.   What is the impact of international diversification?
       b.   How might a portfolio be diversified internationally, and what are the risks of international diversification?

8-9.   a.   Summarize the problems of portfolio theory.

8-10. A diversified portfolio of stocks is expected to generate a return of 15 percent with a beta of 1. A diversified portfolio of long-term bonds offers an expected return of 11 percent and has a beta of .3. A diversified portfolio of short-term debt securities has an expected return of 8 percent and a beta of .1. How can you combine investments in these choices to
       a.   maximize expected return
       b.   minimize risk
       c.   provide a beta of .5 and a maximum return for that beta level (ignore portfolios consisting of all three investments)

Self-Test Questions

T   F   8-1. Overall, market risk is the most important risk that affects the price movements of common stock portfolios.

T   F   8-2. The weak form of the efficient market hypothesis (EMH) states that the past history of price information is of no value in assessing future changes in stock prices.

T   F   8-3. The efficient market, as the term is used in investments, is concerned with making security transactions at the lowest unit cost.

T   F   8-4. Characteristics of efficiency in the market are that information is widely available and that it is generated in a random fashion.

T   F   8-5. A market that is semistrong-form efficient is also weak-form efficient.

T   F   8-6. The semistrong form of the EMH states that stock prices reflect all public and nonpublic information.

T   F   8-7. In a semistrong efficient market, investors cannot act on new public information after its announcement and expect to earn above-average returns.

T   F   8-8. The semistrong form of the EMH refutes technical analysis but supports fundamental analysis.

T   F   8-9. The Sharpe index assesses a portfolio's total return relative to its total risk.

T   F   8-10. The Treynor index assesses a portfolio's excess return relative to its alpha.

T   F   8-11. When comparing large, broad-based equity mutual funds, both the Sharpe and Treynor indices generally provide identical or almost identical rankings of the funds.

T   F   8-12. Tests of technical trading rules generally conclude that past price and volume strategies cannot consistently outperform a simple buy-and-hold strategy.

T   F   8-13. Results of studies concerning the trading activities of corporate insiders generally support the validity of the strong form of the EMH.

T   F   8-14. A market anomaly is an exception to what is expected in a totally efficient market.

T   F   8-15. If the stock market is efficient, then money (portfolio) managers need not be concerned with portfolio diversification and risk.

T   F   8-16. A portfolio's beta differs depending on the benchmark portfolio used in its determination.

NOTES

1. This is the version found on the CFP^{TM} Formula Sheet.
2. This is actually a *joint test* of the accuracy of x_i, β_i, and the selection of the market index. The principle is that we can test beta estimates for their reliability, but the actual test is a bit more complex than described here.
3. M. E. Blume, "On the Assessment of Risk," *Journal of Finance,* March 1971, pp. 1–10.
4. Barr Rosenberg, "The Capital Asset Pricing Model and the Market Model," *Journal of Portfolio Management* (winter 1981), pp. 5–16.
5. K. Brown, S. Tinic, and V. Harlow, "Risk Aversion, Uncertain Information, and Market Efficiency," *Journal of Financial Economics*, vol. 22, 1988, pp. 355–358.
6. E. Fama and K. French, "The Cross-Section of Expected Stock Returns," *Journal of Finance,* June 1992, pp. 427–465.
7. A recent innovation, exchange-traded funds (ETFs) are exchange-brokered funds based on foreign market (stock) indexes. These funds permit easier diversification with higher liquidity and lower expenses than equivalent mutual funds.

9

Security Analysis and Selection Techniques

Learning Objectives

An understanding of the material in this chapter should enable the student to

---

9-1. Explain the components of fundamental analysis and how they influence stock performance.

9-2. Explain how macroeconomic analysis is used to evaluate the economy's effect on industry and firm fundamentals.

9-3. Explain how industry analysis assesses the outlook for particular industries.

9-4. Explain how company analysis examines a firm's relative strengths and weaknesses within its industry or industries.

9-5. Explain the dichotomy between fundamental analysis and market efficiency as they relate to stock market prices.

9-6. Describe the various screening techniques investors use to screen out unattractive stocks so that only those deserving closer scrutiny remain.

9-7. Explain the Graham and Templeton integrated approaches to investment selection that simultaneously analyze several different selection criteria.

Chapter Outline

As discussed in chapter 4, the value of an investment can be estimated by discounting its expected income stream. Both the theory and the evidence supporting this approach to valuations are unimpeachable. Applying this approach, however, requires estimates of that future income stream, as well as assessing the risks associated with these projections. Forecasting earnings even one year ahead is difficult enough, to say nothing of projecting both earnings and the dividend payout ratio a number of years into the future.

This chapter surveys the issues associated with fundamental analysis. It discusses both macroeconomic analysis and industry analysis. Specific approaches to economic and industry analysis are presented. Then company analysis is considered, giving particular attention to the evaluation of a company's competitive position, management quality, financial strength, and profitability. The chapter examines the relevance of this analysis to the market price and the efficient market hypothesis (EMH).

A comprehensive analysis of the economy, industry, and firm may be useful, but most investors do not have the required time, skills, and resources to perform such an analysis. Operational approaches that enable analysts to screen a lengthy list of stocks and thereby reduce the number of prospective investments to a manageable number are necessary. This chapter examines screening techniques that identify and eliminate unattractive stocks so that only the stocks that deserve closer scrutiny are left. Finally, the chapter explains Graham's and Templeton's integrated approaches to fundamental analysis, which simultaneously analyze a variety of selection criteria.

OVERVIEW OF FUNDAMENTAL ANALYSIS

macroeconomic analysis

Fundamental analysis traditionally takes a "top down" approach, which consists of breaking the analysis into three parts: (1) macroeconomic analysis, (2) industry analysis, and (3) company analysis. *Macroeconomic analysis* seeks to evaluate the current economic setting and its effect on industry and firm fundamentals. Industry analysis assesses the outlook for particular industries, whereas company analysis examines a firm's relative strengths and weaknesses within its industry or industries.

These three categories correspond to the three principal influences on stock performance. Clearly, each is important, although studies show that, in terms of both firm profits and the total return on stocks (dividends plus price changes), market/economy and firm-specific factors are the dominant influences, with industry factors accounting for only about 10 percent of the variability.

Three Categories of Fundamental Analysis

- Macroeconomic analysis: evaluates current economic environment and its effect on industry and company fundamentals
- Industry analysis: evaluates the outlook for particular industries
- Company analysis: evaluates a company's strengths and weaknesses within its industry(ies)

MACROECONOMIC ANALYSIS

Publicly traded firms make up a large part of the economy. Profitability, a major determinant of share prices, is closely tied to the nation's economic health. When the economy is depressed (as in a recession), most firms operate well below their capacities. For example, in the 1982 recession, which had an inordinate effect on the agriculture sector, John Deere's sales fell by 14 percent, while its profits declined by 97 percent. At the same time, many of its competitors (International Harvester, Allis-Chalmers, and Massey-Ferguson) were losing money and, in International Harvester's case, threatened with bankruptcy.

The general tendency for profits to drop more than economic activity in a recession is illustrated in table 9-1. During these recessions, personal consumption generally increased (an average of 4.62 percent), employment dropped modestly (–.92 percent), and profits fell appreciably (–15.91 percent). A rapidly growing economy, in contrast, leads to above-average employment, sales, and profit increases. Although investors generally fare better in booms than recessions, the relationships are complex. The economy's primary impact on stock prices relates to its effect on their expected income streams. The dividend decisions made by corporate managements tend to reflect long-term (not annual) earnings trends. Investors do, however, expect that earnings increases will eventually lead to higher dividends. Thus, an earnings increase is still a favorable sign even if the dividend response is slow. If invested productively, earnings that are retained should produce still higher earnings. Eventually, these higher earnings should lead to both increased dividends and a higher stock price. Similarly, losses or reduced earnings are likely to lead to reduced dividends and stock prices.

TABLE 9-1
Percentage Changes in Economic Activity for Postwar Recessions: Change in Profits, Civilian Non-Farm Employment, and Personal Consumption Expenditure

Year (Period)	Change in Profits	Change in Civilian Non-Farm Employment	Change in Personal Consumption Expenditure
1948–1949	–18.4%	–.66%	+.01%
1953–1954	–1.8	–2.47	+3.16
1957–1958	–22.3	–1.91	+1.27
1960–1961	–12.2	–.9	–.64
1970–1971	–11.4	+.08	+8.27
1973–1975	–34.2	+.71	+12.60
1979–1980	–17.8	–.83	+6.38
1981–1982	–24.3	1.40	+7.05
1990–1991	–0.8	–0.9	+3.5
Average	–15.91	–.92	+4.62

Source: Economic data obtained from the Economic Report of the President for various years.

In other words, causation runs from the economy to companies' profits and then to stock prices. That is, the state of the economy affects the performance of individual companies. Company performance, in turn, is the major determinant of the stock price. Economic activity is reflected in such data as the gross domestic product (GDP), industrial production, and the employment (or unemployment) rate. The level of economic activity has a major impact on the sales and prices of individual companies. Their sales revenues minus their expenses then determine income. A portion of net income is paid out in the form of dividends, and the remainder is retained earnings. Dividends provide immediate cash flow to investors, while retained earnings are used to finance the resources needed to produce future growth. Thus, current profitability coupled with an understanding of the firm's expenses and revenues may be used to formulate a guide to the company's expected future stream of cash flows.

Relationships between Stock Market and Economic Outlook

Because macroeconomic activity has a major impact on company sales, profits, and dividends, the investment community pays close attention to the business cycle. According to conventional Wall Street wisdom, stock prices reflect the expected condition of the economy approximately 6 months later. Indeed, the National Bureau of Economic Research rates the stock market as one of the primary leading indicators of economic activity. The economy generally moves in the same direction for much longer than 6 months, so the economy and the stock market often move together. They may, however, move in opposite directions just before a turning point in the business cycle. At still other times, the market may incorrectly forecast business behavior and move in a direction inconsistent with future changes in the economy until there is a correction. However, in the last three decades, stock prices have tended to decline in reaction to increased inflation, high interest rates, and Federal Reserve credit tightening during the so-called boom-bust phase of the business cycle.

Not all market moves are related to changes in the economic outlook. What might be termed emotional factors sometimes influence the market. For example, unfavorable news, such as the fall of France in 1940, the assassination of President Kennedy in 1963, the Cambodian invasion in 1970, the Iranian hostage crisis of 1979–1980, and the attack on the World Trade Towers in 2001, were shocks to the stock market. Such noneconomic influences are superimposed on the basic stock market-economy relationship.

A Specific Approach to Economic Analysis

Investment analysts perform economic analysis when they use their knowledge of the economic environment to assess the outlook of the stock market. One approach to this task begins with the basic valuation models. Recall the dividend discount model and the P/E (price-earnings) ratio model that were introduced in chapter 4. As we have already seen, in equilibrium the price of a stock or other investment equals the present value of its expected income stream. When the growth rate of that income stream can be approximated by a constant defined as g, the (dividend discount) valuation formula may be expressed as follows in equation 9-1:

$$P_0 = \frac{d_1}{(k - g)}$$ (Equation 9-1)

where: P_0 = stock price at time t = 0
d_1 = anticipated dividend over coming year
g = expected long-term growth rate for dividends
k = the appropriate discount rate for the stock

Most investors prefer to relate stock prices to expected per-share earnings (P/E ratio). Thus, a more usable form for this relationship brings in the expected earnings per share for next year e_1, the anticipated dividend payout ratio p (= d_1/e_1), and the P/E ratio as shown in equation 9-2:

$$PE = \frac{p}{(k - g)}$$ (Equation 9-2)

Both equations will generate relatively accurate valuations when reliable long-term average values for p, k, and g are used (assuming that the values for individual years are generally relatively close to these averages). In many circumstances, therefore, both equations express the determinants of the price and P/E ratio of a stock.

Although equations 9-1 and 9-2 are expressed in the form of a single share of stock of a single company, the same basic relationship can be applied to the entire stock market. The market is usually represented by an index value, which is designed to represent a diversified portfolio of stocks. For example, the New York Stock Exchange (NYSE) constructs an average of stock prices called the NYSE Composite Index. The Standard & Poor's 500 Index (S&P 500) is another broad-based index of stock. A number of other popular indexes are also reported in the financial press.

When applied to the market, equation 9-2 implies that aggregate stock prices relative to aggregate earnings (as reflected by the P/E ratio of a broadly based market index) are a function of the overall dividend payout ratio, the expected growth rate for aggregate dividends, and the appropriate discount rate for the stock market (the risk-free rate plus the market risk premium).

The level of stock prices is the product of the market's average P/E ratio and its average earnings per share (or the corresponding earnings for the index). A forecast of the market could thus be decomposed into two tasks: forecasting the earnings of the market (or an index) and forecasting its corresponding P/E ratio.

Forecasting the Market P/E

Many analysts predict the market's earnings and then derive a forecast for the market's price level by applying their earnings forecast to the current market P/E ratio.

Example: In mid-1987, the NYSE Composite Index stood at about 180 with a P/E of about 21 and most recent 12-month earnings of $8.60. If year-ahead earnings are expected to be $10, a P/E of 21 implies an index value of 210.

Such a simplistic approach, however, ignores the possibility that the market P/E may change. It often does. Indeed, the market did change dramatically shortly after June 1987. The great stock market crash of October 1987 saw the market fall by more than one-third in the space of a few weeks. By late November, the NYSE index was down to around 135. That level corresponded to a P/E of 16. Had the NYSE index generated 1988 earnings of $10, a P/E of 16 would imply a value for the index of around 160. Clearly, market forecasts need to explore the factors that may cause the average P/E to change.

Recall the determinants of the P/E reflected in equation 9-2:

$$PE = \frac{p}{(k - g)}$$

Thus, the market P/E ratio is largely a function of p, the dividend payout ratio; k, the appropriate discount rate; and g, the expected growth rate in dividends. The overall market dividend payout ratio has averaged close to or somewhat above .5. A given year's variations relative to that average are largely a response to departures from the normal growth in earnings.

The long-run growth rate in the economy is around 3 percent to 4 percent in real (adjusted for inflation) terms. Although the growth in earnings will vary greatly from year to year, the long-term growth rate will be similar to that of the economy. The growth rate in nominal terms would tend to be increased by the inflation rate. That is, the expected nominal growth rate should approximately equal the long-term real growth rate plus the expected inflation rate. In periods of rapid inflation, however, the nominal growth in earnings is likely to be somewhat less than the inflation rate plus the long-term real growth rate. Rapid inflation tends to depress the real value of earnings and discourages investment in long-term growth.

The appropriate discount rate is a function of several factors. Suppliers of capital seek a return that will compensate them for both risk and the expected rate of inflation. Thus, k should equal the real risk-free rate plus a premium for risk and an amount to compensate for expected inflation. Therefore, a real risk-free rate of 3 percent and risk premium of 4 percent would produce a market discount rate of 7 percent plus the expected inflation rate.

Note that inflation plays a role in all three components of the P/E equation. A rise in the inflation rate tends to depress p, thereby reducing the P/E. That is, the higher the inflation rate, the larger the fraction of reported earnings represents of unsustainable profits. For example, profit sources, such as sales from inventories carried on the books at long-out-of-date cost levels, tend to be greater at high inflation rates. Firms are unlikely to increase their dividend rates when their earnings increases are expected to be temporary.

A rise in the inflation rate also tends to increase both k and g, but the greater impact is on k. Thus, (k − g) tends to increase as inflation rises, thereby reducing the P/E. Overall, an increase in expected inflation tends to decrease the numerator and increase the denominator of the P/E ratio equation, thereby tending to lower its overall value.

It is important to remember that the risk premium and its impact on the required rate of return (discount rate) are based on perceived risk. Although it takes time for the dividend payout ratio, growth rate, or even the inflation rate to change, investors' perceptions of riskiness can change rapidly, often in response to a single piece of information, or even a rumor that turns out to have no factual basis. Investors tend to overreact to bad news, and the market sometimes reacts to events that have no economic significance. The volatility of perceived risk applies to the market as a whole, as well as to individual firms. In fact, it might be safe to say that one of the most powerful causes of rapid market declines, such as the one that occurred on October 19, 1987, was a sudden increase in investors' perception of market risk.

Steps to Obtain the Market P/E Multiple

- Estimate the market's overall dividend payout ratio p from past data, the stage of the business cycle, and expected inflation rates.
- Estimate the aggregate stock market discount rate k as the sum of the real risk-free rate, the market risk premium, and the expected inflation rate. Alternatively, add the appropriate risk premium to the current nominal (no inflation adjustment) risk-free rate (for example, the rate of return on T-bills).
- Forecast the nominal long-term growth rate in the market's earnings g. The real long-term growth rate is largely a function of the stage of the business cycle. The nominal rate is the sum of the expected long-term real growth rate and a percentage (close to but probably less than 1) of the expected inflation rate.
- Apply the values for p, k, and g to equation 9-2 to obtain the forecasted market P/E.

INDUSTRY ANALYSIS

Economic analysis assesses the general environment and its impact on firms and industries. Industry analysis, in contrast, examines the specific environment of the markets in which different industries compete. Investors might begin a search for attractive investments by either evaluating the component companies of a selected industry or analyzing a particular firm first and then its industry and competitors. With either scenario, both company and industry analysis are undertaken. In the discussion that follows, the process is assumed to begin with industry analysis. (This is consistent with the top-down approach.)

Before proceeding, we should establish the relevance of industry analysis to investors. The evidence is rather clear on one point: Individual industries have, over time, provided very different returns to investors. Consider, for example, the returns of the banking industry in the late 1980s and early 1990s versus the software industry and the telecommunications industry. Over specific periods, some industries show much higher returns than others. On the other hand, there is wide dispersion in the performance of individual firms within particular industries. Furthermore, when assessing a firm's financial data, it is important to see how the firm performs relative to other firms in the same industry in order to make a meaningful comparison.

Michael E. Porter's research indicates that a critical factor affecting the profit potential of an industry is the intensity of competition in the industry.[1]

He believes that the competitive environment of an industry determines the ability of the firm to sustain above-average rates of return on invested capital. Porter discusses five competitive forces that determine the intensity of competition among firms; these factors can vary greatly among industries: rivalry among existing competitors, threat of new entrants, substitute products or services, bargaining power of customers, and bargaining power of suppliers.

Looking at industry analysis from a global perspective, firms active in foreign markets will be affected by global competition. Clearly, the U.S. automobile industry faces competition from firms in Japan, Germany, and Korea. Thus, any analysis of the auto industry must be extended to include global factors.

Their independent movements notwithstanding, attractively performing industries contain a disproportionate number of profitable investments. Therefore, we would like to know how to identify industries that will show the highest future returns. One possibility might be to select industries with strong recent records. This assumes that the same forces that produced the past record will continue, at least for a while longer. Projecting past industry performance, however, involves uncertainties similar to those of extrapolating past earnings growth. Past growth may imply some momentum but also establishes a higher base. The central issue is whether past growth reflects the industry's stage of development or isolated circumstances. Knowing the industry's stage of development is a good indicator of whether its recent rate of growth is likely to continue. Thus, identifying an industry's development stage may help assess its growth prospects.

Stages of Industry Development

Industries are thought typically to pass through several developmental stages. Initially, many new firms are established (start-up stage), and growth is rapid. A shakeout then reduces the number of firms (consolidation stage) as the less efficient firms tend to merge or go bankrupt. After the adjustment, growth slows to that of the economy (maturity stage). Finally, new industries begin to grow at the expense of the existing industry (decline stage). Predicting evolution from one stage to another is not easy. In fact, some industries follow different schemes from the typical one just described. For example, the solid waste disposal industry experienced modest performance until the ecology movement brought it to life.

Some experts question the validity of the life cycle approach to industry analysis. They note, for instance, that the Coca-Cola Company has been a successful competitor, deriving much of its revenues from a product that has changed relatively little in 100 years. However, Coca-Cola has achieved its most recent profit momentum through the effects of globalization and international growth. As of 1999, Coke derived over 60 percent of its revenues from outside the United States.

In general, globalization may offer new life to some mature and declining industries. Products that have already saturated the market in the United States and other industrialized countries might find substantial new marketing opportunities in less developed nations.

Life Cycle of an Industry

- Start-up stage: many new firms; grows rapidly (example: genetic engineering)
- Consolidation stage: shakeout period; growth slows (example: video games)
- Maturity stage: grows with economy (example: automobile industry)
- Decline stage: grows slower than economy (example: railroads)

A Specific Approach to Industry Analysis

The same basic methodology that was examined in the section on economic analysis can be used to analyze an industry. That is, the market performance of an industry can be forecast from an analysis of its earnings and P/E potentials. This analysis is easier to perform when the industry is represented by an index. In addition to the broad stock indexes, a number of indexes are compiled for the stocks of individual industries. Data on these indexes and the stocks that make them up allow investors to forecast their earnings and P/Es. If no industry index is readily available, a quasi-index can be formed from the stocks of the principal companies that make up the industry.

Analysts would like to be able to accurately forecast future levels of industry sales, expenses, and profits. Relevant governmental policies should be assessed. The interrelationships with competing and complementary supplier and customer industries should all be considered. This analysis is relatively difficult to perform accurately. Nonetheless, industry analysis yields superior returns only when it is superior to the market's assessment.

As with market analysis, investors should bear in mind the relative nature of the process. Although the prospects of individual industries need to be evaluated, the most attractive industries for investment are not necessarily the ones with the brightest profit and growth prospects. Rather, investors seek investments with greater potentials than the market recognizes. In other words, the market may have already taken account of these prospects in the prices of stocks of companies in that industry, so that investors cannot earn superior risk-adjusted returns by investing in that industry. Thus, an industry with bleak prospects may contain attractive investments if the market is even more pessimistic than the true outlook justifies.

COMPANY ANALYSIS

Once industry analysis has identified a potentially attractive area for investment, the companies within that industry need to be evaluated. Three important company characteristics are competitive position, management quality, and financial soundness. Each relates to how successful a firm is likely to be within its industry or industries.

Competitive Position

While somewhat more difficult to evaluate than its financial strengths and weaknesses, a company's competitive position is an important performance determinant. How able is the firm to withstand competitive pressures? How vigorous are its rivals? What is the government's treatment of the company? Clearly, these are interesting questions.

Management Quality

A perceptive, aggressive, forward-looking management improves the odds of realizing a company's full potential. The following characteristics are relevant: motivation, research and development activity, willingness to take risks, long-term orientation, success in integrating merged firms, effectiveness in delegating authority, use of information systems, use of a board of directors, and relations with financial analysts. Several studies note that managers who are especially interested in stockholder welfare generally outperform those more concerned with their own well-being.

Financial Soundness

An attractive industry environment, strong competitive position, and effective management are all important components of a company's fundamental position. Only companies with adequate financial resources, however, can fully exploit their opportunities. Accordingly, much of fundamental analysis involves assessing the company's financial strengths and weaknesses.

Basic Accounting Concepts Used in Fundamental Analysis

balance sheet

Because accounting data are utilized extensively in financial analysis, we shall briefly review the principal types of financial statements. First, a *balance sheet* reflects the financial status of a company at a point in time. A listing of assets appears with current assets reflected first. Plant and equipment are valued at cost less depreciation, whereas most other assets are valued at the lower of cost or market value. Liabilities (both short- and long-term debt) and net worth (the stockholders' residual ownership position) appear next. Total assets equal the sum of liabilities and net worth (see table 9-2).

TABLE 9-2
Basic Balance Sheet

Assets	Liabilities and Net Worth

Current Assets
  Cash
  Inventories
  Accounts receivable
  • • •
Long-Term Assets
  Plant
  Equipment
  Land
  Market value of patents and
    royalties
  • • •
Other Assets
	Current Liabilities
	  Accounts Payable
	  Short-term notes
	  • • •
	Long-Term Liabilities
	  Corporate debt
	  • • •
	Net Worth
	  Stockholders' equity

Total Assets = Total Liabilities and Net Worth	

Think of the balance sheet as identifying the firm's assets (listed on the left-hand side) and how those assets are financed (listed on the right-hand side). The greater the percentage of the firm's assets that are financed by debt, other things being equal, the greater the firm's financial leverage. Too much debt (financial leverage) increases the risk of default.

income statement

The *income statement* reflects the results of operations for a period of time. It starts with total sales or revenues. Various expenses are then subtracted until only the company's earnings (income) remain. The income statement helps answer questions such as these: How much did the company make or lose in the recent period? How do current earnings compare with past results? Every year (unless the company sells or buys back some stock) the company's net worth will change by the net change in that year's retained earnings. The change in retained earnings normally equals net income minus dividends. The income statement and balance sheet are thus connected by changes in net worth.

statement of changes in financial position

The *statement of changes in financial position* (sources and uses of funds), the third of the principal financial statements, helps to analyze the company's liquidity/cash flow position. It shows how the changes in the accounts of the balance sheet and income statement contributed to the net change in the cash position for the year.

Types of Accounting Statements

- Balance sheet: picture of resources (assets), obligations (liabilities), and net worth (equity) at a certain point in time
- Income statement: earnings, calculated as revenues less expenses, over a period of time
- Statement of changes in financial position: cash flow changes

---

Preparing accounting statements necessarily involves many subjective judgments, and subjectivity opens up opportunities for abuse. Unfortunately, the temptation is too great for some managers. Permissible accounting conventions can be misused to distort a company's financial appearance. Nevertheless, the vast majority of accounting statements reflect a consistent and meaningful financial picture.

ratio analysis

Ratio Analysis

Relative magnitudes of financial data are generally more revealing than absolute levels. A company with a bank balance of $1 million could be very rich or very poor, depending on its overall size. Accordingly, ratios of financial aggregates have long been used to assess the financial positions of various sized companies.

Ratios may be grouped into four categories. Liquidity ratios measure the company's ability to meet its short-run obligations. Debt ratios measure the company's financial leverage. And profitability and efficiency ratios are designed to reflect the firm's productivity.

liquidity ratios
current ratio
current assets

current liabilities

Liquidity Ratios. The *current ratio* is an index of the short-run solvency or liquidity. It is defined as *current assets* (cash, short-term investments, accounts receivable, prepaid expenses, and inventories) divided by *current liabilities* (accounts payable, notes due in one year, and the current portion of long-term debt). As with all ratios, the optimal value varies from company to company, industry to industry, and over time. Stable incomes and reliable sources of short-term credit lessen the need for liquid assets and therefore reduce the optimal current ratio level. Indeed, a high current ratio may indicate that resources are being tied up unnecessarily.

**quick ratio
acid test ratio**

The *quick ratio,* or *acid test ratio,* is defined as liquid assets (cash plus receivables) divided by current liabilities. Therefore inventories, which may be relatively difficult to liquidate, are part of the current ratio's numerator but excluded from the quick ratio. A high current ratio and low quick ratio might be a warning sign indicating that the firm is experiencing difficulty moving its inventory. The appropriate level varies among industries, over time, and according to special company characteristics.

**inventory turnover
ratio**

The *inventory turnover ratio* equals the cost of goods sold divided by average yearly inventory. The reciprocal of the inventory turnover ratio, multiplied by 360, represents the average number of days that goods are held in inventory. The ideal inventory level differs with the industry and in some cases with the season and business cycle. A high inventory turnover suggests brisk sales and well-managed inventories. However, a very high inventory turnover ratio might indicate inadequate inventories. A low inventory turnover ratio may reflect idle resources that are tied up in excess inventories and/or a large obsolete inventory component. A low inventory turnover, relative to the firm's competitors, might also be indicative of a marketing problem.

The average collection period (ACP) is the weighted average life of outstanding accounts receivable—that is, net accounts receivable divided by daily sales. The term daily sales is defined as annual net sales divided by 360. The ratio should be compared with the company's stated credit policy. For example, a manufacturer might have a credit policy based on an expectation of receiving payments within 30 days of billing. If the ACP is longer than 30 days, the firm may have a problem with credit extensions. Perhaps the firm needs to tighten credit standards or improve its collection policy. On the other hand, too low an average collection period, relative to the industry, might suggest that the firm is losing potential customers by maintaining an overly stringent credit policy.

Liquidity Ratios

- Current: current assets/current liabilities
- Quick (or acid test): (current assets – inventories)/current liabilities
- Inventory turnover: cost of goods sold/average yearly inventory
- Average collection period: net accounts receivable/daily sales

debt-equity ratio

Debt Ratios. Debt-equity and times-interest-earned ratios are used to assess the prospects for a company's continued success and stability. The *debt-equity ratio* (such as liabilities divided by net worth or long-term debt divided by equity), also known as a financial leverage ratio, varies considerably from industry to industry, company to company, and over time. A high debt ratio can be profitable to shareholders, but it also represents financial risk. As a general rule, a firm whose cash flows are relatively stable, and that experiences very little business risk, can afford to take on a fair amount of financial risk. On the other hand, a firm that is in an early stage of development, or that is engaged in a risky type of business, should avoid adding to its business risk by taking on a substantial amount of financial risk.

Companies that borrow generally do so in an effort to increase their profit relative to their net worth (that is, their return on equity). This is the principle of financial leverage mentioned above. A company that can borrow at X percent and earn $(X + Y)$ percent on the money gains the difference. Financial leverage is, however, a two-edged sword. The company that borrows has thereby incurred debts that must be serviced, regardless of the returns earned with the borrowed funds. Thus, companies that are planning to be heavy borrowers need to be relatively confident that the return that they earn will exceed their borrowing costs. Interest payments must be made when due whether or not a profit was made in that period.[2]

A company's appropriate debt-equity ratio varies primarily with its earning stability. A comparison of debt-equity ratios over time and within the industry may help assess the adequacy of the current level. A rapid rise in the ratio can suggest potential problems. It is of less concern if the increased debt still leaves the firm with a substantial cushion of equity and the firm has profitable operations; the company may simply be taking advantage of heretofore unused debt capacity. If the firm is experiencing losses or only modest profits, however, increased reliance on debt suggests possible problems.

Debt is not the only type of fixed payment obligation. In particular, leases may further complicate accounting statement analysis. Purchasing assets with borrowed funds increases the debt-equity ratio, whereas leasing the same assets does not increase debt *per se*. The long-term obligations are similar, however, whether new assets are leased or purchased with borrowed money. Thus, debt-equity ratios do not always accurately reflect a company's total financial commitments. Investors need to look beyond simply the debt ratios of companies that lease a large fraction of their assets. Companies must show their capitalized long-term lease obligations on their balance sheets.

Some financial analysts prefer to use the debt-asset ratio rather than the debt-equity ratio. As mentioned above, assets equal debt plus equity. Thus, the two ratios are closely related and have the same numerator. The main difference in the two ratios is in their scales. Equity can be a small percentage of assets, a large percentage of assets, or in between. Therefore, the debt-equity ratio can vary from 0 (no debt) to a large number (almost no equity). The debt-asset ratio, on the other hand, lies between 0 (no debt) and 1 (no equity).

times-interest-earned ratio

The *times-interest-earned ratio,* sometimes called the earnings-coverage ratio (earnings before interest payments and tax, divided by interest payments), also reflects a company's debt exposure. Unlike the debt-equity ratio, however, it relates the company's interest obligation relative to its earning power. Obviously, the higher the ratio, the greater the safety of a company's interest payments.

Debt Ratios

- Debt-equity: total debt/shareholders' equity
- Debt-asset: total debt/total assets
- Times-interest-earned: profit before interest payments and tax/interest payments

return on equity (ROE)
return on assets (ROA)
net profit margin (NPM)
asset turnover
equity multiplier

Profitability and Efficiency Ratios. Five important and related profitability-efficiency (or activity) ratios are (1) *return on equity (ROE)*, (2) *return on assets (ROA)*, (3) *net profit margin (NPM)*, (4) *asset turnover*, and (5) *equity multiplier.*

Annual averages are generally used to compute profitability and efficiency ratios. A shorter time frame can be used, but seasonal influences would distort the results.

$$ROE = \frac{\text{After-tax profit}}{\text{Shareholders' equity}}$$

$$ROA = \frac{\text{After-tax profit}}{\text{Total assets}}$$

$$NPM = \frac{\text{After-tax profit}}{\text{Sales}}$$

$$\text{Asset turnover} = \frac{\text{Sales}}{\text{Total assets}}$$

$$\text{Equity multiplier} = \frac{\text{Total assets}}{\text{Shareholders' equity}}$$

There are two key relationships among these formulas. The first is that

ROA = NPM x Asset turnover

The second is that

ROE = ROA x Equity multiplier

Dupont formula

These two equations are part of the *Dupont formula* system. They are frequently combined as

ROE = NPM x Asset turnover x Equity multiplier

$$\frac{\text{Net income}}{\text{Shareholders' equity}} = \frac{\text{Net income}}{\text{Total revenues}} \times \frac{\text{Total revenues}}{\text{Total assets}} \times \frac{\text{Total assets}}{\text{Shareholders' equity}}$$

This last equation allows us to examine the source of any profitability problems by looking at the components of ROE. ROE, as a measure of profit relative to shareholders' equity, is a major determinant of share prices.

The NPM tends to vary inversely with turnover. A high-turnover operation such as a supermarket tends to have a low profit margin, whereas a high-margin operation such as a jewelry store tends to have a low turnover. In other words, the net profit margin and the asset turnover ratio are frequently determined by the characteristics of the industry. The critical factor is *always* the product of the two, not each one separately.

Profitability and Efficiency Ratios

- Return on equity (ROE): Net income/shareholders' equity
- Return on assets (ROA): Net income/total assets
- Net profit margin (NPM): Net income/sales
- Asset turnover: Sales/total assets
- Equity multiplier: Total assets/shareholders' equity

Other Ratios. In addition to liquidity, debt, profitability, and efficiency ratios, investors may find several other ratios useful. Earnings per share (EPS) is the company's total earnings (less any preferred dividends) divided by the number of shares of common stock outstanding. Several different earnings numbers are often reported. Fully diluted EPS assumes the exercise of all outstanding warrants and rights and conversion of any outstanding convertible bonds and convertible preferred stock. In other words, to calculate fully diluted earnings per share, net earnings are divided by the number of shares of stock that would be outstanding if all warrants, rights, and conversion privileges were exercised. In a sense, fully diluted earnings per share provides a "worst case scenario" analysis. Earnings figures may include or exclude extraordinary items and the results from noncontinuing operations.

As we have already seen, the P/E ratio or ratio of the per-share market price to expected EPS is a measure of the relative stock price. The current annual dividend divided by the price per share is the *dividend yield*. The dividend payout ratio (p in the P/E ratio model) equals dividends per share divided by EPS (or total dividends divided by net income). A low dividend payout ratio may indicate a desire to finance growth internally, or it may be a sign of a struggling company. A high dividend payout ratio may suggest few attractive investment opportunities.

dividend yield

Cash flow per share is the sum of after-tax profits and depreciation and other noncash expenses divided by the number of shares of common stock outstanding. The cash-flow-per-share figure reflects an important source of discretionary funds.

book value per share

Book value per share equals the company's net worth (after subtracting that attributable to preferred shareholders) divided by the number of shares of common stock outstanding. The per-share book value is typically compared with the current stock price. A high book value relative to the stock's price may indicate either unrecognized potential or overvalued assets. Railroad book values, for example, are often many times the market price of the stock. Unless the assets can be sold for close to their book values, however, the railroads' modest profit rates justify their low stock prices. For most companies, the per-share book value is a much lower than the price of the stock. In other words, most firms are worth more than just the combined value of their assets. Book value is based on historical costs and generally fails to take into account the impact of inflation. It also ignores intangible assets such as the quality of R&D that the firm is currently undertaking or the value of well-trained and highly motivated employees.

Other Ratios

- Earnings per share (EPS): (Net income after taxes – preferred dividends)/ number of shares
- Price-earnings (P/E): Price per share/expected EPS
- Dividend yield: Indicated annual dividend/price per share
- Dividend payout: Dividends per share/EPS
- Cash flow per share: (After-tax profits + depreciation and other noncash expenses)/number of shares
- Book value per share: Net worth attributable to common shareholders/number of shares

---

Sources of Ratios. A company's ratios are most effectively analyzed by comparing them with those of similar companies. Thus, averages of industrywide ratios are helpful. Robert Morris Associates collects data and computes ratios for a large group of industries. Other sources include Dun & Bradstreet and Standard & Poor's. Individual industry ratios may be computed with appropriate data from several similar companies. It is also important to evaluate trends in financial ratios over time, in order to see whether a company's financial condition is improving or deteriorating.

Example: To see how important the source of a company's past financial results and trends are, consider the following companies. Each company has a 5-year per-share earnings growth of about 10 percent. Firm A's sales and profits have grown proportionately, while its assets have remained nearly constant. Firm B's debt has increased from 10 percent to 40 percent of its assets. Firm C's profit margin has increased from 10 percent to 16 percent. Firm D's assets, sales, and profits have all grown proportionately.

Firm A (little asset growth)

	1994	1999
Assets	$10,000,000	$11,000,000
Liabilities	3,000000	3,000,000
Sales	30,000,000	50,000,000
Profits	3,000,000	5,000,000
Earnings per share	$1.00	$1.67

Firm B (increased debt)

	1994	1999
Assets	$10,000,000	$17,000,000
Liabilities	1,000,000	7,000,000
Sales	30,000,000	50,000,000
Profits	3,000,000	5,000,000
Earnings per share	$1.00	$1.67

Firm C (increased margin)

	1994	1999
Assets	10,000,000	10,000,000
Liabilities	3,000,000	3,000,000
Sales	30,000,000	30,000,000
Profits	3,000,000	5,000,000
Earnings per share	$1.00	$1.67

Firm D (balanced growth)

Assets	10,000,000	17,000,000
Liabilities	3,000,000	5,000,000
Sales	30,000,000	51,000,000
Profits	3,000,000	5,000,000
Earnings per share	$1.00	$1.67

Clearly, the profits of these companies have grown for different reasons. Increased capacity utilization accounts for most of firm A's profit growth. Eventually, existing capacity will be fully utilized. Once that point is reached, expanding capacity further would increase fixed costs. Profit growth would suffer in the process, especially if inflation drives up the cost of expansion.

Firm B's profit rise is largely due to increased use of leverage. A further increase in the debt ratio would probably raise both the cost of borrowed funds and the risk to the stockholders. Thus, a sale of additional equity may be required for continued growth. Such a sale would dilute the ownership position of existing shareholders.

Firm C has either raised prices or reduced its costs. In either case, opportunities for additional profit increases are probably limited. Increasing prices may encourage customers to make their purchases from the firm's competitors; further cost cutting could reduce quality or increase future costs.

Firm D may well continue its growth at the same rate and in the same manner as in the past. Although other factors could intervene, at least the past growth rate has been balanced and is therefore potentially sustainable.

A Specific Approach to Company Analysis

The same basic approach that was explored in the discussion of economic and industry analysis can be applied to individual companies. That is, the investor can direct his or her analysis toward forecasting a company's earnings and its P/E ratio. The product of these forecasts is then a prediction of its stock price. These forecasts should be based on an understanding of the company's competitive position, management quality, and financial soundness, as discussed above.

Various approaches can be used to forecast the company's P/E. One method examines the historical relationship between the company and market P/Es. The forecasted change in the market P/E can then be applied to the current company P/E value.

A second P/E estimate can be obtained by using the predicted change in the industry P/E. Finally, equation 9-2, PE = p/(k – g), can, with appropriate inputs, be used to derive a prediction for the company's P/E. That is, values for payout p, required return k, and expected growth g can be estimated and applied to the equation to generate the forecast. Estimated values for these factors can be derived both from the industry estimates and from an analysis of the specifics of the company.

Keep in mind that this is only an approximation because it assumes that the company's dividend payout ratio, growth rate, and required rate of return remain constant over time.

The forecasted P/E is then multiplied by the per-share earnings forecast. The result of this process is a forecast for the company's stock price. Several of these forecasts can be obtained by using the different earnings and P/E forecasts. Comparing the current price of the stock with the forecasts should indicate whether the stock is appropriately priced. A low current-to-forecast price suggests a buy; a high current-to-forecast price suggests a sale or a decision not to purchase.

Approaches to Forecast the Company's P/E

- Utilize the historical relation between the company and market P/Es. Then apply the forecasted change in the market P/E to the current company P/E value.
- Apply the predicted change in the industry P/E to the current company P/E.
- Use the P/E equation (equation 9-2) to derive a prediction for the company's P/E.

To summarize, one logical approach to forecasting the average level of a company's stock prices is to forecast its earnings and P/E multiple and take the product of the result.

Relationship of a Firm's Fundamental Position to Its Market Price

Stock prices usually reflect the company's economic and industry environment, competitive position, management quality, and financial strength. A company with a strong balance sheet, market position, profit potential, and management team operating in an industry with bright growth prospects is therefore likely to be fully priced—and may even be overpriced. A weaker company, in contrast, may be underpriced if its prospects are viewed too negatively. Accordingly, stock prices should always be evaluated in relative terms.

FUNDAMENTAL ANALYSIS VERSUS MARKET EFFICIENCY

If markets are relatively efficient (semistrong form), the (known) fundamental strengths and weaknesses of companies are already accurately reflected in their market prices. Under these circumstances, it could be argued that fundamental analysis would be a waste of time. On the other hand, if the market sometimes (or frequently) misvalues securities vis-à-vis the available public information, fundamental analysis may be worthwhile. Although the degree of market efficiency is a controversial topic, whatever level is achieved occurs because some important market participants, such as brokerage firms and other investment houses, analyze fundamentals. In other words, fundamental analysts tend to make markets more efficient than they would otherwise be. Indeed, many investors (both large and small) devote considerable amounts of time and money to undertake or buy such research. Moreover, several firms (for example, IBES International) regularly publish consensus estimates of earnings by industry analysts. When these consensus estimates are not met, the market reacts quickly to raise or lower stock prices, depending on the direction of the surprise.

Fundamental analysts believe that, at any given time, there is a basic intrinsic value for the overall stock market, various industries, and individual securities, and that these values depend on underlying economic factors. Thus, fundamental analysis can help to determine the intrinsic value of an investment asset at a point in time by examining the variables that appear to determine value, such as current and expected earnings, interest rates, and risk variables. Fundamental analysts believe that occasionally the market price of a security and intrinsic value differ, but eventually investors recognize the discrepancy and correct it. Therefore, if investors can do a good job of estimating intrinsic value based on fundamental analysis, they can make superior market timing or allocation decisions and acquire undervalued securities, thus generating above-average returns.

earnings surprise

A study by H. Russell Foger (1993) showed that the crucial difference between stocks that enjoyed best versus worst price performance during given years was the relationship between expected earnings estimates of professional analysts and the firm's actual earnings (*earnings surprise*). He found that stock prices increased if actual earnings exceeded expected earnings (positive earnings surprises), and they fell if earnings did not reach expected levels (negative earnings surprises). Thus, if investors or analysts can do a superior job of projecting earnings and their expectations differ from the consensus, then they will probably have a superior investment record.[3]

In analyzing the possible superior returns to performing fundamental analysis, it is important to consider the costs as well as the benefits. Obtaining the information necessary to forecast a company's future sales, profits, and dividends is both costly and time consuming. Even if an investor "beats the market" by performing a detailed fundamental analysis, it might be worthwhile to ask how much time and expense were devoted to that analysis and how much that individual could have earned during that time. It might also be worthwhile to ask whether one's methods of analysis result in *consistently* superior returns or whether there have been only a few exceptionally good, perhaps lucky, investments.

Although a full-blown analysis of the economy, industry, and firm may be useful at times, most investors are unable to undertake such an effort. Even those with the necessary time, skills, and resources require operational approaches that allow them to winnow down their lists to a workable number of prospects. Thus, shortcuts are needed to allow the analyst to identify potentially attractive investments on a first-pass basis. That is, investors need

screening

methods for *screening* a long list of stocks and selecting those that deserve closer scrutiny. Based on the narrowed-down list, investors may then undertake more detailed analysis. Let us now consider how to select securities to analyze.

SCREENING TECHNIQUES

Lists of stocks that have something unusual in common appear regularly in *Forbes*. The discussion that accompanies the lists generally implies that an appreciable number of the listings are undervalued or otherwise attractive. For example, *Forbes* lists firms that sell for a small fraction of the potential values of their underlying assets. The criteria vary over time, but they always include firms that are underpriced relative to their tangible assets.

Most *Forbes* issues contain at least one list of interesting stocks. Examples include stocks with low P/Es and high growth rates, former institutional favorites, companies with dividend reinvestment plans, companies that are expected to emerge from bankruptcy with big profit potentials, potential growth companies, stocks disliked by the experts, cash-rich and cash-poor companies, high-yield utilities, stocks that *Forbes* analysts expect to show substantial earnings increases, and emerging growth companies in a difficult market environment.

Similarly, *Value Line,* using its own analytical techniques, compiles weekly lists for various categories. Some of these categories include

- timely stocks I (ranked #1 for next 12-month performance)
- timely stocks II (ranked #2 for next 12-month performance)
- conservative stocks I (ranked #1 for safety)
- conservative stocks II (ranked #2 for safety)
- high-yield stocks (estimated year-ahead dividends)
- high 3-to 5-year appreciation potential
- biggest free cash-flow generators
- widest discount from book value
- lowest P/E
- highest P/E
- stocks trading at a discount from their liquidation values

Low-P/E Stocks versus Growth Stocks

growth stocks

Many lists are based on one of two concepts: P/E and growth. Indeed, investment analysts have long debated the relative merits of low-P/E versus *growth stocks*. A firm whose profits are expected to grow rapidly will command a high price relative to its current earnings. One with less bright prospects will generally have a lower P/E. The P/E ratio equation illustrates the relation between the P/E and expected growth:

$$PE = \frac{p}{(k - g)} \qquad \text{(Equation 9-2 repeated)}$$

Clearly, P/Es should differ with the firms' prospects (dividend payout ratio, risk, and expected growth).

No one argues with the arithmetic. High growth expectations do justify higher P/Es than lower growth expectations do. The debate over low-P/E versus growth stock centers on how well the market prices securities relative to their actual potentials. According to such well-known fundamental analysts as Benjamin Graham and John Templeton, the market frequently goes to extremes. These two suggested that the market tends to overestimate the growth prospects and underestimate the risks of some stocks (especially the highly touted growth stocks). As a result, the market accords them higher P/Es than their fundamentals warrant. The stocks of less exciting companies, in contrast, may be viewed by the market as having less attractive prospects than they actually do. Stocks that the market views too pessimistically would then end up with unrealistically low P/Es. Once the market realizes the true

low-P/E stocks

potentials of these stocks, the prices of *low-P/E stocks* should rise at a faster rate than the market averages, whereas the high-P/E stocks should do less well. Those who accept this line of reasoning prefer a portfolio that is heavily weighted toward low-P/E stocks and largely avoid stocks with high P/Es.

Growth-stock advocates, in contrast, have contended that stocks with rapid growth potentials are attractive investments even at relatively high prices. A high current P/E may not seem overpriced relative to future earnings, whereas low P/Es may accurately reflect poor potentials. The two views (low-P/E and growth stock) have alternated in popularity.

A best selling book of 1999 titled *Dow 36,000,* by James Glassman and Kevin Hasset, maintains that the Dow Jones Industrial Average (DJIA) was undervalued at about 10,500. Observing the total returns to a portfolio of stocks held for the previous 20 years, the authors contend that a portfolio of all stocks was no more risky than holding bonds. Therefore, they argue that stocks should be priced so that their expected return equals that of bonds. In calculating what they call a perfectly reasonable price for stocks, the authors begin with a 30-year Treasury bond that yields 5.5 percent. Interest on the bond would not grow, they note, while stock dividends tend to rise over time. Given that advantage, the authors calculate what stocks should initially yield to match the return on bonds. To match a bond yielding 5.5 percent, they say, an investor would need the initial dividend yield on stocks and the annual growth rate of the stock dividend to add up to the same as the 30-year bond—or 5.5 percent. Actual dividend yield on stocks has varied over time, but estimates indicate that it should average 5 percent a year. Therefore, the authors assert, to match the future return on bonds, stocks initially need to yield just 0.5 percent, which would place the equilibrium value of the DJIA at about 36,000.[4]

Of course, this claim is based on very questionable assumptions, primarily that stocks and bonds are equally risky. Jeremy Siegel, upon whose original research Glassman and Hasset based their model, contends that his data do not lead to their conclusions. "They are under the assumption," Siegel states, " that those people who have 20- or 30-year time horizons will totally dominate the equity markets and will continue to have faith in their long-run performance, despite poor and possibly disastrous intervening years."[5] Siegel further points out that the Glassman-Hassett model does not handle the possibility of a change in the Dow's forecasted value well. For example, suppose that investors do bid up the DJIA to 36,000 so that stocks offer the same expected return as a 5.5 percent 30-year Treasury bond, but that interest rates rise to 6.5 percent. To match this higher return, stocks would have to yield 1.5 percent. To get to that level, share prices would have to plunge 67 percent. At that point, those who had thought that stock's risk was equal to that of 30-year Treasuries would have to revise their views.

This indicates that the Glassman-Hassett model is extremely sensitive to changes in the inputs, especially interest-rate fluctuations.

Advocates of growth stocks recommend investments in companies with outstanding past records and/or growth potentials. They do not generally seek out stocks with high multiples but are quite prepared to pay a high price (relative to current earnings) when strong future growth is anticipated. Their arithmetic can appear quite persuasive. Earnings that grow at 20 percent will double in approximately 4 years. Should the multiple remain constant, the price will also double over the same 4-year period—but multiples must be justified by *long-term* growth prospects relative to the appropriate discount rate, which is related to the riskiness of the firm.

The companies that tend to grow the fastest are relatively young companies and companies whose products are new or who are in the process of developing new technologies. Yet these are also the companies that tend to be quite risky. While a fair number of new companies may grow at a rate of 20 percent or more during their first few years of existence, a sizable number also go bankrupt. Thus, the same companies that are potentially high-growth companies are also high-risk companies.

Furthermore, very high rates of growth are not sustainable over the long haul. Although it may not be too unusual for a company to grow at 20 percent or more during its first few years of existence, it is unrealistic to expect that rate of growth to persist. As businesses mature, their rate of growth tends to level off. On average, businesses tend to grow at the same rate as the overall economy.

Therefore, while it makes sense for growth stock to have higher P/E multiples than other stock, these multiples should be based on realistic assumptions about the firm's long-term growth prospects. If a P/E ratio appears to be based on the assumption that a new company's high growth rate will persist indefinitely, it seems logical to conclude that the stock is overvalued.

Much of the fluctuation in stock prices reflects a change in the consensus P/E ratio. The change in P/E ratio, in turn, reflects changing views within the market regarding the firm's growth potential. Let us therefore examine more closely just how much differing growth expectations can affect P/E ratios. The following example focuses on the impact of growth.

Example: Assume the payout ratio p is .5 and the appropriate discount rate is 12 percent for both the stock market and individual stocks. An economy-wide, long-term growth rate of 7 percent (3 percent real and 4 percent inflation) would produce an average P/E of 0.5/(.12 − .07) = 10. If a particular company's g is 8 percent, its P/E would be

12.5. A g of 9 percent would produce a P/E of 16.7, while a g of 10 percent would imply a P/E of 25. If g is as high as 11 percent, the P/E would rise to 50.

As the example shows, relatively small changes in the expected long-term growth rate g can have a dramatic impact on the P/E ratio. This impact is particularly great when the P/E is already relatively large. A more realistic example would take account of the tendency for higher values of g to correspond to lower payouts and greater risk premiums (and thus higher discount rates). In his extensive research on security valuation approaches, Aswath Damodaran discusses a number of problems associated with uses of P/E ratios, noting that the volatility of earnings can cause the P/E ratio to change dramatically from period to period.[6]

Advocates of low-P/E stocks note that stock prices rise dramatically when both earnings and multiples increase. Quite possibly, a multiple may more easily increase from 5 to 10 than from 10 to 20 and will have an easier time growing from 10 to 20 than from 20 to 40. That is, the market may well become more nervous about the price of a stock as its P/E rises. Thus, low-P/E stocks may have a better chance of achieving truly outstanding performances than high-P/E stocks, which may be more likely to be fully priced already.

Example:	Suppose a company that sells initially at a P/E of 5 experiences per-share earnings growth of 20 percent per year for 10 years. Its earnings will be six times as high as when it started. Such an earnings growth is likely to lead to an increase in the P/E multiple. Rapid past growth often leads to expectations of rapid future growth. If the P/E of this company doubles, its stock will sell for more than 12 times its earlier price.

The advocates of low-multiple stocks further contend that high-multiple stocks are particularly vulnerable to disappointing news.

Example:	Suppose a growth stock currently earns $2 per share and sells for $50 (P/E of 25). If the following year, it earns only $1.50, a continuation of its P/E of 25 would correspond to a price of $37.50. On the other hand, if the poor earnings led to lower growth expectations and a lower P/E, the price decline would be much steeper. Thus, for example, a fall to a P/E of 10 would imply a price of $15, or a decline of 70 percent.

Clearly, disappointing earnings can severely wound a stock that had sold for a high multiple. In general, the higher the P/E multiple, the greater the impact of an unexpected change in earnings, especially if the change is accompanied by a change in expectations of future growth.

Value Investing

value investing

growth investing

For the period 1975 through year-end 1995, *value investing* (investing in below-average P/E stocks) as measured by the S&P/Barra indices led *growth investing* (investing in above-average P/E stocks) as measured by average annual return. The term value investing refers to Benjamin Graham's philosophy of investing in companies with hard assets whose stock prices are relatively cheap. The average annual return for value investing came to 16.5 percent, compared to 14.0 percent for growth investing. In the latter 1990s, however, the trend shifted, and since 1995, growth stocks moved ahead of value stocks, with a 29.9 percent average annual return versus 25.9 percent for value stocks for the period 1995–1999.

One explanation for value investing's lagging performance is that the payoffs from these two investment disciplines tend to move in opposite directions as investor sentiment shifts. That is, in some years, value investing is the preferred style, while in other years, growth investing is preferred.

Another more profound reason for value stocks' underperformance in recent years is the dramatic changes that have occurred in the U.S. economy. The economy is no longer driven by manufacturing and so-called smokestack industries but by rapidly changing innovations in technology and services. In this type of economy, the big winners are not the manufacturing-type firms such as General Motors, but those that are at the forefront of innovation and implementation of the new technology, such as Microsoft. Of course, not every firm that seeks to implement a new technology becomes a Microsoft. While innovative technology-intensive firms can become big winners, there have been big losers too. Over the past 15–20 years, a number of firms that have sought to implement and develop new technologies have gone bankrupt in the process.

Combining P/E Ratios with Other Factors

Although much of the evidence suggests that low-P/E stocks tend to be underpriced, a more basic relationship may be at work. For example, a disproportionate number of low-P/E stocks may be the issues of relatively small companies.

Firm Size

Suppose that the stocks of relatively small companies tend to outperform the market. Size, not P/E, might then be the true factor to explain the apparent effect of a low P/E. Indeed, Reinganum found that portfolios selected on both P/E and firm size tended to generate abnormal returns (above the risk-adjusted market level). The P/E effect largely disappeared, however, when size was controlled.[7] Other studies found similar results.

The studies hypothesized that the small firm effect was due to a misspecification of the CAPM because CAPM formed the basis for adjusting returns for risk. The positive abnormal returns may simply have been a reward for the extra effort of analyzing small firms (the basis of the "neglected firms" hypothesis discussed below). The apparent abnormal returns may have been due to underestimating their risks, or due to lower trading activity (a measure of marketability). Still other researchers reported that the magnitude of the small firm effect was reduced but could not be fully explained away when adjustments were made for the impacts of risk premium, tax effects, benchmark error, incorrect assumptions about investor risk aversion, nonsynchronous trading, or earnings yield.

analyst neglect (neglected-firm effect)

Analyst Neglect (Neglected-Firm Effect)

The abnormal returns of small firms could be due to either (1) superior performance relative to their fundamentals (current profitability, apparent growth potential, and so on) or (2) underpricing relative to those fundamentals.

Most institutional investors prefer to invest in large firms. They can make meaningful investments in large firms without having an undue effect on the companies' stock prices. Similarly, analysts tend to concentrate on larger firms and therefore draw attention to such stocks. Several studies have found that stocks that analysts ignore (whether large or small) tend to outperform the more closely followed issues. Accordingly, a number of mutual funds have sought to exploit this small firm/neglected-firm effect by assembling portfolios of these companies. Another factor that may be at work is referred to as the low-price effect.

The Low-Price Effect

low-price effect

The results of several studies imply that stocks with low per-share prices tend to generate returns above the market averages. Moreover, this *low-price effect* may well be stronger than both the P/E and the size effects. Exactly why low-priced stocks seem to perform so well is subject to much debate. There are three rationales offered to support this phenomenon. The first is that low-priced stocks are generally believed to be more risky than the average stock. Thus, their higher average return may reflect greater risk. Still, the returns of these stocks continue to be higher when standard risk adjustment procedures are applied. Perhaps low-priced stocks are even more risky than their estimated betas imply. In particular, they may contain a substantially greater amount of nonmarket, and thus diversifiable, risk. We have already seen that, capital market theory notwithstanding, nonmarket risk is generally accorded a premium. That is, stocks with high levels of nonmarket risks are priced to offer higher expected returns than otherwise similar stocks with lower levels of nonmarket risk.

Furthermore, the market-determined risk premium is a function of perceived risk. If investors collectively believe that, all else being equal, low-priced stocks are riskier than higher-priced stocks, then their risk premium and required rate of return will reflect that belief.

The second rationale is that low-priced stocks are also more expensive to trade. The bid-ask spread of low-priced stocks tends to be relatively high. Stocks that are more expensive to trade probably need to offer higher expected returns to attract investors. In addition, the market for low-priced stock may be thinner, so low-priced stock will be less liquid than higher-priced stock.

The third reason is the general aversion of many investors, especially institutional investors, to low capitalization and low-priced shares. The perceived quality of a stock is thought to be associated with the level of its per-share price. If many investors shun a significant segment of the stock market, that group of stocks may tend to be underpriced. The financial performance of some of the group may eventually lead them to achieve quality status and institutional acceptance.

Research by Fama and French in 1995 found that stocks of small firms and those with high book-to-market ratios provided above average return. They point out, however, that there was evidence that there may be risk factors left out of the simple capital asset pricing model. Fama and French suggest a three-factor model in which the expected return on a stock depends on its exposure to the market risk, size, and book-to-market value.[8] Thus, various models of risk and return have their advocates, but most financial economists continue to agree on two basic ideas: (1) Investors require a higher expected return for taking on risk, and (2) they appear to be concerned predominantly with market risk that cannot be eliminated through diversification.

Takeover Candidates

Buying a stock just before it becomes an acquisition target is one of the few ways of making a quick profit in the stock market. Acquiring firms almost always offer a substantial premium over the preannouncement price of the target firm. Moreover, takeover candidates are sometimes bid up in a competition between would-be owners. At times, stock market activity tends to focus on the possibility of a takeover. In the 1980s a number of investors **raiders** (often called *raiders*) became well known for their records of attempted takeovers. Only a relatively small fraction, however, of takeover attempts actually succeed in wresting control from the existing management. **greenmail** Sometimes the target firm buys back the raider's stock at a premium *(greenmail)* over the market price. At other times, another buyer is brought into the picture by management (the white knight), or another raider eventually outbids the initial raider. At still other times, a friendly outsider (the white squire) is sold a substantial minority position. Occasionally, the target tries to acquire the raider company (the Pac Man defense).

Regardless of the buyer (white knight, target company, or another raider), the initial raider usually sells out at a profit. At still other times, the initial raider succeeds in taking control. At that point, it may do one of several things. It may, for example, seek to restructure the company in order to extract value for itself and the other shareholders. Such restructurings usually increase the firm's debt and use the borrowed funds to buy out the public shareholders. This is known as a leveraged buyout, or LBO for short. In other instances, all shareholders may be paid a substantial sum per share (partial liquidating dividend). Once in control, the raider may seek to sell the firm off a piece at a time or as a package. Sometimes selling off unprofitable divisions can make the remainder of the business more profitable, so shareholders' wealth is increased by these divestitures. In some circumstances, the raider may settle in and run the acquisition as a going concern.

Another group of investors called risk arbitrageurs looks to profit from potential and attempted takeovers. They assess the current stock price relative to the proposed or expected terms of the takeover and the likelihood of a successful acquisition. Depending on that assessment, they may purchase shares of the target firm in hopes of selling later at a profit.

Implications of Takeover Trading for Individual Investors

Several studies bear on the activities of raiders and risk arbitrageurs. One study found that, when a firm acquired enough stock (5 percent or more) to file a Schedule 13D, the target's price generally rose, probably in anticipation of a takeover attempt. Schedule 13D, which is required by the SEC, discloses beneficial ownership of certain registered equity securities. Any person or group that acquires beneficial ownership of more than 5 percent of a class of registered equity securities must file a Schedule 13D, reporting the acquisition, together with other information, within 10 days after the acquisition. Furthermore, the market price of the stock of a target firm acts as a rather accurate predictor of the probability that the takeover attempt will succeed. Thus, the activity of risk arbitrageurs generally drives the stock price toward the terms of a takeover that is likely to go through but not toward the terms of one that is likely to fail. Risk arbitrageurs are able to obtain useful information on the probability of a successful takeover and then to earn substantial returns by trading on that information. Such traders not only make profits on their own investments but also generally enhance the wealth of the other shareholders in the firms that they target by driving up the price of the stock.

Managerial Objectives and the Agency Problem

Corporate managers are shareholders' agents and are paid to make decisions that maximize shareholder wealth. Sometimes, however, managers have their own agendas, and they make decisions that serve their own personal interests, rather than those of shareholders. This conflict of interest, called the principal-agent conflict or the *agency problem*, arises from the disparity between the goals of corporate managers and shareholders.

agency problem

The agency problem can take rather blatant forms, such as shirking, diverting corporate funds to personal uses, or awarding contracts and hiring on the basis of personal friendship, rather than seeking out those who are best qualified. It can also take somewhat subtle forms, such as investing in projects that enhance the manager's reputation, rather than those that maximize shareholder wealth. Managers may make investment decisions that entrench their position, even though this may not be the best possible use to make of corporate funds. Managers may also take steps to block corporate takeovers in order to protect their jobs, even though stockholders often benefit when a company is taken over.

Managers' bonuses are often tied to net income, which is the proverbial "bottom line." Therefore, corporate managers may have an incentive to take actions that will make a company look good on paper, even when those actions do not actually maximize shareholder wealth.

Underinvestment in research and development may be a form of the agency problem. R&D investment results in benefits to shareholders, especially in industries that are technology intensive. However, in the short run, R&D investment results in expenses, and therefore lower profits, while the benefits may not be realized until years later. To the extent that managers are concerned primarily with short-term results, there will be a tendency to underinvest in research and development.

Graber (1997) found a positive correlation between length of CEOs' stay with the firm and R&D investment, which is especially pronounced in relatively small companies in technology-intensive industries, such as pharmaceuticals and computers.[9]

There are several market mechanisms that tend to restrict corporate managers' discretionary behavior. Internal incentives to promote shareholders' wealth maximization include stock options/ownership by managers. External factors that encourage maximizing shareholder value include potential takeover bids, outright mergers, and institutional investors' voting or trading in the company's stock.

William Baumol's classic 1967 study contended that managerial salaries and prestige are more closely related to sales than to profits, and managers might therefore sacrifice income for growth.[10] Thus, managers have an incentive for excessive sales promotion and setting low margins. Organizational slack is another potential problem. When not under competitive pressure, firms may allow costs to increase and overall efficiency to decline. Moreover, managers may use the corporation to promote their own social and political goals. Some social and political activity may improve the firm's public image or legal climate, but other actions may reflect the manager's own particular preferences. Also, it is often the individual CEO who receives the public recognition when a company makes a conspicuous contribution to a highly visible charity. It could be argued that the CEO is buying prestige with other people's money.

Even if managers' personal investments in their firms influence their behavior, the potential for conflicting or independent interest exists. Particularly blatant types of abuse include corporate officials who overpay themselves, trade on inside information, dispose of corporate assets at bargain prices to friends or relatives, and favor certain suppliers.

The relevant evidence on the agency problem may be summarized as follows: Managers often substitute their own interests for those of the stockholders. Thus, firms managed in the interest of stockholders generally tend to outperform firms managed by self-serving managers. Finding a direct link between stock market performance and manager orientation has been difficult, however, because manager motivation is not something that can be directly observed or quantified.

How can an investor avoid investing in firms in which managers put their own well-being above that of shareholders? It is easier said than done, because no corporate manager is going to advertise the fact that he or she is not concerned with maximizing shareholder wealth. But there are observable clues that an astute investor can use. In general, when managers own a substantial amount of stock in a company, they are shareholders as well as managers, so they are more likely to take a personal interest in maximizing the value of the company's stock.

Another clue might be the turnover rate among senior management. (High employee turnover in general might be a warning sign. Although employee turnover is not publicly available information, firms are required to disclose the names of their top managers in their annual reports, so turnover from year to year can be detected.) A firm with high management turnover is likely to have a short-term orientation, since managers are unlikely to be concerned with the firm's well-being after their expected departure.

Encouraging a shift toward stockholder orientation is clearly in shareholders' interests. Accordingly, shareholders might consider voting for the dissidents in a proxy fight. A large pro-dissident vote is likely to make existing management more stockholder oriented. Asking pointed questions of managers either by letter or at annual meetings may also signal potential stockholder dissatisfaction. Finally, a thwarted takeover bid or a new compensation scheme that ties salaries more closely to profits or stock performance may favorably affect managerial goals.

Characteristics of Possibly Undervalued Securities

- Low P/E
- Small capitalization
- Neglect by investment analysts
- Low per-share price
- Unrecognized takeover candidates
- Stockholder (as opposed to managerial) orientation

INTEGRATED APPROACHES TO FUNDAMENTAL ANALYSIS

Graham's Approach

Benjamin Graham coauthored the investment text that dominated the market from the 1930s to the 1950s, and he was a frequently quoted authority on investments. Graham advocated investment in financially strong companies with low prices relative to their underlying values. In the last years of his life (he died in 1976), Graham and Dr. James B. Rea listed a set of 10 simple criteria for identifying undervalued stocks.[11] These criteria can be grouped into three categories: low price, strong finances, and growing earnings. Specifically, Graham and Rea suggested selecting securities with the following:

1. an earnings-to-price yield of at least twice the AAA bond yield. Thus, if AAA bonds yield 10 percent, EPS should equal at least 20 percent of the stock's price (P/E of 5 or less)
2. a P/E ratio no higher than 40 percent of its 5-year high
3. a dividend yield of at least two-thirds of the AAA bond yield
4. a stock price below two-thirds of tangible per-share book value
5. a stock price less than two-thirds of net quick liquidation value (current assets less total debt)
6. total debt less than tangible book value
7. current ratio of two or more
8. total debt no greater than twice the net liquidation value
9. compound 10-year annual earnings growth of at least 7 percent
10. two or fewer annual earnings declines of 5 percent or more in the preceding 10 years

Very few stocks ever meet all of these criteria. Those qualifying in seven or more are said to have a high reward-to-risk ratio. Graham and Rea particularly stressed criteria 1, 3, 5, and 6 (a stock price that is low relative to earnings, dividends, and book value, as well as debt that is low relative to book value). They contended that individual high reward-to-risk stocks may not necessarily perform well, but a diversified group of 30 or so such securities should produce handsome returns.

Graham and Rea also suggested that investors should sell a stock whenever any of the following occurred:

- It had appreciated by 50 percent or more.
- It had been held for more than 2 years.
- Its dividend was eliminated.
- Its earnings dropped sufficiently to make it overpriced by 50 percent or more relative to criterion 1 above (too high a P/E ratio).

On the other hand, a stock that an investor would buy on the basis of the original criteria should be held. Little or no research (other than that implicit in Rea's own work) supports the value of these selling rules, however.

Templeton's Approach

If results are any indication of the value of an investment strategy, John Templeton's growth fund deserves careful scrutiny. Unlike Graham and Rea, however, Templeton did not reduce his approach to a series of simple rules. Still, its major elements may be established from the published record, as summarized below:

- a world view to investing. U.S. stocks are only one component. At any one time, stocks are cheaper in some countries than in others.
- a low price relative to current earnings, asset values, and dividend yields (like Graham and a host of others)
- extensive diversification with risky stocks to produce an acceptable portfolio risk (unlike Graham's approach)
- selling when the market is particularly optimistic and buying when it is particularly pessimistic
- assessing emerging socioeconomic trends and their likely investment impact. For example, back in 1977, Templeton saw a growing economic role for government with an especially adverse impact on the visible and, therefore, more vulnerable large firms. Similarly, he saw continued high inflation rates and thus advocated investments in which the returns are most likely to move up with the price level.

Like Graham, Templeton sought conservatively priced stocks that were out of favor. In addition, he tried to assess the future. Would the country offer a favorable investment climate? Would the company be well situated for forthcoming economic trends? Compared to Graham, Templeton was less concerned with the risks of individual companies but focused on the risk-expected return characteristics of the entire portfolio.

SUMMARY AND CONCLUSIONS

This chapter explores traditional approaches to macroeconomic, industry, and company analysis, considering both general and specific approaches. Industries exhibit very different performances, but selecting those with the best prospects is quite difficult. Evaluating the industry's stage in the life cycle may offer some help. Company analysis involves assessing a company's relative strengths and weaknesses within its industry(ies). Management quality, which is another important company characteristic, is especially difficult to judge.

Financial statement analysis utilizes a variety of different types of ratios. Liquidity ratios reflect short-run strengths and weaknesses. Debt ratios relate to a company's longer-run prospects and riskiness. Profitability and efficiency ratios reflect current operating effectiveness with an eye toward the future. Various other ratios such as earnings per share, P/E, cash flow per share, dividend payout, and book value per share may be used to provide additional insights.

When evaluating financial ratios, it is important to look for trends. The changes in financial ratios over time can often convey more information than the absolute value of the ratios themselves. In addition, a company's financial ratios should be compared with those of other firms in its industry. It can be valuable to determine how a firm's liquidity, leverage, profitability, and efficiency ratios compare with those of its competitors.

Although assessing industry and company strengths and weaknesses is one way to search for attractive investments, this approach is useful only if the analysis uncovers overlooked values.

Investment analysts have suggested a wide array of fundamental approaches. *Forbes* lists offer one useful starting point. Low-P/E stocks may tend to be undervalued, and small firms that investment analysts ignore may be a good bet to outperform the market on a risk-adjusted basis. Low per-share price may also be a useful criterion. An unrecognized takeover candidate could handsomely reward a timely purchase. In certain circumstances, knowledge of managers' ability and orientation may help investors. Management ownership of a sizable percentage of the firm's stock may indicate that managers are concerned with the company's long-term well-being. The final fundamental approaches that are discussed in this chapter are the integrated methods of Graham and Templeton. The available—admittedly limited—evidence seems to support their methods' usefulness.

CHAPTER REVIEW

Answers to the review questions and the self-test questions start on page 501.

Key Terms

macroeconomic analysis	times-interest-earned ratio
balance sheet	return on equity (ROE)
income statement	return on assets (ROA)
statement of changes in financial position	net profit margin (NPM)
ratio analysis	asset turnover
liquidity ratios	equity multiplier
current ratio	Dupont formula
current assets	dividend yield
current liabilities	book value per share
quick ratio	earnings surprise
acid test ratio	screening
inventory turnover ratio	growth stocks
debt-equity ratio	low-P/E stocks
	value investing

growth investing   raiders

analyst neglect (neglected-firm   greenmail

  effect)   agency problem

low-price effect

Review Questions

9-1. Explain how economic analysis can be used to forecast the market's performance.

9-2. Assume that the market's dividend payout ratio is .50, the required rate of return is 13 percent, and the expected growth rate is 9 percent.
   a. Compute the market P/E (price-earnings ratio).
   b. What would happen to the market P/E if the payout ratio fell to .45 and all else remained unchanged?
   c. What would happen to the market P/E if the growth rate increased by 2 percent and everything else remained unchanged? Is such a change at all likely? Why or why not?
   d. What would happen if the required rate of return declined to 10 percent and everything else remained unchanged? Is such a change at all likely? Why or why not?

9-3. Explain how economic analysis can be used to forecast the industry's performance.

9-4. Explain how economic analysis can be used to forecast a company's performance.

9-5. Discuss the impact of a company's competitive position on its investment attractiveness. Consider potential antitrust problems.

9-6. The Go Go Corporation currently has a payout of .2 and is accorded a risk premium of 3 percent above the market required rate of return of 15 percent. It currently sells for 35 with EPS of $1.25. What is the implied growth rate?

9-7. Discuss the role of management quality in investment analysis.

9-8. Briefly summarize the three principal types of accounting statements.

9-9. Using the balance sheet and income statement that follow, find the current ratio, quick (acid test) ratio, inventory turnover ratio, debt-equity ratio, net profit margin, asset turnover ratio, return on assets, equity multiplier, and return on equity for both the year ended January 2000 and the year ended January 2001.

Balance Sheet for Review Question 9-9 (Amounts in millions, except share data)		
	January 28, 2001	January 30, 2000
Assets		
Current Assets:		
Cash and Cash Equivalents	$ 167	$ 168
Short-Term Investments, including current maturities of long-term investments	10	2
Receivables, net	835	587
Merchandise Inventories	6,556	5,489
Other Current Assets	209	144
Total Current Assets	7,777	6,390
Property and Equipment, at cost:		
Land	4,230	3,248
Buildings	6,167	4,834
Furniture, Fixtures, and Equipment	2,877	2,279
Leasehold Improvements	665	493
Construction in Progress	1,032	791
Capital Leases	261	245
	15,232	11,890
Less Accumulated Depreciation and Amortization	2,164	1,663
Net Property and Equipment	13,068	10,227
Long-Term Investments	15	15
Notes Receivable	77	48
Cost in Excess of the Fair Value of Net Assets Acquired, net of accumulated amortization of $41 at January 28, 2001, and $33 at January 30, 2000	314	311
Other	134	90
	$21,385	$17,081
Liabilities and Stockholders' Equity		
Current Liabilities:		
Accounts Payable	$1,976	$1,993
Accrued Salaries and Related Expenses	627	541
Sales Taxes Payable	298	269
Other Accrued Expenses	1,402	763
Income Taxes Payable	78	61
Current Installments of Long-Term Debt	4	29
Total Current Liabilities	4,385	3,656
Long-Term Debt, excluding current installments	1,545	750
Other Long-Term Liabilities	245	237
Deferred Income Taxes	195	87
Minority Interest	11	10
Stockholders' Equity		
Common Stock, par value $0.05. Authorized: 10,000,000,000 shares; issued and outstanding—2,323,747,000 shares at January 28, 2001, and 2,304,317,000 shares at January 30, 2000	116	115
Paid-In capital	4,810	4,319
Retained Earnings	10,151	7,941
Accumulated Other Comprehensive Income	(67)	(27)
	15,010	12,348
Less Shares Purchased for Compensation Plans	6	7
Total Stockholders' Equity	15,004	12,341
	$21,385	$17,081

Statement of Earnings for Review Question 9-9 (Amounts in millions, except per-share data)			
	Fiscal Year Ended		
	January 28, 2001	January 30, 2000	January 31, 1999
Net Sales	$45,738	$38, 434	$30,219
Cost of Merchandise Sold	32,057	27,023	21,614
Gross Profit	13,681	11,411	8,605
Operating Expenses:			
Selling and Store Operating	8,513	6,819	5,332
Pre-Opening	142	113	88
General and Administrative	835	671	515
Total Operating Expenses	9,490	7,603	5,935
Operating Income	4,191	3,808	2,670
Interest Income (Expense):			
Interest and Investment Income	47	37	30
Interest Expense	(21)	(41)	(46)
Interest, net	26	(4)	(16)
Earnings Before Income Taxes	4,217	3,804	2,654
Income Taxes	1,636	1,484	1,040
Net Earnings	$2,581	$2,320	$1,614
Basic Earnings Per Share	$ 1.11	$ 1.03	$ 0.73
Weighted Average Number of Common Shares Outstanding	2,315	2,244	2,206
Diluted Earnings Per Share	$ 1.10	$ 1.00	$ 0.71
Weighted Average Number of Common Shares Outstanding, Assuming Dilution	2,352	2,342	2,320

9-10. The GRO Company has a P/E of 25 and EPS of $1.00. Asset Play has a P/E of 8 and EPS of $1.00.

   a. If in the next 5 years GRO's P/E falls to 20 while its EPS increases at 10 percent per year, what will its stock sell for?
   b. Similarly, if in the next 5 years Asset Play's P/E increases to 15 and its EPS grows at a 10 percent rate, what will its stock sell for?
   c. Ignoring the impacts of dividends, taxes, and commissions, what are the rates (HPR and annual) of return for investments in GRO and Asset Play?

9-11. Using the starting values given in question 9-10, assume that the EPS for both GRO and Asset Play has grown at a 5 percent rate (annual) for 5 years.
   a. If GRO's and Asset Play's P/Es fall to 12 and 6, respectively, what will the stocks sell for?
   b. Ignoring the impacts of dividends, taxes, and commissions, what are the rates of return for investments in GRO and Asset Play?

9-12. a. Using the starting values given in question 9-10, assume that GRO's payout and its appropriate discount rate are 13 percent. What is its expected growth rate?

  b. Suppose Asset Play's payout is .5 and appropriate discount rate is 12 percent. What is its implied expected growth rate?

9-13. Summarize the track record of investing in low-P/E stocks.

9-14. Discuss the small firm effect.

9-15. Summarize the neglected-firm and low-price effects.

9-16. Why would an investor want to be able to identify takeover candidates?

9-17. Apply the discounted cash flow approach to the following situation: The Cash Cow Corporation currently generates a net cash flow after all expenses of $3 million. This cash flow is expected to grow at a rate of 5 percent. If the appropriate discount rate is 12 percent, how much is Cash Cow worth?

9-18. In what ways may manager and stockholder goals differ? What is the relevance of these differences to investors?

9-19. How can investors seek firms in which the principal-agent conflict (agency problem) is minimized?

Self-Test Questions

T F 9-1. Profits tend to be less variable than the overall growth in the economy as measured by the GDP.

T F 9-2. Fewer assumptions are necessary to apply the earnings multiplier approach to a firm's valuation than are required to apply the dividend discount model approach.

T F 9-3. The earnings multiplier (or P/E approach) to valuation uses the estimated next year's earnings.

T F 9-4. One relationship that exists when using the dividend discount model to estimate the earnings per share (EPS) for valuation purposes is the higher the expected growth rate of dividends, the lower the estimated P/E.

T F 9-5. The P/E ratio approach to valuation is applicable to the total market as well as to industry and company analyses.

T F 9-6. If the growth estimate for the industry of a firm rises from 6 percent to 8 percent but the risk premium for the firm rises from 10 percent to 13 percent, the intrinsic value for the firm is likely to decline.

T F 9-7. P/E ratios used for the earnings multiplier model are sensitive to changes in the interest rate.

T F 9-8. The basic balance sheet equation is as follows: Assets + liabilities = net worth.

T   F   9-9.   The quick ratio is used to assess the capital structure of the firm's balance sheet.

T   F   9-10.   Raising the debt ratio will lower return on equity, all other things being equal.

T   F   9-11.   Fully diluted earnings per share are not affected by outstanding convertible debt.

T   F   9-12.   Fundamental analysis rests on the premise that a security has an intrinsic value that is based on the firm's underlying variables.

T   F   9-13.   The highest-P/E-ratio stocks listed on the New York Stock Exchange, when held for a long period of time, often underperform the S&P 500 Index.

T   F   9-14.   Analyst neglect arises mainly because some corporations do not publish their results.

T   F   9-15.   Takeovers and acquisitions usually benefit the stockholders of the acquired firm.

T   F   9-16.   The agency problem can be solved by paying corporate executives more.

T   F   9-17.   Graham and Rea's approach to fundamental analysis requires looking at more than three key factors.

T   F   9-18.   According to the semistrong form of the efficient market hypothesis, fundamental analysis should not consistently provide superior returns for an investor.

T   F   9-19.   While Graham's approach provides specific quantitative criteria for evaluating stock, Templeton's approach deals more in general principles for assembling a portfolio.

NOTES

1. M. Porter, *Competitive Advantage: Creating and Sustaining Superior Performance* (New York: McMillan, Inc., 1985), chapter 1.
2. The exception to this statement is the income bond. Interest is due on any income bond *only* if it is earned.
3. H. R. Foger, "A Modern Theory of Security Analysis," *Journal of Portfolio Management,* vol. 9, no. 3 (spring 1993), pp. 6–14.
4. J. K. Glassman and K. A. Hassett, *Dow 36,000: The New Strategy for Profiting from the Coming Rise in the Stock Market* (Times Books, 1999).
5. J. Siegel, *Stocks for the Long Run,* 2d ed. (New York: McGraw-Hill, 1998), pp.105–113; "The Nifty-Fifty Revisited: Do Growth Stocks Ultimately Justify Their Price?" *Journal of Portfolio Management,* vol. 21, no. 4 (summer 1995), pp. 8–20.
6. A. Damodaran, *Damodaran on Valuation: Security Analysis for Investment and Corporate Finance* (New York: John Wiley and Sons, Inc., 1994).

7. M. Reinganum, "Misspecification of Capital Asset Pricing: Empirical Anomalies Based on Earnings' Yields and Market Values," *Journal of Financial Economics* (March 1981), pp. 19–46; "Abnormal Returns in Small Firm Portfolios," *Financial Analysts Journal* (March/April 1981), pp. 52–56; "Portfolio Strategies Based on Market Capitalization," *Journal of Portfolio Management* (winter 1983), pp. 29–36.

8. E. F. Fama and K. R. French, "Size and Book-to-Market Factors in Earnings and Returns," *Journal of Finance,* vol. 50, no. 1 (March 1995), pp. 131–155.

9. R. Graber, "Longevity of Management Employment and Research and Development Expenditures: An Agency Theory Explanation for Under-Investment in R&D in Some Corporations," PhD dissertation presented at University of New Orleans, 1997.

10. W. Baumol, *Business Behavior, Value and Growth* (New York: Harcourt, Brace & World, 1967).

11. B. Graham and D. Dodd, *Security Analysis*, 3d ed. (New York: Whittlesey House/McGraw-Hill, 1951); R. Murray, "Graham and Dodd: A Durable Discipline," *Financial Analysts Journal* (September/October 1984), pp. 18–23.

The Stock Market and the Economy

Learning Objectives

An understanding of the material in this chapter should enable the student to

---

10-1.   Explain several methods of forecasting economic activity.

10-2.   Explain the economic impact of fiscal and monetary policies.

10-3.   Explain the relationship between stock performance and monetary policy.

10-4.   Explain the inflation protection of stocks and of several investments other than stocks.

Chapter Outline

Forecasting stock market movements is virtually impossible to do. Nonetheless, people like to try, and a number of different approaches have been suggested. A solid understanding of stock market-economy relationships assists any investor in understanding both economic forecasting and the relationship between the stock market and the economy.

This chapter considers various ways to forecast economic activity. The discussion includes econometric models, leading indicators, and investor-constructed forecasts. To help investors understand how to formulate a forecast, the chapter also examines the economic impact of fiscal and monetary policies. Then it explores the empirical relationship between stock performance and economic policy, giving particular emphasis to monetary policy. The remainder of the chapter discusses theoretical arguments and empirical evidence on the impact of inflation on returns.

FORECASTING ECONOMIC PERFORMANCE

The business cycle has a major effect on a firm's profits, dividends, and stock price. In an expanding economy, sales increase, inventory moves more quickly, employment and personal income increase, and corporate profits and dividends rise. In a weak economy, the opposite is true. Changes in stock prices tend to precede changes in economic activity.

econometric models

econometrics

Econometric Models

Econometrics is the statistical analysis of economic data. Microeconomics focuses on individual consumers, firms, and industries, while macroeconomics considers the overall economy's performance. Our interest here is largely with macroeconomic data and analysis. A number of econometricians have made a business out of forecasting economic activity. Their forecasts are generated by applying the latest economic information and expectations to their own models. Individuals may subscribe directly to these services, but the cost is substantial. Articles based on econometricians' predictions, however, frequently appear in the financial press. Thus, investors may, with a bit of a lag, learn the forecasters' viewpoints, although perhaps not the reasons underlying those viewpoints, for a minimal cost.

Econometric forecasts of the economy have several noteworthy limitations. First, the predictions are made periodically and therefore do not reflect interim developments. Second, by the time the forecasts become available, stock prices may already incorporate the relevant information. Third, forecasters' past records are far from perfect.

Leading Indicators

leading indicators

Leading indicators are designed to forecast economic activity. Beginning in the 1940s, the National Bureau of Economic Research (NBER) and the U.S. Commerce Department identified 10 monthly data series that tended to lead the business cycle, based on observations going back to the 1920s. Today, the monthly data series are quite similar to the original selection and include stock prices themselves (the S & P 500 Index), average weekly work hours, average unemployment claims, inflation-adjusted manufacturers' new consumer goods orders, vendor performance (companies receiving slower deliveries), new building permits, interest rates spread on 10-year Treasury bonds less federal funds, inflation-adjusted M2 (M2 includes currency and checkable deposits in the hands of the public, plus savings and small time deposits, repurchase agreements, and money market deposit accounts), and consumer expectations from the University of Michigan Survey Research Center.

In addition to the 10 leading indicators, there is a coincident indicator series (four components) and a lagging series (seven components). The list of indicators has been expanded and revised over time and is now published by the Conference Board. Under normal circumstances, updates to the leading, coincident, and lagging indexes incorporate revisions to data only over the previous 6 months. Longer-term revisions that cover changes in components that fall outside the moving 6-month window are incorporated in December of each year.

Economic Indicators

- Leading (10 series)
- Coincident (4 series)
- Lagging (7 series)

Research by Wertheim and Company and by Geoffrey Moore found leading indicators quite accurate at forecasting economic turns but offering about the same amount of lead time as the stock market itself.[1] Thus, by the time the leading indicators forecast an economic turn, the stock market would already have made a corresponding turn of its own.

Investor-Constructed Forecasts

Although both leading indicators and econometric forecasts appear to have relatively limited value in stock timing, many investors seem inclined to make such forecasts, at least implicitly. As they do about the weather, almost

**gross domestic
product (GDP)**

fiscal policy

everyone has an opinion on the economy. These opinions should be based on an accurate understanding of how the economy operates, even though most investors probably prefer not to attempt the implied precision of an exact forecast of such macroeconomic data as *gross domestic product (GDP)*, unemployment, and inflation. Investors may, however, be more inclined to estimate the direction and perhaps the general magnitude of the changes in each. That is, few individuals would have felt comfortable forecasting an increase in real GDP of 4.2 percent in 1999, but many might have been more capable of correctly predicting greater growth than occurred in the prior year. Serious efforts to predict economic activity should account for the important role that the government's economic policy plays. Government spending and taxing policy (*fiscal policy*) and any activity that affects interest rates and the money supply (monetary policy) have important economic impacts. Let's now consider fiscal and monetary policy and their effects on the economy.

Fiscal Policy

fiscal multiplier

leakages

Government spending affects the economy in several ways. First, when the economy has room to expand, increased government expenditures may call forth additional production. Thus, starting a new public works project (for example, a highway, school, or dam) will put people to work to produce the structure and the required inputs (cement, steel, and so on). These newly employed workers will likely spend most of their income on consumer goods and services, thereby creating demands that put others to work. This *fiscal multiplier* process increases employment and production. At each stage, however, a portion of the extra income does not go directly back into the domestic economy. It is saved, taxed, or spent on imported goods. These *leakages* reduce the multiplier's power. Moreover, the additional spending forces the government to increase its borrowing or taxes, thereby crowding out other borrowers and/or reducing other disposable incomes. Thus, proportionately less goes to each succeeding round.

The effect of a tax decrease is similar to a government spending increase. Lower tax rates and reduced withholding increase households' after-tax income, causing consumer spending to rise. This spending increase, in turn, leads to additional production, employment, and income, which cause further increases in spending. Thus, either a government spending increase or a tax decrease stimulates the economy, whereas a government spending decrease or a tax increase restrains the economy. According to Keynesian theory (Keynesians are discussed later in this chapter), a change in government spending has a greater economic impact than a tax change of equivalent size. The multiplier acts on the full amount of the change in government spending to affect the GDP, whereas a portion of the tax change affects savings, leaving the multiplier a lesser amount on which to act.

Stimulative fiscal policy is normally applied when the economy has sufficient room to absorb the resulting increase in spending with increased output. When the economy is already operating near its capacity, however, stimulative fiscal policy can have little or no impact on output or employment. Under these circumstances, the principal effect of fiscal policy stimulation is to increase prices. As we shall soon see, inflation is not a plus for either the economy or the stock market.

How Fiscal Policy Operates through Government Spending and Taxes

- Increased government spending or decreased taxes stimulate the economy.
- Decreased government spending or increased taxes restrain the economy.

Monetary Policy: The Fed's Tools

Federal Reserve Board (Fed) monetary policy money supply

The *Federal Reserve Board* (*Fed*) has primary authority over our nation's *monetary policy*. By largely determining the rate at which the *money supply* expands or contracts, the Fed exercises a considerable amount of influence over the supply of and demand for credit (that is, loanable funds). Interest is the price one pays for the use of such funds. Interest rates are determined by the intersection of these supply and demand functions.

M1

The money supply itself consists of all cash and coin in circulation outside banks, plus all accounts in depository institutions that are subject to withdrawal by check (*M1*). Most of M1 is held in the form of checkable deposits. Federally chartered banks and state banks with Fed memberships are required to maintain reserves (that is, cash and certain near-cash assets) equal to a predetermined percentage of their deposits. This percentage is called the reserve ratio or *reserve requirement,* which is set by the Fed. A bank's required reserves are found by multiplying its deposits by the required reserve ratio.

reserve requirement

Example: Suppose a bank has $5 million in transactions deposits and the reserve ratio requirement is 3 percent. The bank's required reserves would be $5,000,000 x .03 = $150,000. These reserves must be held either as vault cash or deposits at the bank's regional Federal Reserve bank.

The Fed can attempt to expand or contract the money supply by reducing or increasing the reserve requirement. If the reserve requirement is decreased, banks need lower reserves to support their existing deposits and therefore may increase their loans. An increase in the reserve requirement could have the reverse effect, unless actual reserves that banks hold exceed even the increased requirement.

Example: Suppose a bank has $5 million in transactions deposits, actual reserves of $300,000, and required reserves of $300,000 (assume that the reserve requirement is 6 percent). If the Fed lowers the reserve ratio to 4 percent, the bank is now required to have only $200,000 in reserves ($5,000,000 x .04 = $200,000). The bank now has excess reserves of $100,000. The bank's excess reserve amount is found by subtracting its required reserves of $200,000 from its actual reserves of $300,000. The bank is now able to make an additional $100,000 in loans.

When a bank grants a loan, it funds the loan by creating a deposit to the borrower's account. In effect, it implicitly creates the money that it loans. The money that is thereby created is initially retained in an account at the lending bank. Checks written against these loan-created deposits will, in turn, be deposited into the accounts of the people or firms receiving the payments. In this way, most of the money flows into other bank accounts, but some of the funds remain with the bank that made the loan. A relatively small portion of the loan money may go into additional cash holdings. Thus, most of the new money resulting from granting the loan ends up as deposits somewhere in the banking system. The corresponding increase in deposits throughout the banking system creates additional lending power. When this lending power is utilized, more deposits and still more lending power result.

money multiplier (monetary multiplier)

open market operations

The ratio between the initial change in reserves and the resulting change in the money supply is called the *money multiplier* or *monetary multiplier*. Because changing the reserve requirements many disrupt the financial markets more than is desirable, the Fed generally prefers to exercise its influence over the banking system through what are called *open market operations*. These operations utilize the Fed's substantial portfolio of government bonds. The Fed's management of this portfolio has a major effect on the banking system.

The Fed's portfolio management requires buying and selling substantial amounts of government bonds. When it is a buyer, the Fed pays for the bonds with drafts (checks) that increase the recipient banks' reserves. These increased reserves allow a multiple increase in deposits and loans as described above. Similarly, when the Fed sells government securities, reserves are reduced, thereby forcing deposits and loans to contract. The Fed buys and sells Treasury securities virtually on a daily basis and thereby pumps in or takes out of the economy a targeted amount of reserves. Many Wall Street analysts carefully monitor the Fed's open market operations and the resulting changes in the money supply.

As explained earlier, the money multiplier is the ratio between the ultimate change in the money supply and the initial inflow or outflow. For example, if the Federal Reserve Board purchases $100 million in government securities through open market operations and the resulting increase in the money supply is $500 million, we conclude that the money multiplier is $500 million/$100 million, or 5. Although this is something of a simplification, we can say that the maximum value of the money multiplier is the reciprocal of the reserve requirement. For example, if the reserve requirement is 20 percent, or one-fifth, then the money multiplier is approximately 5.

To see how this works, imagine that the Fed buys $100 million in government bonds from Bank A. With a 20 percent reserve requirement, Bank A will have to keep $20 million of the additional $100 million in reserve, but it can loan out the additional $80 million. The borrowers of that $80 million will use the money to purchase a variety of goods and services, so the money will change hands quickly. The sellers of those goods and services will receive this additional money. Many sellers will deposit the additional money in a bank, or they will spend it on other goods and services, in which case other people will receive the money and most likely deposit it in a bank.

Sooner or later, a very large part (almost all) of that extra $80 million will find its way into a bank deposit. For simplicity, let's assume that the $80 million is deposited in Bank B. Bank B must now put $16 million (20 percent of $80 million) in reserve and can lend out an additional $64 million. Once again, an extra $64 million worth of goods and services will be purchased, and the sellers of those goods and services will have an additional $64 million at their disposal. Again, for simplicity, let's assume that the entire $64 million is deposited at Bank C. Bank C can now lend out an additional 80 percent of $64 million, or $51.2 million. The process then repeats itself again and again, increasing the amount of money in circulation each time.

Mathematically, if the Fed makes an open market purchase of P dollars, and the reserve requirement is r, the increase in the money supply is

$$P + P \times (1 - r) + P \times (1 - r)^2 + P \times (1 - r)^3 + \ldots$$
$$= P \times [1 + (1 - r) + (1 - r)^2 + (1 - r)^3]$$
$$= P \times 1/r$$

Therefore, 1/r is called the money multiplier or monetary multiplier.

It was earlier said that the money multiplier is a bit of a simplification. There are two reasons for that. First of all, the reserve requirement is the *minimum* percentage of deposits that banks are required to keep in reserve. Banks can always choose to keep more than the legal minimum amount in reserve. However, banks generally prefer to lend money out in order to earn interest, rather than keep more than required in reserve. Furthermore, not all money ultimately winds up in banks. Some money is kept in the form of currency or held in brokerage accounts.

When the Fed makes open market purchases or sales, it increases or decreases the money supply by the amount of the open market transaction times the money multiplier. When the Fed changes the reserve requirement, it changes the money multiplier itself. For example, if the Fed were to change the reserve requirement from 20 percent to 25 percent, it would reduce the money multiplier from 5 to 4 (1/.25), thus decreasing the money supply.

discount rate

The Fed also lends reserves to member banks, stressing that discounting is a privilege, not a right. It extends these loans only on a short-term basis (as a safety valve) and only to applicants that it views as not abusing this borrowing privilege. The Fed makes discounting more or less attractive by adjusting its interest rate on and its willingness to grant such loans, but it tends to keep the *discount rate* in line with the federal funds rate.

federal funds rate

The *federal funds rate* is recently the most important target rate affecting financial markets. It is the rate that banks charge each other for overnight use of federal reserves in the so-called federal funds market. Federal funds are deposits that commercial banks hold at Federal Reserve banks.

Federal Open Market Committee (FOMC)

Compared with the Fed's other tools, discounting plays a relatively minor role, but changes in the discount rate are used principally to signal changes in Fed policy. At its meeting in February 1994, the *Federal Open Market Committee (FOMC)* began the practice of immediately disclosing its decisions upon making them, rather than waiting until the next meeting to disclose the minutes of the previous meeting. Beginning in October 1997, the Fed announced that its FOMC directive would henceforth specify an explicit

---

The Fed's Principal Policy Tools

- Reserve requirement: Increasing (decreasing) the required percentage reduces (raises) the amount of money that can be supported by a given reserve base.
- Open market operations: Fed purchases (sales) of government securities increase (decrease) the bank deposits available to support the money supply.
- Discount loans: Increasing (decreasing) the discount rate and decreasing (increasing) its willingness to grant discount loans tightens (eases) monetary policy.

target for the federal funds rate. In addition, the directive would express a bias to possible future action in terms of the rate. For a long time prior to the announcement, the Fed had implemented monetary policy by making discrete and frequent small adjustments to its federal funds rate target. Often, changes in the federal funds rate are simultaneous with other changes in the marketplace, such as changes in the various market-determined interest rates.

Economic Impact of Monetary Policy

How does an increase in deposits and loans affect the economy? The supply of money in the form of transactions balances (for example, checkable deposits) and the corresponding amount of the banking system's outstanding loans play key roles in the economy. An increase in the supply of money and loans outstanding tends to reduce interest rates (at least in the short run). The increased supply and lower cost (interest rate) of loanable funds encourage many people to spend more on consumption. For example, households are more inclined to purchase a new car or a new home if it is easier to finance. Similarly, businesses are encouraged to invest more in plant and equipment expenditures and in other long-term projects (for example, research and development). These additional consumption and investment expenditures tend to create more income and jobs and to stimulate even more spending. A reduction in deposits and loans, in contrast, tends to reduce spending and income.

Economic Effect of Deposits and Loans

- Increase in deposits and loans: stimulates spending and income; can increase inflation
- Decrease in deposits and loans: restrains spending and income; can reduce inflation

---

As with fiscal policy, stimulative monetary policy tends to increase real (noninflationary) output when the economy has slack resources, and it tends to increase prices when bottlenecks appear or when the economy is already operating near full employment or capacity utilization. Thus, stimulative monetary policy is often favorable to the economy and stock market. That is, it is likely to increase demand for goods and services and thereby increase profits. Additionally, an increase in the availability of loanable funds may reduce real interest rates. As we shall see, a decline in interest rates is particularly bullish (favorable) for stock prices. When the economy is already operating near its capacity, however, further stimulation is particularly likely to be inflationary. These inflationary pressures are bearish (unfavorable) for both the economy and the stock market.

Monetary and Fiscal Policy: Some Qualifications

As we have seen, the economy may be stimulated by increased government spending, lower taxes, and an increase in the money supply, and it may be restrained by the reverse processes. Now let us introduce some qualifications.

First, the impacts of changes in tax rates and government spending (fiscal policy) or in the reserve requirement, discount rate, and open market operation (monetary policy) take time to work their way through the economy. As a result, changes in the direction of monetary and fiscal policy generally precede changes in the direction of economic activity. This is particularly true of fiscal policy, because it takes considerable time for Congress to enact a new budget or to change the tax rates.

Second, monetary and fiscal policy are both subject to political pressures. Their degree of sensitivity differs, however. Monetary policy is formulated by the Federal Reserve Board of Governors and its Federal Open Market Committee. Members are appointed by the President and confirmed by the Senate for long (14-year) staggered terms. Furthermore, the Fed is not dependent directly on Congressional appropriations. Its own interest income is more than adequate to cover its operating expenses. The Fed, therefore, is generally able to pursue a relatively independent monetary policy. Fiscal policy, on the other hand, is formulated jointly by Congress and the President, and many diverse interest groups may affect the decision-making process. As a result, short-term pressures increase the difficulty of implementing long-run fiscal policies.

Third, the stock market also monitors and reacts to its perceptions of the direction of economic policy. Thus, to obtain an advantage relative to the market's own economic assessment, investors need to have a superior understanding of economic policy/economy-stock market relationships. In other words, investors need to be able to outguess the market in its forecast for the economy's future.

Goals of Monetary and Fiscal Policy

The primary economic goals of monetary and fiscal policymakers are price stability and full employment. Most people have a general idea of what price stability and full employment mean. Nonetheless, the concepts are sufficiently complex and confusing to warrant some discussion.

price stability

Price stability is the absence of either a sharply rising (inflation) or falling (deflation) trend in overall prices. Inflation is a general rise in the price level. Thus, for example, a 6 percent annual inflation rate implies that $1.06 is required to buy the same diverse market basket of goods and services as could have been acquired a year earlier for $1. Inflation of 6 percent does not mean that *all* prices rise by 6 percent. In fact, some prices may actually fall, while other prices may rise dramatically. An inflation rate of 6 percent simply means that, *on average,* prices rise by 6 percent. Deflation, in contrast, is a general fall in the price level. During most of our history, actual inflation and potential inflation have been much more of a problem than the threat of deflation. Furthermore, policymakers (especially at the Fed) frequently state the problem of achieving price stability as a matter of lowering the rate of inflation (rate of change of prices upward), rather than the complete elimination of all price increases.

full employment

It might be logical to think that *full employment* would be defined as 100 percent of the labor force's having jobs. Realistically, however, some people (not necessarily the same people) will always be unemployed, even in the best of times. People change jobs (frictional unemployment), work at seasonal jobs (seasonal unemployment), or are unemployed because of location, background, or training (structural unemployment). These various classes of unemployed people create an almost irreducible floor for reported unemployment. In fact, the absence of frictional unemployment would probably not be a good thing. Frictional unemployment often occurs because some percentage of people are looking for better jobs, where their talents, skills, and training can be better utilized and they can be more productive and earn more money. Society as a whole benefits when individuals work at jobs that maximize their productivity. The height of this floor, however, changes as the economy evolves (see figure 10-1 below). Full employment, therefore, is generally defined as corresponding to some acceptable level of

FIGURE 10-1
Unemployment, Labor Force Participation, and Employment Rates

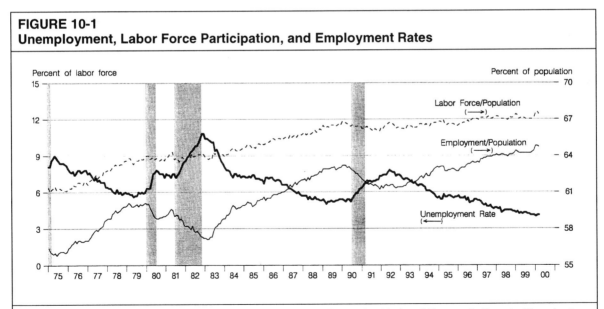

Reprinted with permission of the Federal Reserve Bank of St. Louis, *National Economic Trends.* The chart appeared on page 10 of the May 2000 issue. Lead article was written by Michael R. Pakko.

unemployment rate

unemployment. The *unemployment rate* itself is defined as the percentage of the labor force that is out of work and actively seeking a job. The labor force consists of those who are employed or actively seeking employment. Extensive government statistics are compiled on both employment and inflation.

Currently, the relationship of the U.S. to the international economy is increasing in importance. Thus, as the world economy has grown more interdependent, such matters as the relative exchange value of the dollar (exchange rate), the amount of imports relative to exports (*balance of trade*), and international capital flows (which may take the form of foreigners investing in U.S. securities or U.S. citizens investing in foreign businesses) have become increasingly important to economic policymakers. Moreover, the actions of foreign and other international investors are having an increasingly large impact on U.S. financial markets.

balance of trade

Some of the government's additional economic and quasi-economic goals and concerns include economic growth, freedom, and opportunity; increased productivity; a higher standard of living; environmental protection; energy independence; consumer protection; and product safety. Policies designed to achieve some of these goals may frequently conflict with other goals.

Virtually everyone agrees that price stability and full employment are desirable. Policies to reduce unemployment may, however, accelerate inflation. When the economy is already near full employment and further stimulated by an increase in the money supply, those bidding for the limited supply of labor will cause wages and other prices to rise. However, some stimulation may be administered to a slack economy before the inflation rate is driven upward.

The international situation adds a further complication. During the 1980s, maintaining the value of the dollar and seeking to attract capital to help reduce the budget and trade deficits may have led to a relatively restrictive monetary policy (*tight money*). Such a policy tends to raise U.S. interest rates relative to rates abroad. However, higher interest rates usually lead to reduced domestic economic activity. Thus, policymakers may at times have to choose between doing what is best for the domestic economy and doing what is best with respect to foreign trade.

tight money

The trend of inflation rates in the U.S. has been basically downward from its peaks in the early 1980s, as measured by the Consumer Price Index (CPI). This trend has been matched by other leading industrial countries and regions, including the European Union, Canada, and Japan. Figure 10-2 shows the rate of inflation in the U.S. measured by the CPI and inflation expectations as measured by the quarterly Federal Reserve Bank of Philadelphia, the monthly University of Michigan Survey Research Center, and the FOMC ranges as reported to Congress in the annual Humphrey-

FIGURE 10-2
Inflation and Inflation Expectations

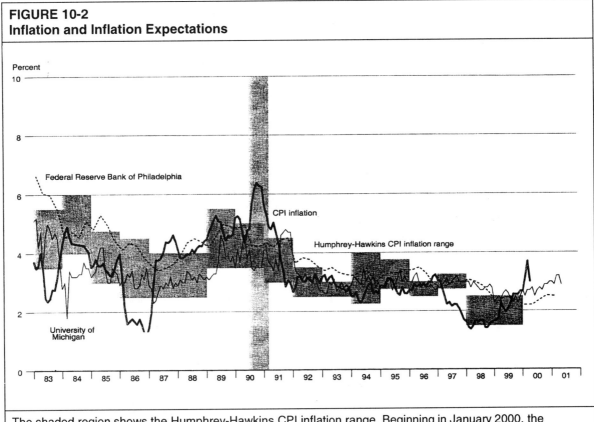

The shaded region shows the Humphrey-Hawkins CPI inflation range. Beginning in January 2000, the Humphrey-Hawkins inflation range was reported using the PCE price index and therefore is not shown on this graph.

Used with permission from Surveys of Consumers, University of Michigan. Reprinted from *Monetary Trends*, June 2000.

Hawkins testimony each year. The downward trend is clearly noted in each of the time series and variables shown since 1990. The CPI inflation rate shown in figure 10-2 is the percentage change from the previous year.

IMPORTANCE OF MONETARY POLICY

Stock market analysts pay particular attention to monetary (as opposed to fiscal) policy for several reasons. First, monetary policy has different industry effects. This is because some industries are particularly sensitive to changes in interest rates. The banking and financial services sector of the economy is an obvious example. In addition, there are industries, such as real estate and utilities, that do a great deal of borrowing to finance their activities. Those industries are quite sensitive to changes in interest rates.

Second, monetary policy is often considered easier to track—and perhaps easier to predict. The Fed's weekly monetary data releases are intensively analyzed by some members of the financial press.

monetarists

Third, an influential group of economists (called *monetarists,* many of whom are associated with the University of Chicago) assert that money drives the economy, while fiscal policy plays a more modest role.

Fourth, monetary policy directly affects the stock market through its influence on interest rates. We will consider each of these matters in greater detail.

Factors Affecting Likelihood of Shift in Monetary and Fiscal Policy

A shift toward greater stimulation is more likely if	A shift toward greater restrictiveness is more likely if
• Unemployment is far above its target.	• Unemployment is near its target.
• The inflation rate is near its target.	• The inflation rate is far above its target.
• Unemployment is increasing.	• Unemployment is decreasing.
• Inflation is decreasing.	• Inflation is increasing.
• The dollar is strong.	• The dollar is weak.
• The trade deficit is large.	• The trade deficit is small, or there is a trade surplus.
• Substantial amounts of capital are flowing into the U.S.	• Foreign capital is threatening to withdraw from or slow its flow into the U.S.

Disproportionate Impact of Monetary Policy

Monetary policy works by rationing credit. Restrictive monetary policy not only raises interest rates (at least in the short run), but it also tends to limit availability of credit to stronger credit risks and thereby influences the allocation of funds among the financial intermediaries.

thrift institutions

Savings and loan associations and mutual savings banks (*thrift institutions)* may be particularly hard hit when interest rates increase. The thrifts have historically maintained a large percentage of their portfolios in long-term fixed-rate mortgages. Thus, in effect, a large fraction of their deposits has been used to fund long-term mortgage lending. Moreover, some portion has been at fixed rates.

The thrifts' deposits, in contrast, have tended to be available to their depositors on demand or to be represented by CDs with relatively short terms. This type of situation implies an imbalance between the maturity structure of thrifts' assets (long term) and their liabilities (short term). The imbalance has tended to make the thrifts more vulnerable to rising interest rates than other lending institutions that do not have a high concentration of assets in fixed-rate mortgages. As interest rates rise, the costs of funds tend to go up, while the rates that the thrifts earn on existing fixed-rate mortgage loans remain relatively constant. The larger the proportion of their assets tied up in fixed-rate loans, the more vulnerable the thrifts are to rising interest rates. Having experienced the adverse effects of rising interest rates a number of times, the thrifts have sought to limit their exposure. The thrifts' sensitivity to increasing interest rates adds to the real estate, construction, building materials, and major appliance industries' vulnerability to tight money.

Over time, a shift to adjustable rate mortgages and the use of various instruments for hedging interest rate risks (financial futures, options, and interest rate swaps) have tended to reduce this vulnerability. Nonetheless, many thrifts (particularly the smaller ones) remain vulnerable to adverse interest rate moves.

Relative Ease of Tracking Monetary Policy

The financial press pays close attention to any news relating to Fed policy. Even the Fed, however, has some difficulty tracking and controlling short-run monetary aggregates. The monetary aggregates, such as M1 (primarily currency plus demand deposits) or M2 (essentially M1 plus other liquid deposits such as savings accounts), are no longer the focus of Wall Street they were in the early 1980s.

Nonetheless, monetary policy is easier to follow than the lengthy, uncertain path of authorizations, appropriation, and implementation of government expenditures. Tax legislation, the other side of fiscal policy, is equally difficult to follow. Moreover, the greater volatility of monetary policy provides more signals than is the case with fiscal policy.

Monetarists versus Keynesians

Keynesians

Since John Maynard Keynes published his *General Theory of Employment, Interest, and Money* in 1936, the monetarists have debated with those who emphasize the importance of fiscal policy (*Keynesians*). Although the Keynesians dominated economic thinking throughout the 1940s and 1950s, by the early 1960s, the debate was again in full swing. The dispute continues, but the issues may be narrowing. During much of the post-1936 period, the Keynesians were far more influential in and out of government. Since the late 1960s, however, both groups have had substantial influence. Most economists now agree that both monetary and fiscal policy affect the economy but disagree on their relative importance, although the "rational expectations" school (originating at the University of Chicago, based on the work of Robert Lucas) argues that both monetary and fiscal policy are useless in the long run.

Direct Effect of Monetary Policy on Stock Market

Monetary policy indirectly influences the stock market through its effect on the economy and on corporate profits. Moreover, the impact of monetary policy on interest rates has a direct effect on the stock market in three related ways.

First, stock prices reflect the present value of their expected future income streams. The rate at which these expected incomes are discounted is affected by the market rates of interest.

Second, investors find bonds relatively more attractive as their yields to maturity increase. As a result, some investors will shift from stocks to bonds when interest rates rise and from bonds to stocks when interest rates fall.

Finally, higher interest rates mean increased borrowing costs for margin investors. These investors will require a higher expected return to justify the greater cost of financing their margin purchases. Falling interest rates have the opposite effect.

How the Impact of Monetary Policy on Interest Rates Affects the Stock Market

---

- The market rate of interest affects the rate at which stocks' expected future income streams are discounted.
- As bonds' yields to maturity increase, some investors may switch from stocks to bonds when interest rates rise and from bonds to stocks when interest rates fall.
- High interest rates result in increased borrowing costs for margin investors, who need a higher expected return to justify their greater financing costs.

INFLATION-STOCK MARKET RELATIONSHIP

Some people see inflation as a purely monetary phenomenon. According to this view, inflationary pressures affect prices but little else. Those who accept this line of reasoning expect investors to seek to maximize their expected risk-adjusted real return without regard to the inflation rate. In their view, inflation just reduces the real (after-inflation) return of anything in which they invest. Thus, these investors choose their investments and manage their portfolios without taking account of the potential impact of inflation.

Others see inflation as more than a simple monetary phenomenon. Therefore, the inflation rate is thought to have an impact that goes well beyond just affecting the price level. These people believe that inflation plays an important role in the determination of the level of economic activity and that it can have rather different effects on the various components of the economy. As a result, these investors consider the different inflation protection of various types of investments. These investors' propensity to spend (particularly on durables) may be affected by what they expect their real returns to be. In addition, different investments may offer varying degrees of long-term inflation protection. Thus, the appeal of some assets may depend on the expected long-term inflation rate. Finally, investors who are able to anticipate changes in the inflation rate may be able to shift profitably between more inflation-resistant and less inflation-resistant investments.

Aside from its impact on prices, volatile inflation rates may increase the uncertainty in the overall economy, and in the stock market in particular. Corporations may be less willing to enter into long-term contracts and to commit to long-term expansion, when there is substantial uncertainty as to what future prices and interest rates will be. This uncertainty itself can have an adverse effect on the stock market.

Wall Street View of Stocks As Inflation Hedge

inflation hedge

real return

Until the 1970s, most analysts thought that the stock market offered substantial inflation protection. Stockbrokers and mutual fund salespeople argued that equity returns would tend to keep up with inflation better than the returns on fixed-income securities (bonds) would. Early thought often confused two rather different *inflation hedge* concepts. According to one view, the market value of an inflation hedge should rise with the general price level. Thus, the *real return* of a perfect inflation hedge should be independent of price changes. A perfect inflation hedge yielding 4 percent with stable prices would return 4 percent plus compensation for the inflation rate.

Although few analysts ever claimed that stocks offered complete protection from inflation, many believed that if consumer prices changed by x percent, average stocks would yield

$$r = a + bx$$

where r = rate of return or yield
       a = a constant value
       b = some positive number less than unity

Thus, if a = 3 and b = .7, then an inflation rate of 5 percent would imply a nominal (no adjustment for inflation) stock market return of

$$3\% + .7\,(5\%) = 6.5\%$$

Such a nominal return corresponds approximately to a real return of

$$6.5\% - 5\% = 1.5\%$$

A real return of 1.5 percent is positive but less than the real return would be at lower inflation rates. This type of behavior relative to the inflation rate would imply that stocks acted as a partial hedge against inflation.

A second form of the inflation hedge concept takes a much longer-range perspective. According to this viewpoint, average long-run stock returns will generally exceed the rise in the general price level. In particular short-run periods, nominal returns may be below the inflation rate. Eventually, however, nominal returns will catch up with and exceed the increase in the price level. If markets behave as this perspective implies, the real value of capital would tend to be preserved in spite of the inflation rate. This form of the inflation hedge concept is less strong because it allows for the possibility that the market will be affected adversely (if temporarily) by high and/or rising inflation rates. In spite of the experience in the 1970s with rapid inflation and poor stock market performance, and in the early 1990s when stock returns were mediocre, the view persists that stocks will still protect investors from inflation in the long run. The work of Jeremy Siegel at the Wharton School of the University of Pennsylvania has reinforced the view that stocks are the best investment in the long run.[2]

Theoretical Underpinnings of Stock Market-Inflation Hedge Hypothesis

To provide effective short- or long-run inflation protection, companies must increase their profits (as measured in nominal terms) or increase their efficiency (that is, lower costs). In periods of rising prices, their own costs are almost certain to be increasing unless offset by productivity gains. Thus, one way that firms might be able to defend their profitability is by raising prices. Because inflation represents an overall increase in the price level, companies should generally be able to increase their prices commensurately with the rate of inflation without losing market share to competitors, who are likely to be raising their prices at the same time. The ability of stocks to withstand the adverse impact of an inflationary environment depends on the underlying company's ability to maintain its profitability. Stocks represent ownership of real assets. The replacement value of these assets and their ability to generate income may well rise with the price level. If firms are able to raise their prices sufficiently, the real (inflation-adjusted) value of dividends and share prices may keep pace with price-level increases. A number of considerations, however, limit firms' ability to raise prices by enough to preserve investment values.

To illustrate, various aspects of our tax system tend to penalize investment income at high inflation rates. First, the IRS requires that companies use historical costs in computing their profits. As a result, they must pay taxes on sums that reflect the difference between the historical cost and the replacement value of inventory, plant, and equipment.

| *Example:* | Suppose a company in a competitive environment that prevents price increases on its own products produces a widget for a recorded cost of $1, based on now out-of-date materials costs. If it then sells the widget for $2, the company must report a profit of $1 ($2 − $1), even if the next widget would cost $1.50 (based on up-to-date materials prices) to produce. |

A high inflation rate increases these differences between accounting costs of goods sold and the forward-looking replacement costs of goods sold. Similarly, a high inflation rate will tend to increase the tax on these reported (phantom) profits. As a result, the real after-tax component of reported profits tends to fall as prices increase. Of course, use of LIFO (last-in, first-out) accounting may reduce or eliminate the difference in accounting cost of goods and replacement cost of goods sold.

Second, inflation tends to push noninstitutional investors into higher marginal tax brackets, further increasing the tax penalty on investments. This effect was a severe problem when our tax system had 11 brackets with a top rate of 50 percent or even higher. The reduced number of tax brackets and lower maximum rate under the Tax Reform Act of 1986, somewhat reversed by the Budget Reconciliation Act of 1993, as well as the reductions in tax rates contained in the Tax Reform Act of 2001, lessen but do not eliminate this effect.

Third, individuals must pay taxes on sums (dividends and capital gains) that often contain a substantial inflation component. Thus, even if the before-tax return rose point for point with the inflation rate, the after-tax return would not.

| *Example:* | A one-third tax rate applied to a 3 percent nominal return and zero inflation (a 3 percent real return before taxes) provides a 2 percent after-tax real return. A 6 |

percent nominal return with a 3 percent inflation rate produces a real after-tax return of only 1 percent. A 9 percent nominal return and 6 percent inflation rate yields a real after-tax return of 0 percent. For nominal returns above 9 percent, a 3 percent before-tax real return corresponds to a negative real after-tax return.

We might suspect that cost and price increases of x percent would (neglecting tax effects) approximately maintain a firm's financial position. In fact, however, higher prices and costs generally require a contemporaneous and disproportionate increase in capital to support inventories, accounts receivables, and new plant and equipment. Moreover, if higher inflation rates are associated with higher interest rates, both the amount and the cost of financing tend to increase with inflation. Thus, to offset the effect of taxes on nominal profits and to finance the increased capital requirements at higher interest rates, prices must be raised proportionately more than the direct cost increase. To offset the increased retained earnings requirement (needed to support the additional borrowings) and the investor's inflation-imposed tax burden, prices may have to rise more than proportionately.

Many firms are unable to raise prices sufficiently to recapture their increased production costs, however, to say nothing of increasing them sufficiently to offset tax and financing effects. Increased competition (including that from substitute products whose costs of production may be more stable), the existence of long-term contracts with customers that lock in a purchase price, or an environment of reduced demand and excess capacity may limit a firm's ability to raise prices and retain the same volume of sales.

International competition may hold some prices down, depending on the interplay of such factors as domestic versus international inflation rates, changes in exchange rates, tariffs and import quotas, and foreign competitors' pricing responses. Similar considerations influence domestic exporters' ability to pass their higher costs on internationally.

Finally, F. Modigliani and R. Cohn argue that investors make two basic errors in pricing securities in the presence of inflation.[3] First, investors are said to capitalize equity earnings incorrectly by comparing the current cash earnings of equity with nominal rather than real bond returns. Bond returns are fixed until maturity, whereas profits and dividends attributable to stocks tend to rise over time. Focusing on stock returns as if they are expected to be constant rather than rise will cause investors to undervalue them. Second, Modigliani and Cohn contend that investors have failed to take proper account of the impact of inflation on the real value of corporate debt. Over time, inflation tends to reduce the real value of outstanding debt. Thus, corporations with substantial amounts of debt outstanding will, in effect, see that debt decline (at least in real terms) in times of rapid inflation. According

to Modigliani and Cohn, these two alleged mispricing effects reduced the
S&P 500 Stock Index by 50 percent in 1977. In 1982, a low point for stocks,
P. Cagan asserted that the market seemed to be as underpriced as it was
alleged to be in1977.[4] The market more than tripled over the next 5 years.
Perhaps the market was mispriced and later realized its error. On the other hand,
the crash of 1987 indicates that the market can also be mispriced on the upside.

Inflation's Adverse Stock Market Impact

- Tax impact
    - Corporate taxes are based on historical costs of plants, equipment, and inventories.
    - Investors are pushed into high tax brackets.
    - Individual taxes are applied to nominal dividend and interest income.
- Cost impact
    - Greater capital is needed for new plants and equipment and for inventories.
    - Higher interest costs are incurred on borrowings.
- Price impact
    - There is resistance to price increases.
    - Competition from substitutes may increase.
    - International competition may increase.

A recent study by Ibbotson Associates (2000) measures the historical
performance of five asset classes of securities over a 74-year period, 1926–
1999. Figure 10-3 shows wealth indices of investments in the U.S. capital
markets as if $1 had been invested in 1925 in each asset, and then
subsequently all dividends or interest was reinvested in the same asset. The
five asset classes are Treasury bills, long-term Treasury bonds, long-term
corporate bonds, the S&P Composite Index (S&P 500), and a portfolio of
smaller-firm common stocks.[5] Table 10-1 shows how $1 would have grown,
adjusted for inflation between 1926 and 1999, if all dividend or interest
income had been reinvested in each of the five asset classes. Of course, these
investments differ in degrees of risk, which accounts for much of the
differences in their respective returns. A dollar invested in the lowest-risk
investment, Treasury bills, would have grown to $1.67 by 1999; in long-term
Treasury bonds, to $4.28; and in corporate bonds, to $6.05 in real terms.
Common stocks were far and away the best inflation-adjusted investment,
with $707.33 for smaller firms and $303.09 for the large-company stocks.

Ibbotson Associates also calculated the compound and average annual
rate of return from the five asset classes for each year over the 74-year
period. This rate reflects both cash receipts, such as dividends and interest,
and capital gains or losses realized during the specific year. Table 10-2

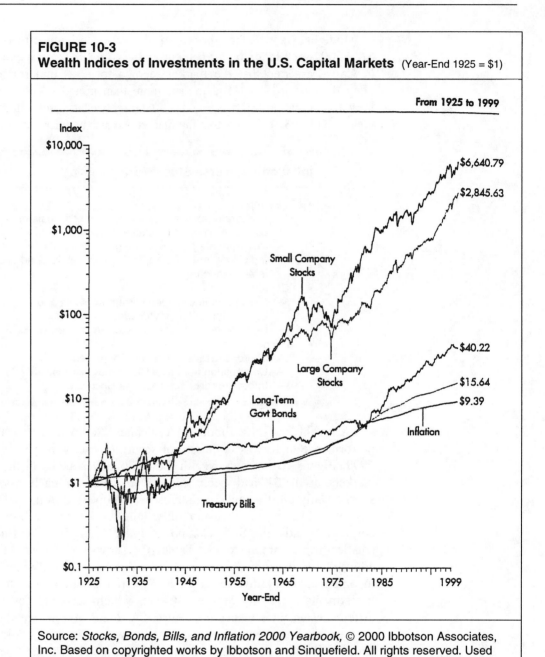

FIGURE 10-3
Wealth Indices of Investments in the U.S. Capital Markets (Year-End 1925 = $1)

shows the averages of the 74 annual rates of return for each asset class. From 1926 to 1999, the Treasury bills provided 3.8 percent per year in nominal terms and 0.7 percent in real terms. The average rate of inflation over the

TABLE 10-1
Total Return: Cumulative Value of $1 with All Interest and Dividends Reinvested

	Nominal	Real
Treasury bills	$ 15.64	$ 1.67
Government bonds	40.22	4.28
Corporate bonds+	56.77	6.05
Large-company stocks	2,845.63	303.09
Small-company stocks	6,640.79	707.33
Inflation	9.39	–
+ Long term		
Derived from figure 10-3.		

period was just over 3 percent per year. The average annual return on common stocks as measured by the S&P 500 was an 11.3 percent nominal rate and an 8 percent real return. This rate of return included a risk premium of 7.2 percent, on average. As might be expected, the nominal rate and real returns for smaller stocks were higher, with a higher risk premium of 8.5 percent. Clearly, over the 74-year period, stocks provided a good hedge against inflation. However, we cannot be certain that this period is truly representative and that the averages are not distorted by a few unusually high or low annual returns. In some given years, such as during the high unanticipated inflation of the mid- to late 1970s, the stock market did not outperform the double-digit inflation rates.

TABLE 10-2
Compound Average Rate of Return (Percent) on Treasury Bills, Government Bonds, Corporate Bonds, and Common Stocks, 1926–1999 (Figures in Percent per Year)

Portfolio	Nominal	Real	Average Risk Premium (Extra Return versus Treasury Bills)
Treasury bills	3.8%	0.7%	–
Government bonds +	5.1	1.9	1.3%
Corporate bonds +	5.6	2.4	1.7
Common stocks (S&P 500)	11.3	8.0	7.2
Small-firm common stocks	12.6	9.2	8.5
Inflation	3.1	–	–
+ Long term			
Derived from table 2-1.			

Assessment of the Evidence

Overall, it seems that stocks tend to provide long-term inflation protection and possibly some short-term protection from anticipated inflation. For investors to know that stock price increases may eventually offset inflation is small comfort, however, if they must sell before the market rebounds. If unexpected inflation rate increases depress stock prices, the real value of investments falls both with the rise in the price level and with the decline in the position's nominal value. Some investors may be able to ride out these market declines, but others may not.

INFLATION PROTECTION OF OTHER INVESTMENTS

The preceding discussion strongly suggests that stocks may not be a particularly effective short-term inflation hedge. Fortunately, some types of investments do offer more dependable inflation protection. Stock-related securities, such as common stock mutual funds, convertible bonds, preferreds, and options, probably behave similarly to stocks. Thus, we expect inflation to affect them in much the same way that it affects stocks. Commodities, real estate, and collectibles, in contrast, may offer different levels of inflation protection. Several studies have found that the returns on fixed-income securities tend to compensate for anticipated but not for unanticipated inflation.[6] This conclusion, while similar to that reached in a number of stock market-inflation studies, has a very different implication. Unlike stocks, debt securities mature. An inflation rate increase that depresses security prices locks in stock investors to a loss, whereas the par value of bond principal may be reinvested at maturity. This may mean a loss of real value but not of nominal value, as with stocks.

Example: Suppose an investor purchases a bond with a yield to maturity of 10 percent in an 8 percent inflation environment. If inflation then rises to 12 percent, equivalent debt yields to maturity might increase to 14 percent. For bonds with low durations, this rise in the unanticipated inflation rate will cause only a modest return loss. Soon the investor's bonds will mature, and the resulting principal can then be reinvested at the new higher market rates. Interest payments can also be reinvested at the new higher rates. The principal of a bond with an even longer maturity will eventually become available for reinvestment.

The fact that debt securities, particularly short-term debt securities, seem to provide a degree of short-term inflation protection leads to concern about their long-run performance. For the 1926–1999 period, Ibbotson finds an average inflation-adjusted return of 8.0 percent, 2.4 percent, 1.9 percent, and 0.7 percent for common stocks, long-term corporates, long-term government bonds, and Treasury bills, respectively.[7] The recent 20-year performance of Treasury bills has been much better, however, yielding 7.2 percent (compounded) versus inflation of 4.5 percent—or a real return of 2.6 percent. Similarly, for the same period, large-company stocks, small-company stocks, corporate bonds, and government bonds have earned real returns of 12.7, 11.1, 6.1, and 6.3 percent, respectively. Thus, the securities that offered the greatest short-run protection (bills) yielded the least long-term real return, and vice versa.

Real estate might provide substantial inflation protection. Replacement costs of developed property vary with labor and material costs (which are correlated with consumer prices). Therefore, real estate construction costs should rise with consumer prices. These increased construction costs should eventually affect existing real estate values, although demand considerations may have a greater short-term effect. Since real estate, however, has its own set of drawbacks (for example, illiquidity), its inflation-protection history is not in itself sufficient justification to invest in real estate.

The same underlying factors that cause consumer prices to rise may increase the prices of collectibles. That is, higher-money incomes chasing a fixed quantity of collectibles should bid prices up more rapidly when the inflation rate is higher. Selected collectors' items did relatively well in the 1980s inflationary environment (for example, rare coins and stamps). With lower inflation, however, the 1990s did not see a similar effect on collectibles.

Regarding precious metals, the value of gold, for instance, peaked in January 1980 at a price of $850 per ounce but subsequently fell 34 percent to about $560 between June 1981 and June 1982. With few exceptions, the investment returns on precious metals continued at a substandard pace through the rest of the 1980s. Gold prices continued to fall throughout the late 1980s and 1990s with the decline of worldwide inflation and the continued demonetization of gold. In the first quarter of 2000, it was below $290 an ounce. Like other forms of precious metals, gold is a highly speculative investment vehicle whose price tends to fluctuate widely. Whereas, historically, gold was regarded as the classic inflation hedge, the luster of gold has faded as a hedge investment since much of its recent movements have depended on relatively unpredictable policy-driven events (for example, decisions by Russia to sell gold from its official stocks or decisions by other central banks not to sell).

SUMMARY AND CONCLUSIONS

Investors who want to understand and/or forecast the market's behavior need to understand how the economy and the stock market are related. Both monetary and fiscal policy have a substantial economic impact. Macroeconomic policy generally seeks to maintain price stability and full employment. Stimulation is designed to reduce unemployment, whereas restraint is applied when inflation is the primary concern. Which is the overriding goal depends on a variety of considerations, including the relative severity of unemployment and inflation and policymakers' judgments.

Investment analysts pay particular attention to the impact of monetary policy on the stock market. Monetary policy affects the stock market both indirectly through its economic effect and directly via its interest rate effect.

Investment analysts also consider the impact of inflation on stock prices. According to pre-1970 Wall Street wisdom, companies could offset the adverse impact of inflation on their earnings (and stock values) by raising prices. Tax effects, government anti-inflation pressure, and international competition often make implementing the necessary price increases difficult, however. Still, to allocate capital properly, the stock market must offer the prospect of a positive real after-tax return.

Some empirical research suggests that, in the short run, unanticipated rises in inflation have been associated with adverse stock market performance. In the longer run, however, average market returns exceed the inflation rate. Both commodities and real estate offer a degree of inflation protection, but they present investors with a variety of other problems, such as risk and illiquidity.

CHAPTER REVIEW

Answers to the review questions and the self-test questions start on page 501.

Key Terms

econometric models	M1
econometrics	reserve requirement
leading indicators	money multiplier (monetary
gross domestic product (GDP)	multiplier)
fiscal policy	open market operations
fiscal multiplier	discount rate
leakages	federal funds rate
Federal Reserve Board (Fed)	Federal Open Market Committee
monetary policy	(FOMC)
money supply	price stability

full employment	thrift institutions
unemployment rate	Keynesians
balance of trade	inflation hedge
tight money	real return
monetarists	

Review Questions

10-1.   Discuss econometric and leading indicator forecasts of economic activity. What are their limitations?

10-2.   Explain how fiscal policy operates through taxes and government spending.

10-3.   Discuss the Fed's three principal tools and how they are used to affect the economy. Address the degree of employment and effectiveness of each method.

10-4.   Why do stock analysts generally give so much attention to monetary (as opposed to fiscal) policy? Discuss its effects on the stock market and role in investment analysis.

10-5.   How would the stock market be expected to react to each of the following developments?

   a.   The Fed, fearing that a recession is threatening, lowers the federal funds rate and expands the money supply. Long-term interest rates fall by over 200 basis points.

   b.   Congress finally gets serious about reducing the budget deficit and raises taxes across the board by $100 billion. The Fed cushions the blow by expanding the money supply. Interest rates fall dramatically, while the GDP continues to grow.

   c.   The Third World countries form a debtors' cartel and offer to negotiate. When the bargaining gets nowhere, they announce a total moratorium on interest and principal payments. The creditor nations respond by cutting off all credit.

10-6.   How and why would unanticipated increases in the inflation rate affect stock prices?

10-7.   Your investment alternatives are stocks, short-term bonds, long-term bonds, and real estate. You expect their returns to follow this pattern:

   - stocks: 8 percent
   - short-term bonds: 3 percent + inflation rate
   - long-term bonds: 5 percent + .3 (inflation rate)
   - real estate: 1 percent + 1.2 (inflation rate)

   You have the following inflation expectations (inflation rate, probability): 2 percent, .1; 4 percent, .3; 6 percent, .4; 8 percent, .2.

a. What is your optimal strategy for maximizing your expected nominal return?

b. How can you best ensure yourself of the greatest expected nominal return with no possibility of receiving less than a 2 percent real return?

10-8.   In a stable price environment, investments A, B, and C are expected to earn 3 percent, 10 percent, and 7 percent, respectively. If they are all perfect inflation hedges, what will their nominal and real expected returns be for inflation rates of 2 percent, 6 percent, and 10 percent?

10-9.   Compute after-tax real and nominal expected returns using the information in question 10-8. Assume that the tax rate on nominal returns is 30 percent.

10-10. Recompute the answers to question 10-9, except assume that the investments are only partial inflation hedges. The degree of inflation protection for each investment is of the form a + bx, where x is the expected inflation rate and b takes on values of .3 and .9. Use the real rates from question 10-8 for the values of a.

10-11. How are bonds, commodities, and real estate expected to behave relative to increases in unanticipated inflation?

10-12. The TUV Corporation is currently selling its product for $40 per unit. Its annual sales amount to 500,000 units. Last year it earned a profit of $2 million. Because of inflationary pressures, its variable costs will increase by $5 (from $20) per unit. If it absorbs the higher inputs costs (keeping the per-unit price unchanged), it can expand sales by 20 percent with existing capacity. Alternatively, it can raise the price to cover the increased variable costs but will lose 20 percent of its unit sales.

a. What is the profit impact of retaining the current price? (Hint: Total costs = total fixed costs + total variable costs. First calculate the total fixed costs, which remain unchanged this year.)

b. What is the profit if the price is raised?

Self-Test Questions

T   F   10-1. Econometricians rely exclusively on macroeconomic data to forecast economic activity.

T   F   10-2. Data series on the average work week, average unemployment claims, and new building permits are examples of leading economic indicators.

T   F   10-3. Increases in either government spending or taxes will stimulate the economy.

T   F   10-4. The multiplier effect causes a $1 increase in government spending to increase the GDP by more than $5.

T   F   10-5. Monetary policy is a function of the Treasury Department.

T   F   10-6.   The M1 definition of the money supply includes checkable deposits and cash and coin in circulation outside the banks.

T   F   10-7.   Reducing the reserve requirement enables banks to increase their loans.

T   F   10-8.   Cash (Federal Reserve notes) is the largest component of M1.

T   F   10-9.   The money multiplier is the ratio of the resulting increase in the money supply to the initial increase in funds (open market purchases).

T   F   10-10.   The federal funds rate is the rate charged by the Fed when it lends reserves to banks.

T   F   10-11.   Fiscal policy attempts to influence the level of economic activity by changing reserve requirements and open market operations.

T   F   10-12.   Monetary policy is formulated by the Federal Reserve's Open Market Committee.

T   F   10-13.   The primary economic goals of monetary and fiscal policy are in conflict.

T   F   10-14.   Price stability implies that individual prices remain the same during the year.

T   F   10-15.   The unemployment rate refers to the percentage of the labor force that is out of work and actively seeking employment.

T   F   10-16.   Monetary policy affects the stock market through its influence on interest rates.

T   F   10-17.   Restrictive monetary policy has no effect on the allocation of funds in the economy.

T   F   10-18.   Investors who see inflation as a purely monetary phenomenon believe that inflationary pressures affect prices but little else.

T   F   10-19.   If the tax rate is one-third, an investor receives a 9 percent nominal return, and inflation is 5 percent, the investor's real after-tax return is 1 percent.

T   F   10-20.   The use of financial leverage will always enhance an investor's after-tax, after-inflation return.

T   F   10-21.   Between 1926 and 1999, small-firm common stocks provided a higher return than large (S&P 500) common stocks.

T   F   10-22.   Securities that offer the greatest short-term inflation protection also offer the greatest long-term real return.

NOTES

1. W. McConnell, *Investment Manager's Review,* Wertheim & Company, Inc., March 23, 1981, 10; G. Moore, *Business Cycles, Inflation and Forecasting,* National Bureau of Economic Research Studies in Business Cycles No. 240 (Cambridge, Mass.: Ballinger Publishing, 1980).

2. J. Siegel, *Stocks for the Long Run,* 2d ed. (New York: McGraw-Hill, 1998).
3. F. Modigliani and R. Cohn, "Inflation, Rational Valuation and the Market," *Financial Analysts Journal* (March/April 1979), pp. 24–44.
4. P. Cagan, *Stock Prices Reflect the Adjustment of Earnings for Inflation,* NYU Monograph Series in Finance and Economics (New York: New York University, 1982).
5. Ibbotson Associates, *Stocks, Bonds, Bills, and Inflation, 2000 Yearbook,* Chicago, 2000.
6. Since 1997, there has been one notable exception to these general results. Beginning in early 1997, the U.S. Treasury began selling TIPS (Treasury inflation-protected securities). The coupon rate on these bonds is reset every 6 months. They have generally been yielding a greater than 3 percent real return, which is much above the 1 percent historical rate as reported by Ibbotson and Sinquefield (see note 7).
7. R. Ibbotson and R. Sinquefield, "Stocks, Bonds, Bills, and Inflation: Year-by-Year Historical Returns (1926–1999)," *Journal of Business* (January 1976), pp. 11–47.

11

Stock Market Forecasting and Individual Security Trading Strategies

Learning Objectives

An understanding of the material in this chapter should enable the student to

11-1. Describe the stock market tendency to overreact to information.

11-2. Explain the use of market timing devices for identifying when to buy or sell stocks.

11-3. Describe several technical market indicators used to predict market moves.

11-4. Explain the meaning and importance of asset allocation.

11-5. Explain the theoretical arguments and empirical evidence on technical analysis as practiced by the chartists.

11-6. Describe the numerous tendencies for prices to behave in a particular fashion.

11-7. Explain the market timing issue in brokerage share performance, dividend reinvestment plans, and dollar cost averaging.

Chapter Outline

Buy low and sell high is great advice, but it is useful only if the investor can identify market tops and bottoms as they are happening. Thus, we would like to know whether the market tops correspond to favorable moods for the market and bottoms to unfavorable ones. If so, can these moods be identified on a contemporaneous basis, and can knowledge of these moods be used profitably?

The chapter first considers the stock market's tendency to overreact, and then it discusses efforts to recognize these overreactions while they are underway. We will consider some of the most commonly suggested timing tools, such as market P/E (price-earnings) ratios and their relationship to interest and inflation rates, behavior during recessions, Dow theory, and investment advisers.

The chapter then discusses various technical indicators (data series or combinations of data series that are purported to forecast market turns). Specifically, short-interest, odd-lot trading, specialists' short selling, mutual fund cash positions, and the Barron's Confidence Index are all explored in the context of several relevant empirical studies. The chapter examines the following additional market indicators: advance-decline patterns, the short-term trading index, the January indicator, and Monday–Friday price patterns.

The chapter then turns to techniques for selecting individual stocks. These include the use of charts, such as bar charts and point-and-figure charts, to look for patterns and predict future stock price movements. The impact of specialized dependencies with respect to block trades, secondary offerings, intraday dependencies, tax-loss trading, and adjustment lags will be explored. We will also consider the impact on stock prices of such events as earnings and dividend announcements, additions to the S&P Index, bond rating changes, and other newsworthy events. The effects of tender offers, mergers, liquidations, share repurchases, and similar transactions on stock prices will be analyzed. We will conclude with a discussion of "passive" market timing strategies, such as dollar cost averaging.

STOCK MARKET OVERREACTION

stock market overreaction

When he was asked to predict stock market performance, J.P. Morgan replied, "It will continue to fluctuate." Anyone who has followed stocks understands the irony of this statement. The market's direction may be difficult to predict, but its continued volatility is not. Stock prices often change dramatically. Specific stock groups frequently go through fads. A stock may rise on a rumor that the firm is entering the Internet market, and later that same industry may be an anathema to the market. News sometimes has almost no impact, while at other times the market may appear to be looking for an excuse to move. To attribute such gyrations to a careful analysis of new information (market efficiency) seems questionable at best. Indeed, stock prices frequently change without any *obvious* pertinent new information entering the picture.

We have already noted that most investors believe that the market has a psychological side, and studies have come up with some supporting evidence. In this regard, Burton Malkiel examined the implications of growth stock pricing in the early 1960s.[1] Malkiel was interested in determining the growth rate in earnings and dividends needed to justify the market price. Very high growth rates must eventually decline. (We have already noted that point in our discussion of the dividend discount model.) For the purpose of his analysis, Malkiel assumed that high growth rates of growth stocks would eventually decline to the overall growth rate of the economy. He then computed how many years of abnormal growth were required to justify the P/Es of growth stocks. From December 1961 to June 1962, the average P/E of Malkiel's sample declined from 62.9 to 24.9. Over that same period, the average required years of abnormal growth fell from 6 to 2 1/2. Changes in the earning prospects of these companies seem unlikely to have caused the drastic reevaluations—both in Malkiel's samples and those that have been observed in past periods of downturns of the market. Further research has determined that changes in real dividends are far too modest to account for the historical pattern of real stock price changes in an efficient market. Neither are news announcements about macroeconomic performance sufficient to explain stock price variation. Finally, several researchers have concluded that qualitative news, even about significant changes in financial policies, does not account for all the return variation that cannot be attributable to quantitative macroeconomic causes.

The widely held view that investors tend to overreact to information has been tested directly by N. Jegadeesh and S. Titman. They found that the trading strategy of buying stocks that have performed well in the past and selling stocks that have performed poorly in the past appeared to generate significant positive returns over 3- to 12-month holding periods during 1965 through 1989. The abnormal returns generated in the first year after portfolio formation, however, dissipated during the following 2 years.[2] The initial positive and later negative relative returns (returns reversals) may be evidence of overreaction.

But there could be other explanations. For instance, one interpretation is that transactions by investors who buy past winners and sell past losers move prices away from their long-run values temporarily and this causes prices to overreact. Another interpretation is that the market underreacts to information about the short-term prospects for firms, but it overreacts to information about their long-term prospects. This is plausible because

TABLE 11-1
Annual Performance of Standard & Poor's 500 Industrial Index

Year	Difference between Index Value at Year End and at End of Previous Year	Year	Difference between Index Value at Year End and at End of Previous Year
1950	18.0%	1975	29.0%
1951	16.3	1976	19.2
1952	11.8	1977	−13.0
1953	−6.6	1978	1.1
1954	45.0	1979	12.3
1955	26.4	1980	25.9
1956	2.6	1981	−9.7
1957	−14.3	1982	14.7
1958	38.1	1983	17.3
1959	8.5	1984	1.4
1960	−3.0	1985	26.3
1961	23.1	1986	14.6
1962	−11.8	1987	2.0
1963	18.9	1988	12.0
1964	13.0	1989	27.2
1965	9.1	1990	−7.0
1966	−13.1	1991	26.3
1967	20.1	1992	4.4
1968	7.7	1993	7.1
1969	−11.4	1994	−1.5
1970	0.1	1995	34.1
1971	10.8	1996	20.3
1972	18.2	1997	31.0
1973	−21.1	1998	26.7
1974	−27.1	1999	19.5

information available for a firm's short-term prospects, such as earnings forecasts, is different in nature from the more ambiguous information that is used by investors to assess a firm's longer-term prospects.

Table 11-1, which reports the annual performance of S&P's 500 industrial index, illustrates the market's volatility. Annual price changes varied from +45 percent in 1954 to –27.1 percent in 1974 and +31 percent in 1997. Only four of 50 annual moves are within 3 percent of the overall average (10.41 percent). Clearly, stock prices fluctuate greatly from year to year. The geometric mean index growth over this time period was 9.22 percent.

This observed volatility does not in itself prove that the market overreacts. It does, however, at least raise the possibility that a mood-based market timing strategy might be effective. This leads into the next topic: How can market extremes be identified, or can they?

BUY CHEAP AND SELL DEAR: WHEN ARE STOCKS CHEAP?

market timing

Buying and selling at the appropriate times is often regarded as being as important to a stock market trader as identifying misvalued securities. The relatively unspectacular performance of most mutual funds illustrates the difficulty of anticipating major market moves. Gary P. Brinson, Brian D. Singer, and Gilbert L. Beebower found that among well-qualified institutional portfolio managers, *market timing* could account for only 1.8 percent of the average return differential, whereas security selection could account for 4.6 percent.[3] Portfolio allocation at 91.5 percent is far and away the most significant cause of the average return differential among these sophisticated investors (the residual interaction term accounts for the remainder 2.1 percent). Still, the potential rewards from accurate timing may encourage some investors to search for any useful evidence.

Investors would like to buy when the market has completed most of its downward movement but has not yet risen much above its low. If the precise bottom is not usually identifiable in advance, perhaps buying can at least be concentrated in depressed periods. This strategy requires some idea of when stocks are near their cyclical lows.

Market Behavior during Recession

Stock market performance during recessions and subsequent recoveries may follow a somewhat predictable pattern. First, there is a pattern of rising markets toward the latter part of recessions. Second, stock price advances tend to be more vigorous after severe contractions than after mild contractions. Investors can sometimes begin repurchasing 6 months after a recession has begun. Buying after the economic recovery begins does not require a forecast. The beginning of a recovery is generally observable within a few months of the bottom. Selling before an economic peak, in contrast, assumes an ability to predict the tops of economic cycles, which is more difficult.

In 1991, Jeremy Siegel examined the reliability of the relationship between stock prices and the business cycle. The stock market is known to have given false signals about future economic activity, particularly with regard to impending recessions. The market has registered many false alarms. For instance, since 1946, there were seven periods during which the cumulative stock returns index fell at least 8 percent and a recession did not occur. The stock market appears to have been a better indicator of coming economic expansions, turning upward on average about 5 months before the economy hits bottom and starts to turn around.[4]

Dow Theory

Dow theory

The *Dow theory* is one of the oldest and best-known approaches to market timing. Its originator, Charles Dow, was also the founder and first editor of *The Wall Street Journal*. Dow developed the key averages quoted widely in the financial pages, the Dow Jones Industrial Average (DJIA), the Dow Jones Transportation Average (DJTA), and the Utility Average. The Dow Jones Industrial Average, commonly referred to as the Dow, is composed of the stock prices of 30 leading industrial companies chosen from sectors of the economy that represent America's largest capitalization industrial (that is, nonfinancial) companies. The Dow relies on a formula resulting from the unweighted average of stock prices of the 30 industrial companies, adjusted for splits and stock dividends. The formula adds up the stocks' daily closing prices and divides by a certain number to derive the average. Higher-priced stocks in the average have greater effect on the average when their prices change by a given percentage than do lower-priced stocks, even though the initial importance of the two stocks was the same when the current index was created.

There are two ways in which the Dow averages and other broad stock indexes, such as the S&P 500, can be useful to the average investor:

- Indexes track the long-term ups and downs of stock prices to aid the investor in determining what the present market is doing, compared with past performance.
- If a stock does not seem to follow the upward movements of the market averages, it may indicate that investigation into the company's health is necessary.

The Dow theory asserts that a continuing trend can be identified by looking first for a new high in a market average defined as primary (such as the DJIA), and then seeking confirmation from a second high (such as the DJTA). Thus, if the Industrials reach a new high followed quickly by a new high for the Transports, the up trend is said to be intact.

Three Basic Ideas behind the Dow Theory

- To make a profit in the stock market, investors should take advantage of the primary market trend, which is the generally upward movement of the market over a period of one to 4 years.
- Whenever a primary trend is up, each secondary trend (a cycle around the basic trend) will produce a peak higher than the last one (*vice versa* for a down trend).
- Any true indicator of a primary market trend will be confirmed relatively quickly by similar action in the different stock price averages.

A study by S. Brown and W. Goetzmann appears to confirm the validity of the Dow theory. The original developers of the Dow theory did not provide an easily testable theory besides the simple rules listed above. Later research, using state-of-the-art artificial intelligence software to identify the precise technical trading patterns associated with the buy-and-sell signals, applied the patterns over 70 years of data. The study found some merit in the Dow theory. For instance, a portfolio that followed the signals to buy or sell identified by the Dow theory software, using an index fund with no transaction costs, would have outperformed a buy-and-hold strategy by about 2 percentage points per year. In addition, the Dow theory portfolio would have incurred one-third less volatility (the researchers' proxy for risk).[5] Brown and Goetzmann found that their version of the Dow theory portfolio beat the market indexes during such bearish periods as the 1970s and even the 1930s. Their model, however, showed the least favorable results during strongly bullish periods, such as the 1980s and the 1990s.

According to the *Hulbert Financial Digest* (a service that monitors performance of investment advisory letters), a portfolio that switched in and out of the market on signals from Dow theorist Richard Russell in the "Dow Theory Letters" would have underperformed a buy-and-hold strategy by about 2.7 percentage points per year since 1980. *Hulbert* found, however, that a Russell-guided portfolio would also have been 35 percent less volatile than the market as a whole. Thus, on a risk-adjusted basis (using volatility as a proxy for risk), the Dow theory-guided portfolio would have beaten the market.

Will the Dow theory work in the future? Only time will tell. But one feature of most timing strategies is that they appear to work for some events but not others. Moreover, they appear to diminish in usefulness over time as pricing arbitrage by investors who anticipate the timing rules eventually eliminates whatever advantage the rules initially display.

Most academics and practitioners remain highly skeptical of technical analysis. The main reason for this skepticism is that thorough tests of technical analysis techniques have failed to confirm their consistency and validity, given all the transaction costs involved, relative to a simple buy-and-hold strategy.

In addition, there are other troubling features of technical analysis. First, several interpretations of a particular technical tool or chart pattern are possible, giving rise to numerous different assessments or recommendations. For instance, those who interpret the signals of the Dow theory are notorious for their multiple interpretations.

A second troubling factor is if a technical trading rule (or chart pattern) proves successful, it will become widely adopted by market participants. If the rule or pattern is widely adopted, it will often prove to be self-defeating. Therefore, stock prices will reach their equilibrium value quickly, taking away profit opportunities from most market participants. Moreover, some market observers may start trying to act before the rest on the basis of what they expect to occur; thus, the prices of affected stocks will tend to reach an equilibrium even more quickly. Eventually, the value of any such rule or pattern will be negated entirely.

According to Malkiel, there are three potential flaws in technical analysis. One, the information and analysis may be incorrect. Two, the security analyst's estimate of "value" may be faulty. Three, the market may not correct its mistake, and the stock price might not converge to its value estimate.[6]

It has proven difficult, if not impossible, to test all the techniques of technical analysis and their variations and interpretations. The techniques are too numerous, and new ones are developed all the time. Therefore, absolutely definitive statements about their validity cannot be made.

Market Forecasters

Rather than try to identify market tops and bottoms, many investors rely on professionals who make their living forecasting the market. But it is not easy deciding which professional to use. Similar difficulties confront investors who rely on market timing experts. Nonetheless, these services are a significant part of the investment scene.

Investors who want to know what market forecasters are saying can subscribe directly to some of the market forecasting letters, or they can read articles that report analysts' opinions on the Internet or in the popular press. Other investors may prefer to assess the data that the forecasters use. Many analysts make at least some use of technical market indicators.

Market Timing Approaches

- Behavior during recessions: The market tends to turn up during in a recession.
- Dow theory: An up trend is confirmed when a high in the primary index (for example, DJIA) is soon followed by a high in a secondary index (for example, DJTA). Down trends are confirmed by the reverse order (DJTA low soon followed by DJIA low).
- Market forecasters: Professional advice on the market is derived from market forecasting services. Most of these services utilize some technical indicators or give some timing advice.

TRADITIONAL TECHNICAL MARKET INDICATORS

technical market indicators

Thus far we have examined market forecasts based on historic relationships during recessions, Dow theory, and market analysts' opinions. The traditional *technical market indicators* discussed below are also used to predict market moves. Specifically, many analysts claim to see timing signals in the behavior of certain data series, or combinations of data series, such as short interest, odd-lot behavior, specialist short selling, and a host of others.

Comparative Market Indices

There are over 3,000 common stock issues listed on the NYSE, not to mention thousands more traded on the American Stock Exchange, regional exchanges, and OTC (listed in financial pages as NASDAQ). You may ask what good the Dow Jones Industrial Average is with only 30 stocks. The answer is partly historic and partly scientific. The Dow Jones Industrial Average began in 1884 with 11 stocks and increased to 30 stocks in 1928. The 30 companies listed for the Dow Jones Industrial are representative of the broad market and of U.S. industry. Except for the utility, transportation, and financial sectors, the companies are chosen because they are major players in their industries and their stocks are widely held by both individual and institutional investors. The 30 stocks in the Dow Industrials represent a fifth of the $1 trillion-plus market value of all stock traded, and about a fourth of the value of stocks on the NYSE.

Research has shown that Dow averages closely mirror broader stock market indicators. By its nature, however, the Dow represents the blue chip or large-capitalization stocks such as AT&T, Coca-Cola, DuPont, GE, and IBM (and more recent additions, including Microsoft, Intel, and Wal-Mart). Other broader market indexes, such as the S&P 500 Industrial Index, represent a much wider array of stocks. Whenever the broader indexes move in a direction opposite from Dow averages, there is a divergence between top-tier (blue chip), high-capitalization stocks and second-tier, lower-capitalization stocks. For instance, if the Dow average moves up while broader indexes fall or remain the same, these conflicting changes may indicate insecurity by market participants and a tendency to seek the security of larger, well-known firms (sometimes called a *flight-to-quality effect*).

Use of widely held and frequently traded companies in the Dow Industrial listing provides an important feature of timeliness—that is, the Dow averages represent major frequently traded stocks. Therefore, these averages represent the direction of current transactions at any point in time, which may not always be the case with broader indexes. The broader indexes, such as NASDAQ/OTC Index, include less frequently traded stocks or stocks that are not widely owned and are therefore not as timely.

Short Interest

short interest

As discussed earlier, short sellers sell borrowed stock that they hope later to replace at a profit. At one time, short sellers were thought to be sophisticated traders who were able to anticipate market turns. Thus, an increase in *short interest* (uncovered short sales) was said to forecast a market decline. Others, in contrast, argued that short interest reflects potential demand from covering short traders. According to this view, a rise in short interest forecasts a market rally. Studies show, however, that short interest is largely unrelated to market rises and falls. Short interest data are published monthly in *The Wall Street Journal*.

odd-lot activity

Odd-Lot Activity

According to some analysts, odd-lot (fewer than 100 shares) traders tend to buy at tops and sell at bottoms. Analysts' rationale is the assumption that people who trade in odd lots, which have a higher per-share commission than round lots, tend to be inexperienced and unskilled traders. Thus, when odd-lotters are buying on balance, the market may be about to fall; when odd-lot investors are mostly selling, the market may be ready to turn up.

odd-lot short ratio

The problem is how to measure this investor sentiment. Traditionally, odd-lot short-selling activity has been measured by the *odd-lot short ratio*, which is calculated by dividing odd-lot short sales over some time period by total odd-lot sales. One difficulty with the ratio, however, is that both the numerator and denominator show degrees of pessimism. An alternative might be to use odd-lot purchases in the denominator. This ratio might be better at recording the differences in expectations between bullish investors (odd-lot purchasers) and bearish speculators (odd-lot short sellers).

The total odd-lot short ratio (TOLSR) can be calculated as follows:

$$\text{TOLSR} = \frac{\text{odd-lot short sales}}{\text{odd-lot purchases/odd-lot sales}}$$

Odd-lot theory suggests observing what the small investor is doing and then doing the opposite. *Barron's* breaks down odd-lot trading on a daily basis in its "Market Laboratory—Stocks" section. It constructs a ratio of odd-lot purchases to odd-lot sales. For example, on December 19, 2001, 8,274,993 odd-lot shares were purchased and 8,786,553 odd-lot shares were sold—a ratio of purchases to sales of about 0.942 (rounded to three decimal places). The ratio has fluctuated historically between 0.50 and 1.45. New York Stock Exchange specialists also reported that there were 445,834 odd-lot short sales on December 19, 2001. Dividing that number by the ratio of odd-lot purchases to sales provides a total odd-lot short ratio of 473,395.

Although the odd-lot theory appeared to have some validity during the 1950s and 1960s, it has failed to be a useful predictor since then. For instance, odd-lotters outperformed many professional money managers by selling on or before the stock market collapses of the 1970s and late 1980s, and they began buying in advance of a recovery during the early 1990s.

Specialists' Short Selling

Some people consider specialists to be especially sophisticated investors who have access to nonpublic trading intention information (the limit order book) and are positioned to react quickly to any emerging developments. Because their profits are largely derived from trading their assigned stocks, much of their success depends on effectively managing their inventory. Specialists generally are supposed to sell short when they expect a price decline and buy when their expectations are positive. Studies have not confirmed, however, that this is a reliable market indicator.

Mutual Fund Cash Position

Equity mutual funds usually maintain a modest cash reserve to meet redemption demands and other needs for cash. They may also hold on to cash when they are undecided about where to invest it. When the cash positions (potential buying power) of equity mutual funds rise to the point at which they become a large percentage of their total assets, the market may have some upside potential. Studies show that mutual funds attempt to time their trading to take advantage of market swings. Mutual funds do not, however, successfully alter the composition of their portfolios over the market cycles.

Barron's Confidence Index

The Barron's Confidence Index (BCI) is the ratio of 10 high-grade corporate bond rates relative to the more speculative Dow Jones Bond Index rates. A high value for the ratio indicates that high-grade yields are relatively close to the yields on more speculative issues. At such times, the market is unwilling to pay much of a premium for quality (or, stated differently, does not require a large premium to hold lower-grade issues). Alternatively, a low ratio implies a substantial premium for quality. The ratio appears in *Barron's* "Market Laboratory" section. This section is a source of many of the underlying data used to compute market indicators. Users of the Confidence Index believe that smart money will move toward quality bonds when the market outlook is unfavorable and toward speculative bonds when the market outlook is favorable. In other words, the risk premium on riskier bonds will increase when the overall outlook for the market is unfavorable. As with most of the indicators discussed so far, the evidence is suggestive but not conclusive. Even in forecasting market peaks, the results are not especially encouraging or useful.

Traditional Technical Market Indicators

- Odd-lot activity: When odd-lot short sales are abnormally high (low), the market is said to be near a bottom (top).
- Specialists' short selling: High (low) specialist short selling is thought to forecast a market decline (rise).
- Mutual fund cash position: Mutual fund cash is an indication of potential future demand for stocks.
- Barron's Confidence Index: The ratio of high-grade to average-grade bond yields reflects confidence of "smart" investors.

OTHER TECHNICAL INDICATORS

Although the indicators discussed in the previous section are quite traditional, they are by no means exhaustive. Let us consider some of the more recent indicators that have developed a following.

Some analysts argue that the market's strength may be gauged by the ratio of the number of stocks advancing to the number declining, especially if there is a tendency for the ratio to persist over some time period.

The short-term trading index, which is derived from the advance-decline ratio, attempts to measure the degree to which volume is concentrated in declining and advancing stocks, and it is defined as the ratio of two other ratios. The first ratio (A) is the *number* of advancing stocks divided by the *number* of declining stocks. The second ratio (B) is the *volume* of advancing stocks divided by the *volume* of declining stocks. The short-term trading index is A divided by B. The indicator is available on most stock quotation machines and on the Internet. A little manipulation reveals that the index is the average volume of declining stocks relative to the average volume of advancing stocks. The lower the ratio, the greater the average volume in advancing stocks relative to the average volume in declining stocks.

January indicator (January effect)

The *January indicator (January effect)* is a rather simplistic tool that often receives a good bit of attention at the beginning of each year. A market that rises in January is expected to rise during the year; a market that falls in January is expected to fall during the year. Because the market generally rises both in January and for the year, the success of the January indicator may easily be overstated. Several other months seem to do about as well.

Regarding the January effect, Donald Keim found, in a landmark study, that small stocks outperformed large ones during the first several weeks almost every year between 1926 and the mid-1970s. One explanation for this was that hard-to-trade small stocks tend to be depressed by investors' tax-related year-end selling. But then small stocks bounce back as investors rebuy them early the next year.[7] However, according to Prudential Securities, small stocks underperformed the market averages each January for the period 1993–1998. One explanation is that fund managers buy small stock in December in anticipation of the January effect, thus offsetting individual investors' tax-loss selling.

Other Technical Indicators

- Advance-decline patterns: Past advance-decline patterns tend to persist.
- Short-term trading index: High (low) relative volume of advancing stocks is a sell (buy) signal.
- January indicator: January performance is said to forecast the year, but the evidence is unimpressive.
- Monday–Friday price pattern: The market tends to rise on Fridays and fall on Mondays.
- Monthly pattern: The market tends to rise in the first half of each month, with much of that tendency concentrated in the months of April, July, and October.

Unusual price behavior has been found for Mondays and Fridays. In the past, the market was consistently more likely to be up on Friday than on Monday. The frequent practice of withholding unpleasant economic news until the market's Friday close may account for the phenomenon. This day-of-the-week price effect suggests that, if no overriding considerations intervene, investors might as well sell on Friday and wait until late in the day on Monday to buy. The Monday after a Friday decline may offer somewhat more attractive buying opportunities.

S. Penman's study of stock market seasonality found that the market tends to be particularly strong in the first half of the first month of quarters two, three, and four.[8] This result appears to be due to a tendency for good earnings reports to be issued at that time; poor reports are released later in the first quarter after most total fiscal year results are fully known. In other words, firms act as if they are hoping to delay bad news until the last possible moment when it becomes legally impossible (due to reporting requirements) to delay any further.

ASSET ALLOCATION

asset allocation

Market timers in their most extreme form seek to be totally in the market when it is going up and totally out when it is going down. Others, however, seek a compromise. An increasingly popular strategy called *asset allocation* has emerged. Although the concept has been around for many years based on the work of Harry Markowitz and others (see chapter 7), its name and popularity are relatively new. Investment advisers and financial planners who are asset allocators seek to vary their proportional ownership of different types of investments based on the outlook for those investments. For example, an asset allocator may divide his or her client's portfolio into several components, such as the following:

- money funds for very low risk and high liquidity
- long-term, high-grade bonds for moderate risk
- junk bonds for speculative appeal in the debt market
- blue chip stocks for low-risk equity market participation
- growth and/or small-cap stocks for greater speculation in equities
- international equities for global diversification
- stock options for short-run speculation in equities

Most asset allocators stick to stocks, bonds, and money market securities. Regardless of which asset categories he or she chooses, the asset allocator varies the percentages invested based on his or her assessment of the investment outlook and the use of portfolio optimizers.

Example: A neutral outlook might imply the following allocations: 20 percent in money funds, 30 percent in long-term bonds, and 50 percent in stocks. A more conservative stance might be 50 percent in money funds, 20 percent in bonds, and 30 percent in stocks.

An extremely bearish outlook might suggest an allocation of 80 percent in money market funds and 20 percent in gold. Alternatively, a more aggressive strategy would move toward greater percentages of assets in growth stocks, small-cap stocks, and options.

TECHNICAL ANALYSIS

charting

Charting, a common tool of technical analysis, is used to assess the market's mood toward specific stocks. Although controversial, chart reading (or its modern-day equivalent, momentum modeling), is still widely practiced.

Types of Charts

bar chart

moving average
relative strength

The two most common types of charts are bar charts and point-and-figure charts. The *bar chart* is used to show the daily price range, closing price, and daily volume. The basic format of the bar chart may be supplemented with a *moving average* line (for example, the average stock price for the past 50 days) and a *relative strength* line. The relative strength line plots the ratio of the stock's price to that of the S&P 500 average or to some other appropriate average or index.

Example: Suppose Standard Widget's daily closing prices are as follows:

May 1, 2001	$30
May 2, 2001	$31
May 3, 2001	$32
May 4, 2001	$31
May 5, 2001	$31
May 8, 2001	$32
May 9, 2001	$31
May 10, 2001	$30
May 11, 2001	$29
May 12, 2001	$30

Assume we wish to calculate the moving average for the past 5 trading days. On May 8, our moving average would be based on the closing prices of May 1 through 5, or ($30 + $31 + $32 + $31 + $31)/5, or $31. On May 9, our moving average would be based on the closing stock prices for May 2 through 8, and so on. For the second week in May, our daily 5-day moving average would be

May 8, 2001	$31
May 9, 2001	$31.40
May 10, 2001	$31.40
May 11, 2001	$31
May 12, 2001	$30.60

Figure 11-1 shows a typical bar chart with share volume for Xerox Corporation during December through October 2001. The moving average lines trace the trend movements over selected averaging periods (typically 90-day and 360-day averages).

FIGURE 11-1
Typical Bar Chart

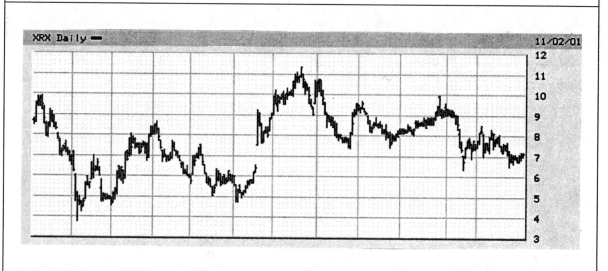

Reproduced with permission. Copyright © 1998–2001 MarketWatch.com <http://cbs.MarketWatch.com>, Inc. Historical and current end-of-day data provided by FT Interactive Data <http://www.FTInteractiveData.com/> Intraday data provided by S&P Comstock <http://www.spcomstock.com/>

point-and-figure chart

A *point-and-figure chart* diagrams stock movements. This chart has no time dimension. The vertical axis measures the stock price. To construct the chart, a threshold level of price movement is determined. One point (dollar per share) is the typical threshold. Every time the stock moves past a whole number level, a mark is recorded. If the move is upward, an X is entered; a downward move calls for an O. As the price rises, Xs are stacked one on top of another. When the price direction changes, an O is entered in the next column. Additional Os are added below as the stock price falls. Point-and-figure charts give a compact presentation of price movements. Figure 11-2 shows a typical point-and-figure chart.

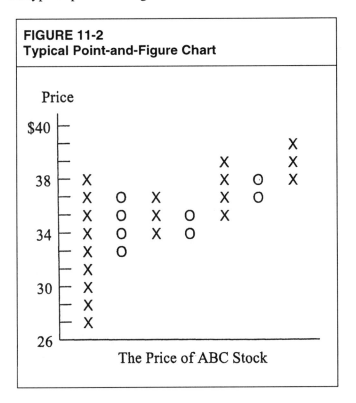

FIGURE 11-2
Typical Point-and-Figure Chart

The Price of ABC Stock

Major Premises of the Chartist's Approach

Much of chartism is based on one very basic premise: Stock prices follow trends. That is, chartists believe that stock prices often behave as if they have a degree of *momentum*. This momentum is expected to carry the price along in its current direction until some new force causes a change in direction.

A second tenet of chartists (in the case of bar charts) is the belief that volume goes with the trend. Thus, in a major up trend, volume will increase as the price rises and decrease when the price declines.

The third major premise of the chartist's approach hypothesizes the existence of resistance and support levels. A *resistance level* emerges as a significant number of investors look to get out when a certain price level is reached. The number of shares offered increases dramatically as this resistance level is approached. Similarly, at a *support level*, a support price

momentum

resistance level

support level

may exist at about the level that the most recent rise began. Investors who missed the first move may be waiting for a second chance to buy if the stock drops back down to that level.

Chartists' Interpretations of Price Patterns

head-and-shoulders formation

Technical analysts seek to identify favorable buying and selling opportunities from repeating price patterns. These patterns include chart formations such as triangles, coils, rectangles, flags, pennants, gaps, line-and-saucer formations, and V-formations. Perhaps the best known pattern is the *head-and-shoulders formation* on bar charts. This pattern, which resembles the human form, shows the following stages of development for a bearish signal:

- left shoulder: The left shoulder builds up when there is a strong rally, accompanied by significant volume. Thereafter, when a profit-taking reaction occurs, the shoulder slopes downward. Volume is noticeably reduced.
- head: Rising prices and increased volume initiate the left side of the head pattern, followed by a contraction, or reduced volume, which extends to the neckline. In this configuration, the head always extends well above the left shoulder.
- right shoulder: When there is another price rally, the left side of the right shoulder slopes upward; finally, when the rally breaks up and prices slide downward, the right side of the right shoulder slopes downward. Volume action is usually decidedly smaller than it was under the left shoulder and head. The right shoulder tends to be equal in height with the left shoulder and it is always well below the head.

According to this interpretation of price patterns, a trader who buys late often has an opportunity to buy a second time on a brief minor rally that pulls prices back to the neckline.

SPECIALIZED DEPENDENCIES

Anxious Trader Effects

Block trades, secondary offerings, intraday dependencies and tax-loss trading may lead to temporary supply-demand imbalances. Initially, the price may be disturbed away from its equilibrium level. Later, as the effects dissipate, the price may move back toward its prior level.

Block Trades and Secondary Offerings

As discussed in chapter 3, block trades are transactions involving 10,000 or more shares. Most block trades reflect a relatively large trader's desire to buy or sell. Sell trades may put some downward pressure on the market. If this pressure is temporary, an investor might profit from it. Most block trades, however, do not depress prices by enough to permit after-commission trading profits on the typical rebound, although those with the greatest price declines offer the most attractive trading prospects.

Several researchers have found price declines that are associated with large secondary distributions on the day of the sale and subsequently.[9] They have also found that secondary distributions of corporate insiders, investment companies, and mutual funds are followed by appreciably greater price changes than when the sellers are banks, insurance companies, estates, trusts, or individuals. Quite possibly, corporate insiders, investment companies, and mutual funds are more likely to base their decision to sell on fundamental grounds to which they are privy but others are not, whereas banks, insurance companies, and others may simply need liquidity.

intraday dependencies

General Intraday Dependencies: Specialists and Limit Orders

It has been argued that stock prices closely resemble a random walk for daily movements. However, temporary intraday barriers to price movements and nonrandom overnight (close to next day's open) price changes have been observed, which may be ascribed to the interaction of specialists' trading and publicly placed limit orders.

Specialists are charged with keeping an orderly market (that is, avoiding excessive volatility) in their assigned stocks. They rely on a combination of limit orders and buying and selling with their own inventory to keep their markets orderly. Limit orders tend to collect at even values (generally whole numbers and halves). A collection of these limit orders at even values may act as temporary barriers to price movements. Once the market has executed a stack of whole-number limit orders, only a few orders may restrict further movement. Continued buying (selling) activity may lead to a rather rapid price increase (decrease) until a new barrier is encountered.

Example: Buying pressure may move a stock price from 18.60 to 18.90. Once 19 is reached, continued buying could quickly propel the price to 19.90, with 20 becoming the next barrier.

Informed Trading

Markets sometimes reflect the activity of informed traders executing transactions with a public that does not know what the informed traders know. For example, someone accumulating a position prior to a takeover attempt will, at the outset, generally have information that is kept secret from the rest of the market. Similarly, an insider may have a much better assessment of the company's prospects than the rest of the market does. Sophisticated traders and investors—particularly specialists—are always aware of the possibility that an informed trader may be on the other side of the market. Accordingly, they become cautious when persistent buying or selling moves a price outside of its recent trading range.

Tax-Loss Trading

tax-loss trading

Yet another area of possible anxious trader impact involves year-end selling to establish a tax loss. *Tax-loss trading* is believed to have dramatically affected some year-end stock prices. The end of the year, therefore, may be an attractive time to purchase stocks that are under tax-loss selling pressure.

Several studies have refined our knowledge on tax-loss trading, especially as it relates to seasonality. A number of studies have found that most of the turn-of-the-year effect—stocks that decline by the largest amounts in December are most likely to rise in January—occurs at the small-firm level.[10] One study tests the hypothesis that tax-loss trading by individual investors is responsible for the January effect. The study examines the ownership structure of a large sample of firms over a 4-year-period and finds

---

Anxious Trader Effects

- Block trades: Prices tend to decline with block trades and regain most of the loss by day's end.
- Large secondary distributions: Prices show modest declines on the day of and following a secondary distribution.
- Intraday dependencies: Bunching orders at certain price points may slow and then exaggerate/accelerate price movements.
- Informed trading: Persistent buying or selling moves the price outside of its recent trading range.
- Tax-loss trading: Issues under year-end tax selling pressure may rise at the beginning of the year; small-firm and low-priced issues are particularly likely to be affected in this way.

that the small firms that usually exhibit high January returns have low institutional ownership. Thus, the study indicates that individual ownership is significantly related to January abnormal returns. One reason that the January effect may concentrate in small firms is because these firms are held by tax-motivated individual investors.[11]

Adjustment Lags

adjustment lags

Adjustment lags are another category of specialized dependencies. Specifically, prices may take time to react to such factors as earnings announcements, dividend changes, additions to the S&P 500 Industrial Index, bond rating changes, corporate crime disclosures, insider trading reports, media recommendations, splits, stock dividends, tender offers, mergers, liquidations, share repurchases, rights offerings, equity sales, debt-for-equity swaps, forced conversions, divestitures, and spin-offs.

Earnings and Dividend Announcements

According to several studies on earnings and dividend announcements, although prices may not adjust instantly to these announcements, the lags appear to be quite short. The reactions seem to be faster for firms with listed options. Firms without listed options take longer to react to quarterly earnings announcements. Moreover, several studies found a relatively slow market reaction to unexpected earnings changes.

Several different studies that focused on dividends have generally found that dividend increases often result in substantial positive price reactions that are usually completed by the day of the announcement or soon thereafter. Favorable dividend announcements tend to be made in a timely fashion, whereas delayed announcements are associated with dividend omissions or reductions.

Additions to the S&P Index

Additions to Standard & Poor's 500 Industrial Index are widely followed by the market. The S&P 500 Index is viewed as a much broader-based index than the Dow Jones Industrial Average. As such, the S&P 500 is the index on which many other financial instruments are based. For example, most stock index futures, options on index futures, and indexed mutual funds utilize the S&P 500. Stocks are added to and deleted from the index in order to preserve or enhance its representativeness. The announcement that a stock is to be added to the index tends to cause its price to rise, whereas a deletion has the opposite tendency.

Bond Rating Changes

According to research on stock price reaction to bond rating changes, there is an appreciable reaction to rating downgrades, but upgrades have an insignificant effect. That may be because the stock's market price already takes into account the positive information about the company that provided the basis for the bond rating upgrade.

Corporate Crime Disclosures

There is a significant negative market reaction to disclosures or allegations of illegal corporate behavior. Virtually all of this reaction occurs at the time of the announcement.

insider trading

Insider Trading

Often, inside information appears to facilitate a relatively accurate stock evaluation. Noninsiders must generally wait until the information is publicly released, but traders can observe insiders' trading decisions and act accordingly.

The inside trades of CEOs and directors appear to be better predictors of subsequent performance than those of vice presidents and beneficial owners.[12] Apparently, CEOs and directors have better access to information.

Insiders must report their trades to the SEC. Thus, investors can consult SEC records to determine insiders' trading on a particular stock. Moreover, some investment services report SEC insider trading data to subscribers. Certain periodicals, including *Barron's* and *Value Line,* report on insider trades, and insider trading activity is sometimes discussed in the financial press, at least on an *ad hoc* basis. However, there can be a time lag of several days or weeks between the time insider trades take place and the time they become known by the investing public. During the intervening time, the market price of the company's stock might change sufficiently so that noninsiders would find it difficult to profit after taking transaction costs into consideration.

There have been several cases related to alleged misused insider information by outsiders who made trades based on it. An important Supreme Court decision in 1997 clarified what constitutes illegal insider trading. The decision upheld the so-called misappropriation theory of insider trading, which states that traders may not trade on nonpublic information even if they are not corporate insiders.[13]

Media Recommendations

According to a study of the daily "Heard in the Street" column in *The Wall Street Journal,* which highlights specific companies' and analysts' opinions of specific stocks, the market appears to react efficiently to published takeover rumors in that column. According to the study, excess returns could not be earned, on average, by purchasing rumored takeover targets at the time the rumor appeared. No significant excess returns occurred on the day the takeover rumor was published, although a positive cumulative excess of about 7 percent occurred in the calendar month *prior* to the appearance of the rumor in the "Heard on the Street" columns.[14]

A 1992 study examined the impact of the insider information scandal related to R. Foster Winans' "Heard in the Street" column in 1984. Winans was giving advance notice to his friend of information that was to appear in the column. The friend was making money on these trades. Following the scandal, the column had a reduced impact on stock prices for both buy and sell recommendations. Several months into the postscandal period, stock price response to information prior to the column's publication day was less. The results seem to indicate that the editors of *The Wall Street Journal* may have become more cautious in guarding against information leaks concerning the column. The scandal did not appear, however, to have altered the column's impact on trading volume.[15]

Another study focused on stock price behavior of firms that were favorably mentioned in the "Inside Wall Street" column in *Business Week*. The study found positive excess returns for favorably mentioned stocks on the day prior to the publication date, the publication date, and the days immediately after publication. There were positive, significant excess returns for long-term holding periods prior to the publication date but significant negative returns for long-term post-publication holding periods.

The study's findings are consistent with the price performance of firms that might have been the subject either of rumors or recent recommendations by analysts or brokerage firms. These results, along with those of earlier studies, suggest that secondary information is valuable only to low-transaction-cost, short-term traders. Investors who buy stock for the longer term based on secondary information generally receive below-market rates of return.[16] By secondary information, we mean the information that tells us how others perceive the stock. This should be distinguished from new information about the firm itself, such as information about the firm's product line or earning potential.

Analysts' Recommendations versus Market Efficiency

The question of whether following analysts' recommendations can consistently lead to superior returns brings us back to the debate over the semistrong form of the efficient market hypothesis versus the efficacy of fundamental analysis. Analysts' recommendations are based on evaluating information that is publicly available, so efficient market adherents would argue that such recommendations should not systematically yield superior risk-adjusted returns.

In a recent study,[17] analysts' recommendations were reviewed for a sample of 3,600 listed companies over a 10-year period. The study constructed hypothetical portfolios based on the consensus recommendations of the analysts. The authors found that an investor who consistently bought stock with the most favorable consensus ratings and sold stock with the least favorable consensus ratings would have outperformed the market on a risk-adjusted basis.

However, due to rating changes, such a portfolio would have had substantial turnover, resulting in substantial transaction costs. Therefore, the study found that once transaction costs are taken into account, one could not consistently earn superior risk-adjusted returns by following analysts' consensus recommendations.

Tender Offers, Mergers, and Liquidations

Tender offers, mergers, and liquidations may present investors with still other attractive trading opportunities. Stockholders often profit when their stock (a target) is tendered for and/or merged into another company. The offering price almost always exceeds the previous level, usually by a substantial margin. Moreover, a variety of people may benefit from such transactions. For example, those who put the deals together are always well rewarded, as are the target firm's advisers. Even the acquired firm's managers are usually well compensated (the so-called golden parachute) when they are forced to leave. Those who know of planned mergers before the announcement may (illegally) trade on that knowledge. Large investors may buy a sizable position in a company and then try either to force a takeover from the inside or to get the company to pay a premium to repurchase their shares (greenmail). The company's own assets are often used as collateral to finance the full takeover (a leveraged buyout, or LBO).

Yet another strategy is to acquire a large position in an undervalued company and then have the company buy out most or all of the small public shareholders. Taking a company private in this way may buy out most shareholders at possibly depressed prices. Of course, the stock may not stay depressed if small public shareholders realize there is new demand for their shares. If the company succeeds in buying out all small public investors, it eliminates much of the stockholder relations cost. Finally, a company whose assets are worth more than the market price of its shares may be bought as a liquidation prospect.

Although these various maneuvers may yield handsome returns, traders need either inside information of planned takeovers (and a willingness to break the law) or the resources to influence the relevant firms. The only realistic strategy for investors is to try to anticipate forthcoming acquisitions. They can then be in the right place at the right time when the target company is put in play. Moreover, once a takeover looks like a success, tendering the remaining publicly held shares is almost always advisable. Small holdings of subsidiaries usually have little speculative appeal.

While some mergers actually occur, others are merely rumored. Stock prices are often influenced by these rumors. Once the real situation is known, the stock will react appropriately. If the stock is truly a target, the announcement will tend to move the price toward the level of the offer. If the rumor is incorrect, the stock will probably go back to or near its price prior to the rumor. Some investors will already own stock of a company that is rumored to be a takeover target. They would like to know whether to hold the stock until the anticipated event occurs or to sell before the rumor turns out to be merely unfounded speculation. Investors who are contemplating buying do not want to be influenced by rumors that turn out to be false. Clearly, for the investor to profit, he or she must know how to assess a takeover rumor.

Share Repurchases, Equity Sales, Forced Conversions, and Exchanges

Earnings retention and minor debt decisions continually alter capital structures. Other actions can appreciably alter the number of shares outstanding and/or the firm's debt ratio. These actions can dramatically affect the shareholders' expected income streams and risks. Moreover, capital structure changes that affect the relative amounts of dividend and interest payments have important tax implications. Thus, the market may well react to such events as share repurchases (which decrease outstanding shares), rights offerings, and forced conversions (both of which increase outstanding shares). According to one study, market reactions to capital structure changes are as follows:

- Changes that affect expected taxes and/or the relative values of stocks versus bonds are associated with significant security price moves in the predicted directions.
- Different classes of security holders are often affected differently by the shift.
- Shareholders are generally adversely affected by a decrease in leverage.[18]

Other studies report that firms use share repurchases to signal their belief that their stocks are undervalued. The studies also found that common shareholders usually benefit from such repurchases and that market reaction to repurchases occurs within one day of the announcement.[19]

Share repurchases decrease shares outstanding and tend to increase per-share prices, while rights offerings and other types of equity sales tend to have the opposite effect. One study found a negative market reaction to the announcement and implementation of equity sales (including the sale of convertible securities).[20] On the other hand, another study found that management requests to increase authorized shares had little or no impact.[21] The impact of the offering on the market price of the firm's stock may depend on the firm's disclosure (required by SEC regulation) of how the proceeds of the offering are to be applied. Still another study indicated that equity carve-outs (partial sales of subsidiaries) and announcements of capital expenditures had generally positive impacts.[22]

Like sales of equity, voluntary exchanges of equity for debt and forced conversions of convertible debentures and convertible preferreds increase shares outstanding and reduce leverage. Thus, these exchanges and conversions tend to lower both per-share earnings and risk. Calling convertibles will force conversion only if the stock price has appreciated sufficiently to make conversion profitable. Therefore, the conversion value must exceed the call price or owners will not willingly convert. When issuers use a call, knowing that security holders will choose to convert, the issuer is said to have forced a conversion.

Adjustment Lags

- Earnings announcements: The market reacts quickly to earnings news.
- Dividend announcements: The market reacts quickly to dividend news.
- Additions/deletions to S&P 500 Index: Stocks tend to rise when added to the index and fall when deleted.
- Bond rating changes: Price reaction is appreciable for downgrades but not for upgrades.
- Alleged corporate crime: The market reacts quickly to news of alleged illegal activity.
- Insider trading: Reports of insider trades appear to provide profitable trading signals.
- Media recommendations: There are short-term positive excess returns for recommended stocks prior to media coverage.
- Tender offers, mergers, and liquidations: Returns can be significant, but investors must anticipate the event.
- Share repurchases: Repurchases often indicate that management believes the stock is undervalued.
- Rights offerings and equity sales: Shareholders generally react negatively to announcements of rights offerings and equity sales.
- Forced conversions and debt-for-equity exchanges: Strong positive performances generally precede forced conversion and debt-for-equity exchange announcements, with negative performances afterward.

forced conversion

A *forced conversion* of debt for equity has a different market impact than a voluntary conversion. The announcement of the swap of stock for debt is sometimes associated with negative stock price performance. Subsequent performance is related to the purpose of the swap. If, for example, the swap is part of a refunding operation, subsequent performance is generally favorable. Swaps of preferreds for common stock and reversions of excess assets (from pension funds to the corporation) tend to have a favorable market impact.

Assessment of Adjustment Lags

The market appears to adjust quickly to most new information. Reactions generally occur within a day or so of the following types of announcements: earnings reports, dividend changes, additions to the S&P 500 Index, bond rating changes, allegations of corporate crimes, share repurchases, and rights offerings. Stock price adjustments actually tend to precede the announcement or event for splits, tender offers, and mergers. Thus, trading based on these relationships normally requires prior knowledge or accurate forecasts. On the other hand, revisions of earnings forecasts, insider trading signals, and forced conversions may produce usable price relationships (that is, those that take place over a long enough period to be exploited).

DOLLAR COST AVERAGING

dollar cost averaging

Dollar cost averaging is a "passive" means of market timing. Most investors prefer not to try to forecast market and individual security movements. Without actually making a forecast, an investor can engage in *dollar cost averaging*, which is the investment of a fixed amount of money at specified time intervals. Investing a fixed dollar amount per period means that investors buy more shares when prices are low than when they are high. The benefit of such a strategy is that it frequently results in a lower average purchase price per share. It also helps some investors who are reluctant to invest a large sum of money in a single shot.

Unless a stock goes into a persistent decline, dollar cost averaging frequently works. It works best when the stock has an early decline and a later rise. It does not, however, protect the investor against a loss of stock values in a declining market.

Dividend Reinvestment Plans

dividend reinvestment plan

One form of dollar cost averaging is a *dividend reinvestment plan*—a program in which stockholders can reinvest their dividends directly into the company's stock. These plans may acquire either existing or newly issued stock. The first plans to be established relied on existing stock purchases. Typically, the corporation sends the dividends of participating stockholders to the managing bank's trust department. This bank maintains an account for each shareholder. Each participant is credited with his or her shares, less brokerage fees and administrative costs. Many plans also permit additional stock purchases for cash. Large round-lot purchases by the plan tend to reduce brokerage fees. Some companies give discounts on their dividend reinvestments. Firms selling newly issued shares charge no brokerage fees on the transactions.

Dividend reinvestment plans have a number of advantages. From the firm's standpoint, the plans add to stockholder goodwill, increase demand for the firm's stock, save some dividend-related expenses, and encourage small stockholders to increase ownership. In addition, plans involving new share purchases reduce the firm's debt-to-equity ratio, provide a regular source of equity capital, and permit new equity to be sold without incurring underwriting fees or other flotation costs.

Some firms also provide dividend reinvestment with regard to their employee stock ownership plans. This offers the additional advantage of increasing employee and management ownership of the company's equity, which should enhance employee and management motivation and concern with maximizing shareholder wealth.

direct purchase plan   Many companies now also offer a *direct purchase plan* (DPP). In a DPP, the investor opens an account and arranges for a regular debit to a checking or savings account to purchase new shares. Such a plan puts the individual's investment program on "automatic pilot."

SUMMARY AND CONCLUSIONS

The evidence reveals a psychological side to the market, which causes the market to fluctuate more than warranted by the fundamentals. Many efforts to identify and predict market peaks and troughs (market timing) have been proposed, but none contain a magic formula.

Stock prices often rise during the later part of a recession and during most of the recovery period. Federal funds rate changes and the Dow theory may occasionally be helpful in predicting market trends. A large number of analysts sell newsletters that attempt to forecast market trends.

Technical market indicators that this chapter discusses include short interest, odd-lot activity, specialists' short selling, mutual fund cash positions, Barron's Confidence Index, advance-decline patterns, short-term trading, and the January indicator. Asset allocation is also discussed as a way of hedging against strong market moves among different asset classes.

The market's perceived volatility and the "mood" of the market in general seem to be very difficult—but perhaps not impossible—to predict. Clearly, this area needs more study. In any event, according the Brinson, Singer, Beebower study mentioned at the beginning of this chapter, the return attributed to asset selection has been higher historically than the return attributed to market timing skills. The jury is still out on whether or not stock market timing and forecasting efforts are worthwhile for the average investor when transaction costs are taken into account.

With respect to strategies for buying and selling individual securities, we found little value in the chartist's methods. Nevertheless, some specialized dependencies associated with anxious trader effects and lags in reaction to new information may well be profitably employed in trading decisions.

Anxious trader effects are observed in the market's reaction to block trades, tax-loss selling, secondary offerings, and intraday interactions of the bid-ask spread with the specialist's quotes. Any adjustment lags are very short for announcements of earnings, dividend changes, additions to the S&P 500 Index, bond rating changes, share repurchases, and rights offerings. Moreover, the market tends to anticipate tender offers and mergers. Insider trading signals and forced conversions may produce exploitable patterns.

Overall, tax-loss selling and insider trading seem to offer the most exploitable price trends. The usefulness of most of the other observed dependencies is largely limited to the investor's ability to select the best times to make a particular trade that he or she intends to make anyway.

Many companies offer a dividend reinvestment plan, which is a form of dollar cost averaging. Investors need to know the pros and cons of participation in such plans. Dollar cost averaging is a low-cost alternative to trying to time individual stock purchases.

CHAPTER REVIEW

Answers to the review questions and the self-test questions start on page 501.

Key Terms

stock market overreaction	asset allocation
market timing	charting
Dow theory	bar chart
technical market indicators	moving average
flight-to-quality effect	relative strength
short interest	point-and-figure chart
odd-lot activity	momentum
odd-lot short ratio	resistance level
January indicator (January effect)	support level

head-and-shoulders formation
intraday dependencies
tax-loss trading
adjustment lags
insider trading

forced conversion
dollar cost averaging
dividend reinvestment plan
direct purchase plan

Review Questions

11-1. Briefly describe investor sentiment around the time of the 1987 stock market crash. What are the implications for market efficiency?

11-2. Discuss the relevance of short interest and odd-lot behavior in market timing. What is the theory, and what is the evidence?

11-3. a. Compute both the odd-lot-short ratio and the total odd-lot short ratio (TOLSR) for the following information: 10-day totals, total odd-lot sales of 1.3 million; odd-lot purchases of 1.6 million; odd-lot-short sales of .07 million.
b. Now recompute the ratios for odd-lot short sales of .24 million.

11-4. Identify the hypothesized relationships for the following indicators:
a. specialists' short selling
b. mutual fund cash position
c. Barron's Confidence Index

11-5. Compute the Barron's Confidence Index for the following values for high-grade and average-grade bond rates: 5.67 percent, 6.01 percent; 7.89 percent, 8.85 percent; 9.50 percent, 11.78 percent; and 10.34 percent, 13.89 percent.

11-6. Identify the hypothesized relationships for the following indicators:
a. advance-decline ratio
b. short-term trading
c. January indicator/January effect
d. Monday–Friday price pattern

11-7. a. Compare the positions of chartists and those who subscribe to the random walk hypothesis.
b. What is the role of the market efficiency concept in this discussion?

11-8. a. How do specialists and limit orders affect intraday stock prices?
b. How can investors interpret and take advantage of this process?

11-9. Discuss the profit potential and evidence for
a. tax-loss trading
b. tender offers, mergers, and liquidations

11-10. Give a brief rationale for and the effect on stock prices of dividend reinvestment plans.

11-11. Explore the effect of dollar cost averaging by performing the following calculations.

a. You purchase $100 of a $10 stock (ignore commissions). The stock's price declines to $5, whereupon you purchase another $100 worth. If the stock's price recovers to $10, what is the value of your portfolio?

b. As before, begin with a $100 purchase of a $10 stock. When the stock price increases to $15, you purchase another $100 worth. If the stock price subsequently declines to $10, what is the value of your portfolio?

Self-Test Questions

T   F   11-1. Stock market overreaction is inconsistent with the weak form of the efficient market hypothesis.

T   F   11-2. Market timing skills have been shown to have an expected payoff about as great as stock selection skills.

T   F   11-3. The Dow theory is still used by technical analysts and chartists.

T   F   11-4. For the purpose of the Dow theory, the most important price movement is that of day-to-day fluctuations.

T   F   11-5. The odd-lot activity indicator is based on the presumption that odd-lotters are relatively unsophisticated investors.

T   F   11-6. One problem with the short interest technical indicator is that more than one interpretation is possible.

T   F   11-7. When mutual funds hold more of their assets in cash, this is a bearish signal, indicating that managers are expecting a downward price movement in the market and are attempting to reduce the risk of their portfolio.

T   F   11-8. The January effect denotes that abnormal returns for small-firm stocks occur largely during the first few weeks of trading.

T   F   11-9. Asset allocators try to avoid overcommitment to any one asset class.

T   F   11-10. Chart reading is a type of fundamental analysis.

T   F   11-11. The resistance level is the price level at which a significant number of investors sell their stock.

T   F   11-12. Profitable exploitation of chart reading and other technical analysis is inconsistent with the weak form of the efficient market hypothesis.

T   F   11-13. Block trades are transactions involving 1,000 or more shares.

T   F   11-14. Announcements of dividend increases have been found to lead to stock price increases.

T F 11-15. Adjustment lags demonstrate that the stock market is not perfectly efficient in adjusting instantaneously to new information.

T F 11-16. Tender offers, mergers, and liquidations may present investors with attractive trading opportunities.

T F 11-17. Shares repurchases, rights offerings, and forced conversions all increase the number of outstanding shares of common stock.

T F 11-18. The decision to participate in a dividend reinvestment plan raises an issue of timing.

T F 11-19. Dollar cost averaging consists of buying a fixed number of shares of stock at regular intervals.

NOTES

1. B. Malkiel, "Equity Yields, Growth, and the Structure of Share Prices," *American Economic Review*, vol. 53 (December 1963), pp. 1004–1031.
2. N. Jegadeesh and S. Titman, "Returns to Buying Winners and Selling Losers: Implications for Stock Market Efficiency," *Journal of Finance,* vol. 48, no. 1 (March 1993), pp. 65–91.
3. G. P. Brinson, B. D. Singer, G. L. Beebower, "Determinants of Portfolio Performance II: An Update," *Financial Analysts Journal* (May/June 1991), pp. 40–48.
4. J. J. Siegel, "Does It Pay Stock Investors to Forecast the Business Cycle?" *Journal of Portfolio Management,* vol. 18, no. 1 (fall 1991), pp. 27–34.
5. S. Brown and W. Goetzmann, "Mutual Fund Styles," *Journal of Financial Economics,* vol. 43, no. 3 (March 1997), pp. 373–399.
6. B. Malkiel, *A Random Walk Down Wall Street*, 6th ed., (New York: W.W. Norton, 1995), chapter 5.
7. D. B. Keim, "Size-Related Anomalies and Stock Return Seasonality: Further Empirical Evidence," *Journal of Financial Economics*, vol. 12, no 1 (June 1983), pp. 13–32; "A New Look at the Effects of Firm Size and E/P Ratio on Stock Returns," *Financial Analysts Journal*, vol. 46, no. 2 (March/April 1990), pp. 56–67.
8. S. Penman, "The Distribution of Earnings News over Time and Seasonalities in Aggregate Stock Returns," *Journal of Financial Economics*, vol. 18, no. 2 (June 1987), pp. 199–228.
9. M. Scholes, "The Market for Securities: Substitution versus Price Pressure and the Effects of Information on Share Prices," *Journal of Business* (April 1972), pp. 179–211; and W. Mikkelson and M. Partch, "Stock Price Effects and Costs of Secondary Distributions," *Journal of Financial Economics* (June 1985), pp. 165–194.
10. M. Blume and R. Stambaugh, "Biases in Computed Returns: An Application to the Size Effect," *Journal of Financial Economics* (November 1983), pp. 387–404; W. Kross, "The Size Effect Is Primarily a Price Effect," *Journal of Financial Research* (fall 1985), pp. 169–179.
11. S. Eakins and S. Sewell, "Tax-Loss Selling, Institutional Investors, and the January Effect: A Note," *The Journal of Financial Research,* vol. 16, no. 4 (winter 1993), pp. 377–384. See also J. R. Ritter, "The Buying and Selling Behavior of Individual Investors at the Turn of the Year," *Journal of Finance*, vol. 43, no. 3, pp. 701–717.
12. K. Nunn, G. Madden, and M. Gombola, "Are Some Insiders More 'Inside' Than Others?" *Journal of Portfolio Management* (spring 1983), pp. 18–22.
13. E. Felsenthal, "Big Weapon against Insider Trading Is Upheld," *The Wall Street Journal* (June 26, 1997), p. C1.

14. J. Pound and R. Zeckhauser, "Clearly Heard on the Street: The Effect of Takeover Rumors on Stock Prices," *Journal of Business* (July 1990), pp. 291–308.

15. P. Liu, S. D. Smith, and A. A. Syed, "The Impact of the Insider Trading Scandal on the Information Content of *The Wall Street Journal*'s 'Heard on the Street' Column," *Journal of Financial Research*, vol. 15, no. 2 (summer 1992), pp. 181–188.

16. I. Mathur and A. Waheed, "Stock Price Reactions to Securities Recommended in *Business Week*'s 'Inside Wall Street,' " *Financial Review*, vol. 30, no. 3 (August 1995), pp. 583–604.

17. B. Barber, R. Lehavy, M. McNichols, and B. Trueman, "Can Investors Profit from the Prophets? Security Analyst Recommendations and Stock Returns," *Journal of Finance*, vol. 56, no. 2 (April 2001), pp. 531–563.

18. R. Masulis, "The Effects of Capital Structure Change on Security Prices: A Study of Exchange Offers," *Journal of Financial Economics* (June 1980), pp. 139–177.

19. T. Vermaelen, "Common Stock Repurchases and Market Signaling: An Empirical Study," *Journal of Financial Economics* (June 1981), pp. 139–183, L. Dann, "Common Stock Repurchases: An Analysis of Returns to Bondholders and Stockholders," *Journal of Financial Economics* (June 1981), pp. 113–138.

20. P. Asquith and D. Mullins, "Equity Issues and Offering Dilution," *Journal of Financial Economics* (January/February 1986), pp. 61–89.

21. S. Bhagat, J. Brickley, and R. Lease, "The Authorization of Additional Common Stock: An Empirical Investigation," *Financial Management* (autumn 1986), pp. 45–53.

22. K. Schipper and A. Smith, "A Comparison of Equity Carve-outs and Seasoned Equity Offerings: Share Price Effects and Corporate Restructuring," *Journal of Financial Economics* (January/February 1986), pp. 153–186.

12

Mutual Funds

Learning Objectives

An understanding of the material in this chapter should enable the student to

12-1.   Describe the various ways of organizing mutual funds, including their sales fees.

12-2.   Describe several types of pooled portfolio arrangements that are similar to but differ from mutual funds.

12-3.   Describe the various types of mutual fund portfolios.

12-4.   Describe three approaches to measuring portfolio performance that take account of risk, and explain how fund performance relates to goals, the market, and individual investor performance.

Chapter Outline

Mutual funds and similar types of investments are designed for people who want to have professionals manage some of their wealth. These pooled portfolio arrangements combine resources from many investors into a single investment medium. The average risk-adjusted performance of pooled portfolios is generally no better than that of the market averages. Nevertheless, mutual funds and the like appeal to many investors because they provide convenience, diversification, record keeping, safekeeping of securities, and portfolio management.

DIFFERENT WAYS OF ORGANIZING FUNDS

Mutual funds and similar investments assemble and maintain pooled portfolios primarily for individual investors who have neither the resources nor the time to manage a portfolio of their own effectively. The ownership of these pooled portfolios is subdivided into shares or units. Each unit represents ownership of a fraction of the pooled portfolio.

Example: Each share of a fund with 10 million outstanding shares represents ownership of one 10-millionth of the fund's portfolio. Suppose that fund's portfolio has a market value of $100 million. Each share would, in effect, represent $10 worth of the portfolio. That is, a one 10-millionth share of a $100 million portfolio would be worth $10.

A share's pro rata ownership of the portfolio is called its net asset value (NAV). If the value of the portfolio in the example above rises to $110 million, the NAV will increase to $11 (assuming that the number of shares outstanding does not change).

Funds also distribute dividends and capital gains to their shareholders. These distributions reflect the shareholder's pro rata share of the portfolio's dividends and realized capital gains.

open-end investment companies   The vast majority of pooled portfolio investments are organized as mutual funds, which are technically known as *open-end investment companies*. They maintain a market for their shares. That is, the company that manages a fund stands willing to buy and to sell that fund's shares at a price based on its NAV.

Selling Fees on Mutual Funds

Mutual funds are marketed in two basic ways: The shares of no-load funds are generally sold directly to investors. The fund charges no sales fee on these transactions. Load funds, in contrast, sell their shares through an agent, such as a stockbroker or mutual fund salesperson. The term "load" refers to the commission paid to the agent.

Load Funds

By law, load charges cannot exceed a maximum of 8.5 percent of the amount invested. There is usually a sliding scale for load charges, whereby large investors may be charged substantially smaller loads (in percentage terms). The average load fund charges 3 percent to 6 percent on the minimum purchase, which itself typically ranges from $100 to $3,000. A 5 percent load on a $10,000 load fund purchase leaves $9,500 for investment. A fee of 5 percent on the gross investment is equivalent to 5.3 percent on the net investment ($500/$9,500 = 5.3%).

Example: Suppose a load fund has an NAV of $20 per share, and an investor must pay a 5 percent load. The formula for computing the price after load is as follows:

$$PL = NAV/(1 - L)$$

where PL = price after load
NAV = net asset value per share
L = load percentage

In this example, the NAV is $20, and the load percentage is .05. Accordingly,

$$PL = NAV/(1 - L) = \$20/(.95) = \$21.05$$

Thus, for an NAV of 20 and a load of 5 percent, the investor would pay $21.05 per share, or $1.05 above the NAV of $20 per share.

Although funds may charge loads of up to 8.5 percent, competition in the marketplace has forced the typical load percentage down. As of this writing, few funds charge loads of more than 5 percent. This sales fee still compares unfavorably with the average commission on direct stock acquisitions (and much less favorably than that of a discount broker or over the Internet).

Some funds have redemption fees associated with them. Redemption fees are generally intended to encourage investors to hold the fund for a longer period of time and to discourage short-term trading. Based on information provided by an SEC staffer, the SEC staff's position is that mutual funds are discouraged from charging redemption fees in excess of 2 percent.

Front-End Loading and Contractual Plans

front-end loading

Investors are sometimes persuaded to sign up for a plan to purchase mutual fund shares periodically over an extended period. This is called a contractual plan. For example, an individual might agree to invest $2,000 per year for the next 10 years. Perhaps the money is to be earmarked for a child's college education. The agent who sells such a plan is rewarded with an incentive commission based on the total amount of the planned purchase. In such a plan, the percentage commission is usually lower (due to the large total purchase), but the commission is also paid out of the investor's initial payments. This is known as *front-end loading*. Not infrequently, the investor decides to cancel the program before all of the planned purchases have been made. Fees charged on front-end-loaded contractual plans can therefore be particularly costly to buyers who subsequently cancel their planned participation.

Concerns raised by the SEC spurred Congress to enact provisions for early redemption and maximum sales load percentages on monthly payments. Contractual plans have declined in popularity.

12b-1 Fees

12b-1 fee

A *12b-1 fee* is an annual fee charged by some mutual funds for distribution and marketing expenses. This fee should not be confused with a load, which is a commission paid directly to the broker selling the fund. Both load and no-load funds can have 12b-1 fees.

The 12b-1 fee is paid directly by the fund out of investors' net assets. The SEC has set a maximum that funds can charge as 12b-1 fees at 1 percent of the fund's net asset value. The NASD has set a maximum of 8.5 percent for the total of load fees plus 12b-1 fees.

contingent deferred sales load

Investors who redeem their 12b-1 shares before the full amount of the selling cost is recouped will generally be charged an exit fee, sometimes called the *contingent deferred sales load* (CDSL). This should not be confused with redemption fees. Redemption fees go directly into the fund, while the CDSL is paid to the fund's underwriter.

Investors should carefully read a fund's prospectus to determine if a 12b-1 fee is charged. (Note that *The Wall Street Journal*'s mutual fund quotations identify funds with 12b-1 charges.)

Some mutual fund companies offer different classes of mutual fund shares, known as class A, class B, and class C shares. The portfolio of securities underlying the different classes of shares is the same. The difference is in the way fees are paid.

Class A shares carry a front-end load, usually between 3 and 5 percent of net asset value. There may also be a small 12b-1 fee, perhaps 0.25 percent of NAV.

Class B shares have no front-end load but carry an annual 12b-1 fee, which can be as high as one percent of net asset value, for their first 7 or 8 years, after which the shares are converted to class A shares. There is also a declining contingent deferred sales load if the shares are redeemed prior to the conversion to class A shares.

Class C shares also have no front-end load and have a somewhat lower annual 12b-1 fee than class B shares, but they do not convert to class A shares. In other words, the 12b-1 fee on class C shares can be regarded as similar to a perpetuity, while that of class B shares can be regarded as similar to an annuity over a specified period of time.

What the Selling Fees Buy

The performance of the investment portfolios of load, no-load, and 12b-1 funds tends to be quite similar, on average. From the investor's standpoint, the principal difference among these types of funds is that those who purchase no-load funds do not incur an agent or sales fee, although they do bear the overall selling expenses that the fund incurs. The pure no-load funds have no agents to compensate. Thus, their selling expenses are relatively modest. Instead of paying a load, a no-load fund investor might incur selling expenses of a fraction of one percent per year.

However, the investor who buys through an agent has access to the services that the agent provides. Agents may advise their clients regarding the risks, potential returns, tax consequences, and other relevant characteristics of the funds they are able to offer through the company or companies that they represent. Mutual fund agents know the relevant features of their product. Some investors prefer, however, to find suitable no-load funds themselves with a bit of research.

Prospectuses for no-load funds may be obtained by responding to advertisements in the financial press or writing to the funds listed in such guides as *Weisenberger's Investment Companies Yearbook* (an annual publication available in most libraries). Several directories are devoted exclusively to no-load funds. Published annually, they list various types of funds, along with their services, minimum investment amounts, addresses, and telephone numbers.

Operating Expenses

The investment advisory fee, which is often called the management fee, is paid to the fund's adviser for portfolio supervision and for general management of the fund's affairs. Sometimes the fee includes an incentive/penalty provision based on the fund's performance relative to a particular benchmark. Administrative costs are the costs of administering the portfolio, incurred largely through record keeping and transaction services (brokerage costs) to buy and sell securities, and are a necessary cost borne by fund shareholders. Other operating expenses include custodial fees, legal and audit fees, and directors' fees. The sum of these three fees constitutes the fund's operating expenses. The operating expenses divided by the fund's total assets is known as the *management expense ratio*.

management expense ratio

Invisible Cost of Transactions

In addition to the operating expenses, investors share in the payment of commissions whenever trades are executed. Another cost investors never see itemized is the loss in share value associated with the price pressures of trading large blocks.

Redemption of Funds

Most mutual funds are set up to facilitate relatively easy redemption at their NAV. Normally, investors can call or write for a partial or full redemption and receive a speedy reply. Most funds also have arrangements for an automatic withdrawal plan. This plan can be structured to provide a monthly income for the fund holder. Thus, the investor can have a fixed sum periodically withdrawn from the fund as long as the balance is sufficient to cover the withdrawal. Some funds do charge a redemption fee. Investors can, however, normally switch funds within the same group (family of funds) without incurring a load or redemption fee or even having to deal with much paperwork. Most funds do limit the number of switches per year and charge a modest fee. Some investors try to profit from market swings by switching between a group's stock and money market funds.

Closed-End Investment Companies

investment companies

Mutual funds are one of a broader class of investment vehicles called *investment companies*. We have already noted that mutual funds are called open-end investment companies. A mutual fund's number of outstanding shares increases or decreases with new sales and redemptions of outstanding shares.

The second most common type of investment company is the closed-end investment company. The number of a closed-end investment company's shares outstanding is basically fixed. The shares outstanding for a closed-end fund would change only if the fund had a public offering, a dividend reinvestment plan (DRIP), a direct purchase plan (DPP), or a share buy-back program.

Unlike purchasers of mutual funds, buyers of shares in a closed-end fund do not receive a prospectus when they consider a purchase. Investors buy and sell their shares in the secondary market in much the same way as with stock in a publicly traded corporation. Like publicly traded stock, their share prices are determined by supply and demand. The shares may sell for a premium or, more commonly, at a discount from their NAV. These discounts can often be 15 percent to 20 percent or more. In fact, some investors believe the purchase of closed-end funds at substantial discounts is a "free lunch" available in the marketplace. Others believe there are real reasons for these discounts.

Large shareholders sometimes force closed-end funds to convert to open end. Relatively substantial resources are required to force such a reorganization. These conversions tend to be quite profitable for the fund holders, even those who hold a relatively small number of shares, especially if they bought their shares at a substantial discount from their net asset value.

Example: Consider a 10-million-share, closed-end fund with a per-share NAV and market price of $10 and $7.50, respectively. This fund might be a tempting takeover target. Although a takeover effort would probably drive the price up, perhaps 3 million shares could be purchased over time at an average cost of $8.50. If the remaining shares are widely dispersed, 30 percent of the outstanding shares should be sufficient for control. The new control group could quickly convert to an open-end fund. By offering to buy back shares at their NAV, the fund would immediately make each holder's shares worth the $10 NAV (assuming that there was no price change while the takeover was underway).

Investment Company Quotations (Closed End)

Closed-end fund quotations can be found in *The Wall Street Journal*, *The New York Times*, and *Barron's,* as well as on the Internet. Funds are grouped into a number of categories, such as general equity funds, U.S. government bond funds, specialized equity funds, and convertible funds. Investment company quotations typically contain the following information:

- name of fund and symbol
- market where traded

- NAV
- market price
- premium or discount of share price relative to NAV
- 52-week market return

An example is as follows:

Fund Name Symbol	Stock Exchange	NAV	Market Price	Premium or Discount	2-Year Market Return
Exwhyzee (XYZ)	N	27.40	25.10	–9	16.7
Abeecee (ABC)	O	42.15	44.20	5	–3.2

Mutual Funds Quotations (Open End)

Daily price quotes for mutual funds can be found in most major newspapers. The information varies from paper to paper. Typically, individual funds are listed under the fund family. For example, funds managed by The Vanguard Group are listed under *Vanguard Funds*.

The New York Times Sunday edition includes the following information:

- fund family
- fund name
- type of fund
- rating
- NAV
- weekly percentage return
- year-to-date percentage return
- 1-year percentage return
- 3-year percentage return

For example, the Vanguard Index 500 Fund is listed as follows:

Fund Family							
Fund Name	Type	Rating	NAV	Wkly % Ret.	YTD % Ret.	1-Yr % Ret.	3-Yr % Ret.
Vanguard Index							
500 Idx	LB	3/4	135.22	+5.0	–0.1	+14.2	+23.2

The meaning of various symbols and footnotes is explained in the newspaper. For example, LB indicates that the fund is a domestic general stock fund that invests in a portfolio described as large blend—the company stocks are generally large capitalization and a blend of both growth and value stocks.

Unit Investment Trusts

Unit investment trusts (UITs), like mutual fund shares, represent part ownership of a common portfolio but, unlike mutual funds, are unmanaged. The absence of portfolio management expenses tends to enhance the return. These trusts are typically set up and marketed by a brokerage firm that receives an underwriting fee from the proceeds of the sale. Once assembled, most debt security portfolios can be left unmanaged until they mature. The secondary market for the ownership units of these trusts is relatively inactive. Thus, UITs are costly to trade prior to maturity, whereas mutual funds are easy to redeem. Most UIT portfolios are composed of debt securities. As the cash flows are received, they are paid to the trust holders (net of any administrative costs). Once all of the cash flows have been paid out, the trust is dissolved.

Some UITs are invested in equities. All equity UITs must have a termination date, at which time the portfolio must be liquidated. There is usually a strategy or theme to an equity UIT. One popular theme has been "dogs of the Dow." People using this strategy believe that the 10 stocks in the DJIA with the highest dividend yields will outperform the other 20 stocks over the next 12 months. Hence, an investor who believes this could regularly repeat this strategy by buying a UIT based on this theme, then rolling the proceeds over into a similar UIT when the old one matures.

Variable Annuities

Insurance companies, banks, and brokerages sell variable annuities. These annuities originate at insurance companies and have much in common with mutual funds, closed-end investment companies, and unit investment trusts. Each of these investment types represents pooled portfolios of assets owned by a group of investors. Unlike the other types of pooled portfolio investments, variable annuities generate a tax-deferred return. Moreover, no tax liability is incurred when funds are shifted from one annuity to another (such as from a stock to a money market annuity). On the other hand, if an individual makes withdrawals prior to age 59 ½, he or she incurs a 10 percent federal income tax penalty.

The drawback to variable annuities is that the expenses and fees tend to be higher with annuities than with similar pooled portfolios. The annuity investor gains some tax advantages but has less flexibility than a mutual fund investor.

Also, annuities have an insurance component that guarantees an income stream for life, depending on the specifications of the annuity contract. This insurance component is funded by the insurer from the funds invested. Normally, the expected value of the payout from the annuity is less than the NAV of the underlying securities. The insurance company's actuarial calculations require consideration of the probability of the annuitant's survival, rather than the probability of his or her death.

Hedge Funds

hedge funds

Hedge funds are a type of pooled portfolio instrument organized for maximum investment flexibility. For example, they may invest in derivatives, sell short, use leverage, and invest internationally. Most hedge funds take substantial risks, seeking correspondingly large rewards. They are typically organized as limited partnerships and allow only "qualified investors" to participate. These investors must demonstrate both the sophistication and the financial resources to understand and take the risks associated with such investments.

Hedge funds can have a substantial impact on the securities markets. (Consider the near collapse in October 1998 of Long Term Capital Management—a large and previously high-flying hedge fund that at its height was leveraged to the tune of more than $100 billion against a capital base of $3 billion.) Most hedge funds are organized offshore to avoid the regulations imposed on U.S. funds.

Types of Pooled Portfolio Funds by Organizational Structures

- Mutual funds: open-ended; price based on NAV
  - Load funds: sold through salesperson for a commission
  - No-load funds: sold directly without a commission
- Closed-end investment companies: corporation-owned; managed portfolio; stock traded on an exchange or OTC, usually at a discount from NAV
- Unit investment trusts: unmanaged; self-liquidating; largely consisting of short-term debt securities
- Variable annuities: mutual fund type of instrument originating at insurance companies
- Hedge funds: typically organized as offshore limited partnerships for qualified investors; maximum investment flexibility

---

Other Types of Pooled Portfolios: Corporations, Partnerships, and Blind Pools

Several other types of pooled portfolios are available to the investor. For example, some ordinary companies hold such large portfolios of stock in other companies that they are, in effect, investment companies in all but name. Among the better known of these firms is Berkshire Hathaway. Berkshire Hathaway was once in textiles but now is primarily an owner of stocks. Its CEO, Warren Buffett, is highly respected for his adroit portfolio management. Buffett is also a multibillionaire as a result of his investments.

Although most investment companies are organized as corporations, a few are organized as partnerships, often limited partnerships. This is to take advantage of the tax treatment and greater flexibility of that form of organization.

blind pool

Perhaps the most risky pooled portfolio device is the *blind pool*. With a blind pool, the investor agrees to finance a venture whose precise purposes are to be revealed later. The prospective investor will, however, be told the pool's general purpose (to finance a program of risk arbitrage, for example). Most people who invest in blind pools do so on the basis of their faith in the investor or group of investors that they are bankrolling. In some instances, the investors are given a clue, such as the intended industry or investment approach. At other times, the investors are truly blind. Blind pools may be organized as shares of stock (usually of a closed-end fund), limited partnership interests, or debt securities (often to be used in as yet undisclosed takeover attempts). Somewhat surprisingly, many people are quite willing to buy these "pigs in a poke."

Alternative Ways of Organizing Pooled Portfolios

- Operating or holding companies: A few erstwhile operating or holding companies hold such large portfolios that their performances are more closely related to their security holdings than to their operations.
- Partnerships: Some mutual funds choose the partnership form, often a limited partnership, because of its greater flexibility and/or tax advantages.
- Blind pools: Investors bankroll enterprises whose purposes will later be revealed; these pools are sometimes involved in takeover financing.

Taxation of Pooled Portfolio Investments

The general principle of pooled portfolio taxation is that if the investment company qualifies for subchapter M treatment under the tax code, then each investor is taxed as if he or she owns a portion of the pooled portfolio directly. The issue is, however, more complicated than it might seem. When shares are bought and later sold, the difference is indeed a taxable gain (long- or short-term gain, depending on the holding period). Funds also generate taxable income (to the holder) when they earn dividends or interest on their portfolio. Similarly, taxable income for the investor results when a fund realizes capital gain on its own portfolio.

To qualify as a regulated investment company under subchapter M of the Internal Revenue Code, the fund must distribute at least 90 percent of its gross income (dividends, interest, and capital gains). Accordingly, virtually all funds comply with the income distribution requirements. The investor is liable for income taxes on these distributions, whose timing and amounts may not always be easy to predict.

DIFFERENT TYPES OF MUTUAL FUND PORTFOLIOS

Mutual fund portfolios generally consist of stocks and/or debt (including money market securities and long-term debt securities). Funds are usually described in terms of their portfolio holdings. The portfolio holdings are, in turn, a reflection of the funds' objectives.

Bond Funds and Balanced Funds

Many different types of bond funds are available in the marketplace. Also, money market funds hold short-term debt security portfolios. Several categories of long-term bond funds include corporates, governments, or municipals. These broad categories are divided into subcategories, such as high-risk corporates and intermediate-term governments. Balanced fund portfolios combine common stocks with bonds. They tend to have slightly riskier portfolios with somewhat higher expected yields than bond funds.

Different Goals of Common Stock Funds

Common Stock Funds

growth funds
income funds

Common stock funds are also classified into a number of categories based on their stated goals. These funds differ principally in their risk orientation. *Growth funds* emphasize appreciation potential and often accept considerable risk. *Income funds* concentrate on high-dividend, low-risk stocks with modest growth potentials. Middle-of-the-road (or "blend") funds tend to place a somewhat higher premium on earnings stability than growth funds do but are more interested in long-term growth than income funds are. A fund's initial risk orientation may be determined from its prospectus. However, many funds drift away from their original goals over the course of a year or two, depending on the fund manager's proclivities. To provide up-to-date guidance to investors as to the general orientation of common stock funds, Morningstar and Lipper have attempted to standardize fund classification, with generally good results.

Differences in Risk Orientation of Common Stock Funds

- Growth funds: stress appreciation potential; accept considerable risk
- Income funds: focus on stocks that pay high dividends; provide low risk and modest growth
- Blend funds: place more emphasis on stability than growth funds do but less than income funds do; seek growth as well as stability

---

Specialized Types of Common Stock Funds

Specialized common stock funds include those that invest in specific industries (for example, Chemical Fund), types of companies (for example, Technology Fund), or regions (for example, Northeast Fund). These types of mutual funds are sometimes called *sector funds*. They come in a variety of categories.

sector funds

international funds
country funds
social responsibility funds

International funds hold both foreign and domestic securities. *Country funds* assemble diversified portfolios of the stocks of a single country. *Social responsibility funds* restrict their portfolio to companies not involved in activities that they consider objectionable (pollution, war materials, tobacco, alcohol, and so on). Penny stock funds concentrate on low-priced stocks.

Index Funds

index fund

One of the fastest-growing types of funds is the *index fund*. Index funds are structured to mimic the performance of an index. Many funds are designed to duplicate (approximately) the performance of the S&P 500 Index. Others may target the performance of some other broad-based index such as the Dow Jones Industrials or the NYSE Composite. Still others may seek to emulate a narrower index, such as that for a particular industry (oil, chemicals, steel, auto, real estate, and so forth). Note that the index fund for an industry is not the same as a sector fund for that industry. An industry index fund will engage in substantially less trading than a sector fund and is therefore likely to have lower transaction costs.

One strategy to managing an index fund is to purchase the securities that make up the index in the exact proportions of the index. Another approach is to purchase the most important components, hoping that the others will perform similarly.

Because of transaction costs, management fees, and frictions in the process, most index funds slightly underperform their indexes. On the other hand, most index funds have low or no loads and much lower fees and expenses (and very low turnover) than more actively managed funds. As a result, the average index fund has a good chance of outperforming the average managed fund on an expense-adjusted basis.

World Equity Benchmark Shares (WEBS)

World Equity Benchmark Shares (WEBS) are index funds designed to replicate the common stock of a single country. There are WEBS for European, Latin American, and Pacific Rim nations. These funds differ from country funds, which are actively managed funds consisting of one country's stock. Since WEBS are index funds, they have far fewer trades—and therefore significantly lower transaction costs—than managed country funds.

MUTUAL FUND PERFORMANCE

The last section of this chapter considers mutual fund performance relative to goals, the market, and individual investor performance.

Measuring Portfolio Performance

We know that risk and return tend to be related. Higher-risk portfolios should, on average, produce higher returns than lower-risk portfolios. Thus, any comparison of portfolio performances should take account of risk. Three primary approaches to these risk-adjusted performance measures have been devised for this purpose: the Sharpe ratio, the Treynor ratio, and the Jensen's alpha measure. Each seeks to measure the return performance relative to the riskiness of the portfolio.

The Sharpe ratio (S_{pi}) is defined as

$$S_{pi} = \frac{p - f}{\sigma_p} \qquad \text{(Equation 12-1)}$$

The Treynor ratio (T_{pi}), in contrast, is defined as

$$T_{pi} = \frac{p - f}{\beta_p} \qquad \text{(Equation 12-2)}$$

The Jensen's alpha measure is

$$\alpha_p = p - [f + \beta_p(M - f)] \qquad \text{(Equation 12-3)}$$

where p   = portfolio return
      f   = risk-free return
      M   = market portfolio return
      σ_p = portfolio standard deviation
      β_p = portfolio beta
      α_p = portfolio alpha

The Sharpe measure relates excess returns (return in excess of the risk-free rate) to total risk (σ_p), the Treynor and Jensen measures relate excess returns to market risk (β_p), and the Jensen measure calculates the percent of return above or below the "expected" return based on the estimate of β_p. The Sharpe measure is more appropriate for an investor whose total wealth is not well diversified. Both the Sharpe and Treynor measures give relative rankings, while the Jensen measure, as noted, gives an estimate of the disparity between actual and expected return.

Why Mutual Funds on Average Do Not Outperform the Market

Most mutual funds do not earn positive abnormal risk-adjusted returns, and many regularly provide negative abnormal risk-adjusted returns. Outperforming a relatively efficient market (such as the U.S. stock market) is difficult. Still, mutual funds do have the resources to hire the best talent, collect the most useful information, and analyze it with the most sophisticated techniques. Furthermore, their large size should facilitate operational efficiency—especially when securities are bought in quantities qualifying for commission discounts. Why then, with all these advantages, do the funds as a group so rarely outperform the market? There are several reasons:

- *Institutional investors constitute a large part of the market.* Outperforming the average would be difficult for any group of investors who make up a large part of the average. Institutions hold at least 40 percent of the total value of U.S. stocks; a still higher percentage of the larger listed issues makes up most of the market indexes.
- *Some other types of large investors have advantages similar to those of the institutions.* Each type of institutional investor (mutual funds, insurance companies, pension funds, college endowments, foundations, and bank trust departments) has access to similar managerial talent, sources of information, and types of analysis. Furthermore, private investment managers, individuals with large sums to invest, and nonfinancial corporations with large stock portfolios all have equivalent advantages. Thus, mutual funds must

compete with other similarly positioned institutional and noninstitutional investors.

- *Mutual funds have a number of disadvantages relative to many other types of investors.* Although mutual funds offer several advantages to investors, they also have a number of disadvantages that tend to lower their return by more than any likely advantage they may have vis-à-vis small unsophisticated investors. The primary disadvantage is their fee structure.

Mutual Fund Advantages

Mutual funds, which are currently the most popular investment vehicle in the United States, provide several valuable services to individual investors that enable them to participate in financial markets with a minimum expenditure of time and effort. Portfolio management, the selection and timing of securities purchases and sales to meet the fund's investment objectives, is an important function best left to professionals. Risk reduction is achieved through diversification—the careful selection of securities whose returns are not closely correlated.

family of funds

Mutual funds provide convenience in a number of ways: Current income and capital gains can be reinvested automatically; some funds allow check writing to facilitate withdrawals; accurate record keeping, especially for tax purposes, is provided automatically. Most funds today are members of families of funds. A *family of funds* is a group of funds with different objectives but managed by the same management company. Fidelity is the largest family, with more than 200 funds. Within almost all families of funds, amounts can be transferred from one fund to another in the fund family by wire, telephone, or on-line. There is no very convenient way to quickly move large amounts of money from one type of portfolio to another.

Advantages of Mutual Funds

- Portfolio management
- Risk reduction
- Diversification
- Convenience

Mutual Fund Disadvantages

The major disadvantage of mutual funds is that owners' returns will exceed the market return only if a mutual fund's portfolio outperforms the market by more than the fund's expenses and management fees. These fees average about 1.3 percent per year for general equity funds.

The second disadvantage—particularly for those funds with large portfolios—is that they sometimes adversely affect the market prices of the stocks that they trade. Sizable purchases tend to be above the most recent market price and large sales below it. Small investors, in contrast, can generally purchase up to several round lots (or even more for an actively traded stock) with little or no price effect. Funds sometimes attempt to counteract this problem by assigning portions of their portfolio to several different managerial groups. Subdividing may reduce, but is unlikely to eliminate, the adverse price effects of their large trades. Furthermore, subdividing may increase management and administrative costs.

The third disadvantage is that many institutional investors must restrict their analysis to a small percentage of traded stocks. Institutions frequently focus on as little as 100 to 500 companies, compared with about 5,000 listed securities and at least 20,000 traded OTC. Institutional holdings are clearly concentrated among the larger firms. The institution is reluctant either to acquire a small-dollar-value position (because it will have little impact on the institution's overall portfolio) or to take too large a percentage position in a small company (because the institution would then risk owning too large a percentage position to be classified as a passive investor). This reluctance tends to remove a large number of stocks from the institution's choice set. Consequently, institutional attention on the large-capitalization segment of the market may reduce the likelihood of finding undervalued stocks. Many smaller-capitalization stocks may remain misvalued because many institutional investors are forced to ignore them. Individual investors are unconstrained when it comes to investing in such stocks.

Disadvantages of Mutual Funds

- Management fees, expenses, and loads for load funds reduce their returns.
- Large investors, such as mutual funds, usually adversely affect the market when they trade.
- Institutions usually restrict their analysis to a small percentage of traded stocks.

Are Mutual Funds Appropriate Investments?

If funds do not generally outperform market averages, should individuals invest in mutual funds (other than index funds)? In other words, should they pay for active professional management that does not increase the risk-adjusted expected return?

Investors who choose to have a fund manage their wealth should do so with their eyes wide open. They should expect no better than average risk-adjusted performance (relative to the stock market). Investors who believe that they can outperform the market may appropriately manage their entire portfolios. Relatively modest resources (for example, $10,000) may be sufficient to construct a well-diversified portfolio. Moreover, investors who are not especially risk averse may properly choose to manage even very small portfolios. However, many investors—even investors with a fair amount of knowledge about securities markets—are not willing to devote the time it would take to actively manage their own portfolio of investments. Risk-averse investors of modest means with little confidence in their investment skills and investors with limited time for investment management may wish to have a mutual fund manage part or all of their wealth.

Investors in mutual funds will find relatively few reliable selection guidelines. For believers in the EMH, there are a few obvious criteria to consider. Clearly, investors should prefer a fund with a risk level corresponding to their preferences. Also, a fund that has a favorable past performance and a low portfolio turnover, a low expense ratio, no load, and no 12b-1 fee may generate a bit better performance than the average fund. Most investors should probably give serious consideration to index funds.

SUMMARY AND CONCLUSIONS

This chapter considers various aspects of mutual funds and related investments. It explores the organizational structures of several types of pooled portfolio arrangements, looking closely at selling fees (load, no-load, and 12b-1), and it discusses the different types of mutual fund portfolios. Finally, the chapter examines mutual fund performance. Mutual funds generally fail to outperform the market for a variety of reasons: Professionally managed portfolios comprise a large part of the total market, their expenses reduce their net returns, they affect the market when they trade, and they are often restricted to a relatively small percentage of companies. Nonetheless, mutual funds offer a convenient and relatively cost-effective way of diversifying. Investors who do not wish to devote a substantial amount of time to managing their own portfolios may well prefer to let a mutual fund handle their investment decisions.

CHAPTER REVIEW

Answers to the review questions and the self-test questions start on page 501.

Key Terms

open-end investment companies
front-end loading

12b-1 fee
contingent deferred sales load

management expense ratio   international funds
investment companies   country funds
hedge funds   social responsibility funds
blind pool   index fund
growth funds   World Equity Benchmark Shares
income funds   (WEBS)
sector funds   family of funds

Review Questions

12-1.   The $$$ Mutual Fund has a portfolio valued at $650 million and 30 million shares outstanding. Suppose over the next 12 months the fund's portfolio value increases to $800 million and shares outstanding increase by 2 million.

   a.   What is the initial NAV?

   b.   What is the percentage increase in the NAV?

12-2.   Assume that the $$$ Mutual Fund in question 12-1 is a load fund that charged a 3 percent front-end load and paid a distribution of $.70 per share over the past year. What would the one-year return for an investor in the $$$ Fund be?

12-3.   Compare load fees with 12b-1 fees.

12-4.   Compare the performance of an investment of $3,000 per year for 5 years in each of the following. Assume that each fund generates a return on its net asset value of 11 percent per year:

   a.   a no-load mutual fund

   b.   a 12b-1 fee of 1 percent assessed at the end of each year

   c.   a front-end load plan assessing an 8.5 percent commission in the first year only

12-5.   Continue question 12-4 as follows: Assume that the no-load fund does generate an 11 percent return.

   a.   How high must the 12b-1 fund's annual return be for it to equal the end-of-period value of the no-load fund?

   b.   Would the return on the front-end load fund have to be higher or lower than the result in 12-5a? Briefly justify your answer.

12-6.   The % Closed-End Investment Company (%CEIC) sells for $25 with an NAV of $33. Suppose 10 million shares are outstanding and the P. Boom Pekans Group proceeds to take over %CEIC. The Pekans Group pays an average of $28 for 35 percent of the stock and then converts it to an open-end fund. Suppose legal costs amount to $500,000 and commissions are 2 percent.

   a.   Compute the percentage discount on the initial NAV.

   b.   If the NAV is $35 at the conclusion of the takeover, what is the gross profit?

   c.   What is the net return after costs and commissions are factored in?

12-7. Briefly describe and contrast open-end investment companies and closed-end investment companies.

12-8. a. What is meant by a sector fund?
   b. What are families of funds and what are their benefits?

12-9. The Scupper Group maintains an extensive list of no-load sector funds. Results for five of the group's funds are as follows:

Fund Name	Prior Year	Dividends	Capital Distributions	Current Year NAV
Good Fund	14.29	.53	.74	13.01
Bond Fund	12.89	1.12	.47	11.98
Go Fund	7.01	.03	.26	13.08
Chip Fund	16.67	.89	.78	17.57
Cash Fund	10.00	.68	.00	10.00

   a. Compute the holding period return for each fund.
   b. The market index return for the year is 22 percent. If you want to compare the performance of the funds, what else, in addition to return, should you consider?

12-10. One year's results can be misleading. A better gauge of a fund's potential performance can be obtained from an analysis of its performance over several years. Consider the fund holding period return below.

Year	Good Fund	Bond Fund	Go Fund	Chip Fund	Cash Fund	Market Index
Year 1	10.5	8.8	17.7	13.5	6.8	12.5
Year 2	−8.5	6.0	−21.6	−3.5	8.4	−5.3
Year 3	15.7	11.4	31.4	23.5	7.3	18.9
Year 4	14.3	9.6	23.4	17.5	5.3	16.2
Year 5	−21.3	−9.1	−32.7	−14.5	11.5	−20.2
Year 6	12.2	10.3	53.4	31.4	7.9	24.3
Year 7	9.0	11.5	−12.3	16.3	7.1	14.5

   Compute the geometric mean return and standard deviation of each of the five funds and market index, using results reported for 7 years.

12-11. Calculate the Sharpe ratios for the market index and five funds in question 12-10. Use a risk-free rate of 4.7 percent.

12-12. a. Compute the Treynor ratios of the funds and index in question 12-10 for the following betas: Good Fund, 1.1; Bond Fund, .6; Go Fund, 1.3; Chip Fund, .9; Cash Fund, .2.
   b. Compare the results with the Sharpe ratios calculated in question 12-11. Describe your method of comparison.

12-13. What advantages and disadvantages do mutual funds have relative to other types of investors?

12-14. a. What types of investors are most likely to find mutual funds attractive?

  b. What mutual fund attributes are valuable to all investors?

Self-Test Questions

T F 12-1. Mutual funds (open-end investment companies) stand willing on demand to buy and sell the fund's shares at a price based on their net asset value (NAV).

T F 12-2. No-load mutual funds are typically sold to investors by salespeople.

T F 12-3. Most load mutual funds charge an 8.5 percent fee on the sale of shares to the public.

T F 12-4. To purchase a fund with an NAV of $20 a share and a 5 percent load, an investor would have to pay $21.05 per share.

T F 12-5. Funds charging 12b-1 fees are technically classified as load funds.

T F 12-6. Closed-end funds typically issue a fixed number of shares for sale to the public.

T F 12-7. The shares of closed-end investment companies typically sell at their NAV.

T F 12-8. Closed-end funds are not permitted to convert to open-end funds.

T F 12-9. Unit investment trusts are typically unmanaged investment portfolios composed of debt securities.

T F 12-10. Variable annuities generate tax-free returns to investors.

T F 12-11. Hedge funds are typically organized as limited partnerships and take large risks in seeking large returns.

T F 12-12. Blind pools may be organized as limited partnerships or closed-end funds.

T F 12-13. To qualify as a regulated investment company, a fund must distribute at least 80 percent of its gross income to its owners.

T F 12-14. Index funds typically have lower expenses and fees than those charged by actively managed funds.

T F 12-15. The Sharpe ratio measures excess returns relative to total risk.

T F 12-16. The Treynor ratio and Jensen's alpha measure excess returns relative to market risk.

T F 12-17. Most studies show that the average risk-adjusted performance of mutual funds usually outperforms the market.

T   F   12-18. The risk-adjusted performance of other institutional investors is no better than that of mutual funds.

T   F   12-19. Large institutions normally trade large blocks of stocks without adverse price effects.

T   F   12-20. Institutional investors typically focus their analysis on all traded stocks.

T   F   12-21. Most stock mutual funds in the 1990s were able to consistently beat the returns on S&P 500 Index funds.

13

Options and Combination Securities

<table>
<tr><td colspan="2" align="center">

Learning Objectives

An understanding of the material in this chapter should enable the student to
</td></tr>
<tr><td>13-1.</td><td>Describe the basic terminology used by option traders.</td></tr>
<tr><td>13-2.</td><td>Describe the markets where option trading takes place, and explain the various factors involved in option pricing.</td></tr>
<tr><td>13-3.</td><td>Explain the basic strategies of option trading.</td></tr>
<tr><td>13-4.</td><td>Explain the mechanics of trading index options and interest rate options.</td></tr>
<tr><td>13-5.</td><td>Describe the basic nature of rights and warrants, and explain how these options are used.</td></tr>
<tr><td>13-6.</td><td>Describe the characteristics of convertible bonds, and explain how their conversion premiums are determined.</td></tr>
<tr><td>13-7.</td><td>Describe the characteristics of convertible preferreds, including their similarities and differences when compared to convertible bonds.</td></tr>
<tr><td>13-8.</td><td>In addition to convertible bonds and convertible preferreds, describe several other types of convertible (hybrid) securities.</td></tr>
<tr><td>13-9.</td><td>Explain the techniques of hedging and arbitraging as they are used in securities trading and other kinds of markets.</td></tr>
</table>

Chapter Outline

DERIVATIVES

All investors need to understand the potential benefits of using options (both put and call options), as well as the characteristics of securities that function like options (rights and warrants) or contain options (convertible bonds and convertible preferred stock). Although the characteristics, terminology, and types of options may appear complicated, the most basic attribute of options' nature is quite straightforward. An option is basically what its name implies: *a choice*. This attribute distinguishes options from other types of securities. An option gives the holder the choice of whether or not to engage in a specified transaction, which involves buying or selling some underlying asset at a specified price at some future time. The choice itself has value, and people are willing to pay a price for options in order to have the choice of whether or not to engage in a specified transaction in the future.

A call option gives the owner the privilege (or choice) to buy a specified asset at a specified price prior to an expiration date; a put option permits the owner to sell a specified asset at a specified price prior to an expiration date. For example, a call option on common stock gives the holder the option to purchase 100 shares of that stock at a specified price until the option's expiration date. An option's value is derived from a combination of the current and potential value of its underlying assets—hence the general name derivative. Calls, puts, rights, and warrants are pure options, whereas convertible bonds, convertible preferreds, and certain other types of securities are combinations. Combination securities derive value from two sources: the potential worth of their convertibility (the option component) and the cash flows that they promise to make (the straight security value). The value of options is based on the characteristics, risks, and opportunities of the particular underlying assets.

A derivative security's value is derived from the value of another asset or financial instrument, such as a stock, stock index, gold, or wheat. Derivative securities represent a *zero sum game*, meaning that each transaction involves a completely offsetting gain and loss.

zero sum game

PURE OPTION SECURITIES

Option Terminology

premium
expiration date

A few terms are key to understanding options. The option price, also called the option *premium,* is the price at which an option trades. The option can generally be exercised any time on or before the *expiration date.* On the expiration date, the option expires and loses any value it may have had before the expiration date. This characteristic of options is so important that many brokers demand from their customers the right to exercise the customers' options on the expiration date if the customer fails to exercise the option when it is economically rational to do so. The price at which the option can be exercised is the *strike (exercise) price.* This price is fixed throughout the life of the option.

strike (exercise)
price

The holder of a call has the right to purchase the underlying asset by requiring the writer of the call to sell the stock at the exercise price. An option to sell an asset is a put. The holder of a put has the right to sell the underlying asset by requiring the writer of the put to buy the asset at the strike price.

in-the-money

When the market price of the stock exceeds the strike price of a call option, or when the strike price of a put option exceeds the market price of the stock, the option is *in-the-money*—it could be exercised to produce a cash inflow. For the call option, this means that the market price of the underlying asset is higher than the exercise price of the option. Conversely, for the put option, it means that the exercise price of the option is higher than the market price of the underlying asset. When the strike price of a call option exceeds the market price of the stock or other asset, or when the market price of the stock exceeds the strike price of a put, the option is *out-of-the-money*. When the exercise price of the option is equal to the market price of the stock, the option is *at-the-money*.

out-of-the-money

at-the-money

Using a profit graph to understand the various aspects of an option is frequently helpful. A profit function shows the potential prices of the underlying asset on the expiration date (which range from zero to infinity) on the horizontal axis and the profit derived from a particular investment associated with each price on the vertical axis. Figures 13-1 and 13-2 demonstrate the profit associated with the purchase of a call option and the purchase of a put option. For simplicity, we will assume the options are each for one share. These two transactions are referred to as *going long* a call and going long a put. Going long means buying and taking ownership.

going long

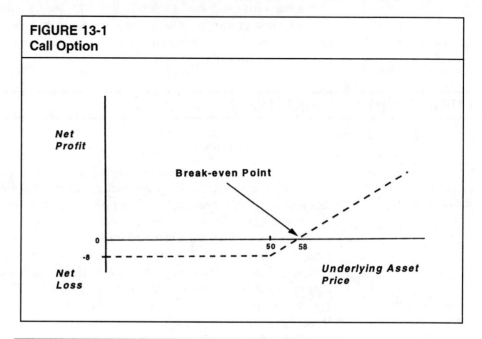

FIGURE 13-1
Call Option

Example: Assume that the options graphed in figures 13-1 and 13-2 both have an exercise price of $50. The call option has a price (premium) of $8, while the put option has a price (premium) of $3. If the underlying asset price is $30 on the expiration date of the options, the call option holder incurs a loss of $8, but the put option holder has a profit of $17 ($50 – $30 – $3). Alternatively, if the underlying asset price rises to $80 on the expiration date, the call option holder earns a profit of $22 ($80 – $50 – $8), while the put option holder incurs a loss of $3. In both cases, the option holder is protected from unlimited losses while remaining able to earn a high profit on the put option and an unlimited profit on the call option.

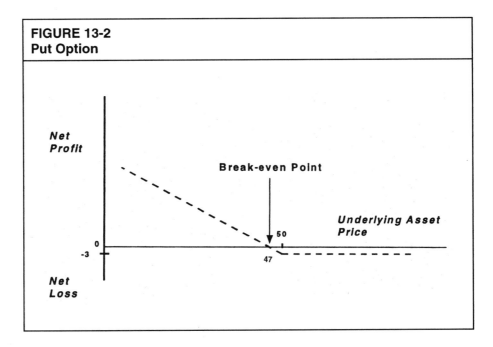

FIGURE 13-2
Put Option

The profit break-even point for going long a call occurs where the underlying asset price equals the exercise price plus the cost of the option. For the call option, a profit is earned when the underlying asset price falls to the right of the break-even point. The profit break-even point for going long a put occurs where the underlying asset price equals the exercise price less the cost of the option. For the put, profits occur when the underlying asset price falls to the left of the break-even point.

It is rational to exercise a call (put) option for a reduced loss just before the option's expiration date when the underlying asset price is just above (below) the exercise price. Failure to exercise in this situation results in the loss of the entire option premium. When the payoff from exercising the option is equal to the cost of acquiring the option, the profit on the exercise is $0. When the payoff from exercising the option is greater than the cost of acquiring the option, a positive profit results.

Example: About 3 months ago, GM stock traded at $72 per share. At that time, you bought a GM call option and paid a premium of $2.50 per share. The option has a strike price of $75 per share. The option expires tomorrow; the stock currently trades at $76 per share, and the option trades at $1.06 per share. If you take no action by the close of trading, the option becomes worthless (expires). What should you do?

You have three choices. First, you could exercise the option and buy the stock for $75 per share (and pay the standard commission for the purchase of stock). Second, you could sell the option today (and pay the standard commission for the sale of an option). Third, you could wait to see what happens on the expiration date. If the price of GM goes up, you could make a fantastic percentage gain. If the price goes down (below $75), the option would become worthless.

intrinsic value

A call option is valuable for three reasons (the put option is valuable for similar reasons). First, when a call is exercised, if the exercise price paid for the underlying asset of the call option is lower than the market price received from the subsequent sale of the asset, a net cash inflow is generated. This cash inflow is called the *intrinsic value* of the option. Although this value is realized only when the option is exercised, the price of the option will always reflect the potential value of its exercise. Second, because the exercise of a call option requires a future cash outflow, the cash outflow is worth less today than it will be on the exercise date because of the time value of money. Third, the call option holder's ability to choose whether or not to buy the underlying asset at a specified price has value in and of itself.

Options are inherently risky assets because the price volatility of an option is magnified with respect to the volatility of the underlying asset price.

Example: Recall the earlier example in which the call option had an exercise price of $50. Assume that an investor can choose between buying a stock outright for $50 today or buying a call option with an exercise price of $50. If the stock price falls to $30, the call option would not be exercised, and the $8 investment in the option would be a complete loss (–100%). If the investor had purchased the stock outright, the loss would be –40 percent [($30 – $50)/$50 = –40%]. Conversely, if the stock price rises to $80, the option could be exercised for a gain of $22. The option holder would receive a return of 275 percent [($30 – $8)/$8 = 275%], while the shareholder would earn a return of 60 percent [($80 – $50)/$50 = 60%].

In both the gain and the loss situations above, the percentage return on the option has a larger absolute value than that of the stock, meaning that the option is inherently and significantly more risky than the stock.

Appendix C at the end of this chapter provides more diagrams, similar to figures 13-1 and 13-2, showing the dollar value of profit and loss from various option and stock ownership positions and their interrelationships. These diagrams may help some readers to gain a better understanding of this material. We will occasionally refer to these diagrams in the remainder of this chapter.

Uses of Calls

The purchaser of a call can benefit from price increases in the underlying security while limiting the risk of loss from price decreases of the security. This enables the investor to benefit from potentially higher rates of return (at much greater risk) on the amount actually invested.

Generally, there are three reasons why an investor may purchase a call option. First, the investor may have borrowed and sold a stock (a short sale). By purchasing a call option, the investor locks in the return on this investment. This process is called hedging, because the risk of the original investment is "hedged" away. Second, an investor may purchase a call when the investor believes the market price of the underlying security is likely to increase above the strike price on or before the expiration date. This is called speculation, because the investor is speculating on future price behavior. Third, if the investor believes that public markets are inappropriately pricing call options relative to the price of the underlying stock, the investor may

arbitrage

engage in a strategy known as *arbitrage*. To engage in arbitrage, the investor buys one security and sells another, so that he or she has no net investment and assumes no risk. Cash inflows resulting from this strategy are possible only when markets fail to price assets consistently, relative to the prices of other closely related assets. In other words, arbitrage takes advantage of temporary mispricings between two different markets.

A variation of the speculation strategy is that an investor may have insufficient cash to purchase an underlying stock but still wants to lock in the price at which the stock can be purchased if and when cash becomes available. Purchasing a call option on this stock does not commit the investor to buy the stock if cash does not become available or if the price of the stock decreases. However, if cash does become available, the investor can buy the stock at the price secured by the purchase of the call option.

Uses of Puts

As with the call option, the put may be used for hedging, speculating, and arbitrage. If an investor expects the price of a stock to fall, the investor can speculate by purchasing a put, allowing him or her to sell the stock at the strike price. However, there is a risk that the price of the underlying asset will increase. With a short sale, the investor could risk a loss of the difference between the market price and the sale price of the asset if the market price increases and the short-seller is forced to cover the short sale by purchasing the asset at the market price. This loss is potentially unlimited because the stock could, in theory, increase to any price. On the other hand, the put option limits the potential loss to the option premium that the purchaser paid because the investor does not exercise the option to sell when the price increases. The profit function for the purchase of a put is shown in appendix C, figure E. The profit function for selling short is shown in appendix C, figure B.

Investors who want to preserve current gains in a stock investment can sell the stock to secure the rate of return at that time. However, selling the stock will trigger gain recognition, ending the potential continued deferral of tax. Alternatively, the investor can purchase a put on the stock and defer the decision to sell the stock, while locking in its sale price should a sale become necessary to preserve current gains. If the market price of the stock declines, the investor can sell the put any time up to and including the expiration date. If the market price of the stock does not decline, the investor can simply let the put expire unexercised. The purchase of a put, in effect, buys the investor time to determine whether there is a need to sell the stock. The investor may continue to hold the stock without triggering capital gains tax at the cost of the put option premium.

Like the writer of a call, the writer of a put may wish to increase portfolio cash flow by the option premium proceeds on the assumption that the market price of the selected underlying stock will remain steady or increase. However, if the market price of the underlying stock declines by more than the strike price, the writer of the put is subject to potential loss of the difference between the market price and the exercise price. The writer may purchase an identical put to "close out" the open position and limit the loss to the difference between the option premium paid and the option premium received. The profit function for writing a put option is shown in appendix C, figure F.

Example: You are closely following the news about DeKalb Manufacturing Company. You believe the company has been getting some bad publicity lately, causing the stock price to decline from $20 to $15 per share. You are confident that the stock has bottomed out, and you decide to write 10 puts at $2 per put. This generates a cash inflow of $2,000 (less commission). You take a week's vacation on the proceeds. Upon returning, you learn that the rumors are true; in fact, the situation is far worse than imagined. The stock drops to $.10 per share as the company declares bankruptcy. What should you do?

You are facing two ugly choices. You can buy back the puts for a price of approximately $15 each ($15,000 total), or you can wait until someone exercises the options and sells you the shares for $15 each ($15,000 total). In either situation, you will suffer a major loss.

Option Markets

Most put and call trading takes place on the option exchanges. Unlisted puts and calls and less actively traded warrants and rights are traded over-the-counter.

Before listed options appeared, all option trading was in the over-the-counter market. OTC options had expiration dates and strike prices that varied greatly. Secondary market trading in OTC options was very haphazard. Virtually all option contract trading now takes place with listed puts and calls traded under rules of the Chicago-based *Options Clearing Corporation (OCC),* which is a not-for-profit corporation established by the options exchanges. Calls and puts represent private contracts between individual buyers and sellers. Technically, the OCC manages and guarantees the option contracts. Thus, each put and call buyer and seller is contracting with the clearing corporation, rather than directly with the opposite party to the transaction. The OCC acts as an intermediary between the two principals in an option trade. Call writers (sellers) must be ready to supply already issued stock (either from their own portfolios or by an open market purchase). Similarly, a put writer must be prepared to purchase existing shares. Options have standardized strike prices and expiration dates. The OCC assures the integrity of the traded option—if one party to the option transaction defaults on its position in the transaction, the OCC stands ready to fulfill the terms of the defaulted side of the option contract.

When listed option trading began in 1973, new option contracts were introduced every 3 months and had an initial maturity (time to expiration) of 9 months. Three sets of expiration dates were traded at any particular time. For example, a company might have options on a January cycle. Its options would be set to expire every 3 months, beginning with January, then in April, July, and October. When the nearest expiration month is January, the other listed options would be April and July. Once the January option expired, a new set of options would be listed for October. Other companies' options were set for February and March cycles.

Options Clearing Corporation (OCC)

Some companies' options still expire only every 3 months. Most companies with listed options, however, now have additional expirations times that fill in the 2 nearest months. Consider, for example, a company with a January basic cycle. In early January, it would list expirations in January, April, and July. In addition, option expirations would be listed for February. Thus, most companies now have a total of four options expirations. Two are in the nearest 2 months; two more distant expirations occur at 3-month intervals. Listed options are set to expire on the Saturday following the third Friday of their month of expiration.

The listed-option market experienced spectacular growth throughout the latter half of the 1970s. Three exchanges—CBOE (Chicago Board Options Exchange), AMEX (American Stock Exchange), and PHLX (Philadelphia Stock Exchange)—now list options on a substantial number of stocks. The value of the options trading in these issues often exceeds the value of the stocks traded for the underlying shares.

American versus European Options

American options
European options

Options are distinguished by whether or not they may be exercised before the expiration date. Options that may be exercised early are called *American options;* options that may be exercised only on the expiration date are called *European options.* Assuming no dividends or tax effects, it would not make sense to exercise an American option prior to its expiration date. Before the expiration date, the option has more value when it is sold than when it is exercised. This must be true because exercising the option eliminates any time value that the option could have retained had it been sold instead. However, cash flows from the underlying asset and tax incentives may induce an investor to exercise early.

LEAPS®

LEAPS®

Puts and calls are normally written for relatively short periods (9 months is typically the longest available); however, a 1990 innovation in the options market called Long-term Equity Anticipation Securities *(LEAPS®)* with expiration dates as long as 3 years—and covering both calls and puts—was introduced on the CBOE and the AMEX. They are now traded on all the options exchanges.

LEAPS® calls enable the investor to benefit from a stock price increase without purchasing the stock outright. In addition, the investor does not have to manage each LEAPS® position daily as a result of taking an initial LEAPS® position. LEAPS® puts provide stockowners with a hedge against significant decreases in their stocks.

LEAPS® also appeal to investors who want to take a longer-term position in some of the options they currently trade. (As mentioned above, expiration dates can be as long as 3 years.) The expiration date for LEAPS® is the Saturday following the third Friday of the expiration month. Equity LEAPS® expire in January.

Option Combinations

Stock options can be combined to create an infinite variety of payoff schemes to accomplish various investment objectives. One of the most popular combinations is called the *straddle*. In a straddle, the investor simultaneously buys or sells a call option and a put option with the same underlying asset and exercise price. The purchase of both options is called longing, or going long, a straddle, and its profit function is shown in appendix C, figure I. The sale of both is called shorting, or going short, a straddle and is shown in appendix C, figure J.

straddle

When long a straddle, the investor loses if the underlying asset price hovers near the exercise price of the two options but gains if the underlying asset price is highly volatile (makes a big jump one way or the other). This strategy is frequently used by investors to profit when they expect unusual volatility in financial markets.

spread

Another strategy is called the *spread*. In a spread, one option is purchased and the other is sold, with each option having a different exercise price or a different expiration date. A bullish spread can be constructed with either two puts or two calls by selling the option with the higher exercise price and buying the same type option on the same underlying asset with a lower exercise price. The profit function for a bullish spread is shown in figure 13-3. This strategy is used by the same investors who would use a regular call option but prefer not to pay for the unlimited potential profits of the call option; the call is more expensive than the bullish spread. The break-even point occurs where the underlying asset price is equal to the lower exercise price plus the difference in premiums between the two options.

Alternatively, the investor who would like to purchase a put option but does not want to pay for the high profit potential of the put option may purchase a bearish spread. The bearish spread can be constructed with puts or calls by selling an option with a low exercise price and purchasing the same type option on the same underlying asset with a high exercise price. A typical profit function for a bearish spread is shown in figure 13-4. Similar to the bullish spread, the bearish spread is cheaper than a related put option. The break-even point is determined in the same way as with the bullish spread.

Tax Effects. The first tax aspect of an option transaction is the tax treatment of the premium received by the writer. No taxable income goes to the writer on the receipt of the option premium. Instead, the writer is taxed on the lapse, exercise, or closing out of the option.

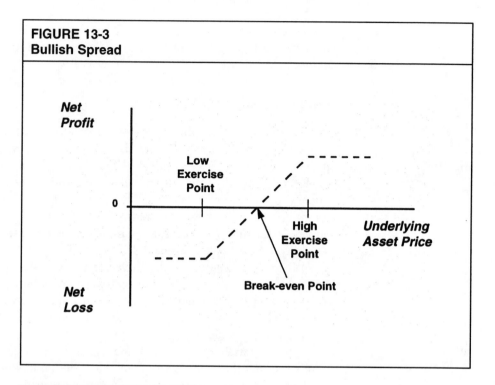

FIGURE 13-3
Bullish Spread

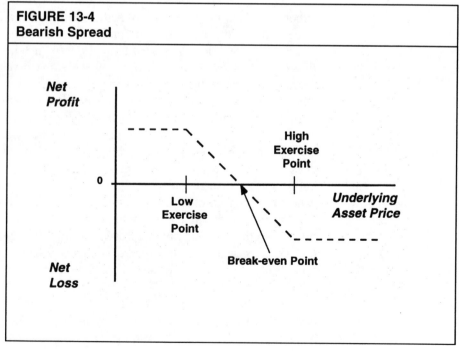

FIGURE 13-4
Bearish Spread

If the option lapses, the writer recognizes capital gain on the date of the lapse. Unless the option is a LEAP®, the capital gain will necessarily be short term. If a put option is exercised, the writer purchases the underlying stock and has a basis equal to the net investment—that is, the strike price reduced by the option premium. The stock's holding period begins with the exercise of the option. If a call is exercised, the writer sells the underlying stock for the strike price. He or she recognizes gain or loss measured by the difference between the sales price and the adjusted basis of the stock delivered to the purchaser. The character of the capital gain or loss depends on the holding **covered call** period of the stock used to cover the call. In a *covered call,* the writer owns at least the amount of the stock at the time the call is written, so the capital gain or loss could be either short-term or long-term, depending on the holding period of the stock used by the writer when the call is exercised. **naked call** However, in a *naked call,* since the writer does not own the underlying stock required to cover the call at the time the call is written, the character will generally be short-term.

Example: Suppose an investor writes a call for 100 shares at $40 per share; the investor also owns 100 shares purchased 6 months before writing the call at $30 per share and 100 shares purchased one month before writing the call at $35 per share. The writer receives a premium of $100 for the call. Nine months later the holder of the call exercises the option. If the writer uses the first block of stock, the writer recognizes $1,100 of long-term capital gain ($4,000 exercise price + $100 option premium – $3,000 basis), because the call is exercised after the stock was held for 15 months. If the writer uses the second block of stock to cover the call, the writer recognizes a $600 short-term capital gain ($4,000 exercise price + $100 option premium – $3,500 basis), because the call is exercised after the stock was held for only 10 months.

If the writer of a put closes out the option by purchasing an identical put, he or she recognizes a short-term capital gain or loss in the difference between the amount paid to purchase the put and the amount received as an option premium in writing the put. Similarly, if the writer of a call closes the option by purchasing an identical call, he or she recognizes a short-term capital gain or loss in the amount of the difference between the amount received as an option premium on the writing of the call and the amount paid to purchase the call.

The second aspect of the option transaction is the tax treatment of the payment of the option premium by the purchaser of the option. Like the writer, the purchaser does not account for the option premium until the option is sold, exercised, or allowed to lapse. If the put or call option is sold, the holder recognizes capital gain or loss in the difference between the sales proceeds and the premium paid for the option. In general, this gain or loss will be short-term because the 9-month limited life of puts and calls does not allow a long-term holding period.

If the purchaser of a put exercises the option, the option premium paid reduces the amount realized on the investor's delivery of stock to the writer. This reduces the gain or increases the loss recognized by the purchaser. If the purchaser of a call exercises the option, the option premium added to the strike price and commissions paid is the investor's basis in the stock acquired by the exercise. The holding period of the stock acquired by the call begins on the day after the date of exercise.

The lapse of a call or put option is treated as if it were sold for zero. The character of the loss depends on the nature of an underlying security. For stocks, it is a capital loss. For a married put, the option premium paid is **married put** added to the basis of the stock identified with the put. A *married put* is a put acquired on the same day the investor acquires the same number of shares of the underlying stock. The holding period of the option is generally short-term.

Setting Strike Prices

Strike prices are initially set at levels that are divisible by 5 or 10 (or in some cases 2½) and closest to the current stock price. Thus, a stock trading at 43 would typically have options listed at 40 and 45. Similarly, a stock trading at 21 would have options listed at 20 and 22.50. Stock prices, however, fluctuate over time. Options with strikes that were near the market price when initially listed will not necessarily remain near the market price. As a stock price moves away from the available strikes, trading becomes less attractive in the existing options.

For example, a call with a strike of 30 on a stock selling for 50 will be priced too high to offer very much leverage. Similarly, a call with an 80 strike on a stock trading at 60 is very likely to expire worthless. Thus, these options have very little speculative appeal because one side of the market or the other has few likely buyers or sellers.

Because stock prices can move quite a bit in a few months, some strikes can differ substantially from the current quote. Accordingly, new strikes are authorized at levels close to the stock's current quote whenever its price changes appreciably. The older options with the original strike prices continue to be traded, but as they expire, the old strike prices are not applied to the new options.

writer

An investor can enter an option contract either as a *writer* or as a purchaser. The writer of a call may own the underlying security to satisfy the holder in case the call is exercised, in which case the option is a covered call, as explained earlier. However, the writer may write the option without owning a sufficient amount of stock to cover the call if exercised (a naked call).

Whether the writer is writing a covered call or a naked call, the writer receives a cash inflow from the option premium. Assume that a trader writes a call option with an exercise price of $40, sells the option for $5, and simultaneously purchases the underlying asset for $38. If the asset price rises to $50 and the option is exercised, the writer's net cash flow will be $7 ($40 – $38 + $5), as we can assume the call would be exercised. However, if the writer does not purchase the underlying asset when the call is sold, the writer's net cash flow is –$5 ($40 – $50 + $5). Conversely, if the underlying asset price falls to $30 and the writer of the call decides to sell the underlying asset, the net cash flow to the writer is –$3 ($30 – $38 + $5) for a covered call; for a naked call, the net cash flow is the option premium, $5. In each case, the range between gain and loss positions is $10, but there is no risk of default on the option contract with the covered call. Also, the stock purchased to cover the call option does not have to be sold when the option expires. The profit function for a naked call writer is shown in appendix C, figure D. For a covered call writer, it is shown in appendix C, figure G.

The writer of a covered call receives cash flows from the underlying asset if the asset pays dividends or when the covered call is closed out (an equivalent option position is purchased and the underlying asset is sold). If the market price of the stock remains at or below the strike price, the option will not be exercised, and the writer will enjoy the extra cash. If the market price of the stock exceeds the strike price of the call option, the option will be exercised, and the additional capital gain in the stock will not be realized.

Example: You own 500 shares of DeKalb Manufacturing Company. The stock currently trades at $20 per share and has not varied from this price much for the last 2 years. Because you bought the stock at $5 per share, you really don't want to sell it and pay the capital gains tax, but you would like to improve your cash flow. You see some March call options with a stock price of $25 are trading at $1 per share. You sell five of these call options to generate a nice cash inflow of $500 (less commission). Everything is fine until late February, when a buyout proposal is presented, causing the stock price to jump to $50 per share. You now wish you had not written the options.

You have several choices. First, you could let the stock be called away in March. Second, you could buy the options back (at a price in excess of $25 each). Third, you could buy back the options and write new options with a higher strike price (this will still produce a negative net cash flow).

Black-Scholes model

Value of an Option: Black-Scholes Model

The valuation of options has long intrigued financial theorists. F. Black and M. Scholes wrote the classic theoretical option pricing work,[1] following earlier work by P. Samuelson and others. Black and Scholes began with the assumption that investors could buy the underlying nondividend-paying stock and write (sell) calls to maintain a fully hedged position. For stock price increases, writing calls can be equivalent to short-selling the stock. With such a hedge, any change in the value of the stock's price could be offset by an equivalent but opposite change in the value of the short position in calls.

Example: Suppose that a $1 change in the stock price was known to cause a $.50 change in the call price. Investors could then construct a fully hedged position by writing calls on twice as many shares as are held. If the investor is short two calls, a $1 increase in the stock price would be matched by a $1 decrease in the value of the call position. Similarly, a $1 decrease in the stock's price would be offset by a $1 increase in the value of the call position. In fact, any small move in the stock's price would be precisely offset by a change in the value of the option position.

hedge ratio

As time passes and stock and call prices change, the appropriate *hedge ratio* (required ratio) will vary. For example, the required ratio of two calls to one share of stock might later change to a ratio of three calls to one share of stock. The investor can maintain a fully hedged position by adjusting the ratio of shares to calls whenever necessary. Thus, if the required ratio changes from two calls per share to three calls per share, the hedger can write (sell) an additional call for each share held. The result of this process is

riskless hedge

called a *riskless hedge*—designed to insulate the investor from market moves in the underlying stock's price. Selling the calls provides a form of insurance against the contingency of market changes in the price of the stock.

In an efficient market, an investment in the combined riskless position should earn the riskless interest rate (approximately the rate on T-bills). Using a model based on the assumptions stated earlier, Black and Scholes developed a mathematical call valuation formula that is a function of five variables. The precise form of the model is rather complex, but the most important results are as follows: Call values *increase* with increases in these four variables: time to maturity, interest rates, the price of the underlying stock, and volatility (or variance) of the underlying stock; they *decrease* as the fifth variable—strike price—increases. Appendix A provides a full statement of the model.

Five Variables in Black-Scholes Model

- time to maturity: The longer the time to maturity, the more valuable the call.
- interest rate: The higher the interest rate, the more valuable the call.
- price of underlying stock: The higher the stock price, the more valuable the call.
- volatility: The more volatile the price of the underlying stock, the more valuable the call.
- strike price: The higher the strike price, the less valuable the call.

The Black-Scholes formula is more than just an interesting theoretical exercise. Option traders often compute Black-Scholes prices to follow a strategy of buying undervalued options (vis-à-vis the model) and writing overvalued ones. The importance of Black-Scholes and its later extensions, therefore, cannot be overstated. It provided a strong theoretical underpinning to the whole development of the derivatives marketplace in the 1970s—the most dynamic part of recent financial markets. It gave investors confidence in what were fair values for options.

put-call parity

Put-Call Parity

The Black-Scholes model effectively deals with pricing call options. Relating call prices to put prices is another theoretical aspect of option pricing. A put-like position can be created from a call and a short position in the stock. (See figures E and H in appendix C.) Such a *manufactured (synthetic) put* will have the same type of payoff matrix as a put. The loss on the short position from a stock price rise is limited by the call, while profits

manufactured (synthetic) put

manufactured call

from the short position will increase as the stock's price falls. Similarly, a long position in the stock plus a put, called a *manufactured call,* has the same kind of payoff as a call. (Combine figures C and K in appendix C.) A loss from a decrease in stock price is limited by the put, while profits from the long position will increase as the stock's price rises. Because a put can be converted into a manufactured call and a call can be converted into a manufactured put, the prices of the two options should be related. Indeed, according to the "law of one price," whenever two assets offer equivalent payoff combinations, their prices must be identical (or within a range permitted by such arbitrage expenses as transaction costs).

conversions

Traders normally prefer to buy puts or calls directly, but some people choose to manufacture puts from calls, or *vice versa*, when prices get out of line. Moreover, some brokerage firms try to profit from apparent price disparities by taking offsetting positions in the manufactured and nonmanufactured puts and calls *(conversions).* This arbitrage activity tends to drive the prices back toward their proper parity.

As with the Black-Scholes formula, the precise form of the put-call parity formula is a bit too complex to discuss in this textbook. Nonetheless, serious option traders should be aware of its existence. (The explicit relationship is presented in appendix B at the end of the chapter.)

OPTIONS ON OTHER ASSETS

Virtually any standardized asset can be subject to the option writing and holding process, provided enough investors are interested in trading these instruments. Assets on which standardized options are written include the following:

- foreign currencies
- stock indexes
- industry indexes
- interest rates (Treasury securities)
- futures contracts

Discussions of stock index, industry index and interest rate options follow. Futures contracts are covered in chapter 14.

Stock Index Options

Mechanics of Index Options

stock index options

Users of *stock index options* are able to buy or sell an entire stock market index, such as the S&P 500 (SPX) or the NASDAQ (NDX) stock exchange index, for the premium paid for the option. Instead of selecting either an index mutual fund (whose portfolio replicates a specific stock market index) or specific stocks (with which to go long if a prolonged market rise seems imminent), the investor "buys" the market by acquiring a call option on the index. Since the gain from the rise in the market is captured for a minimal outlay, the value of the option will rise with the increase in the index. Bearish investors, on the other hand, hold puts to profit from a decline in the market index.

As with stock options, standardized expiration dates and strike prices have been established for index options. Settlement between the writer and the holder takes place on the expiration date. Strike prices are written with 5-point increments on the underlying index. For example, if the SPX (the most popular of the indexes used for option trading) stands at 1141, put and call options at 1140 and 1150 and in ± 5- or 10-point increments from there could be written and traded. When the index rises to new highs or lows, options for new strike prices around those levels are written and traded—often for months to come. The options exchanges will trade index options at strike prices well beyond any recent levels of the indexes (even well above historical highs) as long as buyers and sellers can be matched. Thus, sample SPX-offered options and strike prices could range from December puts of 1100 all the way to December calls of 1175. Suppose the SPX index value closed at 1141 on November 14, 2001. This range of highs and lows in strike prices is not found historically for most of the stocks underlying the S&P 500 for such a short period. (Only volatile high-tech stocks tend to exhibit a similar range in offerings of standard options.)

Table 13-1 shows sample premium quotations for the SPX and NDX options from a typical financial page. This premium quotation is multiplied by 100 to determine how much the buyer pays (or the writer receives) for the option. For example, assume that the SPX stands at 1141 and the premium asked for a December call option with a strike price of 1150 on that specific index is $29. For an index option, the normal lot is 100 units. Therefore, the price for this call option is $2,900 ($29 x 100). Because the index is 1141, this call is currently out of the money and has no intrinsic value, but it has a time value of $2,900.

As with company-specific stock options, writers of index options place margin deposits with their brokers for the period of the option or until the option position is closed out through purchasing an offsetting contract. Unlike the stock options in which settlement of exercised options includes the delivery of the common stocks to the call holder (or to the put writer), settlement for stock index options is made in dollars. The amount of money that will be paid on the settlement date depends on the difference between the exercise price and the index. Multiplying this difference by $100 determines the amount that will be paid by the option writer.

TABLE 13-1
Sample Chicago Mercantile Exchange Index Options Quotes (Figures for November 14)

S&P 500 Index (SPX)			Close 1141	
	Calls		Puts	
Strike Price	Nov	Dec	Nov	Dec
1130	15.50	. . .	3.80	
1140	11	35.50	8.50	32
1150	4.10	29	12	36

NASDAQ-100 (NDX)			Close 3997	
	Calls		Puts	
Strike Price	Nov	Dec	Nov	Dec
1100	41	61	1	18.40
1175	.50	18	33.50	50

Example: Referring to table 13-1, suppose on November 15, 2001, a December call on the NDX with a strike price of 1100 is purchased, and the index closes at 1175 at the end of March (third Friday)—a difference of 75, or approximately 6.4 percent. In this case, the writer's obligation requires payment of $7,500 ([$1,175 – $1,100]) x 100) to the holder. If the holder acquired the call at $61 from the writer for a cost of $6,100 ($61 x 100), the buyer's gain is $1,400, and the holding period return is 23 percent ([75 – 61]/61) over one month. The writer, of course, loses $1,400.

A similar put option at a strike price of 1100 would not be exercised because the index value in the example above exceeds 1100. Holders of puts exercise their options only when the strike price exceeds the index value on the day the option expires. However, if the purchaser of the put had bought the put at the same time as the call buyer, the put purchaser would have paid $18.40 per put ($1,840) and would have lost it all (–100%). Clearly, NASDAQ index options are not for the faint of heart.

Interest Rate Options

interest rate options

Puts and calls on specific U.S. Treasury securities are called *interest rate options*. Usually, these options are written for a relatively large dollar amount, such as $100,000, of a particular issue. These options are based on the average yield of the most recently auctioned 7-, 10-, and 30-year U.S. Treasury bonds. These options are exercisable only on their last trading day. One unique aspect of these options is that their duration is only one trading cycle of 3- and 6-month options. Once these expire, no new options can be written on the Treasury bonds on which these options are based. The rationale for this practice is that most of the bonds are in portfolios that are not actively traded. Sufficient secondary trading does not exist to justify a continuing market for these options.

RIGHTS AND WARRANTS

Actively traded rights and warrants are generally listed on a stock exchange. As pure options, rights and warrants have much in common with calls. The same basic valuation principles and risk-return trade-offs are present with all three types of securities. Nevertheless, each option type has some distinctive characteristics.

Rights

A rights offering to existing shareholders allows a company to raise additional capital and avoid diluting the current shareholders' positions. These rights, which will specify the terms for the stock purchase (price and time frame), give the right of first refusal on the new stock to the existing shareholders. Shareholders who want to maintain their proportional ownership in the company can simply exercise their rights. Most holders of a trivial percentage of a really large company have little or no interest in maintaining their percentage ownership. Thus, they may prefer to sell their rights on the open market. Other shareholders, however, may take advantage of the offering to increase their investment in the company.

Rights usually allow purchase of new stock at a discount from the current market price. In the terminology of puts and calls, rights are in-the-money. They have an intrinsic value. If the stock's price rises, then the value of the right also increases. Rights trading is, however, relatively speculative because most rights have a short lifespan—often only a few weeks.

Usually, one right is issued for each outstanding share, typically giving the holder an option on a fraction (say, one-quarter) of a share. Thus, the holder of 100 shares of the underlying stock might receive 100 rights, which would entitle him or her to buy 25 additional shares. Rights are generally issued for short exercise periods at strike prices that are in-the-money. Accordingly, rights are generally priced very close to their intrinsic values (little or no time value).

Cum-Rights and Ex-Rights

As with dividends, a rights offering announcement specifies a date of record for people who own the stock to receive the rights. Up to that day is the *cum-rights* period. After that date, the stock sells *ex-rights* (no right attached). Setting the record date a few days after the ex-rights date allows time for the company's record keeping. Generally, the shares go ex-rights in the marketplace 4 business days before the record date. Table 13-2 shows the typical timing of a rights offer.

TABLE 13-2 Typical Timing of a Rights Offering		
Date	Day	Event
January 14	Monday	Rights offering announced for shareholders of record on Monday, February 4
January 28	Monday	Last day to buy the shares cum-rights
January 29	Tuesday	Shares go ex-rights
February 4	Monday	Actual record date

Rights Valuation Formulas

The value of the underlying stock depends on whether it is selling cum- or ex-rights. The stock's price will generally drop on the day it goes ex-rights because subsequent buyers will not receive the rights.

Valuation during the Cum-Rights Period. Assume that buying 10 shares of XYZ at $40 gives the buyer enough rights to buy one additional share at $38. Accordingly, the buyer can buy 10 + 1 shares of stock for $438:

$$(10 \times \$40) + (1 \times \$38) = \$438$$

The shares' average price is $438 divided by 11, or $39.82, and the intrinsic value of one right is $40 minus $39.82, or $.18. An owner of 100 shares should be able to sell the rights for $18 (less commission). Thus, the intrinsic value of one right during the cum-rights period is determined by the following formula:

$$\frac{\text{Instrinsic value of one right}}{\text{during cum-rights period}} = \frac{\text{Market price of stock} - \text{Subscription price}}{\frac{\text{Number of shares needed to}}{\text{subscribe to one share}} + \text{One share}}$$

Applying this formula to the above example yields

Intrinsic value = ($40 – $38)/(10 + 1) = $2.00/11 = $.18

The market value of the right may, however, differ from its intrinsic value. That is, rights' prices may reflect some time value.

Valuation during the Ex-Rights Period. As a stock goes ex-rights, its market value usually declines slightly. The adjusted formula for the intrinsic value becomes

$$\frac{\text{Intrinsic value of one right}}{\text{during ex-rights period}} = \frac{\text{Market price of stock} - \text{Subscription price}}{\frac{\text{Number of shares needed to}}{\text{subscribe to one share}}}$$

If the stock drops by $.25 to $39.75 when it goes ex-rights, the intrinsic valued of one right is as follows:

$$\frac{\$39.75 - \$38.00}{10} = \frac{\$1.75}{10} = \$.175$$

Warrants

Firms that might otherwise have trouble raising capital often sell warrants in a financing package that also includes bonds. Frequently, these bonds have an intrinsic value way below par and can be sold at par only because of the inclusion of warrants with the bond.

Exercising the warrants increases the number of shares outstanding (firms almost always use Treasury stock to cover warrants and rights). Therefore, in the normal case, the market price of the outstanding shares of stock before the exercise of the warrants will tend to fall somewhat, other things being equal.

Frequently, start-up firms or firms with somewhat risky (but optimistic) prospects are the main issuers of warrants to aid in financing. Because pure debt issues would have to carry higher yields, the firm would use the bond-cum-warrants approach to lower its initial financing costs. This approach allows the bondholders to share in the firm's growth while providing a more secure return on capital if the firm does not grow.

CONVERTIBLES

Appeal of Convertibles

Hybrid securities derive value both from their yield (interest or preferred dividends) and from the upside potential of the underlying common stock. If the price of the underlying common stock rises sufficiently, it becomes worthwhile for the holder of the convertible security to convert to common, thus acquiring common stock at a price below its market price. The holder might also choose to sell the convertible instrument at a profit that reflects the increase in the underlying common stock's price. A third option is to hold the convertible bond, keep receiving periodic interest payments, and convert only when the dividends on the underlying common stock exceed the interest payments on the debt instrument, or until the debenture is about to mature (or be called). The third option gives the holder the best of both worlds—realizing both the higher interest payments on the debenture and eventually the capital gain from converting to common stock. If the stock's price does not rise sufficiently to make conversion worthwhile, the owner still receives income from the interest payments plus the face value of the debenture at maturity. Thus, convertible debentures offer a combination of the upside potential of common stock and the downside risk protection of bonds.

The conversion feature has a price, however—generally a lower coupon interest rate than that paid on straight bonds of comparable risk and maturity. In the secondary market, convertible debentures sell at a higher price than comparable bonds without the conversion feature. In the event of bankruptcy, straight bonds tend to have a higher priority than convertible bonds.

Terminology

As with pure options, there are a number of specialized terms pertaining to convertible bonds, which are defined below:

conversion ratio

- *conversion ratio:* number of shares of common stock into which the bond is convertible

conversion price

- *conversion price:* face value of the security divided by its conversion ratio

conversion value

- *conversion value:* current stock price multiplied by the conversion ratio

straight-debt value

- *straight-debt value:* market value of an otherwise equivalent bond lacking a conversion feature

conversion premium
premium over straight-debt value

- *conversion premium:* bond price less its conversion value
- *premium over straight-debt value:* bond price less its straight-debt value

---

Example: Suppose a $1,000 par-value bond trading at par is convertible into 50 shares of common stock. The conversion ratio is 50. The conversion price is $1,000/50, or $20 per share. If the underlying common stock is currently trading at $15/share, the conversion value of the bond is 50 x $15 = $750, and the conversion premium is $250 ($1,000 − $750). The conversion value is a measure of what the convertible bond is worth if immediately converted into common stock.

The straight-debt value of a convertible bond is the intrinsic value of a comparable bond without the conversion feature.

Example: Suppose the convertible bond in the example above has a coupon rate of 12 percent and 5 years to maturity, and a straight bond of comparable risk trading at par pays a coupon rate of 13.5 percent. Using a discount rate of 13.5 percent and calculating the present value, we find that the straight-debt value of the convertible bond (assuming annual interest payments) is $947.88.

Consider what happens when the price of the underlying stock rises.

Example: Suppose the price of the stock in both examples above increases to $25 per share. The conversion value of the bond is now $25 x 50, or $1,250. The conversion value of the bond now exceeds its straight-debt value.

The market price of a convertible bond should always be at least the greater of its straight-debt value or its conversion value. This is because the holder has the option of either keeping the instrument as a bond or converting it into stock. The greater of these two amounts represents a floor below which the price of the convertible should not fall.

The market value of the convertible can, however, exceed this floor because of the time value or speculative value of the conversion option. Even if the conversion value is below the current market price of the company's stock, there is a reasonable likelihood that the price of the stock will rise sufficiently before the bond matures to make conversion worthwhile. The size of this speculative value is directly related to the time to maturity and the volatility of the price of the underlying stock, and it is inversely related to the spread between the conversion price and the stock's current market price.

Advantages of Convertible Bonds

There are two principal advantages to investing in convertibles compared with common stock. First, the current yield on the convertible bond is likely to be much higher and more certain than the dividend yield on the underlying common stock. Second, the fixed interest rate gives holders downside protection, because they are legally entitled to receive interest payments and the principal amount at maturity even if the company performs poorly and its stock declines in value. In the event of bankruptcy, holders of convertible debt have priority over holders of common stock.

Like straight bonds, convertible bonds are vulnerable to interest rate risk. If the market interest rates increase, the straight-debt value of the convertible declines. Remember, too, that the convertible bond's speculative value will exist only as long as there is a reasonable chance that the underlying common stock's market price will exceed its conversion price before the bond matures.

Call Feature

During the 1980s with their high interest rates, most newly issued bonds were callable. The convertible bonds were no exception. Convertible bonds always contain some form of call provision. The call feature is especially relevant to holders of convertible bonds, because it can limit the bonds' upside potential. To understand, imagine that the market price of the underlying stock rises above the conversion price. As long as the interest payments on the bonds exceed the dividend payments on the common stock shares into which the bonds are convertible, it would be worthwhile to hold the bonds, continue to receive interest payments, and exercise the conversion feature just before the bonds mature. This means that the issuing company is bearing the cost of interest payments, while the bondholder is enjoying the potential gains from stock appreciation (with little risk), as well as receiving the interest payments.

The issuing company can effectively force conversion, however, by calling the bonds. If a convertible bond is called, the holder of the bond can either accept the bond's $1,000 face value plus call premium or convert. Once the last date of the call period passes, the investor no longer has the option to convert and will not earn any additional interest. It is in the issuing corporation's interest to force conversion once the conversion value of the bond exceeds the call price *and* it is clear that all bondholders will eventually convert. The corporation saves substantial interest expenses (although there may be some incremental dividends), and it can issue more debt.

Conversion Premium

The conversion premium is of great importance to an investor. The conversion premium is at its largest when a bond trades near par value. When the price of the underlying stock is unusually high or low, the conversion premium will be relatively small to nearly nonexistent. When the price of the stock is near the conversion price, then the bond premium is at its maximum. This relationship is shown in figure 13-5. Let us consider why the conversion premium behaves in this manner.

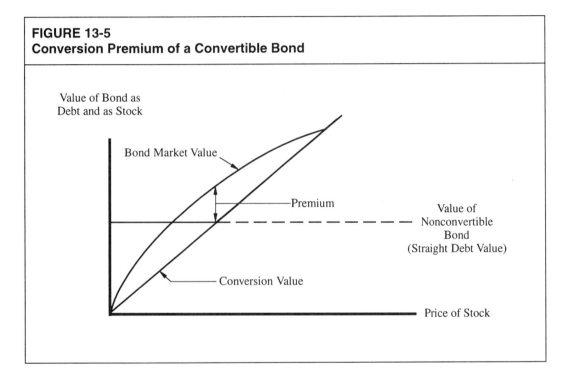

FIGURE 13-5
Conversion Premium of a Convertible Bond

A straight line emanating from the origin represents the conversion value. The slope of the line is equal to the conversion ratio. When the price of the stock becomes large, then it becomes a near certainty that the bonds will ultimately be converted. In fact, the only real question is when the company will force conversion. Thus, when the stock price is high, the bond premium reflects the difference between the interest payments on the bond and the dividend payments on the stock, and the expected amount of time until the company forces conversion. If forced conversion is imminent, the conversion premium will be virtually nonexistent. If forced conversion is believed to be delayed (for example, the company lacks the cash and the ability to raise the cash to pay for the call), there will be some conversion premium in the bond's price.

A horizontal line represents the straight-debt value when the stock price is high. However, as the stock price collapses toward zero, the straight-debt value also collapses toward zero. The bonds of a worthless company are also usually worthless. When the stock price is incredibly low (relative to the conversion price), there is so little likelihood that the bonds will ever be converted that the conversion feature becomes worthless for all practical purposes. Hence, the conversion premium will essentially cease to exist.

Convertible Preferred Stock

There are similarities between convertible bonds and convertible preferreds, but there are also some differences. The downside protection is less certain with convertible preferreds, because there is no legal requirement that the preferred dividends be paid. However, preferred dividends must be paid before common stock dividends are paid, so there is still some degree of downside protection.

The pricing of convertible preferreds is similar to the pricing of convertible bonds. When the market price of the underlying stock is close to or above the conversion price, the conversion value influences the price of the convertible preferreds. When the market price is far below the conversion price, the price of the convertible preferreds is closer to the straight preferred stock value.

As with convertible bonds, the number of common shares that can be obtained by converting one preferred share is known as the conversion ratio. The conversion ratio can change over time. For example, an issue of convertible preferred stock may have a conversion ratio of 4:1 for the first 10 years after issue, 2:1 for the next 10 years, and become straight preferred stock thereafter.

The conversion value of convertible preferred is the market price of the common stock multiplied by the conversion ratio.

Example: If the market price of the underlying common stock is $15/share, and the conversion ratio is 4:1, then the conversion value is $60 ($15 x 4 = $60). If the market price of the convertible preferred stock is $65/share, then the conversion premium is $5 ($65 – $60 = $5).

The conversion premium is often expressed as a percentage: conversion premium divided by conversion value. In the example above, the conversion premium would be $5/$60, or 8.33 percent.

Other Types of Convertibles

hybrid convertibles

Convertible bonds and preferreds are the primary types of convertible securities, but other types of combination securities also bear mentioning. Unlike traditional convertibles, *hybrid convertibles* (also called exchangeable debentures) are convertible into stock of different companies from those that issued them. Companies with substantial stock portfolios or companies that seek to divest shares of a partially owned subsidiary may find hybrids a useful source of funds.

Equity Notes

equity notes

Equity notes (also called mandatory convertible notes) were developed to meet banks' capital needs. These notes are issued as debt instruments that yield a fixed coupon until maturity, when they are automatically converted into common stocks.

Liquidity Yield Option Notes

LYON

One of the most complex of the convertibles is the liquidity yield option note, or *LYON*. LYONs differ from ordinary convertibles primarily in being zero-coupon convertibles. In addition, they are callable and redeemable. Making the security even more complicated, both the redemption and call prices change over time.

Commodity-Backed Bonds

commodity-backed bonds

Commodity-backed bonds are debt instruments whose values are potentially related to the price of some physical commodity. These bonds

---

Types of Combination Securities

- Convertible bonds: debt securities that may be exchanged for common stock at a fixed ratio
- Convertible preferreds: preferred stock that may be exchanged for common stock at a fixed ratio
- Hybrid convertibles: debt securities of one company convertible into the common stock of another company
- Equity notes: debt securities with mandatory conversion to equity upon maturity
- Liquidity yield option notes (LYONs): zero-coupon, convertible, callable, redeemable bonds
- Commodity-backed bonds: debt securities whose potential redemption values are related to the market price of some physical commodity, such as oil

allow the owner to speculate on a commodity price rise while earning a modest return. The bond's price will move up and down with variations in both the commodity price and market interest rates. Mexico has issued 20-year bonds with payments that depend on the price of oil. With options that specially positioned issuers can offer, commodity-backed bonds were designed to appeal to speculative investors. Additional types of innovative combination securities will probably be devised as time passes.

SUMMARY AND CONCLUSIONS

Option securities offer many diverse investment opportunities. Pure options such as puts, calls, rights, and warrants tend to magnify the gains or losses from price changes in the associated stock. Owners of these securities obtain substantial upside potential, while their loss exposure is limited to the price of the options. Put and naked call writers, in contrast, take the opposite side of the trade. They have limited profit potential coupled with substantial risk exposure. Actively traded options are usually listed on an exchange, whereas more thinly traded issues trade OTC. According to the Black-Scholes valuation formula, the value of a call should increase with the underlying stock's price and volatility, time to maturity, and the market interest rate, and it should move inversely with its strike price.

Put-call parity relates the price of puts to the price of corresponding calls. Options may be bought, sold, or exercised. The option writer may write them against owned stock (covered call writing), other options (spreads or ratio positions), or nothing but sufficient assets to cover (naked call writing). Options can be used to reduce a portfolio's risk exposure (hedging), or they can be used as speculative instruments.

Convertible debentures and convertible preferred stock are the most common types of convertibles. Other more obscure types of hybrid securities include exchangeable bonds, equity notes, LYONs, and commodity-backed bonds. Each of these securities combines a fixed-income security with an option (or in the case of equity notes, an obligation) to convert the security into common stock or another asset whose future price is uncertain. As such, these securities offer both upside potential and some downside protection by combining a more volatile security (such as common stock) with a more stable one (such as a bond).

Convertible securities generally have a call feature, which limits their upside potential because it enables the issuing company to force conversion when the market price of the stock exceeds the conversion price. This prevents the holder from receiving the higher interest payment on the bond and converting just before the bond matures. Convertible securities are also subject to interest rate risk and default risk. In the event of bankruptcy, straight debt generally takes precedence over convertible debt, but convertible debt takes precedence over preferred and common stock.

CHAPTER REVIEW

Answers to the review questions and the self-test questions start on page 501.

Key Terms

zero sum game
premium
expiration date
strike (exercise) price
in-the-money
out-of-the-money
at-the-money
going long
intrinsic value
arbitrage
Options Clearing Corporation
   (OCC)
American options
European options
LEAPS®
straddle
spread
covered call
naked call
married put
writer

Black-Scholes model
hedge ratio
riskless hedge
put-call parity
manufactured (synthetic) put
manufactured call
conversions
stock index options
interest rate options
cum-rights
ex-rights
conversion ratio
conversion price
conversion value
straight-debt value
conversion premium
premium over straight-debt value
hybrid convertibles
equity notes
LYON
commodity-backed bonds

Review Questions

13-1.   a.   Distinguish between a put option and a call option.
   b.   Explain the writer's obligations for each.
   c.   Why is purchasing a call not equivalent to writing a put?

13-2.   a.   What kind of option would an investor purchase to protect a profit in a stock he or she owns?
   b.   How would such a strategy differ from simply selling the position?
   c.   What factors should an investor consider when evaluating the two strategies?

13-3.   a.   Explain the meaning of the term strike price.

        b.   How does it relate to intrinsic value, time value, or being in- or out-of-the-money?

13-4. The ASD Company's stock sells for 32; a 6-month option to purchase it at 35 sells for 1 3/4. (Ignore time value in a.–c. Ignore dividends in a. and b.)
   a. What price must the stock reach within that 6 months for the option investor to break even?
   b. What are the percentage gains for each if the stock rises to 45?
   c. How would all of these results change if ASD pays one dividend of $.75 during the 6-month period?

13-5. a. What obligation does the writer of a covered call undertake?
   b. What are the risks and prospective returns of a covered-call-writing strategy?

13-6. a. What is a straddle?
   b. Under what circumstances would an investor be inclined to buy a straddle?
   c. When would an investor be inclined to write a straddle?

13-7. a. Briefly explain what a spread is.
   b. What is the motivation for holding a spread?

13-8. Distinguish between a warrant and a right.

13-9. a. Exercising warrants increases/decreases earnings per share. Explain.
   b. Similarly, what is the impact of exercising rights on per-share earnings?

13-10. XYZ stock is selling cum-rights at $50. The rights entitle the holder to five shares at $47 for every 100 shares owned.
   a. What is their theoretical value?
   b. Compute the theoretical value assuming that during the ex-rights period, the stock price falls by the amount implied by the dilution.

13-11. a. Why is call risk particularly relevant to convertibles?
   b. Under what circumstances are convertibles particularly likely to be called?

13-12. a. Discuss the various factors that affect a convertible's premium over conversion value.
   b. How does the premium over conversion value relate to the time value on a call option?

13-13. The SOM Company convertible debentures sell for 105 ($1,050), while its common stock is priced at $40/share. The convertible's conversion ratio is 20; its annual coupon rate is 10 percent. Its estimated straight-debt value is 90. The stock pays a dividend of $2 per share per year. The bonds mature in 2007 and are callable at 107.

    a. Compute the convertible's
- conversion price
- conversion value
- conversion premium
- premium over straight-debt value
- current yield

    b. If you purchased the bonds at par ($1,000) and the stock subsequently rose to 55 1/2, what is the minimum profit per bond (ignore the impact of commissions and coupon payments)?

13-14. For the convertible debentures in question 13-13, suppose that the stock price rose to $65 and the bonds were called. What would the convertibles sell for after the call, assuming conversion was still possible?

13-15. A share of convertible preferred selling at $100 may be exchanged for two shares of common stock, trading at $40. What is the conversion premium?

13-16. What should the convertible preferred in question 13-15 sell for if the common goes to $60? Assume the preferred stock is callable at $100.

13-17. What do convertible bond investors obtain and what do they sacrifice relative to investors in straight bonds and relative to investors in the underlying stock?

Self-Test Questions

T   F   13-1. Stock options are written by the issuer of the stock.

T   F   13-2. The value of a put will decline as the price of the stock rises.

T   F   13-3. When the market price of the stock is less than the exercise price in the option, a call is in-the-money and a put is out-of-the-money.

T   F   13-4. The time value of an option is the difference between an option's price and its intrinsic value.

T   F   13-5. The largest option premium is for call options that have a strike (exercise) price that exceeds the market price.

T   F   13-6. If the underlying stock is trading at $31, the intrinsic value of a put with a strike price of $30 is –$1.

T   F   13-7. Warrants are long-term call options issued by corporations.

T   F   13-8. The time value of a warrant that trades at $4, carries an exercise price of $35, and whose underlying stock has a market price of $33, is $2.

T   F   13-9. If the market price for the stock is below the exercise price on the warrant's expiration date, the warrant is worthless.

T   F   13-10.   The largest loss that the buyer of an option can suffer is the loss of the intrinsic value of the put or the call.

T   F   13-11.   The profit potential, as a percentage of the initial investment, is greater when purchasing call options than when fully margining a long position in the stock.

T   F   13-12.   Listed options have standardized expiration dates and strike prices.

T   F   13-13.   The purchase of an out-of-the-money call when anticipating a run-up in the price of a stock would be a shrewd but aggressive investment strategy.

T   F   13-14.   At a call option's expiration, the payoff to its holder is zero if the market price of the stock is equal to the exercise (strike) price.

T   F   13-15.   An investor who anticipates a fall in the price of a stock might want to short the stock and purchase a put to protect his or her ownership interest in a particular stock.

T   F   13-16.   Writing covered calls to increase income is a conservative investment strategy.

T   F   13-17.   Buying a protective put on a stock index ensures that the owner of a diversified stock portfolio can limit the potential loss over the duration of the holding period.

T   F   13-18.   When the stock's price exceeds the exercise price, the payoff for the long position in the stock becomes positive, whereas the payoff for writing a naked call remains constant at the amount of the premium paid by the option buyer.

T   F   13-19.   The writer of a put expects the price to stay steady or perhaps fall in the near future.

T   F   13-20.   The risk of a short sale can be reduced by the purchase of a call on the same stock.

T   F   13-21.   A straddle combines a put and a call option on the same stock with the same exercise price but different expiration dates.

T   F   13-22.   When the holder of a stock-index call exercises the option, the writer must deliver a portfolio that represents the index.

T   F   13-23.   Stock index options differ from industry options in that stock index options are written on broad-based portfolios of stocks intended to capture the overall behavior of the stock market, whereas industry options are written on much more narrowly defined portfolios of stocks from specific industries.

T   F   13-24.   A call option is similar to a warrant in that it gives the holder the right to purchase a specified number of shares of stock at a specified price on or before a specified date.

T   F   13-25.   The market prices of both call options and warrants rise when the price of the underlying stock falls.

T   F   13-26.   Rights give existing shareholders the opportunity to buy additional stock at a price lower than the current market price of the shares outstanding.

T   F   13-27.   If four rights are needed to purchase a new share of stock, the shares are currently trading at $50, and the subscription price for a new share is $42, each right has an approximate value of $2.

T   F   13-28.   Warrants earn a higher percentage return to the investor than direct ownership of the stock if the stock rises sharply in price.

T   F   13-29.   The term *conversion premium* refers to the difference between the market price of the bond and its par value.

T   F   13-30.   The bond value or straight-debt value of a convertible is defined as the price at which the convertible would trade if it were nonconvertible and valued at (or near) the prevailing market yields of nonconvertible comparable issues.

T   F   13-31.   Convertible bonds offer the issuer the opportunity to initially offer common stock at a price above the stock's current market price.

T   F   13-32.   Convertible bonds that are called may be either converted into stock or redeemed at the call price.

T   F   13-33.   Because of their risk, convertible bonds carry a higher interest rate than comparable bonds without the conversion option.

T   F   13-34.   Most convertible bonds are callable.

T   F   13-35.   All convertible bonds are convertible until maturity; however, there may be an initial waiting period.

T   F   13-36.   An investor would never be wise to convert a bond when called if the underlying stock was trading at a price less than the conversion price.

T   F   13-37.   There is little correlation between returns on convertible bonds and returns on the stock market.

T   F   13-38.   A convertible's conversion premium is directly related to the price of the underlying common stock.

T   F   13-39.   Assuming that the stock price rises above the conversion price, eventually the conversion value and the market price of a convertible bond will equal each other because of the risk that the bond might be called.

T   F   13-40.   A convertible bond will sell at a price not less than the larger of its bond value or its conversion value.

T   F   13-41.   Convertible bonds have greater price sensitivity to changes in interest rates than nonconvertible bonds do.

T   F   13-42. Hybrid convertibles, or exchangeable debentures, are convertible into common stock of a company other than the company that issued the debenture.

NOTE

1. P. Samuelson, "Rational Theory of Warrant Pricing," *Industrial Management Review* (spring 1965), pp. 13–32; P. Samuelson, "Mathematics of Speculative Price," *SIAM Review* (January 1973), pp. 1–42; F. Black and M. Scholes, "The Pricing of Options and Corporate Liabilities," *Journal of Political Economy* (May–June 1973), pp. 637–654.

Black-Scholes Formula

Note: Knowledge of the Black-Scholes formula is not required for the CFP™ exam. The use of the Black-Scholes formula to estimate option values is appropriate for the more advanced student who is interested in examples of how option prices can be derived. The Black-Scholes formula for call option pricing can be derived precisely, given the following assumptions:

- The capital markets are frictionless—that is, there are no transaction costs or taxes, and all information is simultaneously and freely available to all investors.
- There are no short-sale restrictions.
- All asset prices follow a continuous stationary, lognormal, stochastic process.
- There is a constant risk-free rate over time, at which investors can borrow as well as lend.
- No dividends are paid.
- No early exercise is permitted.

The resulting formula is as follows:

$$C_0 = S_0 N(d_1) \; - \; \frac{S \; N(d_2)}{e^{rt}}$$

$$d_1 = \frac{\ln \; (S_0/S) \; + \; \left(r_f \; + 1/2 \; \sigma^2\right) t}{\sigma\sqrt{t}}$$

$$d_2 = \frac{\ln \; (S_0/S) \; + \; \left(r_f - 1/2 \; \sigma^2\right) t}{\sigma\sqrt{t}}$$

and where
C_0 = option value
r_f = continuously compound riskless annual interest rate
S_0 = stock price
S = strike price of option
e = 2.718 (the natural logarithmic constant)
t = time to expiration of option as a fraction of a year
σ = the standard deviation of the continuously compounded annual rate of return of the underlying stock
$\ln(S_0/S)$ = natural logarithm of S_0/S
$N(d)$ = value of the standard normal distribution evaluated at d

Tables 13A-1 and 13A-2 can be used to find the value of N(d).

TABLE 13A-1
For Values of N(x) When x ≥ 0

This table shows values of N(x) for x ≥ 0. The table should be used with interpolation. For example,

N(0.6278) = N(0.62) + 0.78[N(0.63) − N(0.62)]
= 0.7324 + 0.78 x (0.7357 − 0.7324)
= 0.7350

x	.00	.01	.02	.03	.04	.05	.06	.07	.08	.09
0.0	0.5000	0.5040	0.5080	0.5120	0.5160	0.5199	0.5239	0.5279	0.5319	0.5359
0.1	0.5398	0.5438	0.5478	0.5517	0.5557	0.5596	0.5636	0.5675	0.5714	0.5753
0.2	0.5793	0.5832	0.5871	0.5910	0.5948	0.5987	0.6026	0.6064	0.6103	0.6141
0.3	0.6179	0.6217	0.6255	0.6293	0.6331	0.6368	0.6406	0.6443	0.6480	0.6517
0.4	0.6554	0.6591	0.6628	0.6664	0.6700	0.6736	0.6772	0.6808	0.6844	0.6879
0.5	0.6915	0.6950	0.6985	0.7019	0.7054	0.7088	0.7123	0.7157	0.7190	0.7224
0.6	0.7257	0.7291	0.7324	0.7357	0.7389	0.7422	0.7454	0.7486	0.7517	0.7549
0.7	0.7580	0.7611	0.7642	0.7673	0.7704	0.7734	0.7764	0.7794	0.7823	0.7852
0.8	0.7881	0.7910	0.7939	0.7967	0.7995	0.8023	0.8051	0.8078	0.8106	0.8133
0.9	0.8159	0.8186	0.8212	0.8238	0.8264	0.8289	0.8315	0.8340	0.8365	0.8389
1.0	0.8413	0.8438	0.8461	0.8485	0.8508	0.8531	0.8554	0.8577	0.8599	0.8621
1.1	0.8643	0.8665	0.8686	0.8708	0.8729	0.8749	0.8770	0.8790	0.8810	0.8830
1.2	0.8849	0.8869	0.8888	0.8907	0.8925	0.8944	0.8962	0.8990	0.8997	0.9015
1.3	0.9032	0.9049	0.9066	0.9082	0.9099	0.9115	0.9131	0.9147	0.9162	0.9177
1.4	0.9192	0.9207	0.9222	0.9236	0.9251	0.9265	0.9279	0.9292	0.9306	0.9319
1.5	0.9332	0.9345	0.9357	0.9370	0.9382	0.9394	0.9406	0.9418	0.9429	0.9441
1.6	0.9452	0.9463	0.9474	0.9484	0.9495	0.9505	0.9515	0.9525	0.9535	0.9545
1.7	0.9554	0.9564	0.9573	0.9582	0.9591	0.9599	0.9608	0.9616	0.9625	0.9633
1.8	0.9641	0.9649	0.9656	0.9664	0.9671	0.9678	0.9686	0.9693	0.9699	0.9706
1.9	0.9713	0.9719	0.9726	0.9732	0.9738	0.9744	0.9750	0.9756	0.9761	0.9767
2.0	0.9772	0.9778	0.9783	0.9788	0.9793	0.9798	0.9803	0.9808	0.9812	0.9817
2.1	0.9821	0.9826	0.9830	0.9834	0.9838	0.9842	0.9846	0.9850	0.9854	0.9857
2.2	0.9861	0.9864	0.9868	0.9871	0.9875	0.9878	0.9881	0.9884	0.9887	0.9890
2.3	0.9893	0.9896	0.9898	0.9901	0.9904	0.9906	0.9909	0.9911	0.9913	0.9916
2.4	0.9918	0.9920	0.9922	0.9925	0.9927	0.9929	0.9931	0.9932	0.9934	0.9936
2.5	0.9938	0.9940	0.9941	0.9943	0.9945	0.9946	0.9948	0.9949	0.9951	0.9952
2.6	0.9953	0.9955	0.9956	0.9957	0.9959	0.9960	0.9961	0.9962	0.9963	0.9964
2.7	0.9965	0.9966	0.9967	0.9968	0.9969	0.9970	0.9971	0.9972	0.9973	0.9974
2.8	0.9974	0.9975	0.9976	0.9977	0.9977	0.9978	0.9979	0.9979	0.9980	0.9981
2.9	0.9981	0.9982	0.9982	0.9983	0.9984	0.9984	0.9985	0.9985	0.9986	0.9986
3.0	0.9986	0.9987	0.9987	0.9988	0.9988	0.9989	0.9989	0.9989	0.9990	0.9990
3.1	0.9990	0.9991	0.9991	0.9991	0.9992	0.9992	0.9992	0.9992	0.9993	0.9993
3.2	0.9993	0.9993	0.9994	0.9994	0.9994	0.9994	0.9994	0.9995	0.9995	0.9995
3.3	0.9995	0.9995	0.9995	0.9996	0.9996	0.9996	0.9996	0.9996	0.9996	0.9997
3.4	0.9997	0.9997	0.9997	0.9997	0.9997	0.9997	0.9997	0.0007	0.9997	0.9998
3.5	0.9998	0.9998	0.9998	0.9998	0.9998	0.9998	0.9998	0.9998	0.9998	0.9998
3.6	0.9998	0.9998	0.9999	0.9999	0.9999	0.9999	0.9999	0.9999	0.9999	0.9999
3.7	0.9999	0.9999	0.9999	0.9999	0.9999	0.9999	0.9999	0.9999	0.9999	0.9999
3.8	0.9999	0.9999	0.9999	0.9999	0.9999	0.9999	0.9999	0.9999	0.9999	0.9999
3.9	1.0000	1.0000	1.0000	1.0000	1.0000	1.0000	1.0000	1.0000	1.0000	1.0000
4.0	1.0000	1.0000	1.0000	1.0000	1.0000	1.0000	1.0000	1.0000	1.0000	1.0000

TABLE 13A-2
For Values of N(x) When x ≤ 0

This table shows values of N(x) for x ≤ 0. The table should be used with interpolation. For example,

$$N(-0.1234) = N(-0.12) - 0.34[N(-0.12) - N(-0.13)]$$
$$= 0.4522 - 0.34 \times (0.4522 - 0.4483)$$
$$= 0.4509$$

x	.00	.01	.02	.03	.04	.05	.06	.07	.08	.09
0.0	0.5000	0.4960	0.4920	0.4880	0.4840	0.4801	0.4761	0.4721	0.4681	0.4641
0.1	0.4602	0.4562	0.4522	0.4483	0.4443	0.4404	0.4364	0.4325	0.4286	0.4247
0.2	0.4207	0.4168	0.4129	0.4090	0.4052	0.4013	0.3974	0.3936	0.3897	0.3859
0.3	0.3821	0.3783	0.3745	0.3707	0.3669	0.3632	0.3594	0.3557	0.3520	0.3483
0.4	0.3446	0.3409	0.3372	0.3336	0.3300	0.3264	0.3228	0.3192	0.3156	0.3121
0.5	0.3085	0.3050	0.3015	0.2981	0.2946	0.2912	0.2877	0.2843	0.2810	0.2776
0.6	0.2743	0.2709	0.2676	0.2643	0.2611	0.2578	0.2546	0.2514	0.2483	0.2451
0.7	0.2420	0.2389	0.2358	0.2327	0.2296	0.2266	0.2236	0.2206	0.2177	0.2148
0.8	0.2119	0.2090	0.2061	0.2033	0.2005	0.1977	0.1949	0.1922	0.1894	0.1867
0.9	0.1841	0.1814	0.1788	0.1762	0.1736	0.1711	0.1685	0.1660	0.1635	0.1611
1.0	0.1587	0.1562	0.1539	0.1515	0.1492	0.1469	0.1446	0.1423	0.1401	0.1379
1.1	0.1357	0.1335	0.1314	0.1292	0.1271	0.1251	0.1230	0.1210	0.1190	0.1170
1.2	0.1151	0.1131	0.1112	0.1093	0.1075	0.1056	0.1038	0.1020	0.1003	0.0985
1.3	0.0968	0.0951	0.0934	0.0918	0.0901	0.0885	0.0869	0.0853	0.0838	0.0823
1.4	0.0808	0.0793	0.0778	0.0764	0.0749	0.0735	0.0721	0.0708	0.0694	0.0681
1.5	0.0668	0.9655	0.0643	0.0630	0.0618	0.0606	0.0594	0.0582	0.0571	0.0559
1.6	0.0548	0.0537	0.0526	0.0516	0.0505	0.0495	0.0485	0.0475	0.0465	0.0455
1.7	0.0446	0.9436	0.0427	0.0418	0.0409	0.0401	0.0392	0.0384	0.0375	0.0367
1.8	0.0359	0.0351	0.0344	0.0336	0.0329	0.0322	0.0314	0.0307	0.0301	0.0294
1.9	0.0287	0.0281	0.0274	0.0268	0.0262	0.0256	0.0250	0.0244	0.0239	0.0233
2.0	0.0228	0.0222	0.0217	0.0212	0.0207	0.0202	0.0197	0.0192	0.0188	0.0183
2.1	0.0179	0.0174	0.0170	0.0166	0.0162	0.0158	0.0154	0.0150	0.0146	0.0143
2.2	0.0139	0.0136	0.0132	0.0129	0.0125	0.0122	0.0119	0.0116	0.0113	0.0110
2.3	0.0107	0.0104	0.0102	0.0099	0.0096	0.0094	0.0091	0.0089	0.0087	0.0084
2.4	0.0082	0.0080	0.0078	0.0075	0.0073	0.0071	0.0069	0.0068	0.0066	0.0064
2.5	0.0062	0.0060	0.0059	0.0057	0.0055	0.0054	0.0052	0.0051	0.0049	0.0048
2.6	0.0047	0.0045	0.0044	0.0043	0.0041	0.0040	0.0039	0.0038	0.0037	0.0036
2.7	0.0035	0.0034	0.0033	0.0032	0.0031	0.0030	0.0029	0.0028	0.0027	0.0026
2.8	0.0026	0.0025	0.0024	0.0023	0.0023	0.0022	0.0021	0.0021	0.0020	0.0019
2.9	0.0019	0.0018	0.0018	0.0017	0.0016	0.0016	0.0015	0.0015	0.0014	0.0014
3.0	0.0014	0.0013	0.0013	0.0012	0.0012	0.0011	0.0011	0.0011	0.0010	0.0010
3.1	0.0010	0.0009	0.0009	0.0009	0.0008	0.0008	0.0008	0.0008	0.0007	0.0007
3.2	0.0007	0.0007	0.0006	0.0006	0.0006	0.0006	0.0006	0.0005	0.0005	0.0005
3.3	0.0005	0.0005	0.0005	0.0004	0.0004	0.0004	0.0004	0.0004	0.0004	0.0003
3.4	0.0003	0.0003	0.0003	0.0003	0.0003	0.0003	0.0003	0.0003	0.0003	0.0002
3.5	0.0002	0.0002	0.0002	0.0002	0.0002	0.0002	0.0002	0.0002	0.0002	0.0002
3.6	0.0002	0.0002	0.0001	0.0001	0.0001	0.0001	0.0001	0.0001	0.0001	0.0001
3.7	0.0001	0.0001	0.0001	0.0001	0.0001	0.0001	0.0001	0.0001	0.0001	0.0001
3.8	0.0001	0.0001	0.0001	0.0001	0.0001	0.0001	0.0001	0.0001	0.0001	0.0001
3.9	0.0000	0.0000	0.0000	0.0000	0.0000	0.0000	0.0000	0.0000	0.0000	0.0000
4.0	0.0000	0.0000	0.0000	0.0000	0.0000	0.0000	0.0000	0.0000	0.0000	0.0000

| *Example:* | Suppose we want to use the Black-Scholes formula to estimate the value of a call option, given the following information: |

- The current market price of the stock (S_0) is $23/share.
- The option's strike price (S) is $25/share.
- The option has 3 months until expiration (t = .25).
- The standard deviation of the stock's return (σ) is $1.
- The risk-free rate of interest is 4 percent (r_f = .04).

We proceed to calculate as follows:

$$S_0/S = 23/25 = .92$$
$$\ln(S_0/S) = \ln(.92) = -.0834$$
$$\tfrac{1}{2}\sigma^2 = \tfrac{1}{2} \times 1 \times 1 = .5$$
$$r_f + \tfrac{1}{2}\sigma^2 = .04 + .5 = .54$$
$$(r_f + \tfrac{1}{2}\sigma^2)t = .54 \times .25 = .135$$
$$\sigma\sqrt{t} = 1 \times \sqrt{.25} = .5$$
$$d_1 = \left(-.0834 + .135\right)/.5 = .1032$$

Using table 13A-1, $N(d_1) = .5411$

$$(r_f - \tfrac{1}{2}\sigma^2)\, t = (.04 - .5) \times .25 = -.46 \times .25 = -.115$$
$$d_2 = (-.0834 - .115)/.5 = -.3968$$

Using table 13A-2, $N(d_2) = .3458$

$$rt = .04 \times .25 = .01$$
$$e^{rt} = e^{.01} = 1.01$$

The value of the call option (C_0) is

$$C_0 - (23 \times .5411) - (25 \times .3458/1.01)$$
$$= 12.45 - 8.56 = \$3.89$$

13A-1.   Using the Black-Scholes formula, estimate the value of a call option with 3 months to maturity and a strike price of $30 when the market price of the underlying stock is $28.50, the standard deviation of the stock's price is $2, and the risk-free rate is 5 percent.

13A-2.   Find the value of an in-the-money option with 40 days (1/9 of a year) to expiration and a strike price of $27 when the market price of the stock is $28, the standard deviation of the stock's price is $1.50, and the risk-free rate of interest is 3 percent. What portion of that value represents intrinsic value, and what portion represents time value?

Put-Call Parity

The formula relating the value of a put to that of a call for the same time to expiration can be written as follows:

$$C_0 = P_0 + S_0 - \frac{S}{e^{r_f t}}$$

where C_0 = call value
        P_0 = put value
        r_f = risk-free rate
        e = 2.718 (the natural logarithmic constant)
        S_0 = initial stock price
        S = strike price
        t = time to expiration of the option as a fraction of the year

---

Example: Suppose a stock has a market price of $25, and both put and call options have a strike price of $24 and 6 months to expiration. The risk-free rate is 4 percent. If the put option has a price of $2, the price of the call can be determined as follows:

$r_f t$ = .04 x .5 = .02
$e^{.02}$ = 1.02
C_0 = $2 + $25 – $24/1.02 = $3.47

13B-1.   XYZ Corp. stock is selling for $30/share. Both a put and a call option are at-the-money, with exercise prices of $30 and 3 months to expiration. If the put option sells for $1, and the risk-free rate of interest is 6 percent, use put-call parity to find the value of a call option.

13B-2.   For the stock described in question 13A-1 in appendix A, find the value of a put option with the same exercise price and expiration date as the call option described in that question.

Appendix C

Profit and Loss Diagrams

These examples assume the following: stock price = $100; strike price = $100; call premium = $3; put premium = $2; no dividends

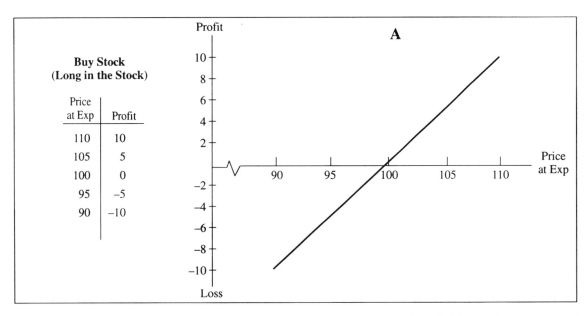

Buy Stock (Long in the Stock)

Price at Exp	Profit
110	10
105	5
100	0
95	−5
90	−10

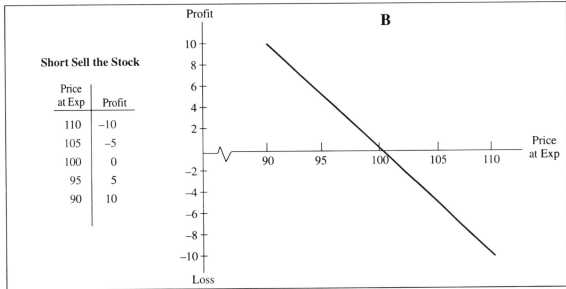

Short Sell the Stock

Price at Exp	Profit
110	−10
105	−5
100	0
95	5
90	10

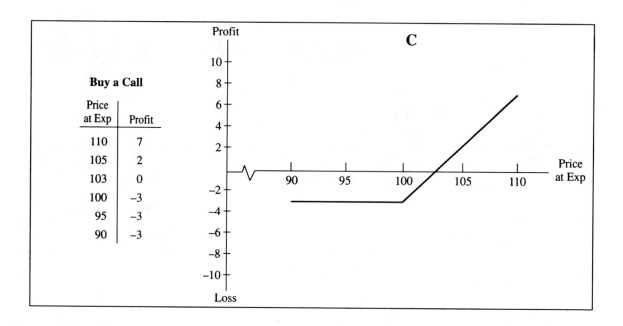

Buy a Call

Price at Exp	Profit
110	7
105	2
103	0
100	−3
95	−3
90	−3

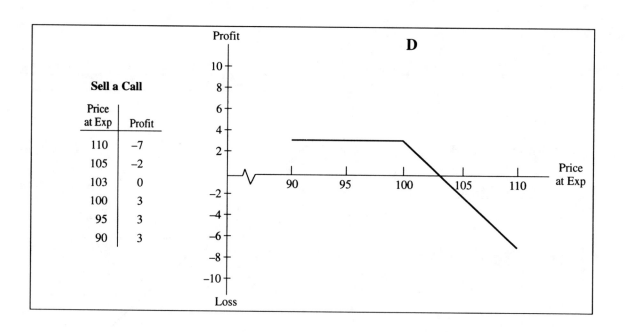

Sell a Call

Price at Exp	Profit
110	−7
105	−2
103	0
100	3
95	3
90	3

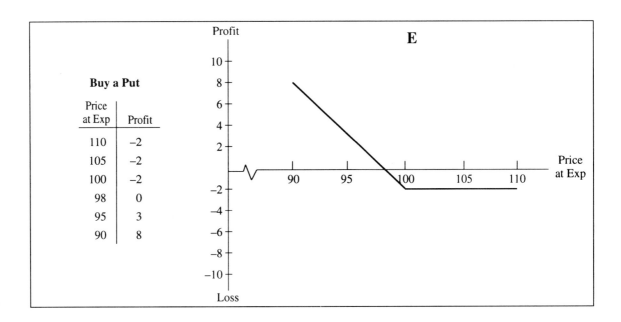

Buy a Put

Price at Exp	Profit
110	−2
105	−2
100	−2
98	0
95	3
90	8

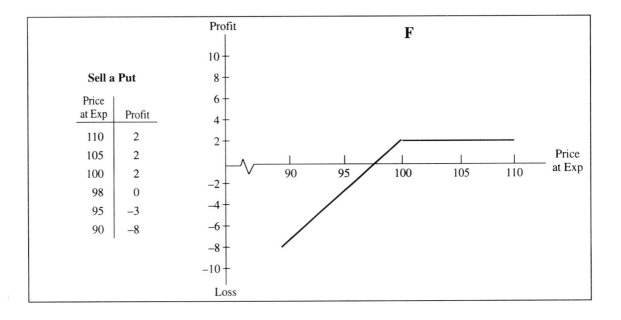

Sell a Put

Price at Exp	Profit
110	2
105	2
100	2
98	0
95	−3
90	−8

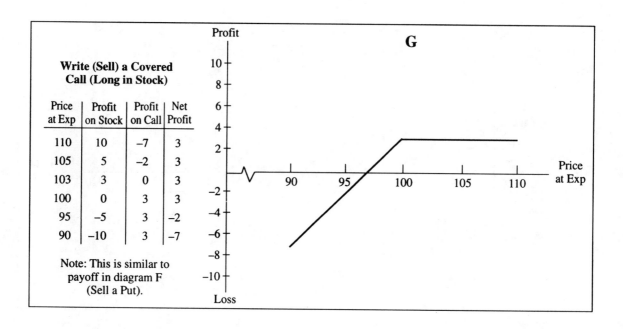

Write (Sell) a Covered Call (Long in Stock)

Price at Exp	Profit on Stock	Profit on Call	Net Profit
110	10	−7	3
105	5	−2	3
103	3	0	3
100	0	3	3
95	−5	3	−2
90	−10	3	−7

Note: This is similar to payoff in diagram F (Sell a Put).

G

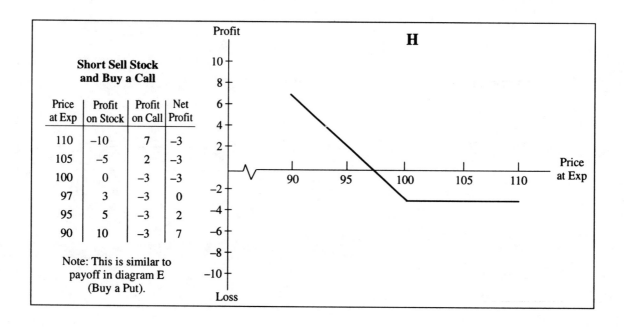

Short Sell Stock and Buy a Call

Price at Exp	Profit on Stock	Profit on Call	Net Profit
110	−10	7	−3
105	−5	2	−3
100	0	−3	−3
97	3	−3	0
95	5	−3	2
90	10	−3	7

Note: This is similar to payoff in diagram E (Buy a Put).

H

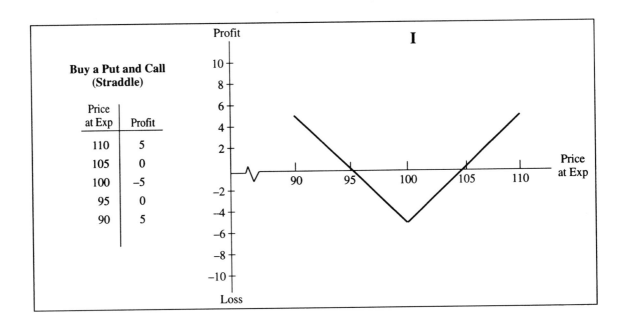

Buy a Put and Call
(Straddle)

Price at Exp	Profit
110	5
105	0
100	−5
95	0
90	5

I

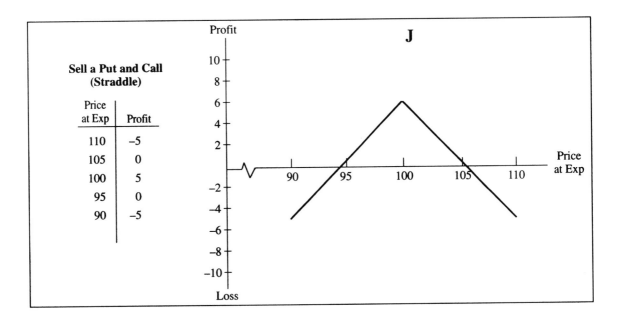

Sell a Put and Call
(Straddle)

Price at Exp	Profit
110	−5
105	0
100	5
95	0
90	−5

J

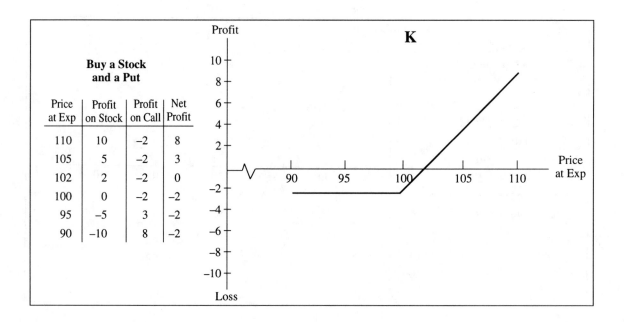

Price at Exp	Profit on Stock	Profit on Call	Net Profit
110	10	−2	8
105	5	−2	3
102	2	−2	0
100	0	−2	−2
95	−5	3	−2
90	−10	8	−2

14

Futures

Learning Objectives

An understanding of the material in this chapter should enable the student to

14-1. Describe the characteristics of futures contracts, and explain how futures contracts are used in trading commodities like agricultural products, materials, and minerals.

14-2. Describe the different kinds of financial futures markets, and explain what is meant by program trading.

Chapter Outline

Commodities are a bit off the beaten path, compared to more traditional investables (stocks and bonds). But futures markets are an important investment area for several reasons. The dollar value of futures contracts traded, including both commodities and financial futures, substantially exceeds that of securities. Moreover, the futures market's dramatic price swings appeal to many speculators. Finally, futures contracts can be extremely beneficial for certain people who would like to hedge away price risk.

COMMODITIES AND FUTURES

The term commodity futures is primarily used to refer to deferred-delivery contracts traded on a futures exchange. A commodity futures contract obligates the short side (the seller) to deliver a specific quantity of a specific type of asset (wheat, silver, and so on) on a prespecified date to a prespecified location or set of locations. The long side (the buyer) promises to pay for the asset upon delivery.

The production of agricultural products to be sold in near and distant markets inspired the practice of commodity futures trading. As in earlier years, at any given moment, a supply of products is available in the market for delivery immediately. In modern terminology, negotiations that end with immediate delivery of a commodity are referred to as the *spot market.* For these transactions, the product must be currently available for delivery. In the *futures market,* a commodity must be available at a prearranged future date and location and meet specified characteristics.

spot market

futures market

Who would be interested in buying products for delivery at some distant date? The obvious answer is a manufacturer whose finished product requires the commodity and who wants to be assured that a supply will be coming to its factory. This reduces the manufacturer's necessity to store raw materials until needed. Since contracts for future delivery establish the delivery price, the commodity producer (seller of the contract) and the manufacturer (buyer of the contract) can make plans based on knowledge of how much each will receive or pay. In this manner, revenues and costs are predictable.

Futures versus Options

Futures and option contracts are sometimes confused. Both involve subsequent events. An option holder has a **right** but not an obligation to buy

---

Difference between Futures Owner and Option Holder

- Futures buyer has the **obligation** to accept and pay for a specified quantity of an asset at a specified price at a specified time.
- Option holder has the **right**—but not an obligation—to buy or sell a specified quantity of an asset at a specified price over a specified time period.

or sell a specified quantity of some asset at a specified price over a specified time period. The holder of a futures contract, in contrast, has the **obligation** to accept and pay for a specified quantity of some asset at a specified price at a specified time. Thus, those who own options have a choice, whereas those who own futures have an obligation to do something in the future.

Forward Contracts versus Futures Contracts

forward contract

A *forward contract* is a customized contractual agreement between parties to accept delivery (buy) and to deliver (sell) a specified commodity or financial instrument at an agreed-upon price, settlement date, quantity, and location. The terms of this contract result from direct negotiations between the parties, and the parties accept the terms of the contract. Because these contracts are nonstandard ones, there is no organized exchange for trading forward contracts.

A futures contract is divided into two contracts—one to buy and one to sell—and it contains standardized features that cover the commodity in question. Because the terms are standardized, active secondary markets exist. Indeed, most futures contracts trade on an organized exchange that sets the terms of the contracts, provides the location for their trading, and monitors their settlements.

Futures contracts allow those who expect later to have or need that asset to establish a price and quantity ahead of time. Standardizing the contract's terms (grade, quantity, delivery location, and date) facilitates active trading. That is, a large number of interested parties can trade the same (standardized) contract.

Futures may be used to hedge spot (that is, immediate delivery) positions or to speculate on commodity price changes. Rather than make or take physical delivery, most hedgers and speculators eventually close out their positions with offsetting trades. Spot and futures market prices that move too far out of line, however, do encourage some traders to make or take delivery. Indeed, the threat of such arbitrage activity generally drives spot and near-delivery futures prices together.

Most futures can be traded with margins of from 5 percent to 15 percent of the contract's value. Thus, even a small change in the price of a contract can produce a substantial profit or loss. Margin percentages are generally set just high enough to limit default risk.

Unlike forward contracts, futures contracts are actually contracts between each contracting party and the exchange. Therefore, neither party to the contract is exposed to default risk, since the exchange is obligated to honor the contract regardless of the actions of the party taking the opposite side of the contract.

Because of the standardized nature of futures contracts, transaction costs tend to be much lower than those of forward contracts. Forward contracts are private, customized agreements between two contracting parties. As such, there can be considerable transaction costs involved in the negotiation of a mutually acceptable agreement between the two parties.

Differences between Forward Contract and Futures Contract

- Forward contract: a nonstandardized (unique) contract between parties to accept delivery (buy) and deliver (sell) a specified commodity or financial instrument at an agreed-upon price, settlement date, quantity and location. There is no organized exchange for trading forward contracts.
- Futures contract: a standardized contract divided into two contracts—one to buy and one to sell—a specified commodity or financial instrument. Futures trade on an organized exchange that sets contract terms, which establish price, quantity, delivery location, and date.

Different Types of Futures Contracts

Listed futures contracts exist for three basic classes of delivery vehicles: agricultural, mineral, and financial assets. The principal foods include cattle, hogs, chickens, wheat, oats, corn, soybeans, barley, sugar, potatoes, coffee, orange juice, and cocoa. The commodity exchanges also trade nonfood agricultural items such as lumber, plywood, cotton, and wool. The minerals traded on futures exchanges include crude oil, natural gas, gasoline, heating oil, copper, zinc, gold, silver, platinum, tin, palladium, and lead. Such financial futures as those for federal funds, Treasury bills, long-term government bonds, several stock market indexes, and various currencies have grown increasingly popular.

The prices of all these items are quite volatile, reflecting their underlying supply and demand variability. No legal or theoretical barriers prevent futures trading in rhubarb or peppermint, but volume would probably be insufficient to justify these listings. Commodity exchanges do, however, frequently try to establish futures trading in new commodities. For example, contracts for turkeys, shrimp, apples, and diamonds were tried and failed. Many other items such as steel reinforcing bars (re-bars), scrap aluminum, returnable drink bottles, uranium, milk, butter, coal, cement, cinder blocks, sulfur, and nails might or might not support futures trading.

Predicting which futures contracts will succeed is quite difficult. Successful contracts have, however, generally possessed most or all of the following characteristics:

- a relatively competitive spot market
- a meaningful standardized contract
- storability or its equivalence (ongoing production)
- sufficient price volatility to attract (or require) speculative and hedging interest

Characteristics of Futures Contracts

Different Instruments

If AT&T issues a series of 7 percent bonds that mature in 2010, these bonds are a different investment instrument than a series of 7 percent AT&T bonds that mature in 2011. Similarly, a futures contract for wheat to be delivered next September is different from one for wheat to be delivered next October. Despite the fact that both bond issues and both wheat futures have many common characteristics, each has different market performance characteristics and thus is a distinct investment instrument reported separately in the financial press.

Long and Short

long transaction

short transaction

Buying a contract for future delivery of a commodity is referred to as a *long transaction*; selling a contract for future delivery is called a *short transaction*. People who take a long position are obligating themselves to take delivery of the specified commodity. People who take a short position are obligating themselves to make delivery of the specified commodity. Thus, when we talk about people who are long a contract or short a contract, we are referring only to the side of the sale to which they are committed.

Required Delivery and Acceptance

When investors purchase stocks or bonds, they anticipate taking delivery of the certificates. With futures contracts, acceptance and delivery of the commodity must be made at the settlement date. Most buyers and sellers of futures contracts, however, do not expect either to take or make delivery. Rather, they plan to close out their position by entering into an offsetting contract. That is, if a futures holder is long (owns) a September wheat futures contract, then the position is liquidated by the holder's placing a sell order (taking a short position) on the same contract. On the records of the exchange, being simultaneously long and short the same contract terminates one's position in that contract.

For someone who enters the contract on the short side (has promised to make delivery), he or she liquidates by placing a buy order for the same contract. Again, being simultaneously long and short a contract abolishes one's position.

Large Dollar Value

Although stocks and bonds normally trade in round lots of 100 shares or five bonds, the dollar value of most buy and sell orders is not all that large. One hundred shares of a $75 stock have a value of $7,500, and five bonds total about $5,000. But the standard futures contract for wheat, for example, contains 5,000 bushels. If wheat is priced at $5 per bushel, the contract has a market value of $25,000. (The size of a futures contract for Treasury bills is $1 million, and, for example, on December 24, 2001, a March contract traded for $982,200.)

Unlike stocks or bonds, the standardized futures market does not trade in odd lots or contracts of less than standard size. Thus, each futures contract has a high dollar value and controls a sizable quantity of a commodity or financial instrument.

Different Types of Commodity Traders

A substantial fraction of commodity traders are professionals. For example, large firms in commodity-related industries (mining, baking, meatpacking, grain, and so on) often maintain representatives on the relevant exchanges. These particular professionals seek to provide a future supply or market for their companies' products. They make it their business to have access to, and a detailed understanding of, the latest information relevant to their particular commodities. For instance, they may be following the latest crop estimates, cost comparisons, weather reports, possible government policy changes, trade figures and the international economy, and a host of other useful data. Access to all of the relevant and available knowledge tends to give these professionals a decided advantage over less-informed traders.

Types of Professional Futures Market Traders

- Firm representatives: hedge needs or outputs of commodity-related firms
- Day traders: short-run traders who close their positions each day
- Position traders: may hold positions for several days based on fundamental or technical factors
- Arbitrageurs: seek to exploit departures from expected relative price relationships

---

Several additional classes of professional commodity traders bear mentioning. They include day traders, position traders, and arbitrageurs. Like stock exchange floor traders and specialists, these traders usually have seats on the exchange and trade for their own accounts.

Day traders usually close their positions by the end of each day. They hope to profit from modest price moves. Unlike day traders, position traders seek to profit from fundamental or technical forces that may manifest themselves over several days. Finally, arbitrageurs try to exploit relative prices that vary from expected relationships.

Trading Futures Contracts

The individuals or firms that generate the majority of the trading in futures contracts do so for the following reasons: hedging, speculating, or spreading.

hedging

Hedging

Many manufacturers purchase commodities and then convert the raw materials into finished products. These firms expect to earn profits from the production and sale of the finished product. The prices of raw materials used in the production process, however, can change significantly from the time they are purchased to the time the finished product is sold to the manufacturer's customers. In many cases, the spot market price at the time the finished good is sold strongly influences that product's selling price. If the spot price falls between the time the raw material is purchased and the time the finished product is sold, the finished product will most likely sell for less than the manufacturer had anticipated. Thus, an unexpected loss will result from holding the commodity during the production cycle. (A gain will occur if the spot market price rises and the finished product can be sold at a price that is higher than expected.)

To protect against this loss, the manufacturer buys the commodity in the spot market as a raw material and simultaneously sells (shorts) the commodity for delivery at the time the finished product will be sold. When the finished product is ready for sale, the manufacturer will close out the short position. If the commodity is then selling for less than the price paid for it as a raw material, a gain will be realized when the manufacturer covers the short position, but less will be realized from the sale of the finished product (*vice versa* if the commodity is selling for more than the price paid for it).

In an absolutely perfect hedge, the gain from covering the short sale is exactly equal to the loss from the sale of the finished product at a lower price. Likewise, the loss from covering the short position due to an increase in the spot price equals the gain that arises from the unanticipated increase in the selling price of the finished product. When used in this manner, most hedges do not provide matching gains and losses, but they do capture most of the adverse price changes and thereby reduce the risk to the manufacturer.

Other manufacturers might have a contract to deliver a finished product at a specified price and date but have no desire to purchase and hold the needed raw material until the time that production starts. To lock in the price of the needed raw material, buying a futures contract that specifies delivery when the raw materials are needed gives the manufacturer the desired protection against adverse price changes of the ingredient.

In other words, manufacturers can use futures contracts to protect themselves against adverse price movements while the manufacturing process is taking place. Likewise, farmers can use futures contracts as a hedge to protect themselves against a decline in the price of crops they are currently growing.

The strategy of hedging with futures can be used with financial futures for stock indexes, foreign currencies, or interest rate futures, as well as for commodities.

Speculating

speculating

Individuals who use *speculating* as an investment tactic anticipate that the price of a commodity or financial future will change during the duration of the contract, and they hold a contract that they expect to benefit from the price movement. Expecting the price to rise, speculators purchase futures contracts (go long). If the market price of the commodity or financial instrument rises, the speculator can sell the contract for a profit. Since the margin deposit is relatively small, the profits can be quite impressive. For example, if an investor pays $1,500 for a wheat contract, a $.25 rise in the price of a bushel of wheat will result in a gain of $1,250 ($.25 x 5,000 bushels) and a holding period return of 83.33 percent ($1,250/$1,500). Of course, if the price of wheat falls, the loss in percentage terms can be just as spectacular.

A speculator who expects the price to fall sells (shorts) the future and gains if the price does as expected. The loss from a rise in the price of the commodity or financial instrument can be virtually unlimited if the speculator is unable to close out the open position during the upward price movement and ultimately has to purchase the commodity in the spot market so that delivery can be made.

Spreading

spreading

Users of *spreading* as an investment tactic buy one futures contract (go long) and sell a second futures contract (go short) that has different terms. In spread positions, the most likely result is that one contract will gain and the other will suffer a loss. This tactic, being both long and short, limits the loss that can result. It also reduces the potential gain. The net result tends to be small gains or losses, but the investor faces less risk than the speculator faces.

Commissions

As described earlier, investors in futures contracts can close out their position without having to deliver or accept delivery of the underlying commodity or financial instrument. *Delivery actually takes place in only a small percent of all futures contracts.* Since the standard procedure is to close out the position by acquiring an offsetting contract, the transaction cost paid at the formation of a long or short futures contract position is a *round-trip fee* that covers the commission at both ends of the transaction. The size of the commission varies, depending on the commodity or financial futures contract and the number of contracts being traded.

round-trip fee

Margin Deposits

Investors can purchase stocks and bonds by paying in full at the time of purchase or by using a margin transaction in which the investor places the initial margin requirement (percentage of purchase price) with the broker and borrows the remainder. When the investor wants to acquire the stock (or bond) in his or her name, the borrowing (the margin loan) must first be paid off. In the futures market, all trades are made with a margin deposit. This deposit is *earnest money* (security) to guarantee the performance by both the buyer and the seller of the futures contract. The transaction does *not* involve any borrowing. The margin deposit stays with the broker through whom the order is placed until the contract is either completed or closed out.

earnest money

Like margin accounts with stocks and bonds, these margin deposits have initial and maintenance requirements established for each commodity or financial instrument. For example, the wheat futures contract with a market value of $25,000 requires an initial deposit of $1,500 and a maintenance deposit of $1,000. Using a procedure called *mark to the market,* the futures contract is valued at the close of business each day, and the investor's deposit is adjusted for the full change in the dollar value of the contract for that day. Under this procedure, losses reduce the investor's deposit, and a margin call is made if the deposit falls below the maintenance amount for that particular futures contract. If the investor fails to meet the margin call, the broker will close out the account by purchasing an offsetting transaction, and the investor must then settle any loss on the account with the broker. If the mark-to-the-market procedure results in a gain to the contract holder, the deposit is increased by the gain. The investor can use the gain, if sufficient in amount, as the initial deposit on

mark to the market

additional futures contracts, thus pyramiding his or her holdings in exactly the same manner as used in margin accounts for stocks and bonds. The investor might also be able to remove cash from the account, as a kind of early distribution of the profit on the trade.

Example: A December wheat futures contract trades at a price of $3.00 per bushel. An investor takes a long position (buys one contract) and places the minimum initial margin of $1,500 in his brokerage account. The next day, the price of the contract falls by $.25 per bushel. The value of the contract has declined by $1,250 (5,000 bushels x $.25 per bushel) from $15,000 to $13,750. The broker removes the $1,250 from the investor's account. Because the minimum margin requirement is $1,000, the investor is now required to come up with at least $750 to get the account back up to the minimum requirement. Failure to do so will result in the broker's selling the contract; the remaining cash in the account ($250, assuming the price of the contract has not changed in the meantime) is returned to the investor.

Had the price of wheat risen by $.25 per bushel, the investor would have been able to remove the $1,250 gain from his account.

Trading of Futures

Trading of all stocks and bonds on an organized exchange takes place from midmorning until late in the afternoon, with extended trading hours recently implemented by the New York Stock Exchange. In the futures market, however, investors have only a short period of time—an hour or two each day—in which to conduct trading in any specific futures contract. Furthermore, because of a unique rule established by the exchanges—the daily price limit—on some days no trading of a particular futures contract occurs at all. The exchanges designed this rule to prevent wide fluctuations in contract prices because of rumors, events, or undue speculation, and to limit the amount necessary in any one day to mark to the market.

daily price limit (interday limit)

The *daily price limit rule* (sometimes called the *interday limit*) prevents more than a specific amount of difference between the closing price (price of last trade) of the previous day and the opening price (price at which the first trade takes place) the next day.

Example: Assume that the daily price limit for wheat is $0.25 and that September wheat futures closed at $5 yesterday. Today's opening price for September wheat futures can be neither lower than $4.75 nor higher than $5.25, no matter what new information might have come to the market between the closing and the opening times. For instance, suppose that during the night, a severe storm ravaged the wheat-growing section of the Midwest and early reports describe widespread damage to wheat crops. This information would make many individuals and businesses seek to immediately acquire wheat futures contracts for September delivery in anticipation of sizable price increases. Without the daily price limit, the price of wheat would skyrocket—perhaps unnecessarily—to as high as $6, but the daily price limit fixes the opening contract at $5.25. Although buyers of September delivery wheat futures would be numerous, sellers would be scarce. If no contract can be traded at $5.25, then no trade takes place for the day. The closing price is set at $5.25 so that all investors can be marked to the market.

The following day, the upper limit of the opening price is $5.50 (lower limit $5). Again, if no contracts are traded, then no trading takes place, and the following day's opening price can rise to $5.75. Following this procedure, the market will eventually open. After a day or so to assess the damage, it may be discovered that the initial information about the storm overstated the crop damage and that wheat will be in greater supply than previously anticipated. In this case, the daily price limit prevented the price of wheat from rising rapidly at first and then falling sharply after a less hasty assessment of the situation.

Each different type of futures contract has a different daily price limit, depending on the price per unit of the underlying commodity or financial instrument. (*Note:* No such procedure exists on the securities exchanges. The specialist will stay at the trading post until a transaction is consummated, and as many as 2 or 3 hours might elapse before a stock or bond opens. Also, there is no limit on the change in dollars or percentage of selling price between the first transaction price and the prior day's closing price.)

Open Outcry

open outcry

The stock exchanges use specialists to maintain an orderly market in the securities, and the auction system is used to match buy and sell orders. By contrast, futures trading uses a system called *open outcry*. In this system, traders shout out their desire to sell (or buy) a contract. In addition to shouting their preferences, traders also use a system of hand and finger signals to indicate the number of contracts they wish to sell (or buy) and how much (in fractions of a cent) they are willing to accept or pay above or below the last-traded full-cent price. When someone acknowledges a willingness to trade at those terms, the contract is formed and recorded. If this sounds somewhat chaotic, it is!

Differences between Commodities and Securities Markets

The futures market has no specialist system. Commodity and option positions must be closed out with the brokerage firm that handled the initial transaction. Stocks and bonds may, in contrast, use different brokerage firms to buy and sell.

In the previous pages, we have noted substantial differences in the markets and mechanics of futures contracts and stocks and bonds. A few more differences should be noted.

Differences between the Markets in Commodities Futures and Stocks

Commodities Futures	Stocks
• Limited term	• Unlimited term
• Maximum daily price moves	• No limit on daily price moves
• Margins of 5% to 15%	• Margins of 50% or more
• Long interest equal to short interest by definition	• Short interest usually small fraction of long interest
• No short selling restrictions	• Short sales not permitted on a downtick
• No interest charged on unpaid margin	• Interest incurred on margin debt
• Market has no specialist system	• Market making by specialists
• Positions must be opened and closed with same brokerage firm	• No restriction on opening and closing positions with different firms

Hedge Trading Results

Another question relating to the futures markets is, Who on balance makes and who loses money? In particular, do those who hedge generally have to pay for the risk reduction that they obtain?

Hedging is akin to purchasing insurance. Thus, those who facilitate hedge trading (speculators) might well be expected to earn a risk premium. Testing this proposition requires identifying those who are seeking to hedge and separating them from those who are speculating. Discriminating between risk takers and hedgers from aggregated data, however, is relatively difficult. Nevertheless, the results of several studies over past years that have attempted such desegregation are that professionals (large speculators) may profit at the expense of small traders, and small speculators do not seem to receive a risk premium for their risk taking.[1]

Disadvantages of Commodity Trading for Amateurs

Professional traders have better access to relevant information, lower trading costs, and/or quicker executions than the vast majority of amateurs. Most small inexperienced investors should be discouraged by this state of affairs. No one wants to compete in a market in which he or she is at a significant disadvantage relative to a large part of the market's participants. Moreover, the number of listed commodities is much smaller than the number of actively traded stocks. Thus, each commodity receives proportionately more attention. Presumably, such attention leads to relatively well-informed pricing, thereby increasing the difficulty of finding misvalued contracts.

In addition, unlike the securities market, each specific futures contract (such as July wheat) has equal numbers of short and long contracts. If the price declines, the shorts gain what the longs lose, and *vice versa*. This is what economists call a zero-sum game. If the professionals make money on balance, the amateurs must lose. Furthermore, both losers and winners must pay commissions.

FINANCIAL FUTURES MARKETS

Transactions in financial futures deal with contracts for foreign currencies, debt securities (commonly called interest rate futures), and stock indexes (index futures). Although the standard size and dollar value of these contracts vary, many of the characteristics and trading concepts of commodity and financial futures are similar. Prior to expiration, all futures positions can be closed out by purchasing the other side of the contract, rather than by delivery of the underlying asset.

Futures on Indexes and Cash Settlement

Traditionally, futures contracts have specified delivery of some specific asset. Although most contracts may be closed out with offsetting trades, those still in force at contract expiration result in the long side's taking and the short side's making delivery. This same practice continues with many of the newer financial futures contracts.

For some contracts, however, the underlying asset would be relatively difficult, expensive, or inconvenient to deliver. Specifically, futures contracts on various market indexes present a potential problem with delivery. Rather than settling by delivery of a physical asset, index contracts are settled with cash. That is, contracts still in existence at the close of trading on the contract's last day are treated as if both parties make the appropriate offsetting trade at the actual closing price of the index on that day. Because of the daily marking-to-the-market prices, this usually requires minimal cash payments. Both parties then have their margins (earned money) returned to them.

Interest Rate Futures

interest rate futures

Trading in *interest rate futures* began in the early 1970s with the Chicago Board of Trade's Government National Mortgage Association (GNMA) futures contracts and the Chicago Mercantile Exchange's (CME) T-bill contracts. The market subsequently expanded to include long-term Treasury bonds, one- and 5-year Treasury notes, municipal bonds, CDs, and Eurodollars. Most of the recent trading has been in Eurodollars, T-bills, and Treasury bonds. GNMA futures are no longer actively traded.

Like all futures contracts, interest rate futures call for delivery of a specific amount of the relevant commodity at the contract's expiration. For example, the Treasury bond contract specifies the delivery of $100,000 face amount of Treasuries with an 8 percent coupon yield. The contract itself specifies the magnitude of the penalties for delivery of bonds with different coupon rates. If someone who is short a Treasury futures contract finds that it is cheaper to deliver bonds with a 7 percent coupon rate even after payment of the penalty, then that is what will be delivered. Price fluctuations in the contract reflect variations in the expected bond interest rate.

Institutions that plan to borrow at some later time can use interest rate futures to hedge against adverse interest rate moves (this is called a short hedge). Similarly, financial institutions with future sums to invest may use the market to establish the rate that they will earn on the investment (this is called a long hedge). Finally, those whose expectations differ from the market may speculate on interest rate futures. A number of researchers have explored the productive use of interest rate futures in hedging and managing interest rate risk.

Example:

Connie James has just learned that she will inherit $500,000 in 6 months. She is elated. However, she likes the interest rates she could invest the money at if she had it today, and she is afraid that rates will decline over the next 6 months. What should she do?

She can look for an interest rate futures contract that most closely represents the type of security she will be most likely to buy when she actually receives the money, and she can buy (go long) $500,000 worth of principal of this contract. Six months later, she can actually take delivery if she wants, or she can sell the contract and buy the appropriate investments in the spot market. If interest rates do go down over the next 6 months as she fears, then the value of her futures contract will have risen. She will end up investing the money at a lower yield, but she will be able to offset that with the profit from her futures position. If interest rates instead go up, then she will lose money on her futures contract, but she will be able to invest her cash at a higher rate than she thought she would. Thus, she is hedged in the sense that the gain or loss on her futures contract will match up with an opportunity loss or gain in her cash position (when she actually receives the money). If the contract she buys is for delivery of the exact security she intends to buy when she receives the money, the hedge may actually come close to a perfect hedge. A perfect hedge is one in which the gain or loss in a futures contract *exactly* offsets the loss or gain in the cash position.

Stock Market Index Futures

stock market index futures

The successful introduction of debt instrument futures spurred interest in equity futures. Today, the most popular *stock market index futures* are the Chicago Mercantile Exchange's S&P 500 Index and the Chicago Board of Trade's (CBT) Dow Jones Industrial Average index. Several European indexes are traded on European futures markets, and the Nikkei 225 stock average of blue chip Japanese stocks is traded on the CME. The CME also trades the Russell 2000 and the NASDAQ 100. The Russell 2000 provides a vehicle for speculating or hedging in relatively small-capitalization stocks; the NASDAQ 100 is heavily influenced by large and small technology stocks. These equity contracts offer a variety of ways to speculate or hedge on the stock market's movement. In particular, the contracts are an ideal way for portfolio managers to hedge either their anticipated funds needs or their portfolios against anticipated market reversals.

Example: Suppose a large common stock portfolio manager anticipates a market decline. To liquidate and later reinvest the portfolio would be costly (spreads, commissions, and so forth). The stock index futures market provides a relatively simple way to protect the portfolio from market moves. First, the manager determines his or her portfolio's beta and then uses the following formula to determine the number of contracts to short:

$$\text{Number of contracts needed for hedge} = \frac{\text{Portfolio value}}{\text{Contract value}} \text{ x } \text{Weighted average beta of portfolio}$$

Consider a portfolio with a weighted average beta of 1.14 and market value of $20 million. The S&P futures contract value is $500 multiplied by the S&P Index future value. Assume the S&P Index future is 1460. Thus, a single contract would be worth $730,000 ($500 x 1460).

Accordingly, the number of contracts needed to short is as follows:

$$\text{Number of contracts needed for hedge (short)} = \left(\frac{\$20,000,000}{\$730,000} \right) \text{x } 1.14$$

$$= 31.23287 \text{ (rounded to 31,}$$
$$\text{the nearest}$$
$$\text{whole contract)}$$

Thus, selling 31 contracts should approximately neutralize the portfolio from market fluctuations. That is, the fluctuations in the value of 31 S&P Index futures contracts should closely approximate those of a $20 million stock portfolio that has an average beta of 1.14. If the portfolio's value declines, a short position in the S&P futures contracts should rise by an offsetting amount. Similarly, an increase in the portfolio's value should be offset by a fall in the value of the futures position. This is called a short hedge because the manager is short the futures contract and long the commodity (the portfolio).

Futures Options

futures option

A commodity option, or *futures option,* is an option on a futures contract. As such, it is an abstraction on an abstraction. The futures contract is itself a deferred-delivery agreement that trades and has a life of its own. An option on such an agreement represents the right, but not the obligation, to enter into such a contract. Thus, a call option on a futures contract is a right to buy such a contract at a prespecified price over a prespecified period. Similarly, a put is an option to sell such a futures contract. The unique feature of options on futures is that they give the investor the opportunity to make a small dollar investment that can control a sizable position in a particular futures commodities or financial instrument. Currently, futures options are listed on a number of agricultural, mineral, and especially financial assets.

Program Trading

program trading

The advent of stock index futures and options has facilitated the rise of a type of trading that generally uses the indexes: *program trading.* In a broad sense, program trading refers to any large-volume, mechanical trading system. This trading is usually based on some computerized model of theoretically appropriate price relationships. Normally, a program involves the simultaneous execution of trades in a number of stocks. The large-capitalization stocks that are members of one of the major indexes, such as the S&P 500, are particularly likely to be involved. These trades also often involve the use of stock index futures or options on these index futures. Program trades for stocks listed on the New York Stock Exchange are facilitated by their *DOT* (designated order transfer) and *SuperDOT* systems. These two systems allow the near simultaneous execution of large trades of a number of stocks. The orders are submitted directly to the system and then transmitted electronically to the specific stock trading posts of each of the securities.

DOT
SuperDOT

By far, the most popular types of program trading are portfolio insurance and index arbitrage. Both involve the use of index contracts (futures or options on futures), and both are primarily used by large institutional investors and traders, including some brokerage firms trading for their own accounts.

Portfolio Insurance

portfolio insurance

The index futures example above illustrates an increasingly popular strategy of portfolio managers. Portfolios, particularly large portfolios, can be managed to limit their exposure to market downturns. The process of limiting a portfolio's market exposure is called *portfolio insurance.* This insurance can be structured to greatly reduce the possibility that losses will exceed some prespecified limit. At the same time, the portfolio will still retain an opportunity to profit from a rising market. The portfolio insurer can use various types of contracts, including index futures, options on index futures, and options on individual stocks.

Under one form of downside protection, the insurer closely monitors the market. When the stock market has a significant pullback, the client's portfolio is hedged. Usually, the insurer sells an appropriate number (for the portfolio's size and beta) of index futures contracts. Alternatively, the insurer may purchase an equivalent number of stock index puts. Either approach largely neutralizes the impact of further downward movement in the market. For example, a short position in index contracts would appreciate as the value of the portfolio declines. Similarly, index puts would place a floor on losses in the portfolio, while upside potential would remain.

Both of these approaches to portfolio insurance (futures or options hedges) generally protect the portfolio against a downturn. Protection, however, has a cost. In addition to the relatively modest direct costs (insurer's fee, commission, and forgone interest on margin deposits), the investor sacrifices some potential gains. Purchasing puts entails a premium paid for the option, while selling index futures contracts shifts any profits from a stock market rise to the purchaser of the contracts. Moreover, the implementation of the strategy requires the availability of sufficient potential supply of/or demand for (at reasonable prices) the hedging contracts. A substantial drop in stock prices may create a major imbalance in the supply-demand relationships for these contracts. Everyone cannot abandon ship at once. The supply of available lifeboats is limited.

In short, portfolio insurance can provide some protection against market downturns. It is not, however, always possible or cost effective to implement, and when it is possible to apply, a portfolio insurance strategy may reduce potential profits from subsequent upturns.

Index Arbitrage

index arbitrage

The existence of stock index futures has facilitated and stimulated another relatively new type of trading. *Index arbitrage* is a strategy designed to take advantage of disparities between index futures prices and the spot market prices of the securities that make up the index.

Suppose, for example, the futures contract on the S&P Index is priced appreciably above the current value of the index itself. The final settlement price of an index futures contract is the closing value of the underlying index. Thus, at the expiration of the index future, the index and the futures contract on the index must have the same value. Accordingly, a long position in the stocks that make up the index, coupled with a short position in futures on that index, will produce a gain that is approximately equal to the difference between the value of the two positions. Some adjustments must be made for the impacts of commissions, bid-ask spreads, and dividends on the underlying stocks. The precise amount of dividends and the level of prices after deducting trading costs are not known at the outset. Moreover, the index programs must be initiated quickly when price disparities open up. Still, when the futures price exceeds the corresponding index, something close to a guaranteed trading profit is possible. If such a profit is attractive compared with alternative risk-free returns, an index arbitrage trade is indicated.

Similar index arbitrage opportunities are available when the futures contract is priced somewhat below the index. In this circumstance, the index arbitrageur shorts the underlying stocks while purchasing the futures contract. This type of program trade is profitable only if the difference in the two prices is sufficient to offset the trading costs (commissions and bid-ask spreads) and dividends on the shorted stocks.

Program Trading, the Brady Commission, and the Crash of 1987

Program trading—particularly index arbitrage—was subject to a substantial amount of criticism in the wake of the stock market's 1987 crash. The exchanges' regulators (and others) have studied the causes of the crash. The best-known of these studies was sponsored by Congress and is referred to as the Brady Commission (named after the commission's chairman Nicholas Brady, later Secretary of the Treasury). Several other institutions also conducted studies. Many financial commentators and some of the committee reports blamed the crash, at least in part, on financial futures trading. Index arbitrage and portfolio insurance received special attention. More generally, trading in financial futures was blamed for the apparent increase in stock market volatility. The commissions, regulators, financial commentators, stock exchanges of New York, and the futures exchanges of Chicago argued vigorously over this and related issues. No one contends that financial futures have no impact on the markets for the underlying financial instruments. Whether the impact is relatively minor, short run, and perhaps stabilizing or is more serious, longer run, and destabilizing remains controversial.

Most critics of the present system would like to restrict index arbitrage, program trading, or, in some instances, financial futures. One possibility is to impose larger margin requirements on financial futures. Another proposal seeks to stop any panic by the installation of so-called circuit breakers, whereby both stock and financial futures trading would stop briefly if the market moves more than some predetermined amount. In fact, circuit breakers were implemented in the late 1980s and then, more recently, scaled back. Other analysts assert that any attempt to restrict or ban financial futures or cash-market trading on U.S. exchanges will simply shift the markets overseas. No doubt, this debate will long continue.

Hedge Funds

Some mutual funds called hedge funds use trading futures and options contracts as their main investment strategy. These funds—and some professionally managed portfolios—typically require minimum investments of $25,000, $100,000, or more. Therefore, they are not available to the investor with modest means. Indeed, some of the wealthiest investors, such as George Soros, are prominently connected with hedge funds. To this point, these funds are relatively unregulated because they are available only to investors who are qualified by virtue of both wealth and financial sophistication. An episode a few years ago with a hedge fund has caused some people to argue that more regulation is needed.

The Long Term Capital Management (LTCM) hedge fund near-debacle in late September 1998 reveals both the power and risks of hedge fund performance and behavior. LTCM was funded by many of the largest investment firms and commercial banks on Wall Street and abroad. In the summer of 1998, the fund managers and partners assumed that abnormal interest rate spreads between U.S. government debt instruments and other debt securities, which were widening, would narrow sooner rather than later. Thus, they bet on this principle by buying options, futures, and other derivatives on the non-U.S. debt instruments.

The widening worsened dramatically, however, after the Russian government's default on its foreign debt and the spill-over effect on Latin American financial markets. This led to a worldwide investor "flight to quality," which meant even more investors fleeing to U.S. government instruments. This, in turn, greatly exaggerated the spread and required the fund managers to cover their positions with even more capital. At the time, they had leveraged some $98 billion of exposure with $4.8 billion of capital. By the end of September, capital had dwindled to some $600 million.

The managers went to their lead lenders and asked for more capital. Enough of the lenders balked that it became necessary to force a bailout masterminded by the head of the New York Federal Reserve Bank. In the end, the lenders (under duress) invested $3.6 billion of new capital, and the original partners' share in the company dwindled to 10 percent.

moral hazard

Debate then raged as to whether the original investors' punishment fit the risks and losses they had caused. The major issue was *moral hazard*—the assumption of risks by one party that causes widespread costs that are not fully borne by that one party, thereby forcing other parties to bail them out. In general, a moral hazard is a situation in which people have incentives to behave in ways that can be detrimental to others or to society as a whole. Taking excessive risks because of the expectation that others will bail one out is a prime example of a moral hazard.

SUMMARY AND CONCLUSIONS

A large dollar volume of futures trading takes place on the various futures exchanges. Commodity futures contracts that are standardized with respect to grade, size, location, and delivery date facilitate substantial hedge and speculative trading. The relatively low percentage margins required to trade futures allow investors to magnify greatly the profits and losses generated by a given price move in the underlying asset. Financial futures markets have grown rapidly because of the opportunity to hedge (and speculate) on the price changes of securities in other financial markets and because of the introduction of a variety of new types of contracts. To succeed in the futures market, a contract requires a basis with sufficient competition, standardization, and price volatility to establish an active trading market.

Financial futures differ from stock trades in a number of ways, including term, trading limits, margin percentages, short restrictions, interest on margin, specialists, commission structure, and opening and closing positions with the same broker. Because of their relatively independent (not related to the stock market) volatility, financial futures contracts may be useful in diversification, but their own volatility limits their appeal to amateurs.

Several different types of professional futures traders compete with the amateur speculator: Scalpers trade on the floor of the exchange, seeking very quick turns; day traders close their positions at the end of each day; position traders may hold for several days; arbitrageurs seek profits from disequilibrium price relations; firm representatives trade for the accounts of firms that deal in the underlying assets. Ultimately, all investors are either hedgers or speculators.

Many commodity and financial futures contracts result in some loss to the traders. In contracts that do realize gains, however, the gains can be substantial. It is the allure of the substantial gains that creates the interest in these contracts. Because of the expertise and time needed to devote to these contracts, they are not appropriate for the casual investor. Futures contracts also encourage new forms of speculation and other practices, such as index arbitrage and hedge fund arbitrage, that have the potential to adversely affect volatility in financial markets as a whole.

Trading in futures contracts has special features. Most important are the daily limits on price changes and the daily marking to the market.

Financial futures instruments include currency, interest rate, and stock market index futures. These instruments are increasingly important and provide opportunities to make markets more efficient and to reduce (or transfer) risks.

CHAPTER REVIEW

Answers to the review questions and the self-test questions start on page 501.

Key Terms

spot market	daily price limit (interday limit)
futures market	open outcry
forward contract	interest rate futures
long transaction	stock market index futures
short transaction	futures option
hedging	program trading
speculating	DOT
spreading	SuperDOT
round-trip fee	portfolio insurance
earnest money	index arbitrage
mark to the market	moral hazard

Review Questions

14-1. Compare commodity futures trading with stock market trading.

14-2. Suppose you start with $5,000 that you invest in silver futures at $5 per ounce, putting down margin equal to 10 percent. A month later, silver rises to $6 per ounce. When your account is marked to the market, you use the excess in your margin account to buy more silver up to the maximum. A month later, silver rises to $7 per ounce. You again buy the maximum amount of silver futures. When silver hits $8 per ounce, you liquidate your position.
   a. How much have you made?
   b. What is the holding period return?

14-3. Suppose that in question 14-2, you had not liquidated your position and that you would receive a margin call when your account fell to 5 percent of the value of your positions.
   a. At what price of silver would you receive a margin call?
   b. Suppose you then sold enough silver to bring your equity up to 10 percent. How much further must silver fall for you to get another margin call?

14-4. What characteristics are needed for a commodity contract to be traded actively on a futures exchange?

14-5. Explain the motivations and advantages that each type of professional commodity trader possesses.

14-6. What factors have led to the recent growth of futures markets?

14-7. a. How do interest rate futures work?
b. What are some of the debt securities underlying such contracts?

14-8. a. How do stock index futures work?
b. How can they be used to hedge a stock portfolio?

14-9. Compute the number of contracts needed to neutralize a $50 million stock portfolio having a beta of 1.07. Assume the S&P Index future is at 1450.

14-10. Explain what a commodity futures option is.

Self-Test Questions

T F 14-1. The buyer of a futures contract is required, if the contract is held at its expiration, to take delivery of the item covered by the contract.

T F 14-2. Only the number of contracts and the price (per unit) are negotiable between buyers and sellers of commodity futures contracts for a specified commodity.

T F 14-3. In contrast with stocks and bonds, margin is hardly ever used in commodity futures contracts.

T F 14-4. The margin requirement for futures contracts is considered a down payment against the total costs of the contract.

T F 14-5. The margin required for futures transactions is a specified dollar amount that varies according to the type of contract and is the amount an investor borrows when making margin transactions.

T F 14-6. Like investors in stocks and bonds, investors in futures contracts must meet two types of margin (or deposit) requirements.

T F 14-7. Futures contracts are marked to the market on a daily basis.

T F 14-8. Recognizing the volatile nature of commodity contracts, the exchanges impose daily price limits for each of the futures contracts traded on the exchanges.

T F 14-9. An investor who holds a portfolio of bonds and plans to sell the bonds within a 6-month period could now sell a futures contract against this portfolio as a short hedge.

T F 14-10. An investor who expects interest rates to decline in the near future would profit by selling interest rate futures.

T F 14-11. If a speculator anticipates that interest rates will rise in the future, he or she might consider buying (going long) interest rate futures to make a profit if interest rates do rise.

T   F   14-12. A short hedge that involves selling a stock index future while holding a portfolio of stocks enables the investor to offset most of a decline in the value of the portfolio should the market fall.

T   F   14-13. The buyer of a futures option has no additional obligation to the seller and is not subject to a margin call as occurs with a futures contract.

T   F   14-14. The biggest difference between a futures option and a futures contract is that the option limits the investor's loss exposure to the price of the option.

T   F   14-15. Index arbitrage seeks to profit by exploiting differences in the prices of stock index futures and the stock index underlying the contract.

NOTE

1. E. Chang, "Returns to Speculators and the Theory of Normal Backwardation," *Journal of Finance* (March 1985), pp. 193–208; E. Fama and K. French, "Commodity Futures Prices: Some Evidence on Forecast Power, Premiums, and the Theory of Storage," *Journal of Business* (January 1987), pp. 55–73.

15

Real Estate Investments

Learning Objectives

An understanding of the material in this chapter should enable the student to

15-1.   Describe the characteristics of people who invest directly in real estate, and identify 10 basic principles of real estate investing they should know.

15-2.   Explain three different ways of estimating real estate values.

15-3.   Describe several aspects of the real estate transaction, including bargaining, financing, and refinancing.

15-4.   Describe several indirect methods of investing in real property indicating the pros and cons of each method.

Chapter Outline

Many investment courses do not cover investments in real estate. Neglecting this important investment medium seems unfortunate. Even investors who prefer other types of investments should consider real estate for its potential diversification benefits. At a minimum, they should acquire some exposure in order to make informed decisions. This chapter gives the reader just such an exposure.

ROLE OF REAL ESTATE IN THE ECONOMY

Real estate ownership is a large and profitable part of the economy. Because most real estate trades in relatively small localized markets, its size and importance are often underrated.

Two-thirds of all dwelling units are owner occupied. Thus, a large percentage of the population is in one way or another involved in real estate investing. Real estate investing has proven quite profitable in the past. Indeed, at times, average real estate returns have exceeded average stock returns.

REAL ESTATE AS AN INVESTMENT

Who Should Invest in Real Estate?

In spite of the real estate market's importance, size, and profitable history, far more people are well positioned to invest in stocks or bonds than in real estate (other than their own homes). Anyone who is serious about becoming a real estate investor should be able to answer yes to each of the following five questions:

- Can you tie up the necessary capital for a minimum of several years? Small investors with only a few hundred to a few thousand dollars to invest are unlikely to find many real estate investments in their price range. Direct investments in real estate often require the owner to have access to additional funds for maintenance or emergencies, such as uninsured damage to the property. Furthermore, real estate is difficult to sell on short notice. Thus, the investor should be prepared to hold properties for an appreciable period (perhaps a minimum of several years).

- Are you likely to remain in the same geographic area for the foreseeable future? Real estate investments usually require frequent attention. Therefore, investors need to be near enough to their properties to supervise them properly.
- Do you have the time and talent to manage property effectively? Rental property often requires a substantial amount of maintenance. New tenants must be found periodically. Rents must be collected. Records must be kept and bills paid. Even if others are contracted to do these tasks, someone still must hire the managers and monitor their work. Moreover, the time and energy spent managing real estate means that the investor gives up the income that could have been earned in other pursuits.
- Can you assume the substantial risk inherent in real estate investing? High leverage and low liquidity both add to real estate's risk. Only those positioned to absorb these risks should expose themselves to them. High leverage results from the customary practice of financing purchases with substantial borrowing. Low liquidity refers to, in this instance, the difficulty of selling real estate quickly in order to raise cash.
- Do you have the credit standing necessary to borrow on attractive terms? Most successful real estate investors use extensive leverage. The investor who is unable to make effective use of borrowed funds may find real estate relatively unprofitable. Because real estate loans are usually secured by the property values themselves, most people can answer yes to this question.

Real Estate Investing Principles

There are 10 principles that all real estate investors should keep in mind.

Principle 1

Real estate values are determined by their highest and best (that is, most profitable) uses. Potatoes could be grown in midtown Manhattan and a flea market operated on Miami beachfront property. These locations could, however, almost certainly be put to much more profitable uses. The Manhattan land would earn more as a site for office buildings, apartments, hotels, department stores, or even parking lots. The Miami beachfront parcel should yield a much higher return as a hotel site.

Investors have a strong incentive to acquire and upgrade underutilized property. Bidding prices up to their most productive use values tends to maximize each property's productivity. Potential buyers and sellers should always evaluate real estate in terms of its most productive use.

Principle 2

The supply of land is largely fixed, while demand tends to increase over time. Heretofore worthless (for human usage) land may sometimes be made useful by draining, clearing, grading, or irrigating. In rare instances, air rights (the right to build over someone else's property) may substitute for high-priced land. However, increasing the supply of usable land is relatively expensive and may encounter environmental (for example, preservation of the wetlands) objections.

A growing population and increasing affluence have tended to raise land values. Similarly, rising materials and labor prices have tended to increase construction costs. Because these trends seem likely to persist, the long-term trend in real estate values is upward.

Principle 3

As with almost any investment, short-run individual price moves may differ substantially from the long-run aggregate trend. During the 1930s, real estate values plunged, along with the price of almost every other investment asset. Much of the property bought in the 1920s remained below its purchase price until well into the 1940s. Some property bought in the Florida land boom of the 1920s is still worth less than the inflated sums paid at the peak of that bubble.

Principle 4

Careful comparison shopping is a useful first step in identifying real estate values. As with all investing, shopping around and bargaining are advisable. Paying more than is necessary or selling for less than top dollar reduces returns. Comparative fundamental analysis of an assortment of available properties is an important aspect of real estate investing. Few fortunes have been made with hasty, half-baked decisions.

Principle 5

Effective real estate investing almost always involves a cautious but extensive use of leverage. Few investors have the resources to buy much real estate for cash. Moreover, property that earns more than the cost of financing yields a positive net return. Therefore, investors should use the collateral value of their property to borrow heavily whenever the expected return safely exceeds the borrowing cost.

Banks, savings and loan associations, and other financial intermediaries are quite willing to lend a substantial percentage (usually up to 75 percent to 80 percent) of the purchase price of developed property. The interest expense is tax deductible (regardless of the type of tax return filed), and any unrealized price appreciation on the property is tax deferred. The lower the down payment on a particular purchase, the more of the buyer's funds that remain available for investment in other properties. Borrowers must normally make a large enough down payment to protect the lenders in case the borrowers default.

Principle 6

Just as they comparison shop for an attractive purchase price, investors should shop around and bargain for the best financing terms. While the amount borrowed, repayment period, and interest rate (or formula for a variable rate mortgage) are all important, other factors such as repayment flexibility should not be overlooked. Since an interest rate decline may make refinancing attractive, the absence of a prepayment penalty is especially desirable. Moreover, *closing costs*, insurance arrangements, and property tax escrow accounts should all be considered in negotiating a loan.

closing costs

Closing costs include fees paid to the lender for granting the loan (points), lawyers' fees, and title search expenses. A *point* is 1 percent of the loan principal. Lawyers charge fees for both drawing up the purchase and sales agreements and for searching and guaranteeing the title. A number of loan provisions are designed to protect the lender from specific contingencies. For example, lenders will normally require fire and casualty insurance on any developed property and perhaps life insurance on the borrower equal to the outstanding loan principal. Any unpaid property taxes are assessed against the property. Thus, the lender may require that an *escrow account* be established for property taxes and insurance and that the pro rata expected property taxes and insurance premiums be added to the mortgage payment. Property taxes are due at specific times (once or twice) during the year. Therefore, borrowers without escrow accounts have greater flexibility in the use of their funds.

point

escrow account

The initial payments of most real estate mortgages (usually monthly) are primarily devoted to covering the interest charge. At first, only a small portion of the monthly payment is directed to principal repayment. Over time, however, the amount of the debt is reduced so that less of the fixed payment is applied to interest and more is available for principal repayment.

At one time, almost all residential real estate mortgages had fixed terms and interest rates. Economic uncertainty and increasingly volatile interest rates in the 1970s led many lenders to prefer to make a variable or *adjustable rate mortgage (ARM)*. ARMs' terms can differ substantially.

adjustable rate mortgage (ARM)

Many ARMs, for example, start with a set rate for the first year and limit how much the rate can vary per period and how high it can go (a cap on the rate). One lender might offer a 6 1/2 percent first-year rate, a rate in subsequent years that varies annually, and a 12 1/2 percent maximum rate. Another might start at 5 1/2 percent and raise or lower the rate no more than 1 percent each year with no cap on the rate over the life of the mortgage.

Several innovative financing methods can reduce the amount of the monthly payments for the buyer. One of these is the shared appreciation mortgage (SAM). In exchange for a lower interest rate, the appreciation mortgage lender receives a portion of the gain that is realized when the property is sold. The lender in effect bets that the property will appreciate by more than enough to offset the lower interest rate. Other types of mortgages include the growing equity mortgage (GEM) and the graduated payment mortgage (GPM). Both types begin with relatively low mortgage payments that increase over time according to a predetermined schedule.

Knowledge of the available range of interest rates or rate formulas, minimum down payment percentages, point charges, escrow terms, available maturities, prepayment penalties, and the like should help the investor to select the most attractive place to begin negotiations. Subsequent negotiations with a number of lenders will likely pay off in better terms that more closely match the borrower's preferences.

Principle 7

Real estate investors should seek to limit all spending on improvements and maintenance to projects that are cost effective. For example, they should not automatically replace a deteriorating roof, repaint the exterior of a faded duplex, or remodel the interior of a now out-of-date office complex. The additional rents the better-maintained property generate may not be worth the higher costs. The expected return, rather than the physical need, should justify any spending on maintenance and remodeling. Rental rates that are depressed by rent control or a deteriorating neighborhood encourage the investor to perform minimal maintenance and eventually to abandon the property. On the other hand, perfectly functional structures may at times be substantially altered or torn down if a different structure would earn enough to justify the conversion.

Principle 8

An investor should never purchase real estate without a careful on-site inspection and comparison with the relevant alternatives. Some companies use a free dinner and slide show to sell Sunbelt property to people living in other areas—especially the Snowbelt. There is no substitute, however, for an on-site inspection. These inspections may reveal a drainage problem;

unpleasant odors from nearby factories, sewage treatment facilities, or garbage dumps; neighboring developments that limit land values; more attractively priced nearby property; and many other unexpected factors. Investors should consider investing only in property that is near enough to inspect. The following are some relevant characteristics to consider in any proposed property purchase:

- location. What changes are taking place? Will they work to the property owner's benefit? Consider road access, utilities and services, and neighboring property development. If property is being bought for business purposes, do surrounding businesses complement it? Are suppliers nearby? Is parking adequate? Will the owner be able to expand to adjacent property if need be?
- competition. What nearby properties have similar uses? Does this choice have any particular advantages or disadvantages? Will competition moving into the area affect the owner?
- facilities and maintenance. Does the physical quality of the buildings compare favorably with neighboring properties? Do the structures have multifaceted use? Are costly repairs likely to be required? If so, does the asking price reflect these projected costs?
- financing. Can the property be financed by both the current buyer and a subsequent buyer? How committed is the original lender to financing the rest of the development? Would other area lenders consider financing the property? If not, why not?
- operating expenses. How stable are the expenses for taxes, management, utilities, and insurance? Might they rise substantially? Are the expense figures provided consistent with the experience of owners of similar buildings? Do long-term leases provide sufficient additional revenues to cover these projected cost increases?
- income. If the property provides rental income, can rents be increased? How do the rents compare with those for similar property? Is the tenancy likely to be stable? What lease terms can the owner offer?
- price asked. How does the price compare with that paid by other property buyers? Could the same dollar commitment buy attractively priced property in a more established area? If the property is income producing, does the price permit a positive cash flow after taxes and mortgage payments? How firm is the asking price?

Principle 9

Owners of real estate should strive to minimize the use of expensive professionals. Real estate investors often require the services of lawyers, realtors, appraisers, architects, accountants, contractors, property managers, and several other types of professionals. These professionals are sometimes well worth their cost. At other times, however, the property owner may effectively perform the task and save the fee.

Realtor commissions are normally set at 6 percent to 7 percent on developed property and 10 percent or more for land. Thus, the sale of a $150,000 house generates a $9,000 to $10,500 commission. Suppose the owner attempts to sell the house directly. He or she might reduce the price by $2,500 and spend $500 on classified advertising. If the effort is successful, the owner would save $6,000 to $7,500. Some buyers also prefer to purchase properties directly. Owners who personally market the property can afford to sell for less.

Most owners can also handle such jobs as bookkeeping, appraising, and property management. Some professional services, however, are practically unavoidable. For example, few nonlawyers know how to do a title search, and the lender is unlikely to accept the work of those who do. Similarly, few laypersons can design and contract major construction. Moreover, an independent appraisal of a large parcel might be well worth the cost. Similarly, large property holdings may benefit from professional management and accounting. The issue really boils down to how highly the investor values his or her time and talent.

10 Principles of Real Estate Investing

- The value of a property is determined by its most profitable uses.
- Land supply is fixed, while demand and, therefore, prices may rise with population and affluence.
- In the short run, real estate prices occasionally fall.
- Comparison shopping and bargaining can lead to the best possible price on property.
- Wise use of leverage enhances profitability.
- Shopping around can result in more attractive terms on interest, down payment, maturity, closing cost, insurance, points, escrow accounts, and so on.
- Expected returns should justify all maintenance or improvement expenses.
- Purchasing any real estate property sight unseen is foolhardy.
- Minimizing the use of professionals whenever it is practical can reduce costs.
- Government actions can have an impact on real estate values.

Principle 10

Investors should continually keep abreast of relevant local, state, and federal agency policies and proposed policies. For example, moving quickly to secure property near new government projects, such as an interstate highway interchange or rapid transit terminal, may yield large profits. Other state or local government actions (for example, rent control) can appreciably depress real estate values.

DETERMINING REAL ESTATE VALUES

Although useful for novice investors, the 10 real estate investment principles summarized above do not come directly to grips with the basic issue of real estate valuation. There are three different ways of estimating real estate values: the market approach, the cost approach, and the income approach.

market approach

Market Approach

Most people would agree that an item is worth what it will sell for. The value of a particular property should not differ greatly from realistic asking prices and recent sale prices of similar real estate. Thus, a check of the market and recent transactions should give some guide to what a particular property is worth. No two properties are precisely equivalent, however. Every property has a different location, and other characteristics (size, condition, and so on) will usually vary, sometimes substantially. Furthermore, a property's market value may differ appreciably from a particular investor's assessment. Therefore, investors should not rely exclusively on the market approach. On the other hand, a price that is above the comparable alternatives is surely too high, while a price that is below the competition is at least worth further consideration.

cost approach

Cost Approach

Real estate values may also be based on the cost of equivalent land and construction. The construction cost should include the cost of funds tied up while the property is being built, and it should allow for the differential values of new versus used structures. When replacement costs are below market prices, investors are encouraged to build rather than to buy. Developed property selling for less than its replacement cost may, depending on demand, be either a bargain or severely outdated or mislocated. Thus, valuations based on replacement costs provide a much better ceiling than floor on true values.

income approach

Income Approach

A Simple Description

Just as common stock values are related to expected future dividend payments, real estate values are strongly influenced by their expected future rental (or other) income.

Example: Suppose an apartment building yields annual rentals of $10,000, is to be purchased for cash (no mortgage), and has expected annual expenses (maintenance, property taxes, insurance, and so on) of $3,000. To simplify the computations, ignore the impact of depreciation on income taxes. Thus, the property is expected to generate a net annual cash inflow of $7,000.

The present value of a constant income stream (a perpetuity) is simply 1/r multiplied by the income stream (where r is the appropriate discount rate). Discounted at 14 percent, the property's expected income stream is worth $50,000.

An even simpler approach, as shown in the following example, utilizes the multiples of gross rents.

Example: If comparable property in the example above is valued at five times its gross rents, this approach would also value the hypothetical property at $50,000 (5 x $10,000 = $50,000).

The appropriate multiple in this approach will, of course, vary with market interest rates. Investors might also take some account of other factors such as risk, leverage potential, net cash flow, and opportunities to upgrade the property.

These very rough-and-ready uses of the income approach can provide a cursory evaluation of a particular property. The potential investor can simply estimate rental income and direct expenses (exclusive of mortgage payments and income taxes) to find the gross income of the real estate. Dividing this sum by the appropriate discount rate will produce a first-pass value estimate. Such an approach can help separate obviously unattractive opportunities from those that deserve further study.

A much more detailed analysis is needed, however, before the investor can make a final decision. Specifically, the investor should consider the cash flows after loan payments and income taxes are paid, take account of the property's expected market price change, and relate the net return to the actual outlay (down payment) rather than the total cost.

A More Realistic Description

Let us consider a more complex, yet realistic, example of the of the income approach. The actual implementation of the income approach involves six steps:

1. Determine the appropriate discount rate r.
    a. Ascertain the current market cost of borrowing funds to finance the contemplated real estate purchase, and adjust this to an after-tax basis.
    b. Estimate the expected after-tax rate of return that could be obtained from a project of comparable risk on the funds required for the down payment.
    c. Determine the weighted average cost of funds: Multiply the percentage to be borrowed by the borrowing rate; multiply the percentage of the down payment by its alternative rate; then add the two values.
2. Forecast future rental income. An established property's current rental rates are known. Rates on similar units provide a guide for newly constructed projects. Forecasting future rates is more difficult. In some cases, the anticipated future rates may be built into the lease. Rental rates on comparable property, vacancy rates, construction costs, and building activity are all relevant factors in rent determination. The investor should usually forecast rent increases conservatively.
3. Forecast the future expenses associated with maintaining the property, including property taxes, repairs, renovations, depreciation, and management costs. Knowledge of the building's structural soundness would be helpful in estimating some of these costs. Current expenses might be projected to rise with inflation. Some adjustments may be required for anticipated needs (such as a new furnace). Note, however, that even experts cannot consistently predict future inflation rates. Since inflation's effects on rents and maintenance costs tend to be offsetting, the investor can at least assume consistent increases for both (factoring in rent control, if present). Mortgage payments are not included as an expense, because they are accounted for in the discount rate. The investor's income taxes must also be estimated.

4. Forecast the property's holding period and value at the time of sale. Again, the investor should try to be consistent. The property's sale price should not normally be expected to rise faster than its ability to produce income.
5. Use these figures to estimate the real estate's value.
    a. Subtract expected cash expenses for each year from anticipated revenues to obtain expected net cash flow.
    b. Use a present-value table or financial calculator to compute the discounted present value of each year's expected net cash flow for the appropriate discount rate.
    c. In like manner, find the present value of the property's expected sale price net of income taxes and selling expenses.
    d. Add the present value of the expected net cash flow to the expected net sales price to obtain the present value of the total.
6. Compare the present value of the expected cash flow plus future net sales price with the price of the property. The higher the income approach valuation relative to the price, the more attractive the potential investment.

Now let us consider a brief application of the income approach procedure:

1. Determine r. (Note that in some market environments these rates may seem high—or perhaps low. They are not meant to be representative of a particular current situation.)
    Borrowing cost: 8%
    Alternative after-tax return on down payment: 10%
    Tax rate: 30%
    Percent down payment required: 25%
    Weighted average cost of capital: .75 x 8% x (1 – .30) + (.25 x 10%) = 6.7%
2. Estimate current and future rental income. (To be conservative, use the current amount for future years.)
    Current rental income: $2,000 per month, or $24,000 per year
3. Estimate current and future property expenses.

Depreciation	$ 6,000 per year
Property taxes	4,000 per year
Repairs	1,400 per year
Miscellaneous	600 per year
Total	$12,000 per year

Estimate income taxes.

Revenue	$24,000 per year
Expenses	–12,000 per year
Taxable income	$12,000 x .30 tax rate = $3,600 income tax

4. Forecast the expected holding period and selling price.
    Expected holding period: 5 years
    Expected net selling price: $164,000 (a modest increase over the current asking price of $160,000)
5. Use figures to estimate the real estate's value.
    a. Net cash flow per year = revenue – expenses – income taxes + depreciation (a noncash expense)
        $24,000 – $12,000 – $3,600 + $6,000 = $14,400
    b. Discounted value of each year's expected net income (determined using HP 12C calculator):

Year	Income	Present Value (Discounted at 6.7%)
Year 1	$14,400	$13,496
Year 2	14,400	12,648
Year 3	14,400	11,854
Year 4	14,400	11,109
Year 5	14,400	10,412
		Total: $59,519

    c. Present value of expected sales price: $164,000 received at the end of year 5 = $118,583
    d. Present value of expected net income plus expected sales price:
        $59,519 + $118,583 = $178,102
6. Compare present value of d. above with asking price. Since the present value is greater than the asking price ($178,102 versus $160,000), the property seems relatively attractive. An investor would certainly want to consider collecting better estimates for the above figures.

Note that while we used greater detail in the example above than in the earlier simplified example, this procedure still focuses on the whole project's expected return. The return on the investor's contribution is a more meaningful figure.

Three Approaches to Valuing Real Estate

*   Market approach: bases value on asking and sale prices of comparable properties
*   Cost approach: bases value on cost of constructing equivalent property
*   Income approach: bases value on present value of expected future net cash flow stream

Combining the Three Valuation Approaches

Attractive real estate opportunities are priced below their market, cost, and income valuations. Real estate priced above any one of these three "values" is probably an unwise investment. If, for example, the price is above either the market or replacement values, more attractively priced properties should be available elsewhere. A price that is high relative to the income-approach valuation suggests that other investments (perhaps outside of real estate) offer higher returns. An investment's attractiveness varies inversely with its price. Moreover, real estate asking prices are often flexible.

THE REAL ESTATE TRANSACTION

Bargaining

Unlike most other investments, real estate transactions often involve some bargaining. Thus, investors should bargain with the seller in an effort to purchase potentially attractive investments as cheaply as possible. Sellers generally expect to receive less than their asking price. Investors should seek to buy at the lower end of the realistic range.

The appropriate level for an initial offer is difficult to prespecify. Some properties are so overpriced that an offer of two-thirds or even one-half of the asking price is realistic. In other cases, an offer 20 percent below the asking price might be insulting. The offer should be high enough to elicit a counteroffer but leave the potential buyer maximum flexibility to continue the bargaining process. Unless the market is particularly strong, the seller will usually counter a reasonable offer. The seller might, for example, drop 5 percent off the asking price. Then the investor could come back with a 5 percent to 10 percent increase in the offer. Once the investor's offer and the seller's asking price are close, one of the parties will usually suggest splitting the difference.

Uninformed sellers can pose both opportunities and difficulties. A seller who wants cash in a hurry or does not fully recognize the property's value may set too low a price. On the other hand, a seller who has an exaggerated vision of property values may try the buyer's patience. Examples of potential uninformed sellers include the following: an out-of-town heir who needs to pay estate taxes, a longtime owner who has not kept up with current prices, and the owner of a run-down property who does not realize that much greater rents could be charged if the property was rehabilitated.

While some uninformed sellers may not know how much their property is worth, others may not know how little it should sell for. Some novice sellers may believe that the real estate market is so strong that eager buyers will meet almost any asking price. Perhaps having the property on the market for a few months will persuade these sellers to be more reasonable.

Seller Financing

Real estate investors may also use the seller to help finance the purchase. For example, a seller who desires a steady income might accept a below-market-rate mortgage on the old property. Most people are unable to earn secure returns on their own investments as high as the rates paid to mortgage lenders. Thus, the opportunity to earn a relatively low (compared to the market) mortgage rate may still seem attractive to them. A seller who receives partial payment in the form of a mortgage will earn a steady monthly income and qualify the transaction as an installment sale, which may reduce taxes.

A buyer who knows the seller's circumstances may be able to work out financing arrangements that are beneficial to both. For example, the buyer might make a 20 percent down payment, assume the seller's existing low-interest mortgage, and give the seller a 5-year note for the remaining debt. The principal amount of the note will, however, need to be refinanced or paid off well before a long-term mortgage would come due. Interest rates then may or may not be lower.

While seller financing is helpful to buyers who need a few years to prepare for higher interest rates and mortgage payments, it should not be viewed as permanent financing. Indeed, borrowers frequently have difficulty paying off short-term seller financing.

The seller should also understand the advantages and disadvantages of entering into a financing arrangement. On the plus side, providing seller financing helps market the property. On the minus side, the buyer's note almost always bears a below-market interest rate. As a "second" mortgage, it should yield more than a first mortgage. For example, if first mortgage rates are 10 percent, the market rate on a second mortgage should be 12 percent or more. A lower rate on a second mortgage is, in effect, a hidden price reduction. Moreover, a buyer who has difficulty paying off the note may pressure the seller into extending the loan. Clearly, seller financing is no panacea for either party.

Negotiation through Intermediaries

Third parties such as realtors or lawyers are frequently brought into real estate negotiations. This approach helps to avoid potential personality conflicts from direct buyer-seller contact. For instance, the seller may become defensive if the buyer directly notes the property's negative factors. The agent earns a commission only if the buyer and seller come to terms. Accordingly, he or she has an incentive to convey the buyer's concerns in a tactful manner. Thus, the agent should be able to comment effectively on the property's condition, location, and/or price relative to that of similar properties.

Closing the Deal

If bargaining reaches an apparent impasse, the would-be buyer should consider low-cost concessions that might push the negotiation to a conclusion. Offering to agree to an early closing date, for instance, might elicit additional flexibility from a seller who is concerned about timing. An early closing means that the seller will promptly receive the proceeds from the sale.

Similarly, relenting on some original demands, such as ignoring certain small problems, offering to buy some of the seller's personal property, or working out a payment plan suitable to the seller, could all clinch a deal at minimum expense to the buyer. If, however, negotiations proceed to different figures that seem firm for both sides, the would-be buyer must decide whether to pay more or look elsewhere.

Negotiating the Loan

Once a price that is satisfactory to both the buyer and seller has been established, the next step is obtaining financing. Finding financing is up to the buyer.

Example: Consider this scenario: The investor begins the financing process by making preliminary inquiries at a local bank. The bank is short of mortgage money, but because the buyer is a long-time depositor, the bank is willing to consider an application. The buyer then applies for a $100,000 loan (80 percent of the purchase price). The bank offers a $98,000 20-year loan at 10 percent with no points. The borrower asks for and receives an option to repay any time after 3 years without penalty, as well as the right to handle property tax and insurance payments without an escrow account. The borrower is required to purchase a term life insurance policy equal to the face value of the mortgage loan.

When both parties are satisfied with the financing arrangement, the loan negotiations are complete.

Completing the Transaction

Once the financing has been arranged, the present owner's clear title must be established (via a title search). The transaction also needs to be registered and taxes paid in the proper locality. At the closing, the buyer, the seller, an officer of the mortgage loan-granting institution, and their attorneys meet and pass the final papers and funds.

Refinancing

refinancing

Refinancing is a useful option in many real estate investment situations. Consider the example below.

Example:	Assume that an apartment building was purchased 5 years ago for $900,000. The buyer borrowed $720,000 and made a $180,000 down payment. Now the property has appreciated, and amortization has reduced the mortgage principal to $650,000. The owner could sell the property for a substantial gain, but significant drawbacks of a sale are that a large part of the proceeds would have to be paid as taxes, and the property still represents a good investment opportunity. Thus, the owner may prefer to extract some funds by refinancing. If, for instance, a reappraisal establishes $2 million as the property's fair market value, the bank might now be willing to increase the loan by as much as $950,000 (to $1.6 million, or 80 percent of $2 million).

REAL ESTATE STOCKS AND RELATED INVESTMENTS

Many investors are not well situated to own, manage, and assume the risks involved with direct real estate ownership. These investors may want to consider other ways of participating in the real estate market. Real estate investment trusts, real estate limited partnerships, and companies with substantial property holdings all represent indirect ways of investing in property. Each offers the opportunity to participate in the market without having management responsibility while limiting risk. Most of these investments are publicly traded companies that own, develop, manage, or sell real estate.

Real Estate Investment Trusts (REITs)

REITs assemble and manage portfolios of real estate and real estate loans. They are organized like, and their shares trade in the same markets as, those of corporations. They are not, however, assessed corporate income taxes if they pay out 95 percent or more of their income as dividends (act as if they are investment companies).

REITs create portfolios of real estate investments with the proceeds from the sale of stock and borrowed funds. Investors purchase shares of the investment portfolio that the REIT holds. By law, at least 75 percent of REIT assets must be invested in real estate, and no less than 75 percent of its income must be derived from real estate.

REITs allow investors to diversify to real estate and mortgages without necessitating active management of the assets. Investors have the benefit of professional management, and, since the REIT's shares are actively traded, investors have a marketable asset that they can sell quickly.

As with all equity investments, returns from REITs vary greatly from year to year, causing them to fall periodically from favor with investors, but investment rose sharply in the 1990s. Investors should evaluate REITs by applying the same methods that they would use to evaluate any stock prior to purchase.

REITs are essentially closed-end investment companies with stated investment objectives that fall into one of three general categories:

equity REITs

mortgage REITs

hybrid REITs

- *Equity REITs* invest in office buildings, apartments, shopping malls, and hotels.
- *Mortgage REITs* are in the business of making both construction loans and mortgage loans.
- *Hybrid REITs* are a combination of equity and mortgage REITs.

Equity REITs are typically the most popular type with investors who want to participate in the growth of real estate values. Dividends should rise if rents increase more than expenses, and share prices generally reflect changes in property values.

Mortgage REITs are similar to bonds. Like all interest-rate-sensitive investments, their prices rise when interest rates fall, and fall when interest rates rise.

Another way to invest in real estate is to purchase the shares of a mutual fund that invests in REITs, typically equity REITs. This approach enables the small investor to reduce risk through diversification.

Especially attractive in this area are REIT index funds. Rather than trying to select REITs that will outperform the sector, index funds purchase the shares of REITs that are included in the Morgan Stanley REIT Index. Investor returns should equal those of the index, minus fund expenses. As with any mutual fund investment, low expenses give the investor a head start.

While less risky than direct real estate investments, index equity REITs are generally considered aggressive investments. They concentrate investment in a sector that can be rather volatile. Investors should expect wide price fluctuations.

Real Estate Limited Partnerships (RELPs)

Real estate limited partnerships, or *RELPs,* are specialized securities that provide investors with an interest in a portfolio of real estate properties. Organized as a limited partnership, these securities have much in common with corporations. Each investor's liability is limited to the amount that he or she initially invests. The management function rests with a group of hired managers. The securities may be freely bought and sold. The principal difference from a corporation is in the way the partnership's income is taxed.

A corporation is an entity that is subject to tax in its own right. The dividends that it pays are taxed a second time as income to the owners (assuming that they are subject to an income tax). A partnership is viewed as a conduit for transferring income to the owner. Thus, the full amount of any partnership income is subject to the investor's income tax. No additional tax is assessed to the partnership itself. Therefore, the partnership's income is taxed only once. Accordingly, the combination of limited liability and favorable tax treatment makes the RELP an ideal vehicle for individual participation in the real estate market.

A number of brokerage firms have sponsored the issuance of RELPs through public offerings. Others have been offered by the syndicator sponsor who is slated to manage the partnership once it is established. All limited partnerships must have a general partner who assumes general liability. Usually, the sponsor takes on this role.

The principal drawbacks to RELPs are their relatively limited secondary markets and their relatively high overhead structure of fees and expenses. Such investments are generally difficult to sell prior to their scheduled liquidation. Moreover, the sponsoring syndicate often structures the deal so that much of the profits go to the sponsor, while substantial risks are borne by the investors. Average returns for RELPs have thus far not been particularly impressive.

Companies with Real Estate Holdings

In addition to the real-estate-related investments, a number of other types of companies have substantial property holdings. In most instances, their properties are related to their primary business. Among industries that hold real estate are the following:

- paper and forest products companies. These firms often have substantial land holdings from which they obtain timber and wood pulp. Some of this land may be worth far more as home sites, for example.
- railroads. Many railroads, particularly those located in the West, own substantial tracts of land, much of which goes back to 19th century

government land grants. Other railroads own valuable downtown property near their terminals. Railroads with poor prospects as transport companies often have depressed share values. If their land holdings are ever liquidated, however, the profits to shareholders could be substantial.

- ranch and farm companies. Some agricultural operations with substantial land holdings are organized as corporations. Frequently, this property is carried on the books at very low historical costs. The liquidation values of these firms are often well above the market prices of their stock.

- oil and mining companies. Generally, their most valuable holdings are their mineral resources, but often these companies, too, own some real estate. As with the other types of firms, the stock price may not fully reflect the property's liquidation value.

- manufacturers. Most manufacturers own only the plants that they operate. Some, however, own valuable office buildings and attractive land holdings that are often overlooked by the market.

- insurance companies. Life insurance companies have huge sums to invest. While most of their funds go into bonds, mortgages, and other debt instruments, some are invested in real estate. Moreover, in many instances, the market seems to undervalue that property.

- movie companies. While most moviemakers have sold off their real estate, some still have valuable studio property in Hollywood. This property may or may not be recognized in the stock's price.

- retailers. Many large retailers have valuable real estate in the form of the store buildings in which they operate. Others have long-term leases at rental rates that are far below the current market levels.

The investment attractiveness of companies with substantial real estate holdings depends both on the extent to which their stock price reflects the holdings and on the likelihood that the property will be sold in the relatively near future.

SUMMARY AND CONCLUSIONS

Real estate investments have unique characteristics that a prospective investor should consider prior to investing. Can he or she afford to tie up sufficient funds for several years? Is the investor likely to remain in the same geographic area for the foreseeable future? Are the talents needed to manage real estate present? Is the investor willing and able to accept the risks?

Among the 10 basic principles of real estate investing are principles that relate to the determination of the price of a given parcel of land by its most valuable uses, the fixed supply of land, the possibility of adverse price moves, the importance of shopping around, the use of leverage, the control of expenses, the inspection of prospective real estate, the use of professionals, and the impact of government actions.

The three approaches to real estate valuation are the market approach, the cost approach, and the income approach. Real estate transactions also usually involve some bargaining, loan negotiation, property management, and refinancing.

In addition to direct real estate ownership, there are indirect ways to invest in real estate, including RELPs, and companies that own substantial amounts of real estate.

CHAPTER REVIEW

Answers to the review questions and the self-test questions start on page 501.

Key Terms

closing costs	seller financing
point	refinancing
escrow account	equity REITs
adjustable rate mortgage (ARM)	mortgage REITs
market approach	hybrid REITs
cost approach	RELPs
income approach	

Review Questions

15-1.   What issues should be considered when determining the suitability of real estate investment?

15-2.   Briefly explain the following methods of real estate valuation:
    a.   market approach
    b.   cost approach
    c.   income approach

15-3.   How might the results of the three approaches discussed in question 15-2 best be used?

15-4.   You are considering the purchase of a home for $179,000. Your local banker will lend you 80 percent of the purchase price. You must, however, pay 3 points for the loan and a $500 loan application fee. Title insurance in your area costs $700, and inspections for structural soundness cost $250. Transferring the title will cost you 0.5 percent of the sale price. You must deposit 12 months' property taxes and insurance into an escrow account;

property taxes are set at about 2 percent of the sale price. Insurance rates in your community are $4 per $1,000 of protection, and the bank requires that you insure your property for 100 percent of the initial mortgage balance. Having a lawyer represent you at the closing will incur a fee of $200. Hooking up various utilities will require fees of $340 and deposits of another $500.

a. What is the total payment for acquiring and occupying the house?

b. Other than the bank loan, how much cash must you raise in order to occupy the house?

c. If we consider the difference between the total payment and purchase price to be transaction costs, what percentage do transaction costs represent of the purchase price?

15-5. A duplex is for sale for $180,000. After expenses, it offers a net rental income (after deducting all out-of-pocket expenses except financing costs) of $28,000 per year. The rents, expenses, and market value of the property are expected to remain constant for the foreseeable future. The borrower may borrow up to 90 percent of the purchase price at 11 percent. Assume a risk premium of 3 percent above the mortgage interest rate. The seller agrees to deduct any closing costs from the purchase price. What is your assessment of the merit of this purchase?

15-6. You are considering the purchase of a parcel of land for $45,000. You can borrow up to 50 percent of the purchase price at a rate of 10.5 percent. Long-term government bonds are yielding 6.5 percent. Briefly discuss the factors that are relevant in determining the cost of capital.

15-7. What alternatives are available to the small investor who likes the general prospects of real estate but is put off by some of the problems of direct real estate investing?

15-8. Suppose that you purchase 100 acres for a cemetery. You estimate that there is room for 1,000 graves per acre. Yearly sales will likely number 100 at $1,000 per sale. Of this amount, $300 will go for preparation and selling expenses and $600 will go into a maintenance trust. The remainder will be profit.

a. Using a 14 percent discount rate, what is the present value of this business?

b. How much would the value change if an 11 percent discount rate is used and the maintenance trust requires only $550 per grave?

Self-Test Questions

T F 15-1. Direct investments in real estate require the owner to provide for management services.

T F 15-2. High leverage is seldom used in direct investments in real estate.

T   F   15-3.   Direct investments in real estate are highly liquid.

T   F   15-4.   A point is one percent of the purchase price of the property.

T   F   15-5.   Lenders may require an escrow account for property taxes and insurance.

T   F   15-6.   Many adjustable rate mortgages have a cap limiting how high the rate may increase over the life of the mortgage.

T   F   15-7.   Realtor commissions are normally the same for developed property as they are for raw land.

T   F   15-8.   The market approach to estimating real estate values relies on an evaluation of the cost to replace the structure.

T   F   15-9.   When seller financing is employed, the rate of interest on the buyer's note is usually above the market interest rate.

T   F   15-10. Refinancing an existing mortgage is a way to obtain additional funds without selling the property.

T   F   15-11. REITs do not have to pay corporate income taxes if they distribute at least 95 percent of their profit as dividends.

T   F   15-12. A REIT is an open-end mutual fund that redeems its shares when investors sell.

T   F   15-13. Hybrid REITs invest exclusively in office buildings, apartments, and shopping malls.

T   F   15-14. All income that a real estate limited partnership (RELP) earns is taxable to the partners.

T   F   15-15. Index REITs are not subject to market risk because they offer a diversified investment portfolio.

T   F   15-16. Purchasing stock in paper and forest products companies is a way for investors to get an equity position in those companies' vast land holdings.

Glossary

12b-1 fee • annual fee paid by investors for the administrative and marketing expenses of a mutual fund, paid as a percentage of the net asset value of the investor's shares of the fund

absolute priority of claims principle • the principle in bankruptcy law that each class of liability claims is to be repaid in full before the succeeding category receives even partial payment

acceptance • *See* banker's acceptance.

acid test ratio • cash and accounts receivable divided by current liabilities; used to measure short-term liquidity (also called quick ratio). It differs from the current ratio by not including inventory in the numerator.

adjustable rate mortgage (ARM) • type of mortgage in which the interest rate is periodically adjusted as market interest rates change

adjusted beta • a statistical correction to beta forecast estimates due to the tendency for historically estimated beta to drift toward 1.0 as later data are gathered. *See also* beta and mean reversion.

adjustment lag • the time it takes for stock prices to react appropriately to new information

advance-decline pattern • technical indicator showing ratio or difference between number of stocks advancing versus number of stocks declining in a particular period (usually one day) on a particular exchange

agency problem • the conflict of interests and disparity of goals between corporate managers and shareholders. This is also known as the principal-agent conflict.

agency security • a debt security issued by federal agencies such as the FNMA, GNMA, or Freddie Mac

all-or-nothing order • an order that must be executed in its entirety or not at all

466   *Fundamentals of Investments for Financial Planning*

alpha • the intercept term in the market model that provides an estimate of a security's return, given a zero market return; also the difference between a security's or portfolio's return and the return that would be expected based on the capital asset pricing model

alternative minimum tax • tax that may be applicable to those with large amounts of otherwise sheltered income (preferences) such as accelerated depreciation deductions; applies when the tax liability computed by disallowing these preferences exceeds the liability when the tax is computed the normal way

American depository receipt (ADR) • a U.S.-traded security representing stock in a foreign corporation, priced in U.S. dollars

American option • an option that may be closed out or exercised at any time prior to or at its expiration date

AMEX (American Stock Exchange) • an organized stock exchange tending to deal in small- to mid-capitalization stocks; merged with NASDAQ

analyst neglect • an alleged anomaly to the efficient market hypothesis that is characterized by the tendency of security analysts to overlook small or obscure firms in their security evaluations

annuity • an asset that usually promises to pay a fixed amount periodically for a predetermined period, although some pay a sum for an individual's lifetime. Certain types of annuities are variable, depending on the issuer's investment experience. Many are sold by insurance companies.

anomaly • condition in the security markets that appears to allow for persistent abnormal returns on a consistent basis after adjusting for risk

anxious trader effects • short-run price distortions caused by sales or purchases of impatient large traders

appreciation • increase in the value of an investment over time; also called capital gain

arbitrage • simultaneously buying in one market and selling equivalent assets in another for a certain riskless profit

arbitrage pricing model • a model used to explain stock pricing and expected return that introduces more than one factor in place of (or in addition to) the capital asset pricing model's market index

arbitrage pricing theory • theory of stock pricing that relies on an arbitrage pricing multi-factor model, rather than the capital asset pricing model

arithmetic mean return • the simple average return found by dividing the sum of the separate per-period returns by the number of periods over which they were earned

ask • the lowest price at which a security is currently offered for sale that may emanate from a specialist (exchange), market maker (OTC), or unexercised limit order

asset allocation (financial planning) • the principal method of portfolio management by financial planners, based on the idea of dividing wealth among different types of assets

asset allocation (market timing) • an approach to market timing. The asset allocator divides his or her portfolio among a number of categories such as low-risk stocks, high-risk stocks, short-term bonds, and long-term bonds. The percentage of the portfolio invested in each of these categories will vary, depending on the asset allocator's expectations of stock market movements. *See* market timing.

asset turnover • ratio of sales to assets. In fundamental analysis of the firm, it is a measure of the "productivity" of assets used by the firm.

at-the-money • when the current stock price is the same as the strike price

at-the-money option • an option whose strike price is equal to the current market price

average tax rate • total amount of income tax paid divided by total income. A person's average tax rate is usually lower than his or her marginal tax rate.

balance of trade • the difference between a country's expenditures on imports and its income from exports

balance sheet • a financial statement showing a firm's or individual's financial position that lists assets, liabilities, and net worth (equity) as of a particular point in time

banker's acceptance • a money market instrument (also called acceptance) usually arising from international trade and containing a bank's guarantee or acceptance

bankruptcy proceeding • a legal process for dealing formally with a defaulted obligation; may result in a liquidation or reorganization

bankruptcy trustee • the person or institution that takes responsibility for the property of the debtor and holds it "in trust" for equitable distribution among the creditors

bar chart • in technical analysis, a type of graph that plots the price over time and typically contains data on the high, low, and volume

Barron's Confidence Index • a technical indicator based on the yield differential between high-grade and average-grade corporate bonds, with a small differential signifying confidence in the future and a large differential signaling a lack of confidence

basis point • one-hundredth of one percentage point; primarily used with interest rates

bear • one who expects a declining market

bearer bond • an unregistered bond whose ownership is determined by possession

bear raid • an attempt to drive prices down by selling short

best-effort basis • a securities offering in which the underwriter acts as an agent for the issuer but is not obligated to purchase the securities

beta • a parameter that relates stock or portfolio performance to market performance. For example, with an x percent change in the market, a stock or portfolio will tend to change by x percent times its beta.

bid-ask spread • the price difference between the bid price and the ask price for an asset

Big Board • popular term for the New York Stock Exchange, the largest U.S. stock exchange

Black-Scholes model • an option-pricing formula based on the assumption that a riskless hedge between an option and its underlying stock should yield the riskless return. The model gives an option's value as a function of the stock price, strike price, stock return volatility, riskless interest rate, and length of time to expiration.

blind pool • a form of investment venture in which the precise purposes of the venture are not revealed until later to the pool of investors

block trade • a trade involving 10,000 shares or more, usually handled by a block trader

bond • a debt obligation (usually long-term) in which the borrower promises to pay a set coupon rate until the issue matures, at which time the principal is repaid; sometimes secured by a mortgage on a specific property, plant, or piece of equipment. *See also* debenture.

bond equivalent yield • the yield on a taxable bond that would be equivalent, on an after-tax basis, to the rate of return on a tax-exempt municipal bond. This value can be obtained by dividing the municipal bond's interest rate by (1 – T), where T is the investor's marginal tax rate.

bond rating • a rating of a bond's investment quality and default risk, usually provided by a rating agency such as Standard & Poor's, Moody's, or Fitch

bond swap • a technique for managing a bond portfolio by selling some bonds and buying others, possibly to achieve benefits in the form of tax treatment, yields, maturity structure, or trading profits

book value per share • the total assets of an enterprise minus its liabilities, minority interests, and preferred stock at par, divided by the number of outstanding common shares

broker • an employee of a financial intermediary who acts as an agent (not a dealer) in buying and selling securities for customers

brokerage firm • a firm that offers various financial services such as access to the securities markets, account management, margin loans, investment advice, and underwriting

broker call-loan rate • the interest rate charged by banks to brokers for loans that brokers use to support their margin loans to customers (usually scaled up for the margin loan rate)

bull market • a rising market

buying power • the dollar value of additional securities that can be purchased on margin with the current equity in a margin account

call • an option to buy stock or some other asset at a prespecified price over a prespecified time period

callable bond • a bond for which the issuing company has an option to repurchase the securities at a set price over a prespecified period (prior to maturity)

call-loan rate • *See* broker call-loan rate.

call premium • the additional amount above the face value that the issuer must pay to redeem a bond prior to its maturity date

call price • the price at which a bond, preferred stock, warrant, or other security may be redeemed prior to maturity; usually begins at a significant premium to the face value and then the premium declines as the instrument approaches its stated maturity (also called redemption price). The call price is equal to the face value plus the call premium.

call provision • a provision in a bond indenture that gives the issuer the option of redeeming the bond prior to maturity

capacity effect • the tendency of inflationary pressures to accelerate when the economy approaches the full employment level

capital asset pricing model (CAPM) • the theoretical relationship that seeks to explain returns as a function of the risk-free rate, market risk premium, and beta

capital distribution • a dividend paid out of capital rather than from earnings. Such distributions are not taxed when received but do reduce the investment's basis (also called liquidating dividend).

capital gains (losses) • an increase (or decrease) in the market value of an asset

capital market line • the theoretical relation between an efficiently diversified portfolio's expected return and risk, derived from the capital asset pricing model

certificate of deposit (CD) • special redeemable debt obligation issued by a bank and other depository institution

charting • an attempt to forecast stock price changes from charts of past price and volume data. This is a form of technical analysis.

chartist • technical analyst who uses price and volume charts to forecast prices

closed-end fund • a type of investment company whose shares are traded in the same markets as other stocks (the price fluctuates from the fund's net asset value). Unlike an open-end fund, the company does not buy and sell shares to investors.

closing costs • expenses associated with obtaining a real estate loan and completing the purchase. These costs may include title search, points, transfer taxes, and various other fees.

CMO (collateralized mortgage obligation) • multiclass mortgage pass-through security that reduces uncertainty about prepayments by specifying time of repayment; a secured bond that is backed by the mortgage payments on real estate

coefficient of determination (R^2) • a parameter that measures how much of the variance of a particular time series or sample of a dependent variable is accounted for (explained by) the movement of the independent variable(s) in a regression analysis. With respect to portfolios, it is a measure of diversification.

collateral • asset pledged to assure repayment of debt. The lender may take ownership of the collateral if the loan is not repaid as promised.

commercial paper • short-term, usually low-risk, debt issued by large corporations with very strong credit ratings

commissions • fees charged by brokers for handling investment transactions such as security or real estate trades

commodity-backed bond • debt security whose potential redemption value is related to the market price of some physical commodity

Composite Limit Order Book (CLOB) • a proposal that would list all orders on all stock exchanges in one composite list that, with free order flow, would allow all orders to be executed in any market where the security is traded

compound interest • interest earned on interest as a result of reinvesting one period's income to earn additional income the following period. (Compounding may take place as frequently as daily.) For example, compounded annually, $100 earning 9 percent will yield $9 the first year. In the following year, the 9 percent will be applied to $109, for a return of $9.81. In the third year, the principal will have grown to $118.81 ($100 + $9 + $9.81), and another 9 percent will add about $10.62. This process continues with the interest rate being applied to a larger and larger principal. In general, when interest rate r is compounded for t periods, the original investment is multiplied by $(1 + r)^t$.

constant growth model • form of the dividend discount model; used to evaluate the intrinsic value of an asset based on the assumptions of a constant growth rate g of cash flow or dividends and a known discount rate k, where k>g

contingent deferred sales load • a fee, as a percentage of net asset value, that investors pay to redeem their shares of a mutual fund. The percentage of net asset value generally declines over time. This is also known as a "back-end load."

conversion • exchange of convertible bond or preferred stock for common stock

conversion premium • the difference between the market price and the conversion value of a convertible bond or preferred stock

conversion price • the face value of a convertible bond divided by the number of shares into which the bond is convertible

conversion ratio • the number of common shares into which a convertible bond or preferred stock may be converted

conversion value • the market price of a stock multiplied by the number of shares for which the convertible bond or preferred stock may be exchanged

convertible bond • bond that can be converted into a specified number of shares of common stock

convertible preferred stock • a preferred stock that may be exchanged for a specific number of shares of the issuing company's common stock

corporate bond fund • a mutual fund that holds a diversified portfolio of corporate bonds

correlation coefficient • a measure of the comovement tendency of two variables, such as the returns on two securities

cost approach • a method of evaluating the value of a real estate investment in terms of the replacement costs of the property or the cost of equivalent land and construction

cost basis • the valuation (book value) of an asset based on the cost of acquiring it. This is also known as historical cost basis and may understate the true value of the asset, especially during periods of high inflation.

country fund • a type of mutual fund that assembles and manages a portfolio of securities in a single country, such as the Japan Fund or the Mexico Fund

coupon effect • the price impact of differential yield components derived from coupon versus price appreciation as a bond moves toward maturity. Thus, a deep-discount, low-coupon bond will offer a yield to maturity that includes a substantial component of tax-deferred capital gains. Such a bond's price will usually be affected favorably by the coupon effect.

coupon rate • the stated dollar return of a fixed-income investment

covariance • the correlation between two variables multiplied by each variable's standard deviation. The covariance of variables x and y is: $COV = E[x - E(x)] [y - E(y)]$, where $E(x)$ is the expected value of x. If x and y tend to be above their means simultaneously and below their means simultaneously, the covariance is positive. If one is above when the other tends to be below, the covariance is negative. If they are independent, the covariance is zero.

covered call • a call option written against stock that one owns

credit balance • a positive balance, as in a brokerage account

cum-rights • sale of common stock with rights attached. Securities that sell cum-rights will reflect the imputed value of the rights to be distributed.

cumulative • a preferred stock for which dividends in arrears must be paid before common dividends can be resumed

current assets • assets that are expected to be used up or converted to cash within the next year or next operating period, whichever is longer (include primarily cash, accounts receivable, and inventory)

current liabilities • liabilities that will become due and payable in the next year or the next operating cycle, whichever is longer (include accounts payable, short-term bank loans, the current portion of long-term debt, and taxes payable)

current ratio • the ratio of current assets to current liabilities (often a measure of short-term liquidity)

current yield • a bond's coupon rate divided by its current market price or a stock's indicated dividend rate divided by its per-share price

daily price limit (interday limit) • the rule established by the futures exchanges for the maximum range of price movement permitted between the closing price of the previous day and the opening price of the next day of trading for any given commodity. Once the limit is reached, trading must stop until the next trading session.

day order • an order that is canceled if it is not executed sometime during the day that it was entered

dealer • a security trader who acts as a principal rather than as an agent and who is considered a specialist or a market maker, not a broker (brokers are agents)

debenture • a long-term debt obligation that, unlike a collateralized bond, gives the lender only a general claim against the borrower's assets. In a default, the debenture holder has no claim against any specific assets.

debit balance • a negative balance in a margin account

debt-equity ratio • the ratio of total debt to total equity

deep-discount bond • a bond selling for substantially less than its par (face) value

default • failure to live up to any of the terms in a bond indenture or other credit agreement

default risk • the risk that a debt security's contractual interest or principal will not be paid when due

depository institution • an institution, such as a bank, that holds deposits and makes loans

derivative security • a security whose value is derived from the value of another security or combination of other securities—for example, options, futures, rights, and warrants

differential return • the difference in returns between a security and the market as a whole

dilution • reduction in value of stock of existing shareholders resulting from issuance of additional shares, exercise of rights or warrants, or conversion of convertible bonds or preferred stock

direct purchase plan • plan by which a specified amount of money is automatically applied toward the purchase of a company's stock at specified intervals (such as once a month); a form of dollar cost averaging

discounting • determining the present value of expected future cash flows based on the discount rate and time until the cash flows are expected to be received

discount rate (for Fed members) • the interest rate charged by the Federal Reserve System on loans to member banks

discount rate (for income stream) • the interest rate applied to an income stream or expected income stream in estimating its present value; the risk-free rate plus the risk premium for that particular source of income (such as a stock or bond)

discretionary account • account over which broker is authorized to exercise discretion with regard to purchases and sales

diversification • the technique of spreading an investment portfolio over different industries, companies, and investment types for the purpose of reducing risk

dividend capture • a strategy in which an investor purchases securities in order to own them on the day of record and then quickly sells them to capture the dividend but avoid the risk of a lengthy hold

dividend discount model • a process of evaluating stocks on the basis of the present value of their expected stream of dividends. Under circumstances where the expected growth rate of dividends is constant at a rate g, and the appropriate discount rate is k (with k>g), the basic formula is $P_0 = d_1/(k - g)$, where P_0 = current stock price, d_1 = following year's expected dividend (based on the growth rate), k = appropriate discount rate, and g = expected growth rate.

dividend payout ratio • percentage of net income (after preferred dividends) paid out as dividends on common stock

dividend reinvestment plan • a company program that allows dividends to be reinvested in additional shares, which are often newly issued and may be sold at a discount from the current market price

dividends • payments made by companies to their stockholders that are usually financed from profits

dividend yield • the ratio of annual dividends per share to price per share

dollar cost averaging • a formula investment plan requiring periodic (such as monthly) fixed-dollar-amount investments. This practice tends to "average" the unit purchase cost of an investment made over time. This is a passive form of market timing because more stock is purchased when the price is low than when it is high.

DOT (designated order transmission) • a system on the New York Stock Exchange in which orders are routed electronically to the trading posts where the securities are traded (often used by program traders)

downtick • a transaction that takes place at a lower price than the immediately preceding price

Dow theory • a charting theory originated by Charles Dow (Dow Jones Inc.). According to Dow theory, a market uptrend is confirmed if the primary market index (such as the Dow

Jones Industrial Average) hits a new high that is soon followed by a high in a secondary index (such as the Dow Jones Transportation Index). A downtrend is signaled in a similar fashion.

dual listing • a security listed for trading on more than one exchange

Dupont formula • a profitability relationship that relates return on equity to several components: ROE = (net income/sales) x (sales/assets) x (assets/equity), where ROE is return on equity. The formula is used for troubleshooting; by breaking return on equity into its component parts, individual ratios can be analyzed to assess a firm's condition.

duration • the weighted average amount of time until the present value of a bond's purchase price is repaid to the investor, based on the time-weighted present value of the bond's principal and interest payments divided by the discounted present value of the bond; used as a measure of a bond's sensitivity to interest rate changes

earnest money • the margin deposit that serves as a security to guarantee the performance of the contract by the buyer or the seller of a futures contract—in general, money put on deposit to guarantee the honoring of a contract

earnings multiplier • the ratio of market price per share to earnings per share. *See also* price-earnings ratio.

earnings per share (EPS) • the net income of a company, minus any preferred dividend requirements, divided by the number of outstanding common shares; provides the investor or potential investor with information on the stability of dividends and capital gains potential; considered one of the most important indications of the value of common stock

earnings surprise • the difference between actual reported earnings and anticipated earnings as measured by the consensus estimates of analysts who make such earnings forecasts

econometric model • a model based on an analysis of economic data, particularly models of the economy. The model uses explanatory variables to estimate future values of dependent variables.

econometrics • the statistical analysis of economic data and the use of statistical analysis to form estimates and predictions

efficient frontier • a set of expected risk-return tradeoffs, each of which offers the highest expected return for a given risk. *See* portfolio theory.

efficient market hypothesis (EMH) • the theory that the market correctly prices securities in light of the known relevant information. In its weak form, the hypothesis implies that past price and volume data (technical analysis) cannot consistently be profitably used in stock selection. The semistrong form implies that superior publicly available information (fundamental analysis) cannot be used to consistently improve stock selection analysis. In the strong form of the hypothesis, even inside (nonpublic) information is thought to be reflected accurately in prices.

equity • common stock, which provides ownership interest in a firm

equity multiplier • ratio of a firm's total assets to equity. This is a measure of leverage, which can increase earnings but can also increase risk.

equity note • debt security that is automatically converted into stock on a prespecified date at a specific price or one based on a formula that is prespecified (also called mandatory convertible note)

equity REIT • a real estate investment trust that invests in office buildings, apartments, hotels, shopping malls, and other real estate ventures

escrow account • in general, an account designed to hold a sum of money for a specific purpose and in particular, concerning real estate, the fund for monthly deposits of the expected pro rata real estate taxes

Eurobonds • bonds that may be denominated in dollars or some other currency but must be traded internationally. They are denominated in a currency other than that of the country in which they are issued.

Eurodollar deposits • dollar-denominated deposits held in banks based outside the United States, mostly in Europe, but some in Asia and other areas

European option • an option that may be exercised only on its expiration date

ex ante • before the fact—for example, a procedure that identifies attractive investments by relying on prior data and generally facilitates a profitable trading strategy

ex-dividend date • the day after the day of record. Purchases completed on or after the ex-dividend date do not receive that period's dividend even if the stock is held on the payment date.

exercise price • *See* strike price.

expected HPR • the expected return on an investment over the holding period

expected return • the most likely return; typically calculated as the arithmetic average of historical returns over a chosen past period or (with stocks) based on the capital asset pricing model

expiration date • date on which an option expires; in standard stock option contracts, the Saturday following the third Friday of the stated month

ex post • after the fact. An ex post approach to identifying attractive investments would not by itself facilitate a profitable trading strategy because the investments would be identified only after the profit had been made.

ex-rights • without rights attached. Stock trades ex-rights after the date of record for a rights distribution.

face value • the principal amount to be paid upon maturity of a bond or other debt instrument; sometimes referred to as the bond's par value

family of funds • group of mutual funds owned and marketed by the same company

FDIC (Federal Deposit Insurance Corporation) • agency that insures deposits at depository institutions up to $100,000 per depositor

Fed • *See* Federal Reserve System.

federal funds market • the market where banks and other financial institutions borrow and lend immediately deliverable reserve-free funds, usually on a one-day basis

federal funds rate • the interest rate charged between banks in the federal funds market

Federal Open Market Committee (FOMC) • the Federal Reserve Board committee that decides on open market policy (consists of all seven of the Federal Reserve Board governors plus five of the presidents of the regional Fed banks, including the president of the New York bank)

Federal Reserve Board • the governing body of the Federal Reserve System, composed of seven members appointed by the President for long and staggered terms

Federal Reserve System • the federal government agency that exercises monetary policy through its control over banking system reserves (also called the Fed)

FHA (Federal Housing Administration) • a federal government agency that insures home mortgages

fill-or-kill order • a type of security market order that must be canceled unless it can be filled immediately

filter rule • form of technical analysis that advocates buying stock when the price rises by a given percent or selling when the price falls by a certain percent

firm-commitment basis • underwriting in which the underwriter purchases the securities from the issuer and makes a commitment to sell them to the public. Most underwritten securities offerings are firm-commitment offerings.

fiscal multipler • measure of the impact of fiscal policy on the economy. Mathematically, it is 1 divided by the marginal propensity to save. For example, if the marginal propensity to save is 20 percent, a $1 million increase in government spending should result in a $5 million increase in the total amount of consumption.

fiscal policy • government use of taxing and spending to stimulate or restrain the economy

fixed costs • costs that do not vary with the firm's output in the short run

fixed-income security • any security that promises to pay a periodic nonvariable sum, such as a bond paying a fixed coupon amount per period. The term is generally used to describe debt instruments, but it can also describe preferred stock.

flat • the trading of bonds for a price that does not reflect any accrued interest

flight-to-quality effect • the tendency of investors to sell off their positions in risky investments and shift toward less risky investments when disturbing news is disseminated

floating rate preferred • a type of preferred stock whose dividend rate varies with market rates

floating rate security • a type of debt security whose coupon rate varies with market interest rates

floor trader • one holding a seat on an exchange who trades for his or her own account (also called registered competitive market maker [RCMM])

FNMA (Federal National Mortgage Association) • a corporation, now privately owned, that operates a secondary market in mortgages and issues its own debt securities to finance its mortgage portfolio; called "Fannie Mae"

forced conversion • the calling of a convertible security to effectively force the holder to exercise the conversion option

forward contract • a customized, nonstandard contractual agreement to accept delivery (buy) and to deliver (sell) a specified commodity or financial instrument at an agreed-upon price, settlement date, quantity, and location

fourth market • direct trading of listed securities between institutions

Freddie Mac (Federal Home Loan Mortgage Corporation) • a government agency that assembles pools of conventional mortgages and sells participations in a secondary market

front-end loading • charging the load (commission) on a mutual fund at the time of purchase

full employment • the unemployment rate that is thought to be the minimum level before inflationary pressures accelerate. This is the level of unemployment that economists generally consider optimal, because a certain percentage of the workforce is likely to be looking for better jobs at any point in time. Opinions on this level have varied over time from about 4 percent to 6 percent.

fundamental analysis • the evaluation of firms and their investment attractiveness based on the firm's financial strength, competitiveness, earnings outlook, managerial strength, and sensitivity to the macroeconomy and to specific industry effects

futures contract • a standardized deferred-delivery commodities or securities contract or promise to deliver a certain quantity of a commodity or security at a specified price at a specified future date

futures market • regulated exchange in which standardized futures contracts are bought and sold—for example, the Chicago Board of Trade, Chicago Mercantile Exchange, and Commodity Futures Exchange

futures option • a call and put option on a futures contract

future value • the value that a certain amount of money today is expected to have at a specified time in the future. The computation of future value takes into consideration ideas of compounding and the expected rate of return on an investment.

general obligation bond • a municipal bond secured by the issuer's full faith and credit and taxing power

geometric mean return • the value of the compounded per-period average rate of return of a financial asset determined during a specified time

Glass-Steagall Act • a 1933 federal act that required the separation of commercial and investment banking; prevented competition between financial institutions in the banking, insurance, and securities industries and established the framework for federal deposit insurance; repealed in November 1999 by the Gramm-Leach-Bliley Act

GNMA (Government National Mortgage Association) • a government agency that provides special assistance on selected types of home mortgages. Securities are backed both by GNMA (Ginnie Mae) mortgage portfolios and by the general credit of the government.

going long • using a futures contract to agree to make a specified purchase in the future

go public • the process in which a start-up or heretofore private firm sells its shares in a public offering

governments • U.S. government bonds issued by the Treasury Department and backed by the full faith and credit of the federal government

greenmail • the practice of acquiring a large percentage of a firm's stock and attempting to be bought out at a premium by threatening to take over the firm

gross domestic product (GDP) • the sum of market values of all final goods and services produced annually in the economy of a country

growth fund • a common stock mutual fund that seeks price appreciation by concentrating on growth stocks

growth investing • investing in stocks that have above-average P/E ratios and are expected to grow rapidly

growth stock • the shares of a company that is expected to achieve rapid growth (often also has above-average risk and P/E ratio)

GTC (good-'til-canceled) order • type of order that remains in effect until executed or canceled

head-and-shoulders formation • a pattern of stock price trends that looks like a head and shoulders and is believed by some technical analysts to forecast a price decline

hedge fund • a type of mutual fund that seeks to offset some of its long positions with short positions, particularly to offset the effects of exchange-rate risk on foreign assets

hedger • one who makes an investment for the purpose of offsetting risk

hedge ratio • in the Black-Scholes model, that ratio of number of calls written that would exactly offset the stock price movement of a number of shares of the underlying stock held. Any small move in the stock's price would be precisely offset by a change in the value of the option position with such a ratio of number of calls to number of shares of stock, so the investor is theoretically holding the equivalent of a risk-free asset.

hedging • taking opposite positions in related securities to reduce or eliminate an existing risk—for example, purchasing put options on a stock one owns

histogram • a discrete probability distribution display

holding company • a company that is set up to maintain voting control of other business enterprises

holding period return (HPR) • the rate of return over some specific time period

holding period return relative (HPRR) • the end-period value relative to the beginning-of-period value for a specific holding period; that is, the holding period return plus one (1)

horizontal spread • short- and long-option positions on the same security with the same strike price but different expiration dates

hybrid convertible • a bond that is convertible into common stock of a company other than the company that issued the bond; also called an exchangeable debenture

hybrid REIT • a real estate investment trust that is a combination of equity and mortgage investments

immunization • the process of minimizing the interest rate risk on a bond portfolio by maintaining a portfolio with a duration equal to an investor's planning horizon

income approach • approach to valuing real estate as the discounted present value of its expected income stream

income bond • a bond on which interest is paid only if the issuer has sufficient earnings

income fund • a common stock mutual fund that concentrates on stocks that pay high dividends; tends to be more conservative than growth funds

income statement • a financial statement of interim earnings that provides a financial accounting of revenues and expenses during a specified period—that is, 3 months, one year, and so on

indenture (bond) • the contract the company makes to its bondholders, including a commitment to pay a stated coupon amount periodically and return the face value (usually $1,000) at the end of a certain period (such as 20 years after issue). A trustee, such as a bank, is charged with overseeing the issuing firm's commitments.

index arbitrage • a trading strategy involving offsetting positions in stock index futures contracts and the underlying cash market securities (stocks making up the index). If, for example, the index future is priced above the stocks making up the index, the arbitrageur would buy the stocks and sell the index. If, in contrast, the index is priced below its corresponding stocks, the arbitrageur would short the stocks and buy the index.

index fund • a mutual fund that attempts to duplicate the performance of a market index such as the S&P 500

inflation • the rate of increase in the overall price level. For example, if on the average, $1.06 will buy what $1 would buy a year earlier, inflation is 6 percent.

inflation expectations • expectations about future inflation rates. The required return (market interest rate) on long-term debt instruments reflects not only the rate of inflation at the time of issue but also collective expectations about future inflation rates over the time the debt is outstanding.

inflation hedge • an asset whose value varies directly with the price level

initial public offering (IPO) • the offering to the public of securities in a firm that previously was privately held. *See also* go public.

insider trading • the buying or selling by investors with access to material nonpublic information relating to the company in question. This practice is illegal.

interest rate futures • a futures contract calling for delivery of a debt security, such as a Treasury bill or long-term government bond. Because the value of debt securities varies inversely with market interest rates, people can speculate on interest rate changes by trading futures contracts on debt securities.

interest rate option • an option to buy or sell government securities

interest rate risk • the risk that an interest rate rise will take place, thereby reducing the market value of fixed-income securities, or that interest rates will fall, reducing the return from reinvesting the periodic coupon interest payments

international fund • a mutual fund that invests in securities of firms based outside the fund's home country

in-the-money • when an option's strike price is more favorable to option holders than the current market price of the underlying security: for calls, when the current stock price is higher than the strike price; for puts, when the current stock price is lower than the strike price. In other words, when one can profit by exercising the option immediately, the option is in-the-money.

intraday dependencies • nonrandom price movements of transactions taking place over the course of a single day

intrinsic value (call, right, warrant) • the price of the associated stock less the strike price of the option, or zero if the difference is negative. *See* in-the-money and out-of-the money.

intrinsic value (option) • amount of money one can make by exercising the option immediately

intrinsic value (put) • the strike price of a put less the price of the associated stock, or zero if the difference is negative

intrinsic value (stock) • the underlying value that a careful evaluation would produce; generally takes into account both the going-concern value and the liquidation or breakup value of the company. An efficient market would always price stocks at their intrinsic values; an inefficient market would not necessarily do so. Under the dividend discount model, the intrinsic value of stock is the present value of the stock's expected future dividends, discounted at the stock's required rate of return.

inventory turnover ratio • the ratio of the cost of goods sold to average yearly inventory

inverted yield curve • a yield curve showing short-term interest rates higher than long-term rates, reflected by a downward sloping yield curve. This reflects an expectation that interest rates are likely to decline in the future.

investment banker • a firm that organizes a syndicate to underwrite or market a new issue of securities

investment company • a company that manages pooled portfolios for a group of owners. The company may be either a closed-end company with a fixed number of shares outstanding, or it can be an open-end company (mutual fund), whose shares are bought and sold by the fund.

investment-grade bonds • relatively high-quality corporate bonds. Investment-grade bonds have a very low risk of default.

January indicator (January effect) • an anomaly detected in past studies of stock market performance that indicates that buying in the small-cap stock market in January tends to produce above-normal returns

Jensen's alpha • a measure of portfolio performance; the difference between the actual return to a portfolio and the return that would have been expected, based on the capital asset pricing model. *See also* alpha.

junk bonds • high-risk bonds that usually promise a high coupon rate but have some risk of default

Keynesian • one who believes in the efficacy of fiscal policy (government spending and taxing) for correcting problems of unemployment and inflation

leading indicators • economic factors whose changes tend to precede turns in the overall economy

leakages • money that becomes absorbed by savings, import purchases, or taxes during each round of stimulatory spending or tax reduction, thus reducing the impact of fiscal policy

LEAPS® (long-term equity anticipation securities) • long-term (expiring in 2 to 5 years, in contrast to 2 near-term and 2 farther away months as with most equity options) equity options that are traded on U.S. exchanges and over-the-counter

lettered stock • newly issued stock sold at a discount to large investors in a private placement prior to a public offering of the same issue. This is also known as restricted stock. In accordance with SEC Rule 144, buyers agree not to sell their shares for a prespecified period.

leverage • using borrowed funds or special types of securities (warrants, calls) to increase the potential return (usually increases both risk and expected return)

limited partnership • a form of business organization that is used by investors in projects that have a finite life and that involve a limited liability partnership as the form of organization. This form of organization has the advantage of being taxed as a partnership, rather than as a corporation, yet, like a corporation, the liability of limited partners generally consists only of their initial investment.

limit order • an order to buy or sell at a prespecified price

liquid assets • assets that can quickly be converted into cash, such as marketable securities or receivables

liquidation • the process of selling all of a firm's assets and distributing the proceeds first to creditors and then the remainder, if any, to shareholders

liquidity • the ease with which an investment can be converted to cash

liquidity preference hypothesis • the term structure hypothesis that asserts that most borrowers prefer to borrow long-term and most lenders prefer to lend short-term (implies that long-term rates generally exceed short-term rates)

liquidity ratio • a ratio (for example, current ratio or quick ratio) of a firm's short-run financial situation that is a measure of the firm's ability to meet short-term obligations

load • the selling fee applied to a mutual fund purchase, similar to a commission

load fund • a type of mutual fund sold through agents who receive commissions

long transaction • contract to make a purchase in the future. *See also* going long.

low-P/E stocks • stocks with low price-earnings ratios. Such stocks tend to be sought out by value-oriented investors.

low-price effect • an alleged anomaly to the efficient market hypothesis that is characterized by the tendency for low-priced stocks to earn above-normal returns

LYON • a complicated type of zero coupon convertible debt security that is both callable and redeemable at prices that escalate through time

M1 • the basic money supply that includes checking deposits and cash held by the public

M2 • a broader-based money supply definition than Ml that includes everything in M1 plus most savings and money market deposit accounts

M3 • a still broader-based money supply definition than M2 that includes everything in M2 plus large certificates of deposit and money market mutual funds sold to institutions

macroeconomic analysis • an analysis of the overall economy, often performed prior to evaluating the prospects for individual firms

maintenance margin percentage • the minimum percentage of equity that an ongoing margin account is required to maintain at all times

management expense ratio • a mutual fund's operating expenses divided by its total assets

manufactured (synthetic) call • a call-like position generated by a combination put and long position in the underlying stock; position with a similar payoff matrix to a call

manufactured (synthetic) put • a put-like position generated by a combination of a call and short position in the underlying stock; position with a similar payoff matrix to a put

margin account • brokerage account partially funded with money borrowed from the brokerage firm; regulated by the Fed. For example, if a 60 percent margin rate is set, $10,000 worth of stock may be purchased with up to $4,000 of borrowed money. Only securities of listed and some large OTC companies qualify for margin loans.

marginal tax rate • the percentage that must be paid in taxes on the last income increment

marketability • the ease with which an investment can be bought or sold without appreciably affecting its price. For example, blue chip stocks are usually highly marketable because they are actively traded.

marketable assets • assets that can be quickly converted to cash without loss of value

market approach • approach to real estate valuation that considers the market price of comparable properties

market maker • one who creates a market for a security by quoting a bid and ask price

market order • an order to buy or sell at the market price that requires immediate execution

market portfolio • a hypothetical portfolio representing each investment asset in proportion to its relative weight in the universe of investment assets

market risk • the return variability associated with general market movements and not diversifiable within the market (also called systematic risk)

market segmentation hypothesis • the theory that there are separate markets for bonds of different maturities, so the interest rates on bonds of one maturity should not be affected by the interest rates on bonds of another maturity

market timing • the effort by portfolio managers to time their allocations of funds in the market as among, say, stocks, bonds, and money market funds to take advantage of perceived differential expected performance among the different assets (asset classes)

mark to the market • to recompute the value of the equity position on a daily basis. This is done to make certain that, as securities prices fluctuate, the amount held in a margin or escrow account remains sufficient to meet minimum requirements. Brokerage firms mark to the market to reduce the risk that a client might default.

married put • a put option held by an investor who also owns the underlying security

master limited partnership (MLP) • a method of organizing a business that combines some of the advantages of a corporation with some of the advantages of a limited partnership.

Shares of ownership trade much like corporate stock, yet the MLP is taxed like a partnership; that is, profits are imputed to the owners and taxed only once.

maturity • the length of time until a debt security must be redeemed by its issuer

May Day • May 1, 1975, the day on which brokerage commission rates were first deregulated and became established by competition among firms

mean • the average or expected value of a sample or distribution

mean absolute deviation • measure of average dispersion from mean

mean absolute return • the average dispersion between each observed return and the average (mean) return

mean return • the average return of a sample distribution of returns

mean reversion • the tendency of an average return to revert to the mean (average) return in the market as the sample size or sample period grows larger

modern portfolio theory (MPT) • *See* portfolio theory.

modified duration • an adjusted measure of duration used to estimate a bond's interest rate sensitivity

momentum • tendency for movement to continue in the same direction, such as a rising trend in stock prices

monetarist • one who emphasizes the economic role of monetary (as opposed to fiscal) policy

monetary policy • government policy that utilizes the money supply to affect the economy and that is implemented by the Fed through its control of required reserves and through open market operations

money market • the market for high-quality, short-term securities, such as CDs, commercial paper, acceptances, Treasury bills, short-term tax-exempt notes, and Eurodollar loans

money market deposit account • a type of bank or thrift institution account that offers unregulated money market rates, requires a minimum deposit of $1,000 (many banks require $2,500), and limits withdrawals to six per month, only three of which may be by check

money market mutual fund • a mutual fund that invests in short-term, highly liquid securities (also called money fund)

money multiplier • the ratio of a change in open market operations by the Federal Reserve Board to the change in the money supply. Thus, a money multiplier of five would imply that a $1 billion purchase by the Fed would result in a $5 billion increase in the money supply.

money supply • generally defined as the sum of all coin, currency (outside bank holdings), and deposits on which check-like instruments may be written. *See* M1.

Moody's Investors Service • a firm that rates bonds and publishes manuals containing extensive historical data on a large number of publicly traded firms

moral hazard • a firm's or individual's incurrance of risks whose full costs are avoided by that firm or individual. In general, a moral hazard is a situation that provides incentives to take inappropriate action, generally in the nature of unnecessary risks. For example, some have argued that deposit insurance gives banks an incentive to make riskier loans than they otherwise would.

mortgage • a loan collateralized by property, particularly real estate. The lender is entitled to take possession of the property if the debt is not repaid in a timely manner.

mortgage-backed security • a debt instrument representing a share of ownership in a pool of mortgages (for example, GNMA pass-throughs) or backed by a pool of mortgages (for example, FNMA bonds)

mortgage bond • debt security for which specific property is pledged as collateral

mortgage REIT • a real estate investment trust that consists of a diversified portfolio of construction loans and/or mortgage loans

moving average • average amount over a specified period of time (for example, average daily stock price over previous 60 days). This average will change over time.

municipal bond • tax-free bond issued by state or local government

municipal bond fund • a mutual fund holding a portfolio of municipal bonds

mutual fund • a diversified portfolio of securities owned by investors, allowing them to indirectly invest in a large number of securities

naked call • a call option written by an investor who does not own the underlying asset. This is very risky, because the call writer is obligated to purchase the asset if the call is exercised, and there is no limit to how high the asset's market price might rise.

NASDAQ (National Association of Securities Dealers Automated Quotations) • an automated information system that provides brokers and dealers with price quotations on securities that are traded over-the-counter

National Bureau of Economic Research • a private nonprofit research foundation that tracks business cycles and sponsors economic research

neglected-firm effect • *See* analyst neglect.

net asset value (NAV) • the per-share market value of a mutual fund's portfolio; total net assets of the fund divided by number of shares outstanding

net equity • with respect to a margin account, the total value of the account minus the amount of debt outstanding

net profit margin (NPM) • net income divided by total revenue. This financial ratio is a measure of a firm's profitability.

NMI (national market issues) • selected NASDAQ securities that represent the largest firms listed on the quotation system

no-load fund • a mutual fund for which no agent or sales fee is involved

nominal rate • the stated interest rate on a bond or other debt instrument

nonmarket risk • risk not related to general market movements. This risk is diversifiable. The total risk of an investment may be decomposed into that associated with the market and that which is not (also called nonsystematic risk).

normal distribution • a distribution corresponding to the shape of the normal (bell) curve

note • intermediate-term debt security issued with maturity dates of one to 5 years

NYSE (New York Stock Exchange) • the largest organized stock exchange based on Wall Street in New York City. Stocks listed tend to be large- to mid-capitalization stocks. *See also* Big Board.

odd lot • fewer than 100 shares of stock. Because commissions as a percentage of the purchase on sales tend to be higher with odd lots, it is generally believed that only unsophisticated investors engage in odd-lot transactions.

odd-lot activity • measure of the amount of odd-lot purchases or sales; said to reflect activity by less sophisticated investors

odd-lot short ratio • a technical market indicator based on relative short trading by small investors. When such trading is heavy, the market is said to be near a bottom.

open-end investment company • a mutual fund or other pooled portfolio of investments that stands ready to buy or sell its shares at their NAV (or NAV plus load if the fund has a load)

open market operations • Federal Reserve transactions (buying and selling) in the government bond market that are intended to influence the money supply, interest rates, and economic activity

open outcry • organization of futures trading on the futures exchanges in which traders shout their desire to buy (sell) a contract, often using hand and finger signals

opportunity cost • implicit cost of an activity or course of conduct, based on forgone opportunities. For example, the opportunity cost to an investor of carefully studying a company before making an investment decision is the income that could have been earned during the time the investor spent studying that company.

option • a security giving the holder the choice as to whether or not to purchase or sell a security at a set price for a specific period

option price (premium) • the price one pays to purchase an option

Options Clearing Corporation (OCC) • the clearing house for listed options that facilitates options trading by guaranteeing execution of trades between options brokers and traders

OTC (over-the-counter) • the market in unlisted securities and off-board trading in listed securities

out-of-the-money • when an option's strike price is less attractive than the current market price of its underlying stock; for calls, when the current stock price is lower than the strike price; for puts, when the current stock price is above the strike price. Such an option has no intrinsic value, but it has time value based on potential stock price movements prior to the option's expiration. In other words, one cannot profit from exercising an out-of-the-money option.

par (value) • the face value at which a bond matures

participating preferred stock • preferred stock that may pay an extra dividend increment in years in which the issuing firm is especially profitable

par value (preferred stock) • the value on which the security's dividend and liquidation value is based

pass-through • a share of a mortgage pool whose interest and principal payments are flowed through to the holders

payout ratio • dividends per share as a percentage of earnings per share

P/E ratio • *See* price-earnings ratio.

P/E ratio model • a model designed to use P/E ratios to identify undervalued or overvalued stocks

per-period return (PPR) • the return earned for a particular period (for example, an annual return)

pink sheets • quotation source for most publicly traded OTC issues

planning horizon (portfolio management) • the time frame in which a portfolio is managed that reflects the length of time before the funds are expected to be needed to meet projected expenses

point (real estate) • one percent of the amount of a mortgage

point-and-figure chart • a technical chart that has no time dimension. An x is used to designate an upward price movement of a certain magnitude, while an o denotes a similar size down move. The x's are stacked on top of each other as long as the direction of movement remains up. A new column is begun when direction changes. Technical analysts attempt to use these charts to predict future price movements.

Ponzi scheme • an investment scam promising high returns that are secretly paid out of investor capital; usually exposed when incoming funds are insufficient to cover promised outpayments. The scam depends on fresh investor capital to pay its promised return. This is also known as a pyramid scheme.

portfolio insurance • a service in which the "insurer" endeavors to place a floor on the value of the "insured" portfolio. If the portfolio value falls to a prespecified level, the insurer neutralizes it against a further fall by purchasing an appropriate number of index puts or selling an appropriate number of index options.

portfolio theory • the combination of the capital asset pricing model (CAPM), efficient market hypothesis (EMH), and related theoretical models of security market pricing and performance. The emphasis is on the importance of diversification.

portfolio variance • a statistical parameter that measures portfolio risk by quantifying the dispersion from the portfolio's average (mean) value

position trader • a commodity trader who takes and holds futures positions for several days or more

posts • 18 horseshoe-shaped locations on the NYSE floor where securities are traded

preferred habitat hypothesis • one of four hypotheses for explaining the term structure of interest rates based on the idea of a tendency for borrowers and lenders to gravitate toward their preferred loan lengths

preferred stock • shares whose indicated dividends and liquidation values must be paid before common shareholders receive any dividends or liquidation payments. Unlike common stock, the amount of preferred dividends is fixed and specified upon issue.

premium (bond) • the amount by which a bond's price exceeds its par or face value

premium (option) • the market price of an option

premium over conversion value • the amount by which a convertible bond's price exceeds its conversion value

premium over straight-debt value • the amount by which a convertible bond's price exceeds its value as a nonconvertible debt security, based on the discounted present value of its cash flows (periodic interest payments and face value at maturity)

prepayment penalty • the fee assessed for early liquidation of an outstanding debt

present value • the value of an expected future sum or sums discounted by the appropriate interest rate or discount rate, which reflects both the risk-free interest rate and an appropriate risk premium

price-earnings ratio • the share price of a stock divided by its actual or anticipated earnings per share. For trailing earnings, the P/E ratio is the stock price relative to the most recent 12-month earnings per share; for ex ante earnings, it is the stock price relative to the next 12-month expected earnings.

price risk • the risk of a bond's price changing in response to future interest rate changes. If rates increase after a bond is purchased, the price for the bond in the secondary market would be below expectations, whereas if rates decrease, the price would be above expectations. Because the direction of future interest rates is unknown, there is uncertainty about the bond's future price.

price stability • the absence or low level of inflation or deflation. While the prices of specific goods would still fluctuate in response to market forces (supply and demand changes), the overall level of prices would be stable.

primary distribution • the initial sale of a stock or bond (new issue)

primary market • the market for initial offerings of securities

prime rate • the borrowing rate that banks advertise as available to their least risky borrowers

principal (of a bond) • the face value of a bond

private placement • a direct sale of securities to a small number of large buyers without the registration requirements of a public offering. There are legal restrictions on who may purchase and on the resale of securities purchased in a private placement.

probability distribution • a distribution of possible outcomes along with their associated probabilities. For example, a normal curve represents a fairly common type of probability distribution.

profit • revenues minus expenses

profitability ratio • a ratio, such as return on sales, that reflects the firm's profit rates

profit and loss statement • *See* income statement.

program trading • a type of mechanical trading in large blocks by institutional investors that usually involves both stock and index futures contracts as, for example, in index arbitrage or portfolio insurance (also called programmed trading)

prospectus • an official document that all companies offering new securities for public sale must file with the SEC. It spells out in detail the financial position of the offering company, what the new funds will be used for, the qualifications of the corporate officers, risk factors, nature of competition, and any other material information.

proxy • a shareholder ballot

proxy material • a statement of relevant information that the firm must supply to shareholders when they solicit proxies

public offering • a security sale made to the general public and registered with the Securities and Exchange Commission

purchasing power risk • the risk that because of increased inflation, expected future cash flows, such as the repayment of the principal of a bond at maturity, will not purchase as much as expected. This is similar to price risk, because increases in the inflation rate also increase the discount rate and lower the market value of outstanding bonds.

pure risk • risk that involves only the chance of loss but no chance of gain

pure risk premium • the portion of the expected yield above the riskless rate that is due to pure risk aversion, as opposed to the expected default loss. In other words, the risk premium represents compensation to investors for the discomfort associated with uncertainty about future cash flows from an investment.

put • an option to sell an asset at a specified price over a specified period

put-call parity • a theoretical relation between the value of a put and a call on the same underlying security with the same strike and expiration date

quarterly earnings • profits, usually per-share profits, for a 3-month period

quick ratio • current assets other than inventory divided by current liabilities. *See also* acid test ratio.

raider • an outside party that seeks to take over a company against the wishes of that company's management

random walk • the random motion of stock prices that are as likely to move in one direction as another, regardless of past price behavior. This type of behavior is called Brownian motion in the physical sciences. It is consistent with the weak form of the efficient market hypothesis (EMH), because if stock prices change randomly, past price movements cannot be used to predict future price movements.

rate of return • a rate that takes into account both dividends and capital appreciation (increases in the price of the security)

rating (bond) • a quality or risk evaluation assigned by a rating agency such as Standard & Poor's or Moody's

ratio analysis • balance sheet and income statement analysis that utilizes ratios of financial aggregates to assess a company's financial position, usually by looking for trends in financial ratios, by comparing a company's financial ratios with the industry average, or both

RCMM (registered competitive market maker) • one who holds a seat on an exchange and trades for his or her own account. *See also* floor trader.

real estate investment trust (REIT) • closed-end investment company that buys and/or manages rental properties and/or real estate mortgages and pays out more than 95 percent of its income as dividends

real interest rate • risk-free interest rate adjusted for inflation. *See also* real return.

real return • a return on an investment adjusted for changes in the price level. For example, if the nominal rate of return is 7 percent, a 3 percent inflation rate reduces the real return to 4 percent. This amount equals the increase in purchasing power resulting from saving or investing money.

real risk-free rate • risk-free interest rate minus the inflation rate. This represents the compensation, in terms of purchasing power, that one receives for delaying consumption and investing the money instead.

record date • the shareholder registration date that determines the recipients of that period's dividends

redemption price • *See* call price.

refinancing • selling new securities to finance the retirement of others that are maturing or being called

regional exchange • a U.S. stock exchange located outside New York City

registered representative • an employee of a registered brokerage firm who is qualified to serve as an account executive for the firm's customers, sometimes called a broker

registration statement • a statement that must be filed with the SEC before a security is offered for sale and that must contain all materially relevant information relating to the offering. A similar type of statement is required when a firm's shares are listed; it generally contains more detailed information than the prospectus.

reinvestment rate risk • the risk associated with reinvesting coupon payments at unknown future interest rates. The yield to maturity (YTM) is generally computed on the assumption that coupons will be reinvested at the same rate as the bond's current YTM. If rates decrease after a bond is purchased, the coupon payments will be reinvested at rates below the computed YTM and the return will be below expectations, whereas if rates increase, the coupon payments will be reinvested at rates above expectations. Because the direction of future rates is unknown, there is uncertainty about the rates at which coupon payments will be reinvested.

relative strength • a technical analysis concept based on an assumption that stocks that have risen relative to the market exhibit relative strength, which tends to carry them to still higher levels.

RELP (real estate limited partnership) • a type of investment organized as a limited partnership that invests directly in real estate properties

replacement cost approach • the valuing of real estate or other assets on the basis of the cost of producing equivalent assets (also called cost approach)

repurchase agreement (repo) • a type of investment in which a security is sold with a prearranged purchase price and the date is designed to produce a particular yield—in fact, an indirect form of borrowing

required rate of return • the rate of return on an investment required by the market to justify the degree of risk incurred; the risk-free rate plus the risk premium. Using portfolio theory, it is the rate of return determined by the capital asset pricing model, which incorporates the relationship between market risk and return. The required rate of return is also the discount rate. In equilibrium (quantity supplied equals quantity demanded), the required rate of return is equal to the expected rate of return.

reserve requirement • the percentage of reserves the Fed requires each bank to have on deposit for each increment of demand or time deposits

resistance level • a price range that, according to technical analysis, tends to block further price rises or declines

retained earnings • after-tax profits less dividends paid

return on assets (ROA) • profits before interest and taxes as a percentage of total assets

return on equity (ROE) • net income after taxes, interest, and preferred dividends, as a percentage of common equity

return on sales • profits as a percentage of sales (also called markup)

revenue bond • a municipal bond backed only by the revenues of the project that it finances

reward to variability (RVAR) • *See* Sharpe ratio.

reward to volatility (RVOL) • *See* Treynor ratio.

riding the yield curve • a bond portfolio management strategy of taking advantage of an upward-sloping yield curve by purchasing intermediate-term bonds and then selling them as they approach maturity

rights • securities allowing shareholders to acquire new stock at a prespecified price over a prespecified period, generally issued in proportion to the number of shares currently held and exercisable at a price that is usually below the current market price. The new shares offered are usually made available from the firm's treasury stock. Rights generally trade in a secondary market after they are issued. Rights bear some similarity to call options, except they are issued by the same company that issued the underlying stock.

rights offering • an offering of rights by a firm wishing to raise additional equity capital while avoiding dilution of existing shareholders' relative ownership

risk • the dispersion of possible returns from the expected return; that is, the degree of uncertainty associated with the investment

risk-adjusted return • the return from an asset adjusted for the degree of market risk associated with the asset. Using the capital asset pricing model, this return is equal to the risk-free-rate + beta x (market return – risk-free rate).

risk averse • the characteristic of preferring certainty and demonstrating a willingness to trade upside potential for relative certainty

risk aversion • the degree of preference for less risky investments, even if they have somewhat lower expected returns

risk-expected return trade-off • tendency for more risky assets to be priced to yield higher expected returns

risk-free rate • the interest rate on a riskless investment, such as a Treasury bill

riskless hedge • a hedge position without risk due to exactly offsetting returns in both directions of price movement of the associated underlying security(ies)

risk neutrality • the characteristic of preferring the highest expected return with indifference to risk

risk premium • the expected return in excess of the risk-free rate that is compensation for the investment's risk

round lot • the basic unit in which securities are traded, consisting usually of 100 shares

round-trip fee • the total commission costs of executing a transaction in the futures market paid at the time of the contract's formation

Rule 144 • an SEC rule restricting the resale of lettered stock

Rule 390 • a NYSE rule (repealed in 1999) restricting members from off-board trading (not on an exchange)

Rule 415 • an SEC rule allowing shelf registration of a security that may then be sold frequently over a 2-year period without separate registrations of each part

run • an uninterrupted series of price increases or decreases

savings bond • low-denomination Treasury issue designed to appeal to small investors

screening • data-analysis technique commonly used by stock market analysts to screen out (or screen in) certain stocks on the basis of their achievement of various numerical or technical criteria—for example, "Pick all stocks that rose more than 15 percent last year and whose P/E ratios are below 20."

secondary distribution • a large public securities offering made outside the usual exchange or OTC market. Those making the offering wish to sell a larger quantity of the security than they believe can be easily absorbed by the market's usual channels. A secondary offering spreads out the period for absorption.

secondary market • the market for already issued securities that may take place on the exchanges or OTC

sector fund • a type of mutual fund that specializes in a particular segment of the market—for example, an industry (chemicals), region (Sunbelt), or category (small capitalization)

Securities Act of 1933 • securities law dealing with the issuance of securities, addressing the registration process, disclosure requirements, and related matters

Securities and Exchange Commission (SEC) • the federal government agency with direct regulatory authority over the securities industry

Securities Exchange Act of 1934 • securities law dealing with existing securities, addressing the filing of periodic reports, the regulation of exchanges and brokerage firms, ongoing disclosure requirements, and prohibiting certain unethical practices, such as market manipulation and insider trading

securitization • the process of turning an asset with poor marketability into a security with substantially greater acceptability—for example, a security that looks like a standard bond but is derived from real estate mortgage loans, auto loans, or credit card balances

security market line • the theoretical relationship between a security's market risk and its expected return under the capital asset pricing model. The equation form is as follows: $r_i = r_f + \beta_i (r_M - r_f)$ where r_i is security i's risk-adjusted expected return, r_f is the risk-free return, β_i is the beta measure for security i, and r_M is the market return.

segmented markets hypothesis • a theory that explains the term structure of interest rates as resulting from separate markets for debt instruments with different maturities

seller financing • a procedure in which the real estate seller arranges for the loan or loans some or all of the purchase price directly to the purchaser

selling short • the act of borrowing and selling a security that belongs to someone else. The short seller covers by buying back equivalent securities and restoring them to the original owner.

semistrong form EMH • the view that market prices quickly and accurately reflect all public information, suggesting that fundamental analysis applied to publicly available information and data cannot systematically yield superior returns

semivariance • a measure of dispersion below the mean. By contrast, variance and standard deviation measure dispersion both above and below the mean.

senior debt • debt that has priority over other (subordinate) debt

separation theorem • the argument (set forth by James Tobin) that the return to any efficient portfolio and its risk can be completely described by an appropriate weighted average of two separate parts: the risk-free rate and the return to the market portfolio. In general, the idea is that there are two separate decisions: what risky investments to include in the market portfolio, and how one should divide one's money between the market portfolio and risk-free asset.

serial bond • a bond issue in which portions mature at stated intervals rather than all at once

settlement • the cash settlement of an exercised option or future

Sharpe ratio • a measure of risk-adjusted performance of an asset, calculated as the ratio of the asset's rate of return minus the risk-free rate divided by the asset's standard deviation. The Sharpe ratio takes all risk into account.

shelf registration • an SEC provision allowing preregistration of an amount of a security to be sold over a 2-year period without specific registration of each sale (permitted by SEC Rule 415)

short interest (stocks) • the number of shares sold short; sometimes used as a technical market indicator of an anticipated market decline (if short interest is believed to reflect well-founded professional traders' opinions) or as an indicator of anticipated market rise (if covering of short interest is expected)

short selling • selling an asset that is not owned with a commitment to purchase the asset in the future

short transaction • entering into a contractual agreement to sell an asset in the future at a specified price; the purchase or sale of a short position

sinking fund • a fund to which a borrowing company makes periodic contributions to ensure that the principal amount of its bond indebtedness will be repaid when due

SIPC (Securities Investor Protection Corporation) • a federal government agency that guarantees the safety of brokerage accounts up to $500,000, no more than $100,000 of which may be in cash

skewed distribution • a nonsymmetrical statistical distribution that is spread out more on one side of its mode than the other; a nonnormal distribution

skewness • the degree to which a distribution is skewed

small firm effect • a possible anomaly to the efficient market hypothesis characterized by the tendency for small firms to earn above-normal rates of return after risk is taken into account

social responsibility fund • a type of mutual fund that avoids investments in allegedly socially undesirable companies, such as those involved with tobacco, alcohol, pollution, armaments, and so forth

specialist • an exchange member who makes a market in listed securities

special offering • a large block of stock offered for sale on an exchange with special incentive fees paid to purchasing brokers (also called spot secondary)

speculating • the act of committing funds for a short period at high risk in the hope of realizing a large gain

speculative bubble • large increase in stock prices that can best be explained by emotional, rather than rational, investor behavior

speculative risk • risk associated with speculation in which there is some chance of a gain and some chance of a loss

speculator • one who engages in risky transactions in the hope of a large return

spot (cash) market • the market for immediate delivery of some commodity, such as wheat or silver

spread (bid-ask) • the difference between the bid and the ask price

spread (options) • purchasing an option and writing an option on the same security with different expiration dates or exercise prices

spreading • creating a combination trade, such as both a long and a short position in the futures market

Standard & Poor's (S&P) Corporation • an important firm in the investment area that rates bonds, collects and reports data, and computes market indexes

standard deviation • a measure of the degree of dispersion of a distribution. As such, the standard deviation is a measure of uncertainty, or risk. About two times out of three, the actual value will be within one standard deviation on either side of the mean value. About 19 out of 20 times, it will be within two standard deviations. One standard deviation is the square root of the variance. *See* variance.

statement of changes in financial position • financial statement showing cash flows into and out of a firm during the reporting period—formerly known as sources and uses of funds statement

stock certificate • document showing ownership of a specified number of shares of a company's stock

stock index option • option on the value of a stock index

stock market index futures • a futures contract on a stock index that does not require delivery of the underlying stock index but is instead settled in dollars according to the difference between the strike price and the actual price of the index

stock market overreaction • an analyst term used to describe the alleged tendency for the stock market to react more than is warranted to news, whether good or bad

stock split • the division of a company's existing stock into more shares (say, 2 for 1, or 3 for 1), usually reducing the price per share in the hope of improving marketability

stop-limit order • an order to implement a limit order when the market price reaches a certain level

stop-loss order • an order to sell or buy at market when a certain price is reached

straddle • a combination put and call option on the same stock at the same strike price

straight bond • bond that has no conversion feature

straight-debt value • the value of a convertible bond as a straight-debt (nonconvertible) bond, based on discounted present value of cash flows

street name • securities held in customer accounts at brokerage houses but registered in the firm's name

strike price • the price at which the option holder can exercise the option to buy (call) or sell (put) shares

strip bond • a coupon bond (with its coupons removed) that returns only principal at maturity and thus is equivalent to a zero-coupon bond

strong form EMH • the view that market prices quickly and accurately reflect all public and nonpublic information (suggests that even inside information will not consistently result in superior returns)

subordination • giving a bond issue a lower priority than other (senior) bond issues

SuperDOT • *See* DOT (designated order transmission).

support level • a floor price that, according to technical analysis, tends to restrict downside price moves

systematic risk • *See* market risk.

taxable income • income on which an individual or corporation is taxed

tax-equivalent yield • the yield on state and local debt instruments after adjustment for the fact that the debt holder is not liable for federal income tax; calculated as $r_t = r_{s\&l}/(1-t)$ where r_t is tax-equivalent yield, $r_{s\&l}$ is nominal yield on state and local debt, and t is the investor's marginal federal tax rate

tax-loss trading • selling a security at the end of the year to establish a capital loss for tax reporting purposes

tax swap • a type of bond swap in which an issue is sold to yield a tax loss and replaced with an equivalent issue

technical analysis • a method of evaluating securities and forecasting future price changes based only on past price and volume behavior

technical default • a technical violation of a bond indenture provision, such as failure to maintain certain financial ratios at a particular point in time. While this technically constitutes a default, it is much less severe than an actual default, such as failure to make an interest payment when due.

technical market indicator • a data series or combination of data series said to be helpful in forecasting the market's future direction (market indicator)

tender offer • an offer to purchase a large block of securities made outside the general market (exchanges, OTC) in which the securities are traded (often as part of an effort to take over a company)

term structure (of interest rates) • a pattern of yields of bonds of differing maturities (risk controlled). *See also* segmented markets hypothesis, unbiased expectations hypothesis, liquidity preference hypothesis, and preferred habitat hypothesis.

term to maturity • the length of time to maturity of a debt instrument

third market • the over-the-counter trading of exchange-listed securities

thrift institutions • institutions other than commercial banks that accept savings deposits, especially savings and loan associations, mutual savings banks, and credit unions

tight money • restrictive monetary policy

times-interest-earned ratio • before-tax, before-interest profit (net operating income) divided by interest expense (a ratio used to detect possible risk of default)

time value (option) • the excess of an option's market price over its intrinsic value

time value (present value) • the value at the present time of (expected) future cash flows, using a discount rate that includes a risk premium, if appropriate

Treasury bill (T-bill) • government short-term debt security issued by the U.S. Treasury

Treynor ratio • a measure of risk-adjusted performance of an asset calculated as the ratio of the asset's rate of return minus the risk-free rate divided by the asset's beta; sometimes called the reward to volatility ratio. Unlike the Sharpe ratio, this ratio takes only market risk into account.

trustee • a bank or other third party that administers the provisions of a bond indenture or that, in general, holds property for the benefit of others

two-name paper • a debt instrument, such as a banker's acceptance, that is issued by one source (for example, a corporation) and guaranteed by another (generally a bank)

unbiased expectations hypothesis • a theory explaining the term structure of interest rates as reflecting the market consensus expectation of future interest rate changes

uncertain information hypothesis • the hypothesis that uncertain information will tend to make investors perceive a higher risk to the firm. Even though the information itself may be positive, the net effect on the firm's stock may be negative due to increased risk perception.

underwrite • to agree to buy all or part of a new security issue, with the intention to sell the securities to the public at a higher price

underwriter • an investment dealer who agrees to buy all or part of a new security issue for resale to the public

unemployment rate • the percentage of the workforce that is actually out of work and actively seeking employment

unit investment trust • a self-liquidating unmanaged portfolio in which investors own shares; a concept similar to a closed-end fund but with a specified liquidation date

uptick • a transaction that takes place at a higher price than the immediately preceding transaction

VA (Veterans Administration) • government agency that provides a variety of services for veterans and their dependents, including the guarantee of repayment of certain home mortgages

valuation • determining the value of an investment as the discounted present value of all expected future cash flows

value investing • assembling a portfolio of stocks that sell at low prices relative to their underlying values, such as their earnings, cash flows, book values, breakup values, and liquid assets

variable annuity • an annuity whose payment is tied to a benchmark, such as a stock market index

variance • a measure of uncertainty or risk; the expected (average) value of the square of the dispersion from the mean: variance of $X = E(X - \overline{X})^2$ where $\overline{X}$ is the mean of X, and E is the expected value

venture capital • risk capital extended to start-up companies or small going concerns that usually requires an ownership interest, as distinct from a pure loan

versus purchase • sale that specifies the purchase date of securities to be delivered for sale

warrants • certificates offering the right to purchase stock in a company at a specified price over a specified period. Unlike options, warrants are issued by the same company that issues the underlying stock and generally have several years until expiration when first issued.

weak form EMH • the view that past stock price return movements cannot be used to predict future price changes; implies that technical analysis cannot consistently provide superior returns

World Equity Benchmark Shares (WEBS) • index funds that replicate the stock market of a particular foreign country

writer (of an option) • one who sells a put or call option and is therefore obligated to make the agreed-upon purchase or sale if the holder chooses to exercise the option

yield • the return of an investment expressed as a percentage of its market value

yield curve • a graphic representation of the term structure of interest rates, or the relationship between yield to maturity and term to maturity (or duration) for equivalent-risk debt securities

yield to earliest call • the holding period return with the assumption that the bond will be called as soon as the no-call provision expires

yield to maturity • a measure of bond yield that takes into account capital gain or loss, as well as coupon interest payments; the discount rate that would make the present value of the bond's cash flows (interest payments plus face value at maturity) equal the purchase price of the bond

zero-coupon bond • a bond issued at a discount that matures at its face value and makes no interest payments prior to maturity

zero growth model • variation of the constant growth model in which the growth rate is zero. This model describes preferred stock and other perpetuities.

zero sum game • situation in which total gains equal total losses

zero sum market • a market such as the derivatives and futures markets where the net gains and losses of buyers and sellers sum to zero after all transactions and expirations of contracts. Also, for each long position, there must be a corresponding short position, which means that the net gains and losses for both parties sum to zero.

Answers to Review Questions and Self-Test Questions

Chapter 1

Answers to Review Questions, pp. 27–28

1-1. *Return* is the gain or loss in value that results from an investment. When we are looking to the future, we are likely speaking of expected return. An expected return is considered to be the most likely outcome or ending value. The range of other possible returns represents risk, which is the possibility that a return will be different from the expected return.

1-2. *Holding period return relative* (HPRR) is the ratio of the final value (including any intermediate payments) divided by the initial value. The time period can be of arbitrary length.

    Holding period return (HPR) is HPRR – 1, which is the percentage change from the initial value.

    Per-period return (PPR) is the standardized version of HPR. The length of time is defined by the context of the situation. PPR may differ from HPR when the time frames do not match.

    Annualized return is an HPR or PPR that has been converted to a one-year statistic, often for comparison.

    Compound interest is interest that accrues to a preceding period's interest. With compound interest, a return is earned on both the initial investment and previous interest payments.

    Arithmetic mean (average) return (AMR) is a single number that is representative of a group of numbers. It is calculated by adding the group's components, which are multiplied by their respective weights. In the simplest case, the weight is 1/n where n is the number of components.

    Geometric mean (average) return (GMR) incorporates compounding when calculating the representative statistic. Calculating multiperiod returns using the GMR will yield accurate results. Using the AMR may lead to inaccurate results because it omits compounding.

1-3. a. HPRR = $7,000/$5,000 = 1.4
          HPR = 1.4 – 1 = .4 = 40%
     b. HPRR = $3,000/$1,800 = 1.667
          HPR = 1.667 – 1 = .667 = 66.7%
     c. HPRR = $228,500/$195,000 = 1.17
          HPR = 1.17 – 1 = .17 = 17%

1-4. Because the holding period is one year, the HPR is the same as the annual return for all parts of question 1-4.
     a. Total value = $11.00 + $0.30 = $11.30
          HPRR = $11.30/$10 = 1.13
          HPR = 1.13 – 1 = .13 = 13%
     b. .07/4 = .0175 (quarterly rate)
          HPRR = (1.0175 x 1.0175 x 1.0175 x 1.0175)/1 = 1.07186
          HPR = 1.07186 – 1 = .07186 = 7.186%
     c. First, we need to compute the coupon income. Eight percent of $1,000 is $80. Half of this amount, or $40, would be received at midyear. At 9 percent (the approximate yield on the bond), that coupon payment would earn another $1.80. At year-end the bond would produce another $40 payment. Thus, the total coupon income would be approximately $81.80. The bond price fell by $40, so the net profit would be about $41.80 ($81.80 – $40).

The current value of the investment would be $931.80 ($850 + $81.80). Thus,
  HPRR = $931.80/$890 = 1.0470
  HPR = 1.0470 – 1 = .0470 = 4.7%
1-5. Annually = 1.1 x 1.1 = 1.21
Semiannually = $(1 + .10/2)^4 = 1.2155$
Quarterly = $(1 + .10/4)^8 = 1.2184$
Monthly = $(1 + .10/12)^{24} = 1.2204$
1-6. a. Arithmetic mean return:
    (7.8% + 9.3% + 4.5% + 11.5%)/4 = 8.275%
  b. If the amounts were in the proportions of .2, .3, .4, and .1, the mean return would be
    .2 (7.8) + .3 (9.3) + .4 (4.5) + .1 (11.5) = 7.30 = 7.3%
1-7. a. We must begin by determining the holding period return relative (HPRR).
    GMR + 1 = $(HPRR)^{1/n}$
    HPRR = (1.056) (.911) (1.100) (1.077) (1.130) = 1.287861
    GMR + 1 = $1.287861^{1/5} = 1.0519$
    GMR = 5.19%
  b. AMR = (5.6% – 8.9% + 10% + 7.7% + 13%)/5 = .0548 = 5.48%
1-8. a. It is a general characteristic of the marketplace that prices are determined that are appropriate for the expected return and risk level of a particular investment. As the risk of an instrument increases, its price declines, thereby increasing its expected rate of return.
  b. Not all high-risk investments offer high returns. This may be due to a market valuation based on reasons other than risk.
1-9. a. Both liquidity and marketability deal with the ease of selling an instrument. The distinction lies in the selling price. If the market price at which an instrument is sold is close to or above the purchase price, the investment is liquid; if it is below the purchase price, the investment is merely marketable. Therefore, liquid investments are a subset of marketable assets.
  b. All liquid instruments are marketable (unless there are external restrictions such as contractual penalties), but not all marketable investments are liquid.
1-10. Investments require varying degrees of attention and effort. For example, selecting and managing some types of investments require little or no special knowledge, facilities, or time commitment, while investments in other assets, such as real estate or soybean futures, require special knowledge, talent, and/or facilities. Likewise, some types of investments may be maintained with little or no effort (bonds), whereas others require constant management (an apartment complex).
1-11. Minimum investment levels can range from a few dollars to open a savings account to millions of dollars for some select mutual funds. Investors should assess the minimum investment level along with appropriateness and affinity. Some investors screen their investments in order to hold only the assets that are associated with products or services that reflect or do not conflict with their belief systems. They may therefore sacrifice return for peace of mind.
1-12. Federal taxes on investments are generally at the ordinary income level (marginal rate) or the long-term capital gains rate. Investments taxed at the marginal rate include interest income (excluding state and municipal securities), rents, royalties, dividends, and short-term capital gains (assets held for less than one year). Long-term capital gains are taxed at a maximum rate of 20 percent. Capital distributions are not taxable but alter the basis that is used in capital gains calculations.

Answers to Self-Test Questions, pp. 28–29

1-1. True.
1-2. False. Marketable assets can usually be bought and sold in quantity at the current market price, while those investments that can be quickly converted into cash at little cost or risk are considered to be liquid.
1-3. True.
1-4. False. An asset's PPR is defined as the sum of that period's income payments and price appreciation divided by its beginning-of-period price.

1-5. True.
1-6. True.
1-7. False. Insurance companies are in the business of selling protection from pure risk. Pure risks involve only the chance of loss or no loss, whereas speculative risks involve the chance of loss, no loss, or gain.
1-8. False. The more distant the redemption date (that is, the longer until the investment's maturity), the less liquid the investment is considered to be. Thus, long-term debt securities are generally not very liquid.
1-9. True.
1-10. False. Itemizing deductions is advantageous to the taxpayer only if allowable deductions exceed the standard deduction.
1-11. False. Deductions are allowed for many types of taxes but not for sales taxes.
1-12. True.
1-13. True.
1-14. True.
1-15. False. The basic rule is that short-term capital gains are taxed as ordinary income.
1-16. True.
1-17. True.
1-18. False. The higher of the regular tax or the AMT is the tax amount that must be paid.
1-19. True.

Chapter 2

Answers to Review Questions, pp. 48–49

2-1. a. The table below shows the dimensions of risk, expected return, liquidity, marketability, minimum size, and effort for various fixed-income securities.

Types	Dimensions					
	Risk	Expected Return	Liquidity	Marketability	Min. Size	Effort
Savings deposits	L	L	H	H	L	L
Savings bonds	L	L	H	H	L	L
Money market funds	L	L	H	H	L	L
Treasury bonds	L	L	L to H	H	M	L
Corporate bonds	L to H	L to H	L to M	L to M	M	L
Municipal bonds	L to H	L to M	L to M	L	M	M

   b. Interest payments of Treasury issues are free from state and local taxes. Municipal bond interest is free of federal taxation and also free of state and local taxes within the issuing state.
2-2. a. Limited partnerships combine the benefits of a corporation's limited liability with the single taxation advantage of a partnership. A single general partner, who is usually the organizer and may be a corporation, *does* have unlimited liability. The limited partners, however, are not liable for the partnership's debts and obligations beyond their initial capital contributions.
   b. Most limited partnerships have one major drawback: Because they are relatively small, their ownership units trade in very thin markets. The master limited partnership (MLP) is designed to overcome this drawback. Most MLPs are relatively large (compared to limited partnerships). Their ownership units are designed to trade actively in the same types of markets as stocks.
2-3. The after-tax yield can be computed from the formula for tax-equivalent yield found in chapter 1. In this case, C is actually the after-tax yield. Keep in mind that only 30 percent of dividends are taxable for corporations.

Solving for C: C = TE (1 – T)

$C_{Individual}$ = .075 (1 – .27) = .0547 = 5.47%

$C_{Corporation}$ = .075 (1 – .36 (.30)) = .0669 = 6.69%

2-4.   a.   Since there is only a single holding period, the overall return is simply the arithmetic mean (average) return:

AMR = (80 – 25 – 15 + 12 + 105 – 80 + 350 – 100 + 0)/9 = 36.33%

    b.   The geometric mean return (GMR) is calculated as follows:

GMR = $(AMR + 1)^{1/5}$ – 1 = $(1.3633)^{1/5}$ – 1 = .064 = 6.4%

2-5.   a.   Warrants, like calls, permit their owner to purchase a particular amount of stock at a prespecified price within a prespecified period. Unlike calls, warrants are generally exercisable for relatively long periods, such as several years. Furthermore, warrants are issued by the company whose stock underlies the warrant. If the warrant is exercised, the issuing company simply creates more shares. In contrast, existing shares are used to satisfy the exercise of a call. Thus, warrants are company-issued securities whose exercise results in additional shares and generates cash for the issuer. Calls are contracts between individual investors that do not involve the underlying company.

    b.   Both rights and warrants are company-issued options to buy stock, and both are traded in the same markets that trade the stocks that underlie them. However, rights differ from warrants in two ways: First, rights are issued for very short-run periods. They generally expire in a few weeks from the time of their issue. Second, rights are generally exercisable at a price that is substantially less than the current market price of the stock. The issuer sets a low enough price to make immediate exercise attractive. Most rights are exercised, therefore, while the exercise of warrants is more uncertain.

2-6.   a.   First, the cost of purchase must be determined. The front-end load involves a charge of $0.85; the total purchase price is $10.85:

HPRR = $12/$10.85 = 1.106

HPR = 1.106 – 1 = 10.6%

    b.   If the fund is no-load, the calculations are

HPRR = $12/$10 = 1.2

HPR = 1.2 – 1 = .2 = 20%

2-7.   Real estate investors have several reasons for being cautious:

- The more debt (leverage) used to finance real estate purchases, the greater the risks.
- The one-of-a-kind nature of individual real estate investments makes such properties relatively difficult and costly to buy and sell. Having to sell real estate on short notice can result in a substantial sacrifice.
- Determining a fair value for a prospective real estate investment requires considerable expertise.
- Managing improved property is a time-consuming task.
- Real estate commissions are considerably higher than those on securities.
- Most real estate purchases require a relatively large initial investment (down payment).

2-8.   The amount originally invested is 10 percent of the value of the contract, or $15,000. If the initial value of the futures contract is $150,000 and it rises to $200,000 when it is closed out, the investor has a $50,000 gain. The gain as a percentage of the amount invested is [HPR = gain/initial investment = $50,000/$15,000 = 3.33 = 333%] 333 percent. This is the holding period return or HPR.

Answers to Self-Test Questions, p. 49

2-1.   False. Depository institutions are no longer subject to maximum rate limitations on their accounts and certificates. Now they are allowed to pay whatever rates the competitive situation calls for.

2-2.   True.

2-3.   True.

2-4.   True.

2-5.   False. Only 23 percent of U.S. households own stock directly, but many more participate indirectly.

2-6.   False. Stock prices generally fluctuate much more than bond prices.

2-7.   False. Preferred stock is not particularly liquid, but it is generally marketable.

2-8.   True.

2-9.   True.

2-10. False. Calls are contracts between individual investors that do not involve the underlying company.

2-11. True.

2-12. False. Mutual funds are classified as open-end investment companies, which may issue new shares as well as redeem outstanding shares.

2-13. True.

2-14. False. Commissions on commodity trades are only a tiny fraction of the potential gains or losses.

2-15. True.

Chapter 3

Answers to Review Questions, pp. 82–83

3-1. Congress set up the Security Investors Protection Corporation (SIPC) patterned after the Federal Deposit Insurance Corporation (FDIC) that protects deposits in banks. SIPC protects brokerage customers against losses that would otherwise result from the failure of their brokerage firm. Of course, customers are not protected against losses due to market fluctuations. SIPC liquidates troubled firms at the SEC's request. Customers are insured up to $500,000, not more than $100,000 of which may be in cash. Any claims above those sums are applied against the firm's available assets during liquidation. Most brokerage firms, however, have purchased additional insurance.

3-2. The National Daily Quotation Service reports the bid and ask prices for all actively traded OTC issues (about 6,000 NASDAQ and 22,000 other issues). These price quotations appear daily in the pink sheets, copies of which are available at most brokerage firms. Investors who want a current quotation of a pink sheet stock need to have their brokers call one or more of the firms listed as making a market in the stock for a price. The phone numbers of these firms are listed in the pink sheets.

3-3. A *market order* requires an immediate execution at the best available price. A *limit order* stipulates the minimum (sell) or maximum (buy) price acceptable for a trade to take place. A *stop-loss order* requires an immediate market trade if the specified price is reached. A *stop-limit order* activates a limit order if a specified price is reached.

3-4. a. The investor's basis in the 700 shares normally is determined under a first-in, first-out (FIFO) approach. This requires that the shares purchased earliest be recorded as the ones sold first. Therefore, the first 700 shares were bought at $15 (300 shares), $18 (300), and $31 (100):

Normal basis = $15 (300) + $18 (300) + $31 (100) = $13,000

    b. Under a specified versus purchase order, the investor can specify which block of stock that he or she holds is to be sold. Therefore, the 700 shares can be allocated to the blocks priced at $40, $31, and $23 per share as follows:

Highest basis = $40 (300) + $31 (300) + $23 (100) = $23,600

3-5. The *third market* is the trading of listed stocks in the over-the-counter (OTC) market. It came about as a result of the former high fixed commissions of the NYSE. The *fourth market* is the direct trading between institutions. The benefit of this method is that prices can be negotiated and commissions bypassed (although there may be a finder's fee for the party bringing the institutions together).

3-6. a. A house call is made when the equity percentage falls below the minimum maintenance level set by the brokerage firm. A Fed call occurs when the equity percentage falls below the maintenance level set by the Federal Reserve Board for margin accounts.

    b. A margin call may be satisfied in any of the following ways:
- adding more money to the account
- adding more collateral to the account
- selling stock from the account and using the proceeds to reduce the margin debt

3-7. After 23 months' experience with the Up Up Corporation stock, Jo Ann's position is as shown below (see table that follows):

    a. She owns 4,583 shares.

    b. Her stock is valued at $229,150.

    c. She owes $68,740 in margin.

    d. Her equity position is $160,410.

Month	Price	Shares	Value	Net Equity	Margin
0	$10	1,000	10,000	5,000	5,000
1	$15	1,000	15,000	10,000	5,000
5	$20	1,500	30,000	25,000	5,000
	Bought	1,000	20,000		
		2,500	50,000	25,000	25,000
11	$30	3,125	93,750	68,750	25,000
	Bought*	1,458	43,740		
		4,583	137,490	68,750	68,740
23	$50	4,583	229,150	160,410	68,740

*Only whole shares are purchased

3-8. When the share price is not specified during a margin call, it must be calculated. With the information we have, we must first determine the portfolio value: Value = margin/(1 − equity %). Next, share price = value/shares owned. Last, the number of shares that must be sold to restore 50 percent equity = (equity − margin)/share price.

   Thus, when Joe liquidates his position in the Down Down corporation stock after the third margin call, he has only $7,806 left out of his original $50,000 investment.

Month	Price	Shares	Value	Beginning Equity	Ending Equity	Margin
0	$50	2,000	100,000	50,000	50,000	50,000
6	$38.46	2,000	76,923	50,000	26,923	50,000
	Sold	600	23,077			(23,077)
		1,400	53,846		26,923	26,923
8	$29.59	1,400	41,420	26,923	14,497	26,923
	Sold	420	12,426			(12,426)
		980	28,994		14,497	14,497
9	$22.76	980	22,303	14,497	7,806	14,497

3-9. The $53,000 balance corresponds to the call rate plus ¾ percent or 9¼ percent. This rate is equivalent to a monthly rate of 9.25/12 = 0.771%. The first month's charge is $53,000 (0.771%) = $408.54. The second month's charge is ($53,000 + $408.54) (0.771%) = $411.69. Continuing with a. and making the necessary adjustments for b. and c. (with relevant rates of 10¼ percent and 10¾ percent respectively):

a.

Month	Charge
1	$ 408.54
2	411.69
3	414.86
4	418.06
5	421.28
6	424.53
	$2,498.96

b.

Month	Charge
1	$230.63
2	232.59
3	234.58
	$697.80

c.

Month	Charge
1	$ 62.71
2	63.27
3	63.84
4	64.41
5	64.99
6	65.57
7	66.16
8	66.75
9	67.35
10	67.95
	$653.00

3-10. The investment banker may choose to act as an agent for the issuing firm, in which case the job is taken on a best-efforts basis. Most underwriting, however, is done on a firm-commitment basis, which means the investment banker buys the securities from the issuer and then resells them to the public.

3-11. The drive for centralization will link disparate markets into one large marketplace. Linkage should lead to greater efficiency with benefits such as narrower spreads and a greater ability to absorb trading volume. In addition, information will flow quickly through the market, allowing for more accurate pricing and thereby limiting arbitrage opportunities.

Answers to Self-Test Questions, pp. 83–85

3-1. True.

3-2. True.

3-3. False. The SIPC protects brokerage customers against losses that would otherwise result from the failure of their brokerage firm.

3-4. True.

3-5. False. Institutional trading makes up a much larger part of NYSE volume than that of either the AMEX or NASDAQ.

3-6. True.

3-7. True.

3-8. False. Since May 1975, each brokerage firm has set its own commission rate schedule.

3-9. False. Spreads tend to represent a smaller percentage of the price for higher-priced and more actively traded stocks.

3-10. False. A limit-order transaction must await an acceptable price because this type of order is executable only at the limit price or better. Some limit orders are never executed.

3-11. True.

3-12. False. The total commission on such a stretched-out trade would appreciably exceed that on a single transaction of the same number of shares.

3-13. False. An all-or-nothing order can be executed only when sufficient volume is available because the order must trade as a unit. However, the order does not have to be executed immediately. It can wait until sufficient volume exists for a single transaction. The type of order that must be either executed immediately or canceled is a fill-or-kill order.

3-14. True.

3-15. True.

3-16. False. The vast majority of trading is done with market and limit orders.

3-17. True.

3-18. False. Listed stocks are generally more marketable than those traded over the counter.

3-19. False. The third market involves over-the-counter trading of listed stocks. Informal arrangements for direct trading between institutions are referred to as the fourth market.

3-20. True.

3-21. False. The initial margin requirement on stocks is set at 50 percent.

3-22. True.

3-23. True.

3-24. True.

3-25. False. Using short sales to drive a stock's price down is considered an illegal attempt to manipulate the market. If the last price change was a decline, a would-be short seller must wait until the price begins to rise again (an uptick) before implementing a short sale.

3-26. True.

3-27. True.

3-28. False. Investment bankers generally agree to sell a new issue on a firm-commitment basis, which means that they buy the security from the issuer and then sell it to the public.

3-29. False. Off-exchange member trading of listed securities is no longer prohibited *per se,* but restrictions still discourage such activity.

3-30. True.

Chapter 4

Answers to Review Questions, pp. 107–109

4-1. An investment entails a current outflow of cash and an expected future inflow. The expected inflow must be greater than the initial outflow; this is compensation to the investor for forgoing the current use of funds. The value of an investment is, therefore, time dependent. This aspect of investment is defined as *time value.* Future cash flows can be valued in current terms (*present value*) if time and risk are taken into account via a discount rate.

4-2. a. The present value of $50 annually, forever discounted at 10 percent is as follows:
PV = $50/.10 = $500

   b. The PV of $1 received annually for 20 years and discounted at 20 percent is $4.87. Therefore, the PV for $200 annually for 20 years, discounted at 20 percent, is as follows:
PV = 4.87 x $200 = $974.00

   c. The PV of $1 received annually for 12 years and discounted at 16 percent is $5.197; $1 to be received in 12 years and discounted at 16 percent is $0.168. Therefore, the PV of a bond with $150 annual coupon for 12 years, maturing at $1,070, discounted at 16 percent, is as follows:
PV = (5.197 x 150) + (0.168 x 1,070) = $779.55 + 179.76 = $959.31

   d. The present values of $1 received in years 1, 2, 3, and 4 and discounted at 8 percent are $0.926, $0.857, $0.794, and $0.735, respectively. Therefore, the PV for a payment stream of $200 in year 1, $300 in year 2, $400 in year 3, and $500 in year 4 is as follows:
PV = (0.926 x $200) + (0.857 x $300) + (0.794 x $400) + (0.735 x $500) = $1,127.40

4-3. a. The PV of $1 received annually for 20 years and discounted at 7 percent is $10.594. The PV of $1 received in 20 years and discounted at 7 percent is $0.258:
PV = (10.594 x $100) + (0.258 x $1,000) = $1,317.40

   b. The PV of $1 received annually for 20 years and discounted at 9 percent is $9.128. The PV of $1 received in 20 years and discounted at 9 percent is $0.178:
PV = (9.128 x $100) + (0.178 x $1,000) = $1,090.80

   c. The PV of $1 received annually for 20 years and discounted at 10 percent is $8.514. The PV of $1 received in 20 years and discounted at 10 percent is $0.149:
PV = (8.514 x $100) + (0.149 x $1,000) = $1,000.40

   d. The PV of $1 received annually for 20 years and discounted at 11 percent is $7.963. The PV of $1 received in 20 years and discounted at 11 percent is $0.124:
PV = (7.963 x $100) + (0.124 x $1,000) = $920.30

   e. The PV of $1 received annually for 20 years and discounted at 13 percent is $7.024. The PV of $1 received in 20 years and discounted at 13 percent is $0.087:
PV = (7.024 x $100) + (0.087 x $1,000) = $789.40

4-4. a. All other things being equal, early cash flows are more valuable than later ones. Cash flow A has most of its flows toward the end of the 5-year period; therefore, it has the lowest present value. The opposite is true of cash flow B, which has the highest value.

   b. The present value of the income streams A, B, and C, discounted at 12 percent, is as follows:
$$PV_A = \frac{\$100}{(1+.12)} + \frac{\$200}{(1+.12)^2} + \frac{\$300}{(1+.12)^3} + \frac{\$400}{(1+.12)^4} + \frac{\$500}{(1+.12)^5} = \$1,000.18$$
$$PV_B = \$1,162.69$$
$$PV_C = \$1,077.76$$

   c. With a discount rate of zero, all cash flows are priced at face value. Each of the cash flows, therefore, is worth $1,500.

4-5. The price of Bond A is computed as follows:

$$PV_A = \sum_{i=1}^{10} \frac{\$80}{(1+.12)^i} + \frac{\$1,000}{(1+.12)^{10}} = \$773.99$$

Similarly, the prices of Bonds B, C, and D are as follows:

$PV_B = \$1,226.01$
$PV_C = \$\ 932.40$
$PV_D = \$1,368.67$

4-6. Two factors must be determined when calculating the present value of a future payment. An examination of the relevant risk leads to an appropriate discount rate. Once the timing of the payment has been determined, the present value can be calculated. This process is repeated for each cash flow until all are accounted for. Their sum is the total present value of the investment.

4-7. The difference in selling price is due to the rates used in discounting the cash flows. A higher discount rate results in a lower price. Lower discount rates lead to higher valuations. The discount rates that would lead to valuations of $600 and $1,200 would have to be of vastly different magnitudes, corresponding to a radically different interest rate environment.

4-8. Inflation affects a bond's price via the discount rate. This occurs through direct and indirect avenues. Inflation is a component of the risk-free rate (the direct avenue). Companies are affected to varying degrees by interest rate changes. Large rate changes can cause operational difficulties that endanger cash flows and ultimately the solvency of the company. These difficulties are priced in the marketplace by adjustments to the risk premium.

4-9. a. Over the 5-year period, dividends will be paid out at the rate of $3.25, $3.50, $3.75, $4.00, and $4.25. At the end of 5 years, the stock will sell for 12 x $4.25 = $51. Thus, we need to compute the present value of the income stream: $3.25, $3.50, $3.75, $4.00, and $4.25 + $51. At a discount rate of 8 percent, the present value factors are 0.926, 0.857, 0.794, 0.735, and 0.681:
PV = (0.926 x $3.25) + (0.857 x $3.50) + (0.794 x $3.75) + (0.735 x $4.00) + (0.681 x $55.25) = $49.55
  b. At a discount rate of 10 percent, the present value factors are: 0.909, 0.826, 0.751, 0.683, and 0.621:
PV = (0.909 x $3.25) + (0.826 x $3.50) + (0.751 x $3.75) + (0.683 x $4.00) + (0.621 x $55.25) = $45.70
  c. At a discount rate of 12 percent, the present value factors are: 0.893, 0.797, 0.712, 0.636, and 0.567:
PV = (0.893 x $3.25) + (0.797 x $3.50) + (0.712 x $3.75) + (0.636 x $4.00) + (0.567 x $55.25) = $42.25
  d. At a discount rate of 15 percent, the present value factors are: 0.870, 0.756, 0.658, 0.572, and 0.497:
PV = (0.870 x $3.25) + (0.756 x $3.50) + (0.658 x $3.75) + (0.572 x $4.00) + (0.497 x $55.25) = $37.69
  e. At a discount rate of 18 percent, the present value factors are: 0.847, 0.718, 0.609, 0.516, and 0.437:
PV = (0.847 x $3.25) + (0.718 x $3.50) + (0.609 x $3.75) + (0.516 x $4.00) + (0.437 x $55.25) = $33.76
  f. With a stable dividend of $3.00 and a discount rate of 8 percent:
PV = (0.926 x $3.00) + (0.857 x $3.00) + (0.794 x $3.00) + (0.735 x $3.00) + (0.681 x $39.00) = $36.50

4-10. Over the 5-year period, dividends will be paid out at the rate of $1.10, $1.20, $1.30, $1.40, and $1.50. At the end of 5 years, the stock will sell for 6.5 x $1.50 = $9.75. Thus, we need to compute the present value of the income stream: $1.10, $1.20, $1.30, $1.40, and $1.50 + $9.75. At a discount rate of 16 percent, the present value factors are 0.862, 0.743, 0.641, 0.552, and 0.476:
PV = (0.862 x $1.10) + (0.743 x $1.20) + (0.641 x $1.30) + (0.552 x $1.40) + (0.476 x $11.25) = $8.80

4-11. a. With a discount rate of 10 percent:
PV = (0.909 x $1.10) + (0.826 x $1.20) + (0.751 x $1.30) + (0.683 x $1.40) + (0.621 x $11.25) = $10.91
  b. With a discount rate of 20 percent:
PV = (0.833 x $1.10) + (0.694 x $1.20) + (0.579 x $1.30) + (0.482 x $1.40) + (0.402 x $11.25) = $7.70

4-12. a. This problem uses the constant growth case of the dividend discount model:
$S = d_1/(k - g) = d_0(1 + g)/(k - g) = 1.1/(.12 - .1) = \$55$
  b. $S = \$2.22/(.12 - .11) = \$222$
  c. $S = \$1.62/(.12 - .08) = \$40.50$

4-13. a. Payout percent = d/e => e = d/(payout percent). With a dividend of $1.10 and a payoff percent of 0.55, we have

  e = $1.1/0.55 = $2.00   PE = $55/$2 = 27.50

  b. d = $2.22   e = $2.22/.55 = $4.04   PE = $222/$4.04 = 55
  c. d = $1.62   e = $1.62/.55 = $2.95   PE = $40.50/$2.95 = 13.75

4-14. To compute the market-implied long-term growth rate, rearrange the PE formula as follows:

  PE = p/(k – g)
  PE (k – g) = p
  (PE x k) – (PE x g) = p
  PE x k = p + (g x PE)
  g x PE = (PE x k) – p
  g = (PE x k)/PE – (p/PE) = k – p/PE

  a. g = 0.12 – 0.40/8 = 0.07
  b. g = 0.12 – 0.50/10 = 0.07
  c. g = 0.12 – 0.60/15 = 0.08

4-15. Firms are reluctant to adjust dividend rates because of the anticipated negative reaction in the marketplace. The other component of earnings is funds that are retained for reinvestment in the firm. Optimal use of retained earnings can enhance the growth of the firm and thereby increase future profitability. Because focusing on dividends can be misleading and ignoring retained earnings results in an incomplete picture, analysis of earnings is by consensus considered to be the best measure of future prospects.

Answers to Self-Test Questions, pp. 109–110

4-1. False. For the vast majority of bonds, the periodic interest payment is fixed at a set amount called the coupon rate.
4-2. False. Any bond with a coupon rate below the discount rate is worth less than its face value.
4-3. True.
4-4. True.
4-5. False. Nominal interest rates are stated in current dollar terms, and real interest rates are stated in inflation-adjusted terms.
4-6. False. The capital gain a shareholder can reasonably expect when selling a stock is based on the discounted present value of the stock's expected future cash flows.
4-7. True.
4-8. True.
4-9. False. Dividend payments on stock tend to increase over time.
4-10. True.
4-11. False. When using the constant growth model, the price of a stock should equal *the next period's dividend* divided by (k – g).
4-12. True.
4-13. True.
4-14. True.
4-15. False. A security identified as undervalued may not necessarily earn a superior return for its owners, especially if the market as a whole declines.
4-16. True.
4-17. True.
4-18. True.
4-19. False. Past earnings growth has not been found to be a very accurate predictor of future earnings growth.

Chapter 5

Answers to Review Questions, pp. 141–142

5-1. The equivalent yield for a one-year T-bill priced at 95 is as follows:

$$\text{Equivalent yield} = \frac{\text{discount}}{\text{price}} = \frac{500}{9,500} = 5.26\%$$

5-2.

	Advantages	Disadvantages
Treasury bills	Low risk, liquid, tax-advantaged	Yield lower than that of riskier investments
Commercial paper	Higher rates	Higher risk, high denominations
Money market mutual funds	Variable rates, liquid, variety of types	Rates not as high as direct investment, variable risk

5-3. a. *Government bonds* include those issued both by the federal government and its agencies (sponsored and not). Risk varies from the essentially riskless Treasuries to low-risk, nonsponsored agencies. Maturities extend from 10 to 30 years. Liquidity ranges from extremely high (Treasuries) to low (agencies). Trading costs vary inversely with liquidity. Most of these securities are tax advantaged in some way. Agencies typically pay higher rates than Treasuries, but the spread can vary by issuer and time. Most trading of government issues occurs in the OTC market.

b. State and local governments raise funds through the issuance of *municipal bonds*. Either a specific revenue source or general taxing authority backs these bonds. The variety of issuers is immense. Because of this, risk and promised return can vary greatly. Risk is occasionally ameliorated by the issuer's purchase of a credit enhancement. A prime feature of these securities is their tax-advantaged status. This feature results in lower yields than would be expected if only risk was considered.

c. Corporations are the third major source of debt securities. Bonds are more risky than Treasuries. The range of risk levels is quite varied. *Corporate bonds* are either secured (mortgage bonds) or unsecured (debentures). Most trading of corporates takes place in the OTC market.

5-4. a. Securitization involves pooling individual assets (for example, mortgages) to create a new asset. The new security may have very different attributes from the underlying assets. This may be due to the pooling (for example, diversification) or to the financial engineering (for example, carving up the cash flows).

b. Pooling assets can lessen undesirable attributes, such as poor marketability, and accentuate positive ones, such as steady cash flow. Securitization benefits the original issuer by freeing it from risk and maintenance costs. This releases resources, thereby expanding their capacity. By extension, this gain translates to greater marketplace capacity, increased liquidity, and more variety of instruments. The individual investor benefits from greater choice of instruments and decreased risk due to diversification.

5-5. a. Ratings agencies satisfy a clear need, given the vast quantity of financial information. Their function is to sift and analyze the information to derive an accurate assessment of default risk. The higher the rating a bond receives, the lower its risk of default.

b. Standard & Poor's and Moody's are the best known bond rating agencies.

c. Ratings may lag in volatile times, leaving the investor with inadequate time to react.

5-6. Riskier bonds generally offer higher yields.

5-7. a. *Income bonds* are primarily (but not always) associated with firms that are experiencing financial difficulty. Because of payment uncertainty, income bond prices are much lower than those of healthier companies. Investors may find the potential for high returns sufficient to offset higher risk.

b. *Floating-rate securities* offer variable coupons that compensate for inflation. This feature leads to a stable real return (nominal return minus inflation) and prices. When contemplating these securities, the investor should consider how the rate is calculated, what it is pegged to, and, as always, what the default risk is.

c. A *zero-coupon bond* is one that offers no coupon. The only payment is the face value at maturity. Purchase prices are well below face value because of the lack of intermediate payments. An investor should be aware that the discount from face value leads to an imputed annual tax liability. Some zero-coupon bonds are derived from coupon bonds through the process of stripping.

5-8.   a.   Investors receive many benefits from the existence of *Eurobonds*. Prime examples are greater instrument choice and portfolio diversification. A prospective Eurobond investor should address the Eurobond's specific characteristics, such as taxes and foreign exchange implications, prior to purchase.

b.   *Private placements* are large blocks of stock that are sold to corporations, closed-end funds, and wealthy investors (bypassing the registration process). Therefore, unless investors are very wealthy, closed-end funds offer the only avenue for participation in private placements.

c.   *Preferred stock* is a hybrid of bonds and common stock. The purchase of preferred stock gives the investor a more stable cash flow than that associated with common stock. The preferred stock owner has a higher priority of claim on the firm's assets than the common stockholder does in the event of corporate bankruptcy. In some cases, missed payments may entitle the owner to voting rights. The individual investor is not entitled to tax breaks that corporations have for owning preferred stock.

5-9.   Mutual funds and unit investment trusts are alternatives to direct investment. These alternatives may confer additional benefits, such as lower minimum investment levels and diversification. Investors should pay close attention to fees and operating costs because of their effect on returns.

Answers to Self-Test Questions, pp. 142–144

5-1.   False. T-bills are issued at a discount and mature at par or face value.

5-2.   True.

5-3.   False. Bids may be entered on either a competitive or noncompetitive basis. All noncompetitive bids are accepted by the Treasury, and buyers who enter these bids agree to pay the average price of all competitive bids that are accepted.

5-4.   True.

5-5.   True.

5-6.   False. Commercial paper is secured only by the issuer's good name.

5-7.   False. Commercial paper issuers are generally able to pay slightly less than the prime rate on their borrowings.

5-8.   False. The principal of negotiable CDs issued by banks and thrift institutions is covered by up to $100,000 of government deposit insurance.

5-9.   True.

5-10. True.

5-11. True.

5-12. False. Because money market funds concentrate on very liquid short-term instruments, adverse interest rate moves are unlikely to affect the fund's share prices significantly.

5-13. True.

5-14. False. Short-term unit investment trusts are unmanaged and mature.

5-15. False. Yields on existing units will not increase when market interest rates rise. The trustholder must wait until the units mature and then reinvest at the higher rate available in the market.

5-16. True.

5-17. False. U.S. Treasury notes are issued with maturities from one to 10 years, while Treasury bonds have maturities greater than 10 years at the time of issuance.

5-18. False. Treasury note and bond price quotations are expressed in 32nds, while T-bill quotes are in hundredths.

5-19. False. All newly issued Treasury notes and bonds are in registered form. Prior to mid-1983, some notes and bonds were issued in bearer form.

5-20. True.

5-21. False. Treasury securities are not subject to state and local taxes.

5-22. True.

5-23. True.

5-24. True.

5-25. True.

5-26. False. The category of municipal bonds known as revenue bonds is backed by revenues from a designated project, authority, or agency, or by the proceeds from a specific tax. General-obligation municipal bonds are backed by the general taxing power of the issuing government.

5-27. False. Corporate bonds known as debentures are backed only by the issuer's full faith and credit.

5-28. False. A bond with a rating of A has less risk of default than one with a rating of B.

5-29. True.

5-30. False. Income bonds pay interest only if the issuer earns it. Specific indenture provisions indicate when earned income is sufficient to require an interest payment.

5-31. True.

5-32. False. A bond separated from its coupons is known as a strip bond.

5-33. False. Zero-coupon bonds have precisely stated maturity values.

5-34. False. Even though zeros pay no coupons, they nevertheless impose an annual tax liability on their owners based on their imputed interest.

5-35. True.

5-36. True.

5-37. True.

5-38. False. Even though preferred stockholders are residual claimants behind all creditors, their claims still have a higher priority than the claims of common stockholders.

5-39. False. Because preferred dividends are not tax deductible to the issuer but interest payments on bonds are, all other things being equal, corporations would generally prefer to issue bonds than preferred stock.

Chapter 6

Answers to Review Questions, p. 177

6-1. Fundamental provisions delineate maturity date, principal, and coupon levels. The investor should also pay close attention to the details of sinking fund and call provisions. Although subordination is always important, it is of greater significance with higher-risk issues..

6-2. The most serious default is a firm's failure to make interest payments when due. However, it can also be in technical default if it has failed to fulfill any of its indenture provisions (in any of its issues). Most defaults are signals of minor financial difficulties and do not result in bankruptcy. However, the investor should actively monitor subsequent events because they may result in the indenture agreement's being altered and cash flows threatened. Default in some cases is just the first event in a worsening situation that subsequently leads to bankruptcy. Markets are therefore very sensitive to defaults. Their reactions can be severe and can exacerbate the company's problems.

6-3. Once liquidation of a company's assets begins, claims are paid according to the absolute priority of claims principle. This method assigns claims to classes, each of which is in a strict hierarchy. The firm's remaining assets are then paid out, beginning with the highest class. The process continues until funds are exhausted. The last class to be paid might receive only partial payment. If this is the case, all claimants within the class are treated equally, thereby receiving proportional payments. In most bankruptcies, some claimants and or classes receive no payment.

6-4. According to the *market segmentation theory,* investors and borrowers have preferred time horizons; therefore, they each occupy a distinct segment along the yield curve. This theory, when it is applied to the normal, upward-sloping yield curve, means that there are fewer people interested in investing in longer time periods; higher yields must therefore be offered to entice investors to lend (as opposed to holding cash).

The *preferred habitat theory* modifies market segmentation with the provision that investors can be induced to leave their preferred segment by the offer of higher yields. In this case, the upward-sloping curve is explained by premiums being offered to entice investors to move from short-term to long-term debt.

Under the *liquidity preference theory*—all other things being equal—investors prefer their money sooner rather than later. To combat this tendency, borrowers must offer interest rates that increase with the length of the loan. This theory best explains a rising yield curve.

The *unbiased expectations theory* explains that the yield curve is based on the market's expectations of short-term rates that will occur in the future. Each long-term rate is, in essence, an average of short-term rates. With a rising yield curve, the market must be expecting future short-term rates to be higher than current short-term rates.

6-5. As expected, both durations declined, but the $100 coupon bond declined .53 years as opposed to .47 for the $60 coupon bond (see tables that follow). In general, the higher the coupon rate, the greater the change in duration when market interest rates change.

Bond A			
Year	Cash Flow	Present Value at 20%	Year x Present Value (Column 1 x Column 3)
1	$ 60	$ 50.00	$ 50.00
2	60	41.67	83.34
3	60	34.72	104.16
4	60	28.94	115.76
5	60	24.11	120.55
6	60	20.09	120.54
7	1,060	295.83	2,070.81
Total	$1,420	$495.36	$2,665.16

Duration = $2,665.16/$495.36 = 5.38

Bond B			
Year	Cash Flow	Present Value at 20%	Year x Present Value (Column 1 x Column 3)
1	$ 100	$83.33	$ 83.33
2	100	69.44	138.88
3	100	57.87	173.61
4	100	48.23	192.92
5	100	40.19	200.95
6	100	33.49	200.94
7	1,100	306.99	2,148.93
Total	$1,700	$639.54	$3,139.56

Duration = $3,139.56/$639.54 = 4.91

6-6. Investors in higher tax brackets often prefer their investment gains in the form of capital gains—as opposed to interest payments—because the rate is lower than that associated with ordinary income. Low-coupon, deep-discount bonds are ideal for this situation, as long as they are purchased in the secondary market and originally issued at par. Because of this, these investors bid up prices, causing corresponding yields to decline. This tax-induced change is called the coupon effect.

6-7. Immunization is the protection of bond portfolio value against interest rate changes. In practice, this might entail matching cash inflows with outflows or simply matching a zero coupon bond's maturity with the investor's horizon. More sophisticated methods involve constructing a portfolio with the desired duration.

6-8. a. *Marketable* issues have lower spreads, thereby lowering trading costs and raising prices, reducing the yield.
       b. *Seasoned* issues are priced higher than new issues and therefore have lower yields.
       c. *Call protection* protects future cash flows, which generally enhances a security's value, so the yield is lower.
       d. *Sinking funds* reduce the probability of default, enhancing value and lowering the yield.

6-9. a. Investors should evaluate their needs and preferences in relation to such factors as risk, expected return, maturity/duration, taxes, diversification, and liquidity. Decisions on these factors will determine the makeup and management of their portfolios.
       b. Bond swapping is the selling and buying of components of a bond portfolio. It is through this method that a portfolio can be maintained or changed.
       c. Transaction costs include commissions, bid-ask spreads, and accrued interest. Although these costs are generally low, they vary with the type of bond and the timing of the transaction.

Answers to Self-Test Questions, pp. 177–179

6-1. True.

6-2. False. The coupon rate is the contractually stated rate on a bond. The current yield is the coupon amount divided by the bond's price.

6-3. False. The yield to maturity is based on the market price of the bond as well as the coupon rate. Therefore, it is possible for the yield to maturity to be higher or lower than the coupon rate.

6-4. True.

6-5. False. Aside from general credit conditions, the most significant factor that influences the coupon rate of a bond is the risk of default.

6-6. True.

6-7. True.

6-8. False. Debentures do not have specific property serving as collateral but are backed by the full faith and credit of the issuer.

6-9. True.

6-10. False. A call provision gives the issuer the option of redeeming the bonds prior to maturity.

6-11. True.

6-12. False. In the case of bankruptcy, unsecured creditors have priority over preferred stockholders.

6-13. True.

6-14. True.

6-15. False. Under the liquidity preference hypothesis, investors prefer to invest in short-term debt securities, while borrowers tend to prefer to borrow long term.

6-16. True.

6-17. False. Duration is a better measure than maturity of a bond's sensitivity to interest rate changes.

6-18. True.

6-19. True.

6-20. True.

6-21. True.

6-22. False. Interest payments on municipal bonds are not taxable, but capital gains are.

6-23. True.

6-24. False. Compared to commissions on common stock transactions, those on bond trades are relatively low as a percentage of the principal amount involved.

6-25. True.

6-26. True.

Chapter 7

Answers to Review Questions, pp. 210–211

7-1. The difference between the popular and the financial definition of risk has more to do with precision than any substantive differences. The financial definition attempts to build a concise definition of risk. All possible outcomes are explored to construct a quantitative description. By moving risk into the statistical realm, risk can be modeled and predictions made.

7-2. a. Mean = $(-5\% + 0\% + 5\% + 10\%)/4 = 2.5\%$
Variance = $[(-5\% - 2.5\%)^2 + (0\% - 2.5\%)^2 + (5\% - 2.5\%)^2 + (10\% - 2.5\%)^2]/4 = .3125\%$

Standard deviation = $\sqrt{\text{Variance}}$ = 5.59%

  b. Mean = $[.1(0\%) + .15(5\%) + .25(10\%) + .25(15\%) + .15(20\%) + .1(25\%)] = 12.50\%$
Variance = $[.1(0\% - 12.5\%)^2 + .15(5\% - 12.5\%)^2 + \ldots + .1(25\% - 12.5\%)^2] = .5125\%$
Standard Deviation = 7.16%

  c. Mean = $10\%/1 = 10\%$
Variance = $(10\% - 10\%)^2/1 = 0$
Standard deviation = 0

7-3. $\overline{R}_i = (.03 + .05 - .01 + .10 + 0 + .01)/6 = .03$

$\overline{R}_j = (.05 + .03 - .05 + .08 + 0 - .01)/6 = .017$

$$\text{COV} = \sum_{t=1}^{6} \frac{(R_{it} - \overline{R}_i)(R_{jt} - \overline{R}_j)}{5} = .00176$$

7-4.   As the number of assets in a portfolio increases, the covariance pairs become the dominant source of risk. Analysis of an asset's covariability with a market portfolio leads to the creation of the beta statistic. Beta is the slope component of the market model that can be used to make predictions of future returns. Beta calculation entails significantly less computation than that of a variance-covariance matrix. The market model, using specific assumptions, can be modified to produce the capital asset pricing model (CAPM).

   Creation of beta and the two associated models was a significant step forward in financial theory, a byproduct of which was a reduction in necessary computing power.

7-5.

Expected Returns for Three Stocks						
		Market Returns				
α	β	0.05	0.1	0.15	−0.05	−0.1
0.01	0.7	0.045	0.08	0.115	−0.025	−0.06
0.05	1.1	0.105	0.16	0.215	−0.005	−0.06
−0.02	1.5	0.055	0.13	0.205	−0.095	−0.17

7-6.   In the market model, *alpha* is the return when the market's return is zero; *beta* is the slope of the regression line. (In other words, alpha is the return to an asset independent of the market return, while beta is the relationship between the asset's return and the market return.) Under CAPM, alpha is the return on a risk-free asset, and beta is the slope of the line linking the risk-free asset and the market portfolio. The lines graphically represent the expected asset return for a given market return and excess market return (above the risk-free rate) for the market model and CAPM, respectively. Covariability becomes increasingly important as the number of assets increases. Beta is a proxy for covariance. It is therefore very useful in portfolio risk determination (due to linearity, portfolio risk is the weighted average of the individual betas). Beta in conjunction with alpha is also used to predict future returns.

7-7.   The market model is the outcome of a statistical regression of an asset's return with the return of a market portfolio. The linear equation that results has a y-intercept alpha and slope beta. The alpha is the asset's return when the market return is zero. The CAPM, by contrast, is based on strict theoretical assumptions. It is functionally different in that alpha is the return on a risk-free asset and beta is multiplied by the market portfolio's risk premium.

7-8.   a. Market risk reflects macroeconomic factors that affect all firms. These include interest rate volatility, inflation, and taxation. Nonmarket risks are specific to a firm or industry. Examples are management performance, labor shortages, legal issues, and funding problems.

   b. Nonmarket risk decreases as diversification increases. This is because the nonmarket risks tend to offset each other. As diversification increases, nonmarket risk diminishes to the point where, for all intents and purposes, only market risk remains (which cannot be diversified away).

7-9.   a. By varying the weights assigned to assets, we can draw a curve in risk-return space. At each point on the curve, no higher expected return can be achieved for a given risk level. Thus, the investment portfolios are efficient. When a risk-free asset is introduced, the efficient frontier becomes a straight line connecting the risk-free asset and the market portfolio (which consists of all assets in their exact value-weighted proportions). To hold a portfolio along this line is to hold both the risk-free asset and the market portfolio in varying proportions (points to the right of the market portfolio involve borrowing to purchase more of the market portfolio).

   b. If only lending is possible, the efficient frontier consists of the line connecting the risk-free asset and the market portfolio. To the right, the frontier is once again the risky asset curve.

   c. If borrowing occurs at a rate higher than the risk-free rate, the line to the right of the market portfolio will be lower and have less slope than in the previous case. This is because borrowing costs diminish returns for incremental increases in risk.

7-10. Because we know that the market portfolio always has a beta of 1.0, we can use the formula $r_i = r_f + \beta_i (r_M - r_f)$ to obtain the return for each of the portfolios.

Expected Returns for Efficient Portfolios					
		β			
Risk-free	Market	0.7	1	1.3	1.6
0.07	0.14	0.119	0.14	0.161	0.182
0.09	0.16	0.139	0.16	0.181	0.202
0.05	0.1	0.085	0.1	0.115	0.13

Answers to Self-Test Questions, pp. 211–212

7-1. False. It is the expected return from an investment that is subject to uncertainties. The realized return is the return that has actually occurred.

7-2. False. Return by itself is insufficient to properly assess and compare the performance of different investments. Risk must also be considered.

7-3. False. In the field of investments, risk is the chance that the actual outcome will differ from the expected outcome. It can be thought of as uncertainty, as the range of possible outcomes, or as the dispersion of possible outcome from expected outcome. Mathematical measures of risk include the standard deviation and the range (highest minus lowest possible outcome).

7-4. True.

7-5. False. A portfolio of securities is less risky than its component securities. This is why diversification is an important investment strategy.

7-6. False. A portfolio's return is the *weighted* average of the returns of its assets. The average assumes that each asset has an equal weight in the portfolio. As relative prices change, the relative impact of each asset on the portfolio return also changes. Therefore, using an unweighted average would result in an inaccurate measure of portfolio return.

7-7. False. A perfectly negative correlation (–1) of the returns between two assets would reduce the variability or risk of the portfolio. This would reduce the standard deviation of the returns to the portfolio. In fact, it would be possible to construct a risk-free portfolio by combining two assets whose returns have a correlation of –1. However, the weighted return of the portfolio would not change.

7-8. True.

7-9. True.

7-10. True.

7-11. True.

7-12. False. If a portfolio is on the capital market line, it is a well-diversified portfolio.

7-13. False. The required return for this investment is 10.6 percent. The market risk premium (10% – 4% = 6%) is multiplied by the stock's beta (1.1) and is then added to the risk-free rate (4 percent) for an expected rate of return of 10.6 percent (6.6% + 4%).

7-14. True.

Chapter 8

Answers to Review Questions, p. 235

8-1. *Fundamental analysis* involves researching factors (for example, earnings, dividends, sales, costs, and capital requirements) that affect a firm's future income stream. The resulting valuation is then compared with the current market price to assess likely future price movement. *Technical analysis* takes place at a more superficial level and seeks less to understand than predict; investor sentiment is more important than theoretical justification. Technical analysis can take into account such factors as price, volume, and market indicators, but it ignores such fundamental factors as a firm's business, product line, quality of management, operating history, and competitive environment.

8-2. The weak form of EMH implies that historical price behavior cannot be used to predict future prices. If true, this view negates the efficacy of technical analysis. Research has indicated that this form of EMH holds, especially when transaction costs are taken into account. Under the semistrong form, all publicly available information is already incorporated into an asset's price; therefore, both technical and fundamental analyses are useless for price anticipation. Evidence supporting this version is mixed. The implication is that astute fundamental analysts may in some cases be able to anticipate price changes. Under the strong form of EMH, all information is incorporated into asset prices; therefore, it is not possible to predict price movement. Financial research has generally not found substantial evidence supporting the strong form of EMH.

8-3. It is possible that the sheer magnitude of data may obscure relevant information. This may delay or prevent prudent investor action. To achieve efficient markets requires ease of access. In practice, investors may not have the resources or understanding to act upon information. Investors may lack the desire to undertake adequate investment research; in other words, other activities may take precedence. It is possible that the market is, for the most part, efficient, but efficiency may not extend to all securities. For example, the information of small firms may be difficult to obtain, thereby making valuation more fraught with error.

8-4. a. According to portfolio theory, nonmarket risk can be diversified away and therefore should be irrelevant to pricing. Market studies have not found this to be the case.

b. Possible causes are as follows: Market participants are unable, for various reasons, to effectively diversify; investors, on occasion, act irrationally; if the borrowing rate is higher than the lending rate, this serves as a barrier to diversification; statistical errors result in the perception of nonmarket risk where, in fact, none exists; and statistical misspecification leads to incorrect models, therefore making interpretation imprecise.

8-5. a. Portfolio theory is predicated on asset returns being normally distributed. Some researchers have argued that if this is not the case, it is of strong enough consequence to invalidate the models.

b. Investigations into investor preferences indicate that the desired distribution is skewed (offering the possibility of very high returns).

8-6. a. Betas are generally calculated by regressing an asset's historical returns on those of a market portfolio.

b. As with many financial statistics, betas tend to be more reliable when applied to a wider perspective—that is, to portfolios as opposed to individual assets. The inaccuracy of individual betas may be due to errors in estimation or an inherent instability of the statistic. Furthermore, a firm's riskiness, as measured by beta, can change over time. Firms expand into new lines of business, enlarge their markets, and divest themselves of unprofitable lines of business. Changes in top management can alter the way a company does business. Competitors enter and leave the market, as do principal suppliers. The regulatory environment facing a particular industry can change. All of these (and other) factors can have a material impact on a firm's riskiness.

c. Many academics have suggested beta adjustments to correct for the tendency to regress toward the average beta of 1. Others have added more input information into the beta calculation. Some researchers hope to improve prediction by examining and revising the assumptions underlying portfolio theory. Despite all of this tinkering, prediction with betas leaves much to be desired.

8-7. Note that the Blume betas are all closer to 1. This reflects the desired mean reversion.

Unadjusted Beta	Blume Beta
1.34	1.26
.57	.74
.78	.88
1.2	1.17

8-8. a. An implication of portfolio theory is that an ideal portfolio is internationally diversified. In comparison to a domestically based one, an international portfolio may in fact be more efficient, providing higher returns with less risk because of its greater diversification.

b. The investor has many available avenues for international investing, including international mutual funds, U.S.-based multinational corporations, and American depository receipts, as well as investing directly in the stocks and bonds of foreign companies. There are, however, many problems associated with international investing: Information is more difficult to obtain; regulation varies greatly; there can be legal impediments, political risk, higher transaction costs, and foreign exchange risk. Despite increasing international integration and the previously mentioned problems, there are still strong benefits to be derived from diversifying internationally.

8-9. Problems have arisen with both portfolio theory and its application, including the following: Markets have not proven to be as efficient as the theory requires, nonmarket risk occurs in valuation, and forecasts have proven unreliable.

8-10. a. The maximum expected return is achieved by purchasing only the stock portfolio. The expected return of this portfolio is 15 percent.

b. Purchasing only the short-term debt securities results in the minimum-risk portfolio with an expected return of 8 percent.

c. A portfolio of bonds and short-term debt cannot possibly have a beta over .3, and its expected return must be lower than a portfolio that includes stock, so we can restrict our search to stock/bond and stock/short-term debt combinations. To compare the expected returns, the relative weights must be calculated. The weights are then used to estimate returns.

<u>Stock and Bond Portfolio</u>
$.5 = X (1) + (1 - X) (.3) = X + .3 - .3X = .7X + .3$
$.7X = .2$
$X = .2/.7 = .29$

$Return = .29 (15) + .71 (11) = 12.16\%$

<u>Stock and Short-Term Debt Portfolio</u>
$.5 = X (1) + (1 - X) (.1) = X + .1 - .1X = .9X + .1$
$.9X = .4$
$X = .4/.9 = .44$

$Return = .44 (15) + .56 (8) = 11.08\%$

Therefore, the maximum return of a .5 beta portfolio is a combination portfolio, 29 percent of which consists of the stock portfolio and the other 71 percent of the bond portfolio. The expected return is 12.16 percent.

Answers to Self-Test Questions, p. 236

8-1. True.
8-2. True.
8-3. False. The efficient market, as the term is used in investments, is one in which the prices of all securities fully reflect all known information quickly and, on average, accurately.
8-4. True.
8-5. True.
8-6. False. The semistrong form of the EMH holds that all publicly available information (including past market data) is reflected in stock prices. However, it does not hold that nonpublic information is also contained in stock prices.
8-7. True.
8-8. False. The semistrong form of the EMH states that neither technical nor fundamental analysis will lead to excess profits.
8-9. False. The Sharpe index assesses a portfolio's performance by measuring the excess return (above the risk-free rate) per unit of total risk. This is accomplished by dividing the excess return (portfolio return less the risk-free rate) by the portfolio's total risk (its standard deviation). Therefore, this measure does not utilize total return.
8-10. False. This measure assesses the excess return of the portfolio relative to its beta.
8-11. False. Fund rankings may differ, depending on which measure is chosen.
8-12. True.
8-13. False. Several studies of corporate insiders found that they earned abnormal returns on their stock transactions.
8-14. True.
8-15. False. Money managers need to be concerned with diversification and risk of the securities; they must also consider transaction costs and taxes in the design and management of the portfolios.
8-16. True.

Chapter 9

Answers to Review Questions, pp. 277–280

9-1.   Economic analysis entails the evaluation of the current economic environment and its effect on market, industry, and company fundamentals. The level of economic activity has a major impact on company sales and prices. A detailed analysis of the historical relationships between the economy, industry, and company should determine the sensitivity of profits to economic activity, inflation, interest rates, and so on. For example, this information along with a forecast of GDP (a proxy for overall economic activity) could lead to a prediction of market sales. This figure is modified by estimates of depreciation and taxes to yield a net profit and earnings-per-share forecast. A new P/E forecast results from estimating each of the variables in the P/E formula. A prediction of market price is the outcome of the product of the earnings-per-share and P/E forecasts. This example illustrates the general process of forecasting the future price level. Whether a simpler or more complicated model is used, most proceed from a macroeconomic model to profit projection to price level prediction. The primary difficulty is deriving accurate estimates of the relationships between intermediate variables.

9-2.   a. $PE = p/(k - g) = .5/(.13 - .09) = 12.5$
       b. $PE = .45/(.13 - .09) = 11.25$
       c. $PE = .5/(.13 - .11) = 25$
            An increase of 2 percent in the growth rate is unlikely except in cases of unstable or new companies. Growth rates tend to stabilize as a company matures.
       d. $PE = .5/(.1 - .09) = 50$
            A decrease of 3 percentage points in the required rate of return in a short period of time is an extremely unlikely occurrence. Such a change can occur gradually over time; as the company matures, its track record of operations shows stability, and its risk premium decreases. However, a decrease in risk premium of 3 percent would normally occur only over the course of several years of stable operations.

9-3.   Economic analysis when applied to an industry uses a similar methodology to that used to predict market performance (see answer to question 9-1). Unless the investor has unlimited time and resources, an index is adequate as representative of the industry. The process begins with a macroeconomic forecast, such as GDP or personal disposable income. This leads to a prediction of sales and, ultimately, earnings. The earnings forecast combined with P/E yields a price estimate for the index.

9-4.   A similar methodology as that employed for market and industry forecasts (see answers to questions 9-1 and 9-3) can be used to forecast company performance. A top-down process is appropriate; market and industry forecasts result in predictions of company sales, earnings, and finally stock price. At the company level, there are a large number of variables that can be used as inputs to the pricing algorithm. The art is in determining relevant variables and their effects. A caveat is that the calculated price should be judged relative to that of other companies.

9-5.   A company's competitive position has a direct bearing on its future growth and profits. Larger firms can, in many cases, achieve economies of scale, which allows them to produce goods more cheaply than their rivals. These economies can extend to other areas, such as distribution and marketing. Competitive position may, in some instances, dictate directions for corporate expansion (vertical, horizontal, or for diversification purposes). But size can bring inefficiencies and management ineffectiveness. Company size and actions may spark government scrutiny. Antitrust activity often varies with the political climate.

9-6.   For the implied growth rate we use the formula: $g = k - p/PE = .18 - .2/(35/1.25) = 17.3\%$

9-7.   The quality of management is difficult for most investors to judge. Investors depend primarily on the media for profiles and data. Companies out of the spotlight—the vast majority—receive almost no coverage. When information is available, investors should pay attention to research and development, marketing, management style, innovation, and responsiveness to shareholder concerns. The percentage of the company's stock owned by top management is also a good indicator of management's interest in the company's long-term well-being. Excessive management turnover can be a "red flag." The psychological element should not be discounted; the value of much of the news is not in the details but rather in the market reaction.

9-8.   The *balance sheet* lists assets and liabilities; it provides a glimpse of how the assets were financed. The debt side of the ledger yields the debt-to-equity ratio that can be used to assess whether the firm is taking on too much risk. The *income statement* begins with total revenues, then details the expenses that are deducted to reach the final earnings figure. This statement reveals expenses and their relation to each other, and it puts them into a historical perspective. The *change in financial position statement* furnishes financial data that reveal cash flows. The firm's liquidity position can be determined from this information.

9-9.   Current ratio = current assets/current liabilities

   Jan. 2000 current ratio = 6,390/3,656 = 1.75

   Jan. 2001 current ratio = 7,777/4,385 = 1.77

Quick (acid test) ratio = current assets other than inventories/current liabilities

   Jan. 2000 quick ratio = 901/3,656 = 0.246

   Jan. 2001 quick ratio = 1,221/4,385 = 0.278

Inventory turnover ratio = cost of goods sold/average inventory

Average inventory = 1/2 x (beginning inventory + ending inventory)

   Jan. 2001 average inventory = 1/2 x (6,556 + 5,489) = 6,022.5

   Since Jan. 1999 balance sheet items are not available, it is necessary to use Jan. 2000 inventory rather than taking an average.

   2000 inventory turnover ratio = 27,023/5,489 = 4.92

   2001 inventory turnover ratio = 32,057/6,022.5 = 5.32

Debt-equity ratio = long-term debt/stockholders' equity

   2000 debt-equity ratio = 750/12,341 = 6.08%

   2001 debt-equity ratio = 1,545/15,004 = 10.3%

An alternative definition of the debt-equity ratio is total liabilities divided by net worth. (Note that because ratios are used to make comparisons rather than as absolute measures of performance, either definition is acceptable, as long as there is consistency over time and when comparing different companies.)

Using the alternate definition,

   2000 debt-equity ratio = 4,730/12,348 = 38.3%

   2001 debt-equity ratio = 6,370/15,010 = 42.4%

Net profit margin = net income/sales

   2000 net profit margin = 2,320/38,434 = 6.04%

   2001 net profit margin = 2,581/45,738 = 5.64%

Asset turnover ratio = sales/average total assets

   For Jan. 2000, only one asset amount is available, so it is not possible to take an average.

   2001 average assets = 1/2 x (17,081 + 21,385) = 19,233

   2000 asset turnover ratio = 38,434/17,081 = 2.25

   2001 asset turnover ratio = 45,738/19,233 = 2.38

Return on assets = net income/average total assets

   2000 return on assets = 2,320/17,081 = 13.6%

   2001 return on assets = 2,581/19,233 = 13.4%

Equity multiplier = average total assets /average stockholders' equity

   2001 average stockholders' equity = 1/2 x (12,341 + 15,004) = 13,672.5

   2000 equity multiplier = 17,081/12,341 = 1.38

   2001 equity multiplier = 19,233/13,672.5 = 1.41

Return on equity = net income/average stockholders' equity

   2000 return on equity = 2,320/12,341 = 18.8%

   2001 return on equity = 2,581/13,672.5 = 18.9%

9-10.   a.   GRO EPS$_{5years}$ = \$1 $(1.1)^5$ = \$1.61

   New GRO price = New PE (GRO EPS$_{5years}$) = 20 (\$1.61) = \$32.20

   b.   Asset Play EPS$_{5years}$ = \$1 $(1.1)^5$ = \$1.61

   New Asset Play price = New PE (Asset Play EPS$_{5years}$) = 15 (\$1.61) = \$24.15

   c.   GRO HPR = \$32.2/\$25 −1 = 28.8%

   GRO annualized return = $\sqrt[5]{1.288}-1$ = 5.19%

   Asset Play HPR = \$24.15/\$8 −1 = 201.9%

   Asset Play annualized return = $\sqrt[5]{3.019}-1$ = 24.7%

9-11. a. GRO EPS$_{5years}$ = $1 $(1.05)^5$ = $1.28

New GRO price = New PE (GRO EPS$_{5years}$) = 12 ($1.28) = $15.36

Asset Play EPS$_{5years}$ = $1 $(1.05)^5$ = $1.28

New Asset Play price = New PE (Asset Play EPS$_{5years}$) = 6 ($1.28) = $7.68

  b. GRO HPR = $15.36/$25 – 1 = –38.6%

GRO annualized return = $\sqrt[5]{.614}$ –1 = –9.3%

Asset Play HPR = $7.68/$8 – 1 = –4%

Asset Play annualized return = $\sqrt[5]{.96}$ – 1 = –.8%

9-12. a. GRO: p = .13, k = .13, PE = 25

PE = p/(k – g) => g = k – p/PE

g_{GRO} = .13 – .13/25 = 12.48%

  b. Asset Play: p = .5, k = .12 PE = 8

$g_{Asset\ Play}$ = .12 – .5/8 = 5.75%

9-13. During the 1975–1995 period, investing in low-P/E stocks resulted in a 2.5 percent superior return to a strategy of investing in growth stocks. The relationship reversed between 1996 and 2000, with growth stocks experiencing a 4 percent greater return. The performance of growth stocks declined in 2001, relative to low P/E stocks.

9-14. Many econometric studies have found that the P/E effect disappears when also accounting for the small firm effect. Various causes for the small firm effect have been hypothesized; these include misspecification of CAPM, higher rewards for incomplete information, underestimated risk, and thin markets. Research that controls for these factors has not been able to eliminate the effect.

9-15. A lack of information and strong price sensitivity have caused many investors to shy away from low-priced stocks. This neglected-firm effect is an attempt to explain the low-price effect and, as such, could be a rationale for underpricing. The low-price effect appears to be stronger than the P/E and size effects. Possible causes are greater or mismeasured risk, higher trading costs, or the perception of greater risk. If returns are higher due to nonmarket risk, this could be diversified away, thereby generating superior returns. In addition, trading costs are minimized over long holding periods.

9-16. Identifying takeover candidates is desirable because acquisition generally occurs at a premium over the pretakeover price. Early identification allows the investor to enjoy the subsequent price appreciation.

9-17. Valuation of Cash Cow Corporation can be accomplished by using cash flow (CF) in the dividend formula with CF = $3 million, k = 12%, and g = 5%:

P_0 = CF_1 (next year's expected cash flow)/(k – g) = 1.05 x $3,000,000/(.12 – .05)

= $3,150,000/.07 = $45,000,000

Note that we increased the present cash flow by 5 percent to comply with the formula's required next period cash flow. Also remember that cash flow is not the same as long-term dividends and that this result is only a rough gauge of the value of Cash Cow Corporation.

9-18. Stockholders are primarily concerned with stock price—theoretically based on the present value of all expected dividends forever. The stockholder is therefore interested in management's taking a long-term perspective that maximizes return while minimizing risk. A manager's self-interest may clash with this goal. Management might undertake a short-term strategy that enhances its image in order for the manager to secure higher pay or a more lucrative position at another firm. Managers might also seek power, resulting in a large, inefficient company. When management and stockholders differ in their goals, the stock price will often suffer.

9-19. Investors should look for firms in which management and shareholders have the same goals. Positive signals include management ownership of shares, low turnover at the executive level, investment in R&D and employee training, a long-term orientation, and sensible cost cutting. Negative signals include high merger activity, excessive management compensation, low dividend yield, low growth rates, and high management turnover.

Answers to Self-Test Questions, pp. 280–281

9-1. False. Profits are more variable than almost all the components of the GDP.

9-2. False. The assumptions are essentially identical. Indeed, the payout ratio must also be assumed in order to apply the P/E (earnings multiplier) approach.

9-3.   True.

9-4.   False. Using the dividend discount model, the higher the expected growth rate of dividends is, the higher the P/E will be.

9-5.   True.

9-6.   True.

9-7.   True.

9-8.   False. The basic balance sheet equation is as follows: Assets – liabilities = net worth.

9-9.   False. The quick ratio of current assets minus inventories divided by current liabilities is used to assess the firm's liquidity.

9-10. False. Using the Dupont formula (ROE = ROS x asset turnover x debt margin), it is clear that raising the debt ratio would raise return on equity, all other things being equal. The firm's financial risk would be increased, however.

9-11. False. Fully diluted earnings per share are calculated after assuming convertible debt has been converted into shares of stock to establish a conservative estimate of earnings for P/E ratio calculation purposes.

9-12. True.

9-13. True.

9-14. False. Analyst neglect arises largely because many institutional investors are less interested in small firms with low capitalizations. All publicly held corporations must publish their results.

9-15. True.

9-16. False. The agency problem is inherent in modern corporations in which stock ownership is usually separated from management control. Therefore, the firm might not operate as efficiently as it could, regardless of executive pay levels. However, compensating managers with stock as well as cash may help to align their goals with those of shareholders.

9-17. True.

9-18. True.

9-19. True.

Chapter 10

Answers to Review Questions, pp. 309–310

10-1. Econometric and leading indicator models have shown little success in predicting market prices. The shortcomings of econometric models include infrequent updating and the inability to supply information that has not already been incorporated into the market price. On the other hand, leading indicators have shown some predictive ability. Some indicators are more successful at predicting economic upturns; others are better at predicting downturns. The stock market itself appears to be a leading indicator of the economy. Poor track records have not prevented ongoing investment and research.

10-2. The government can act on the economy either through direct transfers (tax cuts or cash payments/vouchers) or indirectly through government programs or projects. Government expenditures are occasionally aimed at increasing production. The theory is that the fruits of increased spending and production flow through the economy, resulting in an overall increase in output. Offsetting this effect is the funding mechanism; taxes and borrowing decrease funds available privately for investment. The tools for spurring the economy are increased government spending and tax cuts. Tax increases and reduced government spending tend to restrain the economy. Keynesians believe that government spending is more effective than tax cuts for economic stimulation. Two caveats should be observed: (1) Spending and its funding work at cross-purposes, thereby partially nullifying each other, and (2) the effect of governmental action depends on the current state of the economy; if the economy is near capacity, inflation may result.

10-3. The Federal Reserve influences the economy via the credit markets. Its primary tools are reserve requirements, open market operations, and the discount window. Changing the reserve requirement is a very powerful but seldom used tool. Open market operations alter total banking reserves that, in turn, affect the level of lending. For the most part, this has been the Fed's chosen economic tactic. When the Fed embarks on an economic policy shift, it signals its intention by announcing a target for the federal funds rate. It then proceeds to alter aggregate reserves through open market transactions. The federal funds rate is determined by the supply of and demand for loanable funds, but these are, in turn, strongly influenced by Fed activity in its open market operations.

10-4.   Reasons for following monetary policy include the following: It has a unique influence on the economy; its effects are easier to model and predict than those attributable to fiscal initiatives; influential economists tout the primacy of monetary policy; interest rate changes have effects throughout the economy. Monetary policy's effect on the stock market occurs through pricing models (via the federal funds rate); rate changes alter the relative attractiveness of various securities; margin costs modify the ability to support the market through borrowing. A sophisticated model of the stock market should include both fiscal and monetary drivers, but as with most models, the devil is in the details. The recent trend among market prognosticators has been to minimize the effect of fiscal policy on the economy. Research has shown that the stock market is relatively efficient in pricing (capitalizing) the effects of monetary action. Opportunity may arise from effective implementation of market expectations as opposed to mechanical rules.

Another factor to keep in mind is that monetary policy can be implemented much more quickly than fiscal policy. For example, the Fed can make a determination to increase the money supply through open market operations and purchase government securities through member banks, which then have money to loan. The impact on the economy is felt within days.

On the other hand, suppose Congress decides to use a tax cut to stimulate the economy. The tax bill will be debated in committees in both Houses of Congress, then debated by the entire House and Senate. A joint committee will negotiate a compromise between the two versions of the bill. The bill will finally be sent to the President, where there will be the risk of a veto. Even when the bill becomes law, it will take time to implement, and even more time for its effects to be felt in the economy. The total lag time might be as much as a couple of years, during which time the economy may have already recovered from the recession.

10-5.   a.   With lower interest rates comes easier credit, which—all other things being equal—should serve as a catalyst for the economy. The stock market should therefore rise.

   b.   A rise in stock prices should be expected.

   c.   The stock market is likely to react negatively to this major disruption in the international credit market, causing a decline in stock prices.

10-6.   When the increase in the inflation rate is unanticipated, there is likely to be an adverse impact on the stock market. Companies that are most likely to be adversely affected are ones that are locked into long-term contracts, wherein they agree to provide goods and services at pre-established prices. Their revenues will have already been determined prior to the increase in inflation, yet their expenses (labor, raw materials, overhead, and so on) will rise with the increase in inflation. The cost of borrowing new funds to repay outstanding debt as it falls due will also rise, as market interest rates increase with the inflation rate. Some companies may even be forced to abandon planned capital expansion as the cost of borrowing rises sharply, making projects that had been thought profitable no longer attractive.

The discount rate rises with the inflation rate. When the increase in inflation is anticipated and planned for, the rate of growth is also likely to rise (in nominal terms). This is less likely to happen when inflation is unexpected. Using the dividend discount model, we can see that when the discount rate rises more rapidly than the growth rate, the market price of the stock can be expected to decrease.

10-7.   a.   To maximize expected returns, you should purchase 100 percent short-term bonds, as shown below.

Expected inflation = .1(2) + .3(4) + .4(6) + .2(8) = .2 + 1.2 + 2.4 + 1.6 = 5.4%

   Expected Returns
   Stocks = 8%
   Short-term bonds = 3 + inflation = 8.4%
   Long-term bonds = 5 + .3(inflation) = 6.62%
   Real estate = 1 + 6.48 = 7.48%

   b.   As the following table indicates, only short-term bonds offer a real return greater than 2 percent at all of the inflation rates shown. You should purchase only these securities if you are unwilling to risk having a real return below 2 percent.

Nominal and Real Returns for Each Possible Inflation Rate				
	Inflation Rate			
	2	4	6	8
Stocks	8 (6)*	8 (4)	8 (2)	8 (0)
Short-term bonds	5 (3)	7 (3)	9 (3)	11 (3)
Long-term bonds	5.6 (3.6)	6.2 (2.2)	6.8 (.8)	7.4 (−.6)
Real estate	3.4 (1.4)	5.8 (1.8)	8.2 (2.2)	10.6 (2.6)
*Real return in parentheses				

10-8. If the investments are perfect inflation hedges, their return in a stable price environment (no inflation) is their real return. Returns in inflationary environments are shown in the table below.

	Real	Inflation		
		2	6	10
A	3	5	9	13
B	10	12	16	20
C	7	9	13	17

10-9. Returns are as shown in the table below.

Nominal (Real) After-tax Returns			
	2	6	10
A	3.5 (1.5)	6.3 (.3)	9.1 (−.9)
B	8.4 (6.4)	11.2 (5.2)	14.0 (4)
C	6.3 (4.3)	9.1 (3.1)	11.9 (1.9)

10-10. Returns where b = .3 and .9 are shown in the following tables.

Nominal (Real) After-tax Returns			
0.3	2	6	10
A	2.5 (.5)	3.4 (−2.6)	4.2 (−5.8)
B	7.4 (5.4)	8.3 (2.3)	9.1 (−.9)
C	5.3 (3.3)	6.2 (.2)	7 (−3)

Nominal (Real) After-tax Returns			
0.9	2	6	10
A	3.4 (1.4)	5.9 (−.1)	8.4 (−1.6)
B	8.3 (6.3)	10.8 (4.8)	13.3 (3.3)
C	6.2 (4.2)	8.7 (2.7)	11.2 (1.2)

10-11. Bonds decrease in value when there is an unexpected increase in the inflation rate. Long-term returns on bonds are historically poor in relation to stocks, especially when unexpected inflation drives bond prices down. Commodities and real estate generally increase in price when overall prices increase; they therefore tend to offer better inflation protection than bonds or stock.

10-12. a. A profit of $2 million and sales of 500,000 at $50 per unit imply that TUV's total revenues and total costs were $20 million and $18 million, respectively. Total variable costs are the product of units sold and per-unit variable costs. Thus, fixed costs must be $8 million. If TUV absorbs the higher inputs costs, it can expand sales by 20 percent with existing capacity. Under these circumstances, its profits will be determined as follows:

Sales revenues = $49 [500,000 (1.2)] = $24,000,000
Total variable costs = $25 (600,000) = $15,000,000
Total fixed costs = $8,000,000
Total costs = total variable costs + total fixed costs = $23,000,000
Profits = sales revenues – total costs = $1,000,000

b. If TUV raises its price to cover the increased variable costs, its profit will be as follows:

Sales revenues = $45 [500,000 (.8)] = $18,000,000
Total variable costs = $25 (400,000) = $10,000,000
Total fixed costs = $8,000,000
Total costs = total variable costs + total fixed costs = $18,000,000
Profits = sales revenues – total costs = $0

Under these circumstances, holding the line on prices and absorbing the cost increase would be the more profitable strategy. Note, however, that such a strategy depends on the existence of sufficient capacity to service the additional demand.

Answers to Self-Test Questions, pp. 310–311

10-1. False. Both micro- and macroeconomic data are typically used to forecast economic activity.
10-2. True.
10-3. False. Increases in government spending stimulate the economy (spur growth); tax increases have a restraining effect on the level of economic activity.
10-4. False. After taking leakages into account, a $1 increase in government spending increases the GDP by less than $2.
10-5. False. The Federal Reserve Board has primary authority over monetary policy.
10-6. True.
10-7. True.
10-8. False. Checkable deposits are by far the largest component of M1.
10-9. True.
10-10. False. The federal funds rate is the rate that banks charge each other for the overnight use (loan) of funds.
10-11. False. The tools of fiscal policy are changes in tax rates and the level of government spending.
10-12. True.
10-13. False. The primary goals of both monetary policy and fiscal policy are the same—full employment and price stability.
10-14. False. Price stability is the absence of either a rising or falling trend in overall prices. It is desirable to have the price level (average) remain stable, while individual prices fluctuate to reflect changing supply and demand conditions for individual goods and services.
10-15. True.
10-16. True.
10-17. False. Restrictive monetary policy raises interest rates and limits credit availability to stronger credit risks, thereby affecting the allocation of funds away from financially weaker borrowers.
10-18. True.
10-19. True.
10-20. False. Only if the after-tax cost of the loan is below the rate of return earned on the investment will the use of leverage enhance an investor's nominal return.

10-21. True.

10-22. False. Treasury bills provide the greatest short-term inflation protection but offer a relatively low long-term real return.

Chapter 11

Answers to Review Questions, pp. 342–343

11-1. The market was bullish until the weekend before the crash. The subsequent precipitous fall does not speak well for market efficiency. Panics highlight an emotional element that is difficult to reconcile and incorporate with the efficient market hypothesis.

11-2. The use of short trading data is often motivated by the belief that short traders have superior market insight. Implementation of this doctrine requires that their actions be mimicked in anticipation of price declines. A spin-off is the belief that short pressure will likely lead to higher demand, thus driving up prices; investors should, therefore, buy when short volume increases. Studies have refuted both of these strategies. Other theorists focus on odd-lot traders and their perceived poor market timing. It is thought that contrary positions should produce profits. Research has found that some positive gains may have been achievable in the 1950s and 1960s, but more recently, this is not the case.

11-3. a. $\text{odd-lot short ratio} = \dfrac{\text{odd-lot short sales}}{\text{total odd-lot sales}} = \dfrac{.07}{1.3} = .0538$

$\text{TOLSR} = \dfrac{\text{odd-lot short sales}}{\text{odd-lot purchases/odd-lot sales}} = \dfrac{.07}{1.6/1.3} = .0569$

   b. odd-lot short sales = .24 million

$\text{odd-lot short ratio} = \dfrac{.24}{1.3} = .185 \text{ and TOLSR} = \dfrac{.24}{1.6/1.3} = .195$

11-4. a. Many assume that specialists have superior market insight. This belief dictates following specialists' short-selling.

   b. A similar market timing method entails monitoring mutual funds' cash position. If the cash position becomes large, a significant market upswing is expected. The implication is that the fund is waiting for the right buying opportunity. Mutual funds have generally not been successful with their cash management timing strategies.

   c. Some investors view the bond market as offering clues about future moves of the stock market. A low value of a statistic such as the Barron's Confidence Index (BCI) indicates that the rate spread between high-grade and speculative bonds is wide, thus revealing that investment is shifting away from speculative bonds. This demonstrates pessimism and does not bode well for the stock market. Results using this method have not been encouraging.

11-5. Barron's Confidence Index = high-grade rates/average-grade rates

$\text{BCI}_A = \dfrac{5.67}{6.01} = .943 \qquad \text{BCI}_B = \dfrac{7.89}{8.85} = .892$

$\text{BCI}_C = \dfrac{9.50}{11.78} = .806 \qquad \text{BCI}_D = \dfrac{10.34}{13.89} = .744$

11-6. a. The advance-decline ratio has been shown to have some persistence. In other words, advances (declines) tend to extend beyond one trading day (sometimes termed momentum).

   b. The short-term trading index uses the ratio of average decline volume to average advance volume. Traders using this statistic have claimed positive results.

   c. The January indicator suggests that if the market rises in January, there is a good chance that it will continue to do so for the rest of the year. The January effect is based on the observation that small stocks consistently outperform the market for the early part of January. This effect may be due to tax implications, and it has diminished in recent years.

d. Some studies have found that there is a disparity between price changes on Monday and Friday. Prices are apt to fall on Monday and rise on Friday. This is based on the idea that bad news is most likely to be revealed after the market closes on Friday.

11-7. a. Chartists' basic premise is that future prices can be predicted based upon observation of past prices and volume. Supporters of the random walk hypothesis believe that this is not possible, that there is no link between past and future price patterns. From this perspective, price movements can be viewed as random.

b. The belief in the separation of past and future prices is a subcategory of the weak form of the efficient market hypothesis. This theory states that a stock's current price incorporates all previously available information. In other words, no abnormal profit can be consistently obtained by analyzing past price movements. Profit opportunities are precluded because price adjustments occur too quickly.

11-8. a. Orders in a specialist's book tend to bunch at certain levels (for example, whole numbers). This bunching can cause price movements to stall and then accelerate. In addition to being disjointed, price movements can become exaggerated. Various researchers have postulated that specialists amplify price changes in the overnight market. The specialist moves prices by trading from his or her account. In this way, limit prices are triggered and still more trades result. The implication is that the specialist might be moving the market to generate commissions.

b. An investor should view the current price and determine likely cluster points for limit orders. This information and a preconception of price direction could signal an opportunity to capitalize on a potentially significant price move. A key factor in the decision process should be the accumulated order volume. With this in mind, the investor should request order sizes in addition to bid-ask prices.

11-9. a. Tax-loss trading primarily involves the stock of small firms at year-end. Price decreases are occasionally dramatic. Evidence for this anomaly is strong.

b. There can be a substantial run-up in the stock's price if a firm is the target of a tender offer, merger, or liquidation. A significant decline may be expected if the action is canceled or proven to be only a rumor. Although a trading strategy based on anticipation of any of these events can be dangerous, it may also present a profit opportunity. Research indicates that companies in these situations often experience price movements well before announcements are made, indicating some insider behavior. The average investor may therefore find that timely action is extremely difficult.

11-10. Dividend reinvestment plans have benefits for both management and stockholders. Increased demand for stock and lower administrative costs benefit management. Stockholders benefit from lower transaction costs. Reinvestment plans are generally viewed in a positive light, thereby contributing to stock value. On the other hand, newly issued shares can dilute the market, thus creating downward price pressure.

11-11. a. The value of your portfolio is determined as follows:

P = $10, buy 10 shares; total shares = 10   Portfolio = 10 ($10) = $100
P = $5, buy 20 shares; total shares = 30   Portfolio = 30 ($5) = $150
P = $10   Portfolio = 30 ($10) = $300

b. The value of your portfolio is calculated as follows:

P = $10, buy 10 shares; total shares = 10   Portfolio = 10 ($10) = $100
P = $15, buy 6.67 shares; total shares = 16.67   Portfolio = 16.67 ($15) = $250
P = $10   Portfolio = 16.67 ($10) = $166.67

Answers to Self-Test Questions, pp. 343–344

11-1. False. The weak form of the EMH allows for random overreaction as a part of the noise in the data.
11-2. False. The return attributed to market timing was shown to be one-half or less of the return attributed to stock selection.
11-3. True.
11-4. False. The Dow theory seeks to confirm if a primary trend, either upward or downward, has emerged. The theory relies on the secondary moves for this purpose.
11-5. True.
11-6. True.

11-7. False. If mutual fund managers are holding more of their assets in the form of cash, this is a bullish indicator. It suggests that the fund managers want to have cash available to make purchases quickly when the upturn begins.

11-8. True.

11-9. True.

11-10. False. Chart reading is a type of technical analysis.

11-11. True.

11-12. True.

11-13. False. Block trades are transactions involving 10,000 or more shares.

11-14. True.

11-15. True.

11-16. True.

11-17. False. Rights offerings and forced conversions increase the number of outstanding common shares, but share repurchases decrease the number of outstanding shares of common stock.

11-18. True.

11-19. False. Dollar cost averaging consists of spending a fixed amount of money on stock purchases at regular intervals.

Chapter 12

Answers to Review Questions, pp. 365–367

12-1. a. The initial NAV of the $$$ mutual fund is $21.67, calculated as follows:

$$\text{Initial NAV} = \frac{\$650,000,000}{30,000,000} = \$21.67$$

b. The increase in the NAV is 15.37 percent, as shown below:

$$\text{New NAV} = \frac{\$800,000,000}{32,000,000} = \$25.00$$

$$\text{Percentage increase} = \frac{\$25.00}{\$21.67} - 1 = 15.37\%$$

12-2. Suppose the investor purchases one share. The one-year return can be determined as follows:

$$\text{Cost} = \frac{\text{NAV}}{1-\text{L}} = \frac{\$21.67}{1-.03} = \$22.34$$

Final value = Final NAV + Distributions = $25.00 + $.70 = $25.70

$$\text{Return} = \frac{\$25.70}{\$22.34} - 1 = 15.04\%$$

12-3. Load fees can be either front end or back end. Front-end loads can be up to 8 1/2 percent, but they are usually 3 percent to 6 percent of NAV and deducted upon purchase. Back-end loads occur upon redemption. They are generally lower than front-end loads and frequently decrease as the ownership period lengthens. 12b-1 fees are annual fees, not in excess of 1 percent of NAV per year, to cover a fund's marketing and distribution expenses.

12-4. a. The best way to proceed is to examine each year's investment. The performance of the no-load mutual fund can therefore be determined as shown below:

Year 1 = $3,000 $(1.11)^5$ = $5,055.17
Year 2 = $3,000 $(1.11)^4$ = $4,554.21
Year 3 = $3,000 $(1.11)^3$ = $4,102.89
Year 4 = $3,000 $(1.11)^2$ = $3,696.30
Year 5 = $3,000 (1.11) = $3,330.00
Final value = $20,738.57

b. To calculate the performance of the 12b-1 mutual fund with a 1 percent fee at the end of each year, we can proceed as in question 12-4a., but a little algebra will make things simpler. The rate of increase can be combined with the 12b-1 fee to arrive at a single annual rate as follows:

Annual rate $= (1 + \text{return})(1 - \text{fee}) - 1 = (1.11)(.99) - 1 = 9.89\%$
Year 1 $= \$3,000\,(1.0989)^5 = \$4,807.42$
Year 2 $= \$4,374.76$
Year 3 $= \$3,981.03$
Year 4 $= \$3,622.74$
Year 5 $= \$3,296.70$
Final value $= \$20,082.65$

c. To determine the performance of the front-end load with an 8.5 percent commission in the first year only, we can use the figures from a. after adjusting the first year's figure as follows:

Year 1 $= \$3,000\,(1 - .085)(1.11)^5 = \$4,625.48$
Final value $= \$20,308.88$

12-5. a. Assume that the unknown annual rate is r. The 12b-1 fund's annual return must be 12.12 percent to equal the no-load fund's end-of-period value, as calculated below:

$(1 + r)(1 - \text{fee}) = 1.11$
$(1 + r)(.99) = 1.11$
$1 + r = 1.11/.99$
$r = (1.11/.99) - 1 = 12.12\%$

b. The answer to question 12-4 tells us that the final value with a front-end load is higher than that associated with a 12b-1 fee. The annual rate can therefore be lower.

12-6. a. The percentage discount on the initial NAV is determined as follows:
Discount $= (33 - 25)/33 = 24.24\%$

b. Pckans Group purchased 35 percent of the 10 million shares. These 3.5 million shares were purchased at an average per-share cost of $28. With a final price of $35, the gross profits are $24.5 million, as calculated below:
Gross profits $= 3,500,000\,(\$35 - \$28) = \$24,500,000$

c. Since this is a takeover, we can assume that only purchase commissions are involved. The net return, therefore, is 22.49 percent, computed as follows:

Commissions $= .02\,[\$28\,(3,500,000)] = .02\,(\$98,000,000) = \$1,960,000$
Total costs $=$ Legal costs $+$ Commissions $= \$500,000 + \$1,960,000 = \$2,460,000$
$$\text{Net return} = \frac{\text{Gross profits} - \text{Total costs}}{\text{Outlay for stock}} = \frac{\$24,500,000 - \$2,460,000}{\$98,000,000} = 22.49\%$$

12-7. Mutual funds are examples of open-end investment companies. Open-end companies have a flexible number of shares that can expand or shrink with demand as the fund buys shares from and sells shares to investors. The price of open-end shares is determined by the value of the underlying shares—in other words, NAV. Closed-end investment companies have a fixed number of shares that are determined at the inception of the fund. The share price of a closed-end fund is determined by supply and demand; it is therefore generally different from the NAV. Purchase of closed-end shares occurs in the open market, unlike the purchase of open-end shares, which ultimately come from the issuing company. Closed-end companies can decide to become or be forced into becoming open-end companies. The change from a closed-end to open-end company results in shares selling at NAV. This usually involves a price increase.

12-8. a. The stocks in a sector fund generally have a unifying theme. The number of sector funds is vast, as are the variety of themes. Examples of sectors include such themes as industry, geographical region, and investment philosophy.

b. A single investment company manages families of funds. By offering a variety of funds, the investment company hopes to appeal to as wide a market as possible. Exchanges between family funds generally have much lower transaction costs than exchanges outside the family. In this way, the investment company hopes to attract and retain customers.

12-9. a. The holding period return for the Good Fund is computed as follows:

$$\text{Good Fund} = \frac{13.01 + .53 + .74}{14.29} - 1 = -.07\%$$

Thus, the holding period returns for the remaining four funds are as shown below:
Bond Fund = 5.28%
Go Fund = 90.73%
Chip Fund = 15.42%
Cash Fund = 6.8%

b. The riskiness of the fund, as well as the return, needs to be considered in evaluating the fund. The Sharpe ratio, Treynor ratio, and Jensen's alpha all provide risk-adjusted measures of fund performance. Investors should also consider fees and taxes.

12-10. The geometric mean return and standard deviation for the five funds and the market index are as follows:

	Mean Return	Standard Deviation
Good Fund	3.67%	12.94%
Bond Fund	6.70%	6.77%
Go Fund	4.43%	28.99%
Chip Fund	11.00%	14.65%
Cash Fund	7.74%	1.77%
Market	7.62%	14.56%

12-11. The Sharpe ratios for the five funds and the market index using a risk-free rate of 4.7 percent are as follows:

	Sharpe Ratio
Good Fund	−.080
Bond Fund	.295
Go Fund	−.009
Chip Fund	.430
Cash Fund	1.718
Market	.201

12-12. a. Using the betas shown for each fund and the market index, the Treynor ratios and Sharpe ratios are as shown in the following:

	Beta	Treynor Ratio	Rank	Sharpe Ratio	Rank
Good Fund	1.1	−0.009	6	−0.080	6
Bond Fund	0.6	0.033	3	0.295	3
Go Fund	1.3	−0.002	5	−0.009	5
Chip Fund	0.9	0.07	2	0.430	2
Cash Fund	0.2	0.152	1	1.718	1
Market	1	0.029	4	0.201	4

b. Treynor ratios and Sharpe ratios are not directly comparable because the formulas are different. Probably the best method of comparison is by ranking the ratios (putting them in the order of their magnitude). For both measures, the rankings are the same.

12-13. Mutual funds compete with other similarly equipped institutions such as banks. It is in comparison to individual investors that disparities become pronounced. For example, funds have lower trading costs, superior analytical means, and vast credit resources. An additional benefit is lowered risk through diversification. On the other hand, individuals are exempt from the costs associated with fund management and enjoy total freedom in asset choice.

12-14. a. Investors of modest means are probably the greatest beneficiaries of the existence of mutual funds. Funds can be found that allow small initial and/or continuing contributions. Participating in a large pool of investments lowers risk.

b. All mutual fund investors receive the benefits mentioned in 12-14a. Additional benefits include time savings, record keeping, and choice of risk level and fund specialization.

Answers to Self-Test Questions, pp. 367–368

12-1. True.
12-2. False. No-load mutual funds are typically sold directly to the public without a sales force.
12-3. False. Few funds charge a front-end load of 8.5 percent of the purchase price of the shares. Most front-end-loaded funds charge less than 5 percent, with the majority in the 3-percent-to-4.5 percent range.
12-4. True.
12-5. False. A 12b-1 fee is an annual charge for marketing and distribution expenses, and it is different from a load.
12-6. True.
12-7. False. The shares of closed-end investment companies are sold in the open market at prices determined by supply and demand. They may sell at a premium or discount to their net asset value.
12-8. False. Closed-end funds may convert into open-end funds.
12-9. True.
12-10. False. Variable annuities allow funds to grow and accumulate tax deferred. During the distribution phase, however, all gain is taxed as ordinary income.
12-11. True.
12-12. True.
12-13. False. At least 90 percent of gross income must be distributed to shareholders for the fund to qualify as a regulated investment company.
12-14. True.
12-15. True.
12-16. True.
12-17. False. On average, mutual funds underperform the market, especially when fees are taken into account.
12-18. True.
12-19. False. Large block trades by institutions often result in adverse price effects.
12-20. False. Typically, institutional investors restrict their analysis to a small percentage of traded stocks.
12-21. False. In the 1990s, few mutual funds were able to consistently beat the returns on S&P 500 Index funds.

Chapter 13

Answers to Review Questions, pp. 399–401

13-1. a. A call involves the right to buy (from the option's writer) at the strike price, whereas a put grants the right to sell (to the writer) at the strike price. Calls participate in the underlying security's price appreciation; puts participate in its depreciation.
   b. A call writer must deliver the promised asset at the specified (strike) price if the call is exercised prior to expiration. Similarly, the put writer must purchase the underlying asset upon exercise.
   c. The holder of a call has a choice whether or not to exercise the option. The writer of a put has no choice but must purchase the underlying asset if the option holder chooses to sell. A call derives its value gains from those of the underlying asset. The call owner's loss is capped by the call's price if the asset's value is unchanged or declines. A put writer's profit is capped at the put premium and not affected by increases in the price of the underlying asset. The put writer's loss increases as the underlying asset's price decreases. The lack of equivalency between purchasing calls and put writing is demonstrated by the differences in profit patterns. (See diagrams C and F in appendix C to this chapter.)

13-2. a. Purchase of a put will protect the investor from decreases in the stock's value and allow the investor to continue to receive dividends.
   b. Selling the stock protects the investor from price decreases, but the investor forgoes dividends and any profits from subsequent price increases.
   c. If the put were free, its ownership would clearly be the superior strategy. This strategy's value varies inversely with the put's price. The investor should also consider transaction costs and the time horizon (puts expire). On the other hand, the put still allows the investor the upside potential of holding the stock.

13-3. a. The strike price is the price at which a transaction in the underlying asset will take place if an option is exercised.

    b. The intrinsic value for calls is the maximum of (1) the difference between the market price of the underlying asset and the strike price or (2) zero. In the case of puts, the intrinsic value is the strike price minus the market price, but not less than zero. Time value is the difference between the option's market price and its intrinsic value. The strike price determines whether an option is in- or out-of-the-money. If the price of the underlying asset is above the strike price, a call is in-the-money and a put is out-of-the-money. If the underlying asset's price is below the strike price, the positions are reversed.

13-4. a. The investor breaks even when the call's intrinsic value (C_1) is equal to its purchase price (C_0):

$$C_1 = S_1 - S$$
$$S_1 = C_1 + S = C_0 + S = 1.75 + 35 = 36.75$$

    b. $HPR_{Stock} = (45/32) - 1 = 40.63\%$

       $HPR_{Call} = [(45 - 35)/1.75] - 1 = 471.43\%$

    c. The dividend must be added to the stock's price when calculating the stock's returns in b. above. This is not the case with the call's calculations; only the market price is used.

13-5. a. In exchange for the premium, the writer is obligated to turn over the stock (receiving payment at the strike price) if the call is exercised.

    b. Covered call writers receive the premium and dividends but forgo any future gains from stock price appreciation above the strike price. Stock price gains are canceled out by losses on the call (assuming exercise). Writers retain the risk of price declines. As is evident, covered call writers desire that stock prices remain stable or rise; this optimal result allows retention of the premium and any dividends that were received. (See diagram G in appendix C to this chapter.)

13-6. a. A straddle is simultaneously buying a put and a call on the same asset.

    b. Straddle buyers are anticipating price movement in the underlying asset. The straddle begins to pay off whether prices move up or down.

    c. Investors who feel that the underlying asset's price is stable are likely to write straddles. If their predictions are realized, all or most of the premium is retained.

13-7. a. The holder of a spread possesses a call and writes a call on the same security. The calls have different strike prices, expiration dates, or both.

    b. A spread holder expects the purchased call's value to rise faster than that of the written call. The two positions can be seen as a form of insurance that limits gains and losses. (See diagrams C and D in appendix C to this chapter.)

13-8. A right is essentially an option, but it is issued by the same firm that issued the stock. The shareholder receives one right per share that entitles him or her to an additional fractional share. The stated price is frequently below market levels. Rights can be traded. Warrants can also be traded but are usually initially tied to bonds, rather than equity. Warrants are generally much longer term than rights and are way out-of-the-money when first issued.

13-9. a. New shares are issued when a warrant is exercised. Per-share earnings decrease if earnings remain constant and shares increase.

    b. Rights also increase the number of shares outstanding, thereby decreasing per-share earnings.

13-10. a. Initial stock price = S_0 = $50

       Subscription price = S = $47

       Number of shares required = N = 20

$$\text{Cum-right } \frac{S_0 - S}{N + 1} = \frac{50 - 47}{20 + 1} = \$.14$$

    b. The number of shares increases 5 percent [(21/20) − 1]. This implies that the new share price (S_1) should be 20/21 of what it was previously (S_0):

$$S_1 = S_0\left(\frac{N}{N+1}\right) = 50\left(\frac{20}{21}\right) = \$47.62$$

$$\text{Ex-right} = \frac{S_1 - S}{N} = \$.03$$

13-11. a. The call provision gives the issuing company the power to limit conversion value. This limitation of upside potential reduces the value of the convertible, because an investor loses the ability to keep receiving interest payments until the bond is about to mature and then converting to common stock.

b. Convertibles are more likely to be called when the conversion value exceeds the call price. This likelihood is slightly lower in the period immediately after issuance. This is because companies are reluctant to terminate securities so soon after being created.

13-12. a. The conversion premium decreases as the stock price rises, as shown in figure 13-5. This is primarily due to the fact that as the stock price rises, the market price of the convertible takes on more of the characteristics of the stock and less of the characteristics of the bond. This effect is even greater for convertible bonds with a call feature (the majority of such bonds are callable). This is because a call becomes more likely as the stock price rises. A drop in interest rates will raise the bond's straight-debt value. With this comes a decrease in the conversion premium. This is due to the conversion option's becoming relatively less valuable, thereby decreasing the "extra" amount investors are willing to pay for the conversion privilege. A rate rise causes the opposite result.

b. The time value of call options and the conversion premium of convertibles are similar. Both are the difference between market price and intrinsic value, and they are based on expectations of an increase in the price of the underlying stock.

13-13. a. The computations are as follows:
* Conversion price = $1,050/20 = $52.50
* Conversion value = $40 x 20 = $800
* Conversion premium = $1,050 – $800 = $250
* Premium over straight-debt value = $1,050 – $900 = $150
* Current yield = $100/$1,050 = 9.52%

b. In this case, the minimum value is the conversion value because the option is in-the-money. The profit could be even greater because of the conversion premium. Conversion value = 55.5 x 20 = $1,110; profit = $1,110 – $1,000 = $110.

13-14. The investor has the choice of converting or receiving the $1,070 call price or the conversion value of $65 x 20 = $1,300. The market would logically gravitate to the higher price, which is $1,300.

13-15. Conversion premium = market price – (conversion ratio x price of underlying common stock) = $100 – (2 x $40) = $20.

13-16. If the common stock rises to $60, the conversion value = 2 x $60 = $120. Since this exceeds the call price, the bond is likely to be called, so there should be no conversion premium.

13-17. The owner of a convertible bond gains an option to exchange the bond for a predetermined number of shares of common stock. This option gives the bond some of the upside potential of common stock. Convertibles offer lower coupon rates than otherwise comparable straight bonds because of this feature. From the straight bondholder's perspective, convertibles offer more upside potential, but a call feature often limits this potential. From the stockholder's viewpoint, convertibles offer more downside protection because of the bond portion. Also, interest rates tend to be higher than dividend rates. Offsetting this are the interest rate risk and default risk.

Answers to Self-Test Questions, pp. 401–404

13-1. False. Options are written by investors and sold to other investors.
13-2. True.
13-3. False. If the market price is in excess of the strike price, the call is in-the-money and the put is out-of-the-money. When the market price of a stock is below the strike price, a call option is out-of-the-money but a put option is in-the-money.
13-4. True.
13-5. False. A call option whose strike price exceeds the market can expire without the market's ever reaching that price. One with an exercise price below the prevailing market price has intrinsic value, however, because the underlying stock can be purchased at a price less than market. Therefore, the option premium will be much higher for the one with a strike price less than the current market. This price relationship holds true, regardless of the expected growth in the price potential of the underlying stock.
13-6. False. The intrinsic value of an option can never be less than zero.
13-7. True.
13-8. False. Because the stock is currently trading at a price below the exercise price, it has no intrinsic value. Therefore, its entire $4 price is its time value.
13-9. True.

13-10. False. The maximum amount that can be lost is the premium, or price paid, for either option.

13-11. True.

13-12. True.

13-13. True.

13-14. True.

13-15. False. An investor anticipating a drop in the price of a stock might want to short the stock but would not use a put to hedge the position. If a hedge is desired, the investor might purchase a call that would allow the purchase of stock to cover the short at a known price should the stock price not move as anticipated. An alternative would be to simply buy a put.

13-16. True.

13-17. True.

13-18. False. In this situation, the writer of the uncovered (naked) call would suffer a dollar-for-dollar loss as the market price of the stock subject to the call rises. The result described in question 13-18 would occur had it been a covered call. Then the writer would have retained the option premium but would have forgone any further gain on the long position in the stock.

13-19. False. The writer of a put expects the price either to stay steady or to rise so that the option holder will not exercise the right to sell the shares.

13-20. True.

13-21. False. With a straddle, the stock, exercise price, and expiration date are identical. The investor does not care in which direction the stock moves, provided it moves by a sufficiently large amount. The investor who uses a straddle loses if the stock's price does not change by an amount that is enough to compensate the investor for the premiums paid for both the call and the put.

13-22. False. With the exercise of any index option, the settlement is made in dollars, not in actual delivery of the securities. This settlement is $100 for each point difference between the stock index close and the strike price of the option on the index.

13-23. True.

13-24. True.

13-25. False. The price of a warrant or a call option will rise when the market price of the underlying stock rises.

13-26. True.

13-27. True.

13-28. True.

13-29. False. Conversion premium refers to the difference between the market price of the bond and its conversion value.

13-30. True.

13-31. True.

13-32. True.

13-33. False. The conversion option is a feature that is favorable to the bondholder. As such, it gives the issuing corporation the opportunity to sell the bonds for their face value, while at the same time paying a slightly lower interest rate than would be required for comparable bonds that lack the potential gain from convertibility.

13-34. True.

13-35. False. There is no waiting period. The conversion period typically extends for the life of the bond. In some cases, however, the issuing corporation may wish to limit the conversion period. At the end of the conversion period, the convertible reverts to a straight-debt issue with no conversion privilege.

13-36. True.

13-37. False. The performance of convertibles depends heavily on the price of the underlying stock.

13-38. False. The conversion premium tends to be greater when the price of the stock is lower. As the price of the underlying stock rises above the conversion price, the conversion premium declines; the value of the convertible approaches the value of the underlying stock. In essence, the conversion premium represents the amount the investor is willing to pay to have downside protection (provided by the bond value) while retaining upside potential. As the conversion value further exceeds the bond value, the downside protection becomes less important. Therefore, the conversion premium declines.

13-39. True.

13-40. True.

13-41. False. Due to the presence of the conversion option, convertible bonds typically are less sensitive to interest rate changes than nonconvertible bonds are.

13-42. True.

Answers to Appendix A and Appendix B Questions, pp. 408 and 409

13A-1. The estimated value of the call option is $10.57, calculated as shown below:

$S_0 = 28.50$

$S = 30$

$S_0 / S = 28.50 / 30 = .95$

$\ln(S_0 / S) = -.0513$

$\sigma = 2$

$\frac{1}{2} \times \sigma^2 = \frac{1}{2} \times 2 \times 2 = 2$

$r_f = .05$

$r_f + \frac{1}{2} \times \sigma^2 = 2.05$

$t = .25$

$(r_f + \frac{1}{2}\sigma^2) t = 2.05 \times .25 = .5125$

$\sigma\sqrt{t} = 2 \times \sqrt{.25} = 1$

$d_1 = (-.0513 + .5125)/1 = .4612$

$N(d_1) = .6776$

$r_f - \frac{1}{2}\sigma^2 = .05 - 2 = -1.95$

$(r_f - \frac{1}{2}\sigma^2)t = -1.95 \times .25 = -.4875$

$d_2 = (-.0513 - .4875)/1 = -.5388$

$N(d_2) = .295$

$rt = .05 \times .25 = .0125$

$e^{rt} = e^{.0125} = 1.0126$

$C = 28.5 \times .6776 - (30 \times .295)/1.0126 = 19.31 - 8.74 = \$10.57$

13A-2. The value of the in-the-money option is $5.98, calculated as follows:

$S_0 = 28$

$S = 27$

$S_0 / S = 28 / 27 = 1.037$

$\ln(S_0 / S) = -.0364$

$\sigma = 1.5$

$\frac{1}{2}\sigma^2 = 1.125$

$r_f = .03$

$t = 1/9$

$(r_f + \frac{1}{2}\sigma^2) t = (.03 + 1.125) \times 1/9 = 1.155 \times 1/9 = .1283$

$(r_f - \frac{1}{2}\sigma^2) t = (.03 - 1.125) \times 1/9 = -1.095 \times 1/9 = -.1217$

$\sigma\sqrt{t} = .5$

$d_1 = (.0364 + .1283)/.5 = .3294$

$N(d_1) = .6291$

$d_2 = (.0364 - .1217)/.5 = -.1706$

$N(d_2) = .4323$

$rt = .03 \times 1/9 = .0033$

$e^{rt} = 1.003$

$C = (28 \times .6291) - (27 \times .4323)/1.0033 = 17.61 - 11.63 = \$5.98$

The intrinsic value of the call option is $1, so its time value is $4.98.

13B-1. The value of the call option is $1.44, as follows:

$S_0 = S = 30, P_0 = 1, t = .25, r_f = .06$

$e^{rt} = e^{.015} = 1.015$

$C_0 = P_0 + S_0 - S/e^{rt} = 1 + 30 - 30/1.015 = 31 - 29.56 = \$1.44$

13B-2. Using the put-call parity formula, the value of the put option is $11.70, determined as follows:

$C_0 = \$10.57, \ S_0 = \$28.50, \ S = \$30, \ e^{rt} = 1.0126$

$P_0 + \$28.50 - \$30/1.0126 = C_0 = \$10.57$

$P_0 - \$1.13 = \$10.57$

$P_0 = \$11.70$

Chapter 14

Answers to Review Questions, pp. 438–439

14-1. Commodity market trading hours are much more restricted than those of equity markets. Commodity exchanges restrict futures price movements. Commodity price changes can trigger a shutdown in trading, which is extremely rare in equity markets. Commodity futures have limited lives and much lower margin requirements than are permitted with stock transactions. There are an equal number of long and short futures trades, while short sales of stock constitute only a small fraction of stock transactions. There are no short-selling restrictions on futures trades. Futures positions must be opened and closed with the same brokerage firm.

14-2. a. You have made $92,144, as calculated below.

$5/oz.	Portfolio = $50,000	Loan = $45,000	
	Equity = $5,000	Ounces = $50,000/$5 = 10,000	
$6/oz.	Portfolio = $60,000	Loan = $45,000	
	Equity = Portfolio – Loan = $15,000	Ounces = 10,000	
Buy:	Portfolio = $150,000	Loan = Portfolio – Equity = $135,000	
	Equity = $15,000	Ounces = 10,000 + ($90,000/$6) = 25,000	
$7/oz.	Portfolio = $175,000	Loan = $135,000	
	Equity = $40,000	Ounces = 25,000	
Buy:	Portfolio = $400,000	Loan = $400,000 – $40,000 = $360,000	
	Equity = $40,000	Ounces = 57,143	
$8/oz.	Portfolio = $457,144	Loan = $360,000	
	Equity = $97,144	Ounces = 57,143	

Profit = final equity – initial equity = $97,144 – $5,000 = $92,144

b. The holding period return is calculated as follows: HPR = $92,144/$5,000 = 1,842.88%

14-3. a. You receive a margin call when the loan value increases to 95 percent of the portfolio value—in other words, your equity has fallen to 5 percent. The new price of silver is calculated by using the new portfolio value and the number of ounces owned. The equations below indicate that you would receive a margin call when the price of silver is $6.63 per ounce.

.95 Portfolio = Loan

$$\text{Portfolio} = \frac{\text{Loan}}{.95} = \frac{\$360,000}{.95} = \$378,947.37$$

$$\text{Silver} = \frac{\text{Portfolio}}{\text{Ounces}} = \frac{\$378,947.37}{57,143} = \$6.63/\text{oz.}$$

b. You must sell enough silver to bring your equity up to 10 percent. To double your equity percentage, you must half the portfolio value. This is because all proceeds reduce the loan value while leaving your equity unchanged:

$$\text{Portfolio} = \frac{\$378,947.37}{2} = \$189,473.69$$

and

Loan = .9 ($189,473.69) = $170,526.32

To accomplish this you must sell half (ounces = 57,143/2 = 28,572) of your holdings. As in 14-3a., you must calculate a new portfolio value that will trigger a new margin call. The corresponding silver price can be determined as follows:

$$\text{Portfolio} = \frac{\text{Loan}}{.95} = \frac{\$170,526.32}{.95} = \$179,501.39$$

$$\text{Silver} = \frac{\$179,501.39}{28,572} = \$6.28/\text{oz.}$$

14-4.   An initial condition is an active and competitive spot market. Another good attribute is a standardized contract that reduces trading costs. Price volatility will attract participants who want price protection (hedging) and those who wish to speculate. These participants make for a deeper market. Some commodity futures are predicated on the existence of storage. In these cases, storage must be available at a reasonable cost.

14-5.   *Firm representatives* are active traders who seek either to promote the market for their firm's output or to obtain good prices on inputs; they are generally knowledgeable and experienced. *Day traders* try to take advantage of short-term price movements in the futures market and close all positions at each day's end. *Position traders* rely on fundamental or technical analysis and are not tied to any specific time frame. *Arbitrageurs* are also analytical but concentrate on relative prices; they search for deviations from historical pricing patterns between commodities or contracts.

14-6.   Much of the recent growth in futures markets can be attributed to the creation of innumerable new types of financial futures. Interest rates have a direct effect on financial institutions and, to a lesser degree, on a vast number of other markets. An increase in interest rate volatility has increased demand for interest rate futures for both hedging and speculation. Rapid futures innovation has attempted to satisfy demand for hedging and speculation in this area. Global trade and corporate expansion have increased the need for currency futures. Booming investment in stocks and other financial assets has sparked demand for related instruments, such as index futures. These are just a few examples that are fueling the growth in financial futures.

14-7.   a.   Interest rate futures are similar to other futures in that they lock in a future price for a commodity—in this case, debt instruments. Setting prices for a date in the future is equivalent to locking in interest rates (which determine the present value of bonds). This basic relationship is augmented by the variety of underlying instruments. Bets can be made on interest rate spreads (different yield curves associated with different classes of instruments—for example, corporate securities and municipals), a foreign country's rates, and credit card rates, to name just a few.

   b.   Some of the underlying debt securities are Treasuries, municipals, CDs, and Eurobonds.

14-8.   a.   Stock index futures are comparable to other futures except that there is no delivery of the underlying commodity. This cash settlement is based on the change in the price of the index.

   b.   With perfect immunization, writing index futures essentially locks in the current portfolio price. A decline in portfolio value is offset by an increase in the future's value. In a similar manner, increases in portfolio value are canceled out by money owed on the futures. (This analysis ignores transaction costs.)

14-9.   The number of contracts needed to neutralize a $50 million stock portfolio with a beta of 1.07 is as follows:

$$\text{Number of contracts} = \frac{\text{Portfolio}}{\text{Contract value}} \times \text{Beta} = \frac{50,000,000}{500\,(1,450)} \times 1.07 = 74$$

14-10. A commodity futures option is an option on a futures contract The owner, therefore, possesses the right but not obligation to buy (sell) futures contracts at a specified price within a prescribed time limit. This instrument gives the owner a great deal of leverage and means that the owner risks only the premium. Prospective owners should be aware that determining whether the option's price is fair is difficult because a commodity option is a derivative of a derivative; any errors in the input estimates compound the error in the resulting price.

Answers to Self-Test Questions, pp. 439–440

14-1.   True.
14-2.   True.

14-3. False. In fact, all commodity futures are traded on margin.

14-4. False. Margin, as used in futures contracts, is a good faith deposit (earnest money) made by both the buyer and the seller to ensure the completion of the contract.

14-5. False. The margin required on commodity futures transactions usually ranges from 5 percent to 10 percent of the value of the contract, depending on the underlying asset. However, the investor is not required to borrow the remaining balance to complete the transaction. Margin on futures transactions is actually a deposit (or earnest money), because the commodity is not actually bought or sold until the contract expires. (Most futures contracts are closed out before the contract expires. Therefore, most commodity futures contracts never involve the actual purchase or sale of the commodity.)

14-6. True.

14-7. True.

14-8. True.

14-9. True.

14-10. False. If the investor follows this tactic and interest rates fall as expected, the investor will need to either close out his or her position or deliver the securities. In either case, with the decline in interest rates, the prices of the bonds and the futures contracts will have risen, and there will be a loss on the transaction. If an investor expects interest rates to decline substantially in the near future, it might be advisable to purchase interest rate futures. Like the underlying bonds, interest rate futures increase in price when interest rates decline.

14-11. False. When interest rates rise, the price of bonds (or other fixed-return instruments) falls. If interest rates are expected to rise, the speculator should sell (go short) these futures contracts, because the actual instrument being contracted for is a bond or loanable funds whose price will *decline* if interest rates rise.

14-12. True.

14-13. True.

14-14. True.

14-15. True.

Chapter 15

Answers to Review Questions, pp. 461–462

15-1. The potential investor should first determine whether he or she has the necessary capital and credit. Risks and related financial liabilities for the life of the investment should be added to this assessment. Some real estate investments entail management and necessitate a location near enough for easy access. These and the likely length of involvement are all factors for consideration.

15-2. a. The *market approach* involves researching the current asking and recent sales prices of comparable properties. Careful attention should be paid to similarities and dissimilarities; it is often from these that a unique price estimate can be determined.

   b. *Cost approach* valuation takes into account what the costs will be if land is purchased and a new building is constructed. This estimate is usually used as a ceiling on what amount the investor should pay for an existing property.

   c. If the investor desires a more analytical method, the *income approach* may be the most appropriate. This method involves determining all cash inflows, outflows, and future property values. The present values are then added to ascertain the overall project value and return. A number of alternative methods give rough approximations of this technique.

15-3. Properties that are priced above the results using the three valuation approaches in question 15-2 should be examined very thoroughly because they are probably overpriced. A price that is above the price yielded by the income approach is a signal that there are most likely alternative investments that offer the investor higher returns for comparable risk. Prices that are above the market and replacement figures should prompt the investor to consider other properties. These assessments should always take into account possible further bargaining concessions.

15-4.   a.   Total costs are $190,833.80, as shown below.

House Cost	$179,000.00
Other Costs	
Loan points	4,296.00
Loan application fee	500.00
Title insurance	700.00
Inspections	250.00
Title transfer	895.00
Escrow	4,152.80
Lawyer	200.00
Utility fees	840.00
Total:	$190,833.80

   b.   Your funding responsibility is $47,633.80, determined as follows:
        $190,833.80 – $143,200.00 = $47,633.80
   c.   Transaction costs represent 6.61 percent of the purchase price, calculated as follows:
        ($190,833.80 – $179,000)/$179,000 = 6.61%

15-5.   You are given enough information for a rough back-of-envelope calculation using the income approach:
        Value = income stream/discount rate = $28,000/.14 = $200,000
The calculated value is much higher than the asking price; therefore, this transaction definitely merits further consideration.

15-6.   The weighted average cost of capital (WACC) is .5(10.5%) + .5(6.5%) = 8.5%. The desired discount rate (cost of capital) should then add a risk premium to the WACC. The premium can be somewhat arbitrary but should at least cover that of the loan. Therefore, the absolute minimum risk premium and total cost of capital are 2 percent and 10.5 percent, respectively. The actual premium and discount rate should be comfortably above these figures.

15-7.   Investors can choose from a wide variety of REIT mutual funds, many of which have low minimum investments. REIT funds offer the added benefit of diversification, especially in the case of index funds. Investors can also search for individual companies that have significant real estate holdings. They should assess whether the stock's price adequately reflects the holding's value and whether sales are imminent.

15-8.   a.   The present value is $71,428.57, calculated as shown below.
        Costs = $300 + $600 = $900/grave
        Per-grave profit = Sales price – costs = $1,000 – $900 = $100
        Annual profit = (per-grave profit) (number of graves sold) = ($100) (100) = $10,000
        Present value = annual profit/discount rate = $10,000/.14 = $71,428.57
   b.   The value has increased $64,935.07, determined as shown below.
        Costs = $300 + $550 = $850/grave
        Per-grave profit = $1,000 – $850 = $150
        Annual profit = $150 (100) = $15,000
        Present value = $15,000/.11 = $136,363.64

Answers to Self-Test Questions, pp. 462–463

15-1.   True.
15-2.   False. High leverage is typically employed because investors desire to put as little of their own cash in the investment and borrow as much as possible.
15-3.   False. Direct investments in real estate offer investors low liquidity. The investments may take a long time to sell at a fair price, depending on market conditions.
15-4.   False. A point is one percent of the loan principal. If a property is purchased for $100,000 and the buyer takes out an $80,000 mortgage that requires 3 points, the cost of the points would be $2,400 ($80,000 x .03 = $2,400).
15-5.   True.
15-6.   True.

15-7. False. Commissions for raw land and undeveloped property are usually higher than commissions for developed real estate.

15-8. False. The market approach simply relies on an analysis of recent sales of similar properties to estimate the current value of a particular property.

15-9. False. The rate of interest is typically below market.

15-10. True.

15-11. True.

15-12. False. A REIT is essentially a closed-end investment company whose shares trade on an exchange or OTC.

15-13. False. In addition to direct investments in property, hybrid REITs make construction and mortgage loans.

15-14. True.

15-15. False. Index REITs are subject to market risk. If investment in the real estate sector declines, the prices of the individual REITs included in the index will decline.

15-16. True.

Index